The Complete Guide to Experiential Psychotherapy

Books by Alvin R. Mahrer, Ph.D.

Dream Work: In Psychotherapy and Self-Change (1989)

How to Do Experiential Psychotherapy: A Manual for Practitioners (1989)

The Integration of Psychotherapies: A Guide for Practicing Psychotherapists (1989)

Therapeutic Experiencing: The Process of Change (1986)

Psychotherapeutic Change: An Alternative Approach to Meaning and Measurement (1985)

Experiential Psychotherapy: Basic Practices (1983/1989)

Experiencing: A Humanistic Theory of Psychology and Psychiatry (1978/1989)

Creative Developments in Psychotherapy (1971, Editor with L. Pearson)

New Approaches to Personality Classification (1970, Editor)

The Goals of Psychotherapy (1967, Editor)

The Complete Guide to Experiential Psychotherapy

Alvin R. Mahrer, Ph.D.

John Wiley & Sons, Inc.

New York • Chichester • Brisbane • Toronto • Singapore

© 1996

Copyright © 1996 by John Wiley & Sons, Inc.

Library of Congress Cataloging-in-Publication Data:

Mahrer, Alvin R.
    The complete guide to experiential psychotherapy / by Alvin R.
Mahrer.
        p.   cm.
    Includes bibliographical references.
    ISBN 0-471-12438-9
    1. Experiential psychotherapy.   I. Title.
RC489.E96M34   1995
616.89'14—dc20   95-7302

Printed in the United States of America

10 9 8 7 6 5 4 3 2 1

Contents

Preface

This book presents practitioners with the complete theory and practice of the experiential psychotherapy I have been trying to develop for some time. This is a therapy that:

- *Enables virtually any person to become a qualitatively new person.* It enables the person to discover what is deeper, what is inside, what they are capable of experiencing, the kind of person that they can become. This therapy enables the transformation into being this new person. The change is from inside out; it is an in-depth qualitative shift in who the person is, what this person experiences, feels, thinks, and is, in the new world in which this person exists.
- *Enables the qualitatively new person to be essentially free of the painful bad feelings of the old person.* The new person is free of the pains and hurts, the anguish, the suffering, and the bad feelings of the old person. The new person is essentially free of the old ways of being; the old scenes and situations; the old ways of acting, behaving, relating; and the bad feelings that go with all that.
- *Invites the person to undergo these changes in each session, whether there is to be just one or many sessions.* Each session is its own complete minitherapy. Each session provides an open door into a world of being a whole new person. Each session opens the door to being free of the scenes and situations of painful feelings that are part of the person and the person's world.
- *Invites the field of psychotherapy into a genuinely new departure, both in the theory of psychotherapy and in the science of psychotherapeutic practice.* Experiential psychotherapy looks at change in a fundamentally different way from most psychotherapies. It represents a dramatic departure in ways of understanding what psychotherapy is and what it can achieve, the ways that therapists can be in psychotherapy, the kinds of changes that can take place, and the ways in which these changes can occur. This new departure is also an invitation for the field of psychotherapy to provide practitioners with a workable, useful framework for carrying out the session, a "science" that is from and for the practitioner— a *science of psychotherapeutic practice.*
- *Provides a four-step framework for the practitioner to follow in each session of powerful, in-depth, sensitive, gentle change toward being the new person.* The essential core of experiential psychotherapy is a four-step sequence to be followed in each

session. These four steps represent the theory and the practice by providing a way toward fundamental, in-depth change toward becoming a new person, freed of the pains and hurts, the bad feelings, of the old person.

This book can show you what to do and how to do it. It is a complete guide. However, this book cannot give you competence and skill. For you to have successful and effective sessions, you must improve your experiential skills gradually and continuously. Study with a fine teacher of experiential therapy. Work with a partner in trying to improve your skills. Study tapes of your own sessions, those of your partner, those of experienced therapists—and practice. Learning the skills takes careful, diligent, actual practice of selected specific skills. This book will bring you to the point where you can practice, train, and improve your skills.

It is up to you to go beyond that point. More bluntly, being familiar with this guide is probably not enough to have successful sessions. Knowing what to do is not the same as having enough competence to do it adequately, to have successful sessions. You need training and sheer practice to be at a good enough level of competence. Furthermore, training and practice could be and should be a lifelong enterprise.

THIS THERAPY HAS EVOLVED AND CHANGED

As a practitioner I use theory to help the practice get better. While experiential psychotherapy was growing, so was its underlying theory of human beings (Mahrer, 1978/1989d). This relatively comprehensive theory still makes sense to me today. But the actual practice is a different story. I described this in two books (Mahrer, 1986d, 1983/1989e) and a manual (Mahrer, 1989f).

These two books and the manual were my attempts to put together a way of doing psychotherapy that has grown, in bits and pieces, since 1954 when I first started doing psychotherapy. The therapy has evolved out of and beyond the earlier versions and is quite different now. It has gone about as far as I can develop it. The steps to be followed in each session are different. The methods for achieving each step have both expanded and become better organized. The therapy is gentler, more sensitive, and yet more powerful and change-enabling.

WHAT IS APPEALING ABOUT THIS THERAPY?

When psychotherapists wrote to me about this therapy, or when we met at workshops and conventions, I was interested in what they found appealing about this approach. I want to share some of their responses with you:

1. It seems to open up genuine changes in just about every session. From the very first session, changes start occurring right away, and continue during and after most sessions.
2. This therapy seems to be helpful, applicable, and useful for just about all patients, no matter how the patient is described in terms of problems, mental disorders, psychopathology, or anything. It seems to be a way to become a whole

new person, free of the scenes of bad feeling, rather than a therapy for certain kinds of patients.

3. This therapy seems to appeal to therapists who are attracted to doing deep-seated work, with effecting change at deeper levels of personality, with getting at the more basic and fundamental levels within the person.

4. The therapy seems to work; there are changes, both at the behavioral level and also at deeper levels. Occasionally, there are impressive, wholesale transformations.

5. The therapy seems to be powerful; yet it is sensitive, with comparatively little pressure on the patient.

6. There is a workable method; therapists can use a relatively simple four-step program to guide their work in each session.

These themes seem to occur over and over again when therapists tell me about this therapy. These are not research findings or the results of surveys. Nevertheless, if any of these attributes appeal to you, then I invite you to read this book and to try out this therapy.

WHAT ARE THE ROOTS AND FAMILY KINSHIPS OF THIS PSYCHOTHERAPY?

I was most strongly drawn to the writings of existential philosophers and clinical therapists such as Binswanger, Gebsattel, Straus, Kuhn, Angel, Buber, Camus, Ellenberger, Goldstein, Heidegger, Husserl, Jaspers, Kierkegaard, Minkowski, Scheler, Tillich, and, of course, Freud. My theory of human beings (Mahrer, 1978/1989d) grows out of the roots of their work, rather than the traditional Rogers-Maslow humanistic psychology (Mahrer, 1989a). Nevertheless, if theories of human beings are roughly organized into psychoanalytic, biological, learning, and existential-humanistic theories, experiential theory would probably fall under the latter family.

How would I situate this experiential psychotherapy in the field of psychotherapies? If we concentrate on the actual methods and procedures, it is very hard to relate this therapy to others. Or, rather, its methods and procedures may also be found in many other kinds of therapies. In those terms, this therapy is not especially unique. However, it may be distinguished from some other therapies on the basis of what is regarded as the key to therapeutic change. Most therapies rely on factors such as insight and understanding, the development and use of the therapist-patient relationship, exposure to the problematic situation or complex of stimuli, or modification of the internal and external variables (Mahrer, 1978b). This therapy does not rely on those means, but instead views "experiencing" as the working avenue toward change (Mahrer & Fairweather, 1993).

There are at least a few dozen therapies that formally identify themselves as experiential psychotherapies, and at least another dozen or more that place themselves into an experiential family (Mahrer & Fairweather, 1993). The phrase "experiential psychotherapy" was perhaps first used to refer to the approach of Carl Whitaker, John Warkentin, Thomas Malone, and Richard Felder (Whitaker & Malone, 1953, 1969). That phrase is frequently used, and experiential psychotherapy and "experiencing" can take on different meanings as shown in the following examples:

- For Gendlin (1961, 1962, 1973, 1974, 1981, 1984), experiencing starts with focusing on oneself, on the directly felt meaning that goes with a selected personal problem; then it refers to having the feelings, words, and pictures that arise from this inward focusing, and attending to the feelings that thereby occur; finally, it refers to the staying with and receiving whatever then comes, a shift or release, an opening up of something more, a carrying forward into further elaboration, a further internal sense. This meaning of experiencing is cast within a larger client-centered framework.
- A second meaning of experiencing refers to the processing of feeling-affective-emotional material to bring about a change in cognitive organization. The processing may consist of discussion, examination, or expression of the material under consideration. This meaning is generally associated with Rice, Greenberg, Safran, and Toukmanian (Greenberg & Safran, 1987; Rice, 1974, 1984; Rice & Greenberg, 1990; Toukmanian, 1990) and has roots in the client-centered approach, but bridges into the cognitive approach.
- A third meaning is the pioneering meaning of Whitaker, Malone, Warkentin, and Felder. Experiencing refers to the encountering-meeting of one's whole self and another's whole self, with each participant having access to the conscious, preconscious, rational, irrational, and unconscious dynamics of the other. This meaning has remained the core of Whitaker's family approach and the experiential approach of Malone, Warkentin, Felder, and their colleagues in the Atlanta group.
- In my meaning, experiencing refers to inner potentials or ways of being, and consists of accessing, integratively welcoming and appreciating, and being and behaving on the basis of the inner experiencing or way of being. This meaning forms the basis of the therapy that will be described in this book.

HOW TO LOOK AT PSYCHOTHERAPY IN TERMS OF FUNDAMENTAL ISSUES AND QUESTIONS

Much of this book is organized around some fundamental issues and questions in the field of psychotherapy. When I read the psychotherapy literature, I try to formulate the more or less basic questions that the writer is answering, or the basic issues on which the writer is taking some position. What can be exciting is not only identifying the positions that lots of writers take, but trying to identify the fundamental issues and questions in our field. I organized this book around some of these fundamental issues and questions.

For each issue, I will give the position of experiential psychotherapy. Most of you have your own positions and answers on these fundamental issues. Some of you will look at psychotherapy in compatible ways that fit well with my own way. But some of you will have ways of looking at psychotherapy that are quite different from mine. By adopting this format, I hope that you will more easily be able to see your own position on these issues and questions and to see how experiential psychotherapy is and is not like your position. We may agree or disagree on our positions, but perhaps we can acknowledge that most of us are taking some position or other on these fundamental issues and questions.

THE FOUR STEPS IN EACH SESSION OF
EXPERIENTIAL PSYCHOTHERAPY

Every session is to go through the following four steps; the working substeps are shown under each step:

1. *BEING IN A MOMENT OF STRONG FEELING: ACCESSING THE INNER EX-PERIENCING.* This step enables the person to live and be in a newly discovered moment of strong feeling, and to access, be in touch with, sense, the deeper inner experiencing.

    Give opening instructions. The person is shown how to look for scenes of strong feeling, how to attend to whatever is accompanied with strong feeling.

    Find a scene of strong feeling. Find a scene (time, incident, situation) in which the feeling is quite strong.

    Live and be in scene of strong feeling, and discover the precise moment of strong feeling. Enter into, live and be in, the scene of strong feeling. Search for and discover the moment, the precise instant, of strong feeling.

    Access the inner experiencing. In the moment of strong feeling, access (receive, be open to, be in touch with, sense) the deeper inner experiencing.

2. *INTEGRATIVE GOOD RELATIONSHIPS WITH THE INNER EXPERIENCING.* This step enables the person to welcome, appreciate, accept, have integrative good relationships with the accessed inner experiencing. Therapist and patient use a package of methods to attain integrative good relationships with the inner experiencing.

3. *BEING THE INNER EXPERIENCING IN EARLIER SCENES.* This step enables the person to undergo the qualitative, radical change into being the inner experiencing in the context of earlier life scenes.

    Find an earlier life scene. Find an earlier life scene by using the scene of strong feeling and accessed inner experiencing from Step 1.

    Be the inner experiencing in the earlier life scene. The person is to shift into being the inner experiencing in the context of the alive, real, immediate, earlier life scene.

    Find other earlier life scenes, and be the inner experiencing in these other life scenes. Find other scenes throughout the person's life, appropriate for being the inner experiencing. The person is to fully be the inner experiencing in these scenes.

4. *BEING THE NEW PERSON IN THE PRESENT.* This step enables the person to be the qualitative new person, the inner experiencing, in the present and prospective future, and to be free of the bad-feelinged scenes of Step 1.

    Select prospective scenes and behaviors for being the new person in playful unrealistic ways. Select extratherapy scenes from the present and from the prospective future. Select ways of being and behaving. The selected scenes and behaviors are to enable the person to be the whole new person, with emphasis on playful unreality.

    Be the new person, in playfully unrealistic ways, in scenes of the present and prospective future. The patient is the new person, the inner experiencing, in scenes of the present and prospective future, and within a context of playfulness, unreality, pretense, and fantasy.

> *Rehearse and refine being the actual new person in present and prospective future scenes.* Rehearse and refine ways of actually being the new person in the extratherapy world of the present and prospective future.
>
> *Commitment to being the new person in extratherapy world.* The new person is committed to the selected, rehearsed, refined new way of being and behaving in the selected extratherapy present and prospective future scenes.

Use this shorthand summary as your guide throughout this book. If the whole book can be condensed into a single page or so, this is it. If someone asks what experiential psychotherapy is, this summary is the answer, plus indicating that the goal of the four steps, in each session, is to enable the person (a) to become a qualitatively new person, and (b) to be free of the bad-feelinged scenes that were front and center in this session.

The first step is to enable the person to *be in a moment of strong feeling*. The moment may be within a current scene or situational context, a scene from the past, or one that has yet to occur. The moment may be real or perhaps merely possible, or fantasized. The accompanying strong feeling may be of any kind, and it may be a good feeling or a bad one. In any case, the person is to be wholly living and being in this moment, wholly caught up in this immediate, vivid, alive moment. Once the person is living and being in this moment of strong feeling, something deeper is activated, brought forward, made more accessible. This is a deeper quality or characteristic, an inner and deeper "way of being," a way that this person has available. I call this an *inner experiencing*.

In each session, the therapist shows the person how to find some scene or situation that is accompanied with strong feeling. It may be a problem or concern, some worrisome recent incident, any attentional center that comes to mind, anything at all that the patient can attend to with some feeling. We may stay with the opening scene or go from there to find another one that is even more compelling or gripping. Often we start with one scene and follow the same or varying feeling until we arrive at a scene that seems to arouse the strongest feeling.

Once we find the scene of strong feeling, we can *enter into this scene*. We can make it alive and real. We can literally be in this scene. When we are in this scene, we then look for when the feeling is strong. We discover the *moment* of strong feeling in this scene. This is a discovery because ordinarily we do not know what this moment is until we actively look for it. Once we find it, we can freeze the moment and enter into it, live and be in it.

This moment of strong feeling is a crucible that enables us to access the inner experiencing. In this moment, the inner experiencing is activated, brought closer, made more alive, opened up, and aroused. You can now sense the inner experiencing, feel it, have it, undergo it, and be reached and touched by it. When this happens, when the inner experiencing is accessed, you have attained Step 1.

The second step enables the person to feel good in relating to this accessed inner experiencing, to welcome and appreciate it. I refer to this change as *attaining an integrative good relationship*. It means that the person feels loving toward it, rather than having to stay away from it, to keep it down, or even to avoid and not be intruded into by it. There are methods that the therapist and patient can use to accomplish this integrative good relationship with the inner experiencing that was accessed in the first step.

The third step enables the person to *be the inner experiencing*. When the person attains a generally good integrative relationship toward the inner experiencing, Step 3 gives the person a chance to get inside, and to live and be from within this inner experiencing. This is a very big change, for the person is to let go of or disengage from, the ordinary, continuing person that he or she is in everyday life, and to be and become this whole new person, the inner experiencing. If the inner experiencing is quite a different way of being, and if the person is this new person to a great extent, then this can be a radical change—a transformation.

To make this Step 3 doable, the change into being the inner experiencing is done in the context of earlier life scenes. First, the person is to be in some general period of earlier life. This period may be relatively recent, or from a few years ago, or many years ago, or when the person was a child, or a baby, or even further back. Generally we go to childhood or to some relatively recent period. Then we look for a life scene or situation that we can use. The earlier scene may or may not be related to the scenes in Step 1. In any case, there are several ways of finding some earlier life scene, event, situation, or incident. Once we find it, the person is to live and be the inner experiencing in this alive and real scene. The aim is for the person to be the inner experiencing as fully as possible, and with wholesome good feelings. Once this is accomplished, then the person can find all sorts of other incidents for being inner experiencing. There are usually lots of incidents and situations where the person was the inner experiencing, or was not but could or should have been. Often these scenes include the ones used in Step 1 (usually scenes accompanied with bad feelings). The goal is for the person to have plenty of opportunities to be the inner experiencing.

Step 4, the final step, enables the person to get a taste, a sample, of what it is like to *be and to behave as the new person* who is the inner experiencing. Instead of being the inner experiencing in the context of earlier life scenes, the new person is now living and being in the context of scenes from tomorrow, the imminent future, and beyond. The person gets an opportunity to sample what it is like to be and behave as this inner experiencing in the extratherapy world. As the new person who is this inner experiencing, the new person feels better, is more integrated and actualized, is closer to being an optimal self, but the bonus is that the new person is essentially free of the bad-feelinged scenes from Step 1.

The fourth step begins with therapist and patient selecting scenes and behaviors in which the new person can truly be the inner experiencing. The context is one of play, pretense, unreality, because the first aim here is to enable the new person to gain a sense of what it is like to be this whole new person in the extratherapy world. Once the new person is fully here, and with good feelings, there can be a shift toward perhaps really being this way, actually being this new person, and behaving in these ways in present and prospective scenes. You rehearse and refine how the new person is in these scenes. When the new person feels good being this way, when it feels right and appealing, solid and appropriate, then the final substep is a self-commitment to actually be this new person, and to behave in this way, in the present and in the future.

These are the four steps that guide how each session unfolds. By the end of this session, the person has tasted what it is like to be a qualitatively new person who is free of those scenes of bad feeling. And these are the goals of the session, the aims and objectives of experiential psychotherapy: (a) to be the qualitatively new person, and (b) to be free of scenes of bad feeling.

A PREVIEW OF THE MAIN POINTS OF EACH CHAPTER

Chapters 1 and 2 deal with the experiential theory of human beings. Chapters 3 through 5 cover the experiential theory of practice. Chapters 6 through 10 show how to do experiential psychotherapy. I will preview each of the chapters, but if you are inclined toward either getting to know experiential psychotherapy or doing it, Chapters 1 through 5 should be read before the rest of them.

The first chapter provides a way of taking friendly perspective toward the basic foundation of experiential psychotherapy. By "basic foundation," I am referring to some of those issues ordinarily contained in the philosophy of science. This field of knowledge may seem somewhat unrelated to the practice of psychotherapy, but many of these issues are absolutely and directly pertinent to practice. This chapter describes the position of experiential psychotherapy on some basic issues in the philosophy of science, and therefore provides the working foundation for the balance of the book.

Chapter 2 provides a sketch of the experiential model of human beings. To do experiential psychotherapy, the practitioner should have a way of picturing human beings and making sense of how human beings are put together—what accounts for the way they are, how they can feel bad, what their worlds are like, how they relate to these worlds, what they can become over their lifetimes. This chapter highlights these and related issues and is designed for the working practitioner who needs a picture or model of what human beings are like from the experiential perspective.

Chapter 3 explains the in-session goals, objectives, and directions of change of experiential psychotherapy. These principles go to the core of the therapy. They define what a session can accomplish. Accordingly, these principles determine what initial sessions are like, how you identify the work for a specific session, what the helpful information is, how the past can be used, and how to see if change is taking place.

Chapter 4 describes how this therapy is useful for just about any person, no matter how the individual may be categorized or labeled in most other therapies. It also shows how to determine if the person and therapy are a good fit for one another in any particular session.

Chapter 5 answers two questions: For what kinds of therapists is experiential psychotherapy suitable? What determines that the session can be successful?

Chapters 6 through 10 concentrate on the actual practice, the handbook or manual for carrying out this therapy. Accordingly, they detail enough of each step to enable you to do this work. Chapter 6 deals with the bulk of the practical issues that the experiential psychotherapist would likely face. Some of these practicalities are almost required groundwork for effective sessions.

Chapters 7 through 10 constitute a complete manual for the four steps of the session. The methods for attaining each step are described in detail and are illustrated through numerous clinical examples.

TERM USED IN THIS BOOK: THERAPIST, PATIENT, AND PSYCHOTHERAPY

I have never known what to call the person that I work with. The issue became even harder to resolve when I gave courses and workshops on dreams, and wrote about people working with a partner: Each person worked on his or her dream in one session and then exchanged roles for the next session. In Europe, some professionals have a tradition of exchanging roles in dealing with the whole range of personal material, and they refer to it as "co-counseling." The word "client" did not bring the right pictures to me, nor did the word "patient." Neither did the word "student," which is often used in the learning of meditative and contemplative methods. The term "analysand" strikes me as rather pretentious. I am inclined to stay with the word "patient" until someone introduces a better word.

I also use the word "therapist" in this book, even though that does not seem quite fitting either. I am not drawn toward phrases that indicate a particular approach, such as "psychoanalyst" or "behavior modifier." Nor do terms such as "helper" or "counselor" even come close. There are lots of considerations for not using the word "therapist," but I use that word because I cannot think of a better one.

In the following chapters, I also use the term "psychotherapy," even though I sometimes wonder if that is the best word for this approach. Some of the patients I worked with were practitioners of other approaches. For example, one was a psychoanalyst and one was a dyed-in-the-wool behavior therapist. I recollect these two in particular because both spontaneously said something like this when leaving a session: "I look forward to these sessions. But I don't consider them psychotherapy. More like opening myself up and changing . . ." Whatever we call it, that is the ultimate goal of each experiential session.

The random use of "he" and "she" represents my effort to avoid gender bias as well as tedious repetition of "he or she." Unless stated otherwise, the material herein is equally applicable to both sexes.

I should also use the term "grateful." I am grateful to the interns and postdoctoral trainees who helped me to see where this growing therapy needed little tinkerings and some big improvements. I am grateful to all those with whom I spent so many hours listening to and learning from each others experiential tapes. I am grateful to those who turned error-filled typewritten and penciled batches of pages into a pretty manuscript: Kibeza Kasubi, Jeannine Cameron, Isabelle Mayrand, Béatrice Dugué, Anick Tourangeau, Marie Rainville, Nancy Marcus Land, and Peggy J. Kleinplatz, PhD. And I am especially grateful to Kelly A. Franklin. Her skills at editorial fine-tuning, deft trimming, extensive rewriting, creative reorganization, and whole-chapter amputation converted the overly ample convoluted manuscript into a readable book.

SECTION I

The Guide to Experiential Theory

How to Take a Friendly Perspective: Philosophy of Science and the Field of Psychotherapy

For you to do experiential psychotherapy, you need to have some idea of its theory of psychotherapy. And to gain this understanding, it is probably important that you appreciate the position of experiential psychotherapy on some basic issues in what is called the philosophy of science. This chapter identifies some of these basic issues and spells out the experiential position on each of them.

Knowing these basic issues seems to make it easier to take a friendly perspective in reading this book. Whether or not you agree with my position, we are at least taking positions on fundamentals that we may both respect.

ISSUES IN THE PHILOSOPHY OF SCIENCE GENERALLY MAKE LITTLE DIFFERENCE TO MOST PSYCHOTHERAPISTS

In 1958, Feigl bemoaned what he saw as a general indifference, among psychologists, to the philosophy of science. He focused mainly on the mind-body problem when he complained that psychology first lost its soul, then its consciousness, and then finally lost its mind altogether. Others have also noted how little genuine interest most psychologists had in the philosophy of science (e.g., Brown, 1936; McGeoch, 1933; Woodger, 1952).

In the field of psychotherapy, most practitioners still appear to have very little concern for issues in the philosophy of science. Indeed, many psychotherapists have little or no idea that just about everything they think and do is inextricably linked to an underlying position on some of these topics. Even further, lots of therapists have little or no idea of many issues on which they hold almost rigid positions (Mahrer, 1962a, 1989f). Even if lots of psychotherapy theorists, researchers, and clinicians generally agree with one another, that does not necessarily mean they acknowledge the underlying concerns in the philosophy of science or recognize that there are other viable positions on these matters.

In this chapter, as I focus on these issues, and the position of experiential theory, you will have a chance to see where you stand on these issues.

WHAT IS THE BASIC NATURE OF WHAT PSYCHOTHERAPISTS DEAL WITH IN THE FIELD OF PSYCHOTHERAPY?

Psychotherapists deal with things like unhappiness, sexual feelings, frustration and irritation, yearnings, pleasure, and excitement. They deal with mental illness, personality disorders, stimuli and reinforcements, ambivalences, and precipitating stresses. They deal with the unconscious, egos, helping alliances, transferences, cognitions, and emotions. Some of these things are in the patient, and some are in what we call psychotherapy. Regardless of what they are or where they are, you will tend to think of them as having a particular kind of basic nature. Furthermore, whatever basic nature you assign to them will likely have some rather profound implications for what you actually do as a psychotherapist. What are some different positions that most psychotherapists take on the basic nature of psychotherapeutic things?

What Positions May Psychotherapists Take on the Issue of the Basic Nature of What Psychotherapists Deal with in the Field of Psychotherapy?

In Figure 1.1, I have outlined six different positions on this issue. Whether you are dealing with a headache, a personality disorder, or a patient being excited and happy, you generally function on the basis of just one of these six positions.

If you hold to a Class 1 position, your way of thinking is that you may assume or have a model in which there is only one kind of basic thing. However, the way to clarify its supposed basic nature is by means of careful description. You describe by using words and terms from a body of constructs—a relatively organized system of terms. For example, you might use an experiential system of constructs such as "potentials for experiencing," "integrative relationships" between potentials for experiencing, and "deeper potentials for experiencing." Or you may hold to some other body or system of constructs. In this Class 1 position, you may use helpful and useful constructs to get at and to describe the basic nature of things. In this position, however, that is about as close as you can come to basic things. Basic things are mere "events," and you cannot come any closer to the basic nature of these events because they have no basic nature, other than being mere events (Kantor, 1942, 1957; Mahrer, 1978/1989d; Rotter, 1954; Stevens, 1935, 1939). You "construct" their supposed basic nature, and the constructs you use may be helpful and useful for your purposes, or not especially helpful or useful. Very few psychotherapists hold to the Class 1 position. Experiential psychotherapists do.

Psychotherapists who maintain a Class 2 position also believe that what they deal with consists of one kind of basic thing. However, they analyze it or get at the fundamental nature by means of reductionism. That is, you are to penetrate deeper and deeper until you arrive at the basic foundation of whatever you are dealing with. In the Class 2 position, the things you deal with have both physical and mental components. "Physical" refers to neurological, chemical, biological, physiological things, and so on. "Mental" refers to things like ideas, cognitions, reinforcements, and ego structure. The distinguishing feature of Class 2 is that physical and mental things can be even further reduced to a third irreducible basic thing that forms its essence. It is neutral. That is, some neutral basic thing underlies the physical and the mental. Very few psychotherapists use the Class 2 position.

On the other hand, most psychotherapists take the Class 3 position. They believe that there is only one kind of basic thing. You get at the basic nature of

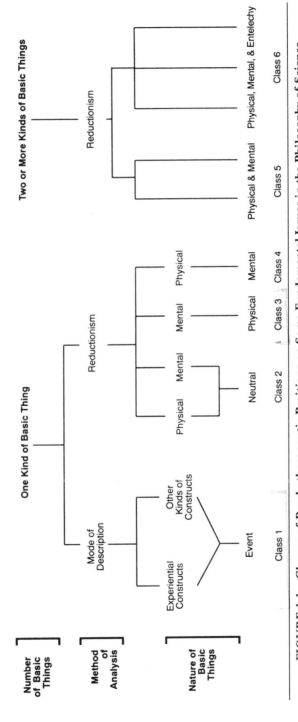

FIGURE 1.1   Classes of Psychotherapeutic Positions on Some Fundamental Issues in the Philosophy of Science

psychotherapeutic things by reducing them further and further into their more basic components. The nature of basic things is physical: neurological, chemical, physiological, biological, and so on. All mental things can be further reduced to their physical bases. What is absolutely basic is physical.

In the Class 4 position, there is only one kind of basic thing. The way to get at the fundamental base is by means of reductionism. In this position, however, the nature of basic things is mental, psychic, spiritual. The physical level of things can be further reduced to its underlying basic mental nature. Very few psychotherapists use the Class 4 position.

In the Class 5 position, there are two kinds of basic things. You get at the basic nature of things by means of reductionism. At the most fundamental level, things consist of both physical and mental irreducible basic elements. Some psychotherapists take this position, but nowhere near the proportion who hold to the Class 3 position.

In the Class 6 position, there are three kinds of basic things. Reductionism is the way to get at the nature of these basic things. At the most basic level, there are three kinds of core elements: One is physical, the second is mental, and the third is called an entelechy. "Entelechy" refers to an element or force that is neither physical nor mental, such as an élan vital or spiritual third thing. Very few psychotherapists maintain the Class 6 position.

If we stop here, these six positions seem to be irrelevant. So I take some position. So what? Let us take a step closer to how these positions may make a difference in what you do and what you do not do as a psychotherapist.

There Is a Single Basic Truth versus There Are Alternative Systems of Constructs

Classes 2 through 6 all agree that there is a single basic truth. Each class has its own notion of what that basic truth is like, but they all agree that basically it is like this or like that. When we ultimately get at the real foundation of schizophrenia, or stuttering, or the emotions, or the unconscious, it will be chemical or electronic or physiological or neurological or something. There is a single basic truth, and we must constantly search for the basic nature of what we deal with in psychotherapy.

Psychotherapists in these classes know that the things we deal with in psychotherapy are real. The thing we call schizophrenia really exists. Likewise stuttering, the unconscious, behavior, emotions, cognitions, ambivalence, mental illness, personality disorders, precipitating stress, sexual impulses, transference, reinforcement, are all real things with real basic natures.

Psychotherapists who hold to a Class 1 position look at these things in a different way. These psychotherapists maintain that we may assume that there are events, but we construct their basic natures. Whether we are talking about paranoia, emotions, or the unconscious, these are mere constructs, and we use other constructs to describe what we construe as their basic natures. The closest we can get to events is to use constructs to describe them (Feigl, 1953; Kantor, 1942, 1953, 1957; Mahrer, 1962a, 1978/1989d; Pratt, 1939; Rotter, 1954). There are alternative systems of constructs, but there is no underlying single basic truth to either these systems or their constructs. For example, there may be experiential, Adlerian, biological, cognitive behavioral, neurophysiological, and psychoanalytic systems of constructs. But their constructs are not truths. Nor is there a single basic truth to compare these various systems of constructs against. Any event is open to construction from an experiential psychoanalytic, or biological perspective, but none of these are more real or true than the others. Basic natures are constructed, rather than being psychological, chemical, spiritual, neurological, experiential, or physiological.

Constructs Are Related to More Fundamental Constructs of That System versus Psychological Constructs Are to Be Reduced to the Constructs of the Hard Sciences

In the experiential system, we talk about potentials for experiencing, and we try to distinguish between on-the-surface "operating potentials," which are tied to the way the person behaves, and "deeper potentials," which are not directly tied to behavior. Operating or deeper potentials are explained or further described by means of other experiential constructs. Some experiential constructs are perhaps more fundamental than others and can be used to explain or further describe less fundamental constructs. In the Class 1 position, psychological constructs are explained or further understood in terms of more fundamental constructs of that system (Kantor, 1953; Mahrer, 1962b, 1971b, 1978/1989d; Rotter, 1954).

On the other hand, most psychotherapists accept that there is a genuine, real, basic thing at the bottom of what we deal with in psychotherapy. Furthermore, at the very bottom, what we deal with in psychotherapy is reducible to things of the hard sciences. Psychotherapeutic concepts, like experiencing, archetypes, transference, reinforcement, and everything else that we deal with in psychotherapy can and will be reduced to neural circuits, chemical resistances, electron-proton aggregates, electric fields, or to the other things of the truly basic hard sciences.

The Class 1 position allows me to decline that way of thinking. We relate psychological constructs to more fundamental psychological constructs, and not to the concepts of what other positions accept as the more basic sciences (Binswanger, 1958b; Buytendijk, 1950; Cantor & Cromwell, 1957; Krech, 1950; Mahrer, 1978/1989d, 1990e; Marx, 1951; Schwab, 1960; Watts, 1961).

WHAT ARE SOME PRACTICAL CONSEQUENCES OF ACCEPTING A SINGLE TRUTH MODEL OR A MODEL OF ALTERNATIVE SYSTEMS OF CONSTRUCTS?

There are important practical consequences of holding either to the model of a single basic truth or to a model of alternative systems of constructs. You can believe that there really is something called schizophrenia, and that it has a basic true nature. Or you can believe that schizophrenia is merely a construct in a system that includes that particular construct, and that each system of constructs is free to describe whatever it construes to be the basic nature of schizophrenia, or even to decline the very notion of schizophrenia.

Approaches Must Include My Universal Basic Truths versus Each Approach May Have Its Own Body of Constructs

In the single truth model, there really are truths. Because the truths exist, any worthwhile approach has to include these truths. However, another position holds that there are alternative systems of constructs. The whole notion of "truths" is a fiction that is accepted as true only in the single truth model. There are serious differences depending on whether you believe approaches must include universal truths, especially yours, or whether you believe that each approach may have its own body of constructs.

A truth is a truth versus shift construct systems and the truths disappear.   If you believe that there are truths, then you can identify them. They exist. They are contained in the body of scientific knowledge about psychotherapy. They stand as truths, apart from any particular psychotherapeutic approach. Good research established the validity of these truths, and good research may confirm them, disconfirm them, and modify or replace them with other sets of truths. Here are some truths: When a client is depressed, there are certain things to look for in the assessment. There are research-based treatments of choice for particular diagnostic conditions. Egos vary in integrative capacity. There are universal basic needs and drives. There are stages of psychological development. There are symptoms of a borderline condition. Every therapist-patient relationship has elements of transference. The brain is a basic determinant of behavior. Emotional expression is dangerous in fragile personalities. Psychotherapeutic change requires the right kind of relationship. There are mental illnesses and diseases. Psychopaths do not do well in intensive psychotherapy. Insight and understanding are essential for psychotherapeutic change. There are laws of human behavior. There are learning deficits. Patients come to therapy for treatment of their problems.

There are hundreds of these universal truths in the field of psychotherapy. Psychotherapists who hold to these truths honestly believe in borderline personalities and basic drives. They are simply true. Schizophrenia would exist even if there were no theories of psychotherapy. It is simply true. Experiential theory has to accept the truth of schizophrenia because there is a real and true thing that is schizophrenia.

However, if you move from this position to one that accepts alternative systems of constructs, then you are free of all these universal truths. The experiential position does not accept the truth of notions like depression, and therefore we do not look for "suicidal ideation" in "depressives." We do not accept the truth of diagnostic conditions, and therefore we do not identify treatments of choice for diagnostic conditions that do not exist in our construct system. We do not include the truth of universal basic needs or drives. Stages of development are not accepted as universal truths. Our construct system does not include the universal truth of symptoms or borderline conditions. Transference is not held as a universal truth. Asserting that the brain is a basic determinant of behavior may hold in cordial construct systems, but not as a universal truth in our construct system. The notion of fragile personality is not accepted as a universal truth. Psychosis is a construct in particular approaches, rather than a universal truth. Our construct system does not include the construct of mental illnesses and diseases. Since we have no construct of psychopath, we do not accept the universal truth that psychopaths do not do well in intensive psychotherapy. Nor do we accept the universal truth that insight and understanding are essential for psychotherapeutic change. In our construct system, there are no universal laws of human behavior.

If you take the right position on some of these issues in the philosophy of science, then all these things are universal truths. Every approach has to accept them. But if you hold to another position, and we do, then all these true things and asserted truths become mere constructs in cordial and friendly construct systems. How you stand on some issues of the philosophy of science can make a practical difference to psychotherapists.

There are universal basic needs and drives versus each system has its own version of what is basic. In Classes 2 through 6, it is easy to assume that there really are basic needs and drives, and that all persons have them. Furthermore, each approach accepts whatever basic needs and drives that theory holds as true. There are all sorts of lists of these universal basic needs and drives, and although we may not have found a list that is generally accepted, it is accepted as true that there are universal needs and drives. The list may include needs and drives for food, sleep, oxygen, sex, aggression, belongingness, social interest, survival, intimacy, and so on. Whatever the list of the moment, each person has the same set of basic needs and drives. Each of the five classes, from 2 through 6, will accept that there are universal basic needs and drives, and that, whatever their nature, everyone has them.

As a Class 1 approach, experiential theory holds that a construct system is free to accept or to decline a construct of universal basic needs and drives. We are not constrained to believe that there is something basic in all people. Indeed, in experiential theory, there are no universal needs or drives.

Inside most people are some things that are bad and dangerous, and should be controlled versus what is inside is described as deeper potentials for experiencing that may be integrated and actualized. According to one position, deep within human beings lie such real things as needs, drives, impulses, wishes, instincts, psychodynamics, pathological processes. Some of these are bad and dangerous.

If what is inside is violence, destructiveness, physical abuse, then the person just may do all sorts of things that justify controlling the violence, the destructiveness, the physical abuse. Picture the person killing others, savagely raping poor victims, shooting innocent babies, blowing up convents. You certainly don't want to encourage such uncivilized, inhumane acts. Therefore, therapists should do what they can to control the violence, destructiveness, physical abuse that is in all or some persons.

According to the experiential position, what is inside people are potentials for experiencing. To begin with, there are no deeper potentials that are intrinsically bad, evil, dangerous, and are found in most people. In this model, there is no bad, evil, dangerous potentials for experiencing, and there are no universal ones anyhow, good or bad.

Nor is there any coterminality between the potential for experiencing and the concrete behaviors that may or may not be related to it. If the deeper potential is described as the experiencing of being strong, firm, hard, tough, you are quite free to picture this as a set of behaviors that can worry you, bother you, make you want to inhibit and control them, or you can see behaviors that are valued, pleasing, happy, and cherished.

In the experiential model, what is inside most people does not include things that are intrinsically bad, evil, dangerous, and deserve to be watched over, controlled. There are ways in which the deeper potentials can be accompanied by bad feelings, but they are not universal, they are not intrinsically bad or evil or dangerous, and they do not warrant control.

Here are two somewhat different positions on the nature and content of, and on what may be done with, whatever is held as deeper in human beings. Each position may be justified and defended. Your class position goes a long way in determining which option is yours.

If your approach does not include my universal truths, then your approach is incomplete, inferior, unscientific versus there are no basic universal truths, and each approach is free to

of course the approach that has no truth honors those that do – all things are valid.
Are we falling into the "there are no rules" rule?

have its own constructs.   Many psychotherapists know that there really is psychosis and that a good therapist-patient relationship must include heavy doses of warmth and empathic understanding. Any approach that does not accept these universal truths must be incomplete, inferior, unscientific, and wrong. If a patient is depressed, then assessment is to look for recent environmental changes that produced decreases in available reinforcers (Nelson & Barlow, 1981). If you accept neither these constructs nor the axiomatic truth, then your approach is incomplete, inferior, and unscientific. Something must be fundamentally wrong with approaches that do not include the universal truth of basic needs and drives. Because there are universal truths, approaches that do not include them are incomplete, inferior, unscientific, or far out, weird, perhaps dangerous.

I have tried to talk seriously with people who have read about, heard, watched experiential psychotherapy, and who are fairly galvanized into rejecting it. Many of these people have an honest sense that their deeply felt truths have been violated. I did not interact with the patient in the way that these therapists know is the truth of how therapists are to relate to patients. What I did with the patient violated what these therapists know are the truths of how a therapist must be with a patient with that problem, or what a therapist should do in the beginning of the initial session. What concerns me is not so much that many of these persons have such deeply entrenched truths about therapists and patients and psychotherapy. What concerns me much more is that if a psychotherapy does not conform to their deeply felt truths, then the therapy is bad, wrong, incomplete, inferior. Many of these people have little or no idea that they hold to such a tight package of universal basic truths until they are face to face with a psychotherapy that does not conform to or accept those truths.

In the initial experiential session, I did not do a psychodiagnostic assessment. I did not even do a case history. My colleague, who wonders how I would be able to gauge the patient's degree of abnormality, cites a transcendent truth: "To know what background topics to pursue in a diagnostic interview, the therapist needs to be broadly knowledgeable about normal and abnormal personality development . . ." (Weiner, 1975, p. 56). I confess that my system of constructs does not include "psychodiagnosis," "normal," or "abnormal." My colleague pronounces my approach as wrong, bad, inferior, unprofessional, and dangerous because of the truths that it lacks.

All of this makes sense in positions that accept that there really are basic truths. However, the Class 1 position says that each approach is free to have its own constructs, and there are no universal basic truths. If your approach does not include my constructs, your approach may be just fine. It is not inferior, incomplete, or unscientific because it does not include my constructs. Nor is my approach inferior, incomplete, or unscientific because it does not include your universal basic truths. To be adequate and scientific, approaches need not contain the truths that are regarded as real and universal in your particular approach.

In the field of psychotherapy, most therapists seem to hold to a position in which approaches that do not accept the current body of supposed truths are judged as incomplete, inferior, and unscientific. From this perspective, the field of psychotherapy may be inferior to and less scientific than the field of religion. The reason is that many theologists allow for quite different construct systems, without, for example, insisting that to be scientific some other religion must accept a specific universal truth about how men and women came about. In this sense, religious bodies of thought are more sophisticated than psychotherapeutic bodies of thought. Maybe we too can advance to a level where we can accept different belief systems.

Expose yourself to other belief systems. If you are a devout Jungian, study experiential theory. If you are a devout cognitive behaviorist, study psychoanalytic theory. Most therapists know precious little about alien approaches. I would like to suggest two reasons for studying approaches other than the one you believe in. One is that you can, if you allow yourself, thereby come closer to seeing the underlying issues on which you hold different positions. If you believe in the *Diagnostic and Statistical Manual of Mental Disorders,* study approaches, such as experiential theory, that do not. Before you reject approaches that believe in psychodiagnoses, allow yourself to discern the underlying issues on which you take different stands. Perhaps the issue has to do with pictures of personality. Perhaps the issue deals with how you conceive the structure of personality. When you are confronted with an alien approach, you have an opportunity to come closer to identifying the underlying issues and questions that both approaches address, even though they may hold different positions on these issues.

A second reason to study alien approaches is simply to acknowledge that there indeed are varying positions on these issues. Throughout this book, you will be given sets of alternative positions on underlying issues. You may, of course, prefer your position. You may find several ways in which your position is preferable to other positions. But at least you will be able to appreciate and to acknowledge that yes, there are indeed alternative positions on these shared underlying issues.

In the field of psychotherapy, with most therapists accepting that there are universal basic truths, it is easy to understand that a few approaches would become dominant and popular, and that their universal basic truths would be forced on others through licensing examinations, ethical codes, professional standards and the supposed research-based knowledge of psychotherapy. If you do not know these universal basic truths, you fail the professional examination. When a student accepts these universal basic truths, the student graduates. When a patient accepts the universal basic truths held by the therapist, the patient is gaining insight and understanding. In the Class 1 position, there are no basic universal truths, and each approach is free to have its own constructs. Your approach is not incomplete, inferior, or unscientific just because it fails to include my universal basic truths.

If therapists believe in the same basic truths, the truths become authoritative, universal, codified, and standardized for all therapists versus each construct system contributes its own codes and standardized practices. Therapists whose positions fall into Classes 2 through 6 accept that there are basic truths. Because their beliefs are held as universal, rather than being restricted to their own construct system, something generally happens when most therapists share the same set of basic truths. Something even worse happens when these therapists set the rules, establish the codes, write the books, develop the standards, determine the policies, lobby the lawmakers. Their basic truths burst out of their particular construct systems, and become apotheosized as universal, authoritative truths, the codes and standards for all therapists. It is one thing when a group of therapists at a case conference agree that this patient is schizophrenic and do not acknowledge that they are sharing a common construct system outside of which there may be no schizophrenia. It is another thing when these therapists are setting the rules for managed care systems, licensing examinations, codes of professional conduct, and standards of accreditation, without acknowledging that they are imposing the truths of a dominant approach on therapists who may not share that approach.

If a program does not train its graduates in these assigned areas, then the program will not be accredited. Licensing examinations include hundreds of "asserted truth" questions that have correct answers. There are practical consequences when the dominant approaches put their own basic truths into the authoritative codes and standards that are to be followed by all therapists, not just those who subscribe to those truths.

All therapists must therefore use the standard diagnostic system. This includes behavior therapists who must give up their own ways of categorizing patients (e.g., Adams, Doster, & Calhoun, 1977; Cautela & Upper, 1975; Dengrove, 1972; Ferster, 1967; Nelson & Barlow, 1981; Suinn, 1970). All therapists are to be trained to carry out standard intake assessment and evaluation on presenting problems, precipitating stresses, coping mechanisms, intelligence, self-concept, defenses, ego strength, pathological functioning, degree and severity of psychopathology, and so on (Korchin, 1976; Nelson & Barlow, 1981; Weiner, 1975). All therapists are to know the signs of depression, are to determine whether the depression is serious, and are to follow the established guidelines if the depression is severe. All therapists should obtain the presenting problems and should know the treatment of choice for the presenting problem. All therapists must know the signs of mental illness, and should pursue the signs and symptoms to check them out. All therapists should have foundational knowledge in psychobiology, neurology, and physiology. All therapists should obtain case history information, and this information should cover standard areas and topics. All therapists must know the standard stages of personality development and should gather relevant information on how the patient proceeded through these stages (cf. Noyes & Kolb, 1967).

All of this comes from therapists knowing that there are basic truths, knowing that these truths are for all approaches, and putting into stone what these universal truths are. In contrast, Class 1 approaches have constructs, not truths. There can be codes and standards for experiential therapists, but they certainly are not imposed on behavior therapists. According to this position, each approach may well have its own codes and standards, and practitioners of each approach may well acknowledge and respect those of other approaches.

Does this mean that there should be hundreds of sets of codes and standards? No. It means that codes and standards are to incorporate contributions that reflect non-dominant approaches. Codes and standards need to be arrived at by means of a process that acknowledges and respects different positions on issues in the philosophy of science, and different approaches to psychotherapy. Licensing examinations can do what they are intended to do, without consisting of hundreds of multiple choice questions based on the universal truths of the dominant approaches. Standards of accredited training programs can be framed that represent more than the imposed requirements of dominant approaches. The entire list of things that therapists are to do can reflect honest differences between approaches and can give up the notion that these are absolute necessities for all therapists in all approaches. Yes, this will mean that there is no more diagnostic system of mental illnesses and diseases imposed on all therapists, no more standard intakes, no more standard assessments and evaluations, case histories, stages of development, axioms and truths about patients, and how-to-do psychotherapy, all imposed on therapists outside the dominant approaches. Beware of therapists who share the same dominant position. Beware of their universal truths that become the laws of psychotherapy. Work toward general codes and standards and practice guidelines that acknowledge different positions.

There are basic therapeutic skills common to most therapeutic approaches versus each approach is free to have its own package of therapeutic skills.   If you believe that there is a common underlying truth, then it is easy to presume that there is a single foundational package of therapeutic skills. Regardless of therapeutic approach, all students are to learn the basic skills of, for example, empathic reflection, simple interpretation, establishing the relationship, and problem identification. Once students have acquired these basic skills, they can go on to learning the more advanced skills of particular therapeutic approaches.

The experiential position is that each so-called basic skill is intimately bound into its enveloping construct system. Empathic reflections and interpretations come from, and fit into, construct systems that provide meaning to those skills. If construct systems do not include the fitting conceptual envelope, then the skills are not sensible or useful. If construct systems differ, and if there is no common, underlying core to the systems, then it is likely that systems will not use the same skills. In short, each system is free to have its own package of therapeutic skills.

If this is so, what guidelines can we use to train our students in rudimentary skills? One way is to acknowledge that different approaches will likely have different sets of foundational skills, and to provide a representative sampling of sets of foundational skills. Another way is to identify common categories of skills, such as listening, coaching and instructing, or relationship-building, and then to acknowledge that within each category the specific skills are linked only to certain approaches rather than to all or even most of them.

Neurobiophysiological Things Are Basic to Psychological Constructs versus Experiential Constructs Are Basic to Other Experiential Constructs

In the Class 3 position, physical things are basic. I refer to neurobiophysiological things, but I mean to include things that are also chemical, anatomic, and all the other physical things that have even a slight bearing on what psychotherapists deal with. Whatever it is that you want to work with, to understand, to have knowledge about, basically and fundamentally it is physical, and you should know its neurobiophysiological base. In the Class 1 position, the constructs of each system are basic to the constructs of that system. The experiential constructs are fundamentally understood in terms of basic experiential constructs. Neurobiophysiological things are simply not assumed to be basic to experiential constructs. The constructs of experiential theory are not assumed to be reducible to more fundamental neurobiophysiological things (Mahrer, 1986b, 1989d). These differences make for some rather practical differences.

For those who accept the Class 3 position, it is sensible that all psychotherapists should have knowledge of, be familiar with the theories of, and know the main research findings of sciences held as basic. This means that psychotherapists are to have a basic understanding of pharmacology, neurology, biology, and physiology, and such fields as cognition, sensation, and perception. Programs that train psychotherapists should include required courses in these basic fields. Here is a practical consequence of believers in one class or position imposing that position onto all psychotherapists.

In contrast, the Class 1 position would suggest requiring courses in neurobiophysiological fields only for approaches which accept that neurobiophysiological things are indeed basic to psychological constructs. Their theories, research findings, and knowledge are not basic to experiential psychotherapy; rather, they are innocently irrelevant. Experimental psychology is not basic to experiential psychotherapy, and basic knowledge of the foundations of experiential theory has nothing to do with neurology, cognition, learning, perception, chemistry, anatomy, physiology, or biology. Once your position declines the assumption of basic neurobiophysiological things, a great deal of what is traditionally required simply washes away.

In medical hospitals, it is generally assumed that neurobiophysiological things are basic. Psychologists have been trying to get into medical hospitals for about a hundred years. In perhaps the first professional symposium on this issue, John B. Watson (1912) and Shepherd I. Franz (1912/1979) presented arguments stating why psychologists deserve a place in medical settings. One of the problems is that medicine owns the body because basic medical sciences are, in the Class 3 position, the foundation of bodily things. A few hundred years ago, theology owned the human body. Medicine fought with theology, and medicine won. Except for sciences that lay claim to dressing the body, fixing the teeth, making the hair look nice, and providing glasses, medicine owns virtually each part of the body. Psychology does not have any body part that it owns—not the nose, stomach, heart, lungs, brain, nerves, arms, or feet. Nevertheless, psychologists can hold to a Class 3 position, accept that neurobiophysiological things are absolutely basic, claim that they do have knowledge of these basic fields, and thereby can try to have a place in medical settings (cf. Mahrer, 1986b, 1978/1989d; Stone, 1979).

In contrast, those who accept a Class 1 position ordinarily decline to fit into medical settings, except perhaps as guests in settings owned by other sciences because we accept that what is basic consists of experiential constructs, not neurobiophysiological things.

If you hold to a position in which the things you deal with as a psychotherapist really have a physical, neurobiophysiological base, then you should either conduct physical examinations or get the results of physical examinations. You should use the results of neurological examinations to see if there is any disease or injury of the central nervous system, and you should check out biochemical dysfunctions (cf. Benton, 1971; Hersen, 1986; Hersen & Bellack, 1988; Lief, 1972; Rebec & Anderson, 1986; Sands, 1972). If you hold to a Class 1 position, however, you do not need supposedly basic chemical, anatomic, neurological, or physiological data. You do not do or rely on physical examinations.

There are some quite practical and far-reaching implications of either believing that neurobiophysiological things are basic to psychological constructs, or, on the other hand, believing that what is basic to experiential constructs are other experiential constructs.

The Body Is a Biological Thing versus the Body Is an Event, Open to Relevant Construct Systems

If you believe in a Class 3 position, then the body is a biological thing. Basically and fundamentally, a description of a bodily thing must consist of biological terms. If you are going to work with bodily things, then basically and fundamentally you must use concepts that are biological, chemical, anatomical, neurological, physiological.

Unless you accept a Class 1 position. Then the body is merely an event. It is open to construct systems that are psychological, biological, or of any kind whatsoever. Actual, real, hard, specific things that you are looking at, on or inside the body, are as open to experiential constructs as they are open to anatomic constructs. You may also describe and understand them in terms of the constructs of Jungian theory, learning theory, or psychoanalytic theory. The funny little growth or the blockage or the hole in this part of the body are just as open to experiential constructs as to chemical constructs. The bodily referents of what is called cancer or diabetes, in one construct system, are exceedingly open to description and understanding by means of experiential constructs. Anything in and of the body is fair game for experiential work because the body is just another event that can be described and worked with in an experiential construct system.

On the other hand, which kind of construct system is more useful for particular purposes is a whole different matter. An experiential construct system may well be useless in getting rid of a growth or a red blotch on the skin. Other construct systems may be far more appropriate. In the Class 1 position, the body is merely an event that is open to description from any relevant construct system, including the experiential system and a biological system of constructs. But one system of constructs is almost certainly more useful than another for particular purposes.

Each Construct System Is an Alternative Way of Describing "It" versus Add up the Basic Parts to Know What "It" Is Really Like

In the Class 1 model, there may be an experiential construct system, and there may be other construct systems such as biological, Adlerian, or cognitive construct systems. Each construct system is an alternative way of construing or describing whatever you are dealing with. In the models for Classes 2 through 6, what you are dealing with is composed of parts that are physical and parts that are mental. You may be dealing with neurological parts, learning disorder parts, chemical parts, cognitive parts, cultural anthropological parts, and emotional parts. The more you know about the parts, the more you know what it is really like.

$x\%$ physical parts $+$ $y\%$ mental parts $=$ what it is versus work within your own construct system.   He has a headache. She becomes gloomy and cries. He is jealous of men who are not fat. She craves to be the head of a law firm. Psychotherapists who fall into Classes 2 through 6 believe that the more you know about the parts the more you know about what these things are really like. Understanding, assessing, diagnosing the headache means seeing how much of it is physical, somatic, organic, neurological, and how much of it is mental, emotional, psychological (Lief, 1972). The formula is that this person's headache is x percent physical plus y percent mental. Therefore, if tests indicate that neurological factors are quite evident, then the headache is only minimally psychological. If no neurological factors can be found, then the headache is probably psychological. If a child tends to be gloomy and to cry a lot, the simple formula may be that there are x percent genetic-hereditary factors plus y percent environmental factors. If you cannot find evidence of conspicuous genetic-hereditary factors, then the child's gloominess and crying are probably due to environmental factors.

Whatever is lumped under physical or genetic or environmental or mental or psychological can also be broken down into components. Therefore, the headache may comprise parts that are neurological, chemical, physiological, cultural, stress-related, and psychoanalytic. Yet the same formula applies. The more you know of the component parts, the more you know of the whole thing. If you want to understand his seeing things that others don't see, then you should assess all the relevant factors: religious, chemical,

the — yes the parts make the whole, but this
breakdown of parts eliminates the synergistic
effects of the whole — this is a key that is
missed

16   The Guide to Experiential Theory

genetic, anthropological, psychoanalytic, psychiatric, emotional, neurological. There
can be a whole set of factors with each linked to the others (e.g., Barrios, 1988; Kanfer,
1985). Nevertheless, the underlying formula is that the parts make up the whole, even
in somewhat complicated ways.

Our Class 1 position regards each construct system as its own, separate, alternative way of making sense of an event. The experiential construct system may be applied
to any event, and we may find that it is open to our mode of description a great deal,
moderately, very little, or not at all. The extent to which the experiential construct system is applicable does not depend on, nor does it determine, the extent to which it may
also be open to constructs that are cognitive, psychodynamic, Jungian, behavioral, genetic, neurological, or physiological. The headache of a particular person may be fully
described experientially and also fully described neurologically. With another person,
experiential constructs may or may not be applicable to the headache. Even further, experiential constructs may have no applicability at all in making sense of eye color, blood
in the urine, or nail growth rate.

If the person has a headache or is complaining about her boss, we can apply experiential constructs. If we combine or integrate bits and pieces of four construct systems, are we closer to the truth than if we use just one of the four construct systems? The
answer is yes, if you believe in much of the integrative or eclectic movement in psychotherapy. The answer is probably no, if you accept the Class 1 position. Building a new
construct system from four separate construct systems is merely building a new construct system. It may be closer or further from the truth, if you like trying to get close
to the truth. It may be more or less useful, if you like construct systems that are useful.

The integrative or eclectic movement is based on the positions represented by
Classes 2, 5, and 6. The idea is that the more pieces you assemble, the closer you get to
"it." These therapists believe that they know more about the headache or the complaining about her boss when they put together psychoanalytic, behavioral, and experiential
theory. How can you know the truth about the headache if (a) a headache comprises
psychological and biophysiological parts, and (b) you only use a psychological perspective, and only one of the many psychological perspectives at that? The answer is you cannot, if you accept the Class 2, 5, or 6 position. In contrast, if you accept the Class 1
position, then each construct system provides its own way of making sense of and describing the event. There is no "truth" that is arrived at by combining component parts.
The integrative or eclectic movement is sensible or not sensible, something to pursue or
not to pursue, depending on your position on these issues (Mahrer, 1989g).

Because most therapists fall in Classes 2 through 6, their way of thinking will almost naturally lead them toward integrating various approaches. First of all, they would
think that there is an underlying truth. There is a psychoanalytic theory and there is a
social learning theory. If there were a perfect theory, it must, therefore, include the
viewpoints of both psychoanalytic theory and social learning theory. The two theories
just provide different perspectives on the underlying reality. Furthermore, since each
perspective gets at the underlying truth, each has a piece of the truth. Accordingly, it
makes eminent good sense that combining what psychoanalytic theory provides and
what social learning theory provides gets you that much closer to the real truth. Opti-
mally, if you combine the good parts of all the good theories, you can almost get at the
real truth of psychological problems, personality structure, psychotherapeutic change,
and all the important things that psychotherapy deals with. Hence, therapists who want
to get at the real truth should look for the very best ways of integrating the very best
theories. This makes very good sense, provided that you fall into a Class 2 through 6

approach and you know that the best way to know what the whole is really like is to add up the basic parts.

The experiential Class 1 position shares none of this way of thinking. Our mission is not that of integrating with other theories, other systems of constructs. We must decline the whole enterprise of integrating approaches, largely because we share none of the underlying reasons that fuel the integrative moment.

In the Class 1 position, we do the best job we can in applying the experiential construct system. We presume that the person may also be exceedingly open to a construct system that is object-relations or Gestalt, Sullivanian, or behavioral, neurological, sociological, or physiological. Each construct system may be applicable independent of any other construct system.

The therapist is to be competent in, and able to shift between, the component parts versus the therapist works within the single construct system. In Classes 2 through 6, whatever you are working with comprises several parts that together make up the whole. This means that the therapist should be relatively competent in these component parts, and should be able to shift in and out of the various parts. It makes sense, for example, that ". . . an initial evaluation is not complete until the therapist has (determined) whether the presenting symptoms are primarily psychogenic in origin or instead related to organic brain dysfunction or some toxic condition . . ." (Weiner, 1975, p. 58). Indeed, the therapist should be sufficiently knowledgeable about component parts such as the nutritional, gynecological, linguistic, neurological, pharmacological, kinesthetic, vocational, dental, physiological, sociological, and endocrinological. Certainly, the therapist should be competent in and able to utilize and shift among components that are Adlerian, Sullivanian, cognitive behavioral, Daseinsanalytic, rational-emotive, Jungian, personal construct, client-centered, humanistic, transpersonal, Gestalt, strategic, bioenergetic, psychobiological, ego analytic, and on and on.

In the initial evaluation, the therapist gauges how much of the problem is toxic and how much psychogenic, how much neurological and how much physiological. Then the therapist applies Gestalt treatment, switches to desensitization, moves to psychodynamic, with a brief interlude of client-centered, and finishes off with cognitive behavioral. To do all this, the therapist is competent in all these fields and approaches, and has some way of knowing how and when to shift from one field and approach to another. When the problem has components, and when the more you know about each part the more you know about the thing you are dealing with, then this is the way you operate.

In the class 1 position, there are simply alternative construct systems. If yours is experiential, then you work within the experiential construct system. You are competent in your particular construct system, in your particular approach. There are some genuinely practical implications of whatever position you hold on this issue.

Understand by Going Further into It versus Understand by Rushing Away from It

In the Class 1 approach, understanding means staying with whatever you want to understand. You go further into it. Your attention focuses more and more on it. You look more closely into it. You poke around inside it. You see how its working parts fit with one another. Your attention is on something that you want to understand, to grasp more, to know more deeply.

A woman complains about her husband's older sister calling her by her given name Ophelia, when everyone else calls her Sam. She likes "Sam," and she hates "Ophelia." A man gets nauseous when he is in fast-moving cars, whether or not he is the driver. Knowing more about these things, understanding them, means staying with them and going even further into them. The keys to understanding lie within the events themselves, so go deeper into the events. Clarify scenes and situations in which the sister-in-law calls the woman Ophelia. Describe these scenes more carefully. Penetrate into what is occurring in her when this is happening. Go further into what is taking place inside and outside when he gets nauseous in the fast-moving car. Clarify what is happening.

In the Class 1 approach, you stay within your construct system, and you get closer and closer to understanding the event by getting closer and closer into the event. You study the attended-to phenomenon itself.

In the approaches of Classes 2 through 6, you get an understanding of the phenomenon by rushing away from it. The keys lie elsewhere. Historical events usually contain the keys to understanding. Something in the woman's past helps to explain why she is so bothered by someone calling her Ophelia, or why the sister-in-law bothers her by calling her Ophelia. Perhaps her sister-in-law reminds her of her mother. Perhaps she was teased unmercifully when she was a child, and other children taunted her by calling her Ophelia.

Understanding comes when you get at the real, the basic, level of explanation. Perhaps the explanation of his becoming nauseous in fast-moving cars lies in neurophysiology. Check out inner and outer variables that determine the nauseous reaction. Check out precipitating causes. Get information that is cultural, sociological, genetic, biological, linguistic, psychopharmacological, chemical, auditory, psychoanalytic, cognitive, perceptual.

In the Class 1 position, you are inclined to understand by going further into it, by applying your constructs to get closer and closer into whatever you want to understand. In the other positions, you are inclined to understand by rushing away from the phenomenon, and by going to whatever you regard as the more fundamental level of explanation, or to the parts that make up the whole, or to other domains that lend understanding.

There Is a Real World of Objective Facts and Data versus Therapists and Patients Are Continuously Engaged in World-Construction

In the Class 2 through Class 6 positions, there are real things. There may be different kinds of physical things and different kinds of mental things, but basically they are all real. Therefore, psychotherapy can deal with objective facts and data. In the Class 1 position, therapists and patients are continuously engaged in constructing their worlds, and this may be done with or without a presumed real world of objective facts and data.

The person responds to the determining real world versus the person constructs the personal world.   If you believe in a real world, then it is easy to hold that this world determines the person, provides stimulation and influence, exerts stresses and pressures, fashions the person into being the way the person is, and is that to which the person must respond, adjust to, cope with. Throughout supposed growth and development, the way the person is depends on the external world's demands, stresses, opportunities, series of developmental stages (Sands, 1972). The world can be divided into various kinds of determinants and influences—genetic, traumatic, familial, biological, social, cultural, sociological. Whether in the past or in the present, there is a real world that determines the person and to which the person responds.

However, if you accept the Class 1 position, your construct system may be one in which it is the person who organizes, defines, architects, fabricates, and builds the world in which that individual exists (Buhler, 1971; Heidegger, 1963; Kierkegaard, 1944; Mahrer, 1971b, 1978/1989d; May, 1958a). There are several ways to do this task. In one of the ways, the person actively constructs the world to determine and control as well as to stimulate and influence the person. But it is the person who constructs the world in this way and invests the world with this power. In another way, a person may construct the external world with building blocks that are exceedingly real, but again, it is the person who organizes and uses the external world, even when that external world is quite real. The person constructs his situational contexts and gives meaning to these situations. Which position you hold makes for some serious and far-reaching implications.

The reporter as objective, accurate, and factual versus patient and therapist as world-constructors.   Psychotherapists who hold to one position believe that some reporters are more or less objective, accurate, factual, reliable. Generally, these psychotherapists accept that other professionals tend to be relatively accurate, objective, and factual. Accordingly, these psychotherapists use reports from lawyers, physicians, social workers, psychometrists, psychologists, psychiatrists, vocational counselors, guidance counselors. Sometimes the patient is judged to be a poor reporter, especially if judged as paranoid, depressed, schizophrenic, undergoing sexual or marital difficulties, retarded, a character disorder, having thinking difficulties, confused, in a panic state, and so on (Nelson & Barlow, 1981; Ripley, 1972). Then it is best to interview the spouse, children, siblings, parents, relatives, friends, colleagues, neighbors, employer (Korchin, 1976; Nelson & Barlow, 1981; Ripley, 1972; Sands, 1972). If you want to know what the patient is like, or what actually happened, get the information from reliable and objective witnesses. Then you can get at the facts.

In the experiential approach, there are no objective, real, factual data to be reported by reporters who are objective and reliable. Instead, there is a constructed world, and the therapist wants to know what this world is like. We emphasize the world described and lived in by this person, and not whether she is an objective and reliable witness of that objective, factual world. Reports from the psychiatrist or sister, whether accurate or inaccurate, are merely indications of the kind of world these individuals constructed with or about the patient. Whether these reports are otherwise judged to be accurate or inaccurate, they merely tell about the reporters' worlds, even though these worlds may include the patient as constructed by the reporters. If I read a report by the psychologist or psychiatrist, or if I interview the spouse or relative, I get a picture of how that person construes the patient. I do not look for what the patient is "really" like, or what "really" happened. Instead, I look for how this particular patient organizes and fashions the particular world in which he lives. In this approach, we do not need reports from objective and reliable witnesses, and the main reason is that we are looking for the way the reporter constructs his world, not whether the reporter is objectively factual.

The reported data as objective, accurate, and factual versus patient and therapist as world-constructors.   According to one position, there are objective facts and data. On the basis of these facts and data, psychotherapists draw inferences about the patient. They rely on objective data about the patient's endocrine system, educational background, recall, intelligence, the neurological basis of the hand-trembling, whether or not the patient has orgasms, what happens when he and his wife have those arguments, whether the boss was sexually harassing him, whether the patient's husband is aggressive and controlling, whether the patient has a learning deficit, whether the child is retarded or lies about where she goes in the afternoons, whether the patient's mother is cold and uncaring. Important inferences are to be drawn from the case history, from what happened in infancy and childhood. These therapists get objective information about the patient's life and then draw conclusions about the patient. Interestingly, the patient often is regarded as an objective reporter, on the basis of which the therapist concludes that the patient has a mental illness and therefore lacks objectivity. Whether or not the father had sex with the child, or the parents had raging fights during the patient's childhood are very important, because the adult patient is then called an incest survivor, a product of child sexual or aggressive abuse, or the adult patient is labeled as having delusions or distorting reality or having inaccurate childhood fantasies (Masson, 1984, 1988). It is important to know whether or not those earlier events really occurred.

If you shift to the Class 1 position, what is important in the experiential approach is how the patient constructs his world. The nature of that world replaces a concern with whether parts of the constructed world are objectively true or not. We do not check on whether or not she really completed two years of university, whether her mother really is obnoxiously domineering, whether he scores low on internal control or had termination problems with the former therapist. Nor do we check on whether her childhood included affectionate parents or a mean older brother, whether her father did those awful things or she was rendered deaf for almost a year before she was six years old. We are interested in the world that the patient constructs, and not whether the data are accurate, reliable, factual, and objective.

You may hold various positions on some of these issues in the philosophy of science, and the position you hold can make substantial differences in what you actually do as a psychotherapist.

What Is the Test to See If Your Truths Are So Rigidly Fixed That You Must Retain Them No Matter What?

Lots of therapists pour out unending strings of truths, whose foundations are harder than rock or steel. Some of these truths are at the level of comparisons among therapeutic approaches. Psychoanalysis is the deepest therapy, and gets at the foundations of personality. Behavior therapies are the treatment of choice for simple phobias. "Simple, nonpsychotic symptom patterns tend to respond favorably to a wide range of psychotherapies . . ." (Thorpe, 1987, p. 729). In long-term, intensive therapy, there is a termination phase, complete with its own issues and problems (Buxbaum, 1950; Blum, 1989; Ekstein, 1965; Ferenczi, 1955; Firestein, 1978; Fleming & Benedek, 1966; Gillman, 1982; Glover, 1955; Levy, 1986; McWiliams, 1986; Shane & Shane, 1984; Ticho, 1972; Weiss & Fleming; 1981). You know that early reinforcement and punishments determine basic behavioral patterns, that there are hereditary and environmental determinants of schizophrenia, that there are fundamental differences between men and women, that the therapist-patient relationship is essential for psychotherapeutic change (cf. Patterson, 1968, 1974).

Once truths are embedded as truth—once you hold to a philosophy of science position where there really are truths—then they may very well be absolutely fixed, rigid, stuck. What is the test to see if your truths are so rigidly fixed that they must be retained no matter what? One answer is to ask the therapist what kinds of evidence would be sufficient to give up the "truth" that psychoanalysis is the deepest therapy, that there is something called schizophrenia, that the therapist-patient relationship is essential for psychotherapeutic change. If there is no such reasonable evidence, then the belief is so rigidly fixed that it will be kept no matter what, for nothing can disprove it (cf. Popper, 1968). Most therapists would have a very hard time even considering the possibility of reasonable evidence, sufficient for them to give up their truths, because the very act of trying to find evidence violates the immutable and undislodgeable truth and forces therapists to conceive something other than that truth. A very great deal of what therapists believe and hold dear is beyond any reasonable evidence that would suggest giving up those cherished truths. If you do hold as true that there is something called schizophrenia, or that the therapist-patient relationship is essential for psychotherapeutic change, then try to mark down the reasonable evidence that would lead you to relinquish these concepts. If you can assemble such evidence, then these truths are open to being given up, and they are not so rigidly fixed that they must be retained no matter what. However, for many therapists, the very attempt is almost unthinkable, goes against their grain, and therefore these are truths that are so rigidly fixed they will assuredly be retained no matter what.

Am I talking about fringe therapists, around 3 to 5 percent of therapists who cling rigidly to a few notions, and who would continue clinging to matter what you showed them? No, I am talking about perhaps 90 to 95 percent of therapists. Furthermore, I am talking about most of the beliefs they hold dear. These truths are put into formal operation. On insurance forms, there is a place for diagnosis. Our secretary inquires about the patient's problem. If the caller has a "severe psychopathology," they are seen by certain therapists with certain approaches. Examination boards and journal editors ask about the kind of relationship you will establish and the nature of the treatment for this patient's bruxism, especially since he is out of touch with his feelings. Engage with just about any therapist and you will be flooded by a whole system of rigidly held truths. The whole system is most evident because such practitioners are operating with psychotherapeutic truths that are beyond disproof and that are rarely if ever subject to disproof on the basis of any reasonable evidence.

Most of what most therapists hold as truths is unable to pass this test. If their rigidly held truths are not really true, then what is the alternative? One alternative is chaos. If there is no such thing as schizophrenia, then the field of psychotherapy becomes chaotic nonsense. How can you even seriously entertain any alternative to the importance of the therapist-patient relationship? Again, one alternative is chaos. Another alternative is a shift to some other rigidly held truth.

If most of what most therapists believe is unable to pass this test, then most of what therapists believe is beyond reasonable evidence of their giving it up. Yet, if patients—not therapists—rigidly hold cherished beliefs beyond any reasonable evidence for giving them up, then therapists call these patients psychotic, paranoid, and similar nasty words (cf. Laing, 1982). Therapists are supersensitive to patients who are convinced that their notions are correct, that the world is the way these patients know the world is. There is no evidence the therapist can offer that has a chance at dislodging what these patients are absolutely convinced is true. Furthermore, they may well insist that others accept these truths. If patients are this way, then therapists may well call them psychotic, paranoid, schizophrenic. If, however, therapists are absolutely convinced that their own truths are true, if others must accept what these therapists know is true, if they too hold these truths beyond any disconfirming evidence, then they are scientific, right, accurate, objective. Maybe these therapists should be called psychotic, paranoid, schizophrenic.

Interestingly, many therapists, whose truths cannot pass this test, value research. Once again, however, these therapists almost certainly could not spell out the reasonable research evidence that would lead them to give up these truths. In general, these therapists and researchers accept and do research on matters that are outside their body of truths, and this body of truths is rarely endangered by the results of research (Mahrer, 1988b). If therapists know that there is something called resistance, and that some patients have a lot of resistance, then these therapists could identify virtually no reasonable research evidence that would lead them to give up this truth. Research may perhaps be done on distal propositions deduced from the truth of patient resistance, but the results of such research would not sacrifice the truth of patient resistance. If these therapists deduce that there are common themes among resistant patients' psychodynamics, demographics, and clinical and psychiatric histories, then it would be exceedingly difficult for researchers to soundly disconfirm these deduced common themes (Glatzer, 1972; Neil, 1979; Robbins, Stern, Robbins, & Margolin, 1978; Robertiello & Forbes, 1970; Saretsky, 1981). And even if the overwhelming weight of research failed to confirm common themes, it would be highly unlikely that this would endanger the truth of patient resistance.

Most accepted truths are safe from research. For one thing, it is the rare researcher who would dare to study a preciously held, accepted truth. Even if a researcher somehow decided to study such an accepted truth, which is difficult to imagine, it is unlikely that the study would be published, and in a journal that is supported by therapists who hold to that truth. In any case, few therapists would ever read the study and then dutifully give up the precious truth because probably no evidence would be sufficient for them to abandon the truths to which they cling. The sad truth is that few of these truths are ever put on the research block and they are almost immune to research.

DEVELOP THEORIES BASED ON PSYCHOTHERAPEUTIC KNOWLEDGE VERSUS CONSTRUCT PSYCHOTHERAPEUTIC MODELS THAT ARE USEFUL

I use the word "theory" in talking about the experiential theory of human beings and the experiential theory of psychotherapy. But I should use the word "model." I think there are big differences between developing theories of psychotherapy and constructing models of psychotherapy. More importantly, these dissimilarities are significant for the theorist, the psychotherapy researcher, and especially the practitioner.

You Want a Good Explanation and Understanding of It versus You Want to Find Useful Connections Between Working Things

If you hold to the positions of Classes 2 through 6, then whatever you deal with in psychotherapy has a real and knowable foundation. Accordingly, it makes sense that you try to find the explanation and understanding of it, whether it is your patient's overdependency or borderline condition, his being tense or his staying in treatment for just two sessions or two decades.

As a Class 1 position, experiential psychotherapy works with constructs about events. The aim is to look for connections between events, especially connections that are useful for achieving the goals of experiential psychotherapy. Useful connections tend to bring you to a relatively practical level. If you do this, that happens. When the patient is being like this, here is the consequence of the therapist doing that. The emphasis is on looking for working, practical connections, and this tends to keep you from ever higher levels of generality.

It is common for therapists to start with relatively big constructs such as borderline personality disorder or schizophrenia or social misfits. If you function in Classes 2 through 6, you will not only believe in the truth of these terms, but you will seek explanations and understandings of them. You will search for ways in which they are somewhat similar and consider these similarities as one kind of explanation and understanding. For example, you will compound your truth perspective by assuming that what is similar about borderlines or bipolars is that they have basic unfilled needs for taking from others, or are essentially empty, or are terrified of getting too close. You will then develop a theory of what explains and provides an understanding of borderlines on the basis of their similar underlying early histories or their shared psychodynamics. You start with a term such as schizophrenia, and you search for the explanation or understanding in the blood or in the genes. Your goal is to get a good explanation and understanding of borderlines, or bipolars, or schizophrenics.

According to the Class 1 position, you have committed one error by holding that there really is such a thing as borderline, as bipolar, as schizophrenia. Then you compound the error by seeking an explanation and understanding of it by looking for common needs, drives, early histories, blood chemicals, or genes. Yet this is what the positions of Classes 2 through 6 incline you toward pursuing. In contrast, in the experiential Class 1 position, we simply look for useful connections between working things. We frame constructs that are parts of useful models. We neither start with nor believe in the truth of borderlines, bipolars, or schizophrenia, and we certainly would not engage in a search for their explanation or understanding by looking for common needs, drives, early histories, blood chemicals, or genes.

There is, therefore, a very big difference between a program of trying to develop theories that provide good explanations and understandings of some "it" that you identify or construct and, in contrast, building psychotherapeutic models that provide useful connections between psychotherapeutic things.

We Need Theories That Depict the True State of Things versus We Need Models That Are Useful

Lots of psychotherapists like to develop theories. Theories are depictions of the true state of things. They usually consist of strings of asserted truths: Masochists are like this; patients with low internal control are characterized in this way; schizoids are like this; here are the stages of development; here are the mental illnesses; there is a growth force in people; here is the structure of personality; these are the things that determine behavior. In the field of psychotherapy, we have lots of theories.

My aim is to be able to accomplish quite practical things in psychotherapy. I want to find useful connections between things. I do not need higher order conceptual explanations and ways of understanding phenomena. Instead, I prefer to construct models that are useful. Models are not depictions of the true state of things. They are simply ways of picturing things, of organizing various connections in helpful ways.

The emphasis is on determining the truth versus the emphasis is on usefulness.   When you are working at the level of doing things in psychotherapy, it may be easier to think in terms of models that are useful. When you are thinking in terms of what human beings are like, it may be easier to think in terms of theories that depict the true nature of things. At the level of psychotherapy operations, it is easier to see if something works. My picture of psychotherapy can be seen as being useful or not, as working or not. When I finish a session, I doubt very much if I would be inclined to give up seeing human beings in terms of potentials for experiencing. Nor would I expect other therapists to give up notions about early learning being important, stages of development, the brain as related to behavior, the importance of cognitions, or the notion of an unconscious. Pictures of what human beings are like are too loose and general to be easily changed, too far removed from what occurs in psychotherapy to be altered by what seems to work or to be useful in psychotherapy (cf. Armstrong, 1982; Brush, 1974; Danziger, 1985; Feyerabend, 1975; Gould, 1981; Kuhn, 1970; Lakatos, 1976; Orne, 1969; Popper, 1968; Rosenthal, 1966). Pictures of human beings are easily pulled toward becoming depictions of the true state of things. They can easily become theories rather than models. In contrast, pictures of psychotherapy can more easily be seen as useful or not so useful. They can become models rather than theories. When it comes to psychotherapy, I believe we need models that are useful, and not theories that purport to depict the true state of things.

Once you take a position that there are truths, and that theories should depict the true state of things, then it is easy to become anchored in some approach that you believe is right. In contrast, if you take a position that you are looking for models that are useful, then you are probably less anchored and more free to shift from one model to a different one. If there have been few if any breakthroughs in the field of psychotherapy over the past few decades or so (cf. Mahrer, Freedheim, Norcross, Stern, & Weitz, 1989), it is perhaps due in part to our sticking with theories that are supposed to depict truths. If more therapists could shift to a Class 1 position, then it would be easier to sample different kinds of basic paradigms (Kuhn, 1970), to adopt models that may prove to be useful. Simply in terms of promoting breakthroughs and advancing the field, I am much more inclined toward models that are useful than toward theories that try to depict what we believe is true.

If you step back and look at the field of psychotherapy, does it seem that the field is able to accomplish more than 10 years ago, 30 years ago, 100 years ago? If we concentrate on what we can do as psychotherapists, my impression is that we cannot do much at all, and we have not progressed a great deal over the years. Attend to the end product. Look at what therapists can actually accomplish nowadays, compared with years ago. If you agree with me that we cannot accomplish much more than we could 50 years ago, then I am inclined to take the "body of knowledge" less seriously. The hallowed truths of psychotherapy seem to count for very little when therapists cannot do much, have little to show as advancement over the past 50 years or more. If psychotherapy as a field had been able to accomplish impressive changes, then I would be more inclined to take our accepted truths more seriously. But we have so little to show for all the supposed knowledge that we have. The net result is that it is much easier for me to dismiss the so-called truths of psychotherapy, to take the body of psychotherapeutic truths with a large grain of salt, and to look elsewhere for models of human beings and psychotherapy that might enable us to accomplish much more than the field of psychotherapy has been able to accomplish so far. When you salute the importance of usefulness, it seems easier to conclude that our supposed truths have not paid off. So perhaps we can drop the truths and look for more useful models.

If a theory is not a depiction of truth, then (a) anyone can describe anything in any way they want, or (b) you are free to construct models that are judged in terms of usefulness. In the beginning of the session, the patient says, "I went to the pond where I usually go when I feel like life isn't worth living, and I cried all afternoon. I thought about killing myself. That thought kept coming and I couldn't get rid of it. Finally I summoned up all my will and beat it. But I know it's going to come back, and maybe I won't have so much strength. I know it's going to come back." A therapist who listened to the tape provisionally diagnosed the patient as having severe depression. I listened to the tape in my way, and said that experiential listening yielded a feeling of being afraid of a weakness, a giving in, a vulnerability.

We talked about our different ways of making sense of what we heard. The other therapist believed in his theory as depicting truth. Of course the patient was a depressive. Of course there is a diagnosis of depression. There is a single truth, and his theory depicts this single truth. I said that his theory is a fine way of making sense of what the patient said, but it is only one way of making sense, at least in my position on this issue. Furthermore, since my goal would be to find a scene of strong feeling, the alternative to his concern with whether or not the patient was "really" depressed would not be just any old description, but one that could be useful to enable this patient to be in such a scene.

Therapists who hold to the approach of Classes 2 through 6 can easily believe that there is one theory that best depicts the truth. These therapists can easily believe that the alternative is sloppy phenomenalism. Anyone can believe whatever they want to believe, and that is not science; it is chaos.

According to the Class 1 position, you may very well construct any model you wish. But you can also adopt a criterion of usefulness. If you want to attain the four steps of experiential therapy, then which theory or model is most useful? Which theory or model of emotions is more useful if you want to attain Step 1, in which the patient is being in a scene of strong feeling? One alternative to believing in some theory that depicts truth is constructing a model that is useful to accomplish your goals.

We should contribute to a body of psychotherapeutic truths versus we should develop a science of psychotherapeutic practice. Theories try to frame the truths, and research should turn these into testable hypotheses and then see if they really are true. By means of good theorizing and good research, we can add to the body of knowledge that is psychotherapy. Theory and research work together. Start with the overarching theory. It is supposed to comprise an organized network of propositions. Apply logical reasoning and deduce hypotheses that can be tested (cf. Brodbeck & Feigl, 1968). When good research tests these hypotheses, you are able to confirm or disconfirm the propositions that constitute your theory of what is true about psychotherapy.

Suppose we take a closer look at the body of psychotherapeutic knowledge that is framed in our theories and is tested by our research. It seems to contain at least two bodies of truths (Mahrer, 1988b). One comes from the truths found in the theories of those who set forth the main systems of psychotherapy: Adler, Alexander, Ellis, Frankl, Freud, Jung, Kelly, Laing, May, Perls, Rogers, Sullivan, Wolpe, and others. The second is the body of truths from fields that are presumed to be basic to psychotherapy, such as learning, perception, motivation, cognition, biology, physiology, neurology, and the social sciences (Kiesler, 1971; Stigliano, 1986). Good theory and good research should contribute to our cumulative body of psychotherapeutic knowledge. This is one position.

There is an alternative position: We should work toward the development of a science of psychotherapeutic practice. This means that we should construct models that are useful and do research that helps to discover working connections in the clinical practice of psychotherapy. The aim of helpful research is to discover how psychotherapy works, what the working connections are (e.g., Elliott, 1984; Hill, 1990; Mahrer, 1988b), rather than to augment a supposed body of truths. The worth of a model is in relation to the state of the science of psychotherapeutic practice. The model is a useful picture, not a depiction of truth.

A key issue is whether you start with a theory-driven and theory-generated concern or with a quite practical and essentially simple matter. If you seek to develop a science of psychotherapeutic practice, you are inclined to start closer to the level of practical matters (e.g., what I say to patients at the very beginning of a session, how long a session is to be, what I do if a patient is silent). I want to know how to enable a person who seems to be on the verge of tears to be free to cry. I want to know how this person can be free of this headache. When I start at this more practical, naively simple level, I turn to models that may be useful tools for what I want to accomplish. Some models are more useful than others. If you start with simple practical events, you work toward a science of psychotherapeutic practice, and you are inclined to develop models that are useful. If you start with theory-driven and theory-generated issues and interests, you are more likely to be involved with theories and with contributing to and drawing from a body of psychotherapeutic truths. I prefer the former perspective.

Theories of psychotherapeutic truths (a) can, or (b) cannot, be improved by apotheosizing scientific rigor and research.   The field of psychotherapy is virtually filled with Class 2 through Class 6 theories that seek to define truths based on the idea that there are truths, and that seek to prove what they assume is true. Just about every approach to psychotherapy and every theory of human beings that goes with each approach assumes all sorts of psychotherapeutic truths. Yet these theories of ours are, I believe, almost uniformly loose and vague, far removed from the actual events that occur in psychotherapy. Even more deadly, our theories of human beings and of psychotherapy are essentially unable to show practitioners how to bring about convincing, effective, or useful consequences. The theories provide plenty of loose-fitting rationales and justifications for what practitioners do. We can explain, theorize, and rationalize; we can cast just about anything within the vocabularies of our theories. But the theories cannot seem to produce much that practitioners can do to bring about concrete and specific effects. Our theories fall short in terms of practical usefulness.

It is little wonder, therefore, that so many people in the field of psychotherapy apotheosize and deify scientific rigor and scientific research. Because our psychotherapeutic theories are so poor and so inadequate, so loose and vague, so insistent on asserted truths, it is as if the desperate effort after scientific rigor and scientific research can somehow hide these defects. We thump our collective chests in proclaiming how important scientific rigor and research are. We insist that ours is a science. We adopt what we proclaim are highest standards of scientific rigor and research. Our scientific journals are filled with studies that presumably have logically derived hypotheses, rigorous methodologies and designs, sophisticated statistics and mathematics.

However, no insistence on highest standards of scientific rigor and research can substantially improve these theories of psychotherapeutic truths. They are just too loose, too full of asserted truths, too calcified and immune from change, too far removed from concrete psychotherapeutic events.

If you must prove the truth of what you assume is true, of what you accept as true, then you will worship science, logic, and mathematics. They did this in the Middle Ages, and psychotherapists do the same thing today. It almost seems that if your truths are exceedingly loose and vague, worlds away from concrete practicality, then you are powerfully inclined to proving their truth by logic, research, and science. In the Middle Ages, the truths involved God, sin, goodness, the natural order. Today, the truths involve schizophrenia, personality disorders, cognitive frameworks, and the relationship. In the Middle Ages, theologians worshipped science, research, logic, and mathematics as grand justifications for the truths in which they unwaveringly believed. In the field of psychotherapy, we do the same today. It seems to me that our theories of psychotherapeutic truths cannot be improved by apotheosizing science, research, logic, and mathematics.

What Are Some Actual Uses of Theories of Psychotherapy?

Theories of psychotherapy typically are intended to depict the true state of psychotherapeutic things, and to provide therapists with a good explanation and understanding of those matters. Do theories of psychotherapy have any other uses? If we take a closer look, we will see that these theories serve other purposes.

Theories of psychotherapy are ways of dressing up common notions in technical vocabulary. Psychotherapists are not the first ones, nor are they the only ones, to have notions about what people are like and how they change. Most people have fairly well organized notions about what people are like, how they got to be that way, and how change can occur. What "theories" usually do is to take these common notions and dress them in uncommon vocabulary—in terms that make the so called theory seem scientific, special, technical, something that psychotherapists know.

If we forget about psychotherapists' technical sounding theories, and talk to just about any group of people, today or hundreds of years ago, it would be easy to see their "theories" of psychotherapy. Suppose that we listen carefully to barbers and athletes, bus drivers and nurses. These men and women probably have well worked-out notions about human nature, the kinds of troubles most people have, what it is that pushes people from inside, how the outside world can affect people, what makes them get mad or do dumb things or make their own lives miserable, what makes them go berserk or out of their minds, how things in people's early childhood help make them the way they are today, how much and what kind of things are already inside a person at birth, what kinds of stages people go through from birth to death.

There are probably 5 or 10 or so common notions of how people change, what you can do to help them change or to get them to change. In fact, many of these common notions are quite sophisticated and have a long history. There are common and sound notions of how to use groups to get people to change, how to use suggestions and persuasion, how to expose people to the scary thing so they are not so scared, how to get them to see things the way you know they should see things, how to cajole and sweet-talk them into doing what you want, how to win people's trust and confidence and how to make them like you so you can then get them to change, how to be their good friend or the kind of special person they value so that you can persuade them to change, how to dispense potions and ointments and herbs that will cause people to change, how to put them in special places that are good at providing the right context for change, how to use other people in their lives to get a person to change, how to use higher causes, big principles, and uplifting callings to get them to change, how to dress yourself in special robes, special positions, or special titles that help people change, how to use rewards and punishments that can get them to change, how to use tricks and ways of fooling people into changing, how to have them do special things that you get them to believe will help them to change, how to put people through special rituals that they believe will enable them to change, how to get people to "let it out" and "open it up" so that "it" is no longer inside and troublesome, how to get them to confess the terrible secrets so that they can feel better, how to understand all the important forces and influences that made them the way they are.

"Theories of psychotherapy" typically are these commonly held notions or theories, dressed up in uncommonly technical jargon and vocabulary. What is new is the jargon vocabulary, not the essential ideas and notions. Regardless of the kind of therapy or the amount of experience, psychotherapists seem to have notions about what people are like and how they can change that are essentially common notions wrapped in technical jargon and vocabulary (cf. Elke, 1947; Fiedler, 1953; Mahrer, 1962c).

Theories of psychotherapy are helpful ways of justifying the acts that therapists carry out; does theory beget practice, or does practice beget theory?   Most therapists like to think that first there was a theory, and then someone deduced how to do psychotherapy. According to theory, there is all this business about psychopathology and defense mechanisms, and therefore you do a diagnostic evaluation. The theory tells you all sorts of things about how patients change, and what helps and hinders change. It tells you that this kind of patient needs that kind of treatment, and doing this to that other patient is best because of that theoretical reason. The theory shows that this patient is to change in this way, and that patient is to change in that other way. Theories enable therapists to reason toward the things they do with this patient.

All of this is one way of looking at theories of psychotherapy. If you think in terms of models, then it almost seems as if a theory is used to justify or rationalize the acts that therapists find important to carry out with their patients. If you are surprised when the therapist, in the first session, forces the patient to admit to sexual feelings toward his baby daughter, the therapist justifies this as a trial interpretation to gauge the patient's ability to look inward and to seek psychic connections. How can you justify getting rid of a patient whom you don't like or are tired of after such a long time? Turn to theory: ". . . if he feels in need of a block of free time, he may give his patient an 'interruption': or, if he tires of a patient, he may terminate his treatment" (Szasz, 1965/1988, p. 129; cf. Mahrer, Howard, & Boulet, 1991). Providing an "interruption" or "termination" can easily be justified by theory. Therapists justify all kinds of acts by saying they did it because it strengthens the ego, builds a helping alliance, removes the patient's blocks, or is needed because of the patient's bipolarity or neurological deficit or low construct permeability. Assessment and evaluation are big business. "All too often, assessment practices are driven by the needs of the assessors, not the needs of the assessed" (Peterson, 1987, p. 28). However, psychotherapeutic theory is almost never at a loss to justify virtually any kind of assessment practices.

The doctor routinely tells patients over the phone that he does "psychoanalysis." He sits face to face with patients, holds their hands throughout the session, insists that patients keep their attention directly on his eyes, and always hugs patients after the session. How come? The answer is not given in terms of how doing this will help attain this working, in-session consequence. The answer is given by turning to "theory." Patients need to know that therapists are right here with them. Patients have to see both my professional and my human side. Neurotics have trouble being close. Patients need reassurance about their needs for closeness. It is important to build trust. These propositions sound pretty good, and therefore therapists find that theory is rather effective at justifying almost anything.

Theory is commonly used to justify what you do, and to justify your rejection of what another therapist does. If you do not like hugging your patients, then how can you explain why you do not hug your patients? One effective way is to turn to theory. Hugging patients is a denial of the therapist's deep-seated fear of patients. Hugging patients is dangerous for patients who have problems controlling sexual impulses. Hugging patients disrupts the establishment of a therapist-patient relationship. If a behavior therapist gives homework assignments, turn to theory to justify why doing that is bad. It takes time for patients to be ready to undertake behavior change. Suggesting new behaviors for patients leads to premature change. If the behavior therapist suggests that the patient might give roses to her sick friend, that may be all right. If the therapist suggests that the patient try anal intercourse, that is disgusting. But your rejection of that particular suggestion can be justified by calling on theoretical propositions. Just about anything that other therapists do and you are opposed to can be declined or even attacked on the grounds of theory. This is a fine use for theory, and it works.

Therapists do all kinds of things that they justify by theory. If you skip the elaborate theorizing and skip to the bottom line, you can usually see what is important for the therapist to do. Suppose that it is important for this therapist to be gentle, a good friend, one who sees patients for a long time by being easygoing and friendly. Does the therapist admit that he likes being this way with patients? Perhaps, but that is rare. Typically, the therapist justifies this with a whole string of general truths presented as theoretical reasoning: (a) This patient was viciously abused as a child, is quite paranoid, and has suicidal ideation; (b) the particular kind of therapist-patient relationship is a sound determinant of therapeutic change; (c) the helpful therapist role is the opposite of the one played out by the significant figures in the patient's childhood; (d) if therapists exert "too much stress," then that is "dangerous" for paranoid or suicidal ideation. The conclusion to this line of theoretical reasoning is that the therapist should be gentle, a good friend, one who sees patients for a long time by being easygoing and friendly. The four conceptual truths can be seen as an elaborate series of justifications for the final act. When it is important for therapists to do what they find important to do, they can easily justify their actions with theory.

In actual practice, therapists typically use theories to dress up common notions in technical vocabulary, and also to justify loads of acts that they carry out or do not want to carry out. I prefer trying to construct models that are useful for the actual in-session work of psychotherapy.

Theories of psychotherapy are ways to stake our claim over the territory.   By having a theory about it, we legitimate our right to it; we can have a piece of the action. Professions fight over who gets to do "it," and so each profession's theory can try to call it the social history, the case history, the psychiatric history, or the psychological history. We get to work on it if we can frame a theory of midlife crisis, family squabbles, a "lifestyle transition problem," or bodily aches and pains. If the person is divided into mind and body, and we are denied access to the body, frame theories about psychosomatics, about behavioral medicine; call it a theory of health psychology. Then we can have a legitimate claim to the territory.

If your theory of behavior means that others own thinking and feeling, just change your theory so that behavior includes thinking and feeling, and just about everything else (cf. Buffery, 1987). If doing a "behavioral analysis" prevents you from access to psychodiagnoses, then expand the theory of behavioral analysis to include psychodiagnoses. If you are still excluded from having a legitimate stake to psychiatric psychodiagnoses, have a theory of psychological diagnoses. You can own methods that are several thousand years old by having theories of what you call negative practice, contingency contracting, or intermittent reinforcement. Once you have a theory of it, you thereby stake your claim over it. There is very little that psychotherapists cannot create theories about.

How Do You Decide If "That" Is or Is Not a Part of Your Therapy?

By "that," I mean diagnostic assessment, or using archetypes, or working with dreams, or using the two-chair technique, or developing a transference, or assigning postsession homework. Some of these are relatively small and specific, and others may be relatively large and general. Some of the "thats" may be relatively routine and standard parts of your general therapy, such as doing a particular kind of diagnostic assessment. Others may be parts of your repertoire that you use when appropriate, like the two-chair technique. In any case, how do you decide if "that" is or is not a part of your therapy? I am going to suggest that what you include and what you exclude in your therapy come from at least two considerations.

Neither of these considerations has much to do with logical deduction from some theory of human beings. You might try to picture a general theory of human beings, such as a cognitive behavioral or a psychoanalytic or a psychobiological theory of human beings. Then picture someone reasoning carefully down to a theory of psychotherapy, and then even further down to using a method of thought-stopping or the two-chair technique. I do not believe that many therapists use most of their methods because some wise person logically deduced the methods from a general theory of what human beings are supposed to be like. On the other hand, most therapists would have little trouble justifying whatever methods they use (e.g., thought-stopping or two-chair technique) by relating them to notions about human beings. Then how do most therapists decide if any particular methods are or are not to be a part of their therapies? Here are two considerations that answer this question.

If your theory or model includes the concept or construct, then you will be inclined to do things based on that concept or construct. You have some kind of theory or model of human beings and of psychotherapy. If it includes a particular concept or construct, then you will likely do things based on that concept or construct. But if it has no place or makes no sense in your theory or model, then you will probably not do things based on that concept or construct.

Does your theory or model include concepts or constructs of mental illness, psychosis, psychoneurosis, sexual deviate, mental disease, personality disorders, schizophrenia, psychopathology, hebephrenia, paranoid schizophrenia? If your theory or model includes these concepts and constructs, if these words make solid conceptual sense, then you will likely do lots of things based on them. However, these words are not constructs in the experiential model of human beings or of psychotherapy. They make no sense in this model. Accordingly, we do not do "assessment and evaluation." We do not label patients with these words. Experiential psychotherapy is not a "treatment" for "mental illness." "Psychotherapy is the only form of treatment that, at least to some extent, appears to create the illness it treats" (Frank, 1973, p. 8.) We do not solicit the kinds of information you need to label a patient as having a mental illness or to determine how severe the disorder is (cf. Schlesinger, 1976). We do not try to see how it arose, what precipitated it, or what its prognosis is. Because there is no construct of "phobia" in our model, we do not go further to see if the patient is a behavioral responder, a physiological responder, or a cognitive responder in relation to that phobia (cf. Hugdahl, 1981; O'Leary & Wilson, 1987). Because there is no construct of psychosis, we do not assess, evaluate, or observe related constructs such as the patient's ideas of reference, depersonalization or derealization (cf. Nelson & Barlow, 1981).

We do not assess the patient's "need for therapy" on the basis of the "severity" of the "psychopathological condition." We do not do an "intake interview" to determine the "diagnosis." If you believe in psychopathology coming from fixations at early stages of development, you may ask how your patient fared through the anal-retentive stage. However, if none of those key terms make any sense in your system, then you will not be exploring the person's early history to look for "fixations" at the "anal-retentive" stage. If the diagnosis of "passive-aggression" is not a meaningful construct in your system, then you will probably not be diagnosing it, trying to figure out its etiology, or figuring out a treatment plan to use on it (Mahrer, 1983a). It makes little sense to do an intake evaluation or to do assessment and evaluation when what you assess and evaluate are not part of your construct system. Therapists can choose among hundreds of forms and instruments and questions designed for patients to fill out or answer before therapy: Did you play a musical instrument as a child? What was your father's occupation? These questions make sense if the constructs they are supposed to shed light on also make sense. If the constructs are not part of your system, then you will not gather all that information.

If the concepts and constructs are sound elements in your system—if they make good sense—then you will likely do all these things as part of your therapy. On the other hand, if the concepts or constructs are not in your system, and make no sense in it, then you will not do these things, and they will not be a part of your therapy. But this is only one way of deciding if "that" is or is not a part of your therapy.

If doing "that" is useful in attaining your aims and objectives, then you will be inclined to include "that" as part of your therapy.   This is the criterion of usefulness. If a method or procedure or operation is useful in attaining your aims and objectives, then including it makes sense. I use whatever is helpful in attaining the four steps. If a method or procedure or operation seems to have little or no use in attaining the four steps, I do not include it as part of experiential therapy.

My aim is to know the immediate world in which the patient is living, and to know the feelings and experiencings occurring right now in this person. If it is useful for me to close my eyes, allow the person's words to be as if they are coming in and through me, and to see the world that is created by those words, then this is what I do. If being face-to-face with the person is not especially useful, then that is not a part of my therapy.

In the opening of the initial session, I do what is useful for the person to move toward being in a moment of strong feeling. If telling a little bit about the therapy I do might be useful for that purpose, I would do it. But it is not especially useful. Nor is gathering information about the patient's intelligence, brain dysfunction, or schooling useful for that purpose. Nor is it useful to start by getting information about the patient's mental status, vocational history, social support system, family structure, or early traumas.

If you are going to help make some decision regarding this patient, then you need to do things to provide a basis for that judgment. The decision may be whether this person should be hospitalized, be removed from a particular job, allowed to stay in that school class, be admitted to a program, be with one or another parent. If I do not make those kinds of decisions, then I need not do what you do to get the information you need (cf. Szasz, 1965/1988). If I seek the underlying experiencing in the person right now, I would probably not try to get a social history or interview the spouse or get a psychiatric workup (cf. Ekstein, 1976). If assessment and evaluation would facilitate the four steps, I would use it, but I doubt it would be especially useful. Nor would it help achieve the four steps in this session to have some psychiatrist or psychologist write an evaluation of the person (cf. Breger, 1976).

In general, assessment and evaluation are of little or no explicit use in achieving the working aims and objectives of experiential psychotherapy. These are not achieved by having the patient subtract numbers, explain the meaning of proverbs, or tell the kinds of jobs she has had. It is of no use to see whether the therapist thinks that the patient has "delusional" thoughts or a "diffused identity," should be called an anorexic or bulimic or an attention deficit disorder, has moderate intelligence, is a product of a broken home, is not sure of the date, or is high on introversion.

If the Gestalt two-chair technique can help attain the four steps, I will use it; if not, I will not include it in my therapy. The same criterion holds for the doubling technique, self-talk, assertion training, or any other method or technique.

According to this perspective, specific and concrete techniques and methods are simply part of the public domain. No particular therapy owns any of these techniques and methods. Therapists are quite free to select whichever ones they want, and to try them out. If they are useful, then they may be used. According to this perspective, not only does no therapy own or have exclusive rights over any specific and concrete techniques and methods, but no therapy is properly defined on the basis of its current set of techniques and methods. Gestalt is not defined in terms of the two-chair technique. Psychoanalysis is not defined in terms of interpretation. Client-centered therapy is not defined in terms of restating what the therapist believes the patient is feeling.

If establishing a transference or building a therapeutic alliance is useful in attaining the four steps, I will use it. In fact, I find that virtually all these relationship methods and techniques are of little actual value in attaining the four steps, and therefore they are not part of experiential therapy. If having a good relationship is useful for explicit aims and objectives, then make it a part of your therapy (cf. Bernstein, Bernstein, & Dana, 1974; Morgenstern, 1988; O'Leary & Wilson, 1987; Peterson, 1968; Rimm & Masters, 1974). The criterion is working usefulness.

If you adopt this criterion, then you should have some relatively easy indicator of whether or not something proves to be useful. You may accept an outcome measure that inclines you toward being empathic, using the two-chair technique, or developing a helping alliance because studies seem to suggest that these methods are related to good outcome. You believe these methods are related to the kinds of follow-up test scores or patient interviews, or symptom checklists, or whatever you accept as indicators of the kind of outcome that you value. On that basis then, you may well include those methods and techniques. My indicators include the four steps, and also the presence of the new way of being and the reduction of the scenes of bad feeling in the beginning of the next session. Using my indicators, I would not be inclined to be empathic, or to use the two-chair technique, or to try and develop a helping alliance. You have your choice of what indicators to use, and you have a choice of whether to use these indicators or simply to accept established therapeutic principles and axioms.

How may you decide whether to make "that" a part of your therapy? How do you decide whether to include or to exclude some method, technique, some principle or proposition? If you accept this position on some of the issues in the philosophy of science, then there are at least two guidelines. One is that the constructs make sense in your construct system. The second is that the method or principle is useful.

How Do You Judge Whether a Theory or Model Is Any Good, Is Better Than Some Other Theory or Model of Psychotherapy?

Most therapists like to think that their theory or model of psychotherapy is good, and is probably better than others. The problem is how to compare theories and models to see which one is better or whether they are any good.

It is almost impossible to compare several theories or models by seeing which are better at grasping or depicting the true state of affairs. This would mean deducing hypotheses that can be tested to see whether or not they depict truth, and this enterprise is easily regarded as not feasible (Danziger, 1985; Feyerabend, 1975; Greenwald, 1975; Mahrer, 1988b; Newton-Smith, 1981). Quite aside from deducing and testing hypotheses, a common way of judging whether some other theory is as good as yours is to see whether the other theory includes your truths. If you hold to the truth of schizophrenia, the unconscious, and the therapist-patient relationship, and if the other theory does not, then typically you judge that the other theory is not as good as yours.

Maybe there are better ways of judging whether one theory or model is any good, or is better than another.

Figure out what a good theory or model should contain, and use these criteria to judge theories or models. There are formal properties of good theories, whether they are in the field of physics, mathematics, or psychotherapy. Relevant as these formal properties are, I am more concerned with what good theories or models of psychotherapy should contain, and here we have no substantial body of writings. There seems to be little agreement on what should be included in good theories or models of psychotherapy (Mahrer, 1987f, 1989g).

I am concerned about what a good theory or model of psychotherapy should contain because it would be nice to have something to work toward, some set of criteria. Accordingly, here are my suggestions for the components that should be present if a theory or model of psychotherapy is to be a good one:

1. It should place itself within some encompassing, larger theory or conceptualization of human beings.
2. It should identify the nature of the useful material to be elicited from patients.

3. It should tell how and for what the therapist is to listen and to observe.
4. It should provide a framework for higher-order description of patients.
5. It should provide a framework of its therapeutic goals and directions of change.
6. It should provide a set of principles of therapeutic change.
7. It should provide general therapeutic stratagems and programs of therapeutic change.
8. It should outline the patient conditions under which given therapist methods and operations can achieve given consequent patient changes and objectives.

To the extent that the theory or model includes these components, I suggest that it is a good theory or model of psychotherapy.

The theory is to fit well with the body of psychotherapeutic knowledge versus the model is to be useful in showing practitioners what to do.   One position is that there is a body of knowledge, of hard facts. We know that these things are true because of research. Theories are good to the extent that they fit well with the body of psychotherapeutic knowledge. Theoretical statements square with research and lead to hypotheses that are tested by research. For example, here are two principles of a cognitive theory of depression: "The first principle of cognitive therapy is that all your moods are created by your 'cognitions,' or thoughts . . . . The second principle is that when you are feeling depressed, your thoughts are dominated by a pervasive negativity" (Berne, 1966, pp. 23–24). This theory is good to the extent that these theoretical statements are reasonably accurate, objective, true, and square with research.

If the body of scientific knowledge includes things like depressive ideation, childhood abuse, and psychosomatic causality, then the theory is good to the extent that it includes these three things, and everything else that is part of that body of knowledge. If the body of scientific knowledge confirms that there is an inborn drive toward healthy functioning, and that removal of the obstructions frees people to move toward health, then a theory is good if it includes these notions and principles. Which theory can be shown to come closer to truth, to the way things really are, to reality, to research-confirmed objective, scientific knowledge? That is the best theory.

In this way of seeing whether a theory is any good, what is referred to as the body of knowledge contains what we accept as truths, as factual knowledge, as statements about the way things really are, and these statements are based on research.

But this is only one position. A quite different position is for "models" of psychotherapy. Models are good to the extent that they are useful, that they can enable the practitioner to know what to do. A model that fails to meet the test of practitioner usefulness is not so good. The connection between the model and its practical use may be loose or tight, close or distant, but the model has to be linked to its practical usefulness. The test of a model is the degree to which it contributes to a science of psychotherapeutic practice.

If the model cannot be shown to make any difference in what the practitioner does, then its usefulness is low. If it makes no difference whether the model includes or excludes constructs of deprivation motivation and biological instincts, then those constructs have little value. If the model can be used to spell out such things as goals and objectives, and how to reach them, then the model is useful. If two models include the same goals and objectives, and one yields more effective ways of attaining these goals and objectives, then that model is better.

Judge success and effectiveness in terms of your criteria, their criteria, or shared criteria.
You can judge whether a theory or model is any good, or better than some others by looking at criteria of the degree to which the theory or model is successful or effective. This
means that a theory or model would first have to spell out its goals, its aims, and objectives, and in a way that would allow someone to judge the degree of success and effectiveness in obtaining these goals, aims, and objectives. There are at least three ways of
using these criteria.

One way is for any theory or model to spell out its goals and objectives, and to see
whether they are generally accomplished. For example, in each session, I want to accomplish the four steps, and I want the person to (a) become the qualitatively new
person who is (b) free of the scenes of bad feeling. By looking at this session and the
next, you can judge the extent to which I was successful and effective (Mahrer, Gagnon,
Fairweather, & Coté, 1992). Ask each theory or model to specify its goals and objectives, and then you may be able to judge whether the theory or model is successful or
effective. I like this way of judging a theory or model. But it does not provide very well
for comparing different theories or models.

You can compare several theories or models if their reasonably important goals and
objectives are quite similar. If several theories or models actually hold similar goals and
objectives, then you can see whether one is better at attaining them. I am impressed when
researchers compare several theories or models on criteria that are truly shared as important ones by all the proponents of the theories or models. This is not easy to accomplish. I think it would be worthwhile to have more research like this.

I am not impressed by efforts to judge the success or effectiveness of one theory
or model using the criteria of another. It is far too common for one theory or model to
impose its goals and objectives onto other theories and models. The conclusion is typically that your theory or model is not as good as mine because it fails to accomplish my
goals and objectives. This is usually coupled with declarations that my criteria are universal, and that all theories and models are to achieve what I declare are the goals and
objectives for all theories and models. If I were to judge other theories and models on
their ability to bring about integrative relationships with deeper potentials, my impression is that experiential therapy would emerge at the top of the heap. Of course,
most of the other theories or models would probably not recognize the criterion.

Suppose that we start with the criterion that the therapy itself is successful or effective. That sounds good so far. Now we become more explicit. After each session, we
should be able to see whether there was a significant change in the patient. There is to
be a significant new way of being and a significant washing away of scenes of strong
bad feeling. Furthermore, we start using this criterion in the first session. If we use this
criterion, then most therapies would not do too well, but experiential therapy and a few
others would be at the top of the heap. The reason is that most therapies would not accept my criterion. If I state the criterion in a general and abstract way, most theories and
models would almost have to agree. That is, a theory or model is good if its therapy is
effective. The only ringer is that I have my own special meaning of "effective," which
most therapies would not accept. Whatever criteria you use to compare several theories
or models should be accepted by all the theories or models.

Some judges hold that the test of a fine criterion is the degree to which you can
logically deduce from the theory down to the actual practices carried out by the therapist. It would be almost ideal if you could state the propositions and logically deduce
the operations of the practitioners. If you wish to use such a criterion to see whether

10 or 30 theories are any good or are better than their neighbors, then you must make certain that the evaluated theories subscribe to that criterion. If they do, fine. But it simply is not playing fair to apply your criterion to theories that do not accept it and thus have good reason to decline being judged by it.

I am especially sensitive to this issue because the specific goals and objectives of experiential therapy seem to differ so much from the goals and objectives of many other therapies. However, when I took a careful look at the goals and objectives on which various therapies generally were compared, I was impressed that (a) rarely did all the therapies seem to share the same specific goals and objectives, and (b) most of the goals and objectives came from dominant or favored theories or models. It is probably best to judge success and effectiveness in terms of openly shared criteria, rather than just your criteria.

I believe that experiential theory and therapy can offer a new departure for the field of psychotherapy, can enable it to have a new foundation in the philosophy of science. The positions that you hold on these issues of the philosophy of science can make for fundamental differences in just about everything you do in psychotherapy, and everything you think about what human beings are like. We now turn to the experiential model of human beings.

CHAPTER TWO

A Thumbnail Sketch of the Experiential Model of Human Beings

This chapter describes the experiential model of human beings. Because ours is a model and not a theory of the true state of affairs, and because ours is an experiential model and not a behavioral or psychoanalytic one, the test of whether our model is any good includes the usefulness of the kind of therapy that goes with this model. The test is not whether this model includes the truths that you believe in. The test is whether this model works, not whether its parts are true or not.

Although this is only a thumbnail sketch of the experiential model of human beings, this chapter should be sufficient for matters of practice. If you are interested in a more detailed account of the experiential "theory" of personality, human development, or social change, there is an earlier book on these and related topics (Mahrer, 1978/1989d).

WHAT ARE THE BASIC WORKING PARTS OF PERSONALITY?

To describe human beings from an experiential perspective, it is helpful to sketch out some basic, working components.

Potentials for Experiencing

In the experiential model of "personality," human beings are made up of *"potentials for experiencing."* These are inner ways of being—ways that this person is capable of, or has available for, being. Each potential for experiencing is a way of being that is distinctive from other potentials for experiencing in this person. By "way of being," I am referring to something that has its own identity and characteristics, but it is not some kind of specific behavior, nor does it include some specific situational context.

Each potential for experiencing is no more than a mere potential, an available way of being. It has no property of a drive, a need, a push, or a pull. It has no intrinsic characteristic of being satisfied, fulfilled, or consummated. It has no properties of activation, force, arousal, or energy.

How to use words for proper description of potentials for experiencing.   It is important to know how to describe potentials for experiencing. Use words that refer to ways of being, but make sure that you do not use words that point toward specific behaviors, concrete actions. The words may include classes or categories of behaviors, but not particular behaviors. You may describe a potential with words and phrases such as being passive, moved about, giving in. Do not use phrases such as floating in water, being picked up by a powerful person who lifts you in the air as if you were a feather. You may use words such as being violent, explosive, destructive. But do not use behavior-filled and situation-filled phrases such as screaming at the child, smashing the old man against a wall, throwing a bomb into the crowd. Use words such as being gentle, loving, soft, but do not use words such as caressing the face of the loved one, cupping the rose in your hands, kissing away the tears of the child.

The words you use are critical. Think of the words you might use to give a thumbnail sketch of how an actor is to be in this particular scene. The words should define the character or way of being of the actor. Generally you would need to use a set of words to get closer to defining that particular way of being. The more words you use, the closer you come to grasping the exact nature of this potential. There is simply too much error and slippage in using single words such as the experiencing of isolation, sex, competitiveness, acquisitiveness, autonomy, achievement, aggression. Single words do not provide a good enough picture. You might use three or more words to identify the way of being.

Furthermore, describing a particular potential for experiencing means being located somewhere when you describe it, and relating to it in some way. If you are inside the potential for experiencing, or if you are outside but relating to it in an accepting or good way, the words you are likely to use will be different than if you are outside and describing the potential through a relationship in which you dislike it, recoil from it, or are bothered and disturbed by it.

The words should portray the potential either as if you are within, undergoing the way of being, and feeling generally good as this is occurring, or as if you are outside but relate to the potential in a good way. The words should not convey a picture of your disliking the potential, of your fearing it, disapproving of it, hating it, recoiling against it. The same potential may be described positively, with words such as strong, firm, being a leader, or, negatively with words such as pushy, domineering, taking over. The experiencing may be described as standing up for oneself, standing one's ground; or if you dislike it, the words may convey a picture of being childish, disobedient, resistant. The experiencing may be portrayed as being independent, autonomous, self-reliant. Or you may convey a disapproving picture by calling it narcissistic, arrogant, exclusive. The experiencing can be described by words such as tough, cracking through barriers, hard, firm. On the other hand, if you draw back from this experiencing, you may refer to it as sadistic, cruel, torturing.

Nor can you get a picture of the potential as bad, negative, hateful, disapproved, and then try to convert it to a picture that is acceptable, pleasing, appealing. Once you see a potential as bad, you have failed to grasp what it is. You cannot say, "What is the 'good form' of killing or sadism or violence?" You have missed the nature of the potential.

See if you can get a picture of different potentials for experiencing or ways of being from the following words: being mischievous, mean, nasty; being soft, gentle, tender; being excited, aroused, titillated; being dominant, controlling, in charge; being cold, hard, metallic; being drawn toward, attracted to, compelled by; being defiant, refusing, oppositional; being withdrawn, pulled away, distanced, removed; being free, liberated, opened up; being controlled, manipulated, dominated; being risky, adventurous, daring; being wicked, bad, roguish, irreverent; being independent, autonomous, self-reliant; being explosive, blasting, violently outbursting; being the authority, boss, the one in charge; being firm, tough, strong; being docile, compliant, yielding; being vital, alive, energetic; being playful, silly, whimsical; being delicate, brittle, fragile; being captivated, wondrous, in awe; being provocative, stimulating, arousing; being close to, one with, intimate; being invaded, entered into; being attacked, assaulted, harmed; being seen, exhibited, shown off; being the jewel, the precious one, the special one; being nurturing, succoring, caring for; being judged, evaluated, assessed; being encountering, confronting, directly facing; being confident, capable, competent; being honest, straightforward, candid.

Each of these sets of words refers to and describes a potential for experiencing, a potential way of being. A potential for experiencing may be accompanied with some kind of feeling, but the potential for experiencing is distinguished from the feeling. At any moment, a potential for experiencing may be accompanied by feelings that are good or bad, happy or unhappy, enjoyable or bothersome, pleasurable or painful. Yet the particular potential for experiencing is distinct from any kind of accompanying feeling.

Operating potentials for experiencing.   Some potentials for experiencing are more or less on the surface and are connected with behavior and with being in the external world. The person behaves, lives in the world, functions, operates on these potentials. They are given as "OP1" to "OP3" in Figure 2.1.

Any person may have any kind of operating potentials. If we look at a number of patients, there is no basis for most or even many patients to have similar operating potentials. Especially if we describe operating potentials carefully, it is likely that

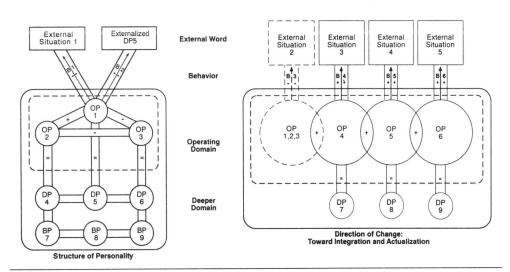

FIGURE 2.1   The Experiential Model of Structure of Personality and Direction of Change

virtually every patient may have a somewhat distinctive set of operating potentials. Nor do patients necessarily have the same number of operating potentials. Figure 2.1 includes three operating potentials. But any patient may have five or eight or just about any number of operating potentials.

As indicated in Figure 2.1, the person is being, behaving, and experiencing on the basis of operating potential 1. Yet this person may also operate on the basis of operating potential 2 or operating potential 3. While the person right now may be operating on the basis of OP1, in a few minutes or so, the person may be operating on the basis of OP2 or OP3. There is a consistency over time in that the person will tend to operate on the basis of the set of operating potentials. In Figure 2.1, this set of operating potentials is indicated as composing the person's "operating domain."

When the person is being one operating potential, the person is being an "I." This "I" is the voice and identity of this particular operating potential. The broader sense of self, the larger picture of who the person is, the sense of identity, can extend to the other operating potentials. Because the person rarely leaves the operating potentials, the picture of who and what the person is is limited to the domain of operating potentials. In Figure 2.1, OP1 may well be conscious of, knowledgeable of, aware of, OP2 and OP3, but that is about the extent of it. In other words, when a person who is talking about himself, says, "I am a whining little baby" or "I am an aggressive sonuvagun," the person is being one of the operating potentials and may be referring to other operating potentials, because his awareness or consciousness is essentially limited to the operating domain.

In this model of personality, there is no separate "I." The person who is talking is always coming from some operating potential. No matter which operating potential is giving voice, it can speak as an "I." In this picture of personality, the one who is talking and saying "I" is the alive, active, operating potential. There is no place, in this model, for a separate, intact "I." Almost every other theory has an explicit or implicit "I" that is almost a free-floating entity, somehow separate from everything else that is you, like a removed, executive control center. It is alluded to when a person says, "I am aware of my aggressive impulses" . . . "I have some irrational thoughts" . . . I have a problem with my dependency" . . . "I am a loyal and trustworthy friend" . . . "I have a choice about whether to be accepting of her or to be furious" . . . "I am changing my behavior" . . . "I have a low self-regard and self-esteem" . . . "I am conscious of my ambivalence." In many theories, there is indeed a presumed separate "I" that can talk about, be conscious of, and can describe, the rest of personality. In experiential theory, there is no such separate "I." The speaker, in talking, is being an active operating potential. There is no separate "I" that is removed and of a different order from an operating potential.

In many theories, this free-floating, executive "I" does such important things as have insight and understanding about oneself. After all, someone has to be the speaker when the person says, "I feel scared." Many theories have some kind of explicit or implicit thing that is this center of self, this "I-ness." In the experiential model, it is a given operating potential that is talking. In other words, operating potentials have the quality of speaking as a self, as the center of I-ness.

Deeper and basic potentials for experiencing.   Some potentials for experiencing are not directly tied to behavior. They are not directly connected with the way the patient acts, interacts, relates, and is living and being in the world. They are not the ones on which the patient directly functions or operates. They may be described as being deeper in the structure of personality. Some of these are described as much deeper, as basic. In Figure 2.1, deeper potentials for experiencing are represented as "DP4" to "DP6," and basic potentials for experiencing are represented as "BP7" to "BP9." Ordinarily, the person will not experience deeper or basic potentials.

Any person may have any kind of deeper or basic potentials. In any particular patient, a potential for experiencing of a given kind may be at the operating level or at the deeper or basic levels. What is at the operating level for one person may perhaps be at the deeper or basic level in another patient, if their potentials happen to be similar. Just knowing the nature of the potential does not allow us to say that it is an operating, a deeper, or a basic potential.

Basic potentials may well be, and probably are, quite different in each person. In other words, there are no universal basic potentials. All "basic" means is that they are further removed from actual behavior—from the operating level—than are deeper potentials. Basic does not imply that we know their nature or content. Even if we were to take a peek at a potential in one person, we would have no way of knowing whether this particular potential is at the basic, deeper, or operating level. Basic potentials for experiencing do not have to do with sex or aggression, with survival, or with anything that is assumed to be basic in other approaches. Basic potentials are not basic biological needs. They are not qualitatively different from deeper potentials, nor are they qualitatively different from operating potentials. They do not consist of instincts or grand forces such as actualizing tendencies or growth forces.

No special principles characterize basic potentials or describe how they function. The same principles that apply to basic potentials also apply to deeper potentials and to operating potentials. The only difference is that operating potentials work with the external world, and neither the deeper nor basic potentials have such direct contact with the external world.

Relationships between Potentials

In addition to potentials for experiencing, the experiential model of personality includes the ways these potentials relate to one another. The relationships may be good or bad, friendly or unfriendly. They are indicated as the plus or minus signs in the relationships between potentials in Figure 2.1. For example, there is a negative sign in the relationships between OP1 and OP3. This indicates that these two operating potentials have a bad relationship toward one another. They hate one another, fear one another, want to seal off and push away one another. Such relationships are fractionated, disjunctive, abrasive, opposed. The word I use is disintegrative.

On the other hand, relationships may be good ones. This is indicated as the plus sign in Figure 2.1, between OP1 and OP2. These two potentials feel good with one another, like and love one another, are complementary, harmonious, unified, peaceful, accepting. The word I use is integrative.

The nature of the potentials has nothing to do with whether their relationships are integrative or disintegrative, whether they feel good or bad about the other. OP1 (Figure 2.1) may have to do with being soft, gentle, tender, and OP2 may have to do with being firm, tough, strong. Yet their relationship may be integrative. This means that when the person is being and behaving on the basis of OP1 (being soft, gentle, tender), OP2 feels good toward the person, likes and loves the person, and the feeling relationship is integrative. On the other hand, if OP3 is the experiencing of being nurturing, succoring, caring for, and if relationships between OP1 and OP3 are disintegrative, then when the person is experiencing being soft, gentle, tender, OP3 relates with hate and fear, in opposition and disjunctiveness.

Potentials whose content may appear to be opposite or contradictory, or mutually exclusive may relate integratively or disintegratively. One potential may involve being dominant, controlling, in charge of. Another may consist of being submissive, controlled, giving in to. These may seem to be opposite when we look at things as being opposite. But the relationship between these potentials may be integrative or disintegrative, regardless of whether they are also judged to be opposite. The same holds for potentials of being outgoing, with others, a part of a group, and being pulled in, alone, by oneself. No matter whether two potentials appear to be opposite, their relationship may be integrative or disintegrative.

In this model, personality consists only of potentials for experiencing and their integrative or disintegrative relationships. These are the basic working parts of personality.

WHAT GETS AND KEEPS PEOPLE IN MOTION?

What gets people going? What activates them? What gets people to do things and to keep on doing these things? We can think in terms of motivating forces. We can believe in underlying drives and needs that serve as the power source, the battery that drives a person along. Maybe basic forces are built into people. Maybe external things stimulate people, get them going, provide motivation and direction. Perhaps social forces get people moving and keep them moving along. Perhaps there are some kinds of grand missions fueled by things like social belongingness or survival or biological development or growth forces or actualization.

Our answer is that all the variables that get and keep a person in motion are contained in the system itself. In this model, the short answer is that the person is put into motion and kept in motion by the system of potentials and their relationships.

Operating Potentials Use the External World to Enable Experiencing to Occur

Operating potentials have a job to do. They act on the external world to enable experiencing. Operating potentials do things in and to the external world, build and construct the external world, make the external world into whatever it has to be for experiencing to occur. In doing so, operating potentials use behaviors to build and construct the external world, and to enable the kinds of relationships that are important for the person to have with the world. In Figure 2.1, these behaviors are indicated as "B1" and "B2." Given a system of operating and deeper potentials, the operating potentials set things in motion by using the external world to enable experiencing to occur.

Operating Potentials Relate Disintegratively to Deeper Potentials

Relationships between potentials in the operating domain may be good or bad, integrative or disintegrative. However, relationships between operating and deeper potentials are almost certainly bad. The job of operating potentials is to maintain the very disintegrative relations toward deeper potentials. Whatever the nature of the operating and deeper potential, no matter how much you might think their respective contents are complementary or harmonious, relations are quite disintegrative. Operating potentials struggle to keep deeper potentials down, to block them off, to keep them out of the operating domain. Operating potentials fear and hate the deeper potentials, even though operating potentials cannot say exactly what the deeper potential is. Operating potentials work to keep themselves intact, and that means keeping distance from the deeper potentials, barricading against them, sealing them off. As far as the operating potential is concerned, deeper potentials are trouble. This disintegrative relationship is indicated in Figure 2.1 by the two negative signs in the relationship between OP1 through OP3 and the deeper potentials. It should be noted that the negative signs are in the operating domain. All this indicates is that disintegrative bad feelings occur in the person who is being the operating potential.

Operating Potentials Both Provide for and Prevent the Experiencing of Deeper Potentials

Operating potentials have two essentially equal and opposing functions. One function is to provide for and to enable some experiencing of the deeper potentials. In this sense, operating potentials are the agents of the deeper potentials. They serve the deeper potentials by enabling a measure of experiencing of the deeper potentials. For example, suppose that DP5, in Figure 2.1, is the experiencing of being hostile, hurting, mean, aggressive. Suppose that OP1 is the experiencing of being dominant, controlling, owning. To the extent that OP1 does its job, there is some experiencing of the deeper potential. The person behaves in and on the external world to enable being dominant, controlling, and owning in such a way that also enables some measure of the deeper experiencing of being hostile, hurting, mean, and aggressive.

The operating potential provides only a small amount—a glimmer or whisper—of experiencing of the deeper potential. Even if the operating potential is being experienced to a large degree, there is only a little bit of experiencing for the deeper potential.

Nor does it matter what the nature or content is of the operating and deeper potentials. They may appear to be opposites. The operating potential may seem to be a subclass of the deeper potential. The two may seem to be coupled together in some sort of complementary fashion. None of this matters. The operating potential will still provide for a measure of experiencing of the deeper potential. But this is only one function of operating potentials.

An equal but opposite function is for operating potentials to prevent the experiencing of the deeper potentials, to ensure that the experiencing is reduced, constrained, truncated, diluted, kept down to a soft glow at most. Operating potentials block off the deeper potentials, keep them sealed off and distant. If operating potentials did this job well, the deeper potentials would be barricaded and pushed so far down that they would be buried forever and never heard from. In a sense, operating potentials accomplish some of this second function by their sheer presence between the deeper potential and the external world. A deeper potential for being hostile, hurting, mean, aggressive could be experienced directly if it were an operating potential, directly opened to the external world. Because there is an intervening operating potential, the deeper potential can only be experienced somewhat.

The operating potential also prevents experiencing of the deeper potential by building an external world that provides little opportunity or even virtually no chance at all for the experiencing of the deeper potential. If the deeper potential is the experiencing of being hostile, hurting, mean, and aggressive, how could the operating potential and external world be so that there is almost no possibility for such an experiencing? The technical question is what kind of operating potential would be able to construct an external world designed to prevent the experiencing of such a deeper potential? One answer is for the operating potential to be almost the polar opposite, and for the person to build an external world that wraps itself around the operating potential and has essentially no place for the deeper potential. The operating potential may be that of being genuinely nice, sweet, delicately shy. The external world fits well with this operating potential, and has virtually no place for the experiencing of being hostile, hurting, mean, and aggressive. Indeed, to carry out this function, the operating potential and its external world may be seen as denying the deeper potential, disproving the deeper potential, demonstrating convincingly that this person is absolutely not hostile, hurting, mean, and aggressive. Any operating potential will do if it can carry out this function. The operating potential need not be the polar opposite. It merely has to ensure that there is little or no opportunity for the experiencing of the deeper potential.

Operating Potentials Fluctuate between Carrying Out Their Experiencing-Enhancing Functions and Preserving Their Existence

As operating potentials go about their functions, one of the consequences is that operating potentials may thereby close out their very existences. The changes that operating potentials bring about through their work could have the dangerous effect of ending the existences of the operating potentials. The net result is that operating potentials carry out their functions—but not too much. There is a kind of balance, a governing of just how far to go, a back-and-forth within relatively narrow limits.

Suppose that the operating potential (OP1, Figure 2.1) is the experiencing of being dominant, controlling, owning, and that its deeper potential (DP5) is the experiencing of being hostile, hurting, mean, aggressive. As the operating potential carries out its role of providing for its own experiencing, that experiencing increases. There is increasing depth and breadth of this experiencing. It gets stronger, fuller. However, OP1 is also related to DP5. It provides for the limited experiencing of the deeper potential. This means that the more the person achieves experiencing of being dominant, controlling, owning, the more the deeper potential is activated, made alive, given a measure of experiencing. Here is where the trouble starts.

If you look at Figure 2.1, DP5 is situated outside and below the domain of the operating potentials. The deeper potential may be situated just a little below, or moderately below, or quite a bit below. As the operating potential does its job, it enlivens the deeper potential and gives it experiential life; there is some little experiencing of being hostile, hurting, mean, aggressive. Picture the deeper potential rising. As the person experiences more of being dominant, controlling, owning, the deeper potential is lifted toward the outer boundary of the operating domain. The deeper potential begins to intrude into the operating domain, to poke its head through, to begin to enter into the operating domain. Here is the trouble.

The operating potential bears disintegrative relationships toward the deeper potential as indicated by the two negative signs in the relationship. As the deeper potential comes closer to approaching and even to intruding and entering into the operating domain, those two negative signs increase to three or more. The person will undergo heightened bad feelings of disintegration, terror, sheer anxiety, falling apart, going to pieces—feelings of the ending of one's very existence. The person feels these awful feelings in relation to the monstrous, grotesque, twisted deeper potential; instead of the experiencing of being hostile, hurting, mean, aggressive, it looms as the worst possible form of what it is. Even worse, the operating potential, caught in the throes of the terrible disintegrative relationship of its own making, senses the end of its very existence, because that is what a truly disintegrative relationship means (Ellenberger, 1958; Laing, 1975; May, 1958b).

Here is where the operating potential must function to prevent the experiencing of the deeper potential. It switches from providing for, to preventing the further incursion of, the deeper potential. The operating potential ceases its work of enhancing, experiencing, and shifts to truncating experiencing. The operating potential may easily accomplish this by shutting down, or by giving way to another operating potential. For example, there is a movement to OP2. This switch solves the problem of the intruding DP5. However, the scenario then continues between OP2 and DP4.

The continuous fluctuation between the operating potentials carrying out their experience-enhancing functions and preserving their existence results in a relatively limited range of allowable experiencing. The sheer degree or intensity or saturation of experiencing of the operating potentials is kept within a limited safe "normal" range, with normal defined as the degree of experiencing above which the deeper potential enters the domain of the operating potentials. There is continuous movement toward and away from experiencing, toward increasing and decreasing experiencing, but never too far.

This scenario occurs regardless of the nature or content of the operating and deeper potentials. It occurs when the operating potentials seem to be instrumental means of providing for the deeper potential. It occurs when the operating potential seems to be effective ways of hiding, opposing, preventing, and shoving down the deeper potential. It occurs when the operating and deeper potentials seem to be polar opposites of one another.

Here is the experiential answer to the question of what gets and keeps the person in motion. Essentially, the operating and deeper potentials are related to one another so that the system gets itself into motion and keeps itself in motion. Because there are potentials for experiencing, there is movement toward experiencing. Because these potentials are in relationship, there are consequences of experiencing. There is no single grand plan, no long-range mission, no driving forces, no forces to keep the system in equilibrium. There is predominantly the enabling of experiencing and the truncating of experiencing.

TO WHAT EXTENT AND IN WHAT WAYS DOES THE PERSON CONSTRUCT THE EXTERNAL WORLD?

One common answer is that there is a real external world which acts on the person; and the person responds and reacts to the external world in his own ways, depending on such things as his state, condition, and history. In this common answer, the person is regarded as "constructing" the external world minimally, except when in some kind of extreme state or condition in which the person "constructs" an unrealistic or distorted personal external world. This is not the answer in the experiential model.

The experiential model sees human beings as being the constructors of their worlds. In saying that human beings are at work "constructing" their worlds, I am using the word in both its active and more passive meanings. By constructing, I mean actively creating, fashioning, causing, architecting, establishing, building, designing, moulding, organizing, and bringing about their worlds. I also mean constructing in perhaps more passive meanings of processing, utilizing, perceiving, selecting out, giving meaning to, and capitalizing on their worlds.

However, because the emphasis is on patients, I am excluding how young children or infants may or may not construct their worlds, and I am also excluding how groups of people construct social phenomena (cf. Mahrer, 1978/1989d).

In the experiential model, human beings are described as using four different modes or ways of constructing their worlds. This can make things rather complicated because many other theories tend to favor a single main way that they see human beings as constructing worlds. Furthermore, in the experiential model, a person may use any or all four modes, may favor one mode for a while, and may easily shift from one mode to another.

In this model, the building blocks for constructing the person's world may well be "real" and also may be "unreal." The person may use building blocks that lots of people can see, that can be identified, weighed, touched, and so on. The person may use a pencil, a car, another person. Or the person may use building blocks that are exceedingly unreal, such as an inner voice, a person whom no one else can see, or an image of something that no one else can touch, see, locate, or describe. Nevertheless, there are four ways, in this model, by which human beings construct external worlds.

Does the external world affect the person, act upon, mold, do things to, determine, impinge on the person? Yes it can. In each of the four ways, the person may construct an external world that acts on the person. The person may actively construct an external world that can hurt the person, make the person feel awful, constrain, and restrict the person. The person can create an external world that is all-powerful and that renders the person helpless. This can occur through each of the following modes by which the person constructs and uses the external world.

The External World Acts on the Person, and the Person Receives It in His or Her Own Way

In this mode, there is a real external world. The external world presents itself to the person, acts on the person. The person does not make this external world, does not cause it or construct it into being. The person does not activate the external world. The situation or the external thing is simply there, presenting itself to the person, serving as an external cue or "stimulus."

However, it is the person who actively takes on the passive role of being the one on whom the external world acts. Not every person lives in the external world in this way, by means of this mode. Not every person necessarily adopts a position in which the external world acts on the person. A person may or can live in this way, but there is no law that this is the way the person must be in relation to the external world.

Even more important, once the external world presents itself to the person, acts on the person, at that very point it is the person who actively determines how the intrusive external world is to be received and what the presented external world "means." The person defines the presented external world.

The patient's baby may reach out and grasp the patient's finger. How the patient receives this is determined by the patient's potentials and their relationships. The patient may well have nothing at all to do with the fellow racing out of the corner store and knocking her and her friend onto the sidewalk as he screeches by. But how the patient receives the knock-down, how the patient experiences this, comes from within the patient. When the patient's mother dies or when the patient's brother says, "Can I come stay with you for four or five months?" the patient may have no hand in arranging for these events. But it is the way the person is that determines how the patient will receive the mother's death or the brother's question.

The external world can include real things that are inside the person's body: a baby, inside the womb; or a virus; or some chemical or drug (Mahrer, Young, & Katz, 1960). The external world may very well be responsible for introducing these things inside the person. But the way the person receives them is a function of the individual, who determines how to respond to this thing inside, regardless of how it got there or what it is.

This means we have to be careful when describing the external world. It is all too easy to describe the external world by including how the person is supposed to receive it. We cannot, in this approach, say that the baby was loving or friendly. The patient may instead have received the baby's reaching out and grasping the patient's finger with pride in the baby's strength of grip, or as an indication of the baby's preciousness. We cannot say that mother's death was a "stress" because the patient may receive it in ways other than as stress. We must be exceedingly careful to describe the external world only in so far as it presents itself to the person, and to grant the person the right to receive it in his or her own way.

The External World Is Merely Available, and the Person Uses It in His or Her Own Way

In this second mode of constructing an external world, the person uses whatever may be present and available to build whatever kind of external world is important to that person.

The person can use the external world simply by the way he perceives it: The room is filthy or casual; the acquaintance is self-confident or arrogant. It is the person who actively selects out this or that element of the external world to perceive in this or that way. It is the person who selects out the little pimple on the nose of the friend and sees it as disfiguring or distinguishing. It is the person who selects out the rise in volume of the other's voice and perceives it as irritation or uncertainty.

The person may use the external world by selecting out the aspect to engage with. Audrey selects a series of unsure and confused men and uses them to infuse with her inner strength. As William walks along the street, he selects out the oncoming huge fellow to gape at. The couple selects out this particular street of manicured lawns as the place to buy their home. The series of unsure and confused men were simply there, so too was the huge fellow walking along the street, and so were the manicured lawns. These are merely available parts of the external world, available for the person to use in whatever way is important for the person. The lovely stand of trees is merely present, and different people can use it in their own ways.

The external world provides plenty of readily available resources, some simple and some complex. Some of these resources are ready-made. All the person does is to use them. Stone walls are hard; if you smash your head against a stone wall, your head will probably hurt. Penny is cold and unfeelinged; if you try to get concern and love from her, you will probably fail. Babies usually cannot cook and provide food for themselves; if you want babies to be reasonably healthy, you will likely have to provide food for them. Umbrellas usually keep rain from getting you wet; if you use an umbrella properly, you will probably not get wet.

There are lots of available building materials that people might use to build a house or a bridge or a tower. The materials might consist of a cave in the woods. A person can use this cave as a place to live. Or the materials might consist of nails and wood and steel. It takes more work to build a place to live with these materials.

In this second mode, the person constructs the external world simply by using what is already there.

The Person and the External World Can Work Together to Construct Something New

In the first and second modes, you are limited to the part of the external world that impinges on you or is available for you to use. In this third mode, there are far more possibilities for creating new external worlds. But it requires far more activity.

It is as if the person and the external world work on one another to see how they can create something new. You and another person each rotate one another, try out different ways of fitting together, work together so that the two of you construct something that may not have been there before. It took the two of you, working conjointly on and with one another, to construct the new thing. You and the other person may change one another or the two of you may remain somewhat the same, but you and the other person have constructed something that was not there before. I induce you to be some way, and you do the same to me. If we succeed, then we have conjointly constructed something new.

There are lots of ways of describing this third mode. It may be referred to as codefining, coconstruction, conjoint construction, or as mutual role induction; and we may choose terms to signify that the whole is more than its parts, that the group is something more than the persons who are its members. You and the other person can work together to evoke something that lies available in each of you. You and the other person can conjointly construct a partnership or an opposition, a team or a group that was not there before. We can create our group, and thereby create some other group that is not us, that perhaps is our enemy. None of this was there before. We constructed it, and we constructed it by our working together.

The possibilities are enormous. Even if it is just you and I, what we can create together is almost without limit. We can do all sorts of things to one another, each creating the other as the external world. If we do this by fashioning a dyad, a group, then we have increased our power manyfold.

The Person Can Actively Create an External World

In this mode, the person is even more active in constructing an external world. Indeed, in this mode, the person is essentially the complete and wholesale builder of the external world, the creative inventor, the complete manufacturer.

You may create something that is real or not real. You may actively create a business where there was none, a political party, a dam, a whole city, spaceships, a work of art, a lovely garden. You created these things, and they are real. They were not there before. Now they are there. Or you may actively create new external worlds that are unreal. You may create creatures from outer space, snakes that are under your bed, a world of elves and gnomes, walls that undulate, gods and goddesses that cavort in mountain valleys.

I can create a beautiful garden where there was none before by digging the ground and putting in the flowers. I can also create a beautiful garden in fantasy, in my own imagery. This garden may be private, and no one may be able to see it. Yet I created it. You may call my garden a delusion or a distortion of reality, or a thing of beauty, but none of this detracts from my having actively created it.

Everyone can, and almost everyone does, actively create their external worlds. It is not the exclusive priority of truly imaginative people nor of people who are peculiar and out of their minds. Rather, it is a process that most people carry out most of the time.

You can actively create an external world that is powerful, that does things to you, that renders you passive. You can actively create an external world that is a gigantic complex of stimulations, and you are merely a complicated set of responses. In this constructed world, your attitudes, your coping skills, even your ways of thinking, are brought about by forces and processes that are beyond you. You can create a world in which the way you are today is a function of how your family treated you, of powerful psychological, biological, and social forces. You are the passive product of forces and processes that molded and shaped you from before you were born, throughout your childhood, and on into the present day. You have actively created a world in which you are the passive product. We actively construct a world in which things influence us; mold and shape us; affect and effect us; fill us with behaviors and actions, thoughts and ideas, feelings and emotions. This powerful world is our own personal creation; we actively constructed it so that it leaves us passive.

We can affirm that there really is a powerful world that influences and determines us. We can firmly believe in and insist on its truth. We can find this truth in our textbooks. It is scientifically proven, understood, established. We have the power to construct a world in which we are passively done to.

These are the four ways that people construct and affect their external worlds, and get their external world to affect them. None of these ways are exclusive to the experiential model. However, what does seem rather unique is that the experiential model accepts all four modes of constructing external worlds.

WHAT ARE THE PURPOSES OR FUNCTIONS OF THE CONSTRUCTED EXTERNAL WORLD?

The simple answer, in the experiential model, is that the external world is constructed to enable experiencing of the person's potentials, and also of the person's relationships between potentials. As indicated in Figure 2.1, the external world is constructed to contain external situations—situational contexts—and to contain externalized deeper potentials. Using the four modes described earlier, the person constructs an external world to serve as external situations for the experiencing of operating potentials, or to serve as externalized deeper potentials with which the person can relate in disintegrative ways.

Making sense of and understanding this person's external world means seeing the ways in which the external world is used as situations to enable the experiencing of operating potentials. It also means seeing how the external world is used to contain externalizations of the person's deeper potentials, and how the person relates to these externalized deeper potentials.

From this viewpoint, the person works hard at constructing an external world in which to feel good or feel bad. Feeling good or bad is therefore both a cause and a consequence of the person's effort to construct the right kind of external world.

The External World Is Used as the Context for Experiencing

An operating potential is a readiness for experiencing. Consider the experiencing of loving, cherishing, being close to, sharing. This experiencing calls for some kinds of appropriate external contexts. The function of the external world is to provide the situation that is appropriate for this experiencing. You may construct a situation involving a mother who holds your hand and looks at you in love, or a little baby who falls asleep in your lap, or a wife who belts out your name as she opens the door and runs into your arms.

At just about every moment, no matter how the person is constructing the external world, the world is a situation for the experiencing of operating potentials. Suppose this is the experiencing of being insignificant, part of the landscape, unintrusive. The situation may occur in subtle little circumstances, such as being in a group of four people, who are animatedly engrossed in talking about an important election. The person says something on another topic, and trails off at the end, so that no one hears the complete sentence. There is an experiencing of being outside, insignificant, overlooked, a nothing. Or the situation may be bigger and more dramatic, such as entering a race for an elected position, and listening to the results by yourself, at home, hearing that the winner received almost 4,000 votes, and you came in last, with barely 100 votes.

The operating potential may be accompanied with feelings that are good or bad. In the preceding situations, the experiencing may be accompanied with painful feelings. But the same experiencing may be accompanied with good feelings, and then the person will build other kinds of situations. He sits with friends and listens, is genuinely interested in them. There are three friends, sitting, having coffee. He is generally quiet, but attentive. He lives by himself in a small house on the outskirts of a small village. He enjoys fishing. At church, he is typically quiet. The feelings in him are soft and pleasurable. The situations of his life enable an experiencing of being insignificant, part of the landscape, unintrusive, in a way that feels peaceful and nice.

The external world may be used as a good-fitting, effective situational context for experiencing the potential. Or it may be only slightly appropriate, slightly effective. In any case, one prevalent use of the external world is as contexts, situations providing for and enabling the experiencing of operating potentials.

The External World Is Used as Externalizations of Deeper Potentials

The external world is also used to house or to be deeper potentials. No matter how the world is constructed, it can be used as the externalization of the deeper potentials. Because relationships with deeper potentials are disintegrative, what faces the person is the awful, grotesque, monstrous, bad form of the deeper potential. It is the deeper potential seen through the channel of the disintegrative relationship. The tragedy is that human beings are hard at work, constructing the world into monstrous externalizations of their own deeper potentials. In Figure 2.1, this is indicated as "Externalized DP5."

The deeper potential may occur as a generalized outer world, the society, the group, traditions, rules, the organization. Or it may occur as a concretely specific thing: my spouse or child, my parent or sibling, my colleague, car, hatchet, dog, or garden. Whatever it is, it is there in the external world. We may call it projection, hallucination, delusion, ideas of reference, but at its core it contains the deeper potential, and its occurrence enables a measure of its experiencing.

Typically, there is a special affinity between the person and that thing out there which is the hated and feared deeper potential. You know it well, even though it is so awful. When your deeper potential is extended into the external world, or looms back at you from the external world, there is a special kind of bond between you. Through this bond, you gain a token measure of experiencing of what it is.

Not only does the person gain a measure of experiencing of the deeper potential, out there in the external world, but there is a second use. The person can establish with the externalized deeper potential the same negative, disintegrative relationship that occurs between the person and the deeper potential. Suppose that the deeper potential is the experiencing of being the leader, the head, the chief, the big boss. And suppose that the operating potential is the experiencing of being open, guileless, transparent. Throughout this man's life, he has populated his external world with a series of people who were the externalizations of his deeper potential: his mother, a college teacher, a superintendent, a union head, and his wife. Relationships with these externalized deeper potentials were uniformly nasty, tense, hateful, tormenting.

The person works at constructing the external world into being the deeper potential, and then caps this off with having the relationship be exceedingly disintegrative. No matter how the person constructs the world into being the externalized deeper potential, it is predetermined that relationships will be fearful and hateful, filled with pain and unpleasantness. It may take a long time, and the person may accomplish this almost singlehandedly. For example, the mother conceives a baby, and gradually shapes it into being the one who orders her about, issues commands, acts like the big boss, while she fears and hates the monster she created. On the other hand, the person may walk into a room and be filled with instant hateful loathing toward the supreme commander sitting over there, issuing orders to the passive followers. In any case, the external world commonly constitutes the externalized deeper potential so that the person can relate to it in the same disintegrative way that the person relates to the deeper potential.

The two purposes or functions of the constructed external world are given in Figure 2.1. There are no grand or glorious purposes, no magnificent aims. The person uses various modes of constructing the external world into all sorts of situational contexts for experiencing, or into externalizations of deeper potentials, to enable experiencing and to undergo the relationships between potentials.

WHAT ACCOUNTS FOR BAD FEELINGS?

What accounts for the person's feeling bad, awful, miserable, rotten, anguished? What can a person do to practically ensure that feelings will be bad? There are different ways of accounting for bad feelings, but all are indicated in Figure 2.1. Whatever words you use to describe bad feelings, they are mainly the consequence of disintegrative relationships between potentials. Bad feelings are not caused by the external world, but by the person who constructs and uses the external world in ways that are accompanied by such feelings. The determining agent is not the other person or the situation. Bad feelings are not caused by external stress or pressure, trauma, or precipitating factors. They are caused by the person who uses the other person or situation, who constructs the external world into being a stress, pressure, trauma, or precipitant. Here are the several determinants of bad feelings.

Painful Behavior: Bad Feelings Are Behaviors That Provide for Experiencing

Some bad feelings are right out on the surface. They show. They are manifest. Picture a person with a look of being hurt. The look is on display and is a look that most of the audience can see. It is a good look, a compelling look. Some children and some adults are very competent at showing looks of being hurt.

When a bad feeling is manifest, it may very well do the same job as other kinds of behaviors; it may provide for experiencing and is indicated as B1 and B2 in Figure 2.1. Bad feelings can serve as behaviors because they enable experiencing of operating potentials. Grandmother is sitting at the table. The family is talking about what she wants them to talk about, namely, people they have all known for many years. Sam and Edna start talking about their respective law firms. Grandmother throws angry darts at them with her eyes. Her face is drawn and tight. Grandmother feels bad. The feeling is real, and it enables the experiencing of being angrily controlling, making others do what she wants, being the absolute boss.

Florence and Edgar have been living together for three years. Sex has become infrequent. They both work. He comes home, and they make dinner. Around bedtime, Edgar becomes anxious and tight about work. Things are going wrong. He frets. He moans. He feels bad. He is so tense that he cannot get to sleep. The bad feelings enable the experiencing of pulling away, keeping distance from, not being too close. The bad feelings are real, and so too is the experiencing they serve.

There is an experiencing of being cared for, attended to, nurtured. One way of enabling this experiencing is by having feelings of being sad, blue, gloomy, especially as a sharp contrast to the way one usually appears. These bad feelings are effective in constructing the appropriate situational context for the experiencing, and also in keeping others nurturantly attentive.

Kelly has bad feelings of being frustrated about decisions, choices. She feels like a fool, like a child who can't ever make up her mind. Others always seem to be able to make decisions. She can't. When Kelly is with others, they rarely expect her to make a choice. But they all like her. The experiencing is being a lovable character, a klutz, a likable nut. The bad feelings effectively enable this experiencing.

When the person does something wrong, bad, or cruel, bad feelings may provide a channel for important experiencings. He did not mean to bruise the kid when he was driving the car. He put his head down on the steering wheel and cried. When he came over to the terrified little boy, he was so abysmally guilt-ridden that these awful feelings enabled the experiencing of being let go, excused, safe from retribution.

Bad feelings can be awful. But they serve as the behavioral means of building the right external situation and provide for the experiencing of operating potentials.

Painful Experiencing: Bad Feelings Occur When the Experiencing Is Disintegratively Painful

When operating potentials are surrounded by bad relationships with other potentials, the nature and content of their experiencings can easily be painful, harmful, twisted, menacing, unpleasant, and therefore accompanied by bad feelings. In Figure 2.1, OP3 is surrounded with negative, disintegrative relationships with other potentials. When this occurs, bad feelings will almost certainly accompany the experiencing of OP3.

This means that the person may experience being a failure, passed over, never good enough, in a way that is accompanied by bad feelings. Or the experiencing is being rejected, unwanted, hated, pushed away, and with accompanying bad feelings. If these potentials were related to in integrative ways, their very nature and content would shift, and the experiencing would no longer be associated with bad feelings.

Suppose that the operating potential is being helpless, unable to control, at the mercy of others, and this is accompanied by bad feelings. To undergo this painful experiencing, the person sets about constructing external worlds that will enable this kind of experiencing. To the extent that the person succeeds in building appropriate situational contexts, there will be this painful experiencing, and attendant bad feelings.

No matter how painful is the experiencing, no matter how bad are the accompanying feelings, there is a kind of bonus. That is, the operating potential is keeping the deeper potential down, sealed off. Suppose that the deeper potential is being free, liberated, autonomous, able to leave. What kinds of operating potential, even though painful, can disprove the deeper potential, can prove that the person is absolutely not the deeper potential, can ensure that the deeper potential does not have breathing room? The operating potential may involve being caught, stuck, hemmed in, blocked. Even though this may be painful, and associated with bad feeling, the operating potential is nevertheless disproving and blocking off the deeper potential.

Painful Reactions: Bad Feelings Are Disintegrative Relationships toward the Experiencing

When operating potentials relate disintegratively toward one another, the experiencing of one means that the other will be unhappy, upset, tense, worried, angry, disjointed, bothered. Bad feelings may be the expression of one operating potential toward another operating potential that is undergoing experiencing. The nature or content of either operating potential is irrelevant. All you need is one operating potential being experienced, and there will be bad feelings coming from the other. In Figure 2.1, when there is some experiencing of OP1, OP3 will be disgruntled, bothered, upset. It will have bad feelings.

If OP1 is being friendly, kindly, loving, good feelings cannot fully accompany the actual experiencing because OP3 will provide bad feelings. This unfortunate state means that the person can seldom feel good as long as some other operating potential bears a disintegrative relationship. Even as there is an experiencing of being friendly, kindly, loving, some other potential may not like that, will feel bad about that, will dislike and fear and hate the person for being friendly, kindly, and loving. It is like living with a person who fears and hates everything about you, everything you do, except that this person is within you, is another part of you. Whatever you are experiencing, some other part sees it as bad, dangerous, hateful, objectionable.

You carefully note when that person you are so attracted to comes out of the bathroom. Then you sneak in the bathroom and sit on the toilet where you are sure that she sat. Now the bad feelings come. Another operating potential is distraught. How could you do such a twisted thing? What is wrong with you? You ought to feel ashamed of yourself. The feeling is quite bad.

The more that the operating potential enjoys itself, the more other potentials may object, oppose, be disgusted at, and thereby hide, close off, seal off the good feelings. Suppose that the operating potential is the experiencing of being cruel, vengeful, getting even. At the wedding, you inadvertently nudge the victim so that the cherry juice gets all over his white tuxedo. Inside, all sorts of good feelings accompany this experiencing, feelings of wicked pleasure, arcane and devilish pleasure, secret pleasure. However, some other potential rushes through its disintegrative relationship and fills you with awful feelings. The former operating potential is kicking its heels in wicked pleasure, and the person is caught in the throes of gloomy bad feelings.

At the party, an acquaintance introduces you to a group of people and cracks a nasty joke about your political obtuseness. It was a cruel slap, but you act as if it was nothing. The other part of you is incensed at you. You should have punched him in the belly! What kind of a simpering wimp are you? What is wrong with you? The feeling is quite bad. Whatever you do or do not do, whatever is the nature of the experiencing, if some other operating potential relates disintegratively, there will be bad feeling.

Painful End-of-Existence: Bad Feelings Occur When the Deeper Potential Intrudes

Bad feelings occur when the deeper potential starts to intrude into the operating domain, and the operating potential is thereby in imminent danger of being destroyed. The person has bad feelings when what has been deeper, what he has worked long and hard to keep deeper, now is practically right on top of the person.

The nature or content of the deeper potential does not matter. As long as the deeper potential starts to rise, and especially when the deeper potential starts to enter into the operating domain, the feelings will be bad. Let us begin with a deeper potential for being violent, destructive, assaultive. Suppose this is DP5 in Figure 2.1. Suppose that OP1 is the experiencing of being sweet, appealing, loved. Even with a disintegrative relationship, there may be little if any bad feeling as the person experiences OP1 to a slight degree. He is undergoing this experiencing as he is alone with the older woman, but there is only a slight degree of this experiencing. He is listening to her sad story about her deceased husband, and she is appreciating his genuine interest.

However, as the person does whatever enables heightened experiencing of being sweet, appealing, loved, the net result is that the deeper potential is activated—made alive—and it rises closer to the operating domain. This is when there may be some bad feelings of tension, unease, anxiety, fractionization. He is exuding sweetness, being appealing, and he is undergoing a good measure of being loved as the older woman gazes at him trustingly, shares ever more personal secrets with him, and seems sincerely appreciative of the special way that he is. The bad feelings begin to rumble. He is becoming more tense and uncomfortable because the deeper potential is stirring, coming closer to the operating domain.

If the operating potential is even more fully experienced, the deeper potential will be even more activated, will come even further through the operating domain.

Now he is undergoing an enormous intensity of being sweet, appealing, loved. Here is the danger point. The deeper potential for being violent, destructive, assaultive is cracking through the operating domain, starting to envelop and invade it. The person is filled with bad feelings of extreme fear, fright, dread. It is the awful feeling of collapse, terror, closing out one's existence, dying, no longer existing.

This way of bringing about bad feeling is perhaps especially ironic or wry because it is due to the very success of the operating potential. At the very moment the operating potential is being experienced, the sheer experiencing sets into motion the deeper potential, which is brought closer and closer until it is able to eclipse the operating potential. The operating potential comes closer and closer to ending its own existence as there is greater and greater experiencing of being, for example, sweet, appealing, and loved.

Painful Relationships: Bad Feelings Are Disintegrative Relationships with the Externalized Deeper Potential

The person works effectively to establish an externalized deeper potential in the world. This means that some other person or thing will constitute the person's own deeper potential. Furthermore, it means that the person will establish the same disintegrative relationship with the externalized deeper potential as exists between the person and the deeper potential. The consequence is bad feelings accompanying this disintegrative relationship.

Suppose that the operating potential is being sweet, appealing, loved, and the deeper potential is being violent, destructive, assaultive. This person may well include in the external world someone who is violent, destructive, assaultive. Furthermore, the person's relationship with the other person will be disintegrative, and the feelings will be bad feelings such as tension, anxiety, unhappiness, anger, and fear in relationship with the other person. If the deeper potential is being authoritarian, cold, manipulating, then there will be this kind of person or agency in the person's world. Her uncle will be like this, or her husband, or her supervisor at work. The relationships with that person will be disintegrative, and there will be bad feelings whenever the person is engaged with that other person.

Through the disintegrative relationship, the man's deeper potential was dimly sensed as an absolute unreachability, a cold remoteness, unapproachability. It was this quality that he saw in his father. It drove him crazy, made him terribly upset, frustrated, torn apart. These feelings were present nearly every time that he was with his father. In his world, his father was the externalization of his own deeper potential, and his own disintegrative relationship with that deeper potential set the contours of how he related with his father. Throughout his life, his father remained the essence of absolute unreachability, cold remoteness, and unapproachability. Furthermore, relationships with his father were forever marked by bad feelings.

If the person fears and hates her deeper potential, she will likely build some part of her external world into being the externalized deeper potential, and then fear and hate that part of her external world. If she goes to another country, she will likely establish some new person or agent as the externalized deeper potential, and then have the same kind of fearful, hateful relationship with that person or agent.

The work may take some time. Or, it may take a few moments. If the deeper potential is sucking dry, draining, enervating, a woman may take years to work out a conjoint relationship with her niece, starting with their becoming buddies, then bringing the niece to live with her and her husband, then helping the niece to become a sculptress and finally, years later, succeeding in constructing her niece into a wholly parasitic leech, sucking her dry, draining and enervating her. Now the feelings are bad ones because there is a disintegrative relationship with the niece. In contrast, the moment the woman is told that she is pregnant, she sees the fetus as a thing that sucks her dry, drains her, leaves her enervated. Her immediate feelings toward that thing inside are disintegrative, bad.

There are different ways of having bad feelings. There are different things that account for bad feelings. Yet they all involve potentials for experiencing and the disintegrative relationships between potentials. Once the person is having a bad feeling, the determinants lie in the person's own potentials and their disintegrative relationships.

If These Are the Ways That Account for Bad Feelings, What Is the Way toward No Longer Having Such Bad Feelings?

Let us look at each way of accounting for a person having bad feelings, and see if the model or picture gives us any clues about how to be relatively free of these feelings. The answers may then serve as a foundation for an experiential psychotherapy to help people become free of bad feelings.

When bad feelings are behaviors that provide for experiencing of the operating potential. Bad feelings can provide for the experiencing of an operating potential. They may be a more or less direct means for the experiencing of the operating potential, or may be a means of constructing a situation that is helpful or useful for that experiencing. In either case, these bad feelings usually are shown, are public, are exhibited, are manifest behaviors.

He is genuinely having a very bad feeling as he is sitting with the group, but a little outside it. His body posture, facial expression, and words display a sense of being hurt. He is feeling bad. He is experiencing the operating potential of being alien, outside, not wanted. Her operating potential is the experiencing of being cared for, attended to, nurtured. One way of constructing an appropriate situational context is by having bad feelings of being terribly depressed, exceedingly gloomy, and ready to end it all. The feelings are bad, but when they are properly displayed, they help construct the appropriate situational context for the experiencing of the operating potential of being cared for, attended to, nurtured.

What change might result in the person being relatively free of these kinds of bad feelings? Some therapies are based on the sensible notion that the person can replace these behaviors with other behaviors that do not include bad feelings. However, the experiential model offers another way. When that operating potential is no longer a part of the operating domain, then those bad-feelinged behaviors will no longer be present. The person will no longer behave that way either to undergo the operating potential or to construct the appropriate situational context for experiencing that operating potential. You are no longer a person with that operating potential and therefore are essentially free of this kind of bad feeling.

How can a person let go of some operating potential? Can a person detach or disengage a particular operating potential? Perhaps. I find that the most effective way of letting go is by bringing the deeper potential into the operating domain. To the extent that the deeper potential becomes a part of the operating domain, the operating potential will atrophy, will be let go, and the person will be free of it, together with its bad-feelinged behaviors. Essentially, you can choose to remain the person you are or become the new person who includes the deeper potential. It is a hard choice to make, but the pay-off is being free of the bad feelings.

When bad feelings occur because the operating potential for experiencing is disintegratively painful.   When relationships with other potentials are disintegrative, the operating potential itself can be painful, hurtful, twisted, unpleasant. Bad feelings then accompany its experiencing. As indicated in Figure 2.1, when both OP1 and OP2 bear disintegrative relationships toward OP3, then OP3 will tend to be disintegratively painful. Its hurtful nature and content are brought out by its neighboring potentials.

Accordingly, the operating potential will consist, for example, of being a failure, passed over, never good enough, and its experiencing is attended by bad feelings. The operating potential will consist of being invaded, destroyed, attacked, and bad feelings accompany the sheer experiencing of this operating potential. Undergoing or experiencing disintegratively painful operating potentials will tend to be associated with bad feelings.

The operating potential may well arrange for appropriate situational contexts to enable the painful experiencing, along with the bad feeling. So the person constructs an external world appropriate for experiencing being invaded, destroyed, attacked, and then undergoes the painful experiencing and the bad feelings.

What is the way out? What kind of change may mean no longer undergoing this kind of bad feeling? There are two avenues for accomplishing this change. The bad feelings will let go when the person is no longer the person with that operating potential, and when that operating potential is no longer related to disintegratively. Picture the deeper potential becoming a part of the operating domain. To the extent this occurs, the operating potential may no longer be a part of the operating domain; the person is a new person who is free of that operating potential. Picture the deeper potential not only becoming a part of the operating domain, but also bearing integrative relationships toward the operating potential. This state is shown on the right of Figure 2.1. To the extent that this occurs, either the operating potential is no longer present, or the relationships of other potentials toward it are now integrative. When this occurs, there are no longer such bad feelings. The person no longer is the same person with the operating potential for experiencing being a failure, passed over, never good enough. When the deeper potential becomes a part of the operating domain, and especially as the deeper potential relates integratively toward that operating potential, the person no longer has bad feelings accompanying the experiencing of being a failure, passed over, never good enough.

When bad feelings are the expression of disintegrative relationships with other potentials.   When potentials bear disintegrative relationships, the experiencing of one will bring forth bad feelings from the other. The sheer experiencing of one operating potential means that some disintegratively related other potential will be upset, bothered, dismayed, and there will be bad feelings. You are experiencing being friendly, kindly, loving. Yet some other potential is so disintegratively related that this experiencing is turned bitter, is never allowed to be enjoyed, is made twisted and awful, by the disintegrative relationship. Accordingly, instead of merely undergoing the experiencing of being friendly, kindly, loving, you have bad feelings of being upset, gone too far, tense about being that way, bothered by the way you are. You are undergoing the bad feelings of the disintegrative relationship.

What can be done to be free of these bad feelings? Because these bad feelings are the expression of the disintegrative relationships between potentials, the way out is to undergo a change toward more integrative relationships. When you are able to love, treasure, play with, have wonderfully integrative relationships toward the operating potential, no matter its nature or content, then these bad feelings wash away, and you are free of them. *[handwritten annotation]*

When bad feelings are the "end-of-existence" reactions to the intruding deeper potential. Bad feelings will tend to occur when the deeper potential intrudes more and more into the operating domain. There is a point where the deeper potential is so close that you are almost drawn into the deeper potential. Your very existence seems to be coming to an end, and you are on the verge of becoming the dreaded deeper potential that you have continuously worked to keep down, barricaded, sealed off.

This is when you start to lose your identity, your existence. You are headed toward falling apart, becoming unglued. This is when you have the bad feelings of crumbling, dying, exploding. This is the tension or the terror of the end of your existence.

You have spent your whole life being solid, strong, dependable, trusted, self-confident. You have been successful in never feeling, and always having safely sealed off, a deeper potential for being sexually done to, a sexual victim, sexually used. Now this deeper potential is activated. It is becoming more intense, more alive. It is coming closer and closer to invading you, intruding into you, imploding into you so that you are on the verge of no longer being you, of surrendering to the terrible inner, deeper potential. Your very existence is coming to an end. The feelings are bad, horrendous, catastrophic.

What is the way out? What can you do to no longer have this kind of bad feeling? One answer is to throw yourself completely into being the deeper potential. Give in thoroughly to the deeper potential. Be it and undergo it all the way. Be it to the fullest extreme. Have fun being it. Be ecstatic in being it. Be wildly joyful in being it. Wallow in being it. Let it totally take you over. Surrender totally to it. In this new being, in being this new person, the bad feelings are let go. You are no longer having the bad feelings because you are no longer the person who fends off and pushes away the monstrous deeper potential. *[handwritten annotation]*

When the bad feelings are the disintegrative relationships with the externalized deeper potentials. Bad feelings occur when you construct your external world to include the externalized deeper potential, and you have the same bad-feelinged relationships with that potential that you have with the inner, deeper potential. There are, then, things in your external world that hate you, bear evil toward you, want you hurt and unhappy, and these things are the externalized deeper potentials. Your own frightening, awful, monstrous version of the deeper potentials are out there in your world, menacing you, threatening you, and your relationships with them are woefully disintegrative. What you fear and hate and seal off in you as the inner, deeper coldness, remoteness, unreachability now is here in your world. It is your spouse, your feared and hated enemies, the grotesque and monstrous things in your own world.

How can you be free of these bad feelings? What is the way out? The answer lies in no longer being the person who bears such disintegrative relationships toward the deeper potentials. It means no longer being the person that you are, and much further, it means being the deeper potentials. When you undergo the magnificent change into being the deeper potentials, then there are no more such disintegrative relationships toward them, and they no longer loom at you from your external world. Such disintegrative relationships no longer populate and constitute your external world.

In summary, here are the ways toward no longer having such bad feelings. With each kind of bad feeling, with each way of making sense of how and why you have bad feelings, there is a common thread among the various ways of no longer having these bad feelings. The common thread is the increased integration and actualization of the deeper potential. This is the way of moving from the left to the right in Figure 2.1, the royal road toward letting go of all of these ways of having bad feelings. Even though there are several ways of accounting for bad feelings, there is only one underlying way of letting go of them—the integration and actualization of the deeper potentials.

You are faced with this momentous choice of who and what you are. It is a powerful, catastrophic choice:

1. You can remain essentially the same person that you are, and this means that the bad feelings will almost certainly remain with you.
2. You can undergo what amounts to a powerful, momentous, radical, wholesale, catastrophic change into being the whole new person, including the integrated, actualized deeper potential, fully letting go of the very person that you are, and letting go of the bad feelings that are inevitably melded into the person that you are.

If you are willing to let go of and sacrifice the person that you are, you can let go of the bad feelings. If not, then you are essentially choosing to remain the person with the bad feelings. The choice is yours.

WHAT IS THE VALUED, OPTIMAL DIRECTION OF CHANGE?

In its simple form, the valued, optimal direction of change occurs when there are increasingly good or integrative relationships between potentials, and what is deeper in the person becomes a part of the operating domain. In Figure 2.1, DP4, DP5, and DP6 become, on the right, OP4, OP5, and OP6, and the relationships between operating potentials become positive, integrative. If the direction of change keeps on going, then all the potentials inside the person become operating potentials, and the relationships between all the potentials become positive and integrative.

These changes are good. In the value system of this therapy, what is valued, desirable, good, is for relationships between potentials to move from disintegrative to integrative, and for deeper potentials to become operating potentials.

Integration

There is no built-in force that pushes the person toward some ideal state in which the potentials get along well with one another. There is no process of development that will end up in a state of integration, provided there is no blockage or deflection. Moving in the direction of good relationships among potentials is an achievement, the consequence of work.

Figure 2.1 displays a change in the direction of increasing integration. The person is far from perfect or ideal because there are deeper potentials where relationships are disintegrative. What I talk about in this section describes a person who is significantly along the road, who is moving along the direction of increasing integration.

Greater feelings of integration, and lesser feelings of disintegration. As relationships between potentials become more integrated, friendlier, more welcoming and accepting, there will be greater feelings of integration. Inside your body, there will be changes in bodily sensations, in bodily feelings. There will be greater feelings of inner peace, oneness, wholeness, unity, tranquility, togetherness, inner harmony, inner centeredness. These good feelings are indicated as the plus signs in the relationships between the operating potentials on the right (Figure 2.1). Furthermore, with increasing integration, these good feelings become fuller and deeper, they occur over more of the body, and they last a longer time.

Similarly, feelings of disintegration decrease. As relationships between potentials become more integrative, there is less feeling of tension, threat, anxiety, dread, disjunctiveness; of being in pieces, being fractionated, fragmented, torn apart; of inner turmoil, disharmony, disjointedness. There are fewer bodily aches and pains as well.

Greater willingness to let go of self, and lesser having to preserve self. On the left, in Figure 2.1, the person consists of operating potentials 1 through 3, and the external world consists of external situation 1 and externalized deeper potential 5. On the right, none of this exists. Operating potentials 1 through 3 are indicated by dotted lines. External situation 1 is gone, and so is externalized deeper potential 5. This change represents the change from maintaining, clinging to, and preserving one's self, to letting go of one's operating potentials and the external world that goes along with these operating potentials (Binswanger, 1958a; Byles, 1962; Ellenberger, 1958; Kierkegaard, 1944; Laing, 1962; Watts, 1960).

When relationships between potentials are truly integrative, each potential is willing to fuse or merge into another potential. Essentially, each potential is willing to let go of its own existence and to enter into the other potential, or to allow the other potential to enter into it. Each potential can say that it is prepared to surrender its own existence, to die, to become one with the other potential. My self is the operating potential that I am right now. Integration means that I am willing to close out my very existence in becoming the other potential, or in letting the other potential become me.

When this willingness faces the external world, it means letting go of being the person who must have this particular external world. I can let go of my car, my city, my home, my children, my family, my garden, everything that goes with being the operating potentials that I am now. When this willingness faces what lies within, the deeper potentials, it means letting go of who and what I am and allowing whatever is within to be me, and for me to be it.

There is a symmetrical washing away of the absolute necessity of clinging to being me, to preserving my self. I need not have some part of me that is my very essence, my core identity, the heart of the very person that I am. With integration, the person is increasingly ready, willing, and able to let go of the core sense of self. There is no grim necessity of ferociously clinging to it, of preserving it at all cost.

Increased integrative relationships toward oneself.   The person will have, and be able to show and act on, increased integrative relationships toward oneself. The person will be able to have more of a sense of loving, appreciating, letting be, taking in, welcoming and acceptance toward oneself. As the person is being and behaving on the basis of one operating potential, other potentials will relate in these integrative ways. This means that the person will be able to shift easily into another operating potential and have integrative relationships toward oneself. Even when moving into being operating potentials that seem opposite to or conflicting or incongruous with one another, the person can be any of these operating potentials and can enjoy integrative relations in doing so.

There will be a greater sense of owning how one is and what one does, of accepting that it is all of and from the self. There is a greater sense of playing with the way one is, of integratively reacting to oneself, of chiding and kidding oneself, of stepping aside from and being able to take the other's view of oneself, but in an integrative manner. The person can even respond negatively and critically toward oneself, be appalled and shocked by oneself, but always within an integrative relationship.

The person will be increasingly aware of and receptive to what is going on within. When there are good or bad feelings inside, the person is more attuned to them, able to receive them, and more able to act on them in integrative ways (Gendlin, 1962, 1964, 1981; Rogers, 1970; Wilhelm, 1962). Each operating potential is more attuned to the other operating potentials, even to the deeper potentials, and the receptivity is more welcoming, accepting, and integrative.

The cessation or radical change of some operating potentials.   When relationships between potentials become integrative, that usually means either some operating potentials will no longer exist or they will be radically changed. Operating potentials relate disintegratively toward deeper potentials. As indicated on the left of Figure 2.1, relationships between OP2 and DP4 are disintegrative. If these relationships become integrative, then most of the purpose and function of the operating potential go away. Operating potential 2 no longer is there to oppose deeper potential 4, no longer is needed to hold it down, keep it sealed off, prevent it from coming into the operating domain. This means that there is a good risk that operating potentials will fade out of existence, and that state is indicated by the dotted lines around operating potentials 1 through 3 on the right in Figure 2.1.

At the left in Figure 2.1, most of the relationships between the operating potentials are negative. At the right, all the relationships among the operating potentials are positive. This change makes for a qualitative change in the manifest nature of the operating potentials. If we are located within the core of the operating potentials, there is little or no change at the heart of its nature or content. However, there may be a significant shift in the manifest nature and content of the experiencing. The operating potential of being childlike, naive, open, may take on a further quality of sensitive receptivity, a nonjudgmental knowing, a pure candidness. The former operating potential of experiencing a sexual rush, a wantonness, licentiousness, now may acquire an added quality, for example, a sensuous appreciation, a mutual eroticism, a languorous sexual excitement.

More integrative relationships with the external world.   Because relationships between potentials are generally negative, relationships with the external world are typically disintegrative. This occurs especially when the person relates to the externalized deeper potential. But it also may well occur in relationships with the external world as situations and contexts for experiencing. The direction of change is toward more integrative relationships with the external world. In Figure 2.1, relationships between operating potentials 1 through 6 and external situations 2 through 5 will become more friendly, pleasant, welcoming, accepting. On the left, in Figure 2.1, relationships with the external world are disintegrative, as indicated by the negative signs. On the right, relationships with the external world are integrative, and these are indicated by the positive signs.

This direction of change means that other persons are related to with a greater sense of letting be, of freedom to be however they are. There is little or no forcing of other people into being the externalized deeper potential. The pressure is gone. One is freer to allow the other people to be themselves, to have plenty of space.

The change means that the person can get closer to another person. There is a heightened sense of intimacy and bondedness. This may occur as love, as warmth and affection, or it may occur as getting close enough to play and be played with, to touch and be touched, to reach and be reached, to affect and be affected. There is also a quality of openness, honesty, candidness, guilelessness, transparency.

Just as the person can shift from one potential to another, the person is able to lose herself in the other. There is a willingness to become, to be, to merge or fuse with the tree, the rippling water, the lover, the precious infant. The person is able to enter into the other, and to know what the other is undergoing, feeling, experiencing. I can give up me, and I can be you. I can know how you are in your world, what it is like to be you in your world.

Less construction of externalized deeper potentials and disintegrative relationships with them.
There will be less constructing of the external world as externalized deeper potentials. Behavioral means of constructing the world into what lies deeper in the person will tend to fade away. The person will be less inclined to shape the other person into being the deeper potentials that lie within.

In addition, there will be less behavioral work to establish disintegrative relationships with the externalized deeper potential. The person's deeper potential consisted of being defiant, refusing, standing up for himself. When he selected people for his department, he was always drawn toward those whom he saw as having some spirit, quick on the draw, alive and crackling. Soon he would begin picking at them for not being loyal, for refusing to be dedicated. He would be frustrated by their not doing what he wanted. Relationships with them were made unpleasant and nasty by his being cold toward them, giving them last-minute work, imposing unrealistic deadlines, and lecturing them because they were not team members, they were defiant, they were uncooperative. The change was toward a washing away of all these behaviors, together with the disintegrative relationships that were established by these behaviors.

In more passive ways, the person declines to construct externalized deeper potentials, and to engage in disintegrative relationships with them. When the semblance of the person's own deeper potential presents itself, the person can decline granting it the status of an externalized deeper potential, or to engage with invitations toward disintegrative relationships (Jung, 1962). It is as if the person says, "I decline to construct you into being my externalized deeper potential, and I decline to participate in a disintegrative relationship with you."

An external world that is less populated with externalized deeper potentials. As indicated on the right of Figure 2.1, there are no externalized deeper potentials in the external world. It gradually loses these externalized deeper potentials, as integration moves along, and the person will less and less be faced with an external world that contains them. Since these deeper potentials are typically related to in a disintegrative manner, they are sensed as monstrous and grotesque, as evil and awful. Because these parts of the external world are the live deeper potentials, they are strong, they overwhelm and control, they loom as powerful controlling forces that own the person and that determine how the person is to be. Deeper potentials that are externalized emerge as powerful forces. With integration, the external world is less populated with these potentials, which brings about enormous changes in that world.

Does this mean that the person's external world is mere sweetness and light, free of agony and misery and painful unhappiness? No. All it means is that the external world no longer contains the person's own externalized deeper potentials. What is left is a world that the person constructs without those potentials. The inhumanity and the suffering that may be in the external world is free of being the person's own externalized deeper potentials. The person constructs the world and uses the inhumanity and suffering that is there on the basis of something other than the person's externalized deeper potentials.

Less likelihood of disintegrative deeper potentials occurring as bodily phenomena. Disintegrative deeper potentials turn up in the external world, and relationships with these parts of the external world are also disintegrative. In a symmetrical way, disintegrative deeper potentials can manifest themselves as bodily phenomena, and they reflect the disintegrative relationships between the person and these deeper potentials. Experiential theory offers its own way of describing the human body in terms of experiential constructs rather than the constructs of biology, neurology, anatomy, and physiology (Mahrer, 1978/1989d). Looking at the human body through an experiential model, some bodily phenomena and events are understood as manifesting disintegrative deeper potentials and the disintegrative relationships between the person and these deeper potentials.

This means that with increasing integration there is a decrease in the occurrence of these bodily phenomena. It is difficult to describe these bodily events, partly because they are already described in terms such as olfactory bulb, basilar membrane, or myoneural junction. Perhaps it would be clearer to say that there will be a decrease in the bodily events that are referred to by words such as cancer, asthma, miscarriage, skin rash, headache, tumor, internal bleeding, back pain, muscle cramping, vaginal infection, inflammatory lesion, obesity, blood vessel constriction, heightened fluid retention, diarrhea, stomachache, epileptoid fit, or high blood pressure. However they are described, with increasing integration disintegrative deeper potentials are less likely to occur as these bodily events.

Actualization

The key feature and meaning of actualization is that deeper potentials become operating potentials. The potentials that were deeper within you become a part of the way you are, the way you function or operate (Allport, 1955; Angyal, 1941; Bertalanffy, 1966; Boss, 1963; Buhler, 1968a, 1968b; Fromm, 1947; Gendlin, 1964; Goldstein, 1963;

If you eliminate your DPs do you get new ones?

Jung, 1933; Mahrer, 1967b, 1971b, 1978/1989d; Maslow, 1963, 1968, 1970; May, 1958b, 1961; Rogers, 1951; Schachtel, 1959; Van Dusen, 1957). In Figure 2.1, DP4 through DP6 become OP4 through OP6. As with integration, there is no built-in force toward actualization, no actualization battery or contained energy. Nothing is there to push or pull actualization along. In this model, the structure of personality allows for deeper potentials to become operating potentials, and that is about that.

If a deeper potential is going to become a part of you—a part of your operating domain—it helps if you are on good terms with the deeper potential. Having a fairly good relationship toward the deeper potential is important for a deeper potential to become an operating potential; achieving some degree of integration is one condition for actualization (cf. Byles, 1962). This is one reason I talked about integration first, and why Step 2 comes before Steps 3 and 4 in the fourfold steps of the session.

In Figure 2.1, the basic potentials on the left became deeper potentials on the right. If Figure 2.1 were to portray some idealized person, then the basic potentials on the left would end up as operating potentials on the right. That may be ideal. Nevertheless, any change from the left to the right can itself represent an enormous amount of successful work.

This direction of change toward increasing actualization stands as a value in experiential theory. Becoming more actualized, being and behaving on the basis of one's own inner ways of being and inner possibilities, is good. It is desirable, at least in this approach. *It is good because you are being your own self?*

What follows is a more detailed picture of the changes that constitute actualization.

Deeper potentials become operating potentials. The direction is toward each deeper potential becoming an operating potential. One way of describing this change is to say that you are now able to experience the deeper potential, to be and behave on the basis of this formerly deeper potential. But this sounds as if you are essentially the same person that you were, only now you can have some new kind of experiencing. That picture is not accurate. A more accurate description is that you are a qualitatively new and different person. Because you are the body of operating potentials and their relationships, the presence of the formerly deeper potential means that you are a new you, a new person, even if only one deeper potential becomes an operating potential. There is a wholesale new identity. The sense of I-ness, the sense of self, is significantly and radically altered, whether you are being the new operating potential or are being some other operating potential.

It also means that the deeper potential is present in its own form, and not in the form that was sensed by the former person whose relationship with the deeper potential was disintegrative. The experiencing is what it can be, from within the deeper potential itself, and no longer whatever it seemed to be as you drew back from it through your disintegrative relationship. The experiencing seems to change drastically from its deeper, disintegrative form to its integrative, actualized form. This is an impressive change.

When these potentials are deeper, it is easy to draw back from them as being dangerous, uncivilized, crazy, primitive, animalistic, grotesque, and monstrous. However, the move from disintegrative deeper potentials to operating potentials means that the operating potentials shift apparent form, shape, and content. They are softer, more friendly, more integrative, and less disintegrative. The change is considerable, although from within there is little or no change in nature and content.

Do you welcome and approve of deeper potentials becoming a part of the operating domain? A lot depends on whether you think of deeper potentials as good or bad, essentially desirable or undesirable. In the experiential model, deeper potentials are merely inner possibilities, ways you are able to experience. They are neither intrinsically good nor bad, wonderful or wicked. Their real and true nature, what they are really, depends on where you are when you answer the question. If you are inside the deeper potential, you will undergo feelings of actualization, and the nature of the deeper potential will be much closer to what it can be. The deeper potential, for example, occurs as being autonomous, independent, competent, self-reliant. If you are outside with an integrative relationship, the deeper potential may appear as a sense of being on one's own, self-contained, self-sufficient. However, if you are outside with a disintegrative relationship, you may see that deeper potential as being cold, hermetic, rejecting, antisocial. Since each of the three vantage points has its own accurate picture of the deeper potential, they are entitled to have quite different answers to the question of whether or not it is good or bad, welcome or dangerous, for the deeper potential to become a part of the person. From the disintegrative perspective, such a direction of change is bad, and the pictures of what the person is liable to become are enough to justify that such a change is bad. However, my choice is to grasp the deeper potential from the integrative perspective and especially from a perspective of being inside the deeper potential. Accordingly, movement from deeper to operating stands as the pinnacle of a change that is valued, welcomed, and desired.

Experiencing is stronger, fuller, and broader.   Whether the operating potential is a new one, a former deeper potential, or an old one, the direction is toward stronger and fuller experiencing. If the potential was deeper, it moves from little or no experiencing to being experienced with strength and fullness. In any case, actualization means that the potential is able to be experienced much more strongly and fully. Ordinarily, experiencing is relatively low, with occasional peaks of strength and feeling. Ordinarily, the person behaves in ways and in situational contexts that do not enable powerful experiencing. If the experiencing is being playful, silly, whimsical, this occurs seldom, and with a restricted degree of intensity. However, the change is toward increased amplitude, saturation, strength, and fullness of experiencing. You simply experience it more.

I am not talking about how this experiencing feels, or how the person feels in relation to it. I am talking about the sheer degree of experiencing itself. If there were a sensitive experiencing meter attached to you, it would indicate greater strength and fullness over longer and longer periods.

I want to distinguish between increased experiencing of the potential, and the undergoing of feelings. Many persons can undergo intense feelings of hurt, tightness, dread, or excitement, aliveness, pleasure. But this is quite different from the experiencing of a potential. At this moment, there may be quite intense feelings of anxiety or excitement, while there is little experiencing of the potential for being playful, silly, whimsical. It is common that the experiencing of potentials is relatively muted or enveloped even as accompanying feelings may be intense. The change is toward the stronger and fuller undergoing of the experiencing, as contrasted with the feeling.

There is another reason why experiencing is stronger and fuller. Operating potentials are there both to provide for and to truncate the experiencing of deeper potentials. They are means to an end, and the end is to allow a measure of experiencing of the deeper potentials, while ensuring that they are kept down and sealed off. In general, operating potentials have a job to do, and that job reduces sheer experiencing. As the deeper potential becomes a part of the operating domain, there is much less of this reason for the operating potential. It is as if the governor of "too much" experiencing is removed. The net result is that the sheer degree of experiencing of the formerly deeper potential is generally greater than that of its operating potential.

In addition to greater depth of experiencing, more potentials undergo more experiencing more of the time. In other words, there is greater breadth of experiencing. Over a day, a week, a few months, each operating potential will be experienced more frequently. Instead of a given potential being experienced for about 40 seconds over a week or two, this kind of experiencing may well occur for several hours or more over that period. Just because a potential is part of the operating domain doesn't necessarily mean that it will be experienced, or experienced more than rarely. With actualization, experiencing of each operating potential occurs more often.

There are greater feelings of actualization.   As deeper potentials become operating potentials, and as relationships between potentials become more integrated, and as the operating potentials engage with the external world, there are greater feelings of actualization. More feelings are described by words such as tingling, energy, excitement, lightness, buoyancy, vibrancy, vitality, aliveness, exhilaration, ecstasy, joy, happiness, satisfaction, pleasure. These feelings occur over more of the body. Not only is there heightened experiencing, but it is accompanied by heightened feelings of actualization.

Former operating potentials may no longer remain.   One of the main reasons for the operating potentials is to simultaneously provide for and keep down the deeper potentials. In other words, as long as the deeper potentials are indeed deeper, the operating potentials exist. When the deeper potentials become a part of the operating domain, there is little or no reason for the former operating potential. Hence, it tends to evaporate, as indicated in Figure 2.1 by the dotted lines around OP1 through OP3.

It is interesting that the solution to problems, to bad feelings, is to no longer be the person with the problems and bad feelings. The problem is not the target, nor is the bad feeling. Instead, it is the operating potential who is or who has the problem, the operating potential in which there is the bad feeling. When you become the new you, then the old you tends to evaporate, and with that evaporation go the problems and bad feelings.

The target or focus of change is the operating potential that is responsible for the behaviors which construct the external situation and enable the experiencing there. The target is not the behavior alone, nor the way the person thinks, the actions that the person carries out, or the situations that enable the experiencing. The target is not what the person does or the situation in which the person does it. Instead, the target is the operating potential that is the organizational structure leading to the behaviors and to the situational contexts.

In the experiential model, many problems that are ordinarily thought of, as agonizing ways of being, as being twisted and weird, crazy and deranged, as being indicators of some terrible inner state, are found in the operating potentials. Being suicidal or homicidal or "psychopathological" are the manifestations of some kinds of operating potentials. When these are washed away and no longer present, the impression may be that what has changed is the very inner foundation of the person, some inner core that was awful, primitive, crazy. Yet all of this is simply the shining forth of the operating potentials. When these former operating potentials no longer remain, the change has occurred at the surface operating level, even though it may appear that there has been a much more profound inner and deeper change.

However, bad feelings need not accompany the operating potential. It may be pleasant and rather enjoyable, such as experiencing a sense of substance, being of worth, being solid and strong. Yet the risk is that this operating potential also may fade away. Experiencings that feel good, that are accompanied with good feelings, are just as likely to extinguish as those coupled with bad feelings, troubles, and sufferings.

Former behaviors and situational contexts may no longer remain.   As the former operating potentials tend to fade out of existence, so too will their behaviors and those parts of the external world that served as their situational contexts. For better or for worse, a great deal of change goes along with the extinguishing of the former operating potentials. As indicated in Figure 2.1, neither behavior 1 nor external situation 1 are present on the right.

The former behaviors may be little ones, such as wearing a gaudy gold ring or allowing old people to leave the elevator before you do, or big ones, such as owning a large home or remaining married. The behaviors that go with the former operating potential may well go out of existence because the operating potential no longer is present. There is no further need to build situational contexts for the old operating domain. All those behaviors extinguish. All kinds of behavior tend to go away when the former operating potentials no longer exist.

External situational contexts are used mainly to provide for the experiencing of the operating potentials. As the operating potential fades, there can be significant changes in the person's external world. When there is no operating potential for being secure, stable, anchored, then whole chunks of a person's continuing external world may no longer remain. Not the career in the government, nor the marriage, nor the big old house, nor the living in the same place where his family has been for nearly 150 years. When she no longer has the experiencing of being demeaned, kicked around, put down, then she may no longer require her husband, his aggressive family, that employer. The external world undergoes change—sometimes big and dramatic change—when the operating potential is no longer present.

If the old operating potentials remain, the integrative relationships mean that actualization can provide new behaviors and new situational contexts. What had existed as wicked and tabooed sexuality was coupled with his secret masturbations in public toilets, in exposing himself to women when he went out after midnight. If the operating potential remains, now in its integrated form, actualization outfits it with new behaviors and new situational contexts. He and his woman companion revel in being naked at home, trying out all sorts of delightful sexual and erotic acts, and all with a much more wholesome sense of wicked and tabooed sexuality. The former painful behaviors and the former painful situational contexts tend to extinguish away.

Even operating potentials accompanied with good feelings may wash away, together with their behaviors and situational contexts. The fellow whose operating potential consisted of being of substance, being of worth, being solid and strong, spent his youth as a big and powerful boy, adolescent, and young man. An athlete, he played football, worked in a gym; he married a petite woman; he enjoyed being well over 6 feet tall and over 250 pounds. Later, he experienced this operating potential as he assumed increasing positions of power and responsibility in the administration of football, in local politics, and in his large family business. Throughout his life, the deeper potential had been sensed as a worthlessness, as being second rate and discounted, or at least this is what was dimly sensed through a disintegrative relationship toward what was deeper. With integration, the deeper potential emerged as a friendly fumbling, an easygoing ineptness, an honest unsureness and uncertainty. As this became an operating potential, there were changes in both behaviors and situational contexts. There were fewer one-on-one confrontations, less having to be right, less defending his decisions as the right ones, more openness at committee meetings, more consultation with others. In general, there was a considerable lessening in the former behaviors and situational contexts in relation to being of substance, being of worth, being solid and strong.

New behaviors will construct and enable experiencing in new situational contexts. Merely being in the operating domain is not enough. For actualization to occur, for experiencing to take place, the experiencing has to happen in the external world. This means there is an essential role for new behavior, for new situational contexts. There has to be provision for the operating potential to live and be in the external world.

The external world has to include appropriate situational contexts for that experiencing. If the operating potential is being admired, looked up to, respected, this occurs most easily in appropriate parts of the external world, in appropriate situational contexts. This means that the direction of change is toward new external situations. On the left, in Figure 2.1, OP1 through OP3 existed in an external world consisting of external situation 1. If you look on the right, there are altogether new external situations. Quite literally, this person is living and being in a new and different world. In addition, there will be changes in the behaviors that served to construct these situational contexts, and also to enable and provide for the actual experiencings. On the left, in Figure 2.1, these behaviors are indicated as B1. On the right, these new behaviors are indicated as B3 through B6. This kind of change is quite substantial. It includes changes in behaviors and also in the external worlds in which the person lives and exists.

If the deeper potential consists of being nurturing, providing care and comfort, the person will now behave in ways that construct appropriate new situational contexts and will see portions of the world differently, as further opportunities for this new experiencing. Or the person will restructure the world to include contexts for this experiencing. New people and new relationships will be brought in, and the person will behave in new ways that enable this new experiencing.

Formerly, the person's world was built around the operating potential for being of substance, being of worth, being solid and strong. The deeper potential was a friendly fumbling, an easygoing ineptness, an honest unsureness and uncertainty. In his daily life, he was able to be this new way, to enjoy the skill of the mechanic who worked on his car, to assist his wife in making special meals for guests, to enjoy offering his ineptness to his neighbor who was trying to fix a broken window. As a local politician, he had fun admitting that he never did understand nuclear power and the dangers of nuclear waste. He spent less time being the boss of the large family business holdings but enjoyed bringing in effective administrators and being much more ready to admit his mistakes.

All of this constitutes the meaning of actualization and integration. Together, they define the valued directions of change in the experiential model. This is what the person can become, whether we are looking at a little movement in the right direction, or taking the long look at what the person may become.

WHERE DOES IT ALL COME FROM? WHAT IS THE ORIGIN OF THE KIND OF PERSON THAT YOU ARE?

Just about every theory of personality provides an answer to these questions. The answers, in many theories, involve consideration of such issues as genetics, early traumas, social values, events during pregnancy, the circumstances of birth, early learning experiences, various kinds of biological and psychological developmental processes, the child's growth and development over these stages, and environmental influences. Most of these issues, and the experiential position on these issues, are discussed in another book (Mahrer, 1978/1989d). The purpose here is merely to give the highlights of the experiential answers to questions of where it all comes from in the first place, and the origins of the kind of person that you are.

How Is an Infant Constructed?

Earlier in this chapter, I described some ways in which people construct the external world. Each person works continuously to build and construct the kind of external world that he or she finds important. People use the same methods to construct an infant as a part of their external worlds.

By "constructing an infant," I am referring to what is called actual biological conception, but I do not limit it to this. I mean that an infant is constructed as part of the person's world. Picture an infant who is still inside the womb. Picture an infant who is 4 days old or 18 months old. Picture a woman who thinks about an infant, a woman who perhaps wants to have a baby. In each of these ways, what we may call an infant is now present in the external worlds of these people. This is what I mean by constructing an infant.

The simplified picture is given in Figure 2.2. In this model, the persons who construct the infant are mainly a mother and a father. However, the principle is that the

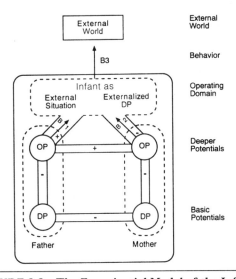

FIGURE 2.2   The Experiential Model of the Infant

infant is constructed by those persons for whom an infant is important. This means that an infant may be predominantly constructed by a mother alone, or by a woman and a man, or by any group of people for whom the infant is a significant part of their external world (Kahn, Mahrer, & Bornstein, 1972). How do these people construct an infant? They do it in the same ways that they construct any other parts of their external worlds.

One way is for the external world to act on the person, to present the infant or even the idea of an infant, to the person. Then the person receives this in her own way. One day, a friend says that she is pregnant and she does not want the baby. Would you want a baby? With that, the idea of having a baby intrudes into your world. It may be important for you to accept this idea, and the baby, or perhaps to dismiss the idea on the spot. Or you have been married for five years, and family and friends bring up the idea that it is time for you to have a baby.

A second way to construct a baby is for the person to use resources that are merely available in the external world. Adopt a baby. If you are a woman, you can use sperm to construct a baby. You can assist in being with a woman who is pregnant. You can work in an agency that houses babies. You can spend a lot of time with a baby that someone else conceived.

Third, you can work conjointly with another person to actively construct a baby. You and another person may work with one another so that suddenly there is the idea of a baby. There may be no actual physical baby, but the couple has conceived the idea of having a baby or getting a baby or becoming involved with babies. A couple may have intercourse and conceive a baby, or use medical technology to construct a baby.

By using these ways, people can construct babies as parts of their external world. The time frame stretches from approximately a year or so before what is ordinarily referred to as conception, to approximately a few years after birth.

What Functions Are Infants Constructed to Serve?

Parents construct infants to serve the same functions as any other constructed parts of the parents' external worlds. The first function is to serve as external situations so that parents can undergo their operating potentials. By bringing the infant into the world, the parent is thereby able to experience the operating potentials in external situations involving the infant. The second function is to serve as the externalized deeper potentials of the parents. By constructing infants, parents are able to make infants into their own externalized deeper potentials, and to establish the same disintegrative relationships as occur between the parents and their own deeper potentials. In the experiential model, these are the two functions that infants are constructed to serve (Figure 2.2).

Suppose that the father's operating potential is being capable and competent. One way of undergoing this experiencing is by producing a baby whom the father regards as a healthy indication of his masculine virility, sexual capability, and competence. The baby is thereby endowed with being the manifestation of capability and competence. Suppose that the mother's operating potential is being better than, competitive, a winner. She constructs the infant as the appropriate situational context for this experiencing. This baby is exceedingly healthy and well-developed. The pregnancy and birth were as fine as could be. The infant is smart, active, intelligent, more appealing, and more attractive than other infants. Suppose that the father's deeper potential is not belonging, being outside of, being by oneself. He may construct the baby into being the externalized deeper potential and draws back from the baby as alien, as not wanting to be touched or held, as fearing strangers, as being strange. Suppose that the mother's deeper potential is being a jewel, special, godlike. In constructing the baby as the externalized deeper potential, her disintegrative relationship leads her to recoil from the baby as too delicate, fragile, something too different, too self-centered, too preening, self-absorbed.

Parents will work efficiently and effectively to mold and shape the infant into whatever is important for them to have the infant be (Bell, 1963; Boszormenyi-Nagy & Framo, 1965; Haley, 1963; Haley & Hoffman, 1967; Jackson, 1957; Laing & Esterson, 1970). Parents accomplish this by making the infant into an external situation or into an externalized deeper potential.

Parents construct and use the infant for experiencing virtually any kind of operating potential. Picture what the infant is to be like if the parent is to experience being inadequate, unable, incompetent; protective, keeping away bad things, taking care of; ripeness, being fructiferous, fertile. If the parent is to experience being protective, keeping away bad things, taking care of, then the infant is to be something that needs protection, is unable to care for itself, is unable to defend itself against bad things. You can easily proclaim that the "basic nature" of infants is that they are unable to protect themselves, to care for or to defend themselves. Or, infants may be seen as basically needing food, sleep, and needing these things now. From before she was pregnant, the mother experienced a sense of being drained, used, taken advantage of. Lots of things in her world grabbed at her, wanted things from her. She constructed the baby as a fine external situational context to enable this same operating experiencing. Even before conception, the very idea of having to have a baby wouldn't let her go. Once pregnant, the baby owned her, took advantage of her, drained her. From the time that her daughter was born, she demanded, wouldn't leave the mother alone, needed things, drained her mother.

By constructing infants as external situational contexts for experiencing, parents assign infants roles such as the needy one, the treasured one, the special one, the confidante, the enemy, the devil, the hateful one, the beautiful one, the secret lover, the little king, the violently angry one, the sickly one, the delicate and frail one, the parent, the wise one, the proof of fertility, the murderer, the leader, the bearer of hopes, the protector, the devil. In each of these, when the infant is being this way, is being this external situation, then the parent is enabled to experience the operating potential. The mother always knew that she would be led astray by her baby, that she would be unable to resist him, that he would malign and poison others, that she would be irresistibly drawn into his evil net. The infant's role is thereby defined. He is this situational context.

Alternatively, parents turn the infant into their own externalized deeper potentials, and bear the same disintegrative relationships as they bear toward their own deeper potentials. In this way, the infant is molded and shaped into being crazy, bizarre, having something wrong, and the parents relate to the infant in hurt and fear, guilt and loathing. The infant is the mother's passivity, helplessness, wimpishness; and she relates to the baby in the same way she relates to that deeper potential within herself, by denial, fear, discounting it, refusing to acknowledge it. In this same way, the father fears and hates his own deeper dullness, dumbness, uncomprehendingness, and thereby constructs his infant into being dull-witted, slow, underdeveloped, dumb. Mother has spent years sealing off her deeper sensuality, her being lustful and erotic. Her daughter is the essence of erotic stimulation, and from the very beginning mother feared and

hated her baby for being so lustful, sexual, erotic, sensual. Whereas the father is dutifully loyal and dedicated to the upper-class family, his deeper potential for rebellion,
defiance, and refusing occur in the infant toward whom he relates with distance, sep-
aration, and disgust.

These are the two main functions that infants are constructed to serve: external
situational contexts or externalized deeper potentials. From some time before the
child's conception to well after birth, parents and key other persons actively construct
the infant to enable experiencing of the persons' operating potentials and relationships with the deeper potentials.

What Is the Origin of Basic Potentials, Deeper Potentials, and Operating Potentials?

The simple answer is that the operating potentials of the infant or young child are the
external worlds of the parents. If the infant-child is constructed into being an external
situation of demandingness, insistence, pressing at, then this is an operating potential
of the infant-child. If the infant-child is constructed into being the externalization of
a parent's deeper potential for being delicate, soft, tender, fragile, then this is another
of the infant-child's operating potentials. The infant-child starts out with these operating potentials. The original set of operating potentials arise out of the external worlds
that the parental figures construct the infant-child into being.

Look at Figure 2.2. If we take the vantage point of the mother, it may be important for her to undergo the experiencing of standing up for herself, not taking it, being
able to refuse and say no. How can she construct a situation appropriate for this operating potential? She works her infant into being the proper external situation. The
daughter is constructed into being too demanding, too insistent, always pressing at. In
this situation, mother can complain bitterly about her daughter and refuse to respond
to every cry. Mother can demand some free time, and her husband has to take care of
their daughter while the wife rides a bicycle or has coffee with a friend. Now let us
switch over to the vantage point of the daughter. From this other perspective, the
daughter now comprises an operating potential for being demanding, insistent, pressing at. These words refer both to the external situation of the mother and also to the
operating potential of the infant. The mother has constructed and molded the daughter into having an operating potential of being demanding, insistent, pressing at.

In the same way, the father may construct the daughter into being the externalization of his own deeper potential. This may consist of experiencing a sense of being
soft, delicate, tender, fragile. The disintegrative relationship toward this deeper potential means it is important that the father construct some part of his external world
into being this deeper potential. His infant is appropriate. From the beginning, he regarded her as too soft, delicate to the point of being sickly, tender and fragile, easily
disrupted, ready to be harmed. This is the way she was for him, and he hated her, drew
back from her, could never warm up to her. However, this way of being also constituted
her operating potential. From the very beginning, the daughter's operating potential
consisted of being soft, delicate, tender, fragile. Father's externalized deeper potential occurred as the daughter's operating potential.

How do the infant-child's deeper potentials originate? The short answer is that
the operating potentials of the parents are the deeper potentials of the infant-child. As
indicated in Figure 2.2, parental operating potentials are responsible for constructing
the infant-child into being this external situation or into being that externalized deeper

potential. When the infant-child starts out, the original set of deeper potentials are the parental operating potentials that constructed the infant into being what the infant is constructed into being.

The bedrock of the infant's personality, the basic potentials, are the deeper potentials of the parents as the parents are shaping, molding, building, and constructing the infant. All of this is indicated in Figure 2.2. During this period when the parental figures, and perhaps others too, are actively constructing the infant-child into being their own external worlds, the deeper potentials in these figures are the basic potentials of the infant-child.

During this "primitive field" when the infant-child is being constructed, there are relationships between potentials. These relationships are present within the father and within the mother, and between the potentials of father and mother. All these relationships are indicated in Figure 2.2. It is almost certain that relationships between operating and deeper potentials will be disintegrative. However, the relationships between the operating potentials of the parental figures, and between the deeper potentials of the parental figures, depend on this particular couple. Similarly, there will be relationships between each parent and the infant as external situations or as externalized deeper potentials. The latter will almost certainly be disintegrative. Whether relationships between the parent and the infant as external situations are positive or negative depends on that particular parent.

This is not especially the traditional picture of the origin of personality, and the comparison of this picture with some of the more traditional ones may raise searching questions. I have discussed these issues elsewhere (Mahrer, 1978/1989d).

In the experiential picture, there is a kind of "primitive field" during which some people, typically mother and father, are working on constructing the infant into being external situations and externalized deeper potentials. During this period, according to the experiential model, those people are being themselves. In addition, and at the same time, these people are being the infant's own deeper and basic potentials. In many theories, these early figures act on, influence, determine what the infant is. In the experiential model, these early figures are what the infant is. I am not trying to assert a set of truths about the origin of the infant's personality; I am only setting forth a model of how the infant's personality is constructed. Figure 2.2 represents what may be termed a "primitive field" in which the infant is constructed. All the parts of this primitive field are the foundations of the infant-child, the wellsprings of where it all comes from, the origin of the psychological structure of the infant-child.

Picture mother undergoing an experiencing of preciousness and wonder as she attends to the baby in her womb or to the baby who is sitting on her lap, looking at mother's eyes. Mother sees her baby as her best friend, her special confidante. In the experiential model, if we freeze these moments, we can hold that being a best friend, being a special confidante, is a part of the infant's personality. We can also hold that the experiencing of preciousness and wonder, occurring in the mother, is also a part of the infant's personality. As indicated in Figure 2.2, if we draw a line around the mother's personality, it encompasses her operating and deeper potentials, as well as her external world. At the same time, if we draw a line around the infant-child's personality, it includes the infant-child as the external world of the parents, and it also encompasses the operating and deeper potentials of the parents.

In most theories, the infant is a separate being from the parental figures. Once the infant is assumed to be separate, then the wellsprings of the infant, the sources of the infant, the answer to where it all comes from, typically consists of things inside the physical infant as well as effects and influences from outside the infant. Things inside the infant usually include inborn human nature, biological foundations, genetic structures, and so on. Things outside the infant usually include a wealth of effects and influences such as events that occur to the infant-child, early interactions between the infant-child and all the things around the infant-child. In the experiential model, the infant-child and the "primitive" persons who construct and mold the infant-child are all part of a primitive field that is, that comprises and constitutes, the basic foundations of the infant-child.

What Is the Origin of Infant and Child Behavior?

Picture an infant of one day or four months of age. The parental figures are actively working on that infant to make him into the kind of external world that is important for the parents to construct. Suppose that the parent is going to make that infant into an external situation or an externalized deeper potential, and that the infant is to be demanding, pressing at, insisting; or is to be a part of the parent's external world that is delicate, soft, tender, fragile; or is to be a best buddy, a special confidante. These ways of being describe the kind of person that the infant is to be, and they also involve actual behaviors of the infant. By constructing and building the infant into being the particular kind of external world that is important, the parents will thereby get the infant to behave in ways that may be described in words such as demanding, pressing at, insisting; delicate, soft, tender, fragile; best buddy and special confidante. The parental figures activate the infant into appropriately fitting behavior. They bring the behaviors into actuality.

Parents can bring forth the right kind of behaviors in lots of ways. They can organize and determine a great deal of the immediately encompassing world so as to induce, determine, pull, shape particular kinds of infant behaviors. They can literally arrange the immediate conditions so as to virtually ensure particular kinds of infant behavior. Parents can determine how the infant's immediate world will react and respond to all sorts of given infant behaviors. Parents can force the infant to behave in certain ways by doing this or that to the infant. They can keep the infant's immediate world relatively stable or can make drastic changes that compel all sorts of symmetrical infant behaviors. Not only can parents determine and organize the infant's world, they can effectively constitute that world and thereby pull for and close off lots of behaviors. Parents can seize on a rudimentary nubbin or little bud of behavior, a beginning movement or slight gesture, identify or label it as a full-blown behavior, and proceed to develop it into the actual full-blown behavior. Parents develop behaviors by receiving and responding to them over a relationship that is integrative or disintegrative. There are powerful ways in which parental figures can bring forth actual infant behaviors that make the baby into the alive and actual external situation or externalized deeper potential of the parents.

Parental figures also can originate actual behaviors in the child. Parents are the activating potentials of the child, who is the external situation or externalized deeper potential of the parents. All in all, parents bring forth behaviors in the child in the same ways as they bring forth behaviors in the infant. The main difference is an expanded repertoire of behaviors. The child of 4 or 10 years can manifest a broad range of behaviors for being demanding, pressing at, insisting; of being delicate, soft, tender, fragile; of being a best buddy and special confidante.

Parental figures pull the strings of the puppet child by being the child's inner potentials. Even if the physical parents recede out, however, they nevertheless remain within the child as the activating deeper and basic potentials. This means that the child's own deeper potentials activate the operating potentials into behavior. The system can function even if the parental figures are no longer present. Indeed, once the system—the potentials and their relationships—is established, appropriate behaviors are produced. The child can therefore keep on behaving in ways that are demanding, pressing at, insisting; or being delicate, soft, tender, fragile; or being a best buddy and special confidante. And the parental figures need not be present at all, neither as the activators nor as the external world in which the child behaves. In this model, the system itself originates infant and child behavior.

Over the Course of Life, to What Extent and in What Ways May There Be Changes in Operating, Deeper, and Basic Potentials?

Some theories of personality are based on a sequence or stages of biopsychological development. There is assumed to be a conflux of biological, genetic, psychological, and social factors that yield a set of stages of human development. To a large extent, human beings become the kinds of persons they are because of the way they proceed through these assumed stages of development. In contrast, the experiential model does not include stages of development (Mahrer, 1985b; Mahrer & Gervaize, 1985). In this model, the question is to what extent and in what ways may there be changes in operating, deeper, and basic potentials. In other words, if the infant-child starts out with a personality structure as indicated in Figure 2.2, does the person essentially remain that way throughout the course of life?

The simple answer is that there is likely a fair measure of change in operating potentials, some measure of change in deeper potentials, and little or no change in basic potentials.

Three ways that operating potentials change over the course of life.   Suppose that we look at one operating potential of the mother. During this period of approximately a year or so before conception to several years after birth, the mother's interactions with her baby included her operating potential of experiencing superiority, achievement, being better than, looked up to. Given this operating potential and its deeper potential in mother, the baby was constructed as her own external world in very particular ways. As the external situation, enabling this operating potential to be experienced, mother constructed the baby into being tough, hard, undeviating, self-confident. In addition, as an externalization of mother's deeper potential, the baby was constructed into being awkward, slow, dumb, uncomprehending.

At the very outset, then, the infant starts out with a deeper potential for experiencing being superior, achieving, looked up to, better than. The baby has at least two operating potentials. One includes being hard, undeviating, tough, self-confident, and the other includes being awkward, slow, dumb, uncomprehending. We are concentrating on one of the infant's deeper potentials and two operating potentials, as indicated in Figure 2.2.

During this early period, the infant has been described as mainly the external world of the primitive figures, such as mother and father. Throughout the infant's life, at age 6 years, 16, 36, or 76, the person may always serve as the external world of the parental figures. Throughout mother's life, she may see the son as hard, undeviating, tough, self-confident, and also as awkward, slow, dumb, uncomprehending. Throughout his entire life, the son may remain as the external situation and externalized deeper potential of the mother.

But what about the son's own external world? If we start with the infant, the two operating potentials and the one deeper potential will be continuously at work building some kind of external world. And herein lies the key to changes and developments in both the one deeper potential and the two operating potentials.

Let us start with the operating potential for being tough, hard, undeviating, self-confident. Suppose this is the operating potential from the period of somewhat before conception to a few years or so after birth. One way in which new operating potentials come about is when the person is being in the external world, is actually behaving, is working on and constructing an external world. This particular operating potential facilitates, but only to a point, the experiencing of the deeper potential. In this case, the deeper potential is being superior, achieving, better than, looked up to. This person's program is that he will enable a bit of this experiencing by being tough, hard, undeviating, self-confident. When he clamps hard on the nipple, he is behaving on the basis of this operating potential. He is undergoing this experiencing as he grabs the bars of the crib and won't let go, when he falls down and hits himself but nothing phases him, when he walks directly toward where he wants to go, even if there are things in his path.

However, when he is somewhat older, in his working on the external world, providing for a measure of the deeper superiority, being better than, achieving, and being looked up to, a new operating potential comes into being. He gains the experiencing of being stronger, athletic, physically capable. He throws well, runs fast, is acknowledged as a fine athlete. This newly emerging operating potential also serves the deeper potential. As he continues to work at and to construct his own external world, the deeper sense of being superior, better than, achieving, looked up to, is moderately activated by yet another operating potential: being a leader, the one in charge, the big boss, the head of the group. This potential was not present before, but it occurs in the course of working on the external world on behalf of the deeper potential.

What started out as a single operating potential has led to two additional ones. How long does this take? It takes as long as it takes the person to construct an external world in ways that do the job. The development of new operating potentials slows down or stops when the external world is good enough to enable the operating potentials to do their job. Most of the development of such new operating potentials is over by the time the person is an older child or young adult. But it may be earlier or take longer. There is no law.

One way that operating potentials develop is over time as some new operating potential becomes able to do the job even better than the old one. Another way consists of serving as a means or instrumental avenue for enabling the original operating potential. Let us look at the original operating potential of being awkward, slow, dumb, uncomprehending. This is the way the infant is to be from the very beginning. As the child works at building his own external world, this single operating potential may do its job all by itself. On the other hand, there likely will occur periods when a new nucleus or pocket develops as there is a glow of experiencing being numb, frozen, empty, dead. Here is a means by which the child can undergo being awkward, slow, dumb, uncomprehending. He falls into these states of being vacuous and numb every so often. In the same way, as he is busy working on the external world, something new starts to develop. There is a sense of being second rate, a loser, no good. Here is another operating means of being awkward, slow, dumb, uncomprehending. From one operating potential, now there are three, with two originating as working means of providing for the one that was there from the beginning.

How long does this take? Is there any schedule? It occurs until the person has generally succeeded in building the kind of external world that is important to build. This may be done in childhood. It may take longer. When the person has constructed an external world that enables the operating potentials to do their job, there will likely be little or no further change. For most people, my impression is that the development of new operating potentials is generally over in childhood and a little beyond.

There is a third way of developing new operating potentials over the course of life. The principle is that the person may develop additional operating potentials to avoid, deny, fend off, disprove the deeper potential. Given the deeper potential for being superior, achieving, being looked up to, better than, the child started out with one operating potential. It consisted of being awkward, slow, dumb, uncomprehending. Over the course of his life, there may well develop additional ways of proving that he is not superior, achieving, being looked up to, better than.

In later childhood, there is something quite special about hooking up with a best friend and being loyal, trusted, a follower. When he is part of small groups, he also experiences being loyal, trusted, the follower. In adolescence and as a young adult, this experiencing occurs when he is in organizations, departments, groups. What has developed is an operating potential born of disproving and effectively avoiding the deeper potential of being superior, achieving, looked up to, better than.

As a young child, there were special moments of undergoing a sense of taking it easy, not expending much effort, being lazy; the specialness of this emerging experiencing lay in its fending off, sealing down, avoiding, and disproving the deeper potential of being superior, achieving, looked up to, better than. In effect, this fellow became a person whose operating potentials, at least some of them, were explicitly developed to ensure that he did not experience the deeper potential. He became a person whose essence was to avoid and disprove being superior, achieving, looked up to, better than.

One way that deeper potentials change over the course of life. All of this developing of further operating potentials has been with regard to one deeper potential (being superior, better than, achieving, looked up to). This deeper potential was present as the mother's operating potential, and existed from the very beginning. Does this deeper potential change? Are new deeper potentials added? If there is any change, what accounts for it? In the experiential model, there can be some change. The deeper potentials that were present at the outset may not necessarily be the package throughout life.

As an infant or child or young adult actively constructs the external world, there is always some little effect on the deeper potential. It is touched or affected just a bit. Constructing and being in the external world, undergoing the experiencing of the operating potentials, does something to the deeper potential. It is as if this potential slowly evolves, reorganizes, or undergoes differentiation. It started out as being superior, better than, achieving, looked up to. As the operating potentials do their work, carry out their functions, and engage in the external world, the deeper potential may evolve and differentiate so that where there was just one, now there may be two. One is a deeper potential for being omnipotent, godlike, mystical. The other is owning, having control over, fully influencing. These evolved deeper potentials bear family kinship to one another, and both share a common root of being superior, better than, achieving, looked up to. Yet they are different from one another.

Without directed, active, focused efforts to change the potentials, there is still some reason and room for a bit of change. Starting from the original package, there may be a fair measure of change in the operating potentials, some change in deeper potentials, and little or no change in the basic potentials.

This model of human beings fits with doing experiential psychotherapy. It allows me to carry out the steps and methods of this way of doing therapy. It provides the enveloping context, the picture of what human beings are that is good enough for me to conduct a session. I do not think of the experiential model as truth. I do think of it as helpful and useful in undertaking experiential psychotherapy.

SECTION II

The Guide to
Experiential Psychotherapy

CHAPTER THREE

In-Session Goals, Objectives, and Directions of Change

The chapter deals with this question: In the actual session with the patient, what are your goals, your objectives, the directions of change you want to pursue?

The experiential session goes through a series of steps (cf. Hill, Carter, & O'Farrell, 1983; Lennard & Bernstein, 1960; Mahrer, 1978a, 1983a, 1986d; Mahrer & Gervaize, 1986; Mahrer, Nadler, Gervaize, & Markow, 1986; Malan, 1982; Selvini-Palazzoli, Bascolo, Cecchin, & Prata, 1978, 1980; Simkin & Yontef, 1984; Snyder, 1945). In experiential therapy, each session goes through the same steps, as indicated in Figure 3.1. The first change, or objective, or direction of change, is that the patient is living and being in some specific moment of strong feeling, and deeper potential 4 is raised up, brought closer, activated, much more available and accessible. In Step 2, relationships between the person (OP1) and the accessed deeper potential (DP4), are more welcoming, accepting, integrative. In Figure 3.1, this is indicated by the change from negative signs, in Step 1, to positive signs, in Step 2, in the relationship of the person toward the deeper potential. In Step 3, the person is now being the deeper potential. In other words, the deeper potential is now an operating potential, and the person is literally being this experiencing (OP4, Figure 3.1), and doing so within the context of earlier life situations. In Step 4, the final step, the person is also being the new potential, but now the person is being this new potential within the context of the prospective world. In effect, the person is a new person, able to be this new person in the world out there. Furthermore, not only is the world different, but the new person's relationships with other operating potentials are more positive and integrative, the person is able to be and behave in ways that are fitted for and to the new experiencing, and the former operating potential may well diffuse away, together with its painful behavior and the painful situational context in which it had existed.

These four steps represent the goals, objectives, and directions of change for each session. But why? What is the further or consequent goal, objective, or direction of change from going through these four steps? The answer is:

1. The person can be a qualitatively new person whose potentials for experiencing now include the integrated deeper potential. The person has become a

qualitatively new person, perhaps only for a few moments or for a while or from now on.

2. The person is now free of the scenes of bad feeling that had been front and center in the beginning of this session. These bad-feelinged scenes are no longer a part of the qualitatively new person.

If this therapeutic model sounds different, so too is the tone and atmosphere in which it is practiced. Later in this book, I will describe, in detail, how to carry out the four steps. The balance of this chapter explores how this experiential therapy relates to most other therapies in regard to the goals, objectives, and directions of change.

The chapter is organized around a number of questions or issues. For each question, I will describe the experiential answer and some other ways of answering the

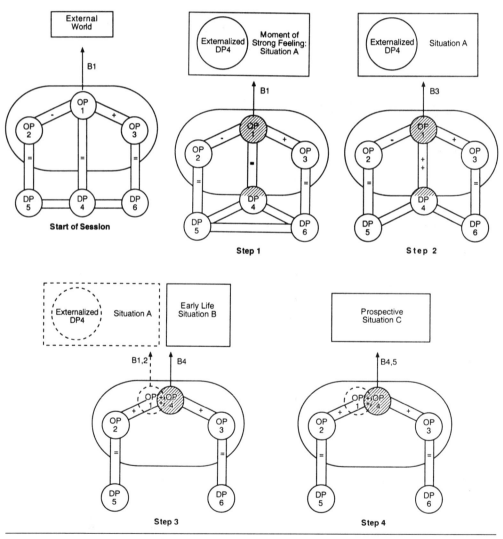

FIGURE 3.1   The Four Steps in a Session of Experiential Psychotherapy

question. For each issue, I will present the experiential position on the issue, and common contrasting positions. As you go through this chapter, you will see some of the important questions and issues that therapists face regarding in-session goals, objectives, and directions of change. You will also see what the experiential answer and position are, especially in comparison with alternative, perhaps more common, answers and positions.

THERAPY IS TO REDUCE PROBLEMS AND PROBLEM CONDITIONS VERSUS THERAPY IS TO ENABLE THE PERSON TO BECOME THE KIND OF PERSON HE OR SHE CAN BECOME

Most therapies may be described as a way of reducing problems and problem-conditions. Some therapies, and experiential psychotherapy is among these, regard psychotherapy as a way of enabling the person to become the kind of person that he or she can become, and to be free of scenes of bad feeling. You may think of therapy in either of these two ways, but it is hard to accept both at the same time. Or, you may have some altogether different way of thinking about psychotherapy.

Therapy Is To Reduce Problems and Problem Conditions

You may think of therapy as a way of treating what you refer to as problems, and the explicit emphasis may be on the patient's problem behaviors. You see the patient as having such problem behaviors as compulsive hand-washing, vomiting several times a day, getting freaked out in airplanes, drinking too much, always getting into fights with her husband, having nightmares, getting words all mixed up when he is upset. Problem behaviors may include behaviors that are seen as abnormal or deficient. The patient is not assertive enough, does not have orgasms, does not get physically close to anyone.

Problem behaviors may also include making decisions and choices, such as about the kind of job the person wants or is suited for, whether or not to have the abortion, whether or not to live with the lover. Problem behaviors may be stretched to include bodily things such as jaw pains, headaches, skin rashes, scratching the head and face, low back pains, being fat.

You may see therapy as a way of treating a "condition." You regard the patient as having a mental illness or disease, some kind of psychopathology. The patient is sick, maladjusted, disturbed. Therapy is to treat the problem condition of bulimia, depression, phobia, the borderline condition, lack of impulse control, ambivalence over sexual orientation, being out of touch with her anger, or having problems with authority figures.

In the middle ground between problem conditions and problem behaviors are all sorts of feelings and emotions. These may be seen as having behavioral aspects, and also as being part of some problem condition. Accordingly, therapy is to treat the patient's anxiety, depression, fearfulness, mood changes, loneliness, and lots of other kinds of feelings and emotions.

Whether it is a problem or problem condition, the usual idea is that something is wrong, malfunctioning, not working properly. There is a sickness or disturbance. One or more of the parts are faulty. Whatever it is, something is wrong. Therapy is to reduce it, fix it, repair it, ameliorate it, get rid of it, make it normal.

You may look for what is wrong and try to do something about it. In this way, you can reduce the problem or problem condition. Sometimes, you may work on the problem or condition as well as the way to reduce it. For example, the trouble may lie in the kinds of thoughts that bother the patient (e.g., Anthony & Edelstein, 1975; Gullick & Blanchard, 1973; Hackman & McLean, 1975; Ownby, 1983; Stern, 1970). The solution also lies in the realm of thoughts, in altering thoughts, in changing cognitive structure (Adler, 1927, 1969; Dreikurs, 1956, 1967; Ellis, 1962, 1967; Kelly, 1955, 1967). In any case, your aim is to reduce whatever is, or causes, the problem or problem condition.

The problem or problem condition is typically something about you, yet distal to and separate from you. In medicine, the problem or condition may refer to the colon, heart, stomach, the tumor. Similarly, in psychotherapy the problem or condition is something about you, yet separate from you: your thoughts, your behavior, your reinforcements, your history, your mental illness, conflicts, psychopathology. But there is an alternative approach.

Therapy Is To Enable the Person to Become the Kind of Person He or She Can Become

Some therapists see patients in terms of inner, deeper qualities, characteristics, processes, possibilities. The emphasis is on becoming a person based on and determined by these inner possibilities. Instead of working to reduce problems and problem conditions, these therapists try to enable the person to become the kind of person that he or she can become. Some therapists who see therapy this way do experiential therapy, client-centered therapy, Gestalt therapy, psychoanalytic therapy, and other kinds of therapy that focus on changes in the person rather than the problem or problem condition.

According to this position, these changes include alterations in how the person thinks and feels, relates and interacts, constructs and lives in the external world, and especially in how the person behaves. In other words, becoming the kind of person that the patient can become carries with it changes in much of what may be regarded as problems and problem conditions (Mahrer & White, 1988; Schefft & Lehr, 1985).

Becoming the kind of person that the patient can become seems to involve changes in the very core of the person, who otherwise may be seen as behaving in a particular way, as having the tumor, as feeling helpless or tense. The change is in the essence of who the person is; it is not limited to behavior, thoughts, reactions, body parts, feelings.

If you think of therapy as a way of treating or reducing problems and problem conditions, then you probably think of specific diagnoses and ways of identifying problems. This fellow is a sexual abuser, and I am going to treat his problem. If you switch over to the other approach, therapy is a means of enabling personal change, a way for the person to become the kind of person he can become. We think of this person in terms of potentials for experiencing, in terms of the kind of life he is constructing for himself, in terms of the nature of his deeper potentials. We do not think of him as a drug abuser any more than we think of him as having light brown hair or as having graduated from Hendricks Elementary School. Here are two quite different ways of seeing patients.

Therapy enables the person to become more integrated and more actualized. In the experiential model, therapy enables the person to have more integrated relationships between potentials (integration), and to bring deeper potentials into the operating domain (actualization). This means that the person becomes a new person who feels different, behaves in different ways, and exists in a different external world.

Our work begins with whatever is inside, with inner, deeper experiencings. Then our work proceeds toward integrating and actualizing whatever that inner, deeper experiencing is, and enabling all the accompanying changes in feelings, in behaviors, and in the person's external world. This is how therapy unfolds. These are our aims and goals.

Other approaches may object, and with good reason. Aren't human beings basically sitting on primitive impulses? If we open up what is inside, most people would be killing, raping, doing all sorts of awful things. People are basically savage, monstrous, evil, sinful, animalistic, uncivilized. Right? Here is where we must acknowledge that different theories or models of human beings have altogether different notions of what is deep inside people. If you believe that most people have basic instincts to murder like-sexed parents and to sexually possess the opposite-sexed parents, then this is probably not something you might want to foster. Are human beings regarded as basically good or bad? In the experiential model, deeper and basic potentials are fundamentally merely potentials for experiencing. When they are integrated and actualized, they are everything that is wonderful in this person.

Therapy also enables the person to no longer be the person with the bad feelings and all that provided for the bad feelings.   The main focus, the major change, is becoming the new person. But this change brings with it a bonus. The person is no longer the person with the bad feelings, the behaviors that provide for the bad feelings, and the external world that enables the bad feelings (Mahrer, 1978b, 1978/1989d). At the end of the session, the patient is to be a new person, and is to be and behave in the external world as this new person. By letting go of being the old person, the new person is able to leave the bad-feelinged scene or situation behind, and behave in ways that no longer preserve and maintain it.

Experiential therapy is therefore in accord with other therapies that likewise work toward effecting deep changes in the very person that the person is and have, as one of their consequences, the washing away of whatever the patient had been troubled by, suffering about, had bad feelings in relation to. We join with some of the psychoanalytic therapies, Jungian therapies, client-centered therapies, and others (cf. Frankl, 1960; Gerz, 1966).

Is this framework merely another way of "treating" problems and problem conditions? The answer depends on what you mean by problems and problem conditions. Some therapists may be satisfied that the problem is washing hands compulsively, having nightmares, lacking assertiveness, being uncertain about a career choice, lacking impulse control, being depressed, being a borderline. In the experiential model, the problem is the bad feeling that is occurring in some scene of strong feeling, the way of being and the behavior that are occurring in this scene of strong feeling, and the particular situation that is the scene of strong feeling. Typically, the problem that emerges in an experiential session is not at all the same as the problem and almost certainly not the problem-condition that is arrived at in the other, more common, framework.

You have a choice. You may see therapy as a way of reducing problems and problem-conditions. You may see therapy as a way to enable the person to become the kind of person he or she can become, including no longer being the person with the bad feelings and all that provides for the bad feelings. My option is the latter.

INITIAL SESSIONS

If we call the first meeting between therapist and patient the initial session, then this section deals with some of the issues around the goals and objectives of this session.

You May Use the Initial Sessions for Relatively Standard Purposes versus Using Initial Sessions for One Purpose Means That You Cannot Use Them for Most Other Purposes

In the initial session, the experiential therapist and the patient will probably go through the four steps. But most other therapists have different programs. One of the more common positions is that the initial session has a relatively standard set of goals and objectives based on getting some sort of assessment and evaluation of the patient: mental status, presenting complaints, history, physical state, coping mechanisms, significant people in the patient's world, precipitating stresses, self-concept, defenses, psychopathology, motivation, prognosis, diagnosis, and lots of other kinds of information from the interview or from tests or from both (e.g., Korchin, 1976).

It seems hard to go through the four steps of an experiential session, and also to do a relatively standard assessment and evaluation. Indeed, a case can be made that you cannot do both. At the end of an initial experiential session, we have essentially no information that is obtained by a more or less standard initial session (Mahrer, Edwards, Durak, & Sterner, 1985), and this is also the case for others who do not choose to use the initial session for some kind of relatively standard assessment and evaluation (cf. Breger, 1976; Rogers, 1951, 1957). Together with some others, we take the position that there are options and choices of goals and objectives for the initial sessions and that our option is to decline the relatively standard set of goals and objectives. In any case, it is hard to proceed through the four steps of an experiential session when you use the first session to get information about the patient's problem, personality, and psychopathology.

What Do You Want the Patient to Do in the Opening Part of the Initial Session?

Perhaps the most common answer is that the patient is to tell about the problem, the worry or trouble, the complaint (Nelson & Barlow, 1981). This makes sense when therapy is to treat problems. The patient comes to therapy for help for the problem, and therefore it is eminently sensible to start by finding out what the problem seems to be. Once the patient states the problem, the therapist is to learn about whatever it is. Look for the circumstances under which it occurs, see how serious it seems to be, inquire into its history. Get the problem-related information.

Another answer is that the patient is pretty much free to talk about whatever seems important for the patient to talk about. The main thing is that the patient can talk; the therapist is mainly to be there to enable the patient to talk, and the patient may talk about just about any topic (Benjamin, 1969). In psychoanalytic therapies, patients were shown how to talk about whatever would come to mind. This was called free association. Some psychoanalytic therapists (e.g., Deutsch, 1949) merely wanted the patient to talk freely, about any topic, and this remains the pattern with many therapists (e.g., Szasz, 1965/1988). Some therapists have a list of topics that should be covered in the initial session, but the patient may be free to start with any topic as long as most of them are covered during that session (Ripley, 1972). In this way, you can track and guide the patient so that if he seems to be getting too far afield, you can guide him back to the topic at hand.

In the experiential model, you want the patient to concentrate on scenes of any kind of strong feeling. The emphasis is on strong feelings, bad feelings, and the scenes and situations that go with these feelings. The patient is to do quite different things in these options.

The Purposes of Initial Sessions Include Getting the Problem, the Case History, the Assessment-Evaluation, and Establishing the Relationship versus the Purpose of the Initial Session Is to Enable Personal Change

These are usually two different purposes of initial sessions. However, one is not the good way and one the bad. One is not true and the other false. The purposes simply differ from one another. Which one do you prefer? With this patient, which of the choices do you prefer?

The purposes of initial sessions include getting the problem, the case history, the assessment-evaluation, and establishing the relationship.   Initial sessions are for particular purposes, goals, and objectives. Perhaps the main purpose is to find out about the patient's problems, difficulties, troubles, presenting complaints, or symptoms. You are to do an assessment-evaluation. This may emphasize the analysis of the patient's problem behaviors, or it may emphasize getting a more psychodynamic picture. Look for signs of psychopathology and mental illness. Examine the type and extent of symptomatology. Get a psychodynamic picture of the patient. Arrive at a formulation of the provisional psychodiagnosis. The assessment-evaluation should provide a picture of the patient's problem, problem condition, and personality structure (Korchin, 1976; Leon, 1982; Sands, 1972; Weiner, 1975).

The initial sessions should include a history of the patient and the patient's problems. It should provide a picture of the patient's background, development, the origin of the difficulties, the precipitating stresses, how the patient coped with the stages of development.

An important purpose of initial sessions is to lay the groundwork for the therapist-patient relationship (Argelander, 1976; Fine, 1971; Gregory & Smeltzer, 1977). Rapport is to be established. Develop the patient's sense of trust in the therapist and in therapy.

On the basis of the initial sessions, the therapist should be able to develop a treatment program, a plan of action, including the possibility of referral. Some idea of prognosis should be formulated.

The purpose of the initial session is to enable personal change.   The experiential model does not include case history, assessment-evaluation, laying the groundwork for a therapist-patient relationship, or looking for a problem condition. Instead, the goal is to enable personal change, right off, and in this, the experiential model joins with other approaches that likewise use the initial session to obtain as much personal change as the patient is ready and willing to attain (Rosenbaum, Hoyt, & Talmon, 1990).

In the very beginning of the session, the purpose is to enable the patient to arrive at some scene or situation that is accompanied with strong feeling. Then we proceed through the four steps, and complete the fourth step with the person able to be and behave as the accessed new person. This is the way we use the initial session.

The aim is to use the initial session in this way regardless of who the person is, regardless of whether this is to be the only session or whether we will have another one subsequently. There is an important choice of purposes for the initial session.

The Goals of Initial Sessions Are Substantially Different from Those of Later Sessions versus the Goals of Initial Sessions Are Substantially Similar to Those of Later Sessions

Here are two quite different ways of looking at the goals of initial sessions. Although there is almost always some middle ground, each way of looking at the goals of the initial sessions regards the other as improper, inappropriate, and probably wrong.

The initial session is one of an extended series; its goals are different from those of later sessions.   The therapist thinks in terms of an extended series of sessions. The series may be relatively brief or rather long. The total number may be defined beforehand, such as a program of 4 or 8 sessions, or the total number may be open-ended so that the actual series may run for 5 or 30 sessions, or in the hundreds. When there is a fair number of sessions, especially over a long time, the therapist may think of a set of phases or stages of therapy. In any case, this is the first session of an extended series.

The goals and objectives of the initial session may be so different from those of later sessions that someone else may do the initial session, especially when it is for screening patients, assessment-evaluation, "intake." In any case, the initial session has its own distinctive goals. It establishes the groundwork for the later therapist-patient relationship (Lazarus, 1976; Szasz, 1965/1988). Build up the patient's readiness and inclination for the extended series of sessions (Brammer & Shostrom, 1982; Gill, Newman, & Redlich, 1954). Determine the patient's need for therapy. Establish the patient's expectations and goals, and tell the patient about the various options (Cormier & Cormier, 1979). Get the information you need to decide on the right treatment, the nature of the problem and problem-condition, the length of the trial period if there is one (cf. Tennov, 1975).

Change is generally to occur later, during and after the treatment program. Although you may start building the foundations for later change, any that occurs in the initial session is suspect. It is called a flight into health, or a counterphobic reaction (cf. Sifneos, 1987). Change is unlikely to occur in an initial session, in part because you do not use methods aimed at trying to bring it about; so if changes do occur, it may mean that something is wrong. Change methods are typically reserved for later sessions, especially when the problem and problem condition are serious, highly pathological, or deep-seated.

Initial sessions do not deal with things that are more appropriate for later sessions. In initial sessions, you tend to play down or to avoid many kinds of interpretations, the pointing out of certain inconsistencies in what the patient says, or deficiencies in the patient or the patient's ways of seeing things (Ripley, 1972). There is plenty of time later to probe into sensitive, painful, or well-defended topics, or to get further information about some important topic (Korchin, 1976).

The initial session is its own minitherapy; its goals are similar to those of later sessions. The therapist looks at this session as a complete minitherapy. Rather than encompassing an extended series of sessions, the scope is limited to this single session. Indeed, the model is that of single-session therapy (Talmon, 1990; cf. Alexander & French, 1946; Mahrer, 1988a; Sarason, 1988; Rice, 1990). If the patient is ready and willing, significant changes can occur in this session.

You and the patient work one session at a time to accomplish what can be done now, here, in this session. If you both wish to have a further session, or many further sessions, that is fine, but while you are proceeding through this initial session, this is the whole minitherapy.

This means that the initial session, like all other sessions, is geared toward as much change as the patient is ready and willing to attain. Quite explicitly, each of the four steps is directed toward change, and the methods of the initial session are methods of change. The culminating changes may be significant and deep, making for broad and sweeping changes in the person (Mahrer, 1991b); or the changes may be slight, quite limited, and narrow (cf. Rosenbaum, Hoyt, & Talmon, 1990).

Some therapists are entitled to hold that you should not try to promote change, certainly not deep-seated change, until you have a fairly broad and comprehensive picture of the patient's intrapsychic dynamics. This may take 10 to 20 sessions. In some approaches, such as psychoanalytic therapy, it may take a year or so. If the question is how much do you need to know to work toward significant changes in initial sessions, then some therapists hold that you need to know enough to conclude that significant changes probably should not occur in initial sessions. The experiential position is that you need to know the deeper potential that is accessed in this session. That is all. Accordingly, you can aim toward the same degree of change in initial sessions as in later sessions.

These goals are for virtually all patients. All patients are invited to go through the same four steps, regardless of whatever strong-feelinged scenes we start with. In other single-session therapies, these kinds of changes are to occur with a broad span of patients and problems, but not especially with all patients and problems (Talmon, 1990).

In general, the goals and objectives of the initial session are essentially those of later sessions, for they all proceed through the same four steps.

There is an emphasis on postsession changes versus there is little or no emphasis on postsession change. In initial experiential sessions, the fourth step includes providing the patient with an explicit opportunity to undertake postsession changes. The patient is shown how to consider, try out and rehearse, refine and modify, and determine the degree of readiness and willingness for the new way of being, and also for specific kinds of new behaviors. Postsession changes are valued and important, and in this sense, experiential therapy joins with a number of other approaches that likewise emphasize postsession changes in initial sessions (de Shazer, 1985, 1991; Goulding & Goulding, 1978, 1979; Mann, 1973; Rosenbaum, Hoyt, & Talmon, 1990; Talmon, 1990; White, 1993; White & Epston, 1990).

In contrast, many approaches explicitly deemphasize postsession changes as a goal of initial sessions, and they generally have a set of therapeutic axioms to justify why such changes are to be actively discouraged. Changes are to be postponed until later. You may come to some agreement on what therapy is to accomplish, what goals are to be reached, what the patient wants out of therapy (Coyne & Segal, 1982; Greenberg & Johnson, 1988; Ripley, 1972). These agreements have some slight hintings toward new ways of being, but typically the initial session is almost routinely associated with little or no emphasis on changes following the initial session. Changes will come later.

There is one category of changes that some therapies highlight in the initial session. It has to do with changes to accommodate getting ready for the extended therapy program. For example, the therapist decides that the fee is to be a little more than insurance pays for, and therefore the patient is to make arrangements to get the extra money. The patient will be seen once a week on Thursdays, at 4:00, and the patient is to rearrange his working hours to allow him to leave at 3:30 on Thursdays. The patient is to tell his wife that she is to help him in some aspects of the behavioral program, such as not having sex as a punishment for his carrying out the problem behavior, or letting him gamble up to $25 on Saturday afternoon as a reward. The patient is to see if her husband is willing to join a group conducted by the therapist on Wednesday evenings. If the therapist decides that the patient's condition is seriously pathological, postsession changes may involve going to the psychiatric hospital, or knowing that the therapist is calling the patient's brother to stay with the patient and be there in case the depression reaches suicidal proportions. These examples fall under a special category of postsession changes that involve the patient's state and preparation for treatment.

In general, some approaches emphasize postsession changes, and other approaches explicitly deemphasize postsession changes. Experiential psychotherapy represents the position that the goals of initial sessions are substantially similar to those of later sessions, and both initial and later sessions end with a serious consideration of the kinds of changes that can be carried out after the session. Many other therapists explicitly avoid postsession changes after the initial session. There is a choice.

What do you do with strong feeling in the initial session? Strong feeling is to be avoided in initial sessions versus use strong feeling to enable personal change.   Picture the patient starting the initial session in a state of quite pronounced feeling (cf. Spiegel, 1972). He is shaking and trembling. He is boisterous and agitated. He is crying and sobbing. He is yelling and screaming. He is so tense and anxious that he can barely speak. He is abysmally morose and depressed. What do you do with the presence of quite strong feeling in the initial session?

The common position is that strong feeling is to be generally avoided. You certainly do not work toward explicitly bringing about strong feeling. Do things in the beginning of the session so that the patient can be relatively relaxed and comfortable. Ask simple questions on relatively safe topics. Get demographic information rather than going to emotionally charged topics. Your goal, in the initial session, is to keep away from strong feeling, keep it within bounds, minimize its occurrence, avoid arousing it.

If the patient is getting too emotional, is starting to be overcome with affect, is actually having strong feeling, do what you can do to reduce it. Help the patient relieve the strong feeling with breathing and relaxation exercises (Korchin, 1976; Leon, 1982; Morgenstern, 1988). Introduce a time-out, a pause, to reduce the strong feeling. Change to a safer topic. Pay attention to what seemed to have accounted for the strong feeling, and make a mental note to examine that material in later sessions (O'Leary & Wilson, 1987; Ripley, 1972). Instead of letting the strong feeling continue, have the patient talk about the strong feeling, inquire into its history, assess and evaluate things about the strong feeling, try to understand the strong feeling, inquire into why the patient might be having it right now, check how the strong feeling occurs in the patient's extratherapy world (Nelson & Barlow, 1981; Weiner, 1975).

If the patient becomes overwhelmed with the strong feeling, becomes assaultive, is on the verge of falling apart, is becoming psychotic, homicidal, suicidal, then take appropriate professional steps. See that the patient is made safe, can get medication, is hospitalized.

In later sessions, therapy may deal with strong feeling in its own way. But in the initial session, the goal is essentially to avoid it. This is quite common position.

Many critics hold that there are disadvantages in avoiding strong feeling in initial sessions, and perhaps some genuine advantages in actively promoting and using strong feeling (Beier, 1966; Davis, 1971; Frank, 1959, 1961, 1973; Haley, 1963; Janov, 1970; Labov & Fanshel, 1977; Mahrer, 1983/1989b; Stieper & Wiener, 1965). The experiential position joins with others that seek to use strong feeling, in the initial session and in later sessions, to promote personal change. In the beginning of the initial session, the patient is shown how to find a scene of strong feeling, and how to enter into this scene, undergoing the strong feeling so as to access the underlying deeper experiencing.

The undergoing of strong feeling is one of a number of methods for accomplishing each of the steps in the initial experiential session. The goal is to foster strong feeling, to use it to enable change to occur, both in the initial session and in each subsequent session.

What do you do in initial sessions? What are your packages of goals and objectives in initial sessions? A common approach is to get information about the patient's problem or problem-condition, and to pave the way toward the later series of sessions. The experiential approach represents an alternative set of answers. In the initial session, the purpose is to undergo personal change, to go through the same four steps of change as occur in any session. You have a choice, and the choice makes a big difference in what you do in initial sessions.

THE NOTION OF "PROBLEMS": ESSENTIAL FACT, USELESS FICTION, OR REPLACEABLE FOCUS OF THERAPY?

The notion of "problems" is central in almost every therapeutic approach and for most therapists. Patients have problems. Therapy is to treat problems. Problems are the core feature of therapy, its essential justification, just about the main reason for a field of psychotherapy. From the experiential perspective, the notion of problems is a gigantic fiction, a myth, a construct with the status of an unquestioned truth largely because so many therapists share that belief. Instead of problems, experiential therapy focuses on the patient's pain, hurt, bad feeling, on strong feelings and the scenes in which they occur, and on the underlying deeper experiencings in this person in this session.

Problems Are Real, Objective, Enduring; Therapy Is Treatment of Problems

Of course there are problems. Patients have problems. Problems are real; they exist. You may quibble about the best words to use in describing this patient's problems, but everyone agrees that patients have problems. The patient has hebephrenia, lacks identity, rebels against authority, is afraid of furry animals, gets anxious in enclosed places, is suicidal, is out of touch with deeper impulses, has obsessive thoughts, is unsure of gender choice, is depressed, steals things from stores, is afraid of speaking in groups, blushes too easily, is afraid of crossing streets or seeing blood, is unable to have orgasms, has an eating compulsion, masturbates excessively, has periods of incontinence, lacks intimate relations, is unassertive, engages in excessive picking of skin, nail-biting, or pulling of hair, has tension headaches, exhibits and exposes himself, is schizoid or borderline or alcoholic, abuses drugs, is an incest survivor.

Problems are real. They exist quite separate from this particular patient and therapist. They are as real as a wart on the nose or a rash on the skin or blood coming out of a wound in the leg. Different therapists can determine that there really is a wart on the nose or that the patient's problem really is a phobia of enclosed places or being unable to get along with his son.

The patient's problems are real and objective even though they may be formulated in different vocabularies. They may be framed differently by an Adlerian or a Jungian, by a behavior therapist or a cognitive therapist. Yet what these different terms refer to is a real and objective problem, even though we may talk about it in different ways.

Problems are real and objective because you can get information about their characteristics. You can describe problems in terms of their severity, the amount of personal discomfort they cause, the precipitating stresses that led to their onset, whether their onset was gradual or sudden, the background factors that provided the foundation for their occurrence, previous attempts to treat them, the patient's ways of coping with them, their frequency, persistence, strength, and prognosis (cf. Cormier & Cormier, 1979; O'Leary & Wilson, 1987).

Because problems are real and objective, you can describe the distribution and prevalence of different kinds of problems in different kinds of groups, such as old people, divorced people, immigrants, nuns, boys, and athletes. You can compare different cultures in terms of their main problems. You can talk about how the common problems have changed over the years, how the main problem in Freud's time was hysteria, how the main problems in North America in the 1950s and 1960s involved the quest for identity, and how the main current problems involve power and powerlessness.

Because problems are real and objective, you can organize treatments around them so that there are specialized programs for depression, stress reduction, phobias, incest survivors, bereavement, low assertiveness, or alcoholism. You can compare different treatment programs to see which one is best for tension headaches or lack of impulse control.

Because problems are real, you can describe and label patients in terms of their problems. This patient is a borderline, that one is a severe depressive, he is an anxiety reaction, and she is schizophrenic. The labels carry administrative weight so that insurance companies and government agencies will allow so much compensation for a simple phobia and a different amount for psychosis. You are allowed this many sessions for a tension headache, and up to this number for a patient with obsessive thoughts.

Problems are real and objective because they possess durability. Once you determine that the problem is an inability to have orgasms, or a borderline condition, it is presumed that your treatment is for this problem in the next session and in the ones after that. The borderline is diagnosed in the early sessions and presumably stays a borderline in the next session and in the later sessions too. Once you do a proper assessment-evaluation, that is that. You may see if the problem is changing, but you do not do a complete assessment-evaluation in the third session and again in the fifth and eighth and so on. Problems have a good measure of durability, stability, and enduringness.

Problems are real and objective because they form the basis for what therapy is to accomplish. You can have goals, you can determine whether your treatment is successful and effective, once you see what the problem is. If the problem is hebephrenia, treatment should get rid of that condition. If the patient's problem is lack of identity, treatment should end with the person having an identity. If the adolescent has a problem of rebelling against authority, treatment should mean the youth does not rebel against authority. If the patient's problem is being afraid of furry animals, treatment should mean that the person is no longer afraid of furry animals. If the problem is that the patient gets anxious in enclosed places, then treatment is successful when the patient is no longer anxious in enclosed places. Once you know the problem, you generally know what treatment is to accomplish. The notion of problems makes a great deal of sense. Problems are quite real, objective, and the basis of treatment.

A "Problem" Is a Therapeutic Artifact, a Construct, Not a Real Thing

For most therapists, it is almost essential that there are "problems," that patients are seen as having problems, and also that therapy deals with these problems. The whole field of psychotherapy revolves around this notion, although different words may be substituted for the term problems. If the term were to be erased, another one would have to be put in its place. It is all but unthinkable that there could be a field of psychotherapy without patients' problems. If I asked most of these therapists what evidence would be sufficient for them to give up their notion of problem, it is almost certain that there could be no such evidence. Most likely, there would be a pause, during which the therapists would perhaps be trying to figure out if I am joking, or if there is some kind of trick.

I know that the meanings of problem are rather loose so that a great deal can be included as a problem. Even so, I would like to suggest that the term problem is just that, a term, a construct. By itself, the construct does not necessarily refer to anything real. If the problem is hebephrenia or lacking an identity, the therapist is going to have to believe in things called hebephrenia and an identity that someone can lack. In the experiential system, there is no such thing as hebephrenia or lacking an identity, deeper impulses, obsessive thoughts, phobia, assertiveness, tension headaches, schizoid, borderline, child abuse, incest survivor. These constructs, and the construct of problem, are outside the experiential system. They are real and true and universal only in some perspectives, not in all of them.

Most therapists accept the reality of whatever problem they assume they are treating. The therapist says, "I am treating her compulsiveness . . . In this session we focused on her ambivalence . . . Right here I am working on his depression . . . I am treating her lack of empowerment . . . At this point we are working on his exhibitionism." There is typically little or no doubt about the truth of the problem. Compulsiveness exists, and the patient can have this problem. There is a slender possibility that the therapist is "wrong," and the patient is not really compulsive. But there is virtually no room for a wholly different perspective in which all those words are understood as constructs, and the issue is no longer whether or not the patient is really and truly compulsive or ambivalent or depressed.

There is a way of thinking about therapy that does not necessarily have to use the term problem. Some therapists may regard therapy as a means of enabling a patient to achieve a relatively specific consequence such as gaining about 5 to 10 pounds, being able to take naps on airplane flights, being able to study school material after supper, or being able to have an orgasm. These therapists may think about their therapy without relying on problem, although most therapists would likely think of these as a weight problem, a nap problem, a study problem, or a sexual problem.

In the experiential system, the closest that we come to what is ordinarily meant by problem is (a) the immediately present bad feeling, (b) that accompanies a specific way of being and behaving, (c) in an immediately present and specific scene, situation, or context. Admittedly, this is our meaning of problem. However, from the experiential perspective, very little of what is ordinarily regarded as problems would qualify. With rare exception, virtually all the ordinary kinds of problems lack one or more of these three parts. Saying that the problem is one of hebephrenia, alcoholism, or drug abuse lacks all three parts. So too does saying that the patient has a problem of lacking identity, is out of touch with deeper impulses, has obsessive thoughts, is phobic, or is an incest survivor. When problems are stated in somewhat behavioral terms, what is lacking is the very specific behavior, a description of the "way of being," any mention of the immediately present bad feeling, and an immediately present and specific scene, situation, or context. Thus our problem would not be excessive masturbation, nail-biting, exposing oneself, fear of furry animals, or being incontinent. At a working, practical level, our meaning that comes closest to problems has very little in common with its ordinary meanings. We drop the term, problem, and instead talk about when and how the person feels awful.

Instead of a problem being something real that exists in the patient, like a growth on the buttocks, therapeutic problems are seen as a conjoint product of the therapist and patient working together. Problems do not exist by themselves. Often the work starts with the therapist. The therapist can organize services in terms of problems so that the patient is presented with a predetermined set of problems to select from. For example, when the patient calls, the secretary or someone presents the caller with the system of problems. The person who answers the telephone asks what the patient's problem is. If there are several kinds of services, the secretary may ask if the problem is a personal problem or a career problem, if it is a speech problem or a couples problem, a family problem or a crisis problem. As soon as you contact the place, you have to think in terms of categories of problems. If you get to the clinic or office, you may be given all sorts of tests, told to answer all sorts of questionnaires. These are full of "problems." You are given inventories of problems, checklists of problems. When you finally see the therapist, the first questions you will answer will be about your problems. "What brought you here? What can I do for you? How may I help you? What seems to be troubling you? What is the problem?" Problems do not simply exist. They are fabricated by therapists who think in those terms and who impose a whole system of problems onto the patient. Maybe the whole notion of problems can be dropped, in some approaches at least.

Because lots of therapists think in such terms, the early sessions are propelled and guided by their search for problems. But then the patient says something that provides a clue, and from that point on therapist and patient can work well together to come up with whatever they both are pleased to acknowledge as the problems. They are the conjoint creation of the therapist and patient, who negotiate and refine problems into existence: I talked with the doctor, and I have a problem of lack of acceptance, a problem of insecurity, a learning problem; I get low grades on my tests because I have an expressive disorder; I get drunk because I have a drinking problem. Observe the therapist and patient as they talk with one another, and you can witness the problem being constructed before your very eyes.

However, if the therapist backs off a bit and allows the patient to talk, by the end of the first session and certainly in the first few sessions, the patient will generally roam all over the place. Given half a chance, patients will become specific and general, they will mention this and that, they will cover this aspect and that one, they will mention so many worries, troubles, concerns, bothers at so many levels of abstraction that it would take a highly focused and determined therapist to remain zeroed in on a single problem, or even three problems. Given half a chance, the patient can easily tell about how he and his wife discovered kinky sex lately, he is proud of his sexual prowess, there is this delicious woman at work, he and his wife used to swim naked in lakes, he loves masturbation, he is recovering from an accident on his motorcycle, his construction work is getting better lately and he worries about whether to get side jobs to make more money because his buddy Jack is starting his own renovation work and maybe he can go in with Jack. After all of this, what is his problem or problems? The therapist is going to have to do a fine job of constructing one or more "problems" out of this mass of material.

Not only will different therapists likely find and define altogether different problems, especially if each therapist conducts the session or sessions from the beginning, but also each therapeutic approach will tend to organize and construct quite different problems, not merely dress up essentially the same problem in its own particular terminology (cf. Morgenstern, 1988). A social learning therapist and a deconstructivist therapist would organize and define quite different problems. A feminist therapist will likely locate different problems than a classical psychoanalytic therapist. Problems do not merely exist. Instead, different theories and different therapists will literally construct different problems.

Therapists and patients work together to construct problems because, according to an experiential system, talking about this problem may be quite important for each of them. Suppose that it is important for a patient to find someone who can see her as special, of real interest, a worthwhile human being. When the therapist inquires about her problem, and when some problem is mutually acknowledged, the specific problem that they build is much less critical than its being talked about in this important way. If the therapist can work with whatever the problem is taken to be, the patient probably can work with it too, provided that the inner sense is one of being regarded as special, of real interest, a worthwhile human being. Problems are, in this view, grist for the kind of experiencings that are important for patient and therapist.

An important part of the notion of a problem is that it tends to be relatively stable over sessions. If the patient's problem is depression or stealing things from stores, then that problem will be present for the next session. The idea is that a problem is like a doorbell that doesn't ring, a heater that won't turn on, or a splinter in the leg. If something is not done about it, the problem generally remains. One of the difficulties with looking at problems in this way is that it is often hard to define a "main" problem or two, unless you assert that there really is some main problem (Mahrer, Mason, Kahn, & Projansky, 1966). Even in behavior therapies, the selection of a main problem is often full of unsystematic imprecision and somewhat arbitrary choice (Klein, Dittman, Parloff, & Gill, 1969). The whole idea of a main problem is perhaps more in the therapist's conception than in the patient.

In the experiential approach, each session opens with the patient starting with some attentional center, some scene of strong feeling. Each patient is quite free to have the same opening scene of strong feeling over a series of sessions, or to find ones that are slightly different, or even quite different. I am impressed with the remarkable shifts from session to session (cf. Mahrer, 1963). When there is no therapist-determined consistency and stability, when the therapist does not impose a stable problem, then there often is a vast shift in the actual scenes, an impressive range of bad feelings, a great many changes in ways of being and behaving, and even a fair measure of variability in the inner or deeper experiencings. In the experiential system, there is no notion of a main problem that persists over a series of sessions, and, accordingly, one is rarely present.

However the problem is labeled, whether it is some manifest thing such as smiling a lot or is described intrapsychically such as ambivalence toward authority figures, it generally focuses on just one way in which the person feels bad. Virtually every patient is entitled to have lots of ways of feeling bad, gradations and nuances of similar or altogether different kinds of bad feelings. Identifying one problem, however accurately, misses so many other ways in which this person feels unsure or hurt, worried or troubled, bothered or upset. It seems unfair and also inaccurate to select a problem, hold the patient to it, and prevent other concerns, frettings, and unhappiness to take center stage.

So what can you do if a nonexperiential therapist asks what your patient's problem is? How do you avoid getting caught in that therapist's own notions about problems and still try, at least a little, to answer a question that is close to this therapist's fixed meaning of problem? I may ask, "in which session?" to indicate that I do not assume a stable, continuing problem that endures over the sessions. I may also describe the scene of bad feeling that is present in this session. This is as close as I can get to what many therapists mean by problems, and I usually try to acknowledge that we may differ in what we mean by this notion.

From the experiential perspective, problems are therapeutic artifacts, largely manufactured by and for therapists. A problem is a construct and is real only within construct systems that accept problems as real. Therapists bandy about the word problem as if they share a reasonably precise meaning of the term is. But if you take a closer look, problem is more of a fanciful myth, a construct used as if it had some specific meaning. In the experiential approach, we talk about times when the person is being and behaving in ways that feel bad. We decline most common meanings of problems.

How Do You Know Whether You Have Identified the "Problem"?

If you believe in the notion of problems, you almost certainly have to arrive at a point where you can say that you now know what the problem is. How do you go about identifying the problem?

There are some different ways of answering this question, and each comes up with a different notion of what the problem is.   Each one of these ways may well come up with a different kind of problem, and a different way of deciding that you now have enough information to decide what it is.

One way is simply to ask the patient what his problem is. The idea here is that you will tend to accept what the patient says it is, at least in a general way. The patient says her problem is that she can't let people get too close. You inquire into this a bit, and you conclude that her problem is indeed that she gets tense and upset when just about anyone gets physically close to her. This includes handshakes, any kind of physical contact, and it includes being within about a foot or so, as in crowded elevators or airplanes. This is one way: Ask the patient. This way is a favorite of behavior therapists (e.g., Woody, 1976).

A second way is for the therapist to listen to whatever the patient describes as the problem, and to impose her own label on it. Your own particular approach defines what the problem is, based on what the patient says. If the patient says that the problem is that the FBI is after him, the therapist may identify the problem as delusional thinking (cf. Nelson & Barlow, 1981). Regardless of how the patient identifies the problem, your approach may mean that you identify the problem as some kind of condition, some mental illness or disease, some kind of emotional disturbance. The problem is labeled as agoraphobia, a borderline condition, or repressed aggression. The patient did not say that; you do. Identify whatever you see as something that is to be reduced, treated, gotten rid of, based on the patient's identification of the problem. The patient is to stop clinging to her grown-up son. The patient is to be more assertive. The patient is to be on a more equal footing with his wife. In labeling the problem in her own way, the therapist may rely on a system that admits only certain things as qualified problems. For example, what is admissible is something that can be regarded as a behavioral excess or a behavioral deficit (Kanfer & Saslow, 1969). In any case, listen to whatever the patient says, and then identify the problem.

There is a third way of arriving at whatever you identify as the problem. First you and the patient talk together for a while. It may be only for 10 or 15 minutes, or it may be for a whole session or more. On the basis of all the material the patient provides, you then come to some decision. The patient may tell you lots of possible problems, from which you select one or two. You conclude that the problem is her obsessive thoughts about constipation, his ambivalence about getting married, her migraines, or his acting out aggressive impulses. You may try and put together most of what the patient has said for the session or so, and organize most of this material into a problem. He mentions that he has trouble getting out of bed in the morning, has stopped having dreams, is not having sex, and gets tired in the afternoon. By putting it all together, you conclude that his problem is depression. You may actively check out other symptoms and other information to see if this or that diagnostic inference is supported. Build up a series of diagnostic inferences. Get more and more information so that you can weigh this and that inference. Then arrive systematically at your notion of what the problem is. He starts with talking about a fear of driving through tunnels. An hour or so later, you have built up enough information to identify his problem as homosexual impulses.

When you use this third way of identifying the problem, you may well come up with two or four problems, even though they may be related to one another. Then you are faced with the issue of which problem to work on first. There are choices. Should you work on the one that is closest to the one the patient seems to want to work on? Should you go directly to the "core" problem? Should you decide on the basis of one that you think is more distressing, more debilitating, more life-threatening, the one with greatest legal ramifications (Fishman & Lubetkin, 1983; Morgenstern, 1988; Wolpe & Lazarus, 1966)? Identifying the problem can mean determining which problem to work on first.

There is a fourth way of knowing what the problem is. First you have to know what the problem-creating circumstance is, the situation in which the patient is caught. Then you use your knowledge of the problems patients have in that life circumstance. You know the kinds of problems patients have who just had their first baby, who lost their loved one, who are facing life-threatening surgery, who face menopause, who are recent immigrants to a strange country. Just find out the problem-engendering life circumstances, and you know what the problems are.

There is a least one more way of knowing that you have found out what the problem is. You have completed your search when you are ready to turn to the next step after identifying the problem. For example, you are ready to use desensitization, or to use bereavement counseling, or assertion training. Or you have gone far enough in identifying the problem when you are ready to get such information about the problem as when it first started, when it was worse, how it has been treated in the past, what seemed to precipitate it. Once you are ready to do what you do after identifying the problem, you know that you have gone far enough.

Here are five different ways at arriving at a point where you know that you have identified the problem. Each way would likely come up with its own kind of problem. Your identification of the problem varies with the method you use to get at it. A therapist who says that the patient has this particular problem could perhaps state more accurately that when he uses this particular way of trying to identify a problem, here is what he gets.

If you still insist that there is a quite real problem—a main problem that this patient has—then you are almost forced to see each of these ways as getting at a slightly different aspect of the single, main, true, stable, and enduring problem. A behavior therapist may do an elaborate "behavioral analysis" and come up with a specific idea of the problem behavior (Kanfer & Busemeyer, 1982; Kazdin, 1985; Mash & Terdal, 1981; Wilson & Evans, 1983). A psychoanalytic therapist may spend many sessions developing a picture of the infantile conflicts between intimacy and autonomy. You may try to find some ways in which these are merely slightly different aspects of essentially the same problem. Or, perhaps each way of arriving at what the problem is may understandably come away with its own, quite distinctive, meaning of problem.

In experiential therapy, the whole notion of "problem" is of little or no use; instead, the focus is on scenes of strong bad feeling.   In this approach, the question is, When is it, what are the times, what are the scenes and situations, when the feelings are strong? Once we find this time, we use it to access the inner, deeper experiencing. We start by showing the patient how to look for the times, the scenes and situations, when the feelings are strong and typically bad. Almost certainly, this puts the patient on a different path than using any of the ways of trying to identify a "problem." When the experiential therapist and patient find a scene of strong bad feeling, most other therapists may be puzzled because they are left not knowing what the problem is.

When most therapists feel they have some idea or grasp of the problem, the experiential therapist usually just starts at that point and proceeds to look for when the feeling is strong. Typically, there is no scene, or there is a soft allusion to some general class of loose situations. Lots of problems are given in terms of psychodiagnositic condition. The patient's problem is a borderline condition, a personality disorder, a phobic condition, and so on. Identifying the problem as the borderline condition tells you essentially nothing about a strong-feelinged scene or situation, especially since the situation may or may not have anything to do with the "condition." What about behavioral problems? The same story unfolds. Identifying a behavioral problem usually tells you very little about strong-feelinged, explicit situations. Try to get the specific content of the bad feeling and the specific scene in which following behavioral problems occur: binge eating and vomiting, fears of public speaking, blushing, eating too much fattening foods, fear of blood, sexual dysfunctions, thoughts of impending catastrophes, fears and worries about being in public places and having to have bowel movement, fear of bats, anxiety about not being able to have orgasms, face-picking, tension headaches, generalized anxiety, nail-biting, pulling hairs from scalp, urges to expose penis in public, test anxiety.

When many therapists would be satisfied that the problem is obesity, the experiential therapist would have no idea of what the bad feeling is nor in what situational context the bad feeling occurs. Therapists arrive at a notion that this woman is too fat, is overweight, is obese. Given half a chance to say what bothers her, she says, "My weight." These therapists are satisfied that she has a "weight problem," has a condition called "obesity." In contrast, the experiential therapist has no idea of the bad-feelinged scene. The experiential therapist looks for the nature of the bad feeling, in relationship to the weight, or anything else, and the situation in which this bad feeling occurs. When she talks about her weight, the feeling is one of almost whining, complaining, moaning. When does she have this feeling about the weight or perhaps anything else? The worst times are when she actually meets the men she talks to on the telephone at work. She is a secretary who does a lot of in-house calling. She gets excited when the caller is an attractive man in the department. When he meets her, perhaps in a meeting, and says, "Oh, you're Kathy," she has the bad feeling. The problem is not her weight or her condition of "obesity." The focus of therapy with this woman, in this session, is the feeling of being a big pretense, of not being attractive, of being a painful disappointment, in situations involving men who are turned off by seeing how fat she is. We look for the situation in which the bad feeling is occurring.

Looking for the scene of strong bad feeling is a rather exciting adventure of discovery. Neither the therapist nor the patient will likely know what situation of strong bad feeling will be found. You may start with her rebellious adolescent daughter and end up with a scene in which she is shaking with rage at her sister's accusations. Starting with her uncertainty about having an abortion, the scene may be the recent appointment with the nurse who seemed to look down on her as just another young pregnant kid, or the journey may culminate in a cavernous feeling of loss and loneliness last year, when she sat home, in her bedroom, after her mother was buried, and gripped her face so tautly that she drew blood. We rarely can anticipate what the scene of strong, bad feeling will be, even if we start from what other therapists would be satisfied is a fair identification of the problem.

At some point, the usual therapist almost always gets a fair notion of what the problem is. The therapist now knows that the problem is the patient gets anxious in elevators, or the patient is uncertain about whether or not to have the abortion. The next thing to do is to get more information about the provisionally identified problem. Check out the patient's support system. How long has the problem lasted? What has the patient done about the problem so far? Is the patient put together rather well, or might the patient fall apart in dealing with this problem? You may look for all sorts of relevant information once you have a fairly good idea of what the problem is. However, at the point where nonexperiential therapists might decide that they have some idea of what the problem is, the experiential therapist has essentially no idea of the scene in which there is some bad feeling. Saying that I get anxious in elevators or that I am worried about whether or not to have an abortion does not identify the scene in which there is some bad feeling. We have a great deal more work to do because we are looking for a scene of bad feeling, not a "problem."

Picture about a dozen therapists, representing a variety of approaches, listening to a tape of an experiential session. Right after the initial instructions, the patient says, "I know that I'm depressed, most of my life. I'm my own worst enemy . . . I've been in therapy before, but I don't do well. I expect to be treated. The doctor is supposed to make me better. People are supposed to take care of me. I always wait for someone to do something for me and then I sabotage it . . . That's why I'm so depressed lately. Only it's getting worse. This depression is going to kill me. I was thinking of killing myself when I was driving to work this morning. With thoughts like this, how can I function?" Most of the therapists tend to agree that the patient's problem is depression.

The experiential therapist is looking for some scene in which a feeling is strong. But which feeling? Depression? The experiential therapist listens for the feeling in the person who is talking, and gets a feeling of being self-critical, bitching about himself, being annoyed at himself. Not "depression." When is it that there is such a feeling of being so self-critical, bitching about yourself, being annoyed at yourself? We arrive at a scene. "Two colleagues, see? Veronica and Claude. They hate me, and I hate them. A couple of days ago, they come into my office. Come in! Don't knock. And they tell me that they think it's best if I quit! Fuck! I could kill them! I really could! I could have killed them!" You can say that this fellow has a problem of depression, and you can cite evidence. Or you can say that the bad feeling is being furious, violent, assaultive, in a scene when two colleagues are in his office and telling him to quit his job and get out. Which is "correct"? I would say that both are. And they are quite different from one another.

Looking for the scenes of strong feeling can start with just about anything that most therapists regard as problems. Wherever you start, look for the feeling, the scene or situation, and for when the bad feeling is truly strong. The person opens with a troubled feeling about his stuttering. You may arrive at scenes and situations of awful feeling in regard to the stuttering, or of some other kind of terrible feeling in regard to the stuttering or in regard to other situational contexts having little or nothing to do with the stuttering (cf. Mahrer & Young, 1962).

When problems are custom fitted to this particular patient, it is easy to give up on the idea of trying to compile lists of problems. Almost from the beginning of attempts to frame problems in the patient's own words, or particularized to this patient right now, the ventures ended up with loads of items (e.g., Kempf, 1915; Plant, 1922). When I began assembling such a checklist for hospitalized patients, with heavy emphasis on how it was for this specific patient, I quickly arrived at 300 items (Mahrer, 1967c), and could have gone on to 3,000 items. If the focus shifts to the precise feeling in a precise situational context, it is hopeless to try and organize all this into a workable list of categories. But that is neither necessary nor useful. What is useful is to arrive at the specific bad feeling in the specific scene in this session (Mahrer, 1970a).

Many therapists look for the "problem." Experiential therapists look for the scenes of strong feeling, including scenes of strong bad feeling. From some problem-oriented perspectives, the two ventures are similar. From the experiential perspective, the two enterprises are altogether different.

Once You Have Some Idea of What the "Problem" Is, What Else Do You Want to Know about It?

Sooner or later, regardless of the method you use, you will probably arrive at some idea of what the problem is. What then? What further information do you want about the identified problem, provided, of course, that your mind-set is one that thinks in terms of "problems?"

One answer is that you do not especially need more information about the problem. Now that you have some idea of the problem or problem condition, you can use the appropriate intervention, treatment, therapeutic program. You may apply the appropriate treatment yourself or refer the patient to the proper specialist. You can determine the appropriate treatment if the problem or problem condition is hebephrenia, schizo-phrenia, bulimia, or if the patient steals things from stores, cannot communicate with the spouse, has a tension headache, pulls hairs from eyebrows, or has a particular kind of depression. In any case, you know what the problem is, and now you can go ahead and see which treatment program to apply.

But suppose that you think in terms of pathological conditions, mental illnesses, psychodiagnoses. Then you may try to find out whether the problem is a symptom of some pathological condition, whether the condition you think the patient has is really the one you suspect, is severe or not so severe, has a long or short history. If the prob-lem is a facial tic, check out other symptoms to see what syndrome is present. Then you can know the kind of psychodiagnosis that fits. If he is depressed, check out the kind of depression by getting pertinent other information. If the problem is that he stutters, Coriat (1915) showed how to get further information about the underlying pathologi-cal condition. Psychoanalytic therapists see stuttering as an intriguing symptom with all sorts of underlying pathological conflicts and possible conditions (e.g., Fenichel, 1945; Froeschels, 1943; Glauber, 1943, 1953). When you identify the problem as be-reavement, there are lots of things to check out concerning the nature, severity, and scope of the underlying pathological condition (e.g., Bequaert, 1976; Buchanan, 1974; Crosby & Jose, 1983; Heyman & Gianturco, 1983; Hyde, 1989; Rohrbaugh, 1979).

You can also get lots of information to help you in the treatment. The kind of in-formation that you look for depends on the kind of treatment that you are providing. For example, if you think in terms of mental illnesses, pathological conditions, and psy-chodiagnoses, then you might want to get a case history and a history of the patholog-ical condition. This information can help you in giving interpretations and having the patient gain insight and understanding about similarities between things in his past and in his present. In fact, lots of therapies like to turn to information about the his-tory of the problem. Then the therapist not only can provide insight, but can complete the unfinished business, provide a corrective emotional experience, catharsis or abre-action, can desensitize, reframe, relearn.

Once you identify the problem, you can see the patient's areas of strength, the situations when the problem is not a problem, and some of the patient's own useful so-lutions (de Shazer, 1985, 1991; Rosenbaum, Hoyt, & Talmon, 1990; Talmon, 1990). You gather all sorts of information on the causes of the problem. To what extent and in what ways is the headache or hair-pulling or depression caused by chemical or pharmaco-logical factors, by neurological factors, by physiological factors, by psychological fac-tors? If the problem is marital stress, check out the specific causes such as mutual unfulfilled expectation (O'Leary & Wilson, 1987). If the problem is stealing things from stores or inability to maintain an erection, then get more information to check out different inferences about what causes the problem.

If you follow a behavioral approach, you may look for information about the an-tecedent, stimulating conditions and consequent stimulating or reinforcing conditions. You look for the things that bring about, maintain, and control the problem behavior (Nathan, 1981). Almost from the beginning of therapeutic treatment of stuttering, it was looked at as a learned behavior, and therapists found all sorts of things that helped bring about and maintain this learned behavior (e.g., Hill, 1945; Rosenberg & Curtis, 1939; Rotter, 1942; Wischner, 1950).

Practitioners of experiential therapy would not identify any "problem" such as in-somnia, stuttering, stealing things from stores, or inability to maintain an erection. In-stead, they look for times when the bad feeling is strong. Suppose that the scene is one in which the stolen perfume is in her purse, she is paying for a hairbrush, the manager is standing near the checkout counter, and she is terrified, her heart pounding, her face tight. Once you identify the scene of strong feeling, you can see how inappropriate it might be to think in terms of further information about a problem. Instead, most of what you want is contained in the scene itself. Somewhere in this scene is a moment in which the bad feeling is strongest. That is what we look for. Once we know that moment, the prize is the inner, deeper experiencing that is now accessible. The experiential therapist needs no further information about the "problem" but instead uses the scene to access the inner, deeper experiencing. Instead of looking for the history of her stealing problem, the experiential therapist identifies a scene of strong feeling and then uses it to access the deeper potential or inner experiencing.

From the experiential perspective, there is little or no use of what is ordinarily called problems or problem conditions. These are not central to our goals and objectives. Indeed, from this perspective, there are lots of serious problems with the notion of problems. Experiential psychotherapy does not aim at reducing or resolving problems. Its directions of change include the washing away of bad feelings of pain, hurt, suffering; the ending of scenes of bad feelings; no longer does the person behave in ways that construct and use the situational contexts to undergo painful experiencing accompanied with bad feelings. This direction of change is outside what most therapists mean by problems and by therapy as the treatment of problems.

HOW DO YOU ARRIVE AT THE GOALS, OBJECTIVES, AND DIRECTIONS OF CHANGE FOR THIS PATIENT?

Almost every therapist arrives at some notion of the goals, objectives, directions of change for patients. These objectives may be more or less firm or loose, may be more long-range or short-range, but there are almost always some goals, objectives, and directions of change. How do you arrive at them? How do you determine what they are for each patient?

The Way You Describe or Identify Patient, Problem, or Problem Condition Contains a Built-in Set of Goals, Objectives, and Directions of Change versus Describing or Identifying the Patient, Problem, or Problem Condition Is Separate from Setting the Goals, Objectives, and Directions of Change

Many therapists believe that the description and identification of the patient, the problem, or problem condition are separate from determining the goals, objectives, and directions of change. First do a diagnosis, an assessment-evaluation of the patient, problem, or problem condition. Then figure out appropriate goals, objectives, and directions of change. Although that sounds sensible, the way you describe and identify the patient, the problem, or the problem condition practically defines the goals, objectives, and directions of change. The two enterprises are almost always intimately intertwined so that therapists who label patients, problems, and problem conditions in a particular way have also set the goals, objectives, and directions of change.

If you identify the problem in terms of "being that way is bad," then the built-in goal is that the patient is not to be that way. The label defines the goal as doing it less, not being like the label says he is. If you say that the patient is alcoholic or has a drinking problem, then the goal is that the patient is to drink less. If the problem is overexcitement, the patient is to be less excitable. If you decide the patient is oversexed, then the goal is less sexuality in whatever ways the patient is too sexual. If the problem is called kleptomania, the patient is to not steal. If the patient is a binge-eater, the goal is to not eat in binges. A patient who has a blushing "problem" is to stop blushing so much. If the problem is depression, then the goal is not be so depressed. If you say the problem is aggression, then the goal is for the patient to be less aggressive. If the patient is said to have a phobia, then the goal is for the person to be less fearful of whatever it is. The way you identify the problem contains the directions of change—the patient is not to be that way.

If you identify the problem in terms of what the patient lacks, then what the patient should have and show more of is built into the way you label the problem. His problem is a lack of assertiveness. The objective is that he should be assertive. This other fellow's problem is a lack of identity. He needs an identity. The patient is immature. The goal is to become more mature. The patient is an unliberated woman. The goal is that she should be liberated (cf. Feldman & Peay, 1982; Morgenstern, 1988).

If you identify the problem in terms of too little, too much, and a valued midrange, then your definition has a built-in-goal of the midrange as proper, appropriate, normal, adjustive, healthy. If you label the person as a sexual deviate, the goal is to move toward the midrange. You may identify the problem as one of being an underachiever or an overachiever. The direction of change is toward the middle. By having a list of what males and females should be like, you can identify the problem as one of gender-inappropriate behavior, and the built-in objective is to become normal, more gender-appropriate.

You have some idea of what normal, midrange, adequate sex is. You come to the conclusion that this person is above what you think is normal for her. She says that she masturbates 8 to 10 times a day. You say that her problem is one of "excessive masturbation," or "compulsive masturbation," and the goal is for her to cut back to perhaps two or three times a day. In contrast, this young fellow says that he and Sarah used to have sex two or three times a week, but over the past couple of years they have sex at best two or three times a year. You define this as a sexual problem, as lack of sexual desire, as blocked sexuality. Your goal is that he should have sex closer to two or three times a week. The built-in goal is for patients to move toward the valued midrange.

If you describe the problem in terms of some issue that patients cope with, then the goal may be to work through the "psychodynamics." Patients coping with that issue have similar psychodynamics, so once you know the problem, you know the goals of therapy. For example, the patient is a bereavement case, an incest survivor, a postpartum depression, or the patient is coping with AIDS, a recent catastrophe, cancer, old age. You have some idea of the psychodynamics of patients with these problems, and working through these psychodynamics constitutes the goals, objectives, and directions of change. You know that incest survivors have a great deal of repressed rage, and therefore the goal is for these patients to work through their repressed rage. Bereavement cases suffer from pain, stress, loneliness, and depression, and they must go through the stages of inner loss and grief (Buchanan, 1974; Clark, 1982; Crosby & Jose, 1983; Hodge, 1972; Peterson & Briley, 1977; Schoenberg, 1970; Schuchter, 1986; Schwartz-Borden, 1986; Silverman, 1981; Volkan, 1975). Once you label the problem or problem condition, the psychodynamics of those patients tell you the goals, objectives, and directions of change.

If the problem is defined in terms of the patient's being a member of an agency or institution, then that agency or institution typically sets the goals. If the patient is in a residential treatment center, then that particular center may have as its goal that its patients are to be able to function in ordinary community settings (Paul, 1987). If the patient is in a palliative care unit, then the goal of that unit may be to make the remaining months of life reasonably serene. If the patient is in a psychiatric unit or hospital, then the goals may include not "acting out" in a disruptive, harmful, crazy manner. Patients in an alcohol treatment center are generally to stop drinking.

If you define the problem in terms of the patient being psychotic, then that label may set the goal as being placed into an institution or psychiatric unit. You have defined a similar goal if you say that this patient is too agitated, is unable to control suicidal or homicidal impulses. In addition, not only are you defining the goal as being in a psychiatric facility, but you may be restricting the treatment to "supportive therapy" (cf. Schlesinger, 1976) or to simple behavioral treatment (Nelson & Barlow, 1981), by the words you use in defining the problem.

I doubt very much if most therapists arrive at the goals, objectives, and directions of change by reasoning from whatever this patient's problem or problem condition is. Many therapists like to think that this is how they arrive at goals and objectives, but generally I believe that labeling the problem and identifying the goals occur at the same time. The actual words you use to identify the problem generally contain the goals of therapy.

Who Determines the Goals, Objectives, and Directions of Change? One Perspective Is That It Is the Therapist

Many therapists like to believe that the goals, objectives, and directions of change come largely from the patient, or at least from a process of negotiation in which both therapist and patient work together. This position is often so deeply entrenched that there would be little or no evidence that these therapists would accept as sufficient for them to admit that they were wrong. Nor would I try to convince these therapists otherwise. However, I would like to outline an alternative perspective in which it is indeed the therapist who almost singlehandedly determines the goals of treatment.

The therapist is the direct determiner of the goals, objectives, and directions of change. Typically, the therapist directly and openly determines what therapy is to try and bring about. Picture a "case conference," which is usually a small group of people who gather together to determine the goals and objectives, the "treatment plan." Sometimes the goals and objectives are relatively loose, but they can be quite definite. These people may decide that the patient should be prevented from living with that fellow, should not be permitted to have artificial insemination, should be pushed toward becoming more understanding of his sister, should stay in the marriage, should get out of the marriage, should have or should not have a baby.

Should the therapist work on the patient's problems with letting men dominate her, her problem of repressed anger toward her mother, her concern with keeping fit, exercising, and being slender, or her occasional states of severe depression? He could talk this over with a few colleagues, or with his consultant. Or he could decide himself. Which of these problems is most bothersome to the patient? Which may be the one with greatest professional or legal dangers? Which one is perhaps easiest to start with at this point in treatment? Which seems uppermost at this point, as far as the patient is concerned? Which one is easiest to resolve? Based on these kinds of considerations (cf. Nelson & Barlow, 1981), the therapist makes a deliberate and determined choice of which goals and objectives to pursue.

Typically, the therapist decides on the goals and objectives because the therapist knows best. The therapist—with advanced knowledge and training—is the doctor, the professional, the specialist. If the doctor decides that the patient should give up this idea of the six-month excursion into the jungle, then that is the best goal. The therapist is more realistic, has a more mature outlook, sees things more accurately, has infinitely more knowledge about pathology and how to change behavior and resolve personal problems. Trust the therapist.

This professional, therefore, is the one to determine that an individual "needs" therapy. The person is behaving abnormally, has peculiar ideas about life, and therefore should benefit from treatment. Many therapists call patients and pressure them to come for counseling because of this or that. Your son is in trouble. You are accepted into the sexual dysfunction program and therefore your physician wants you seen for counseling. You are diagnosed as having cancer, and therefore you need therapy. Your supervisor has some concerns about your personal problems interfering at work, so you should come in for therapy. Your daughter is behaving funny at school, and I would like to talk this over with you. Therapists are good at going after clients and having explicit goals in mind. Indeed, these goals and objectives are the basis for getting the potential clients to come in the first place.

Many therapists make it their professional responsibility to determine the goals and objectives. Your husband, who is my patient, needs constant care and understanding, so I would like you to rearrange your life and make sure that you are with him in this particular way. The therapist determines that this patient is competent to stand trial, or that patient is incompetent to manage her daily affairs. That patient has severe depression, and therefore here are the things that have to be done to make sure there is no suicide. This older woman is to be evaluated for brain damage. On the basis of my professional opinion, you should have the abortion, or it would be better for your mental health if you did not have the abortion. Because of these considerations, the goal is hospitalization (Gregory & Smeltzer, 1977).

The therapist is the subtle, indirect, but persistently powerful determinant of the goals, objectives, and directions of change.   The therapist is always guiding the patient in one direction or another, influencing, shaping and molding what the patient talks about. Virtually everything the therapist says and does, and does not say and do, exerts a subtle, indirect, but persistently powerful effect in determining the goals and objectives.

From the very beginning, the therapist works quite carefully with the patient to label, to identify, to put into focus, the nature of the problem. Arriving at the nature and content of the problem is a delicate and sensitive negotiation in which the therapist exerts a powerful hand. Starting from whatever the therapist guides the patient into framing as a provisional statement of the problem or difficulty, the therapist shapes and molds it into the problem that the therapist sees it as being. The therapist is largely responsible for arriving at the patient's defensiveness in his relation with his adolescent daughter, and the possibility of a sexual problem here. The therapist guides the problem into being her "excessive" grieving over her dead husband. The therapist guides him into seeing his problem as his aggressive tendencies. Even more powerfully, once the patient accepts this as the problem, there is a set of built-in-goals, objectives, and directions of change. Merely by working to define the problem or problem condition in this way, the therapist has succeeded in exerting a strong influence in determining the directions of change.

Almost from the beginning, and certainly throughout the sessions, the therapist has a picture of how the patient should be and should not be. On the basis of this picture, the therapist continually blocks this avenue, avoids that topic, deflects the patient, influences the patient toward this and away from that. The therapist sees the patient as a lesbian, living with another woman, as having a daughter from a previous marriage, and as making noises about wanting another baby. The patient feels she is entitled to artificial insemination. The therapist uses subtle means of dissuading her. After a few more sessions, she abandons the idea.

Throughout the sessions, patients will make overtures toward this or that direction of change; they will indicate inclinations and leanings toward doing this, being like that, engaging in this or that. In response, many therapists have loads of ways of either approving or disapproving, of encouraging or discouraging. Therapists easily serve as judges, and they use ways of saying yes or no that are persistent, powerful, subtle, indirect, but usually quite effective.

If the patient seems inclined to switch from one sexual orientation to another, therapists may introduce plenty of considerations that subtly but powerfully advise the patient against doing so (cf. Davison, 1977; Feldman & Peay, 1982; Morgenstern, 1988; Silverstein, 1977). If the therapist is not in accord with what the patient seems to want, then the therapist is to "reeducate" the patient (Cormier & Cormier, 1979). Many therapists believe their professional responsibility includes the approval or disapproval of what the patient seems to be heading toward.

If the therapist decides that what the patient seems inclined toward is dangerous and harmful, then a subtle but effective maneuver is to introduce a consideration of the effects on others. If the patient introduces the possibility of sending roses to her grandmother on the anniversary of her grandmother's winning a ribbon at the flower show, the therapist does not think of the negative consideration on others. However, if a patient is inclined to have sex with her boyfriend's father, quit her fine job, or to show up at her mother's formal lawn party wearing a dog collar and leash, the therapist may well confront the patient with the importance of thinking about the negative effects on others. This maneuver is powerful. It can be carried off with subtlety, but its effect is clear. Do not do it.

When a patient takes the initiative in determining the goals, objectives, and directions of change, many therapists must reassert their mandate. Furthermore, the therapist can always cite extreme instances of patients carrying out wild and dangerous behaviors to justify therapists being in control. What if the patient wants to shoot people, blow up a building, beat up old people? The conclusion is that the therapist must approve of, judge the acceptability of, and generally be in charge of the goals, objectives, and directions of change. Patients cannot be left alone to carry out whatever behaviors they may want to do. *but they are — they would be ill*

In this perspective, the therapist predominantly determines the goals, objectives, and directions of change for this patient.

How Does the Therapist Determine the Goals, Objectives, and Directions of Change?

Therapists write a great deal about how to arrive at goals. My first serious concern with this issue led to an edited book where many therapists addressed these issues (Mahrer,

1967a). However, what follows comes from listening to tapes of actual sessions conducted by hundreds of therapists representing lots of different approaches and combinations of approaches, from many hours in case conferences and talking with colleagues about particular goals for specific patients, as well as from reading what therapists write about how they arrive at their goals. There are at least three ways that most therapists use to arrive at goals.

The patient is to conform to the therapist's personal value system of disapproved ways of being and behaving. Therapists generally have personal value systems that include particular ways of being and behaving as bad, as disapproved. Accordingly, the goal, the objective, the direction of change, is that the patient should not be or behave that way.

Many therapists are incredibly judgmental. They see or find or come across particular ways of being and behaving and simply disapprove of the patient being and behaving in that way. The therapists do not like it. Being and behaving in that way is a violation of their personal value system.

Therapists almost never would openly admit that they disapprove of that way of being or behaving. Instead, therapists call it sick, pathological, maladjustive, problematic, self-defeating, immature, symptomatic of a personality disorder or an emotional illness, unrealistic. It shows that the patient is too rigid, too lacking in control, too sexual, irresponsible, narcissistic, lacking feeling, indecisive, passive-aggressive. In other words, instead of saying outright that they disapprove of this way of being and behaving, therapists mask their disapproval with jargon words that provide professional justification.

Another way of justifying what therapists disapprove of is to assert that such a way of being and behaving is dangerous, can lead to harm, can hurt oneself or others. Keeping five guns in the house is therefore bad not because it is "pathological," although you could make such a case, but rather because children might hurt themselves or others with the guns. Lots of ways of being and behaving can be called dangerous. It is safer and more justifiable to say that something is dangerous than to say that you object to it, you dislike it, and it is on your list of disapproved ways of being and behaving.

Many therapists operate with such a list. As soon as a patient displays something on that list, it is instantly labeled as disapproved, sick, pathological, perhaps even dangerous. From listening to a few sessions conducted by one therapist, I noted the following items from her list of disapproved ways of being and behaving: staying on welfare, stealing a chicken from a store, lying about where you were that afternoon, leaving a well-paying job, having an affair with a married person, talking publically about fucking, being a 47-year-old woman who is slender, being late for appointments and not feeling guilty, having sex with your sister's boyfriend, quitting high school.

The process is twofold and swiftly automatic. The first step is finding the thing that is bad, that is on your value system of bad things. As the patient talks, the therapist finds the bad thing. "He is sadistic!" "She is abusive!" Once the therapist spots a sadistic streak or abusiveness, that is that. Not only is there really a sadistic streak or abusiveness, but it is bad. In fact, it is bad even before the therapist spots it. It is truly as if these therapists are the values police, out to find the bad patients. The second step is then automatic. The goal is to do something about the sadism or the abusiveness. Therapeutic machinery is lined up to get rid of the sadism and the abusiveness. There is, something scary about this way of operating, no matter how common it is, or especially because it is so common. My value system says that that value system is bad.

What is also scary is that many items on lists of disapproved ways of being and behaving become official. If a number of therapists share similar items of disapproved ways of being and behaving, it can be institutionalized. You can even organize it into an official and standardized nomenclature of mental illnesses and diseases. If enough therapists have it in their disapproved list, then it is the accepted basis for putting people like that into hospitals. It is not your personal list; it is "the" professionally mandated list of disapproved ways of being and behaving, reading as the handbook of psychodiagnostic disorders.

Is being homosexual to be disapproved? It used to be a mental illness. Officially, being homosexual is not disapproved. Then what do therapists do if they still disapprove of homosexuality? The answer is to disapprove of it anyhow. Many therapists "regard homosexual behavior and attitudes to be undesirable, sometimes pathological, and at any rate in need of change toward a heterosexual orientation" (Davison, 1977, p. 4).

How do many therapists determine the goals, objectives, and directions of change? They maintain a personal list of disapproved ways of being and behaving. The aim is to stop those ways of being and behaving.

The patient is to conform to the therapist's personal value system of approved ways of being and behaving.   Symmetrically, many therapists have a personal list of approved ways of being and behaving. It is the good list of valued, desirable ways of being and behaving. From this list, therapists can determine this patient's goals, objectives, and directions of change.

Patients are to move toward increased contribution to social values and benefits (Nelson & Barlow, 1981), to women's rights and feminist values, toward social good and social norms (Kratochwill, 1985b). Patients are to become more self-approving and self-liking (Braaten, 1961; Dollard & Mowrer, 1947; Raimy, 1948). Patients are to act in ways that are mature (Haigh, 1949), to show more focus on immediate experience (Gendlin, Beebe, Cassens, Klein, & Oberlander, 1968), to show more cooperative behavior (Horowitz, Sampson, Siegelman, Weiss, & Goodfriend, 1978), to evidence more emotional expression, self-exploration, ownership of their own feelings, behaviors, and thoughts (Schauble & Pierce, 1974). The list can go on and on. Some lists are more or less shared by therapists of a given orientation. Other lists are shared by large groups of therapists from different orientations.

Some lists are highly personal to the given therapist. Good ways of being and behaving include leaving the family at a particular age, eating properly, having a job, paying alimony, using birth control devices, being plump, being skinny, having a baby, having a career, having a career and a baby, having sex with your spouse.

The therapist declares that her patient got in trouble by stealing some clothes from a store, the patient is quite an intelligent girl but she works cleaning people's houses, she has a bunch of boyfriends with whom she has sex, and she left high school about six months before graduation. The patient should, therefore, not do things that get her into trouble with the law, she should finish high school and do something more in keeping with her intelligence, and she should not be having sex with so many of those guys. Once the therapist has a chance to describe the patient, what she describes tends to come from her personal value system, and the related directions of change come straight out of that same value system.

The approved goals and objectives may be presented to the therapist by others, such as the treatment team, the parents of the patient, a probation officer, social worker, physician. Indeed, the patient is referred with these goals and objectives in mind. Once these other sources set the goals and objectives, the therapist is free to accept or decline them. Generally, if these goals and objectives conform to the therapist's personal value system of approved ways of being and behaving, then they become the goals and objectives of treatment. Before and during treatment, the parents want you to get this adolescent girl to study more, to stay in school, and at least to pass. She brings you letters from her family. They called you before they even sent her to you. They pay your bill. These become the goals and objectives for treatment. In a similar way, this other patient is to be less alcoholic, to stop beating his child, to get a job, to take her medicine, to let her grown-up children leave home, to stop dressing that awful way, to start bathing regularly. Hundreds of objectives and goals are given to therapists by external sources who have a stake in the patient being the way they want him to be, and as long as these conform to the therapist's own value system of approved ways of being and behaving, they are accepted as the goals, objectives, and directions of change.

The patient is to adopt the therapist's perspective.   Most therapists have a perspective, a way of looking at things. The goal, the objective, the direction of change is for the patient to adopt the therapist's perspective. The therapist's way of looking at things may be a general life philosophy, a way of looking at oneself, at one's world, at one's interpersonal relations. It may be ways of living the good life. It may consist of ways of dealing with problems in general or with this particular problem the patient is facing. The perspective may be personal, or it may be shared with other therapists who likewise are humanistic, behavioral, cognitive, Jungian, or psychoanalytic.

If the therapist looks at things from a psychoanalytic perspective, then one of the directions of change may be for the patient to look at things through a psychoanalytic perspective. They would both look for the childhood connections, unconscious mechanisms, and psychoanalytic dynamics. Sometimes, the therapist's perspective consists of prescriptions for living the good life, little homilies on the rules for living: Most people need an adequate support system, you need an interest of some kind, it is good to have friends, it's not good to overdo things, you need something stable in your life. These are not Jungian or cognitive ways of making sense of the world. They are the therapist's own wisdoms. Nevertheless, the goal is for the patient to adopt this perspective.

When patients face some issue, some trouble, the aim is for the patient to adopt and carry through the therapist's favorite recipe for resolving that kind of problem. If the problem has to do with the husband's younger brother staying with them much too long, then the patient is to adopt the therapist's perspective. For example, the therapist believes that the problem relates to the whole group, and therefore the whole group should have some sessions. Or the therapist may hold the perspective that the important thing is what all this means to the patient, how the patient participates in this problem, the patient's relevant psychodynamics. Or, the therapist's perspective is all for honesty, saying it like it is, being open. Instead of grumbling and becoming upset, the best thing is to tell the brother-in-law how she really feels. The aim is for the patient to adopt the therapist's perspective on what to do about this kind of problem. Look at the problem my way.

If the patient begins looking at things from the therapist's perspective, this is an important goal, a worthwhile objective. It shows that things are going in the right direction. It indicates progress, improvement. So important is this to the therapist that the patient's adopting the therapist's perspective is elevated to one of the highest goals and objectives of therapy. When patients see things the way the therapist does, that is dignified as insight and understanding (Beutler, 1981; Claiborn, 1982; Frank, 1973; Hobbs, 1962; Mahrer, Dessaulles, Gervaize, & Nadler, 1987; Rosenbaum, Hoyt, & Talmon, 1990).

Most therapists arrive at the goals, objectives, and directions of change by getting the patient to adopt their own perspectives on things, or by calling on their own value system of approved and disapproved ways of being and behaving. I don't have much respect for these particular ways of deciding what can be accomplished with the patient. There are other ways at arriving at the goals of therapy, but these three ways account for the major goals of most therapists. In the experiential system, how does the therapist arrive at the goals, objectives, and directions of change?

How Do You Arrive at the Goals, Objectives, and Directions of Change for This Patient? What Is the Experiential Answer?

The experiential answer is that in each session, the therapist and patient look for the deeper potential or inner experiencing that is here; the goals are determined by that inner experiencing. The aim is to enable the patient to be and to behave on the basis of this integrated and actualized inner experiencing. This is the purpose of Steps 2 through 4. This is the main answer. A secondary answer deals with whatever scene of strong bad feeling the patient identifies in the first step. The goal is for the new person to be free of that scene.

The aim is to be and behave as the integrated, actualized inner experiencing. Every session enables the therapist and patient to find some inner, deeper potential or experiencing in this patient. The patient is to become a new person based on this inner experiencing. The deeper experiencing is to be welcomed and appreciated, is to be on good terms with the other potentials, is to enjoy good relationships with the other potentials. This is called integration. The deeper experiencing is also to become a part of the operating domain, a part of the person that the patient is. More important, the patient is to become this new person. The new person is the new experiencing, is being and behaving on the basis of this new experiencing. This is called actualization.

Suppose that Jenny is living and being in a scene in which her husband is once again being unfriendly, removed, pulled in, distant. Her feeling is outright annoyance and irritation. She is bothered and upset both by her own present annoyance and irritation, and also by the disgusting way that her husband is being. Some therapists are inclined to frame goals right here. They may say that the direction of change is toward learning how to cope with her own feelings of annoyance and irritation, or toward being able to do something so that she can have reduced feelings of annoyance and irritation, or toward preventing the situation from occurring so that the husband is less inclined to be unfriendly, removed, pulled in, and distant.

The experiential therapist may start with this scene, but go further and deeper into this scene. If the therapist and patient go further, living and being in this scene even more, searching for and being in a particular moment when the feeling is especially strong, only then is it likely that she will arrive at something that may lie deeper. Here is an inner experiencing, a deeper potential. Whatever it is, whatever its nature, we are usually surprised because we simply find whatever we find, access whatever is accessed. There is no reasoning from the bad-feelinged scene to the nature of the deeper potential. However, it is this deeper potential that serves as the basis for the direction of change. We search for what is inside, and its integration and actualization provide the goals of this session.

In some approaches, what is inside, deeper, is the way the person is to be. Experiential therapy falls in this group. Even when I first started working with patients and did lots of intelligence testing, I was drawn toward possible other answers that these patients had available but did not give. I was attracted to what I called their "potential intelligence" (Mahrer, 1957, 1958; Mahrer & Bernstein, 1958; Thorp & Mahrer, 1959). I still regard what lies within, the person's deeper potentials for experiencing, as the touchstone for arriving at directions of change.

However, many therapists and therapies go in the opposite direction. They regard what is deeper as bad, as dangerous. What is inside consists of primitive impulses, archaic instinctual material, bad stuff that has to be controlled, watched over, kept in line. You have to keep reality in mind. You have to consider the rights and needs of others. The goals of therapy are to make sure that the bad insides are kept inside. Patients are to see their bad insides and to know what they are. Patients are to have insight and understanding of the nasty things inside like unconscious impulses and behavioral tendencies that would get most people thrown into jails or mental hospitals. The main direction of change is toward keeping the lid on the inner material. You may have insight and understanding of what is inside, but just make sure the bad stuff stays there. In experiential, the aim is to be the integrated and actualized deeper experiencings. In many therapies, the aim is to seal off, keep down, and to be in charge of the monstrous, dangerous inside material.

Getting the directions of change from the deeper potentials is different from saying that the goals are for patients to scream and yell, let it all hang out, fully express all kinds of feelings, behave any old way that you like. I regard all of this as referring mainly to operating potentials, not to deeper potentials. Our directions of change are toward being and behaving on the basis of integrated and actualized deeper potentials, and not doing whatever you happen to feel like doing, and justifying it as being authentic, open, or showing your feelings.

Does experiential encourage ways of being and behaving that are dangerous, harmful, bad, crazy, uncivilized? If the patient is going to be and to behave on the basis of deeper potentials, wouldn't we have to be very suspicious of the ways the person might be? My answer is no, and I have the following reasons:

1. In the experiential system, deeper potentials have natures that are themselves neutral. The nature is bad if you see what the deeper potential is through a disintegrative relationship. The nature of what is deeper is bad if you truly believe that whatever is deeper in this person or in most people is bad, dangerous, harmful. However, in the experiential system, every deeper potential is wonderful when you are inside it and when your relationship to that deeper potential is integrative.

2. The purpose of Steps 2 through 4 is to enable significant changes toward establishing integrative good relationships with the deeper potential, and toward the person actually moving within the deeper potential. These steps minimize the likehood of dangerous, awful consequences.

3. In Step 4, when the person is considering actually being and behaving in new ways in the extratherapy world, both therapist and patient go through a process of rehearsal, tryout, of checking how it feels, of expressly weighing the risks and dangers. This tends to reduce the risk of such dangerous behaviors, especially since there is such focused attention on precisely how the person is to be and precisely what the person may actually carry out.

4. The payoff lies in what seems to have actually happened after experiential sessions. How frequently have patients killed themselves or others, shown up the next time in a state of lunacy or derangement? By whatever measure seems sensible, I am not aware of any sessions having propelled patients into doing things that are dangerous or harmful, bad, crazy, or uncivilized.

In the experiential system, there is no judging of some deeper potentials as acceptable and some as unacceptable, there is no list of approved and disapproved ways of being and behaving, there is no list of healthy or mature ways for people to be. The experiential therapist is not a judge who labels this deeper potential as acceptable and that as unacceptable. The directions of change are determined by the patient's own deeper potentials, and not by the value system of the therapist who pronounces this as acceptable and that as unacceptable.

Being and behaving as the new person means letting go of the scene of strong bad feeling. In the beginning of the session, there often is some scene of strong bad feeling. The goal and objective are to become the new person, and this direction of change means the end of the patient constructing such scenes, having bad feelings in the scenes, undergoing painful experiencings and painful behaviors in these scenes. If this session is effective, there will be no more such scenes of bad feeling, or at least they will occur less frequently and with less bad feeling. These scenes of bad feeling are our target, our goal, objective, direction of change.

In the experiential approach, it is not enough to ask the patient what he sees as the problem and wants as the goal, and to accept these as your objectives. Doesn't it make sense to accept that the goal is to get rid of the depression when the patient starts the initial session by saying, "I am depressed. I want to get rid of my depression"? We would likely start with this statement, and look for some scene of strong feeling. I know that some therapists might very well conclude that the goal is to reduce the patient's depression, but I would not. With the person who actually opened in this way, the feeling was one of being almost helpless as she seemed to be constructing her enemy, the depression. As we pursued times when she may have felt helpless, unable to overcome, being overwhelmed by, some strong and relentless enemy, perhaps the depression, we arrived at a scene. She was sobbing as she was staring at the cancer, seeing it as hard and powerful, small and impenetrable, uncaring and coldly destructive. Accompanying the sobbing was a feeling of utter weakness, giving in, the complete victim. Here is the scene of strong feeling. The direction of change is to be free of being in such scenes, together with the accompanying bad feeling.

Interestingly, another patient also began with almost the same words: "I am depressed and I can't stand it any longer." By searching for the scene of strong feeling, we arrived at a scene in which she is in the kitchen, hurt and downcast, quiet, clenched, as her husband is once again coldly and surgically forcing her to admit how bad a mother she is to their children, and the intense feeling is being terrified of losing her own self, her own way of seeing things, and fully giving in to his relentless accusations. The direction of change is toward being free of these scenes of strong bad feeling.

In the experiential system, there is no preset list of problem behaviors that are disapproved and looked on as symptoms of psychopathology or some serious diagnostic condition. Our aim is not to get rid of those behaviors. The goal is not to prevent the patient from flushing the toilet five or more times whenever she uses the toilet, or to get him to go back to work instead of sitting under the tree in the park, reading stories to the squirrels. The goal is always the scene of strong bad feeling and not some isolated behavior.

The experiential therapist does not have a set of solutions to particular kinds of problems, nor is there any favorite set of prescriptions for dealing with, resolving, reducing, or attacking "problems" with given interventions and treatment programs. Instead, the goal is first to identify the scene of strong feeling, then to enable the patient to become the new person, and finally to give this new person an opportunity to let go of the scene of strong bad feeling.

In the experiential system, who determines the goals, objectives, and directions of change?   In one sense, it is the therapist. The therapist guides the patient toward identifying the inner experiencing that is here in this session and also guides the patient into looking for the scene of strong bad feeling. So there is a sense in which the therapist determines the goals, objectives, and directions of change.

In another sense, however, the directions of change are determined by the content of this person's inner experiencing in this session. The experiential value system places the emphasis on the patient's inner experiencing, but the patient's own inner experiencing provides the specific content of the directions of change for this patient in this session.

At the end of Step 1, the therapist and patient have identified some scene of strong feeling, typically a strong bad feeling. They have also identified an inner experiencing. Once these are found, the directions of change are just about set. The avenue of change is toward the patient's being and behaving on the basis of the integrated and actualized inner experiencing, and toward a washing away of the scene of strong bad feeling. Ideally, another therapist can replace the one who completed Step 1, and the directions of change, the goals and objectives, will remain essentially the same. In general, the therapist has very little impact on determining the particular goals and objectives with this patient.

Although the goals, objectives, and directions of change are determined by the nature of the person's deeper potentials, an exceedingly heavy premium is placed on the patient's immediate state of readiness and willingness to proceed with each substep. While it is the inner experiencing that determines the directions of change, it is the patient who is responsible for whether or not to do the work. This heavy emphasis on the patient's state of readiness and willingness starts from the very beginning of the session and carries through each of the four steps.

Going even further, if the therapist uses a nonexperiential way of arriving at goals and objectives, he will have real trouble carrying out the steps of an experiential session. For example, suppose that the therapist, during the first step, or even before, reasons that this woman has strong aggressive tendencies, occasionally loses patience, and hits her mentally deficient child; the desired direction of change is that she should look at her child differently so that she can be better with her child, and certainly should stop hitting him. Having arrived at these goals and objectives, the therapist will almost certainly have a very hard time accessing a deeper potential in Step 1, and successfully accomplishing Steps 2 through 4. This predetermined set of goals and objectives for the woman blocks the therapist from achieving the experiential steps and the goals and objectives that go with these steps.

One way of arriving at the goals, objectives, and directions of change is that the patient is simply to come to adopt the therapist's own way of looking at things, or is to conform to whatever ways of being and behaving are on the therapist's personal list. These ways of arriving at the goals are quite common. In the experiential system, the direction of change is toward being and behaving on the basis of the integrated and actualized deeper potential that is accessed in this session, and this includes the washing away of the scene of strong bad feeling from the first part of the session.

Diagnose the Problem or Problem Condition, and Select the Treatment of Choice versus Experiential Therapy Is Appropriate and Useful for All Patients with All Kinds of Bad Feelings

Many therapists believe that there is a best treatment for whatever problem or problem condition the patient has. First you diagnose the problem or problem-condition, and then you select the treatment of choice. The experiential position is that this therapy enables the person to open up deeper potentials, to become a person who can be and behave on the basis of these integrated and actualized deeper potentials, and be free of the scenes of bad feeling. These goals and objectives are open to, available for, and useful to any person whatsoever, and for any kind of bad feeling.

Diagnose the problem and prescribe the treatment.   This conventional way of thinking has the appeal of common sense. There are at least three ways of applying this strategy (Mahrer, 1989f). In the purest form, the therapist does not follow any special school of therapy but instead uses a method that includes or represents many of the major schools. This usually is called being eclectic or integrative. Furthermore, the therapist should not follow any particular kind of integrative-eclectic approach. Using this overall eclectic-integrative approach, the therapist diagnoses the problem or problem condition and then prescribes the treatment of choice. The strategy is incorporated into this dictum: "*What* treatment, by *whom*, is most effective for *this* individual with *that* specific problem, and under *which* set of circumstances?" (Paul, 1967, p. 111). Some have worked out comprehensive schemas of answers so that, once you diagnose the problem, you can choose the most effective treatments (e.g., Goldstein & Stein, 1976; Halgin, 1985). For example, if you diagnose the problem as a simple phobia, then you can select from such treatments as flooding, desensitization, insight-understanding, in vivo exposure, or other proven treatment modalities or programs (Beck, 1976; Clark & Jackson, 1983; Ellis, 1962; Levis & Hare, 1977; Marshall, Gauthier, & Gordon, 1979; Meichenbaum, 1977; Paul, 1969b; Wolpe, 1969).

A second way of diagnosing the problem and selecting the treatment is to work within one approach. Instead of an overall eclectic-integrative approach, you stay within a cognitive approach or systems approach. Within your approach, there are various treatment options, and you select the best one for that problem, all carried out within your explicit therapy. For example, if you are a behavior therapist, you first diagnose the behavioral problem and then you select from such behavioral treatments as systematic desensitization, assertive training, role-playing, modeling, or in vivo desensitization (Goldfried & Pomeranz, 1976).

A third way is to choose several therapeutic approaches, and to go back and forth from one to the other. When you run into some issue or problem, it may be appropriate to switch to the other approach. Since psychodynamic and behavioral approaches are so common, there have been lots of attempts to show how they can be combined so that you can use whichever one is best for that issue or problem (Bernstein, 1984; Birk, 1970; Brady, 1968; Cohen & Pope, 1980; Feather & Rhoads, 1972; Marmor, 1971; Rhoads & Feather, 1972).

Club rules for those who believe in diagnosing the problem and prescribing the treatment. Therapists generally accept certain rules in order to belong to the very large club that diagnoses a problem and prescribes the treatment (Mahrer, 1989f, 1991a). Not all therapists belong to this club. Experiential therapists are not members.

One rule is that you must believe in the more or less official lists of problems and problem conditions. One such list is from the current version of the mental illnesses and diseases, approved by the American Psychiatric Association (DSM-IV; APA, 1994). You believe that there really are official problems and problem conditions. It is not enough for the patient to say that he feels rotten or that he is tired of screwing up all the time. There should be some defined problem or problem condition, and furthermore, whatever it is, it persists from session to session until it is cured or treated effectively.

A second rule is that you believe it is important to diagnose the problem or condition. Typically, this is the aim of initial sessions. Third, you believe that once you identify the problem or condition, you then define the goal, the objective, the aim of treatment. In short, first you diagnose, then you set the treatment goal. I suggest that even within the club, this is not the case. Instead, the therapist's own approach largely determines what problem or problem condition is identifiable, and the treatment goals are intrinsically built in to the way you name that problem or condition. Once your approach allows you to identify the problem condition as a simple phobia, it is already predetermined that the goal is to reduce or get rid of the simple phobia.

A fourth rule is that there are treatments of choice for particular problems or problem conditions (Cone, 1988; Cormier & Cormier, 1979; Kiesler, 1971; Paul, 1967, 1969a, 1969b). These treatments of choice do not come from a large range of therapies, but are restricted to those that fall within, and are thereby cordial to, the therapist's overall approach. Any particular therapist will have a limited number of therapies as candidates for a particular problem. For example, suppose a therapist identifies a problem of anxiety and we ask what therapies are reasonable choices for treatment. This therapist would likely have her own limited repertoire of possible treatments, and all others would automatically be out of the running.

A fifth rule is that all treatments of choice must share the same goals. Suppose that a therapist describes the problem as this fellow having poor sexual relations with his wife, or as this woman being uncertain about being a lesbian. If the therapist is going to select the most effective treatment, the choice is made from treatments that share the same goal. If the goal is for the patient to give up her lesbian life style for a heterosexual life style, then the package of possible treatments may well be quite different from those effective in enabling her to become more certain of her choice of a lesbian life style. Treatments of choice must share the same treatment goal, rather than merely relate to the same kind of defined problem.

The final rule is that the therapist is to be reasonably knowledgeable and competent in the selected treatment of choice. In actual practice, this usually means that the possible candidates are further restricted to those the therapist is fairly good at.

If you are going to diagnose the problem and prescribe the treatment, then you should believe in and follow these rules. Experiential psychotherapy graciously declines.

Experiential psychotherapy is appropriate and useful for all patients, with all kinds of bad feelings.   The four steps are the best way that I know to access a person's deeper way of being or inner, deeper experiencing, and then to enable the person to be and behave as this new person, including the washing away of whatever scenes of bad feeling were there. These changes are available to any patient at all. In this sense, experiential therapy, together with some other therapies, is universal. Such therapies are appropriate and useful for any and all patients. Remember, the key is the scene of strong feeling and the inner experiencing. Any patient can be free of the scene of strong bad feeling. Any patient can be and behave on the basis of the integrated and actualized inner experiencing.

Our aim is to enable this patient to be free of this bad feeling in this situational context and to be able to be and to behave on the basis of this inner experiencing or deeper potential. I know of no other therapy or treatment program that can do these jobs better than experiential therapy. If I found other therapies that accomplished these two jobs better than experiential therapy, I would try to modify the present experiential methods and include those other methods. Accordingly, this therapy is appropriate for all patients for whom these two aims apply and ought to be the very best approach for accomplishing these two aims.

If you think in terms of therapies being effective for particular kinds of problems and problem conditions, then it makes sense to hold that particular interventions, programs, and treatments are better for some kinds of problems and problem conditions. If you think in terms of inner experiencings and scenes of strong bad feeling, then it makes sense that any patient can benefit from this therapy.

HOW DO YOU ARRIVE AT THE GOALS, OBJECTIVES, AND DIRECTIONS OF CHANGE IN AND FOR THIS SESSION?

Suppose that it is the very beginning of the 1st session, the 5th session, the 45th session, any session. How do you arrive at the goals, objectives, and directions of change for this particular session? Do you start the session with some kind of plan or program? Suppose that you are partway into a session. How do you determine what to do next, what you might want to accomplish next in the session?

For Each Session, Therapist Starts with a Continuing Picture of Patient, and a Plan for What This Session Should Accomplish versus Therapist Starts Each Session Afresh, Ready to See What Deeper Potential Accesses, and What the New Person Can Be

It is just before the session. Do you have a plan for what to cover, for what you want to accomplish? Do you have a continuing picture of the patient, the problem, the problem-condition, where you are in the course of treatment?

Approach this session with a treatment plan.   For many therapists, the initial sessions provide the therapist with some picture of the patient. You have an idea of the patient's problem, the problem-condition, the psychopathology, and the psychodynamics. On the basis of this picture, you can frame some idea of what you are to work on in the next sessions; you have a notion of what you might want to accomplish. It may be that you and the patient have arrived at a kind of contractual understanding of what should be accomplished. He is moderately depressed, and he is painfully unsure whether to remain in theater or to join his two brothers in the restaurants that they run. As you get ready for this next session, you have some general idea of the direction you want to go, generated by the assessment and evaluation of the initial sessions.

Getting some idea of the direction you want to take and what you want to do in these sessions is typically called case management, case planning, treatment programming. You formulate a treatment plan or program. This may be for the next session, or for the next four or six sessions or so. The plan may be relatively explicit, or it may be general and loose. It may have been developed by the treatment team, the chief of the unit, you and your supervisor. Often the general contours of the treatment plan are already built into the goals and purposes of the agency, the service, the unit, the program. You know what the in-session goals are because the program is to reduce substance abuse or spouse abuse, or to keep patients in the halfway house from having to go back to the hospital.

You keep a more or less stable picture of this patient's problem, problem condition, and personality. This relatively enduring picture goes a long way toward defining what you should cover and accomplish in this particular session. Before the session, what is in your mind is that this is a pain-management case, a case of obesity, an eating problem, a phobic, a young offender, a marital problem. You know that she has trouble with aggressive impulses and needs further strengthening of her controls. You know that he is alcoholic, and is slowly moving toward recovery so that he needs lot of support. You know that she is resisting the termination of the incest survivor program, and exhibiting symptoms of a schizoidal nature. With this picture, you can do this session because you have some notion of what to cover and what to work toward.

It helps that you know where you are in the overall treatment program. You are in the trial phase of long-term therapy. You are heading toward the final phase of the 12-session treatment program for stress management or weight control. By keeping this in mind, you have some idea of what to cover and where to go in this session.

You have some agenda for what area or topic to deal with in this session. The agenda may be somewhat loose or rather focused. You may explore her relationships with her boyfriend, now that she is standing up for herself more. The last session finally touched on his rage toward his father, and this area would be a good one to talk about. Because she missed the last session and is starting again to accumulate a balance of owed fees, it is time to look at what may be happening in the therapist-patient relationship. The plan is to go further into his early competitive relations with his brother. If the patient does not talk about these topics, that is to be regarded as avoidance, and perhaps the reasons for the avoidance should be explored (Bokar, 1981; Zaro, Barach, Nedelman, & Dreiblatt, 1977).

Approach this session afresh.   The experiential therapist approaches this session afresh, looking for whatever deeper potential accesses in this session, and using this inner experiencing to determine the goals, objectives, and directions of change in and for this session. This session, as every session, is to cover whatever material occurs during it (cf. Bion, 1967, 1970).

The session opens with your showing the patient how to identify whatever scene of strong feeling is here now. The aim is to see what scene of strong feeling is present, and what inner experiencing is accessed in this particular session. In this sense, each session is an adventure, for you have little or no idea of what will occur in the first step. You have little or no idea of the scene of strong feeling or the inner experiencing that accesses in this session.

Once you access the inner experiencing, the aim is indeed to go through Steps 2 to 4, and for the patient to be and behave on the basis of this inner experiencing. But you have no predetermined idea of what this particular inner experiencing is in this particular session. You have no idea of the content of the directions of change, of the content of the possible new way of being or the content of the likely new behaviors.

You certainly do not have any plan that you will cover this topic or explore that area, that you will accomplish this particular aim, or that you will get into that important thing that occurred recently. Even if you know that the patient's loved one died recently or that the patient found out a few days ago that she has cancer and will probably die soon, you still open the session by giving the person plenty of room to locate her own scene of strong feeling (Mahrer, Howard, Gervaize, & Boulet, 1990). The patient may have started last session with a riveting concern about her son or her cancer or her falling apart during the night, but that was last session. In this session, she is free to start with the same content or with any other scene of strong feeling.

Is each session hopelessly separate from any other? Is there nothing that the therapist carries over from previous sessions? Doesn't the therapist really approach this session with some picture of what the patient is like, with some notion of whatever the patient ought to focus on, with some picture of the way this session should go and what should be achieved? Is the experiential therapist like some computer whose memory is wiped clean of what happened in all previous sessions? In one practical sense, the answer is yes. The therapist has no preprogrammed picture or topics or goals. Whatever scene of strong feeling the patient has for this session comes essentially from the patient and not from the therapist.

However, the therapist reviews a few things before the session to establish carryover or continuity from one session to another and enable the therapist to carry out this session as well as possible. The most important thing that the therapist reviews, before the session, is the inner experiencing, the new way of being, that occurred during the final step of the prior session, and the new way of being and behaving that the patient elected to carry out after the session. The therapist reviews, before the session, that the patient ended the last session ready to be and to behave as this new commanding, this ordering, this being the authoritative boss, and furthermore, she elected to have fun being this way in demanding that her husband learn from her how to do the laundry, and that he absolutely would do this task on Saturday. In the beginning of this next session, this scene may be included as one of a number of possible opening scenes of strong feeling in the first step. But only as one; there can be others.

Second, the therapist reviews the kinds of scenes of strong bad feeling that have been present in the last session or so. Sometimes, there are no opening scenes of bad feeling. Sometimes the same scenes occur over a series of sessions, in the opening step. Nevertheless, the heavy emphasis is on approaching each session afresh.

There is an advantage from accepting each session as its own minitherapy. Whatever inner experiencing you access in this session will likely be different from the inner experiencing that you found in the previous session, and the one you will find in the next one. Consider the point, in the first step, when you believe that you have some idea of the nature of the inner experiencing. You believe that the inner experiencing is being loved, concerned about, cared for. This is your best guess about what it is. But suppose that you are wrong. It is easier just to do your very best in identifying and using whatever inner experiencing you think you have found because you are free to start afresh in the next session. You are only working one session at a time. Starting afresh each session means that the inner experiencing you think you got in this session is not a treatment plan for subsequent sessions. It is not a diagnosis to be retained over the next sessions. It is not a label stuck on the patient from here on.

If your aim is to go through the four steps, then you cannot accomplish that by having a treatment plan for what you want to cover in this session. Once you define the goals and objectives to be attained for this particular patient in this particular session, you sacrifice the chance of attaining the four steps. You have a choice, but, to a large degree, whichever choice you make tends to exclude the other.

Significant Changes Call for a Series of Sessions versus Significant Changes Are Available in Each Session

How much change can occur in this single session? A common position is that the extent of likely change in any single session is quite limited. If significant changes are to occur, that calls for extended series of sessions. How much change can be expected to occur in this given session depends on all sorts of factors, including the patient's diagnosis and problem, but, in any case, the amount of change likely in this particular session is almost always limited.

In the experiential position, a great deal of change may be expected in any single session. More specifically, the experiential therapist regards this session as its own minitherapy (cf. Bion, 1967; Langs, 1979; Rosenbaum, Hoyt, & Talmon, 1990). Each session can go through the four steps. The therapist is ready and willing to go through the four steps. If the patient is too, then it is possible for him to leave the session as the new person. Some deeper potential that was not a part of his operating domain is now a part of it. There is now a new self-confidence, assuredness, self-containment. There is now a new quality of softness, sweetness, gentleness. He is different. He was not that way when he went in, but he is this way when he comes out.

Even further, in one session, she no longer has the scene of strong bad feeling. When she entered the session, she was a person who desperately clung to her son, was annoyed, hurt, made troubled by his outbursts against her. Now she is free of these scenes. She is no longer a person who gets involved in such bad-feelinged scenes and situations. In one session, she is free of the bad feelings and the situations in which she had them. This is the second kind of change that can be achieved in a single session (Mahrer, 1993).

What Determines the Working Goals, Objectives, and Directions of Change Over This Session?

How does the therapist know what to do next in this session? Researchers suggest that many therapists seem to function on the basis of some kind of overall sequence of goals (Cashdan, 1973; Cormier & Cormier, 1979; Craighead, Kazdin, & Mahoney, 1976; Gottman & Lieblum, 1974; Hackney, Ivey, & Oetting, 1970; McConville, 1976; Osipow & Walsh, 1970; Paul, 1978). Even within single sessions, there may be a kind of organized microstrategy or patterned sequence of what a given therapist does (Mahrer, Nifakis, Abhukara, & Sterner, 1984).

The experiential therapist is programmed to proceed through the four steps. Almost without thinking of what is to be done next, the therapist is geared to go through the four steps. This program carries down into the substeps so that, within each of the four steps, the therapist knows what substeps to go through. Occasionally, the therapist will complete a step and be uncertain what the next step is. It may take a few seconds or more to remember that you have finished Step 1 and now you are headed toward achieving Step 2, but generally the therapist merely is programmed to go through the four steps of the session. This is what the dancer does, the boxer does, the baseball player does, and the experiential therapist does.

HOW CAN YOU TELL WHETHER YOU ARE ATTAINING THE GOALS, OBJECTIVES, AND DIRECTIONS OF CHANGE?

When a practitioner is working with a patient, it is generally helpful to have some idea of whether or not therapy is going along well. Over the course of the session or after therapy is over, practitioners and researchers are both entitled to have some concern about whether the goals, objectives, and directions of change have been reasonably attained.

Researchers are especially involved with setting therapists against one another, and coming up with conclusions about which therapy is more effective or successful with this particular kind of patient or problem or problem-condition. As reasonable as this sounds, it is very hard to do unless the therapists agree that they are all sharing the same goals, objectives, and directions of change. The more specific and careful you get about the goals, objectives, and directions of change with regard to this particular patient, the more unlikely it is that the goals of several therapies would fully agree. Although such specific agreement is conceivable, it is extremely unlikely. A related issue is that the therapies would have to agree on the timeframe for attaining the goals, objectives, and directions of change. In experiential therapy, these are obtained during each session, and they typically vary considerably from session to session. The therapies would have to agree on when and how often the goals, objectives, and directions of change would be determined. I am more concerned with how you can tell whether you are or are not attaining the goals and objectives, rather than how to compare the attainments of different therapies.

There is a relatively common way to determine whether you are attaining the goals and objectives. In general, this consists of getting some idea of what the patient is like at the beginning of therapy, and comparing that with how the patient seems to be when therapy is done. You may use some kind of pretherapy measure or evaluation. Or you may get some idea of the problem or problem condition, and then see if it is resolved or reduced. The outcome may be based on the problem, the problem condition, the agreed-on goals and objectives, lots of built-in criteria of outcome measures and instruments, or simply customer satisfaction: the degree to which the client is pleased with the therapy or therapist. You may use a measure or instrument of the sheer number of complaints or problems, although it may be difficult to determine whether an increase or a decrease is necessarily an indication of successfully obtaining the goals and objectives (cf. Mahrer, Mason, Kahn, & Projansky, 1966). These are all ways of seeing if you have attained the goals, objectives, and directions of change over a series of sessions.

You can use this pre-post method when the goal and objective are the same for each session, from the beginning to the end of therapy. That has never occurred with my patients, but many therapists evaluate the attainment of goals and objectives this way.

You may also think in terms of this single session, rather than waiting for a whole series of sessions. I have generated a list of such indicators from what lots of therapists with different approaches named as good or very good moments in their sessions—

moments that indicated attainment, or moving toward attainment, of their goals, objectives, and directions of change (Mahrer, 1985d, 1988d; Mahrer & Nadler, 1986; Mahrer, Gagnon, Fairweather, & Coté, 1992).

When researchers and practitioners think in terms of attaining goals and objectives, they generally think in terms of before and after. But there are other ways.

What Are The Criteria of Successful, Effective Experiential Sessions?

In this approach, the goals and objectives are to be achieved in each session. Typically, the goals and objectives of each subsequent session are quite different from those of the previous sessions. There are two ways of evaluating success.

Have you attained the four steps in this session?   Each session provides the patient with a chance to go through the four steps. A session is successful and effective to the extent that it attains the four steps (Mahrer, 1985a). If you look at the preceding 5 or 10 sessions, and all of them have attained the four steps, then these are good sessions; therapy is going along well with the patient. The sessions are successful and effective. If most of these sessions failed to attain the four steps, then therapy is not especially successful or effective.

This allows a practitioner to tell right away whether this session is going well or not. During and after each session you can see if you attained the four steps. In many other therapies, it is somewhat harder to tell if any particular session has gone well. Even in behavior therapy it is often hard to tell if therapy is proceeding as desired (Woody, 1976).

In each session, the experiential therapist looks for the scene of strong bad feeling and the inner experiencing. Before this session, the therapist does not know what these will be. Therefore, although the therapist can predetermine that attaining the goals and objectives means attaining the four steps, there is little or no way of knowing the particular content of these goals and objectives until Step 1 has been attained (Mahrer, 1982).

Is each session absolutely independent of the ones that precede and follow? Not really. You can look at each session quite independently to see if the four steps were attained, but there are also ways in which what happens in this session is related to earlier and later sessions. Each session can access a deeper potential and enable the person to be and behave on the basis of this potential. In other words, in this session, the deeper potential can become an operating potential. But this alone does not necessarily mean that the deeper potential remains an operating potential. That takes work. It means that the person must actually be and behave as this new operating potential in the extratherapy world. Otherwise, the inner experiencing tends to sink back into the deeper domain. If the inner experiencing is made into a more or less stable part of the operating domain, that paves the way for some other deeper potential to be "next," that is, to be available for accessing in sessions. This process allows the possibility that, over time, the movement of deeper potentials into the operating domain may pave the way for the person to access basic potentials. It also leads to the second criterion of successful, effective experiential sessions.

Is the person a qualitatively new person, free of the scenes of bad feeling?   If the four steps are reasonably effective and successful, the criterion payoff is that the person who was there at the beginning of the session has become a qualitatively new person. That is, the deeper potential that was accessed is to be an integrated and actualized part of the operating domain. Here is a qualitatively new person, changed from the inside out. Here is a deep change, a significant change, a whole new person.

Also, this new person is free of the scenes of bad feeling that were there in the beginning of the session. The new person is free of those scenes, and also of the bad feelings that were part and parcel of those scenes.

These changes may only occur for a flickering few moments at the end of the session when the new person is present. It is better if this new person seems to have some lasting value, perhaps can remain a while. But at least the old person had a taste of what it can be like to be this whole new person. It is a real achievement if these changes can carry over to who and what the person is in the next session.

Look for the changes in the subsequent first step.   The degree to which a session can be regarded as successful and effective can also be determined by looking at the next session or so. There are two things to look for. One is to see if the patient actually carried out the new way of being and behaving that was arrived at in the previous session. If the patient carried it out with good feelings, then this is an indication of the success and effectiveness of the last session. However, if the patient did not carry this out, or if the feelings were bad ones, then using this criterion, the last session was not especially successful or effective. There is a second way of using the first step of the session to see if the preceding session was successful or effective. In this session, you usually arrive at a scene of strong bad feeling. Suppose that it is just about the same scene of strong bad feeling as in the previous session, or even in the past several sessions. The scenes are more or less the same. The strong bad feelings are similar. The ways of being and behaving are similar. In session after session, he is in scenes of being hurt and misunderstood by his wife, he is painfully depressed, and the operating experiencing is being unloved, lost, alone, rejected. If the Step 1 scenes of strong bad feeling are similar, then the previous session or sessions were unsuccessful and ineffective. Even if the four steps were attained, on this important criterion the previous session was no good.

On the other hand, the scenes of strong bad feeling may be roughly similar in the two sessions, and still there are ways that the previous session may be regarded as successful and effective. The accompanying feeling may be different, perhaps even lighter, more pleasant. The scenes may be involve being hurt and misunderstood by his wife, but in the subsequent session the feeling is less painful, lighter, more like being disgusted with oneself. Often there is some evolving change in the operating experiencing. In the previous session, the experiencing was being unloved, lost, alone, rejected. In this session, it seems to become a being picked on, poked at, pushed around. The feeling is still bad, but the experiencing is changing somewhat. These kinds of changes in the feeling and the experiencing, even if they are slight, indicate that the previous session was somewhat successful and effective. It is interesting to follow a particular experiencing over a series of sessions. Typically, it will evolve, modify, give way to somewhat new forms, develop one or another aspect. All of this is testimony to the success and effectiveness of the prior sessions.

You can tell if you are attaining the goals, objectives, and directions of change in experiential therapy by seeing if you have attained the four steps of the session, by seeing if the patient actually carried out the new way of being and behaving, and by seeing if there is a change in the opening scene of strong bad feeling.

CHAPTER FOUR

For What Patients Is Experiential Psychotherapy Useful, Appropriate, and Appealing?

A therapist is entitled to ask what kinds of patients to refer to a colleague who does experiential therapy. An experiential therapist would like to know what kinds of patients are and are not especially suitable for experiential therapy. What patients will find experiential psychotherapy useful, appropriate, and appealing?

The Shorthand Answer

Whether the question is asked by a patient, the therapist, or someone else, the shorthand answer is that experiential therapy is useful and appropriate for virtually any individual adult who (a) has some kind of relatively strong bad feeling, and (b) is reasonably ready and willing to undertake the four steps of this session (Mahrer & Roberge, 1993). This is one way of answering the question. There is another way. Experiential psychotherapy is useful and appropriate for virtually anyone who may want to use a session to move in the direction of becoming a substantially new person who is more integrated and actualized, who is relatively free of the present bad-feelinged scenes and situations.

EXPERIENTIAL THERAPY IS USEFUL, APPROPRIATE, AND APPEALING FOR PATIENTS WHO VALUE A SUBSTANTIALLY LARGE HAND IN THEIR OWN PROCESS OF CHANGE

Some therapies provide patients with a substantially large hand in the ongoing process of the session. Experiential therapy is one of these. Some patients may be drawn toward therapies that put the patient in the driver's seat. Patients who value this sense of control, of being more or less in charge of what happens in the session, are drawn toward experiential therapy.

Does it therefore select-out those who are unwilling to admit their agency causing it to not deal w/ timely mentally ill people?

Experiential Therapy Is for Patients Who Place Paramount Importance on Their Own Readiness and Willingness

From before the first session, and throughout each session, there is a premium on the patient's readiness and willingness. Before the first session, the patient is the one who is ready and willing to have this session. Generally, the patient makes the initial call rather than being "referred" to the therapist without some express indication that the patient wants to have a session.

In the first session and throughout every other session, the patient's readiness and willingness are paramount. Even more pointedly, for each step, and for just about each substep, the therapist says, "Is this all right? Are you ready? Does this seem OK? Are you ready to do this?" The patient has the deciding hand. If the patient is ready to do this next substep, you do it. If the patient is not, you don't. Some patients like this. They want to have a large hand in the moment-to-moment carrying out of the therapy.

So important is the patient's moment-to-moment readiness and willingness that the therapist is virtually saying, all the time, "I will show you what to do and how to do it, but you are the important one, so if you decline, that is fine, and if you are ready and willing, we proceed." In this sense, the therapist does not "intervene," or "use interventions." There is, therefore, very little of what is commonly called resistance, opposition, or lack of motivation (cf. Mahrer, Murphy, Gagnon, & Gingras, 1994). These terms generally indicate the patient is not doing what the therapist wants the patient to do. In experiential therapy, the patient is either ready and willing or not so. The therapist is not here with wantings or demands for the patient to do this or that, to get around her resistance. This therapy genuinely honors the patient's readiness and willingness.

At the end of each session, both therapist and patient must want to have a subsequent session. Typically, the therapist indicates that she would indeed like to have another, but the patient must also be ready and willing. In virtually every way, from the beginning to the end of the session, the patient's readiness is paramount, is honored and respected. Some patients are drawn toward a therapy in which they have such a substantially large hand.

Experiential Therapy Is for People Who Are Drawn toward Self-Change Alone or with a Partner

This therapy is useful, appropriate, and appealing to those who want to undergo self-change, either alone or with a partner. Experiential dream work is expressly for such people, and the book on dream work (Mahrer, 1989c) is designed to enable any person to follow the steps by oneself or with a partner. But the person can also start with any scene of strong feeling, in or out of a dream.

The four steps can be carried out by you, or by you with the help of a partner who knows the four steps and can guide you when you get too far off track. Start with a dream or some bad feeling that occurred recently, in some scene or with regard to some person or thing. Go through the four steps as best as you can. If you work with a partner, it is the partner's job to help keep you on track. But you do the work.

Alternate who does the work and who is the partner. You can do this with someone you trust even if neither of you are experiential therapists. But you have to start. Try it out a few times.

I would like to suggest something that is part suggestion and part challenge. Look over the past day or so. Can you think of some time when there was a rising up of feeling in you? The feeling may have been good or bad, but it is a time when there was a feeling inside you. It may have been a slight incident in which that other person in the department was in the elevator with you, and you were filled, just for a brief few seconds, with sexual feelings. It may have been when your sister was mad at you and said you were a selfish bastard. It may have been an awful feeling when you were driving your car and came so very close to smashing into the little boy crossing the street right in front of you. Whether you work by yourself or with a partner, start with these feelinged scenes and follow the steps. Just about everyone can be the patient. If you are inclined to start with your own scenes of strong feeling, this therapy is designed for you, either by yourself or with a partner.

Experiential Therapy Is for Patients Who Shun Being the Object of Therapists' Own Personal Agendas, Goals, Values, Psychobabble, and Relationships

Lots of people have a healthy skepticism about therapists and psychotherapy, lots of good reasons for declining to be the object of some psychotherapist's ministrations. While psychotherapists are rarely at a loss to explain why these people stay away from therapy, neither are these people at a loss for reasons to stay away from therapists. Yet some of these very people are drawn toward experiential therapy and a few other therapies. There are some considerations that lead these people to choose experiential therapy.

First, experiential therapy has somewhat defined steps in each session, and relatively specific methods for carrying out each step. When these people think of experiential therapy, they think of a more or less organized procedure. They prefer this kind of therapy to being swallowed into a quagmire of interpersonal relationships with the therapist, getting involved with endless talk about their relationship, or having their mutual feelings about one another be a main part of what transpires in the session. Experiential therapy offers explicit steps and methods, rather than yet another relationship, especially one that has to be paid for.

Second, many of these people do not relish being the object, the victim, of therapists whom these people regard as incompetent do-gooders, as self-proclaimed professionals who can and do trap patients in the therapists' own agendas, goals, values, and relationships. Essentially, these people neither trust nor respect therapists as a group. Then why would these people seek to be patients in experiential therapy? Instead of being the object that the therapist treats, so very much is left in the patient's hands. The therapist shows the patient what to do and how to do it, and the patient is the one who does it, provided that he is ready and willing. It is also important that so much of the actual methods involve both patient and therapist attending to a third focal center, something other than one another. Instead of the therapist doing something to the patient, both therapist and patient are attending to this third thing they are working on.

Some people, including some therapists, feel that putting themselves at the mercy of a therapist would be an act of sheer surrender they would later kick themselves for. Then why experiential therapy? In experiential therapy, patients often say that they are in charge of what happens from moment to moment in the session, that they are the bosses, essentially free of the therapist's relationship and all the baggage that goes with these relationships.

Occasionally, patients will begin sessions with feelinged scenes of giving in, surrendering, being vulnerable, being invaded by, being swallowed up by, being the victim of some external force, parent, dominant figure, powerful leader, even some therapist. Experiential psychotherapy is appropriate for these concerns because the patient can use such scenes without having to give in to, surrender to, be swallowed up, or twisted out of shape by the experiential therapist. Patients appreciate this. So do I.

Third, some patients are keenly aware of some distinguishing characteristic, something that may mark them as different from the therapist. I am male; my therapist is female. I am black; my therapist is white. I am old; my therapist is young. I am from a small town in India; my therapist grew up in Montreal. I am a Muslim; my therapist is Catholic. To what extent am I going to be the object of my therapist's own personal agendas, goals, values, and imposed relationships? I do not want my therapist to have predetermined ways that I am to be, because I am black and he is white, because I am male and my therapist is female. I do not want to get caught in my therapist's personal issues with black males. Shouldn't I see a black male therapist? Aren't there loads of good enough reasons for women to work with female therapists? Patients are quite entitled to avoid getting caught in this therapist's life philosophy, this therapist's notions about very short people, heterosexuals or homosexuals, patients with altogether different backgrounds, personal issues, things that are bothersome. If my two babies died, do I really want to see a male therapist?

Such persons are drawn toward experiential therapy because the method reduces these issues to a minimum. The objectives and goals are built into the four steps. Attention is directed toward the personal center of attention, and not on the patient who is black while the therapist is white. With eyes closed, the patient and therapist focus on going through the steps rather than looking at one another's skin color or sex. Because both are attending to that third thing, to what is "out there," they join together, come close to being merged, fused, conjoined rather than each one attending mainly to the other. Patients are drawn toward experiential therapy because there is less chance of the patient's getting caught in the therapist's own personal agendas, goals, values, and imposed relationships.

Fourth, some patients are drawn toward a therapy that seems to be relatively free of what they regard as psychobabble. Many of these patients are somewhat sophisticated about psychotherapy. They have read a fair amount about psychotherapy, and they have strong opinions about psychiatry, psychology, and psychotherapy. They think of most of the field as psychobabble, as pumped-up hoax, as much ado about nothing, as ungrounded frumpery, as mainly silly nonsense. These people do not like being labeled or diagnosed or described by all kinds of psychobabble psychodynamics. They are not taken in by serious allegations about deep-seated problems. They regard the field as a pseudoscience, a professional scam. It is hard for them to call psychiatrists and psychologists "doctor." They simply do not accept what so many psychotherapists believe as psychic truths. Many of these people are drawn toward experiential therapy, and a few other psychotherapies, because they seem to be relatively free of such psychobabble.

The final consideration is that these patients do not want to be the unwilling object of what the therapist is trying to do to them. Whether in the therapist's office, an agency, or a hospital, these patients do not like having someone else decide what label to put on them, and then proceed toward getting them to be the way that is built into the label. The patient does not like being labeled a suicide risk and having the goal be dealing with her unexpressed rage. Experiential therapy is appealing to patients who do not like being treated as if they are labeled like this, and therefore are to become like that.

Experiential Therapy Is Not Useful to Get Patients to Be the Way the Therapist Wants

When therapists ask if a particular therapy is "good" for patients who are dependent, who need pain management, or who are schizoid, the usual meaning is that the patient is to be less dependent, to manage pain better, or is no longer so schizoid. Experiential therapy is not useful to get patients to be the way the therapist wants. If you have a more or less stable and continuing picture of how this patient is to be and to behave, do not use experiential therapy. It probably will not work.

The therapist tries to get the patient to stop hiding the towels, to stop peeing in bed, to stop crying so much, to be satisfied with her job, to complain less about stress, to have less headache pain, to stop biting his nails, to have orgasms, to have fewer arguments, to communicate better with her husband, to have more sex, to stop drinking so much, to keep his job. The therapist says that the patient "needs" to keep emotions in better control, to be more in contact with reality, to do less acting out, to be more aware of her feelings. The referral indicates that the patient needs more autonomy, greater security, more trust in others.

Experiential therapy is a poor choice for accomplishing these goals. Its goals arise from the scenes of strong feeling, and from the inner experiencings that are accessed. Furthermore, the goals almost certainly shift from session to session. The goals do not come from what the therapist wants for and from the patient, no matter how justified these wantings may be.

Other therapists have occasionally referred cases to me in the spirit of a challenge. They say that this patient has "obsessions," and they know that obsessions are notoriously hard to treat (Boulougouris & Rabarilas, 1977; Cawley, 1974; Emmelkamp, 1988; Meyer, Levy, & Schnurer, 1974; Millon, 1981; Rachman, 1982; Rachman & Hodgson, 1980). Let's see if you can be successful with this patient's obsessions. I cannot. Experiential therapy cannot be used to attain goals predetermined by the therapist and enveloped around the patient.

Nor is experiential therapy useful in institutions where patients are given labels with built-in goals. This therapy is unable to get patients to use drugs less, to stop drinking so much, to give old people something to do, to enable dying patients to die gracefully, to reduce criminal acts, to get adolescents to be more "adjusted," to get medical patients to be more "compliant."

Patients often have some conspicuous feature that the therapist targets. The patient has "hysterical" blindness, amnesia for a recent car accident, a baby that the doctor and patient know will almost certainly be born dead or will have no arms or legs. Therapy is to focus on that conspicuous feature. Experiential therapy cannot be used to accomplish what the therapist wants, to do to the patient what the therapist decides to highlight.

It is easy to justify the therapist's intent to cure the medical student of her fear of blood, or the businessman of his fear of flying. Such cases, however, are used to justify the large proportion of cases in which someone does not like the way a person is, and pronounces that the person "needs" therapy to "help" him no longer be that way. Once the person starts having sessions, I am impressed with how exceedingly common it is that what therapists pick on to change is something the therapist doesn't like or disapproves of, something about the patient that bothers the therapist. Therapists are simply too prone to make the patient be the way they want the patient to be. Experiential therapy is not useful under these very common circumstances.

+ he doesn't really expect to
cure depression or sadness patients
does he?

I am proud that experiential therapy is not an effective tool to make the patient be the way the therapist wants the patient to be, no matter how justified the therapist feels. But occasionally I wish that experiential therapy were this kind of tool. I find myself hoping that this therapy could get rid of this patient's cancer, or could lift him out of his seething anguish. When this happens, I am letting myself get caught in a perspective that is not fitting for experiential therapy. This therapy simply does not lend itself to being a tool to accomplish what the therapist wants, whether or not the patient seems to want it too, or so the therapist believes.

EXPERIENTIAL THERAPY IS USEFUL AND APPROPRIATE FOR VIRTUALLY ANY PATIENT VERSUS A PARTICULAR THERAPY IS USEFUL AND APPROPRIATE FOR PARTICULAR KINDS OF PATIENTS, PROBLEMS, AND PROBLEM CONDITIONS

Some therapies hold that they are useful and appropriate for virtually all patients. Experiential therapy is one of these therapies. Many other therapies hold that therapies are more useful and appropriate for particular kinds of patients, problems, and problem conditions. These are two quite different frameworks.

Virtually Any Person May Use Experiential Therapy versus Therapy Is Mainly for Patients Who "Need" Therapy

Experiential therapy is for any person who has times of strong bad feelings. This therapy enables this person to move in the direction of having fewer of these scenes of strong bad feeling. This therapy is also for persons who are ready to begin a journey toward becoming a person who is increasingly more integrated and actualized. These people may not highlight any particular kinds of times that are especially painful, although they usually do. They are simply ready to start their own personal journey.

In contrast, there is a common framework in which therapy is especially geared for patients who need therapy. There is something wrong with them. They have persistent symptoms of underlying pathology. These therapists know that something is wrong and the person needs therapy, or someone else comes to that conclusion, and tells the person that she needs therapy, that she "should" have treatment for her problem or problem condition. A professional person may evaluate the person and conclude that therapy is "indicated." You just don't go for therapy. Something should be wrong. Therapy is to be "needed." Here are two different frameworks. Experiential therapy goes with the former framework.

Virtually Any Person May Use Experiential Therapy versus Prescribe the Appropriate Treatment for the Diagnosed Problem or Problem Condition

Experiential therapy joins with a few other therapies in holding that virtually any person can use and can benefit from the therapy (cf. Fine, 1971). I do not think in terms of particular kinds of "problems" or "problem conditions." I think in terms of whether the person would like a session, whether the person is ready and willing to have a session and to achieve what may be achieved.

I also think in terms of the particular scene of bad feeling that is important to this person in this session. Experiential therapy can work with virtually any kind of scene of strong feeling. The scene may involve something in the body or a recent incident. The scene may be mostly in the patient's head or overt and public. It may involve a child, a spouse, a career, a criminal act, or any kind of content. The scene may be dramatic and serious or mundane and minor. It may include any kind of behavior, those that are common and inconspicuous or explosive and momentous, behaviors that are happy and feel good, or behaviors that other therapists see as symptoms of mental illness (Mahrer, Stewart, Horn, & Lind, 1968), behaviors that other therapists see as being more chemically, genetically, or biologically based. The scene may involve any kind of feeling.

Experiential therapy is for virtually any person because it relies on a single process of change. If you believe that change occurs through a combination of the right kind of therapist-patient relationship and well-done interpretations, then that therapy can be for just about any patient who can benefit from that kind of change process. In the experiential system, change occurs through the four steps for all persons, all inner experiencings, and all scenes of strong feeling. Accordingly, any person can go through the experiential change process.

In general, just about anyone can use experiential therapy. However, an altogether different framework says there are different kinds of problems, such as thinking of killing your neighbor, and lots of problem conditions, such as hebephrenia. There are also lots of therapies and treatments. Some therapies and treatments are better for some problems and problem conditions. You can see which therapies and treatments are most useful and effective for which kinds of problems and problem conditions. If the patient has a simple phobia, there are supposed to be some therapies and treatments that are effective, so use these.

You can use a fine-grained category system of problems and problem conditions, and a fine-grained category system of treatments and therapies. You may use the official nomenclature of mental illnesses and diseases, plus a detailed list of problems and complaints. You may use a detailed list of treatments and therapies, including each kind of drug and all 200 to 400 therapies. You can mix and match both lists so that this particular patient has 14 problems and conditions for which you prescribe a combination of 22 treatment programs. Or you can divide therapies into just two groups. One group includes uncovering therapies, and the other group consists of supportive therapies. The uncovering therapies are effective with patients who are psychoneurotic, and the supportive therapies are for patients who are anything else, mainly psychotic or brain-damaged.

Experiential therapy does not fit into any of these prescriptive frameworks. Our framework does not define which problems or problem conditions experiential therapy is effective for.

IS EXPERIENTIAL THERAPY USEFUL AND APPROPRIATE FOR PATIENTS WHO . . . ?

There are at least two quite different meanings of "useful and appropriate." One meaning is that the patient can go through the four steps and can therefore gain what experiential therapy has to offer to anyone who goes through the four steps. An altogether different meaning is that experiential therapy is useful and appropriate to reduce the patient's problem or problem condition, or to achieve the kinds of specific changes that the therapist wants to achieve. In general, based on the first meaning, the answer is that experiential therapy is useful and appropriate for virtually any person.

How can we describe patients to see if experiential therapy is or is not especially useful and appropriate? It is relatively hard to answer this question when the questioner holds to some picture of human beings and psychotherapy that is quite alien to experiential theory, or when the question is worded in technical terms that are outside the experiential construct system. To answer these questions, there must be a reasonable amount of friendly looseness in translating the meaning into experiential theory, or in helping the questioner to view the picture of human beings or psychotherapy through the experiential perspective. But let us try to take a closer look.

Are Psychotic, Bizarre, Deranged, Crazy, Weird, Mentally Ill?

One way of avoiding a direct answer is to say that these constructs have no place in an experiential system. I do not think in terms of psychoses, and I genuinely would have little or no way of saying that this patient is psychotic. So this question is not easy to answer. Nevertheless, therapists ask if this therapy is good for "psychotics," or they name some particular brand of psychosis. I try to get the therapist's picture of what he has in mind when he says the patient is psychotic. Usually there is a pause, and the therapist will say something to indicate that I should know fairly well what he means. I don't. I usually have a set of very different pictures. The word psychotic has either no meaning to me because it has no place in my model of human beings, or it brings pictures to mind of patients who went through experiential sessions just fine and yet were officially called psychotic.

Many patients have said that they were diagnosed as psychotic. Some of these patients had been in mental hospitals. Many patients are referred by therapists or physicians who tell me that these patients are psychotic. The referral sources say that the patient has a history of doing all sorts of things that qualify as grossly psychotic. Sometimes I give demonstrations and workshops in psychiatric hospitals, and I have a session with a patient who the staff says is diagnosed as psychotic.

Can these patients go through an experiential session? In practical terms, the question is whether they can sit in the chair, close their eyes, and carry out the steps of an experiential session. My experience so far is that they can. What proportion? About the same proportion as patients who are not diagnosed psychotic. Is this surprising? I don't find it surprising. One reason is that there is a sort of screening process. To have a session, the patient should indicate that he wants to have a session. This means that the person must get on the phone and call me for an appointment. When I talk to the person on the phone, all I look for is even a mild readiness and willingness to have one session. I do not look for signs of "psychosis." So there may be many patients, diagnosed as psychotic, who never did contact me for a session even though a professional person wanted them to call.

There are features of this therapy that help make it fitting for patients who are called psychotic. Our attention is out there, on something that is attended to by both of us. I essentially let go of a back-and-forth interaction, with our attention mainly on one another. I am not interacting with the person in a way that would be conducive to the person's carrying on with ways of being and behaving that are regarded as psychotic. By joining with the person, attending to whatever the person selects as meaningful, and by not having a face-to-face interaction, there may well be little or no basis for the person's ordinary "psychotic" ways of being and behaving (Mahrer, 1970b; cf. Ansbacher, 1965; Haley, 1963; Leary & Gill, 1959; Rogers, 1966).

Are Considered Close to Becoming Psychotic, Doing Things That Are Dangerous, Violent, Harmful, Unethical, Unlawful?

Some therapies are regarded as inappropriate because the patients would become psychotic, go off the deep end, act out, kill themselves or others, go into a severe depression or a wild agitated state, end up being worse, in jails or mental hospitals. These patients have brittle defenses, weak egos. They are on the verge of psychotic states. Their personalities are fragile. Some therapies (e.g., Jackins, 1962, 1965; Janov, 1970; Laing, 1962) are supposed to exert too much "stress" on the patients and thereby bring about disastrous consequences. These therapies are certainly inappropriate for such patients, aren't they?

These kinds of worries or fears are rarely voiced by patients who begin experiential therapy but are common in other people, especially in many therapists. There are some reasons why the experiential therapist would probably not have such fears. One is that the experiential model does not include the kind of personality picture that generally goes with such fears. In the experiential model, there are no defenses, brittle or otherwise. There are no fragile personalities, no weak egos, no looming primitive id impulses. Therapists who are worried about patients who are shaky or near to psychosis or close to the deep end generally have a picture of a gyrating maelstrom of primitive psychotic impulses, and a frightened patient desperately clinging to defenses that are becoming weak and punctured. In this picture, the wrong therapy shatters the final defenses, and down the patient goes into the vortex of psychotic impulses. This is far afield from the experiential model of operating and deeper potentials and their relationships. Indeed, a person who is shaky, upset, starting to give in to strong feeling, may be especially suitable for being in a moment of strong feeling and accessing the inner experiencing, and also going through the subsequent three steps. In other words, the experiential model is not one in which the fears of crumbling "defenses" and "surging psychotic impulses" justify fears of becoming psychotic, doing things that are violent, harmful, unethical, and unlawful.

Second, patients who are regarded as "like that," from the perspective of these other therapists, simply do not end up going berserk or doing wild things in or after experiential sessions. It just does not seem to happen.

Third, most of these fears refer to aspects of what I would regard as the operating domain. The patient may well have hinted at killing someone, or even expressed fears of going crazy or doing something dangerous. This kind of talk is part of the way the person functions, part of the operating domain. The whole thrust of experiential sessions is to introduce significant changes into the operating domain, and thereby move away from, not toward, bringing these fears to reality. *Good point*

Fourth, these fears go with a picture of the experiential therapist somehow forcing or pressuring or inflicting on the patient demands for yelling and screaming, getting into "dangerous" material, doing things that shatter or overwhelm the patient. In actual sessions, there are simply too many checks and balances, too much emphasis on the patient's immediate readiness and willingness. It is easy, perhaps, to think of this therapy as forceful, bludgeoning, bombastic, explosive, as grabbing the patient and shoving him into powerful emotions. In actuality, the process is almost always soft, gentle, sensitively fitted to the person's own pace, own immediate readiness and willingness. When the patient goes through the four steps, at his own ready pace, nothing bad seems to happen. The person does not "decompensate," or go to pieces, or do awful things that patient and therapist, and others, feel bad about.

Finally, when these fears are front and center in the first step, when the patient is genuinely focused on falling apart, doing dangerous things, this is grist for the experiential mill. The content is merely one kind of focused center of attention or scene of strong bad feeling. It is simply where the session starts.

All in all, experiential therapy works fine with patients who fear (or therapists fear are close to) becoming psychotic, doing things that are dangerous, violent, harmful, unethical, or unlawful.

Are Highly Emotional or Unable to Have Strong Feelings?

Some therapists regard experiential psychotherapy as a good treatment for patients who have "flattened affect," for patients "out of touch with affect." These therapists think of experiential therapy as forcing patients to "have feelings." In a similar vein, these therapists would probably not refer patients whom they describe as highly emotional or emotionally "labile" because (a) these patients do not "need" experiential therapy, and (b) these patients are already highly emotional, and therefore experiential therapy might be dangerous for them.

Experiential therapy seems to work just fine with patients whom therapists and others regard as "highly emotional" or "emotionally labile" or who "lack control over their emotions." These persons can and do go through the four steps. The same seems to hold for patients whom therapists and others regard as emotionally flat, affectless, unable to have feeling. I know that many therapists use these phrases to describe some patients, but I do not think of patients that way. The closest that the experiential system comes is that such a way of being may refer to a given operating potential in this patient. Her way of being may be that of being unfeelinged, dead, neutral, not showing feelings. Accordingly, some therapists say that they can't get anywhere with this patient, he is cold and distant, unfeeling; see what you can do with this one.

Quite aside from whether or not a therapist or patient considers "not having feelings" as a problem, some patients may talk rather quietly and in a controlled fashion. They do not cry freely or yell or show feelings in the session. They may even say, in a relatively unfeelinged way, that they practically never shout, get flustered, cry, shake, raise their voice, or have feelings. Therapists may conclude that these patients "cannot" have feelings, have "problems showing emotion," are "out of touch with affect." From the experiential perspective, about all we can say is that it may be important for some patients to be this way. They may be described as having an operating potential for being cold, in control, unfeelinged. In the actual session, I find no difference, in the degree of having and showing feelings, when you compare patients who are said to be full-feelinged and to show feelings easily against patients who are said to be unable to have feelings. "Some patients are unable to have feelings" is, from the viewpoint of experiential theory, another one of those many beliefs or myths that are accepted as absolute truths by some therapists.

The net result is that most patients can go through the four steps, whether they seem to be highly emotional or unable to have strong feelings. These descriptions make little or no difference when it comes to the likelihood that the patient can go through the four steps.

Are Focused on Specific Bodily Events That Physicians Treat?

In the first step of the session, patients can focus on any scene of strong feeling. That scene may consist of specific bodily events that are ordinarily treated by physicians. The patient may be attending to the newly installed heart valve, the disk in the spinal cord, the mangled left arm, the paralysis on the right side of the face, the unborn fetus, or the cancer in the lungs.

The main reason such patients are able to use experiential therapy is that attending to the newly installed heart valve is no different from attending to any other scene, time, object, center of attention. We may stay with the heart valve or go to some other scene, some other attentional center. Yet we can easily start with the heart valve, or any other bodily event.

There is another reason that such opening attentional centers are fitting for experiential therapy. I do not recommend experiential therapy as a treatment of choice for a broken arm or a toothache or a blocked colon. I do not believe that experiential therapy can heal a broken arm or a toothache or a blocked colon or cancer. However, my picture of how the body works (Mahrer, 1978/1989d) leaves some room that bodily changes can occur through the kinds of changes that are opened up by the four steps of sessions. I have never seen a cancer, and I have no idea of what cancer is. Nevertheless, it makes some sense to me that some kinds of changes, perhaps similar to those occurring in experiential therapy, may occur in what is referred to as cancer (Mahrer, 1980b; cf., Bowers & Weinstock, 1978; LeShan, 1977; Simonton, Matthews-Simonton, & Creighton, 1978).

I regard the body as quite open to description and understanding from quite different conceptual systems. Of course, the body is open to description from perspectives that are anatomical, neurological, physiological. The body is also open to description from an experiential perspective. Looked at experientially, what is referred to as cancer may be understood in experiential concepts. For example, things that are bodily may be described as ways of enabling experiencing, just as sticking your tongue out may be a way of enabling experiencing. Or, the body may manifest deeper potentials just as easily as your dog may be used as an externalization of your own deeper potentials. When a patient is highly focused on something on or in the body, that scene can be used in Step 1 to access a deeper potential. This is one use of bodily events. A more exciting use is as the possible focus of therapeutic change. To the extent that the bodily event enables experiencing, or the bodily event is a manifestation of a deeper potential, the bodily event may be let go. That is exciting.

"Need" a Therapist Who Is . . . ?

Some therapists think in terms of patients who "need" a therapist who is this way or that way, who has particular kinds of qualities or characteristics, who can offer a given kind of relationship. Typically, the referring therapists predetermine what the therapist should be like, what the therapist should provide.

The reasoning is that because the patient is this way, then the appropriate therapist should be that other way. For example, this patient was abused as a child and is full of paranoid ideation. Accordingly, he needs a therapist who is gentle, will not exert pressure, will slowly build rapport. This female patient lost a baby soon after child-birth. She needs a therapist who can empathize with her hurt, a female therapist who can share the patient's deep-seated pain. This female patient is fragile and blocked by anxiety. She is terrified of male aggressivity and tends to act out impulsively. She needs a female therapist who is solid and secure, and who can provide structure while the patient gains a sense of trust in her ability to control impulses and tolerate anxiety.

Experiential therapists would probably not fit into this framework. They could not easily fit the script for the kind of therapists that are prescribed. In fact, it would seem hard to describe most experiential therapists as being like this or that, or as providing this or that. Even further, the whole framework is both alien and contradictory to experiential psychotherapy. Experiential therapy is not useful or appropriate when therapists think in terms of patients who "need" a therapist like this or that, or who can provide this or that.

Are Couples, Families, or Groups?

I know how popular couples therapy, family therapy, and group therapy are. Perhaps this is why so many therapists have asked me if experiential therapy can be used in this format, and why so many therapists tell me that they have adapted this therapy for couples, families, and groups.

There are certainly plenty of good reasons for working with couples, families, and groups. It is common for patients to say that they would like to be seen in couples or families. Many therapies have solid grounds for saying that treatment of this person is helped by working with the couple or family, or that the problem is indeed the couple or family as a unit or system. The trouble is that I have no experience with these formats and therefore my answer to the question would have to be mere speculation, in which I have little trust. So my honest answer is that I do not know if experiential therapy can be used in these formats.

Actually, I acceded to a few requests to work with couples and families. All I did was to work with one person at a time while the other(s) just sat there in the office. There were two main problems, but I expect these were mainly because of my lack of experience in these formats. One problem was that I became aware, at times, of the other person or people in the office. Sometimes I heard noises, and the noises allowed me to become distracted. But even without hearing noise, I still managed to be aware of the other(s) in the office. The second problem was in the fourth step. If the prospective new ways of being and behaving involved someone in the office, or might conceivably involve that other person or persons, I again became exceedingly aware of the other people in the office. But these, again, were my problems, and not problems of applying experiential therapy in these formats.

I have tried to conduct experiential therapy in front of a group of therapists, perhaps a small group of 10 to 25 or a larger group of around 100. Usually there is a volunteer from the audience. I have watched other therapists do these demonstrations. Many of them seemed to do rather well. I no longer do these demonstrations because I cannot put all my attention out there. I cannot listen in the experiential way. I cannot be with the patient well enough to carry out a session. I am much too aware of the people in the audience, of their sheer presence, of whether I can do even an adequate job. When I am in my office and there is another person watching me and the patient—the spouse, the parent, the sibling—I cannot do my job.

On the other hand, some therapists I have trained, and other therapists who contact me, do use experiential therapy with couples, with families, and in groups. They say that they use all sorts of experiential methods with the couples, families, and groups (cf. McLemore & Hart, 1982). Some say that they modify the methods. Most say that they close their eyes and have the patients close their eyes too. Many work with one person at a time. I encourage therapists to apply this therapy, and to modify this therapy, for use in these formats. My work is with individuals, but you work as you are inclined.

Are Infants or Children?

I have had a fair number of sessions with people as young as 12 to 14 years. However, I have no experience trying to do this therapy with younger children. Once again, I encourage therapists either to try to apply, or to modify, the methods for working with younger children.

Infants are another matter. When I worked with infants (Mahrer, 1978/1989d; Mahrer, Levinson, & Fine, 1976), there had already been other attempts to apply therapeutic principles to working with infants (e.g., Gordon, 1967; Lambie & Weikart, 1970; Williams & Barber, 1971). The actual methods that I worked out were to enable parents to have "sessions" with their 6- to 8-month-old infants in order to accomplish two goals. One goal is for the infant to become free of the primitive field that comprises the parents. In other words, the goal was for the parents to be able to let go of the infants as part of the parental primitive external world. The second goal, the other side of the first goal, is for the infant to be able to gain his own sense of self. Instead of the "center of gravity" lying within the parents, instead of the organizing center of the infant being the parents, the goal was for the infant to get a taste of being his own organizing center, the initiator, the constructor, of his own world.

The clinical methods were for parents or parental figures to be able to be with infants so as to move closer to these twin goals. In a way, I always have thought of this program for infants as having the same spirit as the four steps of experiential therapy. The goals of this infant psychotherapy and experiential psychotherapy have always seemed similar to me. Although the four-step experiential psychotherapy has not been used for children, the clinical methods of the infant program have (Mahrer, 1978/1989d; Mahrer, Levinson, & Fine, 1976). It is possible to modify the methods somewhat so that the goals of the infant program may also be applied to children who are 1 year old, 2 years old, 5, 7, 12, and throughout adolescence.

Nevertheless, this particular four-step psychotherapy is for adults, and perhaps may be used with people around 12 to 14 years of age, but that seems to be about the lower limit.

Have Been or Are in Other Therapies, with You or with Other Therapists?

Many patients have been in other therapies, with other therapists. I find that their having been in other therapies has very little effect on their going through the four steps. Even patients who know essentially nothing about experiential therapy seem to start right off being able to close their eyes and proceed through a session.

What used to be somewhat surprising is that a fair number of patients are in some other kind of therapy while also having experiential sessions. Typically, it seems that these patients have been in psychoanalytic or Jungian therapies, or in therapies with more or less focalized aims, such as reducing smoking or being able to tolerate stress or coping with the death of a loved one. Even when these patients have individual sessions three to five times a week with another therapist, I find that there is surprisingly little difficulty in their seeing two different therapists. It would be easy to think that there should be problems, clashes between the two therapies, but somehow I have not run into problems.

However, I do not believe that experiential therapy can be used well when the therapist has been doing some other kind of therapy with this patient, and then switches to experiential. Tapes of therapists who decided to do this, reveal some serious problems in attaining the four steps when the therapist switches to experiential from just about any other approach. Two reasons seem to account for this. One is that in most face-to-face therapies you will have established some kind of a role for yourself and for the patient. For example, I listened to tapes of sessions in which the therapist was being a good friend, was genuinely wanting the patient to become comfortable with women, told about his own trials and tribulations about finding a woman, was being the kind of buddy that a young fellow might want. Switching to experiential would deprive both therapist and patient of this very important role-relationship. Each time I listen to tapes of a therapist doing psychoanalytic, Gestalt, behavioral, or just about any other kind of therapy, and then I listen to the next session, an experiential one, I wince a little. It seems evident that neither therapist nor patient are comfortable giving up whatever kind of mutual roles and relationships they have so carefully evolved over the sessions. I do not think it is such a good idea to switch.

The second problem is: Why are you switching? Unfortunately, what I am often told is that the therapist was trying to accomplish something, whatever therapy she was using was not doing so well, and maybe a few experiential sessions would work. Typically, when I hear the beginning of the experiential session, therapists introduce it by explaining that this is going to be a little different. They may say that this therapy might help get at what is blocking the relations with women, or it is to open up feelings, or it is somehow to accomplish what the therapist wants to accomplish. In the session, the patient is not free to select any scenes of strong feeling. Instead, there is a preselected focus. The patient is told to start with his difficulties with his girlfriend, or her sense of loss, or his tension whenever he is to perform in just about any way. Experiential therapy cannot be carried out when the therapist has preselected issues, goals, objectives.

If you are inclined to try doing experiential therapy, it is probably easier to start doing it with a new patient. There seem to be some problems in trying to have a successful experiential session when you have been doing some other therapy with this patient.

HOW CAN YOU TELL IF THIS PATIENT CAN HAVE A SUCCESSFUL EXPERIENTIAL SESSION?

Determining the patient's suitability for a particular kind of therapy is a popular game in many therapies. How do you determine if this patient will do well in Jungian analysis or in biofeedback or in the women's group? How can the experiential therapist tell if this patient can have a successful session, or that perhaps experiential therapy is not working with this patient?

See If This Patient Can Have a Successful Experiential Session versus See If This Patient Is Suitable for an Extended Series of Sessions

In experiential therapy, the practical question is whether or not this patient is reasonably likely to have a successful session. You are thinking of one session, just one. You are not thinking of an extended series of sessions. At the end of an experiential session, the question is whether it is reasonably likely that this person can have a successful next session. You focus on one session at a time.

I would have a hard time thinking of what presession information would help me to predict whether or not this patient can have a reasonably successful single session. How could I predetermine that this person would find a scene of strong feeling, would be ready and willing to live and be in whatever strong-feelinged scene we discover, would be ready and willing to undertake each substep? A diagnostic evaluation won't help. Neither will a therapist's description of what she regards as this patient's psychodynamics. I cannot think of how test scores would provide that information.

Indeed, if just about any person can have a successful experiential session, why would an experiential therapist try to obtain some presession information? All we want to do is to see if this person can have this immediate session.

In contrast, the question in many therapies, is whether this patient is a suitable candidate for an extended series of sessions. If you are considering whether or not to accept this person into psychoanalytic therapy, with three to seven or more years of sessions, then it makes good sense to take a close look at suitability (Gill, Newman, & Redlich, 1954). It also makes sense in most therapies, as long as you and the patient are considering an extended series of sessions, whether it is a defined five-session program or an open-ended series of sessions. Then it makes sense to look for the patient's motivation and ability to do what your therapy requires, and to determine whether the patient is in good enough shape to benefit from your extended series of sessions (cf. Weiner, 1975).

Have an Experiential Session and See; Have a Trial Period; Do an Assessment-Evaluation of Suitability

How can we see if this patient can have a successful experiential session? How can you tell if experiential therapy works? A fellow calls up, and he knows nothing about experiential therapy. He is genuinely concerned about whether it can be the therapy he wants. How can he tell if this is the therapy for him? How can these questions be answered? The answer is simply to try a session.

This is a very cost-efficient way to see if this patient is suited for this therapy, and this therapy is for the patient. It is a lot cheaper, usually, than a battery of tests or a pretherapy assessment, or of having a whole series of trial sessions.

Since each session is a complete minitherapy, it makes sense to combine getting as much as possible out of this session, and simultaneously seeing if the patient is likely to be able to go through the four steps in the next single session.

Sometimes a person calls and asks if she can interview me to see if she wants to have me as her therapist. Typically, I say that such an interview would make good sense if we were thinking of lots of sessions over months, but that I work just one session at a time, and that at the end we can both decide if we want another session. Besides, it would probably be quicker and better to have a session or to go as far as we are both ready to go. Then she can get a firsthand sample. This seems to work for just about everyone who calls with such questions. Occasionally, a person wants to read a bit about this therapy. I try to find out what he would like to know and then give whatever references seem to be appropriate.

In other therapies, especially in long-term psychodynamic therapies, it makes sense to have a trial period, (Breger, 1976; Singer, 1965). This may take 3 to 10 sessions or perhaps more. You are seeing if this person is suitable for the long-term period of psychodynamic therapy. In this sense, like a trial marriage, the two people "need to know each other better before they can decide on their future relationship" (Szasz, 1965/1988, p. 168). During this trial period, you can assess the therapeutic alliance (Pollack & Horner, 1985), see how the patient handles interpretations (Malan, 1982), see if the patient does well with dreams, associations, and getting at childhood material (Fine, 1971), and assess the patient's motivation and therapeutic urge (Saul, 1972).

It is perhaps more common to have a pretherapy assessment and evaluation to examine the suitability of this patient for some therapy. Often this takes a number of sessions (Weiner, 1975). The one who does the assessing looks for things such as environmental constraints and limitations, the patient's support system and resources, verbal fluency and intelligence, ego strength and degree of tolerance of anxiety, capacity for social relatedness, the degree and severity of disturbance, the history and nature of precipitating stresses, and loads of other things.

If you are going to have an extended series of sessions, it makes sense to do a pretherapy assessment and evaluation, or to have trial period. However, you can probably best determine if this patient can have a successful experiential session simply by having an experiential session.

In the First Several Experiential Sessions, How Can You Tell if There Should Probably Be No Further Sessions, if This Patient and This Therapy Are Not Especially Suitable for One Another?

The simplest answer is that the four steps were not attained. Typically, you failed to get off the ground. You failed to attain the first step. You may not even have found any scene of strong feeling. This is the most common reason for considering that perhaps there might not be any further sessions. Even if you do attain Step 1, you should attain Steps 2 through 4. If you have a few sessions, and you do not reach Step 1, or you fail to complete the four steps, then I am quite drawn toward letting the patient know that we are not achieving what we should be, so perhaps it would be best to have no further sessions.

At the end of the session, you both may still want to try again. Or both of you may acknowledge that, for whatever reason, neither of you are inclined to continue. Or you may decide to wait a while and try another session in several weeks or so. You are both free to decide whatever seems fitting. Sometimes it takes one or two sessions before you have a session that goes through the four steps. However, if you do have one or two or even three sessions, and none even come close to the first step, and neither of you are especially inclined to try again, then stop. This saves grief and bad feelings on the part of the patient. After all, you are both free to try again later, if you wish.

Whether we stop after one session or several, I try to be clear that we just were not able to accomplish what the session should enable us to accomplish. I almost always believe that this has more to do with me than with something about the patient, and I seem to get this across to the person. I study tapes of these sessions, and I almost always find things that I did not do well. The problem generally lies with me. In any case, however, I try to be clear that we were unable to accomplish this specific thing, such as finding a scene of strong feeling, or being able to live and be in the moment of strong feeling. For whatever reason, usually having to do with me, we failed. So we may as well stop.

A second way of determining if there probably should be no further sessions, if this patient and this therapy are not especially suitable for one another, typically revolves around the failure to get to the first step. In some initial sessions, for whatever reason, the patient may attend fully and consistently to the therapist, rather than following the opening instructions and attending predominantly to something out there, to times and scenes of strong feeling. Some patients will ask about the therapist, his personal life, his training, his being drawn toward experiential therapy. The patient may be single-mindedly persistent in asking why the therapist said that, what the therapist had in mind, what the therapist might have been thinking. All of this defeats the purpose of the opening instructions and means that the first step will probably not be attained.

When patients steadfastly attend directly to the therapist and do not follow the opening instructions, we are unlikely to attain the first step. There may be lots of reasons for this, but if the first session consists of the patient's directly attending wholly to the therapist, then neither this nor later sessions seem likely to be successful in getting to the first step, much less getting through the four steps. If the initial sessions are characterized in this way, I am inclined to end this therapy, at least for now.

I find that the heavy preponderance of patients can have successful sessions; experiential therapy is useful and appropriate for virtually any patient. If, occasionally, the first few sessions are not successful, and we both want to try again, most of these patients can have successful sessions. Occasionally, however, the first few sessions indicate that the patients and this therapy are not suitable for one another. It makes sense to stop.

CHAPTER FIVE

For What Kinds of Therapists Is Experiential Psychotherapy Suitable, and What Determines That the Session Will Be Effective?

In the previous chapter, we questioned: Which patients is experiential therapy is suitable for? In this chapter, we turn our attention to two related questions: (a) For what kinds of psychotherapists is experiential psychotherapy suitable? (b) What determines that the session will be effective? Some of the answers to the first question help to determine if the session will be effective. Accordingly, the chapter is not divided into two main sections, one for each of the two questions. Instead, each of the major points should be read as if it provides an answer to both of these questions, and most of them do.

This chapter has a rather practical flavor because experiential psychotherapy is suitable for some therapists but not others. Actually, this therapy seems to be suitable for just about any patient, but only for some therapists. Similarly, this chapter has a rather practical flavor because if certain things are present, then you can be reasonably assured that the session will be effective. You can be reasonably assured that the session will achieve each of the four steps and that, in the next session, the patient will be more of a person who is able to be and behave on the basis of the inner experiencing that was accessed in the prior session; also in the next session, the person is relatively free of the bad-feelinged scene from the prior session.

What seems to help make a therapy popular, and how likely is it that experiential psychotherapy will become popular? What helps make a particular therapy popular is one of those questions for which there can be lots of good answers covering lots of different kinds of issues. The degree to which researchers decide to study a particular therapy may provide a little push toward popularity. If behavior therapies are much more studied than Jungian therapy or Adlerian therapy, then popularity with researchers may help behavior therapy's popularity a little bit. However, the results of lots of studies are unlikely to be enough to make a therapy popular (cf. Feyerabend, 1975; Kuhn, 1970; Mahrer, 1978/1989d, 1989f; Meehl, 1978; Polanyi, 1958).

On the other hand, I believe there are lots of good reasons why some therapies become popular. Of all these reasons, I want to highlight three which suggest that experiential therapy may well be suitable for and appealing to a proportion of therapists, but is unlikely to become a highly popular therapy.

A therapy becomes popular if it enables therapists to play out popular therapist roles and to undergo popular personal experiencings in the session, and especially if it enables therapists to play out a wide range of therapist roles and to gain a wide range of personal experiencings. Some therapies, like psychoanalysis, may offer a rather narrow range of therapist roles and personal experiencings, but they are popular ones. In the same way, eclectic or integrative therapies can be popular because they probably offer a wide range of therapist roles and personal experiencings. On this score, experiential therapy falls short, because it does not enable the therapist to play roles or gain personal experiencings, at least not to the extent a therapy should if it wants to become popular. Why not? The answers will be given later in this chapter.

A therapy tends to become popular to the extent that beginning practitioners can do it reasonably well. For example, many beginning therapists seem to gain a reasonably good measure of success right away with client-centered therapy. Fine client-centered therapists may be on a higher plateau, but an impressive proportion of new therapists can enjoy a modicum of success early on. Unfortunately, it is rather hard to do experiential therapy at first. Acquiring the skills sufficient to have successful session seems to take time. When a therapy requires some time to master the necessary skills, it is not likely to be wildly popular with lots of beginning therapists.

In some therapies, it is relatively easy to believe that the first three or five sessions are proceeding along rather well. If the patient returns for sessions, if there seems to be a relatively good relationship, and if nothing bad seems to happen, it is somewhat easy to conclude that the therapy is doing all right. In contrast, it is relatively conspicuous whether or not the four steps were attained in an experiential session. Unsuccessful sessions are compellingly conspicuous. This feature can easily stand in the way of a therapy's popularity. It applies with gusto to experiential therapy and therefore hardly qualifies this therapy as a future favorite.

A therapy is inclined toward popularity when its belief system fits well with the popular belief systems of most therapists. By the time most therapists are studying to become therapists, they usually have some sorts of notions of what people are like, how people got to be the way they are, what pushes and pulls people, what is inside most people, how people change, what the directions of change are, and so on. The theory may be rudimentary, not enveloped in technical vocabulary, but the major contours are there. Popular therapies usually contain popularly held belief systems. My impression is that the belief systems of experiential psychotherapy and experiential theory are not especially cordial to the entrenched belief systems in most of those who will become therapists.

Experiential psychotherapy will appeal to a modest proportion of therapists, but I do not believe that it is likely to be one of the exceedingly popular therapies.

How much of experiential therapy is a therapist asked to keep relatively stable, and how much is quite open to modification and improvement? The four steps are relatively stable, solid pillars of this therapy. These four steps provide a program or template for how therapeutic change can occur, and a conceptual framework of how change may be understood to occur. When I think of experiential therapy, I think of the four steps.

Although there is always a window for altering the four steps, they seem to be reasonably stable and anchored at least for a while. The same seems to hold for the two aims or objectives of enabling the person to become a qualitatively new person, free of the scenes of bad feeling.

The theory or model of human beings is another matter. It is quite open to further development or even to radical change. I regard this theory as a heuristically useful model that helps me solve problems in the actual practice. On the other hand, I have the highest trust in what actually occurs in the practice. If what is shown by the practice is at odds with the overall model of human beings, it is the overall model that will change. So far, the overall model has remained relatively stable. But it is only a useful model, and it is quite open to change.

With regard to the working methods, and the substeps for each of the four steps, there is plenty of room for a great deal of change. I welcome therapists to improve the substeps and the working methods. This is where there should be all kinds of new developments and changes. Try out lots of other methods. See which ones are more effective in achieving the four steps.

Experiential therapy may be regarded as suitable for therapists who are willing to accept the four steps and the current substeps and working methods. It is also suitable for therapists who are willing to explore use of better substeps and working methods, all within the general framework of the four steps.

The More Useful Position Is That the Determinants of a Successful-Unsuccessful, Effective-Ineffective Session Lie Almost Exclusively in the Therapist, Not in the Patient

My position is that if the session is a good one, it is because of the therapist; if it is a poor session, it is because of the therapist. I say that this is my position not because it is an assertion of some truth. Rather, I find that this position is much more useful than believing that the determinants lie mainly in the patient, or may well be distributed between the patient and the therapist, or somehow "depend on this or that," which is another way of leaving it open that the determinants may lie mainly in the patient.

I take this position because it is the most useful one for improving the therapy. If the session is a fine one, if there is something outstanding or a little breakthrough in the session, then this position is helpful in guiding me toward finding what seemed to work. When the patient is like this, and I do that, then look at the wonderful consequence, this impressive change. What seemed to help bring that about? What did I do that was different? Similarly, if this session was a poor one, this position enables me to look for what I did wrong. Here is a problem posed by the patient's being this way or doing that; look at the poor way I dealt with it. By taking the position that the determinants lie mainly in the therapist, I can almost always learn something useful to improve the practice.

This means that responsibility for an unusually fine session or for a rotten session lies in the therapist and not with the patient. In many therapies, if you want to get some idea of whether the therapy will be successful and effective, you study the patient. Is the patient motivated? Is the patient appropriate for this treatment? Is the patient compliant, cooperative, a good patient? How serious is the problem? Does the patient have a sufficiently strong ego? Can the patient carry out the postsession behaviors? There are all sorts of questions that focus on the patient. If you switch over to the other position, however, you turn away from the patient, and you focus on the therapist. You look at the things discussed in this chapter to see if the therapist is able to have a successful and effective session with this patient. Whether this session or this therapy will be successful switches over to assessing and evaluating the therapist, not the patient.

If there are problems in this session, if a series of sessions seems to go nowhere or even to make things worse, this position puts the blame on the therapist, not on the patient. If the four steps are not attained, if the therapist and patient do not even attain the first step, the problem lies in the therapist, not in the patient. If the subsequent session shows that the prior session was not very good, then the responsibility lies in the therapist, not in the patient. Again, these are not assertions of truth; they are the consequences of adopting this particular position on what determines if a session is successful or unsuccessful, effective or ineffective.

It is common, easy, and attractive to take the position that the fault may lie in the patient. You can easily assert that this is true and quote research to justify your belief. You can presume all sorts of qualities and characteristics of patients in general, or this particular patient, to explain problems and why this therapy was unsuccessful or ineffective with this patient. However, my position is that this approach is not especially useful if you want to improve the therapy.

Suppose that Steps 1 through 3 seemed to go rather well, but not Step 4. As soon as you turned to the possibility of considering new ways of being and behaving in the imminent world, the step seemed to go nowhere. You can immediately switch to the patient and easily find answers within the patient. Some of these might be general therapeutic axioms, entrenched in the clinical literature, well-accepted as virtual laws. It takes time to effect substantial change. It is not therapeutic to force "premature" change. Superficial changes come more readily, whereas more substantial and deep-seated changes require more time. Other therapeutic axioms may relate more specifically to this particular patient. This patient is too threatened by the possibility of actual change. She is not ready to give up her symptoms. Patients with that diagnosis are resistant to change. The relationship must be sufficiently enduring and strong for the patient to venture change. His external world is not conducive to change. You can debate whether these statements are true or not. I would simply acknowledge that these are perfectly fine ways of putting the blame on the patient, if you are so inclined. However, my preference is to identify what, if anything, can be found in terms of the therapist's contribution to the problem of the poor Step 4. When the patient was this way, what might the therapist have done? What did the therapist fail to do well? What did the therapist do that helped lead to the poor Step 4? Turning to the therapist is more useful, I find.

Lots of therapists find ready excuses in the patient's "resistance." Resistance is a well-established concept in the clinical literature, and is readily called on to justify an unsuccessful and ineffective session or series of sessions. From our position, however, we neither look for nor use the notion of patient resistance to explain a poor session or something not going well in the session. What is referred to as patient resistance we understand as being essentially caused by the therapist, and not the patient (Mahrer, Murphy, Gagnon, & Gingras, 1994).

The same holds for what is referred to as termination problems. In psychodynamic therapies, problems that surface in the terminal stages of long-term therapy are often attributed to both the therapist and to the patient, with a fair share of the responsibility falling on the patient's shoulders (e.g., Atkin, 1966; Bridger, 1950; Ekstein, 1965; Fenichel, 1945; Firestein, 1969; Freud, 1937; Glover, 1955; Greenson, 1966; Robbins,

1975; Saul, 1958). It makes good sense to see a share of the termination problems as involving patient qualities and characteristics, provided that you look at this from a particular position. However, from our position, the therapist is almost single-handedly responsible for such problems (Mahrer, Howard, & Boulet, 1991).

Can you accept a position that virtually all the determinants for the success and effectiveness or lack of success and effectiveness lie with the therapist, and not the patient? To the degree that you can, then experiential therapy may be suitable for you, and you may be able to have successful and effective sessions.

If You Honor the Patient's Readiness and Willingness to Undertake Each Substep, Then (a) This Therapy May Be Suitable for You, and (b) The Session May Be Successful and Effective

Almost without exception, when the patient is to do something, the next substep, you should see if the patient is ready and willing. If you uphold this as paramount, as a requisite, then this therapy may be suitable for you, and the session may be successful and effective. If you are not especially inclined to highlight the patient's readiness and willingness to do this immediate thing, then this therapy is probably not suitable for you, and your session will likely not be able to attain the four steps.

Relying on the patient's readiness and willingness is not honored and upheld because this is a nice way that people should be with one another, or because it is supposed to contribute to some kind of therapist-patient relationship. The reason is that the patient is the one to carry out each substep. The session cannot even begin unless the patient is quite ready to follow the opening instructions. From then on, it is likewise the patient who is to carry out each substep. Quite practically, if the patient is not ready and willing to do it, it will not get done.

The most important thing that the patient brings is readiness and willingness to take this substep. No other patient quality or characteristic is more important than this. You may think of such things as the nature and severity of the "illness," the degree of motivation, all of the many qualities and characteristics that are commonly regarded as contributing to the success of the session. From the experiential perspective, none of these play any substantial role, compared with the singular importance of the patient's readiness and willingness to carry out this immediate substep.

The patient's degree of readiness and willingness is an immediate affair, in relation to this substep. It may fluctuate from this substep to this other one. It may be generally high in this session, and somewhat lower in another session. It is not a more or less stable or continuing quality, characteristic, trait, or parameter of this patient.

Nor does the therapist try to "get" the patient to do this next thing, to be cooperative or motivated. Instead, you merely ask. You invite the patient to do this next thing if he is ready and willing. You leave it up to him. In this way, experiential therapy is perhaps one of the softest sells, for you wholly honor the patient's immediate degree of readiness and willingness.

The patient is the one who carries out the act, who does or does not do it. The patient has veto power. If the patient is not ready and willing to do it, that is all it takes. You honor the patient's decision. You cede virtually all mandate, choice, and decision to the patient (Enright, 1970; Mahrer, 1978c, 1978d). You respect, honor, and abide by the patient's readiness and willingness (Mahrer, Nadler, Dessaulles, Gervaize, & Sterner, 1987; Mahrer, Nadler, Gervaize, & Markow, 1986).

If You Find the Experiential Model of Human Beings to Be Reasonably Sensible, Then (a) This Therapy May Be Suitable for You, and (b) The Session May Be Successful and Effective

Some therapists are able to believe that each theory of psychotherapy is merely its own way of looking at things, its own particular construct system, rather than the single true way of grasping what human beings are really and truly like and how psychotherapy really and truly works. I am referring to what I call the Class 1 position on some of the issues of the philosophy of science discussed in Chapter 1. If you can take this position, then experiential therapy may be suitable for you and you may carry it out effectively. If, however, you believe in a single truth, in one theory being the truth, then this therapy may not be suitable for you, and you will have trouble having successful experiential sessions. In effect, I am asking you to be able to do what experiential therapy invites patients to do—to let go of their established, everyday, common way of seeing things, and to adopt that of a different system. If you are able to do this, then perhaps patients can; if you are unable, then patients will also have a hard time shifting, changing, going through the steps of the session.

Your way of understanding human beings should at least be reasonably consistent, friendly, and cordial to the experiential model. On the other hand, some therapists know that what lies within human beings is essentially unchangeable, is basically bad and uncivilized, should be controlled. There are basic human instincts, fundamental traits. While some may be acceptable, it simply would not do for people to go around acting on the basis of these instincts and fundamental traits. The world would be uncivilized. People would rape, kill, pillage, destroy, do bad things to one another, violate the guidelines of human decency. What is inside is basically bad, evil, wicked, antisocial, sick, dangerous. If you look at human beings this way, then experiential therapy is unsuitable for you. You would almost certainly have ineffective sessions.

Experiential theory pictures an "operating domain," a more or less surface set of operating potentials that are instrumental in the way the person constructs and lives in his world. These operating potentials essentially compose the stable, continuing person, who he is and what he is like. According to the experiential model, this operating domain can be and should be substantially replaced by deeper potentials in a way that is called integration and actualization. However, there are other theories and models that regard the person as one who is as somewhat modifiable and improvable, but certainly not as replaceable by whatever is regarded as deeper. If your way of looking at what I term the operating domain is relatively consistent with the experiential model, then this therapy may well be suitable for you, and sessions may be effective. If, however, your own way of picturing the person is seriously different, then this therapy may be inappropriate for you.

You can give yourself a test. Chapter 2 presents the experiential model of human beings. As you read through this chapter, do the various parts of this picture make sense to you? Is this model reasonably fitting for you? If the answer is yes, then you and this therapy may be suitable for one another, and you may well be able to have successful sessions. On the other hand, it may be that some parts of this model were grating. They violated what you know is true about human beings and the structure of personality. They conflicted with the truths that comprise your own personality theory of what human beings are like. Perhaps the experiential model simply lacks important truths that a theory must have, like psychobiological phases of development or the basic role of neurological determinants of behavior. If there is a fundamentally poor fit between the experiential model and your own set of truths, your own theory, then experiential psychotherapy is probably not suitable for you, and your sessions would likely be unsuccessful.

If You Find the Experiential Model of Psychotherapeutic Change to Be Reasonably Sensible, Then (a) This Therapy May Be Suitable for You, And (b) The Session May Be Successful and Effective

If this therapy is going to be suitable for you, and if you are going to have a fairly good chance of being successful and effective, then you should find the experiential model of psychotherapeutic change to be reasonably sensible.

It should make sense that the direction of change is toward integration and actualization of deeper potentials for experiencing.   The experiential model of psychotherapeutic change is intimately designed around the notion of inner, deeper personality processes. It is based on the notion of deeper potentials for experiencing, inner ways of being, deeper qualities and possibilities. The experiential model of psychotherapy is expressly designed to enable the person to become a substantially new and different person. Deeper potentials for experiencing are to become solid components of the operating domain, of the very substance of who and what you are. This is called actualization. They are to bear good, welcoming, friendly, loving relationships with other operating potentials for experiencing. This is called integration. Does this make sense for you?

It should make sense that the four steps provide a useful avenue of psychotherapeutic change.   There are lots of ways of picturing how and why psychotherapeutic change occurs. In the experiential model, the question of how and why psychotherapeutic change occurs is answered by the four steps that are to be attained in each session. But this is only one answer. There are lots of other models and theories of psychotherapy. If the experiential four steps make sense, then this therapy may well be suitable for you, and your experiential sessions may well be successful and effective. However, if some other theory of psychotherapeutic change seems to be much more attractive and sensible, then experiential therapy may not be suitable or successful for you.

You may hold that one of the requisite components in psychotherapy is the patient's gaining insight and understanding of this or that kind. You may well be convinced that psychotherapeutic change occurs largely through some kind of helpful therapist-patient relationship. You may find it sensible that psychotherapy is to modify the patient's wrong or ineffective or maladjustive thoughts, or that it occurs by modifying whatever the patient's problematic behavior is held as contingent upon. There are many theories of psychotherapy. If your own theory of psychotherapy does not fit with the experiential model of the four steps, then this therapy is probably not suitable for you, and your sessions may not be especially effective.

It should make sense that psychotherapeutic change requires the patient's actually carrying out the new way of being and behaving in the postsession extratherapy world.   The four steps enable the patient to be and to behave as the integrated and actualized inner experiencing, and to gain a realistic taste or sample of what it is like to be and to behave as this new person in the context of the prospective extratherapy world. If the four steps were successful, and if the patient is ready and willing, the consequence is that the patient actually carries out this new way of being and behaving in the postsession extratherapy world. To the extent that this occurs, then psychotherapeutic change has taken place. In effect, the patient has actually carried out the new way of being and behaving that was the culminating fruit of the fourth step in the session. However, if this new way of being and behaving was not carried out, then it is unlikely that psychotherapeutic change has taken place.

Looked at in another way, a session is successful and effective if the four steps were attained in the session, and if the patient actually carried out the new way of being and behaving in the postsession extratherapy world. Quite practically, the indication that the patient actually carried out the new way of being and behaving is typically found in the beginning of the subsequent session. Accordingly, you can determine that this session was successful and effective by looking at this session, to see if the four steps were attained, and also by looking at the subsequent session, to see if the patient actually carried out the new way of being and behaving. If all of this makes sense, then this therapy may be suitable for you, and the session may be successful and effective.

It should make sense that what is to change and how it is to change are largely determined in the first step of each session.   In the beginning of each subsequent session, the therapist looks for two kinds of changes. One is that the inner experiencing from the prior session is now part of the patient's operating domain. The second is that if the first step of the prior session included a painful scene of strong bad feeling, that scene is now washed away, less painful, occurs less readily.

With regard to this immediate session, however, the experiential therapist approaches the first step with a sense of adventure. The first step will identify the scene of strong feeling and will open up the inner experiencing that is accessed in this session. What is to change and how it is to change are largely determined by what the first step of this session reveals. If this makes sense to you, then experiential therapy may be suitable, and your sessions may well be effective.

On the other hand, there are many different ways of determining what is to change and how it is to change. For example you may prefer to identify problems, problem behaviors, or problematic conditions that you are to treat by ameliorating, reducing, changing them. It may be quite sensible for you to label and categorize patients in terms of what you see as their problem or pathological condition, such as saying that a patient is an alcoholic, an incest survivor, has repressed anger, needs assertiveness training, has bruxism, is to be treated for binge eating, is depressed, has a bipolar condition, is a borderline. In each instance, the problem or condition is your continuing target, and the direction of change is essentially built into the identified problem or pathological condition. If these are your ways of determining what is to change and how it is to change, then experiential therapy is not especially suitable for you, nor will the sessions likely be especially effective.

It should make sense that the therapist's psychotherapeutic belief system is an important determinant of the nature and extent of possible change.   According to the experiential model of human beings and of psychotherapy, the therapist's own personal belief system is a powerful determinant of what is open to change, the way it can change, the extent to which it can change, the length of time that such change may require, whether the changes can be narrow or broad, constricted or dilated, with a ceiling that is low or high.

The experiential therapist's belief system holds that the patient has a large hand in constructing his own world, and therefore his world may well be altered to a significant degree, including the real, hard, tangible things in that world. If we can access an inner experiencing, this patient may become a substantially new and different person, with this inner experiencing as an important part of that person. Scenes of bad feeling may no longer be a part of the patient's personal world. Furthermore, these changes can be of such a degree and a nature that they qualify as virtually transformational (Mahrer, 1990c, 1993). Even further, these changes can occur in and following each session.

According to the experiential belief system, these ambitious changes can occur in just about every patient. Indeed, the therapist must be able to conceive and to picture this patient, in this session, as an optimal person, based on the inner experiencing that accesses in this session, a person who is substantially integrated and actualized.

In the experiential belief system, if Step 1 accesses an inner experiencing of being superior, on top of things, in charge, then the experiential belief system holds that this is the way the person can be. Furthermore, Steps 2 through 4 are designed to enable the person to be and to behave on the basis of this accessed inner experiencing. In contrast, some other belief systems say no. Even if there is something deeper in this person, it does not necessarily follow that the patient could, or even should, be and behave on the basis of this deeper quality. These therapists can easily cite considerations that are consistent with their belief systems. There are reality constraints. The patient may not be equipped with the wherewithal to be superior, on top of things, in charge. Being this way is inconsistent with his "character," his "personality makeup." Being and behaving as a new person can only occur gradually, over months or years. The patient's real world may be inappropriate for such a change. Such a change may be "harmful" to the patient, inconsistent with the patient's "best interests." If your belief system is friendly with the patient's being and behaving on the basis of the deeper potential, experiential therapy may be suitable. On the other hand, if you are drawn toward voicing why the patient could not or should not be and behave on the basis of the deeper potential, then your belief system inclines you away from experiential therapy. In any case, if the therapist accepts that the therapist's psychotherapeutic belief system is an important determinant of the nature and extent of possible change, then this therapy may be suitable and the sessions may be effective.

It would be almost ideal if the therapist were to study cassettes of actual experiential sessions. This is what occurs in the first phases of learning to become an experiential therapist. As you watch and listen to what happens in the session, how the session moves along, it is helpful to judge whether what is happening seems to be sensible or whether it seems to violate what you believe or what you know is the way that therapy should occur. By studying the sessions so closely, you can have a chance to see firsthand and up close whether or not this way of doing therapy fits well or poorly with your own notions about what could and should happen in sessions. If you do not have access to cassettes of actual experiential sessions, this volume should enable you to be able to see whether or not what happens in sessions fits well or is grating and violating of your own explicit or implicit notions of what should or should not occur in psychotherapy. In this way you can tell if you and experiential psychotherapy are suitable for one another. If the answer is no, then chances are you would have a hard time having successful sessions.

If the Therapist Is Sufficiently Competent in the Working Methods of Attaining the Four Steps, Then There May Be a Reasonable Likelihood of Achieving a Successful and Effective Session

To attain each of the four steps, you usually must go through a set of substeps. For example, before you access a deeper potential, you should be in a moment of strong feeling. To be in a moment of strong feeling, it helps to be in a general scene of strong feeling. Achieving each step usually means going through a few substeps. If you are not adequately skilled in going through these substeps, it will be hard to attain any of the steps. The therapist must be competent in the methods of achieving the substeps for each of the four steps.

The importance of adequate skill and competence. There is a serious aspect to this guideline. If you have an adequate degree of competence in the working methods, then you are likely to have a successful and effective session. But if you do not have an adequate level of competence, good enough to attain the substeps, then it is quite unlikely that you will attain the four steps. When I listen to a tape of a session, I can easily detect that this therapist lacks even rudimentary competence in the working skills, and seems to have little or no idea of what substeps to go through to attain a given step. Or I can be quite sure that this therapist does have the adequate level of competence in the working methods, and knows the substeps to follow to attain the step.

Every so often I receive a tape of a session from a therapist who says that he is trying experiential therapy. He begins the session by almost pleading with the patient to try this "new kind of therapy" because "I think it will help you to be in touch with your anger." He promises, ". . . if this doesn't work, we'll do what we usually do." The therapist then asks the patient what she is feeling, and spends most of the session trying to get the patient to have this feeling more. This will not work. To attain the four steps, therapists should follow the four-step program and have adequate competence in the working skills. You really must have minimally adequate competence in the experiential methods to achieve the four steps.

Some therapists are drawn toward the experiential methods, but they are drawn more to talking about why they cannot do the methods, rather than developing competency in the actual skills. For example, they may have little or no skill in being aligned with patients, yet they are attracted to interesting discussions about why they may be reluctant to do so. Maybe I am unable to get close to some patients. Maybe I have a fear of intimacy. Maybe some patients are threatened by fusion with a parental figure. Such speculations about why the therapist is not being aligned are easy, compelling, attractive, and fun, but no substitute for sheer learning, sheer practice, sheer development of skills. Doing this therapy calls for competence in the actual skills.

The importance of actual practice to acquire the skills. I am impressed how many skills, usually outside therapy, are accepted as requiring training, learning, practice, and a gradual development of minimal competence. It is hard to read directions about typing and then to be able to start right off typing 60 words a minute. It takes practice. You can read about how to play a violin, but generally you do need some practice to become reasonably competent. Developing a moderate level of skill as a ballerina probably takes some practice. Doing surgery to remove an appendix calls for a period of learning, of training, of practice. It can be embarrassing to document the number of hours spent by psychotherapists in direct skill-learning practice. While a graduate musician may have spent a thousand hours practicing the piano during her schooling, the psychotherapist may have spent up to one hour, perhaps, in direct training-to-criterion in the total package of things the graduate will do in psychotherapy. Virtually all therapists have spent almost no time in sheer practice of a set of skills to attain a level of adequate competence. I am not talking about spending time doing psychotherapy. Spending 2 or 10 years doing therapy is quite different from spending an hour in serious practice, doing it over and over so that you can attain a level of adequacy in this particular skill. There seems to be a discernible level of real competence that the therapist must acquire in the working methods, techniques, and procedures or substeps, in order to have a good likelihood of attaining the four steps.

The importance and the challenge of receiving the inner, deeper experiencing in Step 1. One of the most difficult parts of the four steps, for most therapists, is receiving the inner, deeper experiencing in Step 1. It is one of the most important achievements, for once you identify the inner experiencing, you know what it is that is to be welcomed and appreciated in Step 2. You know what the person is to be in Step 3, and you know how the person is to be in the extratherapy world, the goal of Step 4.

The therapist must master specific skills to receive the inner experiencing in this moment of strong feeling. If the therapist is unable to be in the moment of strong feeling, and lacks sufficient skills to receive the inner experiencing, then the therapist will likely fail to identify the crucial element for the rest of the session. It is essential that the therapist accept the challenge and have the skills of receiving the deeper, inner experiencing. When the therapist is ready to do this and is competent in doing this, then the inner experiencing can be accessed in Step 1, and this is crucial to achieving a successful and effective session.

Do you believe that there are explicit skills that have to be mastered in order to be able to have successful experiential sessions; that acquiring competence calls for hours and hours of actual practice, a period of learning and sheer practice-to-criterion? If the answer is yes, then this therapy may be suitable for you and there may be a reasonable likelihood of achieving a successful and effective session.

If the Therapist Is Sufficiently Competent in Being "Aligned" with the Patient, Then There May Be a Reasonable Likelihood of Achieving a Successful and Effective Session

It is almost essential that the therapist be competent in listening for the experiencings and scenes. The therapist is to be "aligned" with the person, rather than in a "face-to-face" position.

What is the patient mainly attending to?   It is perhaps most common, in most therapies, that the patient's attention is on the therapist, even though the patient may talk about just about any topic. While there may be a little bit of attention on whatever the patient is talking about, probably 90 percent or more of the patient's attention is on the therapist. Even more, it is likely that throughout at least 90 percent of the session, in most sessions, about 90 percent of the patient's attention is on the therapist. This is one sound reason that so many therapists can say that there is always a "relationship" between therapist and patient. If the patient is almost always attending to the therapist, then it makes sense to say that the patient has a relationship with the therapist.

However, the predominance of the patient's attention may be on something other than the therapist (Mahrer & Gervaize, 1983). In meditation and contemplation, the person is to place the bulk of attention on something other than the teacher or therapist. Instead, attention is to be poured onto the gurgling brook or the candle flame or midway between an external object and internal bodily phenomena (Ornstein, 1971; Ouspensky, 1949, 1957; Wilhelm, 1962).

In classical psychoanalysis, a fundamental rule is that the patient is to attend mainly to the flow of associations, rather than talking mainly to the therapist. This is how Freud instructed patients: "So say whatever goes through your mind. Act as though, for instance, you were a traveller sitting next to the window of a railway carriage and describing to someone inside the changing views which you see outside" (Freud, 1913/1958, p. 135; cf. Freud, 1940). Attention is directed mainly on the flow of associations, rather than directed mainly to the analyst.

What is the therapist mainly attending to?   Most therapists spend most of their time attending mainly to their patients. Therapists have face-to-face conversations with their patients. They talk to their patients. Therapists attend mainly to their patients throughout most of the session.

Therapists are usually aware of the referred-to content of what patients talk about. The patient may be talking about the low back pain or her husband's being a slob, and the therapist is aware of the content, but the therapist is attending mainly to the patient who is describing her back pain, or how her husband is such a slob. Regardless of the content, most therapists spend most of their time with their attention mainly on the patient.

In the experiential system, the therapist's attention is almost always "out there," on whatever objects or scenes or images are out there (Mahrer, 1980a). Instead of looking at or attending to the patient, virtually all the therapist's attention is on something else, on that third something. In fact, the therapist is mainly looking "out there" throughout the entire session, and practically all the therapist's attention, not just a little bit, is directed "out there." Whether it is the patient who is talking or the therapist who is talking, just about all the therapist's attention is wholly directed on whatever appears out there, on whatever scenes are present in front of him. At every moment throughout the session, the aligned therapist is seeing whatever is out there, and essentially none of his attention is on the patient.

Out there includes whatever the patient provides for the therapist to see. If the patient is talking about her husband, the therapist may see the husband. In addition, out there can also include things located in the patient's body. She may be attending to the cancer, her infected toe, tired old body, low back pain, or the tension around her heart. Whether it is external or internal, the therapist's attention is fully concentrated on it, on seeing it.

There are some ways in which an emphasis on attending out there is natural and useful, where attention is focused on the work target rather than on being face-to-face with the other person. When a surgeon is busy doing surgery, her attention is ordinarily on the object of her work, and not concentrated on talking to and interacting with the patient. Picture a dentist working on a tooth, an optometrist concentrating on an eye, a speech therapist focusing on the speech pattern. Lots of professions involve concentration on the object of work, and not especially on being face-to-face with the client.

You are face-to-face with the patient who turns his gaze away from you to concentrate on something else. He turns away when he concentrates on the way his father used to lie down on the couch after work, and take a little nap. He is attending mainly to the recent phone call from his daughter, trying to remember just how she said the words, "'I got a surprise for you, Dad' . . . No, something like that . . ." In some ways, it is perhaps natural that therapist and patient would be mainly attending to something other than one another. They need not be attending mainly to one another, even though this is the way it is with most therapists most of the time.

By far, the most common option is for therapist and patient to be face-to-face, each attending mainly to the other. The patient talks to the therapist, with attention mainly on the therapist. The therapist talks to the patient, with attention mainly on the patient. This is the face-to-face way of being together. It is so common, across just about all the therapies, that it is almost taken as standard.

A second option is for the patient to attend to a third thing while the therapist attends mainly to the patient. The patient's attention is mainly on the wonderful baby she had a few weeks ago, or on the embarrassing incident yesterday, or on the memory of her trying to learn the new piece of music when she was a child. While the patient's attention is mainly on this third thing, the therapist is attending mainly to the patient. She observes the patient, notices how the patient says this, notes that the patient has a little catch in her voice, thinks about how the patient seems to be avoiding some important topic.

The third option is when both therapist and patient are attending mainly to the third attentional center or scene. The patient's attention is mainly on that baby, and the therapist is likewise mainly focused on the baby. This is the way that the experiential therapist and patient are with one another. In this option, therapist and patient are aligned, both attending mainly to "it" (Mahrer, Boulet, & Fairweather, 1994).

You can simultaneously engage in a face-to-face relationship and be aligned with patient versus you have to make a choice.   It seems to me that you must make a choice. Your attention cannot simultaneously be focused on the patient and also on whatever the patient is mainly attending to. When you both are attending mainly to his cancer or his mother's expression, you cannot, at the same time, be attending mainly to the patient.

When you are essentially face-to-face with the patient, the two of you may talk about just about anything. Yet virtually everything you say and do tends to lock the two of you into mainly attending to one another. Once the two of you are face-to-face, whatever you say comes from that posture and therefore preserves the two of you in that posture. No matter what the patient says, and no matter what you say, it is as if you are saying, "Talk to me; attend mainly to me; say it to me."

Because you are mainly attending to one another, it is almost inevitable that you will be engaging in some kind of relationship. What most therapists mean by "the relationship" almost necessarily means that the two of you are mainly attending to one another. However, by relating together, by attending mainly to one another, you are almost certainly not attending mainly to some third entity. The patient may be talking about his son, but most of the patient's attention is on you, not on his son, and most of your attention is on the patient, not on his son. You will almost certainly not be able to see the patient's world through the patient's eyes. For one thing, the patient is not mainly attending to his world. Even if he is, you are attending mainly to him, and not to seeing his world. When you are in a face-to-face relationship, you almost certainly sacrifice seeing the patient's world, and especially seeing the patient's world the way he does.

When you are external, separate from the patient, in a face-to-face relationship, you will likely be able to maintain a continuing sense of who you are, a sense of identity. You will have a sense of what is happening right now, and of your being the person that you are. There is self-awareness, self-consciousness.

In the experiential model, the two of you are attending mainly to a third entity, a third something, some object or scene. When you talk, your attention is on that third thing. What you say tends to keep the patient attending out there. Even when your words are addressed to the patient, they are said as your attention remains focused out there. So you say, "That cancer looks kind of dark and hard; is that the way it seems for you?" When you are saying these words as you are looking at the cancer, the net result is that the patient likewise keeps looking at the cancer, is drawn further into seeing the cancer.

When the two of you are aligned, it is hard to be in a face-to-face relationship. What most therapists mean by a relationship is that therapist and patient are mainly attending to one another, and this tends to occur only minimally when the two of you are aligned. A helpful relationship, a therapeutic relationship, a therapeutic alliance, a transference—these almost always call for a good measure of the patient and therapist attending mainly to the other. Being aligned, both attending out there, means that there is very little of what is commonly meant by a relationship.

And yet, it is as if therapist and patient can be somehow closer when they are both aligned, both sharing the same attentional center. Something happens that is different from when the two are face-to-face. I call it "being aligned." Others talk about the two being joined or conjoined, the therapist being plugged in to, merged, or fused with the patient (Binswanger, 1958a, 1958b; Fromm, Suzuki, & Dimartino, 1960; Laing, 1962, 1982; Maupin, 1965). When therapist and patient are face-to-face, there can be a certain package of closeness, intimacy, love, bondedness. This kind of relationship is different from what occurs when patient and therapist are aligned, both attending to the third entity. The distinction between what can occur in a face-to-face relationship and what can occur in the two being closely aligned may well underlie Maslow's (1968) distinction between D and B intimacy-love, Fromm's (1956) distinction between mature intimacy-love and symbolic union, Seguin's (1965) dual or shared intimacy-love, Lewis's (1960) gift or need intimacy, and Binswanger's (1958b) distinction between communication and communion. Without thinking about it, without conscious awareness of it, something special, something more, occurs when therapist and patient are fully aligned with one another. There is a kind of blending or close alignment that is not quite the same as when the therapist and patient are separate, face-to-face, and in a relationship of closeness, warmth, intimacy, and love with one another.

In many ways, it is hard to be both aligned and face-to-face. There does seem to be a choice. In experiential therapy, therapist and patient are aligned. The therapist is almost always looking out there, with most of his attention directed out there. The patient is also looking out there, attending to some object or scene. Most other therapists are rarely in this posture. Most therapists and patients are continuously attending mainly to one another in a face-to-face relationship. The two postures differ, perhaps a great deal. But do the differences make a difference? I think they do.

When you are face-to-face, you listen to what patient says versus when you are aligned, the patient's words occur in and through you.   When you are face-to-face with the patient, the patient is predominantly talking to you. You are external to the patient, generally attending to the patient, and it is in this posture that you listen to what the patient is saying. You may listen with a behavioral system or an Adlerian system or an implosive system, but you will receive whatever the patient says as you and the patient are attending mainly to one another.

In the experiential model, you and the patient are situated so that the patient is attending to some third entity, and not to you. Your attention is "out there." The patient says, "This job is just great—except that most of the staff of the hospital are crazy!" The more your attention is out there, the more something interesting happens to the words spoken by the patient. It is as if these words are coming in and through you! It is as if the patient were located somewhere in you, in an enlarged boundary that includes the patient. "You" enlarge and encompass the patient so that it is somewhat like the patient, in you, is saying these words. You are keenly attentive to seeing the staff of the hospital, as the words are spoken, "This job is just great—except that most of the staff of the hospital are crazy!" Some voice inside you seems to say these words.

The experiential therapist is seeing the images and scenes that are out there, as the words are occurring in and through the therapist. You are attending mainly to what is out there, to the images and scenes created by the words coming in and through you. The experiential therapist is, accordingly, not attending mainly to the words themselves, and even less is the therapist thinking that these words are coming from the separate patient over there.

This is the way the therapist is with the patient. Most of the therapist's attention is out there, on the images and scenes that are created by the words of the patient, with the words almost seeming to come from inside the therapist.

Which Is More Useful and for Which Purposes—Being Aligned or Being Face-to-Face?

Generally, three features define the aligned posture with patients.

1. The therapist's instructions make it relatively clear that the therapist and patient are to be attending to a third entity, something other than one another, usually a focal center or a scene accompanied with feeling.
2. The therapist's attention is to be directed out there as fully as possible, on whatever appears in front of her, and practically none of the therapist's attention is on the patient.
3. The therapist receives the patient's words as coming from the therapist herself, some part of an enlarged, dilated therapist. Rather than being a separate person, outside the therapist, the patient is "inside" the therapist whose outer boundary has stretched out to include the patient.

However, the most common way of being with the patient is face-to-face, with each participant attending mainly to the other. Of these two ways of being with patients, which one is more useful for which uses or purposes? I am inclined to believe that each is generally restricted to its own particular uses and is relatively inadequate for the purposes of the other. What are these purposes? Which one is better for which purpose? When you and the patient are face-to-face, what are you essentially unable to accomplish? When you and the patient are aligned, what purposes have you all but sacrificed?

Face-to-face is better for the patient's providing you with information about standard topics.   There are lots of relatively standard topics that most therapists want information about. For just about all these topics, face-to-face is much better than when patient and therapist are aligned with one another. Therapists want to get information about the problem, what the problem is like, what seems to cause it, when and where it seems to be worse or not so bad, what the patient has tried to do about the problem, how severe it is, when it started. Virtually all the helpful information about the problem is best obtained when the therapist and patient are face-to-face.

There are hundreds of pieces of demographic information that many therapists like to get. Is the patient married, what is the marriage like, how are things with parents, what about friends, what have been the big changes lately, whom does he turn to, what about church, what other problem is she having, what about his sex life, what about work, are there children? Face-to-face is better to get the answers.

By being face-to-face, you can get all sorts of information about the history of the problem, the history of the patient. You get early childhood information, and a great deal of information about school, friendships, work, sex, losses, injuries, accomplishments, and on and on, topic after topic, all about the way the patient was and everything that influenced him. Face-to-face is good for getting this information.

Face-to-face is better for observing the patient.   Most therapists, in most approaches, get a lot of information from watching the patient. A great deal of what most therapists rely on comes from watching the patient, and all of this important information comes much better when you are face-to-face with the patient.

You can see how the patient responds to what you say. You can notice the way the patient sits, including how this way of sitting is similar to or different from the usual way. You can note changes in what she is looking at, how and when her body shifts, telltale little gestures that go with certain kinds of topics. A great deal of psychodiagnostic data is furnished by watching the patient. You can see things that are probably not especially within the patient's consciousness, like the inadvertent clenching of a fist, or playing with a wedding ring, or foot tapping. You can observe changes in facial expression, smiles and frowns, all manner of playing out of feelings. In so many ways, observing the patient is valuable, and this can be done much better face-to-face than when you and the patient are aligned with one another.

Face-to-face is better for using the therapist-patient relationship.   When you are face-to-face, when the two of you are attending mainly to one another, it is almost assured that there will be some kind of interaction, some relationship. For therapists who want to use a relationship, face-to-face is far superior to patient and therapist being aligned, both attending to some third center.

You can establish the relationship, you can develop it, you can use it in the many ways that therapists use the relationship. Whatever the type of relationship, face-to-face is superior to the aligned model. It is almost taken for granted that change requires a special kind of relationship in most approaches, but certainly in psychoanalytic-psychodynamic approaches (Alexander, 1963; Alexander & French, 1946; Caruso, 1964; Fromm-Reichmann, 1958; Jung, 1933; May, 1958a, 1958b; Sullivan, 1953a, 1953b). In classical psychoanalytic work, the patient is lying on a couch and what about a combo - some face to face + some individual exp . . .

156   The Guide to Experiential Psychotherapy

not literally face-to-face, but nevertheless patient and analyst are attending mainly to one another as they converse together.

The face-to-face model is better for the therapist who is interested in understanding how the patient's words can be interpreted as telling about the relationship. The therapist is in a good position to see that what the patient is saying about her parent or boss may shed light on what is happening in the patient-therapist interaction, on how the patient may be understood as talking, directly or indirectly, about the therapist. For therapists who value this kind of material, the face-to-face relationship is superior.

In contrast, the experiential model is not especially effective for using the relationship (Mahrer, 1986a). Most of the patient's and therapist's attention is out there, on something else, and not on one another. Throughout the four steps of the session, the "relationship" of both patient and therapist is much more with whatever they are attending to than with one another. When the patient does address the experiential therapist, and when the therapist does address the patient, it is with most of their attention on that third attentional center, rather than on one another. Rogers (1951) hints at this kind of relationship when he described the client-centered therapist as a kind of companion as the therapist and patient are both engaged in working their way through important personal material of the patient.

Face-to-face is better for the therapist's stream of private thoughts.   Most therapists are face-to-face with the patient, listening to and talking to the patient, and maintaining a stream of private thoughts. This stream of private thoughts contains the therapist's personal notions and ideas, hidden notions about the patient, inferences, observations. Almost all this is private, personal, out of bounds, separate and removed from what the therapist is saying, doing, showing to the patient.

The therapist, who has private thoughts about how the patient is being right now, quietly observes all sorts of things about the patient, and makes sense of them: "She looks away whenever I mention something that gets her defensive." "I notice this slippage in logic; perhaps there is a psychotic process here." These ideas about the patient's illness, the signs and symptoms of pathology, all are put together in a private stream of thoughts (Argelander, 1976; Linn, 1972). These observations and conclusions may be filed away or perhaps gone into later in the session or at an appropriate time in later sessions (Korchin, 1976; Noyes & Kolb, 1967). Most therapists have more private thoughts than things to say to the patient. At the end of the session, many therapists have accumulated pages and pages of private thoughts about how the patient is being and responding in this relationship: "She is starting to trust me . . . He is fighting his dependency on me . . . She is keeping me at a safe distance . . . He is trying to get me to take his side on this." Your private thoughts deal with how you are affected by the patient: "She is making me feel like I was mean to her . . . I am bored with him . . . I think I am feeling like I want to protect her, be her guardian."

Put together inferences about the patient by organizing this piece of information into what you already know. Then you arrive at a picture of what the patient is like, or a picture of how she is changing. As the patient is telling about her taking silverware from restaurants, you privately put this together with other information to arrive at a somewhat more accurate picture of the patient's being the deprived one, or that her problem of antisocial acts is perhaps getting worse. You process this information with what else you know about the patient: "I wonder if we should explore other aspects of her childhood." "We had better work on this because the stealing behavior is getting worse."

When you are face-to-face, you can arrive at private thoughts about what to do with this information that the patient has given you. Should you warn the patient about what you are professionally directed to do with this information? Would you have to report the patient if she tells you that she steals all those valuable things? If the patient indicates that she has abused her child, or is headed toward talking about that, you have private thoughts about your professional responsibilities. All these private thoughts are available to the face-to-face therapist.

You have private thoughts about what you are going to be saying. Indeed, it is the private thoughts that tell you when to say it (Bellak, 1981; Brammer & Shostrom, 1982; Weiner, 1975), whether to talk about it before or after something else (Malan, 1976; Menninger, 1958; Weiner, 1975), just how much to say about it (Colby, 1951; Weiner, 1975), and whether the phrasing of it should be soft and easy or harder and more direct (Claiborn, 1982; Levy, 1963; Morgenstern, 1988; Nydes, 1966; Reider, 1972; Searle, 1976; Troemel-Platz, 1980; Wachtel, 1980).

Many of these private thoughts are concerns about what you are considering saying and doing right now. You think, "I am worried that she is on the verge of losing control. If I do this, she may fall apart." "He is so resistant that if I say this, he'll probably attack me." From the face-to-face perspective, you think about concepts such as loss of control, falling apart, and resistance that are outside the experiential system. Even further, having these kinds of private worries and concerns go with the external, face-to-face perspective. They tend not to be present in the aligned posture.

Even as the therapist is talking, a parallel stream of private thoughts often goes along with what the therapist is saying: "I don't feel good saying this . . . Maybe he'll think of this as too swarmy, too manipulatively sweet . . . I think I am lowering my voice here . . ." Once the therapist says it, the stream of private thoughts may contain all sorts of notions about what the therapist just said.

It is interesting how prevalent this stream of private thoughts is in just about all therapists, yet relatively little is written about how this may be problematic for other aspects of face-to-face psychotherapy. For example, many therapists value a relationship, and yet even as the therapist is relating, a great deal of the therapist is off-limits, out-of-bounds, withdrawn into the removed stream of private thoughts. Many therapists value being open, honest, candid, and yet so many of these therapists maintain a steady stream of private thoughts even as they are convinced that they are being, open, honest, and candid. Many therapists follow a generally unspoken but powerful rule that the therapist has the right, and even the professional obligation, to maintain a private stream of thoughts. However, that same right is not extended to the patient. If the patient is determined to have the same stream of private thoughts, he is being withdrawn, distrusting, removed, withholding, paranoid, psychopathic. Having private thoughts is a sign of pathology, except when the therapist is doing it.

In contrast, the aligned model is poorly designed for enabling and using the therapist's stream of private thoughts. Even worse, when you and the patient are aligned, there is very little room for a stream of private thoughts (Mahrer, 1982, 1978/1989d). If you do have a private thought, the experiential model pulls it out into the open: "For a second, I don't know what to do next . . . I just started having a picture of your mother, sitting, drinking again . . . I just forgot your dad's name. I forgot! What's his name? . . . I like you; you're great!"

This way of aligning with a patient may be exceedingly inadequate at enabling the therapist to use a stream of private thoughts. But it is useful for doing what some existentialists and phenomenologists refer to as giving up your presuppositions and presumptions about the patient (cf. Darroch & Silvers, 1982). If he starts the session by going to a recent scene in which his wife died, lots of therapists may be guided by a stream of private thoughts about what they believe the patient should be feeling, and should be going through (e.g., Barrett, 1979; Buchanan, 1974; Crosby & Jose, 1983; Frieze, Parsons, Johnson, Rubler, & Zellman, 1978; Lopata, 1969; Parkers, 1972; Peterson & Briley, 1977; Rohrbaugh, 1979; Schoenberg, 1970; Urada, 1977). In the experiential model, all of this is given up, you have succeeded in letting go of your presuppositions, your stream of private thoughts, and you have failed to gain the benefits of maintaining a stream of private thoughts.

Being aligned is better for seeing the patient's world.   When you and the patient are aligned, the patient is shown how to place most of his attention out there, on the objects, incidents, and scenes of strong feeling. Throughout the session, both you and the patient are attending mainly out there. This means that you are privy to seeing the patient's world. You see this world immediately, directly, vividly. You are seeing the patient's world as he sees it and as it is for him, whether or not the patient is fully aware of seeing it in the way it is for him (Holt, 1968; Mahrer, 1975b; Mahrer, Boulet, & Fairweather, 1994).

Is there a gradual process of seeing more and more of the patient's world? If the therapist is only aligned to a small or moderate degree, does she see the patient's world, but in some hazy or fragmented way? The answer seems to be no. There seems to be a threshold, at about 80 percent alignment or so, when the patient's world or, more accurately, the world thrown up by the patient's words, is present. When this happens, what the therapist sees out there is quite vivid, real, alive, compelling. In different words, the therapist must be aligned quite fully, perhaps around 80 percent or so, before the therapist can see, live, and be in the patient's world.

When you and the patient are mainly face-to-face, it is much harder to see the patient's world (Mahrer, 1978c). From outside, from being external to the patient, and especially by being in any kind of relationship with one another, you can see the patient's world only secondhand, indirectly, through an obfuscating maze (Gendlin, 1972; Haley, 1963; Laing & Esterson, 1970; Mahrer, 1970b; Rogers, 1966; Szasz, 1965/1988).

Rogers wanted to accomplish this from outside, face-to-face (1951, 1957). He wanted to see the patient's world by trying to get inside the patient's shoes. However, this is hard to do when you are face-to-face. It is quite a challenge to be outside the patient, face-to-face, and to try and leap inside the patient's shoes. Whether or not it can be done, it is much easier to see the patient's world when you start by being aligned with the patient.

Many therapists would perhaps like to see the patient's world, to know what this world is like for the patient. Most of these attempts start with the patient and therapist face-to-face and involve some maneuver whereby the therapist works to remain outside the patient while straining to see the patient's world. I believe it is much easier to see the patient's world when you start by being aligned with the patient.

Being aligned is better for knowing the feelings and experiencings going on in the patient.
Getting a fairly good idea of how the patient sees her world and what feelings and experiencings are going on in the patient make up most of what is referred to as empathy. According to Schroeder (1925) and Schilder (1953), this concept was first introduced by Theodore Lipps in 1897, elaborated by E. B. Titchener, and first used in

the diagnosis of mental disease by Southard in 1918. Although empathy is a corner-stone of many psychotherapies, a review of the actual clinical methods suggests that the face-to-face posture has been largely unsuccessful in enabling therapists to see the patient's world as well as her feelings and experiencings (Mahrer, Boulet, & Fairweather, 1994). The aligned posture can accomplish this better.

Throughout most of the session, the experiential therapist is living and being in the scene with the patient. Most of the therapist's attention is out there. Furthermore, the therapist allows the patient's words to come in and through the therapist. When this happens, the therapist will probably have some kind of feeling or experiencing. If you are truly living and being in the scene of strong feeling, and if you are truly letting the patient's words come in and through you, it would be very hard not have some kind of feeling or experiencing.

You are essentially blended, merged, or fused into the patient (cf. Corcoran, 1982; Havens, 1978; Mahrer, Boulet, & Fairweather, 1994; May, 1989; Vanaerschot, 1990). While this is a somewhat poetic way of describing how the two of you are, it is as if your outer boundary allows the patient to come inside so that the two of you are occupying the same space (Rothenberg, 1987). You essentially are so aligned with the patient that you actually feel and experience, in you, what is occurring in the patient (cf. Havens, 1978, 1986; Mahrer, Boulet, & Fairweather, 1994; May, 1989; Mearns & Thorne, 1988).

What is hard to describe, unless you have undergone it yourself, is what it is like to be almost fully aligned with the patient. If the patient is having a spat with her boyfriend and he walks out of the restaurant, you may be seeing him walk away so fully and vividly that it is as if you are actually being in the scene. Similarly, the patient's words are so inside you that it is as if these words are your own words. When you are fully aligned, it is almost amazing how open you are to nuances of feeling, to a world of experiencings. You are probably more in touch with the feelings and experiencings occurring in the patient than the patient is. Furthermore, the received feelings and experiencings are so very real, so alive. It truly is as if they are your feelings and experiencings, because, by being so aligned, they indeed are your feelings and experiencings.

When you are face-to-face, the relationship itself will make it harder for you to identify the feeling or experiencing in the patient over there, at the other end of the relationship. It is too easy for you to have your own feeling or experiencing as you receive whatever the patient is saying and doing and being like. The relationship will tend to diffuse, distort, and generally interfere with your knowing the feeling or experiencing occurring in the patient. Your own personality may well push away, block, interfere with, knowing what is occurring in the patient, and may very well put it in some bad or twisted form that is different from what is occurring in the patient.

The more the therapist is face-to-face with the patient, engaging in some kind of relationship, the less the therapist seems to be able to get close to whatever is occurring in the patient. More bluntly, by engaging in a face-to-face "relationship," you are probably sacrificing knowledge of the patient's insides. Both Fenichel (1953) and Laing (1975) described how the patient's involvement in the therapeutic relationship is an effective means of avoiding whatever is deeper. Most therapists believe that a good relationship somehow enables the patient to open up what is deeper in the patient, or enables the patient to be on better terms with the insides. This may be a colossal error. "This point must be emphasized because of the common error in many circles of assuming that the experience of one's own being will take place automatically if only one is accepted by someone else" (May, 1958a, p. 45; cf. Mahrer, 1978c).

From outside, being external and face-to-face, you will usually come up with some idea of what the patient may be feeling or experiencing. But when you are aligned, you are in a far better position to know the feeling or experiencing going on in the patient, and this encompasses both those occurring on the surface and especially those occurring deeper in the patient.

Being aligned is better for attaining the four steps of the experiential session.   There is a pragmatic reason for preferring the aligned posture. It is much easier to attain the four steps of each experiential session using the aligned posture as compared with being face-to-face.

Each of the four steps requires that the therapist and patient be in some scene, some situational context. In Step 1, patient and therapist are in some scene, and then in some moment, of strong feeling. They can access the deeper potential when they are aligned. Welcoming and appreciating the accessed inner experiencing, in Step 2, means that patient and therapist are attending to the inner experiencing, and are living and being in scenes. This also occurs in Step 3, in which the patient is expressly to be living and being in earlier life scenes. In Step 4, the patient is to gain a taste of what it is like to be the new person in forthcoming, prospective scenes. Attaining the fourth step is accomplished when the therapist and patient are both living and being in these scenes.

Whether you are looking at attaining each of the four steps, or at accomplishing the substeps for each, you can do it when you and the patient are aligned. You almost certainly would be unable to attain the four steps if the two of you were face-to-face. What the face-to-face model can achieve is practically irrelevant to what has to be done to attain the four steps. The moral is that if you want to attain the four steps, it is just about essential to be aligned with the patient.

Being aligned is better for freeing you of the effects of your own personality.   To accomplish the four steps of the experiential session, it is almost essential that the therapist disengage from his own personality. It may be that accomplishing this all the way is impossible. But it is possible to set aside or to disengage from most of your own personality, to be substantially free of your own particular potentials and their relationships. You can go a long way toward accomplishing this, at least enough to guide the patient through the four steps, when you and the patient are aligned. You will probably not be able to accomplish this when you are in the face-to-face posture.

Disengaging from most of your own personality is not some mysterious, mystical feat. It occurs almost easily when you put most of your attention out there and the patient does too, when you are mainly living and being in the patient's world, seeing what is there for the patient, and when the patient's words come in and through you. In short, the method of being aligned does the work for you and enables you to be free of a great deal of the effects of your own personality.

Before the session, you may be concerned with some things that are troublesome and bothersome. You are filled with a lot of anger because you heard that your daughter had been beaten up and was in the hospital. You are simply feeling fat and bloated, grungy and out of sorts. You have been trying to deal with your husband's worries about his job, and that whole issue is on your mind. When you are aligned, you live in the patient's world and, to that extent, you leave behind your own worries, troubles, uncomfortable feelings, and experiencings.

Outside the session, when you think about the patient, or when you are with the patient before and after the session, you are attending more or less directly to the patient, and you are entitled to have your own personal feelings toward that person. You are attracted to the patient. You think of the patient as a charming and delightful person. You are respectful of the person's important role in the government. You are concerned about the patient's upcoming surgery. All your personal reactions are minimized or even set aside when you and the patient are aligned and working together. I am not talking about extreme instances in which you have violent hatred toward the person, or you are constantly having powerful sexual feelings toward the person. But, the ordinary range of feelings about the person, good or bad, are mostly set aside when you are aligned; your own personal reactions are essentially inert or play virtually no role.

The nice thing about letting go of so much of your own personality is that you can work with whatever comes from the patient. You can receive the feelings and experiencings occurring in the patient and do so without much distortion, selectivity, twisting them out of shape. You can receive what is coming from the patient, not because you have some supreme clinical powers, not because you are especially sensitive or acutely perceptive. Rather, it is because you have freed yourself of your own personality to the extent that you see what the patient puts out there and allow the patient's words to come in and through you.

Suppose that there is no deeper potential in you that is describable as being enveloped, encompassed, enfolded. Or, suppose that there is indeed a deeper potential like that in you, and your relationship is moderately disintegrative. Without any substantial awareness, you steer clear of any such experiencing and of situations that might pull this kind of experiencing in you. Even if this describes what you are like, you will be able to work with this experiencing in the patient. You can work with experiencings that are in the patient, even if you do not have these experiencings yourself, or they are deeper within you.

If you are mainly looking out there, and if you allow the patient's words to come mainly through you, then you may be able to be essentially free of your own problems, of deeper potentials you fend off in yourself. This is an ambitious assertion. But it seems to hold.

Being aligned is better for working with just about any experiencing, any scene, and any kind of patient.   You may never have experienced being crazy, totally out of contact, wholly cut off. But you can know it, grasp it, and even undergo it if you can be aligned with the patient. The patient will offer you the chance to undergo this particular experiencing. You can work with it in each of the four steps, provided that you are well aligned with the patient.

In a way, this is a bit of what makes me look forward to each session as an adventure. It is like being a character in someone else's dream. It is a matter of wondering who and what I am going to be in this upcoming session. I have a limited repertoire of my own experiencings. However, because I have bootlegged so many different kinds of experiencings from my patients, I have had a far richer experiential life in my therapeutic work than in my own daily living.

Being aligned means that you can go through scenes and incidents that you may have rarely or never gone through in your own world. You can be a young child who is forced to have sex with the cruel man. You can play the piano exceedingly well, with your teacher beaming with pride. You can watch your younger brother almost drown out there in the lake. You can rob a neighborhood store and use the money to pay off the tough guy. You can have anal sex, sex in a large cloth bag, sex in the back of the church, sex with the older brother, sex with the prostitute who is older and wiser than your mother. You can have menstrual cramps or a screeching pain in the penis. Some of the scenes and incidents are extraordinary, and some may be quite mundane, and yet they are scenes that are outside your own life. You can go through them right along with the patient because you are closely aligned.

Can a therapist with black skin truly have the experiences, live in the scenes, "be" a patient with white skin? Can a male therapist actually be a female patient, having her feelings of sexual attraction to the fellow sitting across the table at the restaurant? Some therapists will say that the answer is no. If therapist and patient are face-to-face, I am inclined to agree that the answer is no. However, when the therapist is fully aligned, my answer is yes.

This means that you can work with patients who are altogether different than you, on virtually any dimension (Mahrer, 1985b). All you have to do is to be aligned. If you are 27 years old, you can go through the session with the 67-year-old patient; if you are 67, you can work with the patient who is 27. If you are an attractive, slender female therapist, you can work with an ugly, fat man; if you are an ugly, fat, male therapist, you can work with an attractive, slender woman. If you are a male therapist, you will be able to be aligned with the attractive, slender woman as she is sitting on the toilet, having mild menstrual cramps. If you are a female therapist, you can be aligned with the male patient who is almost going crazy as his girlfriend is slowly caressing his penis. If you are a male therapist, you can be aligned with a female patient who is almost ready to give birth in the hospital delivery room.

During the session, you simply are aligned, and you go through the scenes. Afterward, when you listen to the tape, it may be impressive or embarrassing that you were being that person, that you were undergoing those experiencings in those scenes.

Being aligned is indeed better than being face-to-face, it seems, for particular purposes. To do experiential therapy, it is practically necessary that you are aligned. However, for other purposes, it seems to be better to be face-to-face. Each has its special uses.

When Therapist and Patient Are Face-to-Face, (a) Therapy Is Merely a Way in Which the Therapist Gains Personal Experiencings; (b) Experiential Therapy Is Probably Unsuitable for the Therapist; and (c) Experiential Sessions Will Probably Be Unsuccessful

When therapists and patients are face-to-face, and this is what happens almost all the time, psychotherapy is one of the richest and most powerful ways of providing the therapist with preciously important personal experiencings. Looked at through the experiential model, this is just about what most psychotherapy is. When therapists almost insist that they and their patients are to be face-to-face, both attending mainly to one another, then experiential psychotherapy is probably not suitable and their experiential sessions would probably be unsuccessful.

Just like any other situation, therapy is used to enable the experiencing of operating potentials and the construction of externalized deeper potentials. From the experiential perspective, a person is continually at work building, constructing, and using external situations. They are for two main purposes. One is to serve as appropriate situational contexts in which the person can undergo operating potentials for experiencing. A second is to house externalized deeper potentials with which the person has disintegrative relationships. These two principles are used to account for all external situations. When we look at the therapist building, constructing, and using the therapy situation, the same two principles apply.

In the moment-to-moment flow of the session, the therapist is understood as undergoing operating potentials for experiencing. The therapist builds, constructs, and uses this situation as a means of undergoing these potentials in the very same way that the therapist uses all other situations in the therapist's world. In addition, the therapist works effectively to build, construct, and use the patient as the therapist's own externalized deeper potential, to enable the same disintegrative relationship as is present between the therapist and the therapist's own deeper potential. Within the experiential system, there is no reason why the therapy situation is to be understood and explained in ways that do not apply to all other situations in the therapist's world.

The same holds for the patient. From the experiential perspective, the patient is likewise understood as building, constructing, and using the therapy situations as a grand and effective means of enabling the experiencing of operating potentials, and also for building the therapist into the patient's own externalized deeper potential. All of this is understood as going on when patient and therapist are mainly face-to-face with one another throughout the session.

Therapy is predominantly a way in which the therapist gains personal experiencings. What is a definition of psychotherapy? Aside from the many ways that therapy is defined, no matter how conceptual or abstract therapists wax in describing what they are doing, the experiential perspective defines therapy as predominantly a way in which the therapist gains personal experiencings. What do we see when we look at psychotherapy in this way?

With this patient, in this session, there are special moments when the therapist has a wonderful sense of being the one who manages, who controls, who makes the important decisions in this patient's life. Or the therapist enjoys special experiencings of intimacy, closeness, or togetherness. Or she has pleasant moments of being sexually appealing, attractive, or sought after. Or she experiences being the wise one, the sage, the one who knows about life. Or there is an inner sense of being the solid rock, the anchor to reality. Or he has a delicious experiencing of being the one whom the person trusts, confides in, entrusts himself to. Or the therapist gains some precious moments of being the stronger one, the one in better psychic shape, the one who is sounder and better put together. Or the therapist has moments of almost reveling in the patient's admiration, worship, or adoration. Or the therapist experiences the sense of being the patient's best friend, the real buddy, or the loved companion. Or the therapist swells with pride in special moments of experiencing a sense of being the consummate professional, expert, or authority. Or there are wonderful moments of being the omnipotent God with magical healing powers. Or the therapist tingles with being the model of mental health, the exemplar, the kind of person the patient can become. Or the therapist has moments of thrilling with the experiencing of being the main one who offers understanding, sheer interest, unwavering concern and prizing.

Is this kind of personal experiencing just a minor side issue? Isn't there so much more to psychotherapy? Doesn't this only apply to a few extreme therapists? The answer to all these questions is no. From the experiential perspective, most of what is called therapy is little more than therapist constructing situations that provide precious personal experiencings as they and their clients are attending mainly to one another.

From the value system of experiential psychotherapy, it is unfortunate that therapy is predominantly a way in which the therapist gains personal experiencings.   Here are some of the ways in which this is regarded as unfortunate, at least from the value system of experiential psychotherapy (Lawton, 1958, Mahrer, 1970b, 1975b; Mahrer & Gervaize, 1983).

1. Psychotherapy is usually dressed up as being for the welfare of the patient, as a professional service for helping the patient. Not from this perspective. Looked at in this way, therapy is mainly for the welfare of the therapist, a way of helping the therapist get the kinds of personal experiencings that are important for the therapist.

2. Psychotherapy is commonly regarded as a profession requiring years of academic knowledge—calling for years of graduate and postgraduate training based on a solid foundation of science—restricted to practitioners who are qualified, accredited, and licensed. Not from this perspective. Listen carefully to what most therapists actually do in most sessions. What seems apparent is that these working techniques are far from being unique to psychotherapy, are common in many interpersonal relations, and require years of training mainly to gain a technical vocabulary to make these ordinary maneuvers sound impressively professional. Strip away much of the jargon and what shines forth is often the personal experiencings that therapists get from doing things they disguise in professional jargon. The therapist says, "I am desensitizing her conditioned response to stress associated with a poorly differentiated ego structure." The naive nonprofessional may be somewhat puzzled. "It looks to me like you just like having this pretty woman hold your hand and tell you about her sex life."

3. I am not so concerned when therapist and patient have mutual and complementary personal experiencings that feel good, and when this is occurring between two consenting adults who are up front about what they are getting from one another. The patient may have fine experiencings of being important in someone's eyes, of being valued as special, and the therapist has complementary experiencings of being admired, seen as a valued confidante. They are providing for each others' personal experiencings. What does bother me is when the therapist's personal experiencing is obtained at the expense of the patient. The therapist gains the experiencing of safe sex and adoration, and the patient writhes in the pain of unfulfilled longings. The therapist gains a sense of being the superior one who scolds the patient for seeking from the therapist what the therapist does not wish to provide. The patient is promised unconditional love and acceptance that is really full of restrictive conditions. The therapist gains whiffs of being the rescuer at the painful expense of the patient's being pushed into a maelstrom of whirling pathology. The therapist gains the personal experiencing of being the all-powerful one at the expense of others in the person's life who are forced into accompanying the patient in having sessions, or whose lives are bent out of shape by the therapist who tells the sister why she is to let the patient live with her for the patient's welfare.

When I think of the field of psychotherapy, I picture most psychotherapists being face-to-face with their patients, and as mainly gaining personal experiencings.

However, this is only one way of looking at what is happening in psychotherapy. There are many other perspectives that are much more flattering.

On the other hand, the experiential perspective becomes more serious when the question is whether or not experiential psychotherapy is suitable for the therapist and whether or not experiential sessions might be successful. If the face-to-face relationship is too important for the therapist to give up, then it seems relatively clear that experiential psychotherapy is not suitable for this therapist, and this therapist's experiential sessions will probably be unsuccessful. The choice is a serious one. It seems that the therapist may well be sacrificing important personal experiencings when experiential therapy is a suitable choice and when experiential sessions are to be successful.

When Therapist and Patient Are Face-to-Face, the Therapist Tends to Exert Substantial Power and Control

When therapists and patients are in this posture, it is hard to avoid exerting a fair measure of power and control over the patients. Some therapists who use this posture would claim that their methods, usually behavioral methods, do not involve such power and control. Other therapists, notably client-centered therapists, would claim that their approach is so free of power and control that it adopted the title of "non directive" therapy. Nevertheless, while the degree of power and control varies, adopting the face-to-face posture brings with it a good measure of power and control.

By means of a stream of private, hidden thoughts that direct what the therapist does. The face-to-face posture makes it almost inevitable that the therapist has a stream of private, hidden thoughts. Accordingly, the therapist exerts power and control by reserving the right to have such a removed stream of thoughts, by denying the patient the right to have one also, and by the very nature of these private thoughts. Because these thoughts are hidden, the patient is not privy to what they are, and that alone exerts some power and control over the patient. It means that the patient cannot be sure what the therapist is up to, what the real reason is for what the therapist is doing right now. The stream of private, hidden thoughts will never tell.

These therapists typically have a private treatment plan, a personal agenda of what to cover, of how the patient is to change, of how to go about achieving that plan. The therapist has a private idea of what the patient is to talk about, whether to get into that now or later (cf. Ripley, 1972). The therapist develops and uses the relationship through the executive guidance of the removed stream of private thoughts. Discretely maneuver the patient into trusting you, so you can get him to divulge the information you want (cf. Sands, 1972). The private stream will tell you what to do, but the covert advice is hidden from the patient. It tells you when to say what you want to say (cf. Morgenstern, 1988). Ask the patient about his assets and strengths, but do not reveal the reasons for doing this, so that the patient will leave the initial session with some sense of self-confidence (O'Leary & Wilson, 1987). Ask questions that can trap the patient such as, "Have you had the feeling recently that things around you were unreal?" (Nelson & Barlow, 1981, p. 7), but do not tell what you might conclude or what you might do if the patient says yes. The private stream of thoughts goes hand-in-hand with the face-to-face posture, and is a good way of exerting power and control over the patient.

Because this private stream of thoughts, like an executive director behind the lines, is out of range of the patient, the therapist's words can easily contain a load of implied meanings, hidden messages. The patient gets the message that he is out of touch with reality when the therapist asks, "Have you had the feeling recently that things around you were unreal?" The patient is quite justified in being vigilantly wary and chary of what the therapist says. Beware of the implied meanings. "Have you ever thought about your having confusion about your true sexual identity? . . . What do you do to control your aggressive impulses? . . . Are you surprised that your baby is so peaceful and contented? . . . How do you feel about your weight? . . . Are you aware of any prejudice in your section?" Without saying it directly, there are some implied messages and meanings: You thought of yourself as a woman, but perhaps you really have a strong masculine component in your personality. You have aggressive impulses that ought to be controlled. You are so anxious and full of conflicts, that it is hard to believe your baby is so peaceful and contented. You certainly are skinny, or a fat pig. The private stream of thoughts can exert a lot of control by inflicting patients with such devious, implied, indirect messages and meanings.

By administering treatment and applying techniques and interventions onto the patient. Not all therapists who adopt the face-to-face posture do this, but most do. Once the therapist and patient are face-to-face, it is easy for the therapist to do things to the patient as the object of the therapist's treatment, techniques, and interventions. It is easy for the strategy to be one wherein the therapist does things to the patient. The therapist interprets, reinforces, uses conditioning, gives empathic reflections, selects and uses techniques and programs. Whether the intervention is tiny, such as saying "uh-huh" in the proper way and at the proper time, or is a big one such as attacking the patient's system of values, the therapist is exerting power and control over the patient. It is almost always justified as in the patient's best interests, and as "therapeutic," yet it is typically an expression of the therapist's power and control over the patient.

By determining the problem, the goal, and the best treatment.   When therapist and patient are face-to-face, it is easy for the therapist to be the main one who determines what the problem is, who figures out what the goal is to be, and who selects the best treatment to do the job. Looked at the other way around, if the therapist is going to select the problem, identify the goal, and choose the best treatment, it is probably a lot easier to do these things when you are face-to-face than if the two of you are aligned. From the very beginning, face-to-face therapists are generally adept at seeing what the problem is, at guiding patients into talking about problems, troubles, worries, concerns, at finding something they can identify as a problem. The patient mentions that he has a daughter whom he had placed in an institution for retarded children. Then the patient cries hard. He hasn't seen her in years. Quickly, the therapist spots a problem here. The patient is denying the existence of his daughter. He is engaging in denial of a significant relationship. One or both of these are problems.

Behavior therapists generally believe that the problem is presented mainly by the patient, with little intrusion from the therapist. On the other hand, some behavior therapists acknowledge that the therapist often plays the major role in selecting and identifying the specific problem behavior that is to be the target of treatment (Evans, 1985; Franks, 1983; Kanfer, 1985; Kazdin, 1985; MacDonald, 1984; Mash, 1985; Morgenstern, 1988). Since power and control lie in identifying the target problem, it is thereby the face-to-face therapist who exerts the power and control.

Defining the problem usually means that the goal is also defined. If the problem is blushing or not being able to study, then the goal is probably to blush less or to be able to study. Sometimes, going from the problem to the goal takes some figuring out. If the physician's wife cannot find a job that she is excited about, one therapist sees the goal as searching for an exciting job, a second arrives at a goal of not working and doing exciting things that are not part of a job, a third has the goal of trying to show her ways to be more enthusiastic at her current job, and a fourth therapist has the goal of her being less concerned about the problem. In any case, there is considerable power and control in the therapist's arriving at the goal, no matter how closely intertwined the problem and the goal seem to be.

It is almost always the therapist who determines just how to treat the problem so as to achieve the goal. Whether the therapist is a Jungian analyst, a behavior therapist, or an integrative-eclectic therapist, there is plenty of room to decide what to do so that this goal can be achieved. Maybe we should probe the patient's early life to see when it first started. How about using paradoxical intention? What about focusing? Maybe flooding can work here. The therapist decides on the treatment for this problem.

There is considerable power and control in the therapist who defines the problem, sets the goal, and chooses the best treatment. The therapist is judge, jury, and executioner, and it is the face-to-face posture that enables the therapist to determine the problem, the goal, and the best treatment.

By wanting all sorts of things from the patient, without candidly telling the patient what they are.   When therapist and patient are face-to-face, the therapist typically wants many things from the patient but is generally not open or candid about these wants. Instead, the therapist generally disguises them and tries to get them in an indirect or devious way. Therapists try to get all sorts of information from the patient, but exactly what the information is, why the therapist wants it, and what the therapist will use the information for are typically kept vague, masked by other stated purposes, or not disclosed at all. Often the interchange is uncomfortably similar to a detective interviewing a suspect. The therapist reports that the patient has a psychotic process or homicidal tendencies or may be a child abuser or can become violent. How did the therapist arrive at this conclusion? It is on the basis of information that the therapist got from the patient. Therapists rarely warn the patient, "The information you give me may be used against you." Instead, inquiries are justified as helping the therapist to understand the patient, to know more about the patient's case history, psychodynamics. Nevertheless, the therapist wants all sorts of information without being entirely candid about why.

Therapists rarely say, "I am going to do this right now, and I want you to respond in this particular way. I am going to build rapport or establish a relationship or build a helping alliance, and here is what I want from you. I am going to give an interpretation now, and I want you to accept this interpretation, to see it as helpful, to benefit from my interpretation by seeing the connection I am trying to get you to see. I think you are much too aggressive toward me and your parents, and I want you to be less aggressive. You don't seem to want to get a job, and I want you to get a job. I am going to give an empathic reflection, and I would like you to receive it by exploring yourself."

Some therapists want every patient to respond in nice ways to their singular characteristics. She is a lovely young therapist who enjoys working with male patients. They are to be fortunate to be with such an attractive woman. He has a wonderful sense of humor, an infectious laugh, an ability to clown and to see the funny side of things, and his patients are to like being with a therapist like this. She is genuinely concerned, interested, caring. Her patients are to revel in being with a therapist like that. He is a very important therapist, holds important professional offices, is occasionally on television, and is mentioned in newspapers. His patients are to welcome the opportunity to have sessions with someone of his stature. Therapists have all sorts of wantings from their patients, even though they rarely are up front and candid about what they do want. In general, the face-to-face posture seems ideal for therapists who are drawn toward exerting power and control over their patients. Once a therapist assumes the face-to-face posture, it seems hard not to exert substantial power and control.

When Therapist and Patient Are Aligned, the Therapist Tends to Have Very Little Power and Control

The aligned posture enables the therapist to give up power and control over the patient. Even further, it seems quite difficult for the therapist to be powerful and controlling in this posture.

By directing patient to attend out there, rather than to therapist.   In the beginning of each session, and throughout each session, the therapist explicitly directs the patient to put her attention out there. By listening to the therapist's directions, the patient attends out there so that the more the patient listens to and follows the therapist's directions, the less the patient is attentive to the therapist. In other words, the therapist's directions are virtually for the patient not to pay attention to the therapist. In this sense, the therapist's instructions self-destruct. If they are successful, the patient is attending out there, and not to the therapist who is giving the instructions.

The attention of the therapist who is giving the instructions is mainly out there. When the patient follows these instructions, his attention is mainly out there. The therapist and patient are moving into the aligned posture, and departing from a face-to-face posture. The instructions that keep the therapist and patient away from the face-to-face posture deprive the therapist of ways to exert power and control over the patient.

By using change methods that are to be carried out by the patient, not by the therapist. In the face-to-face posture, the change methods are almost uniformly carried out by the therapist. The therapist is the one who carries out the interventions, who administers the procedures onto the patient. When patient and therapist are aligned, the change methods are largely carried out by the patient. The therapist does a lot of showing the patient what to do and how to do it, but the patient is mainly the one to carry out the methods (Mahrer, 1978b).

Each of the four steps of an experiential session is carried out predominantly by the patient. The therapist does not "do" these steps or the substeps to the patient. Being in the moment of strong feeling is carried out by the patient, not by the therapist. Rehearsing likely new behaviors is done by the patient, not by the therapist. This conception of change largely involves showing the patient what to do and how to do it. The experiential therapist declines a great deal of power and control when the patient carries out the change methods.

By emphasizing patient's readiness and willingness to do it.   In the aligned posture, the therapist does a lot of checking on the patient's readiness and willingness. Most of what the therapist does is coupled with giving the patient the right to do it or not, which makes some sense since it is generally the patient who must carry it out.

If the patient is ready and willing to do it, then it can be done. If, however, the patient is not especially ready and willing, or is even reluctant, then the experiential therapist essentially lets go. The patient is ceded the power to do it or not. There are no attempts to "deal" with the patient's "resistance." Throughout the four steps, the patient's readiness and willingness are uppermost, and honored. It is the patient who has most of the power and control.

By being clear in telling patient what, how, and why to do it.   For the patient to carry out the substeps, it helps to be quite clear in showing the patient what to do, how to do it, and the more or less immediate goal or objective in doing it. There is essentially no hidden agenda, no use of devious or indirect means of trying to get the patient to do whatever it is, no hidden aims and purposes.

With many patients, in many sessions, you are naively open about the working aims and goals of the step or substep you are about to undertake. In starting the session, the opening instructions let the patient know what you are looking for. In the Step 1, you first find a scene of strong feeling, and then you are to enter into this scene. The therapist may very well say, "Now we have to enter into this scene to make it alive and real." You tell the person, "We are to enter into the exact moment of strong feeling, and here is how to do this."

Throughout each of the four steps, the patient is told what you are trying to achieve, and how to achieve it. In Step 2, you may say, "The thing to do is to see if you can feel good with this quality in you. So let's see if we can just keep it here for a while and see what the feelings are in the body." You explain each little substep, what it is for and how to achieve it.

There is something so very open about letting patients know what we are intending to do, and how to attain it. Yet, we do this mainly because patients need to know the goals and aims in order to make the best use of the methods and techniques.

This is much more concrete and specific than providing patients with a general understanding of cognitive behavior therapy or how conditioning works or how patients can control anger outbursts by following a behavioral program. Typically, these general explanations are given in the beginning of treatment. In contrast, experiential therapists are clear in telling patients what, how, and why to do it, in each step and substep of the session.

Many therapists might think of times when they do tell a patient what, how, and why to do something. These therapists may find an occasion or two, or some condition under which they might be this open. However, this is standard fare for experiential therapists as they proceed through each step and substep of the session.

By joining with the patient in attending out there, and in going through the four steps.
The experiential therapist joins with the patient in looking out there, and in going through the four steps. Except for when the therapist is giving instructions for what to do next, both therapist and patient are generally carrying out the steps together. It is hard to exert power and control over the patient when you are joined with the patient in standing in line at the take-out counter, when you and the patient are seeing what it is like in your body, when you are holding the baby and loving its facial expression.

There is something very power-diffusing when you say what you say as both of you are attending out there. Therapists who hear about this therapy for the first time sometimes tend to recoil at what the experiential therapist says, and see the words as directive, pushy. When the experiential therapist and the patient are standing in line at the checkout counter, both attending to the big fellow in front of them, the therapist says, "'This is an express line! You got a whole basket full! Get in another line!' Now say all this in your way, and go ahead and have fun belting it out!" From outside, those words are high-powered and controlling, but when you are aligned with the patient, these words are the voice of the inner experiencing in the scene.

When you are joined with the patient it is much harder to be the external, separated, removed therapist who administers a treatment, who wants the patient to change in some particular way, who sees the patient as the object of his intervention.

In general, if you want to exert power and control, it seems better to be face-to-face than to be aligned. By being face-to-face, you will be exerting massive power and control, even though it may be subtle and indirect, but very present. The aligned therapist sacrifices huge chunks of power and control.

If You Find the Aligned Model to Be Preferable to the Face-to-Face Model, Then (a) This Therapy May Be Suitable for You, and (b) The Session May Be Successful and Effective

In general, the aligned model and the face-to-face model are substantially different from one another. The therapist may follow one or the other, but it is usually hard to carry out both at the same time. If your attention is preponderantly "out there," it usually cannot also be preponderantly on the patient. One model is almost certainly preferable. If it is the aligned model, then experiential therapy can be suitable for you, and the session may be successful and effective.

The aligned model should be seen as reasonably sensible and useful. The aligned model can be seen as reasonably natural, as making both conceptual and practical sense, and as a useful way to be with patients throughout the session. Whether the patient's attention is focused on the cancer, the baby, or on some situation, it should be sensible and useful for the therapist's attention to be out there from the very beginning to the very ending of the session (cf. Bugental, 1965; Halpern, 1965; Mahrer, 1978a, 1978c; Mullan & Sangiuliano, 1964; Perls, 1969).

It is so easy for this aligned model to be coupled with a continuous reliance on the patient's readiness and willingness. If this falls below a working level, then the process stops. In this sense, the session is characterized by gentleness, a sensitive reliance on the patient's fluctuating readiness and willingness. Without even trying, there is a minimum of pushing, of effortful trying to get the patient to do this or that.

If the aligned model is alien, strange, and uncomfortable, then the therapist will likely do all sorts of things to instill doubts and misgivings in the patient. Before the session, or even on the phone, the therapist will indicate how bizarre the patient might find it to have his eyes closed during the session. Instead of doing the aligned posture naturally, the therapist will provide all sorts of defensive rationales for not looking at one another, for closing eyes, and this will be done in ways that invite the patient to back off. It is as if the therapist is saying, "You probably won't like talking this way. We should be looking at each other. So when you are not fully satisfied, we can be eyeball-to-eyeball like I would prefer in the first place." If you regard the aligned model this way, then this model is not reasonably sensible and useful for you, experiential therapy is not likely to be suitable for you, nor will your sessions be especially successful and effective.

The therapist should be willing to sacrifice face-to-face therapist roles and personal experiencings. If experiential therapy is going to be suitable for the therapist, and if the sessions are going to be successful, then the therapist must be willing to give up what the aligned model cannot provide. For you to find experiential therapy, suitable, you need to sacrifice face-to-face roles and personal experiencings. In effect, you have to give up some of the powerful attractions in being a therapist.

This is a massive sacrifice, perhaps too much for many therapists. The aligned model is very hard to accept, not so much because of what it enables the therapist to achieve, but mainly because it means sacrificing face-to-face roles and personal experiencings. Beginning therapists are commonly attracted to the aligned model as an idea, intriguing to speculate and to talk about. However, once they get a taste of face-to-face therapist roles and personal experiencings, these are typically too seductive and enticing to give up. A larger proportion of more seasoned therapists seem willing to make this sacrifice. Because they have tasted the joys and have also had opportunity to become somewhat disenchanted with these roles and experiencings, such therapists are willing to let go of them and can find the aligned model a welcome alternative.

The therapist should be ready and willing to be aligned with the patient.   You should be ready and willing to look out there, to see whatever the patient's words construct in front of you. You should be ready and willing to live in this scene, to focus your attention on whatever it is. You should be ready to allow the patient's words to come in and through you, to situate yourself so that the patient's words are as if they are coming from you. You should be ready and willing to have the patient's feelings and experiencings. If being aligned is something you are ready and willing to do, then this therapy may be appealing and useful for you. If not, for any reason, then this therapy is not especially suitable, nor will your sessions be especially successful and effective.

When you are aligned, do you literally give up the essence of the person that you are? Do almost all experiential therapists act and sound alike in the session? In a sense, there is some similarity because they can speak with the voice of the inner experiencing from the end of Step 1 and throughout the balance of the session. It is as if a number of actors are all playing the same role. There can be a core pool of similarity in the person that they are being. Beyond that, you have essentially left behind a great deal of the person that you are when you are aligned with the patient. Even so, if some of your own unique personality qualities and characteristics shine through, it is probably your own way of being the inner experiencing and proceeding through the steps.

When you are aligned, the inner experiencing will shine through your voice. When the inner experiencing is being demonic, evil, wicked, and when you are aligned, what comes through your words is something from the inner experiencing. In other words, your voice is the voice of a person who is demonic, evil, wicked. Put more bluntly, you are not the real you in the session. You are the inner experiencing.

To what extent? Must you be the experiencing almost 100 percent? Do you have to be the ideal character actor, switching from one character to another as the patient moves through Step 1? Would your friends recognize you when you are the demonic, evil, wicked one? It seems that you would have to be the inner experiencing at least to some moderate extent. If the patient is talking about how nice it would be to get rid of her tyrannical grandmother, and then almost hisses, "Maybe I could arrange a little surprise explosion for her," the voice of the therapist is to ooze the sense of being demonic, evil, wicked. The more you can "be" and speak as the inner experiencing, the better. If you cling to being the standard therapist, interacting and relating and sounding much like the standard therapist, you will have a hard time being aligned, and a very hard time having effective experiential sessions.

When you begin a session, you have little or no idea who you will be. By the time Step 1 is done, you know who you will be the rest of this session. The inner experiencing that you are will probably vary from session to session, even with the same patient, because you are being whatever inner experiencing accesses in this session (Mahrer, 1993a).

A relatively important turning point for many therapists occurs when they allow themselves to be thrown into being aligned. They arrive at a point where they no longer have to cling to who they are. The more important leap is into being aligned, and almost wholly so. Take the leap.

Many therapists are convinced that they are, for example, unable to have strong feelings, unable to experience being wild, crazy, abysmally depressed, violently explosive, or many other experiencings. They are convinced that they cannot wholly enter into the patient's scenes. They know that their own personalities would not allow them to merge or fuse with lots of patients. I find that these hesitations are real and make good sense only when the therapists are located outside, external to, and face-to-face with the patients. But I have also found that these therapists are wholesomely surprised when they take the leap into becoming aligned. They are surprised that they can achieve virtually all those things that they were so convinced they would not be able to accomplish. There is an incredible difference between who you are and what you can do, when you are aligned, as compared with who you are and what you are convinced you can and cannot do when you are external to the patient. The critical issue is whether you are ready and willing to learn how to be aligned with the patient.

If you cling to being external, outside the patient, then you will have trouble being aligned, and you will likely not be able to have effective sessions. You will tend to see and hear what the aligned therapist does not see and hear, and you will probably not see and hear what the aligned therapist does. The aligned position will provide the therapist with altogether different material that is useful and workable for attaining each of the four steps. The therapist should be able to be aligned, should be ready and willing to be aligned, and should be aligned, throughout the whole session.

The aligned model may be especially suitable for therapists with conspicuous physical features.   When your eyes are closed, and your patient's eyes are closed, and when both of you are attending out there rather than to one another, then your own conspicuous physical features tend to fade away. As far as therapists are concerned, this may be for better or for worse. Picture therapists who are beautiful, compellingly attractive. Male and female therapists alike are almost forced to deal with this conspicuous physical feature in some way. He is an unusually handsome fellow, and the first thing that strikes most of his patients is that this therapist is gorgeous. She is stunningly attractive. Whether her patients are male or female, the overwhelming physical feature is her beauty. In face-to-face therapy, it is almost certain that their attractiveness will play a large part in the therapist roles and personal experiencings they are almost compelled to undergo. These therapists may enjoy their beauty, and they are entitled to be drawn by what the face-to-face model can therefore provide. On the other hand, some of these beautiful therapists may prefer to do a therapy that emphasizes their concrete competencies, and that deemphasizes their being lovely to look at. For these good-looking therapists, the aligned model enables them to do something more than bathe in the glow of their physical attractiveness.

I remember one doctoral student who was exceedingly beautiful, a stunningly attractive young woman. She did client-centered therapy and, later, behavior therapy, and her sessions were dominated by patients responding to her sheer beauty, even when she was doing her best to be empathic, or to execute some kind of behavioral program. She would not even try experiential therapy because, it seemed, the aligned model would deprive her of the joys of being so attractive. On the other hand, at a workshop I met a therapist in his 50s, a psychiatrist who said that one of the things that drew him to experiential was the aligned model. He explained that he had a fine career doing psychodynamic therapy when he was young, looked like a model, reveled in being exceedingly handsome, and tried hard not to have adoring female patients. Now he is almost completely bald, paunchy, and could no longer enjoy the former face-to-face role and personal experiencings.

You may be well over 6 feet tall, a big fellow, built more for professional football than being a therapist. You may be just a fraction over 5 feet tall, slender, rather frail. You may be in your middle 20s or in your 60s. You may be a therapist whose physical features are rather grotesque. You may have one arm or no legs. You may be blind. Your face is full of pimples. You are an albino. You are confined to a wheelchair. You have a compellingly massive nose, scars all over your face, a conspicuous goiter. Whether you like it or not, there are physical features that are simply compelling. Although you may try to accommodate these features in some kind of face-to-face therapy, it is much easier to adopt the aligned model if one of your wishes is to allow these physical features to play a lesser role in your therapeutic work. Under these circumstances, the aligned model may be suitable for you.

Here are some of the main effects of experiential sessions on therapists. Do these effects make the aligned model appealing or unappealing to you?   If I compare what occurs in most experiential sessions with what occurs in many sessions that other therapists have, I am struck by how few, and how muted, are my own personal experiencings during the session. It is rare that I feel threatened by the patient, or that we are becoming very close, or that the session is going well, or that I wish I had not said what I just said, or that I should watch out because this patient seems to be going off the deep end, or just about any other kind of personal experiencing in the actual session. I lose nearly all the good personal experiencings that many other therapists have in their sessions. I also lose most of the bad personal experiencings that other therapists can have. In general, personal, in-session experiencings tend to be rather rare and quite muted and soft, if they do occur. For me, this makes the aligned model appealing. The loss of personal experiencings may be more or less appealing for you.

When the session is over, and we open our eyes, I frequently feel a little shy and somewhat embarrassed. I was almost literally a part of this person. We went through some very personal scenes and times together, almost as one human being. I may say, "That was something!" or "Hello, nice to see you . . ." when we open our eyes and look at one another. After the session, in this moment of opening our eyes, he becomes the person that he is, and I become the person that I am. We had been virtually one person; now we return to being two separate persons.

When I listen to the tape, or just recollect what I went through in the session, I sometimes can hardly believe who I was and what I went through. It is a little like waking up from a dream, or perhaps more like waking up from having been the dreamer in someone else's dream. I can hardly believe that I was the patient, and did what I did in the scenes. I had feelings that are not my usual ones. During the session, I was a whole different person being the patient in the patient's highly personal world. I am really an old man; in the session I was a young pregnant woman. It is sometimes a little disconcerting, often surprisingly whimsical. I have bootlegged on the patient's experiencings and scenes; I have lived their lives. I have been a little girl who was lovingly held by her mother. I have been an adolescent who was forcefully and violently raped by someone I had trusted. I have almost drowned. I have had cancer that I know is going to kill me. I have been nominated for an international prize. I have had a hundred experiencings that are essentially outside what occurs in my own daily life. I approach each session as a whole new adventure. Who am I going to be? What scenes shall I be in? What will I feel and experience? This whole enterprise may be appealing or unappealing. For me, it is excitingly appealing.

The sessions usually deal with opening feelings and scenes that can be very serious, extremely painful, sometimes agonizing. The first step even goes further into the hurt and the pain to live and be in the actual moment of strong feeling. But, from then on, once the inner experiencing is accessed, the session is typically happy, exciting, and sometimes funny, both for the patient and for the therapist. Accessing the inner experiencing in Step 1 may be exciting, releasing, almost like liberating something that has been imprisoned. Steps 2, 3, and 4 are commonly accompanied with happy, exciting, nice feelings. After all, you are having good feelings as you are welcoming and appreciating the inner experiencing in Step 2. Actually getting inside and being the inner experiencing is exciting and often sheer fun in Steps 3 and 4. Many of the actual working methods are accompanied with the good feelings of being and behaving as the inner experiencing with hilarity, doing it until it feels good, engaging in sheer playful fantasy, being the inner experiencing all the way. It is almost as if the session is designed to maximize integration and actualization, and the methods help to accomplish these with playful fun, excitement, aliveness, vitality, vibrancy, silliness, whimsy, gaiety, robustness, intensity, and fun.

After the session, I often do have personal experiencings. I feel proud of what we both accomplished. I feel like we could congratulate ourselves. Good for us. Look at what we did. Quite personally, I had a hand in some marvelous changes that this patient has achieved. This kind of personal experiencing is pleasing.

There is another state that occurs after the session. When therapists read about the theory of experiential psychotherapy, what occurs in the four steps, how deep this therapy can reach, some therapists expect that the effect on the therapist is exhausting, draining, enervating. They believe that the therapist should be worn out at the end of the session. In contrast, I find that when I am almost completely aligned with the patient, and when we do a good job of going through the four steps, then the opposite usually occurs. At the end of the session, I am much more energized, feel more alive, invigorated, vibrant. It is almost like having engaged in a wonderful dream during a whole evening's sleep. This aftereffect of sessions is quite appealing to me.

The aligned model means that you will almost certainly have plenty of chances to let go of your own personality and to get into the patient's. Do you undergo significant personal change sheerly by being the experiential therapist? You do get practice in disengaging from your own operating domain. You may gain a little from going through the four steps in regard to a particular inner experiencing that is in the patient. But these are softly ineffective ways of your undergoing change. I doubt if there is substantial change in your own personality. The steps do not especially involve your own personal life, and after the session, you do not carry out the important changes in the real world. All in all, my impression is that following the aligned model and proceeding through the steps of the sessions do not have any genuinely substantial effects on the therapist's own personal changes.

If the aligned model is more appealing to you than the face-to-face model, then this therapy may be suitable for you, and your experiential sessions may be successful. However, if the aligned model is not especially appealing, then almost certainly this therapy is simply not suitable for you, and it is virtually certain that you will be unable to carry out effective experiential sessions.

If You Are Sufficiently Ready and Able to Be Aligned, Attend Out There, Have the Strong Feeling, and Go through the Four Steps, Then There May Be a Reasonable Likelihood of Achieving a Successful and Effective Session

You should be sufficiently competent in the aligned model for the session to be successful and effective. You must be ready and able to direct most of your attention out there throughout the session, not merely here and there across the session. Virtually each time the patient talks, your attention is out there. The same holds for when you talk. When you can do this well, then it is easier for the patient's words to be as if they are coming in and through you, rather than from a separate person to whom you are substantially attending.

Similarly, you must be sufficiently competent to enable the patient's attention to be out there. Throughout the session, the patient is mainly attending to some aspect of herself, to her friend's face, to being in the small group, to the pain in her lower back, to seeing herself enjoying a cigarette. You must enable the patient to be in a state of substantial feeling throughout most of the session (Mahrer, Lawson, Stalikas, & Schachter, 1990).

Through virtually all the four steps, you should be able to have strong feelings, whether they are pleasant or unpleasant. You must allow yourself to undergo pain, hurt, turmoil, anguish, all kinds of bad feelings. In the same way, you must be able to undergo strong good feelings. You must be skilled in undergoing scenes, moments, opportunities of absolute silliness, whimsy, laughter, clowning, rollicking, giggling, and chuckling (cf. Ansell, Mindess, Stern, & Stern, 1981; Ellis, 1977, 1981; Farrelly & Brandsma, 1974; Greenwald, 1975; Grotjahn, 1970; Killinger, 1976; Mahrer & Gervaize, 1984; Mindess, 1971, 1976; Narboc, 1981; Rose, 1969; Rosenheim, 1974).

Experiential therapists may not be wildly emotional or feelinged in their actual lives. They may not be screamers or hard laughers. But in the session, they must be able to have strong feeling. They must be more open than the patient to strong feeling, and to just about any kind of strong feeling. Essentially, you should be prepared to have any feeling to a strong degree in the actual session. You must be ready and willing to undergo powerful feeling, so much so that the patient is likewise ready and willing. If you are not ready and willing, then the patient will probably not be. If you can undergo incredible joy, erotic feelings, hatred, primitive wailing and moaning, sheer power, then the patient may also be able to. If you cannot do so, then this therapy is not for you. If you are ready and able to do so, then you can do this therapy. If you are ready to attend out there, to be aligned, to have the strong feeling, and to join with the patient in going through the four steps, then this therapy can be suitable for you and the session can be successful and effective.

If You Are Drawn toward Engaging in Your Own Continuous Process of Experiential Change, Then (a) This Therapy May Be Suitable for You, and (b) The Session May Be Successful and Effective

A large proportion of experiential therapists are in experiential therapy, or engage in their own experiential self-change sessions, or have alternating sessions with a colleague. They are drawn toward moving in the direction of their own personal integration and actualization. It is important for them to have regular experiential sessions, whether by themselves, with a partner, or with a therapist. It makes sense to me that when therapists are drawn toward undergoing what this therapy offers, then this therapy is probably suitable for them.

Undergoing your own experiential change is a lifelong enterprise. Instead of completing a course of therapy, you tend to have sessions throughout your life. Therapists who are drawn toward the idea of a lifelong process of change seem to find experiential therapy suitable.

If you want to have successful and effective experiential sessions, is it helpful to be engaged in your own continuous process of experiential change? I think so. The more you can go through the four steps yourself, the more effective you are likely to be in going through the four steps with your patients. When you have both the skills and a favorable inclination toward going through the four steps, it seems to be easier and more effective for your patient to do so. When you can integrate and actualize your own deeper potentials, there is a gradual increase in the kinds of deeper potentials that you are able to work with in your patients. If a particular deeper potential is no longer something you must block and keep deeper in you, then you can more effectively work with this deeper potential in your patients.

CONCLUSIONS

I believe that experiential psychotherapy is appropriate and suitable for just about every patient, but also that only a relatively small proportion of therapists would find experiential psychotherapy suitable for them. If we look at some of the more general determinants, experiential therapy is perhaps suited especially for therapists with these qualities:

1. They believe that the determinants of a successful-unsuccessful, effective-ineffective session lie almost exclusively in the therapist, rather than in the patient.
2. They fully honor the patient's readiness and willingness to undertake each substep.
3. They find the experiential model of human beings and of psychotherapeutic change to be reasonably sensible.
4. They find the aligned model to be preferable to the face-to-face model.
5. They are drawn toward engaging in their own continuous process of experiential change.

How can an experiential therapist be reasonably assured that the session can be effective and successful, that the four steps can be attained, and that the person will be and behave on the basis of the inner experiencing that was accessed in the session? If these things are present, then there is a fairly good assurance that the session can be effective; if these things are missing, then you can be equally assured that the session will be ineffective:

1. The therapist believes that the determinants of a successful-unsuccessful, effective-ineffective session lie almost exclusively in the therapist, not in the patient.
2. The therapist honors the patient's wholesale and absolute readiness and willingness to undertake each substep.
3. The therapist accepts and uses the experiential model of human beings.
4. The therapist accepts and uses the experiential model of psychotherapeutic change. The therapist accepts (a) that the direction of change is toward integration and actualization of deeper potentials for experiencing; (b) that the four steps constitute the useful avenue of psychotherapeutic change; (c) that psychotherapeutic change requires the patient's actually carrying out the new way of being and behaving in the postsession extratherapy world; (d) that what is to change and how it is to change are largely determined in the first step of each session; and (e) that his or her psychotherapeutic belief system is an important determinant of the nature and extent of possible change.
5. The therapist is sufficiently competent in the working methods of attaining the four steps.
6. The therapist prefers the aligned model over the face-to-face model.
7. The therapist is sufficiently competent in the aligned model.
8. The therapist is drawn toward and engages in a continuous personal process of experiential change.

These are a lot of conditions, but they go together as a package. When they are present, then you can be reasonably sure that the session will be effective and successful.

The Practice of
Experiential Psychotherapy

CHAPTER SIX

Dealing with the Practicalities of Experiential Psychotherapy

Before providing a detailed account of how to carry out the four steps, it will be helpful to address some practical matters in the actual practice of experiential psychotherapy. I will try to deal with the range of practicalities you may face that are over, under, or outside the professional guidelines followed by all therapists.

WHAT KINDS OF SETTINGS ARE RELATIVELY SUITABLE OR UNSUITABLE FOR THE PRACTICE OF EXPERIENTIAL PSYCHOTHERAPY?

I have almost always had my private office in my home. However, my purpose here is to deal with some of the practicalities of doing experiential psychotherapy in other settings.

A Suitable Setting Is Where Most of the Therapists Emphasize Deep-Seated Personal Change and Work with Any Kind of Bad Feeling

This kind of setting is nicely suited for the practice of experiential psychotherapy. I can picture a number of experiential therapists working together in a setting. I can also picture experiential therapists working with other therapists who likewise emphasize deep-seated personal change, and who work with just about any kind of feeling that is bad, troublesome, uncomfortable, upsetting. Many therapists share these emphases, whether they identify their approaches as psychoanalytic, Jungian, Daseinsanalytic, psychodynamic, existential, client-centered, Gestalt, or some combination or integration of these or similar approaches.

In effect, what the therapists identify as their specific approach is less important than their shared emphasis on enabling deep-seated personal change and working with any kind of bad feeling. These therapists tend to share a sense of commonality in what they are working with, in what they are enabling to occur, in goals or directions of change.

Experiential Therapy Does Not Fit Well in a Setting Offering a Collection of Specialty Services

Many settings offer a number of different kinds of mental health specialty services. The setting is private practice or a community clinic or agency. Sometimes, the unit is a freestanding administrative entity. Or, it may be a part of some larger administrative unit such as a university, a hospital, a government agency. Other times, it is a large and variegated unit designed to provide a wide variety of the human relations, mental health, personal services for a community or catchment area (Bolman, 1967; Foley & Sanders, 1966; Mahrer, 1972b, 1973; Rafferty, 1966; Roe, 1970; Schulberg & Baker, 1970). In any case, there are problems in trying to practice experiential therapy in a setting that offers a collection of specialty services.

In these settings, each therapist usually has one or more specialties that may be defined narrowly or broadly. Services may cover women's issues, depression, anxiety, vocational problems, communication skills, stress management, speech problems, pain reduction, learning disorders, hyperactivity, eating difficulties, sexual abuse, social skills training, phobias, study habits, psychosomatic problems, incest issues, alcoholism and drug abuse, assertiveness, and many more, some more general and some more specific.

But this is only one way of identifying what the therapists do. There are other ways. You can specialize in particular kinds of psychodiagnostic entities. The whole nomenclature of mental illnesses and diseases offers another way of identifying specialties. Therapists may select specific diagnoses and have one or more as their specialty areas. You may also define specialties in terms of the number and nature of the clientele. Accordingly, therapists may have specialties involving groups of clientele, all of whom have some sort of problem or problem condition in common, such as all are alcoholic or have been in legal trouble because of spouse abuse, or are recently discharged from mental hospitals. Some therapists work with individuals, some with families, some with couples, some with adolescents, middle-aged, old people, children, infants, adults, women, men, blacks, immigrants. You may specialize in terms of your approach or orientation. Therefore, a therapist may say that she is a systems therapist, Adlerian, Sullivanian, social learning, cognitive, cognitive behavioral, psychoanalytic, client-centered, Gestalt, and on and on, including particular kinds of eclectic or integrative combinations.

How and why would experiential therapists have trouble fitting into such a setting? One way is that experiential therapy would not easily fit into a listing of services on the basis of the number and kinds of clientele served by the unit. Experiential therapists can work with women, with men, with adolescents, with parents, with single or married persons, with middle-aged people, with young people, with old people, with people recently discharged from mental hospitals or jails, with people with different skin colors, with different nationalities, with immigrants. Some experiential therapists work with groups, families, couples. It would be awkward to list the services as including blacks, adolescents, elderly, couples, and experiential psychotherapy.

Not only can experiential therapists work with virtually any way of identifying "problems," but the patient has wholesale freedom to start each session by getting at any scene of strong feeling, any kind of problem, so that the problem in one session is typically substantially different from the one in earlier and later sessions. It would be difficult to present the clinic's services as including career and vocational counseling, women's issues, depression, anxiety, phobias, eating problems, and experiential psychotherapy, which works with all of these.

Once a clinic, facility, or center has a number of different specialty services, there usually is some procedure to direct the patient to the appropriate service. This problem becomes very hard to resolve when, as is almost always the case, the specialties are identified in many different ways that overlap with one another, that are on different levels of generality, and that comprise different dimensions for identifying problems, clientele, orientations, and so on. Consider a clinic that has experiential therapists as well as therapists who deal with career and vocational counseling, stress management, depression, anxiety, problems of the elderly, learning disorders, behavioral therapy, couples therapy, family therapy, children, and speech and communication problems. How does the facility direct a patient to the appropriate specialty?

The most common answer is that the facility has some way of getting enough information to make a reasonable referral to the appropriate staff member or program. The secretary, "intake" interviewer, or some other person has to screen prospective patients. Someone may interview the patient on the telephone or bring the patient in for an interview, and then conclude that this patient is fitting for the therapist who specializes in depression, or stress management, or the experiential therapist. How do you do this? What information is helpful? A common answer is that you try to find out the patient's problem, and then you can decide if anyone in the facility works with that problem. "If patients call in a depressed state, and the therapist finds out on the phone that they drink excessively, the therapist should not see them unless the therapist or someone else in the facility is knowledgeable about chemical dependency and can help the patient in detoxification" (Talmon, 1990, pp. 26–27).

One of the difficulties is that the secretary or the intake interviewer is imposing a framework of designated "problems" that is wholly alien to therapies such as experiential psychotherapy, client-centered therapy, and some other therapies. Another difficulty is that the patient is thereby forced to conform to the secretary's or intake interviewer's framework of problems. Patients who simply feel bad and have trouble fitting into the facility's category system typically are forced to deal with this by pigeonholing their bad feeling into a problem of anxiety, or perhaps a vocational problem, or maybe one of stress, or possibly a family problem. Ordinarily, patients are not encouraged to take all of these options, or even two or three.

Experiential therapy does not nicely fit into a system that first categorizes a "problem" and then steers the patient to the appropriate therapist or program. If the experiential therapist is the treatment of choice for any kind of bad feeling, the other therapists might have as much objection as the experiential therapist does about the ordinary system. A patient who tells the secretary or intake interviewer about his drinking, or his feeling gloomy, or his fights with his wife may well be referred to the alcoholism program, the depression program, the marital program, or to the experiential therapist. While the alcohol specialist, depression specialist, or marital specialist would probably find their appropriate problem and presume that it has a measure of stability, the patient may open the first experiential session with scenes about drinking, the second experiential session with scenes of feeling downcast, and the third experiential session with scenes of fighting with his wife. The whole model of a secretary or intake interviewer trying to slot the patient to the appropriate therapist on the basis of some determination of the patient's supposed problem is simply not appropriate for experiential therapy.

Neither does experiential therapy fit into a system where the therapist is a member of a large group that provides therapy for clients who are also members of the system. This may be called a managed care system or health maintenance system or something else in which client and therapist are members of some larger bureaucratic system. Typically, the client is referred to the particular therapist because the client has a particular problem or diagnostic condition, the therapist treats people with that problem or diagnostic condition, and the therapist has demonstrated that he or she is able to do an adequate job in an adequate number of sessions. Experiential therapy would have a hard time fitting into that setting because it is not designed to identify or treat the standard categories of problems or diagnostic conditions. Whatever concerns or scenes of strong feeling the patient may have in the initial session or so are given full freedom to shift in any subsequent session. The opening step may even deal with scenes and situations of strong feelings that are pleasant, exciting, and happy. Since we work 1 session at a time, the experiential therapist would have a hard time saying that it will take 4 sessions or 14 sessions to "cure" a specific problem or diagnostic condition; it would make little or no sense in the experiential approach.

Experiential therapy, like some other therapies, does not fit in with the guiding notions underlying the managed care or health maintenance systems. Perhaps it makes sense to acknowledge that these systems are restricted to some therapies. Perhaps the systems should be modified to include therapies such as experiential therapy. Perhaps experiential therapy and others are exciting alternatives to the therapies within the managed care systems.

Experiential Therapy Does Not Fit Well in a Setting with a Predetermined Mission, Goal, Direction of Change

In many settings, the facility has its own built-in mission, goal, direction of change. Generally, experiential therapy does not fit well into such settings. Picture settings in which patients are to deal with bereavement, their imminent death, their alcoholism, their spouse abuse, their eating problems, their depression, their anxiety (Mahrer & Bornstein, 1969; Mahrer & Boulet, 1987). Generally, there is a built-in set of goals and objectives. The patients are to drink less, to have less depression, to stop abusing their spouses, to reduce their eating problems, to become less anxious. No matter how they got into the program, the patients are to have the same or similar outcomes, goals, directions of change.

Experiential therapy will not fit into such a setting or facility. For one thing, we work by arriving at the direction of change at the end of the first step. Instead of the therapist's having a predetermined notion of the goal, we start with explicitly leaving the goal or direction of change open until we identify a specific scene of strong feeling, and the underlying deeper potential. Only then can we say that we have some idea of the goal. Only then can we say that the direction of change is toward a washing away of that scene of strong feeling, and toward the patient's being able to be and to behave on the basis of this inner experiencing. To have a predetermined, built-in, program-determined goal acts directly against achieving our goals. Almost always, the goals and directions of change that are arrived at in experiential therapy are not explicitly those of the program. We cannot be restricted to or handcuffed by the mission of the setting.

In addition, we leave the therapist and patient quite free to have the same or different scenes of strong feeling and inner experiencings in each session. Using a stable setting-prescribed set of missions and goals flies directly in the face of our determining these in each session. Imposing a set of predetermined goals and aims almost ensures that the experiential session will not be successful and effective.

If the patient identifies scenes of strong feeling involving his drinking, it may be that by the end of the session the patient no longer is a person who drinks so much or at all. If the experiential therapist happens to be working in an alcohol treatment clinic, the changes would seem to be just wonderful, exactly what the clinic wants. In this sense, experiential fits in quite well because changes may occur right away, and these changes are in line with what the facility wants. However, there is no guarantee that the changes will be the ones sought by the facility. If the patient identifies other scenes of strong feeling, and other kinds of inner experiencings, there is no guarantee whatsoever that the changes, even though they may be significant, will have anything to do with reduced drinking. The moral is that an experiential therapist would probably not fit in with other therapists who are geared to do something about patients' drinking, or any other predetermined mission or goal.

In many such settings, the patient is referred to the facility or program by the child-care worker, probation officer, or physician who determines that the patient is to be "treated" for his depression, his borderline condition, or his obesity. Not only is experiential therapy not suited because it is not designed to bring about depression-reduction, reduction of a borderline condition, or obesity-reduction, but in addition, this therapy counts on the patient's wholesale readiness and willingness to initiate sessions. This therapy probably will not work when the therapist pressures patients into the office, gets patients from the hospital ward, honors the velvet glove of a referral, or makes seeing the therapist part of the standard procedure for the patients to get the medical treatment they want.

In many facilities, the staff gets together to talk about the patients. They plan the treatment goals, make suggestions or decisions about what is to be done to get the patient to move in the direction of the facility's mission. These may be called case conferences, treatment evaluations, team meetings. Sometimes a group of therapists all work on the same patient—there may be a social worker, occupational therapist, rehabilitation counselor, psychologist, psychiatrist. In these meetings, they pool their information and clinical impressions to develop an organized treatment plan. In effect, the members of this group are working together to impose their group-determined direction of change on the patient. They may determine that the patient is regressing, is resistant to treatment, and should be put in a group, should not have so much contact with her sister whose visits seem to be interfering with the treatment plan, and should not be allowed out on weekend passes. Experiential therapy cannot fit in with these group-determined treatment programs. Such a setting is unsuitable for experiential therapy for the basic reason that the goals and directions of change are to come from what occurs in the first step of each session. In so many ways, the experiential therapist would have a very hard time fitting into such a setting.

If the experiential therapist is going to work in a unit or program, it should be one that accommodates inner personal change possibilities and is receptive to any kind of bad feeling. This means the staff may include some client-centered therapists, humanistic therapists, Gestalt therapists, psychodynamic therapists, psychoanalytic therapists, Jungian therapists, and others who are attuned to inner personal change and just about any kind of bad feeling.

HOW DO YOU MAKE ARRANGEMENTS FOR AND UNDERTAKE THE INITIAL SESSION?

Regardless of the setting, there are practical issues relating to arrangements for the initial session and the undertaking of the initial session.

The Patient Initiates Contact with You

It is the patient, not someone else, who initiates contact with the experiential therapist. Generally, it is the patient who calls, rather than some referral source. If a referral source calls or writes about your seeing the patient, simply invite the person to have the patient call. This applies both to more or less formal referral sources, such as some other agency, a counselor for the school system, a referral source for the company, a physician, or a probation officer. It also applies to family members who wish to have a son or brother or spouse see you for therapy. Merely invite the caller to ask the patient to give you a call.

This guideline is followed in some other therapies. For example, ". . . it is a part of the folklore of psychoanalytic technique that the analyst insist that the patient himself make the initial appointment. If someone else contacts the analyst, he should be asked to request the patient to call" (Szasz, 1988, p. 154). From the experiential perspective, following this guideline seems to increase the likelihood of an effective first session. This guideline also puts into immediate practice the policy of relying on the patient's own readiness and willingness and thereby tends to reduce role-relationship problems. If a referral source arranges for the patient to show up for the initial session, the chances are quite high that you are already enveloped in some kind role-relationship game before you even meet the patient.

These considerations almost certainly mean that you do not initiate contact with the patient. You do not go and get the patient. You do not call the patient and try to get the patient to see you. You do not write letters to persuade the person to be your patient. If your patient wants you to see her husband, or if she says that her husband asked her to ask you about having a session, you may simply say, "If he wants to have a session, ask him to give me a call . . ." I do not determine that it would be helpful to my patient if her husband were also in treatment, and therefore do what I can to get him to see me. I do not say, "I think it's a good idea if I had some sessions with your husband . . . . These issues involve both of you, maybe it would be a good idea if I saw both of you . . . . How would it be if your husband also saw a therapist? I can give you the name and number of my associate . . ." I do not call the husband and exert professional pressure for the husband to come in. "We can discuss your's wife's progress . . . . You are involved in the issues just as she is . . . . It would help me to get to know you so that I can better treat Zelda." Unless there are some very exceptional circumstances, it is the patient who is to initiate contact with you for the initial session.

What Do You Say on the Phone?

The general guideline I follow is that outside the actual work of the session, I am the person that I am. Generally, I behave as a reasonably professional psychotherapist. But, aside from that, I merely am the person that I am when we talk on the phone. This may vary somewhat from time to time, and from patient to patient. One relatively constant theme is that I am somewhat brief on the phone, generally attending to the business at hand.

I try to provide certain pieces of information—to make sure that the patient knows where my office is, how to get there, and where to park. We find some date that is convenient for both of us, and I usually try to find one that is relatively soon. I let the person know that I work one session at a time, and that the person is to pay at the end of the session. I tell what my fee is. I let the person know that the session ends when we are done, and that this usually takes around an hour and a half, perhaps more or less. I explain that unless there are some truly exceptional circumstances, the person is to cancel the session at least a day in advance, or there will be a charge for one hour. I ask for the person's telephone numbers, and occasionally their address.

Usually, I schedule only the one session. An exception is when someone comes from far away, usually for a weekend. I typically schedule the initial session, for example, at 7:00 P.M. on Friday, and I tell the person that we can also have sessions on Saturday and Sunday if we both want them.

If I foresee no openings and have a waiting list, I may give the person the names of a few other experiential therapists. If the person wishes, I invite him to give me a call sometime later to see if there may be some openings. Rarely do I offer the names of non-experiential therapists, partly because I do not solicit whatever information might be useful in offering an appropriate referral. If the person asks, I may suggest some resource the person may contact to obtain an appropriate therapist.

Partly because I work one session at a time, I rarely get involved in long conversations on topics that are perhaps more appropriate for therapies that include an extended series of sessions. I seldom discuss my approach. Even if the patient indicates that he knows nothing about experiential therapy, or that she has heard about or is somewhat acquainted with this therapy, I hardly ever have telephone conversations about my work. If he asks what he can read about experiential therapy, I may name a book or two. But this does not happen often.

Because the main purpose is to make the business arrangements clear for the initial session, there is relatively little emphasis on conducting a telephone interview to get a fair amount of information on topics initiated by either therapist or patient. Some therapists, in contrast, do engage in such interviews. "The telephone interview takes considerable skill and patience to identify and respond to the patient's major concerns and to guide him, if necessary and feasible, to venture into the clinic" (Korchin, 1976, p. 172).

Patients have a right to ask questions and to have some idea whether or not to have a session, but the issue loses some of its punch when the arrangements are just for one session, and not for a commitment to an extended series of sessions. Suppose that the patient says, on the phone, "I have problems with homosexuality, and I've been to therapists who tell me that I shouldn't worry about it. How do you feel about these kinds of problems?" Or the patient says, "I have dreams about having been other people in past lives, and I think I did live before. Can you help me with this? I've been in therapy before and my therapist didn't want to talk much about this. Is this the kind of thing you can help me sort out?" I generally let the caller know that we can have a session and see if things work out, and we can easily start with that matter if the person wants to. I much prefer having a session, just one, to having somewhat extended telephone conversations about issues that can well occur in the first part of the session.

Usually, I try to steer a fair middle ground between providing the information that the patient truly wants and has a right to know, and not getting involved in a full-blown telephone interview. For example, a patient may ask if I do hypnosis, bioenergetics, or dream interpretation. Without getting into a long conversation, I may say that I do not do hypnosis or bioenergetics, but dream interpretation is harder to talk about because yes I use dreams but no it is not quite dream interpretation. It is hard to know when to provide the information, when to engage in an extended discussion, and when to simply invite the person to have a session. In any case, I do not launch into lectures about the likelihood of success or failure of hypnotherapy or bioenergetics or other nonexperiential procedures:

> Many request specific techniques such as hypnosis, bioenergetics, dream interpretations, past-life regressions, and a host of other treatments. Although it is probably sound clinical practice to incorporate some of those procedures that the client believes will be most helpful . . . the ethically responsible therapist must assess and communicate to the client the likelihood of success with any of these procedures. (Morgenstern, 1988, pp. 96–97)

What Do You Do in the Initial Sessions?

In the initial session, you have an experiential session. You get to work. You are going to go through the four steps with the person.

You think in terms of this session, not that this is the only session you will likely have (cf. Bloom, 1981; Talmon, 1990), and not that this is the first of an extended series of sessions. You are merely programmed to show the person how to go through the steps of this session.

Since you work one session at a time, most of the questions about such things as suitability are answered in the session itself. You need not look for patient qualities and characteristics to see if the patient is suitable for this therapy or for an extended series of sessions (cf. Alexander, 1965; Barrios, 1988).

The main purpose of the initial session is to go through the four steps as well as you can. Perhaps the main guideline for deciding what you do or do not do is whether or not it helps to attain the fours steps. If the answer is no, then I do not do it. There are lots of things that other psychotherapists do in initial sessions, all of which may be justified in their own approach, but which may not contribute to the effective attainment of the four steps in the session. Accordingly, I do not try to determine whether the patient "needs" short-term or long-term treatment, should be seen by a physician, ought to have changes in his drugs, might be placed in a hospital, ought to have intelligence tests, should be evaluated neurologically or physiologically, or lots of things that are sensible in some other approaches but counterproductive for proceeding through the experiential session.

In the initial experiential session, the opening instructions enable the patient to identify scenes of strong feeling. In contrast, many "intake interviews" include getting some notion of the presenting complaints, the patient's problem, the reason for the patient coming to therapy. That is of essentially no use to the experiential therapist. In many intake interviews, there is a lot of assessment and evaluation, history taking, information gathering. Virtually none of this information is relevant, appropriate, or useful in experiential therapy.

I know that therapists and patients can assemble powerful arguments for a kind of mutual interviewing so that therapists can get the information they want, and so that patients can get the information they are justified in obtaining. For example, therapists and patients can easily justify talking about lots of topics before the patient makes a commitment to this therapist and to this therapy:

> . . . a patient has rights to certain information before he decides about psychotherapy. He has a right to know how the therapist views his psychological problems and what means he recommends for dealing with them; he has a right to know something about the psychotherapeutic process and the nature of the commitment it requires; and he has a right to inquire about the qualifications of the therapist to provide the treatment that is being offered. (cf. Korchin, 1976; Weiner, 1975, p. 74).

Patients are entitled to get some information about the therapist's qualifications and training, and some therapists like to provide such information. Some patients may indicate that they would like to be treated by means of a particular approach, such as Jungian or cognitive behavioral, or by means of a particular method such as dream interpretation or hypnosis. Some therapists discuss the merits and problems in using these approaches or methods for this particular problem. Other therapists may do the best they can to accommodate the patient's request (Lazarus, 1976).

You can easily justify a wide range of topics that could be talked about in initial sessions. However, experiential therapy can proceed effectively without using the initial sessions to cover these common topics, and patients rarely ask about these topics. There are several reasons initial experiential sessions tend to go through the usual four steps without using these sessions to talk about so many topics that are common in many other therapies:

1. Our frame of reference is just this session, rather than for 5 or 20 or an open number of future sessions. If we were contemplating a contract for six months or six years of therapy, many of these other topics would then become pertinent.
2. Many of the patient's concerns and questions are likely be answered in the actual session. After one or two sessions, much of the information is provided. She can see for herself.
3. It is very hard to have a good experiential session if we engage in mutual interviewing about the rationale, the therapist's qualifications, the suitability of this therapy for this patient, and so on.
4. I prefer having a successful experiential session rather than getting embroiled in role-relationship games.

However, there is always the exceptional patient who finds it important to ask you questions in the very beginning of the initial session. She may introduce this by saying, "There are some questions I would like to ask." I typically answer by saying that I would prefer to begin the session, but if she wants to ask a question or so, go ahead. I also indicate that it is easier for me to listen by turning away and closing my eyes so I can see better. So go ahead. I have yet to be "interviewed" with a more or less set of prepared questions.

At the initial session, I do not have a legal contract that the patient is to sign. This may be a serious mistake. Both professional and legal considerations seem to warrant use of such a contract. As a private practitioner, I have not used such a contract. On the other hand, I see the wisdom in having such a legal contract when the patient is being seen through a clinic, center, agency, or facility where professional and legal problems make such a contract almost standard practice.

WHAT SHOULD THE OFFICE AND SITTING ARRANGEMENTS BE LIKE TO ACCOMMODATE EXPERIENTIAL THERAPY?

Your office may be in your home, a private practice center, a clinic or agency, some larger facility such as a hospital. Wherever your office is located, there are some practical considerations in having the kind of office that is suitable for this therapy, and in sitting so as to accommodate the aligned posture.

What Should the Office Be Like to Accommodate Experiential Therapy?

In many respects, the office is similar to the offices for other therapists and other approaches. A waiting room may be situated so that patients can, if they wish, leave your office and the building without passing the waiting room. The actual office decoration varies with the person who is the therapist. Some have personal pictures, books, or artwork. Some do not. How you decorate your office is mainly a function of the kind of person that you are. I find no general guidelines that are helpful for decorating your experiential office.

I use relatively low illumination because patients find it easier to close their eyes and to keep them closed if the general illumination is low. Windows are covered with shades or drapes to keep the illumination low.

I have a tape recorder that is within reach of my chair so that I can turn it on and off. Because my eyes are closed, I take no notes during the session, and I count on going over the tape to help me take the notes for this session. I have been doing this for so many years that it is rare for a patient even to mention the tape recorder. Sometimes I mutter that I am turning on my notes. If a patient asks about my taping, I generally say that I tape because my eyes are closed so I take no notes during the session; I also indicate that I use the same tape over and over again. If the person seems to have reservations about my taping, I do not tape.

What is perhaps more important is the emphasis on soundproofing. Because our eyes are closed and there can be a fair amount of noise, and because sound from outside can have an inhibiting effect, the office should be such that almost no sound comes in or out of the office. Do everything you can to soundproof the walls, floor, and ceilings. Be especially careful about heating and air ducts, which can easily transmit sound from office to office. Make sure that the doors are soundproofed. I find that lack of adequate soundproofing is one of the biggest problems in offices used for experiential work.

In many other approaches, it is common to use comfortable chairs. Some therapists use couches. Some use psychoanalytic couches. More uncommonly, some therapists use big pillows. Sometimes, as in primal therapy, the patient is to lie on the floor, spread-eagled, "because I want the body in as defenseless a physical position as possible" (Janov, 1970, p. 81).

In experiential therapy, both the therapist and patient should be able to lean back comfortably, with their feet up or down, and to be able to move about in their chairs if they wish. The chairs I use are similar to each other. They are big, well-padded, and high-backed, with large armrests and footrests. The chairs are big enough to accommodate small slight people and large tall people.

What Are the Practicalities of Sitting Close, with Eyes Closed?

The chairs are situated about one or two feet from each other, both pointing in the same direction. In each session, including the initial session, I tell the patient to sit down and get settled. I do the same, sitting back, putting my feet up. I ask, "Are you ready to start? If you are, then close your eyes and keep them closed the whole time. My eyes are closed, and they'll be closed the whole time."

If I feel a little defensive, sometimes in the first session, I may explain that it is easier for me to see what the person is talking about with my eyes closed, and it is usually easier for him to see what he is talking about when his eyes are closed. Patients practically never refuse or even quibble, and I believe that this is because I am usually so comfortable sitting this way, with my eyes closed. It really is much easier to follow what the patient is saying and to see whatever the patient's words construct out there, when I have my eyes closed. I find that sitting this way and with eyes closed tends to reduce most of the interferences and distractions with seeing what the patient's words construct for me. I wish that I could actually blend or fuse into the patient; I want her words to come in and through me, so I feel and experience what the person is feeling and experiencing, and can live and be in this scene right along with or as the person herself.

As soon as I get settled in the chair, my eyes are closed. I begin the opening instructions with my eyes closed. Even in the initial session, I sit back, close my eyes, and say, "OK, well my eyes are closed. I'm ready to start. If you're ready, just close your eyes and keep them closed the whole time. It's easier to see this way . . . OK? . . ." Then I proceed with the rest of the opening instructions.

A compromise alternative for therapists who are hesitant.   Some therapists are hesitant to start this way, to sit side-by-side, so close, especially with their eyes closed. They can give all sorts of reasons why this position is not especially comfortable. Therefore, they give the patient all sorts of explanations. They tell about the theory of experiential therapy. They explain that this therapy may be helpful for the patient. They may simply alert the patient that this therapy is a little different because we sit this way and we keep our eyes closed. Some therapists almost plead with patients to at least give it a try, and then the patients can talk about how they like this arrangement. While I can appreciate therapists' hesitancies, these attempts at justification are not especially helpful to having an effective session. There is an easier way to accommodate therapists' misgivings.

Arrange the chairs in a more traditional way, so that you and the patient are more or less facing one another, at an angle. When you start talking, feel quite free to look away from the patient. Make sure that you do not look onto the patient's eyes so that you two are welded eyeball-to-eyeball. Situate yourself so that you are able, if you wish, to glance at the patient's face, but your attention is somewhat away from the patient. Usually, you can be looking down or off or away.

When you start with the opening instructions, let the patient know that it is easier for you if you kind of look away so that you can "see" what the person is talking about. As you say this, you may glance at the patient's face, but mostly you are going to look in the general vicinity of the patient. Ask the patient if this is all right. Say that you might even close your eyes at times, especially when you are trying to see something important, or to follow what he is saying. Tell the person to be free to look at whatever he wants, and to also feel free to close his eyes whenever he wants, for however long he wants. As you are saying all this, you are talking to the patient, but not at the patient, face-to-face.

This is the way you may talk with friends or with just about anyone, when you discuss relatively important things. You might perhaps spend a little time directly looking at the other person, but often you or the other person or both of you will avert your eyes and look away when you are focused on something compelling. The patient may look away to see or concentrate on the special thing he is talking about. When she has this feeling, she may avert her eyes. In general, patients, and therapists too, look down or away or out there when they are concentrating on this or undergoing that.

You can give the opening instructions, looking somewhat away from the patient's face, perhaps with your eyes closed. When the patient starts talking, tell the patient to feel free to look away, to see it more, to put attention on it. The patient responds to your opening instructions by saying, "Well, yes, yesterday. I saw my little daughter. I'm divorced and . . ." You may say, "It's OK. Just see her. I can see her. If it helps, close your eyes and see her . . ." As you continue to talk, you are more or less looking out there, not eyeball-to-eyeball.

When you adopt this position, the chairs are at the usual angle for most therapists. Occasionally, you may glance near or at the patient. But mostly your attention is out there or down there. Your position enables you to concentrate on what the patient is saying, without being face-to-face. You may adopt this position throughout the entire session. Although you are free to look at the patient, most of the time you are looking away, looking at what the patient's words construct there for you. Closing your eyes can feel natural, and you need not be concerned about whether the patient's eyes are closed. Or you may simply invite the patient to go ahead and close his eyes, if he wishes to.

You can conduct a session or two, or even all your sessions, in this way. It is doable. It is a compromise. It is a way for you to reduce some of your hesitancies. Sooner or later, if you wish, you might try being side-by-side, with eyes closed from the very beginning. This aligned posture is not necessarily exclusive to experiential therapy (Mahrer, Nadler, Gervaize, & Markow, 1986).

What are some practical considerations of adopting the aligned position and minimizing the stream of private thoughts?   When you sit side-by-side, close your eyes, and adopt the aligned position, you minimize the typical removed stream of private thoughts. Most therapists are essentially external, and that position allows them to have private thoughts, clinical inferences, observations about the patient, executive and removed thoughts about what is going on, how to respond to the patient, what to do next. The aligned position minimizes most of these thoughts, and the therapist can go through the whole session with little or no awareness of them. The stream of private thoughts is probably there but is so muted that it is of almost no consequence.

More dramatically, the experiential therapist is almost fully open so that what might have occurred as private thoughts instead come tumbling out willy-nilly. The therapist is postured and aligned so that just about everything is said, shown, opened up. Accordingly, the therapist says, "I'm having shivers . . . What do we do next? Oh, yes, we have to feel all right about what we just found . . . I am seeing her looking kind of stern. Is this just me? What do you see? . . . Wait a minute! When you stop, I don't know where we are. I'm seeing the damned cancer. Where are you? . . . I think I'm winding down. But what about you? Are we done for today? . . ."

HOW DO YOU DEAL WITH THE PRACTICALITIES OF SCHEDULING, SESSION LENGTH, ENDING SESSION, FEES, MISSED APPOINTMENTS?

You arrange for the session to start at 11:00, or at 3:00, or at 5:30. The starting time is set. The ending time is open. How do you know when the session is over? It is over when you have finished the four steps. At the very end of the fourth step, he is ready and willing to be this way, to behave in this particular way, and in this particular scene tomorrow or in the next few days or so. This is when your work is over. The fourth step is finished. The session is ready to be ended.

When you have completed the fourth step, there is often a kind of pause, a shifting away from the work. It is as if you become you once again. Your attention is no longer out there. You wake up. Your attention goes to things that are of you and your own immediate world. You are thirsty. You have thoughts about Jean's wanting you to see the outfit she bought today. You become aware of the time, or of a light odor floating about the room, some muted sounds. Once your attention shifts to things other than the work, you are ready to end the session.

What do you actually say to end the session? Say that you are ready to stop, to wind down, ready to end the session, but always check with the patient. "Is this all right? . . . Are you ready to stop? . . . Ready to open your eyes? . . . You're the important one here, so what do you think?" Almost always we are ready to end at pretty much the same time.

I end the session by opening my eyes. "I'm ready to open my eyes. OK?" When our eyes are open, the session is over. Almost always, when I open my eyes, I look over to the patient. This is really the first time that we look at each other in the session.

What do you do if the person simply does not seem ready to have a session today, or perhaps the session begins but it is clear that you are not progressing toward the first step? Most of this is rather conspicuous after 20 minutes or so. There may be little or nothing to start with, or there is little or no energy for work today. I generally accept this as just fine. After all, there are occasions when the patient is not especially ready for a session. Wind the session to a close. The important thing is to accept this and let it be. Do not try to force or pressure the patient to go through a session. Do not dress this up as some sort of problem or difficulty or failure. Do not try to get the patient to go through the four steps. If the patient is not ready, simply wind the session to a close and schedule another one.

Sessions usually take an hour and a half or so. Sometimes sessions take less than an hour. If a session takes much more than two hours, one or more of the steps usually were not well done. I find that most therapists who do this therapy have sessions that take a little over an hour to a little under two hours. When things go reasonably well, it just seems to take about this long to go through the four steps. This means that you have a fair gauge for scheduling the next patient. That is, if you schedule a patient at

8:30, you can be fairly certain that the session will be over around 10:00 or 10:15 or so. When you schedule the next patient depends on how much "in between" time you want. I would schedule the next patient at 11:00. Others might schedule the next patient at 10:45. Therapists in full-time practice tend to schedule patients about two and a quarter hours apart.

Business is done at the end of the session. I make out a bill and patients usually pay by check. Some pay in cash. I charge by the hour, although that means by the half hour. That is, if the session is around an hour, or well under an hour and a half, I charge my hourly fee. If the session is at least an hour and a half, and substantially under two hours, I charge for an hour and a half. If the session is two hours or so, I charge for two hours. I give a statement or receipt at the end of the session. It spells out the patient's name, date, length of the session, the charge, and indication that the bill was paid. I sign the receipt.

The final business is the scheduling of the next session. Ordinarily, I like to have one session a week. But this is relatively flexible so that sometimes the next session is scheduled for two or three days later, and sometimes only after a few weeks. Usually, we work out a somewhat regular schedule, although this may vary a bit.

Most patients have sessions for a year or two. However, many have a batch of sessions for a number of months, and then take a break that may last months or more, and then they return for another batch of sessions. My inclination is both to have lots of sessions stacked together and also to be somewhat loose and flexible. By working on the basis of each session as its own minitherapy, most patients seem to want to have sessions for quite a long time.

Occasionally, a patient will say that he has only an hour or an hour and a half. The session starts at 2:00, and he says that he has to leave at 3:00 or 3:30. This is quite rare, but it does happen. I find that we cannot complete a session with a one-hour deadline. We may try to complete one in an hour and a half, but that it difficult. I usually do not even try to have a session when we have to stop after an hour. An hour and a half is doable.

Although patients seldom fail to keep appointments with the single-session format, it can happen. If it is the first session, I often do not charge. After the first session, especially since patients know that they are to give me at least a day's notice, I usually charge for one hour. I often call when the patient seems to be about a half hour late. We typically arrange another session. However, if the patient does not call, or if I do not reach the patient during the appointed hour, I typically do not pursue the patient. Our working contract is, after all, only for this immediate session, even if we have been having sessions for some time. Almost always, the patient calls and we arrange for another session. If I do not hear from the patient, however, and we have typically just had one or two sessions after which we both were hesitant about having another, then I leave the matter be and do not pursue further appointments. I leave much of the initiative up to the patient.

HOW DO YOU DECIDE WHETHER OR NOT TO HAVE ANOTHER SESSION?

In most therapies, the implicitly accepted idea is that patients are to be seen for an extended series of sessions. It may be for a more or less predetermined number, such as 5 or 12 sessions, or for an open-ended number of sessions that may be relatively short or over many months or years. Yet the implicit or explicit agreement is for an extended series of sessions (Mahrer, 1988a). In experiential therapy, the agreement is explicitly for one session at a time. How do your decide whether or not to have the next session?

After Just about Any Session

At the end of each session, you decide if you want to have another session or if you would prefer not to have one. If you are drawn toward having another session, then you initiate scheduling the next session. The key guideline is that you want to have another session. If you do, go ahead and initiate the arrangements. I may say, "How about the next session being next Thursday, OK?" or I say, "I'd like to have the next one on the 12th, Wednesday. What do you think?" I indicate that I do want one, and here is my suggested date. Almost always, we settle into a routine. First I give the bill, then I initiate scheduling the next session. She is absolutely free to say yes or no, to modify the date and time.

I do not introduce the issue of scheduling the next session by asking if the patient would like to have another session. I know whether or not I want one, and it seems more fitting for me to indicate that, of course, I want one. Also, this sets aside any extended conversations about whether or not to have another session.

Are there occasions when I am leaning toward not scheduling another session, or perhaps not having one for some time? After the first two or three sessions, I find that I almost always do want to have another session, am quite ready and eager to have the next session. Rarely do I have misgivings or hesitancies about having the next session. If the patient is hesitant, however, then I tend to fully accommodate (this issue will be discussed later).

After Initial Sessions

At the end of initial sessions, you have to decide if you do or do not want to schedule another one. Be honest with yourself and the patient. Do you really want to have another session? Do you look forward to having another session? If we have gone through the four steps, I almost certainly do want to have another session. In any case, I check to see if I want to have another session. If my answer is yes, then I initiate scheduling another session. I may say, "I want to have another session. How about Friday? What do you think?" Or I may say, "We have to schedule the next session. I want one. You too? Yes? No? What do you think?" I initiate scheduling of the next session, and I indicate that I want one. Sometimes I even say something about this session: "This was good. Yes. I'd like to have another session . . ."

Suppose that you are truly hesitant about having another session. What impresses you is that you never even came close to achieving Step 1. It may be clear that you did not get to Step 1, and perhaps neither did the prior session. If, for any reason, I am hesitant about having another session, I say so. I am the one who initiates talk about whether or not to have another session. Here is where I try to be as honest and as open as possible. I may say that we did not get to a time when the feeling was strong, or we had a lot of trouble finding something that was filled with strong feeling. I may say, "I'm willing to give it another try, but a lot depends on you. What do you think?" Or I may say, "Well, we've tried three times. Maybe this isn't going to work. But what do you think?"

If I am hesitant and the patient is also not inclined to have another session, we usually do not schedule another session. Sometimes the patient mentions that she would like to wait a while. Could we schedule another session in a month? I usually accommodate. If we are not going to have further sessions, it usually takes only a few sessions or so before we both feel satisfied not to schedule another session, at least not for some time.

I have no recollection of any bad feelings or bad consequences from our deciding not to schedule any further sessions. As long as I do the initiating, as long as I am reasonably open and somewhat concrete about what we failed to do, and as long as I am rather open to trying again if the patient wishes, things seem to go well. Indeed, it usually seems to be a good way of not forcing us to keep trying, especially when all the indications point toward not continuing.

Sometimes interns and postdoctoral trainees are bothered when, after one or two sessions or so, the patient does not show up or leaves a message canceling any further sessions. These therapists are often inclined to feel bad and to talk about the patient's "resistance" or "lack of motivation," or how the therapy was inappropriate for this patient. They tend to put the blame on either the patient or the therapy. While I know that most of these explanations make good sense, I find that it is far more useful to study the previous session or so. Typically, I find that the therapist really did not want to have another session, pressured the patient into scheduling another session, and blamed either the patient or the therapy or both for not attaining the four steps. It is much easier to initiate the matter by indicating your honest and simple readiness to have or not to have a subsequent session right away or at all.

If the patient, after the first session or so, indicates a hesitation to have another session, or does not seem to want one, I honor that concern. We do not have to have sessions, and we can, if the patient wishes, have one at any time in the future. I do not try to get him to have another session. I am not "recommending" psychotherapy, and I am not trying to get patients to have further sessions after an initial session. Other therapists may have somewhat different objectives: ". . . when a patient initially expresses some mixed feelings in response to a psychotherapy recommendation, the therapist should attempt to explore these feelings and resolve them in favor of a decision to continue" (Weiner, 1975, p. 87). In contrast, I do not try to get the patient to have another session.

Experiential therapists seldom get ensnared in games in which the therapist is trying to get the patient to want to have sessions, and the patient is reluctant, going along against his will, or privately getting ready to dump the therapist. This is one of the advantages of working one session at a time, and being open and honest about not being eager for yet another session if the first few were not effective.

By applying these guidelines, especially in the initial sessions, there will be few if any occasions where the therapist truly wants to have another session but the patient does not show up for the appointed session. The whole notion of "dropout" does not fit well into a single-session format where the therapist indicates whether or not she wants another session and is sensitive to the patient's wholesale readiness and willingness or hesitation and unwillingness to have the next session. Indeed, the opposite seems to occur; patients are often drawn toward a single-session format that honors the therapist's and patient's wanting or not wanting to have another session (Fiester, Mahrer, &

Giambra, 1974). On the other hand, because this therapy opens the way toward achieving as much as possible in single sessions, a great deal is often accomplished in just a few sessions, and then both therapist and patient may be ready to discontinue sessions, at least for a while. I do not regard these as dropouts (cf. Silverman & Beech, 1979).

After a Fair Number of Sessions

Not all sessions are effective, are successful in going through the four steps. After a fair number of sessions, one or more may not get through the four steps, or even attain the first step, or even start with any energy or likelihood of getting off the starting blocks. What do you do in regard to scheduling another session? I tend to follow the usual guidelines. That is, I see if I seem to look forward to and want another session. If I do, and if the patient does too, we schedule one.

How do we determine when to have no further sessions, or perhaps to schedule one far ahead, or to keep the door open to scheduling a session at some later date? After a fair number of sessions, we may simply decide to stop. Sometimes, we decide to schedule one for six months or more. Sometimes, we decide to stop and leave it up to the patient to request a session at a later date. Patients can always return later for a session. Often they do. Many patients return every year or more for a package of sessions. I regard sessions as something that should be available throughout the person's life.

I do not think in terms of an extended series of sessions with a termination stage, nor are there the usual problems that are associated with long-term therapy such as psychoanalysis (Mahrer, 1978d; Mahrer, Howard, & Boulet, 1991). Nor does the concept of termination apply well to the single-session format and to these guidelines for scheduling the next session.

After the final session, I generally tell the person to feel free to call for a session whenever he wishes. I invite the person to return in a year or so, or whenever he wishes. Often I go further, and suggest that he return whenever something leads him to think of having another session, or when there are some compelling bad feelings, or when significant changes are in the offing, or when there is any other reason at all. And many patients do.

HOW DO YOU DEAL WITH THE PRACTICALITIES OF REFERRAL RELATIONSHIPS WITH COLLEAGUES?

I appreciate calls or letters from colleagues, referring patients to me. Many therapists know that I do not especially value most of the information that they might give me about the patient, that the main thing I need is for the person to give me a call. However, other therapists want to give me reasons for referring the person, or to provide some pertinent information about the patient. They tell me about their overall psychodiagnosis, the presenting complaints, their notions of the patient's problem, something of the patient's background, what they see as the patient's motivation for therapy, previous treatments, prognosis, the severity of the condition, and impressions of what the patient is like. For several reasons, I neither solicit such impressions nor find them useful. One is that the referrer almost always is using a nonexperiential construct system. Second, the referrer's impressions are, from my perspective, largely determined by the referrer's role-relationship with the patient. Third, the referrer's impressions usually have nothing to do with the patient's scenes of strong feeling or inner experiencings. Finally, the impressions and descriptions make no real difference in what I will do in the sessions.

On the other hand, there are some relatively common conditions under which an experiential therapist may refer the patient to another therapist. If I have no foreseeable openings, and we are talking over the phone prior to an initial session, I generally refer the person to a few experiential therapists. I tell the person that I will call the other therapists and let them know that I gave their names to the person. If the person asks for a particular kind of therapist, such as Jungian therapist or a therapist who specializes in sexual problems, I generally direct them to some resource where they may obtain a more knowledgeable referral.

If I guide the person toward other therapists, it is generally either on the phone before the initial session, or it is after a few sessions, when we did not get through the four steps and this therapy seems not to be especially suitable or appropriate for this patient. Under these two conditions, especially if the patient asks, I do my best to suggest other resources where the person can obtain a helpful referral.

I find it hard to provide what I would regard as a helpful, proper, appropriate, professional, direct referral to nonexperiential therapists. I almost never have seen the actual work of these therapists. If the therapist lists herself as doing psychodynamic therapy or specializing on couples therapy, that tells me very little of the actual approach.

I have no solid way of knowing the degree of skill or competence of the other therapist. Nor do I regard myself as sufficiently knowledgeable in Adlerian therapy or desensitization therapy or treatment of autistic children to trust my evaluation of the competence of these other therapists. Over the phone, or after one or two experiential sessions, I have insufficient technical information to refer this person to a biofeedback specialist or an implosive therapist. I respect that ". . . the referring therapist has the responsibility for ascertaining the appropriateness of the referral, including the skill of the receiving therapist" (Van Hoose & Kottler, 1977, p. 83). Because this responsibility is so daunting and I am unable to assess the skills of the other therapists, I do my best to suggest some resource that can do a much better job of making an appropriate referral.

I am often tempted to refer, not in the usual way, but on the basis of a fitting role-relationship. After a few experiential sessions in which it seems clear that we were unable to attain even the first step because of the patient's compelling role-relationship, I am inclined to refer the patient to a therapist who would be wonderfully suited for that role-relationship. For example, suppose my strong impression is that this person is almost forcing me to take over his life and manage his affairs, or she is trying very hard to have me be a kindly old parental figure who is fascinated with exploring her dearly beloved psyche. We did not even get past the very beginning of the first step because the patients were so geared to establishing these mutual roles for themselves and for me. I would love to refer them to therapists who, I am fairly sure, would be well-suited for fulfilling the kind of role the patient seems to be trying to get me to play. Complementary role-relationships would seem to be a useful dimension for referrals. Both parties would likely be satisfied and pleased, and the welfare of the patient would be served. How mutually beneficial it might be when I am fairly sure that this patient is fulfilling a role of being at loose ends, needing someone to organize and manage his life, almost directly inviting the therapist to take over his life, and I do know a therapist who, I am almost convinced, is adept at having others put themselves in his safe hands, is a fine manager of others' lives, and who loves patients who are at loose ends, needing life management from just such a therapist. In so many ways, they are made for one another. Wouldn't it be mutually beneficial to refer patients on the basis of mutually beneficial role-relationships? The idea is very tempting.

HOW DO YOU RELATE TO PATIENTS BEFORE AND AFTER THE ACTUAL WORK IN THE SESSION?

If the actual work of the session starts when you both are ready and you close your eyes, and the session stops when you both open your eyes, then this section deals with some of the practicalities outside the actual in-session work.

Some Pre- and Postpracticalities

I do virtually no touching, holding, hugging, physical contact with patients. Occasionally, I shake the person's hand. I help the person off and on with the coat or jacket. But I seem to have no routines that involve substantial physical contact. I am not sure why, except that it does not seem to fit the kind of person that I am with patients (Mahrer, 1987e). I know that many therapists often hug their patients or have other kinds of physical contact. I am not aghast or repelled by this, but it does not occur in my way of being with patients.

Partly, I suppose, because my office is in my home, I usually wear slippers, and I invite patients to remove their shoes and put on slippers. I usually have two or three pairs of slippers available, and leave it up to the person to select which ones to use. If I had my office in a clinic or center, I might not use slippers or invite patients to use them.

I do not provide coffee or tea. I have heard tapes of sessions where therapists do offer coffee or tea, and perhaps cookies. Some therapists have special mugs for the patient and know whether the patient likes sugar or milk. I do not do any of that. Mainly, I find that interferes with starting the session. On the other hand, if a patient arrives at the waiting room, which is just outside my kitchen, and says that he is very thirsty, could he have a glass of water, I accommodate.

Preliminary or Post "Little Talks"

I tend to minimize any pre- or postconversational little talks. Once we are in the office, we sit down, close our eyes, and have the session. Most of what the patient is inclined to talk about can be incorporated into the opening instructions. Even if it seems trivial, it is often fed into the opening material. If he comes into the office and talks about a recent trip, the cold weather, his having a cold, being tired, how this office is like his old office where he used to live, I invite him to start here, but the emphasis is on searching for scenes of strong feelings.

Occasionally, someone in the family calls or writes a letter about the patient. For example, a brother may call and indicate that since the patient has just been through a divorce and has gone through bankruptcy, the brother simply wants me to know that he can give the patient enough money to have sessions. Or the sister writes a letter giving lots of information about the patient's childhood just in case the information may be helpful. Aside from how you respond to these phone calls or letters, how do you use the material in the actual sessions? I typically give the letter to the patient in the beginning of the next session and include the letter as a possible object or scene in the opening instructions. If it is a phone call, I generally let the caller know, as quickly as feasible, that I will mention the phone call to the patient, and I almost always include the phone call in the opening instructions.

There are essentially no "aftersessions." I do not initiate discussion of whether this session was a good one, how the patient felt about this session, whether this session was better than others, how the patient feels about experiential therapy, or any other topics that invite a session after the experiential session. Some therapists, although not usually experiential therapists, like to ask the patient what seemed to work in the session, what it was that seemed helpful. They like to engage in conversation about how this session seemed to be for the patient. I tend to avoid such aftersessions, mainly because they draw us into pronounced role-relationships.

It is easy to justify these little aftersessions by saying that the patient seems to want to talk about the session. However, that is rare, especially when the session has ended with the fourth step, and the patient is geared toward the new way of being and behaving. From listening to tapes of sessions, my impression is that these aftersessions are predominantly encouraged by and fostered by the therapist, rather than the patient. I have heard many sessions where a therapist persuades a patient to have an experiential session, to try one out, with the explicit or implicit promise that they will go back to the kind of therapy they had been following if the patient does not like the experiential session. After the experiential session, the therapist essentially says, in effect, "Well, what do you think? Did you like having an experiential session? Should we have another? Better to go back to what we had been doing? Should I look around for something else to try?" Or the therapist has a poor session, and almost says, "Tell me that it wasn't my fault. I did all right, didn't I? You're not disappointed with me, are you? Please reassure me." To a large extent, these aftersessions are predominantly to serve the therapist, even though it is easy to put the responsibility on the patient who is supposed to want them, need them, seek them out.

If you engage in these little talks after the session, if you engage in role-relationships, and especially if you spend a fair amount of time in face-to-face relationships, then it is likely that patients will call you to have telephone conversations about all sorts of issues. Patients will tend to accept your role-relationship offers and call you in keeping with whatever roles you and the patient mutually fostered. She will call you when she feels bad, to tell you how wonderfully something went, the nice thing that happened, how awful she feels, the crisis she is in, and all sorts of appropriate and fitting things so that you both can continue playing out the roles the two of you so carefully built and fostered in the sessions. This tends to happen minimally in experiential therapy because you do not foster mutual role-relationships and do not engage in preliminary or post "little talks."

When we open our eyes, deal with the business of payment, and schedule the next session, I am geared toward leaving the office. What I talk about and how I am are determined by the person that I am at that time.

Being the Person That You Are

How you relate to patients before and after the actual work of the session can be determined by the person that you are. When I meet the patient at the door, I simply am the person that I am. I am not crazy, wild, unethical, immoral, unprofessional. I am usually not cold, mean, brusque, unfriendly, all-business, superprofessional. I am whatever person I am at the time, and I behave accordingly. I may appreciate the way she walks so energetically up to the door. I may play with how he is right on time. I may be drawn toward her shoes, and how attractive they are. I may have fun with his bringing his own slippers. If my trusty old dog is now dead, and the patient always petted him on arrival, I mention my buddy being dead; I may say how much I miss him because I really do. Whatever seems to come from the patient or from me is in accord with my being the person that I am.

What do you do when you see the patient in the waiting room, or at the door, and there is something pressing on your mind about the patient? There was an article about him in the newspaper a few days ago. You just learned that a colleague of yours, who was also the brother of the patient, was injured in a car accident. She just returned to Canada after receiving a prestigious award. Do I initiate saying something about the issue? If mentioning something is front and center on my mind when I first see the person, I go ahead and say something. I am being the person that I am, before I start work.

When I open my eyes after the session, I may comment on how wet my eyes are, or how suddenly aware I am of the light. If I am drawn toward the special pen that the patient uses to write the check, I may ask to look at it. If I get up and my back is stiff, I may mention that. If he checks around to see if anything dropped out of his pockets, I may play with that. If she has a glow on her face or grins at me in some way, I would probably remark on it. If the weather is awful, I may talk about that. If she asks if I saw her picture in the paper, I certainly chat about that. The general guideline I follow is that I am the person that I am in these interactions before and after we are doing the actual work.

Patients seldom ask personal things about me. Sometimes I bring these up myself, though ordinarily I don't. If the patient asks about a trip I was on, I talk about it. If they ask if I have children, I talk about that. If they ask about the house, I talk about that. But always I am the person that I am. I have moods. I am sometimes downcast or excited, serious or silly, happy or sad. I simply am the person that I am, but I do not get involved in a great deal of pre- or posttalk.

Dealing with Your Own Physical-Bodily State

Therapists, like most people, will have more or less temporary physical-bodily states or conditions. Suppose that you are very tired. Suppose that you have an ache or a pain in your teeth, back, head, stomach, or legs. I find that these go away when I assume the aligned position (Mahrer, 1983b). They generally come back when the session is over.

What do you do if you have to wear an eye patch, a neck brace, if you have a cast on your arm or leg, if you are on crutches, if you are in a wheelchair? These may be temporary, but they are compelling and conspicuous. I typically mention these, or talk about them, especially when the patient says something about them. I also find that these tend to disappear as attentional centers once we close our eyes and the patient starts attending to her own material.

This also applies to the therapist's being conspicuously pregnant. When you highlight the therapist-patient relationship, face-to-face conversation, and therapist-patient roles, then the therapist's pregnancy can become a front-and-center topic. You can then make a fine case for bringing up the pregnancy, talking about it, or not having sessions because you are pregnant (cf. Auchincloss, 1982; Bridges & Smith, 1988; Nadelson, Notman, Arons, & Feldman, 1974). Experiential therapists who are pregnant, even conspicuously pregnant, can have effective sessions provided that the therapist is able to carry out the aligned posture and use their bodily sensations in the proper experiential manner (Kleinplatz, 1992).

The general rule is that lots of physical-bodily states can be set aside when you align well, put all your attention out there, and allow the patient's words to come in and through you. The same guideline applies if you just won the lottery, your son was picked up by the police again, you just found out that your car was stolen, you and your spouse were engaged in a championship fight just before your session, or your mother called to say that your father finally ran away with his secretary. You may, of course, cancel a session. Or you may try having a session because many of these compelling immediate crises are indeed set aside when you put your attention out there and allow the patient's words to come in and through you.

WHAT KINDS OF NOTES DO YOU MAKE AND HOW DO YOU USE YOUR NOTES?

At the end of almost every session, I make one or two notes about what I learned about psychotherapy. I mark down what seemed special about some part of this session. What seemed to work? What happened that was so good that I would like to be able to accomplish it again? I also mark down problems and issues that I do not like to think about. I note what seemed to go wrong. I am especially bothered by and attentive to the same old problems and issues that come up again and again. These notes are for me.

I also take notes for and about the patient. I routinely mark down three things after each session. One is the scene of strong feeling. The feeling may be good or bad, and the scene may be quite recent or from long ago. This is the scene we identify in the beginning of Step 1. Second, I mark down the inner experiencing that was accessed and used in the session. To describe the inner experiencing well, I typically use about two to four words or phrases. Third, I mark down the new way of being and behaving that the patient resolved to carry out after the session, including the situational context in which it is to occur. These notes are what I need to do my work. I probably should also take notes to defend myself against imagined lawyers and legal bodies, but I haven't been jolted into adding these kinds of notes.

I also have a single sheet in each patient's file. On this sheet, I have the names of the significant people in the person's current and past life. I have the names of spouses, children, parents, brothers and sisters, and all sorts of significant others such as best friends, the uncle, grandmother, the girlfriend during elementary school, and the hated enemy in junior high school.

On that page, that single sheet, I keep a running diagram of the patient's deeper potentials. For example, suppose that the deeper potential we found in the first session is described by words such as sneaky, devious, hiding. Suppose the deeper potential from the second session is passive, used, wimp. I try to see if this second deeper potential is similar to or different from the first one. If I decide that it is different, I put it elsewhere on the page. Suppose that the deeper potential from the third session is being vicious, nasty, underhanded. Is this something we have already found? I decide that it is in the same general neighborhood as sneaky, devious, hiding. Therefore I add these words (being vicious, nasty, underhanded) to sneaky, devious, hiding. Gradually, I can build up a picture of the deeper potentials that we accessed over the sessions.

Of what use is this? If I find that essentially the same precise deeper potential seems to occur in many sessions, I have a fairly good idea that I have probably not done a very good job, at least with regard to sessions containing that deeper potential. My aim is to enable that deeper potential to become part of the operating domain, to evolve and change toward more integrated forms, and to give way to other deeper potentials.

Relatively often, good work on a deeper potential leads to its occurring in a gradually evolving and more integrated form. For example, in one session, the deeper potential is described in terms of being alone, apart, by myself. In a later session, the deeper potential is staying away, not being a part of, being out of the group. I determine that this is the former deeper potential, but evolving and changing somewhat. So I add these new words. Suppose that I later access a deeper potential described as on one's own, independent, autonomous. Here is perhaps a gradually evolving deeper potential. I can see how the deeper potential is changing. Another example is a deeper potential of losing control, chaotic, falling apart, and its evolving into being spontaneous, free, impulsive. Physical violence, attacking, destroying becomes something somewhat different: stand up to, oppose, defy. Finally it becomes strength, power, firmness. A deeper potential that starts with being passive, used, wimp, may develop into soft, vulnerable, and finally into being reached, open, close to.

I cannot predict how deeper potentials will evolve. Their progress seems peculiar to each person. Nevertheless, I use this single sheet to see how deeper potentials in this patient are moving toward increasingly integrated new forms.

Just before I have a session with this person, I add the deeper potential from the last session to this single sheet. I also look over my notes from the previous session or so to ensure that the opening instructions include something about the new ways of being and behaving the patient was to carry out at the end of last session, and something about whether the bad-feelinged scene from the last session or so is still here in her life. This is how I use my notes to get ready for the present session. Then I am open to whatever seems to be here in this session.

I almost never write reports about patients. However, if the experiential therapist works for a clinic or agency that wants reports, the material is taken from these notes. The experiential therapist is prepared especially to describe (a) scenes of strong feeling, (b) inner experiencings that were found in the sessions, and (c) new ways of being and behaving that the patient was ready and willing to carry out at the end of the sessions. The "standard" topics in most reports don't fit too well in experiential therapy.

IS IT PRACTICAL TO MIX, BLEND, AND INTEGRATE EXPERIENTIAL THERAPY WITH OTHER THERAPIES?

There are at least two ways that you can picture mixing, blending, and integrating experiential therapy and other therapies. One way is to picture the therapist as combining experiential and other therapies, and a second way is for the patient to be in experiential and some other therapy or two at the same time, with different therapists. I will discuss each of these in turn.

Is It Practical for the Therapist to Mix, Blend, and Integrate Experiential Therapy with Other Therapies?

In general, my answer is no (Mahrer, 1989g). Almost no matter what you mean by mixing, blending, or integrating, my impression is that a therapist will essentially be unable to combine experiential therapy and other therapies. I say "almost" because I do find that therapists can blend the methods and procedures of experiential therapy in with some other therapies, and also that the methods and procedures of other therapies may be used in this therapy. I regard experiential therapy as mainly comprising the four steps and the various substeps for achieving each step. I do not regard any of the methods or techniques as even slightly owned by experiential therapy. Many are quite common in a number of other therapies. I regard specific methods and techniques as more or less public property. Therefore, if therapists find the methods and techniques of experiential therapy helpful in their work, I think that is fine. If a therapist finds it helpful to use some additional methods and techniques in experiential therapy, not only do I think that is fine, if the methods and techniques seem useful, I want to know about that.

The main consideration I would have is the degree to which blending or integrating experiential therapy and other therapies (a) contributes to attaining the four steps in the session, or (b) contributes to whatever are your own nonexperiential aims and objectives. If you feel that proceeding through the four steps helps with your own aims and objectives, then you are the judge of that, and you may conclude that it is indeed possible and even helpful to combine experiential therapy into your overall way of working with your patients.

Some therapists tell me that they do experiential therapy with couples, families, and groups. I am interested in how they do it because I find it hard to work with one person when there are others in the room. I am much too aware of the others to be able to do a good job with this patient. Nevertheless, if some therapists use this therapy with couples, families, and groups, I think that is just fine, especially if I can hear tapes of their sessions.

Some therapists tell me that they typically have one or two traditional initial sessions, usually to define the presenting problem. Then, these therapists say, they decide whether it seems wisest to work with the patient experientially or some other way. If they decide to use experiential therapy, they do so. Similarly, if they start with experiential therapy, they may later believe that it is time to switch to desensitization or to cognitive behavioral or to a Gestalt or to a psychodynamic approach. On the other hand, they may start out with behavioral therapy and later decide that it is now reasonable to switch to experiential for a while.

One of the main reasons that I do not integrate experiential therapy with other therapies in this way is that I am not able to switch from one picture, theory, way of understanding patients and therapeutic change to some altogether different one (cf. Mahrer, 1989g). You would have to have some overall framework that made good sense of having an intake interview, looking for psychopathology, psychodiagnosis, presenting problems, precipitating stresses, learning deficits, all sorts of assessments and evaluations. You would have to have a conceptual framework that was friendly not only to all the kinds of information you wanted to collect in the initial interviews, but also to all the therapies you might choose to adopt following the initial interviews. That is some grandiose conceptual framework. I cannot picture it.

The experiential framework is too narrow for me to do an intake evaluation that leads me to decide that this patient needs this or that drug, or has inadequate defenses against inner psychoanalytic impulses, or has a belief system that is too permeable, or is hebephrenic, or is an incest survivor. Indeed, I have a very hard time picturing such an overall framework that can include an experiential model of human beings and therapeutic change, two to five other theories of what human beings and therapeutic change are like, and also can guide me through doing an intake evaluation and assessment. It may be possible to have such an overall framework, but I have yet to come across a superframework that can nicely include experiential therapy as one of the therapies to be chosen after some standard intake sessions.

If integration means doing standard intake sessions and then selecting experiential therapy, or if integration means somehow switching back and forth among experiential therapy and other kinds, then I find integration to be conceptually and practically impossible.

Some therapists say that they integrate experiential therapy and other therapies by blending several approaches, with experiential as one of the approaches. I am pleased that these therapists can develop a way of doing therapy that includes experiential as one component. If experiential therapy contributes to a satisfactory overall blend, then I am satisfied. However, it is hard for me to see how, for example, the four steps of experiential therapy blend in with what client-centered therapy or cognitive behavioral therapy might see fit to accomplish in a session. It seems to me that you either try to achieve the four steps or you do not. If this makes sense, then I have trouble seeing how a therapist could integrate the experiential four steps with what other therapies seek to accomplish in the session.

I do not try to combine, blend, or integrate experiential therapy with other therapies. I do not think it can be done. But I am ready to see actual examples of how such combining, blending, or integrating may be done. Maybe it is possible.

There is another reason I do not try to integrate experiential therapy and psychoanalytic therapy or desensitization therapy or Ericksonian therapy or solution-focused therapy. I am trying to become genuinely proficient at experiential therapy. I am not competent in psychoanalysis, in desensitization, Ericksonian, or solution-focused therapy. I have a healthy respect for therapists who combine three or five therapies when I am still trying to become genuinely competent in just one. It would, therefore, be hard for me to combine experiential and other therapies, if only because I am not really very good at any other therapy.

Is It Practical for the Patient to Mix, Blend, and Integrate Experiential Therapy with Other Therapies?

Every so often, a patient indicates that he is also having sessions with another therapist. This may occur over the phone in making arrangements for the initial session, or it may occur in the course of a subsequent session. The issue I want to deal with is how practical, helpful, confounding, interfering is it for a patient to have experiential sessions and also sessions with another therapist who is doing something other than experiential therapy.

If a person tells me, in the phone conversation before the initial session, that he is seeing another therapist, my usual practice is to suggest that the patient not have an experiential session. The reason is that each time this has occurred, my best guess is that I was being drawn into some kind of role-relationship game. I am not eager to have a session under these conditions.

On the other hand, there have been a few occasions where, usually after a fair number of experiential sessions, the patient mentioned that she was also having three or four sessions a week with a psychoanalyst, or sessions with a therapist for the patient's alcoholism, or for help in deciding what career to pursue, or for her fear of being in airplanes, or that he was in a group for problems around depression or drug abuse or pain management or for coping with problems in getting along with his child. Occasionally, the patient has indicated that he has appointments with a psychiatrist at the hospital from which he was discharged.

I have been reasonably careful in studying the sessions of these patients to see if their being in other therapies seemed to make difference in their experiential sessions. My answer, at least so far, is that their being in other therapies seemed to make little or no difference in what happened in experiential sessions or in the effectiveness of our sessions.

If I apotheosized the patient-therapist relationship, my impression is that the issue of another therapist would be grist for the relationship mill. I would perhaps be drawn toward trying to get the patient to talk about how she is using both of us, or how it fits into the patient's psychodynamics to have two therapists who are serving important roles in her life, or I may work toward being the only therapist the patient sees, or I may seek to have extratherapy professional relationships, of one kind or another, with the other therapist. It is easy to justify the therapist's making it a topic of concern that the patient may be having sessions with another therapist. I have, so far, found that this has been an exceedingly minor point in the few patients who have mentioned this.

HOW DO YOU DEAL WITH THE LIKELIHOOD OF BAD OR DANGEROUS THINGS HAPPENING AS A RESULT OF EXPERIENTIAL SESSIONS?

When I am asked this question, I usually have about three pictures of bad or dangerous things happening from experiential sessions. One is where the session is over and the patient is a blithering lunatic, a crazy babbler, certain to kill someone, minutes away from doing something awful. What are you going to do, now that you are confronted with a patient like this? My way of dealing with this matter would be to study a few times that it happened, and try to figure out how to deal with the next time it happens. But this has not yet occurred in my practice (cf. Mahrer, 1980c), so I have no answer from experiential theory.

Second, the question might refer to experiential patients, after the session, doing bad or dangerous things, even though the therapist had little or no idea, during the session, that something like this might well occur. Once again, as far as I know, this has not occurred in my practice. It may happen. It may have already occurred, though I would think I would have known about it in the next session or so. If I am not aware of actual occurrence that I can study, I can prepare no way of avoiding its later occurrence.

There is a third meaning of the question. If few patients or none have done bad or dangerous things after the session, what are some guesses about what the experiential therapist does to keep the likelihood so low, virtually nonexistent? This section will deal mostly with this meaning of the question.

Who Seem to Be Concerned about Bad or Dangerous Things Happening as a Result of Experiential Sessions? Patients? Experiential Therapists? Other Therapists?

Neither patients nor experiential therapists seem to be especially concerned about the likelihood of bad or dangerous things happening after the sessions. The concern comes almost exclusively from other therapists, who have some entitlements for their worries.

One is that many therapists begin to worry when they learn that experiential therapy invites the patient to give up the person that he is, and to allow something deeper to become a part of the new person. The idea of such a paramount change can be scary for therapists who know that change is to be restricted to how you behave, how you feel, how you perceive and cope with things, but certainly not in the very self that is you. If experiential therapy dares to conceive such a major change in the person's self, that alone is bad and dangerous. Who knows what this new person might be like, might do?

A second way in which other therapists are entitled to be fearful is that they see the experiential therapist giving up control over what is to change, when it is to change, how it is to change. They insist that it is the therapist who is to determine, monitor, watch over whatever changes are to occur. It is the therapist who has treatment plans that screen in allowable changes and screen out changes that are not allowed. When these therapists view experiential therapy, they are entitled to be frightened that they have sacrificed control over change. If they are no longer the determiners and controllers of what changes are permitted, they fear for the consequences. Who knows what bad and dangerous things may occur once these therapists lose control?

Third, these therapists are fearful of a therapy that opens up change in every session. They know that change, especially significant change, must occur only later, after there is a well-developed therapist-patient relationship, only after serious work is done on the patient's psychodynamics. Therapies that open up change, especially significant change, in each session, are suspect. Who knows what bad and dangerous things might be the consequence?

Fourth, many therapists have a healthy skepticism about patients being and behaving on the basis of what is deeper. What is deeper is unhealthy, sick, pathological, suspect. If patients start being and behaving on the basis of what is deeper, of course one would have to worry about bad and dangerous consequences. Patients are to know and understand their basic nature, to be able to cope with it, to control and guard against what lies in the psychic netherworld. Opening up that realm is bad, dangerous, pathological, sick, uncivilized, wild, crazy, psychotic, evil, and most certainly unprofessional, unethical, immoral, and probably illegal.

When other therapists look at experiential therapy through their own theoretical perspectives, they are entitled to have grave concerns about bad or dangerous things happening as a result of experiential sessions.

What Bad or Dangerous Things Do You Picture Happening as a Result of Experiential Sessions?

I picture several kinds of happenings when I think of bad or dangerous consequences from an experiential session. I picture a patient killing himself, or trying to kill himself, or going into an awful state in which he is filled with thoughts about killing himself. I can picture a patient going into a state in which she seems to be weird, bizarre, crazy, inhuman, lunatic, deranged, and in a way that is painful, anguished, awful. I picture a person doing something he later regards as terrible, awful—an action that ruined his life. I picture the person changing dramatically into someone who does mean, cruel, destructive, painful things to others. I picture the patient's victims who are tortured, maimed, killed, beaten up, made to feel agonized and terrorized by the patient. The patient locks a baby in a closet for weeks, rapes a woman and leaves her in a state of intense suffering, breaks windows in neighbors' homes and screams obscenities at them in the middle of the night.

When I picture bad and dangerous consequences, I think of a progressively insidious process in which patients and therapists trap themselves in increasingly painful relationships over months or years. She becomes ever more deeply hurt and wounded in her increasingly painful relationship with her therapist (cf. Elkind, 1992). He slowly gives up everything that was joyous and pleasurable as he makes his therapist the sole centerpiece of his daily life, and there is slowly saturating anguish and pain as patient and therapist work hard to perpetuate a relationship that is mutually harmful and destructive, and moves relentlessly from year to year.

These are the kinds of pictures I have when I think of bad and dangerous things that might result from a session or a whole series of sessions. When I look at these possibilities from a practical perspective, my impression is that the incidence or likelihood of these actually happening in experiential therapy is minimal, and that the four-step, single-session model has checks and balances against the likelihood of such events.

What Does the Experiential Therapist Do to Virtually Ensure That Bad or Dangerous Things Will Not Occur?

One way that I do not use is to screen away patients who just might do such bad and dangerous things after the session. Perhaps because this therapy works on a single-session basis, and with just about any patient, there are lots of patients who may seem frenzied, turned inside out, and wallowing in the distinct possibility of bad or dangerous things. In addition, I welcome a fair proportion of outright "challenge" patients, and these may include some where there may be a risk of bad and dangerous behaviors.

One way of reducing the risk is to decline having further sessions if it is clear that you have never come close to attaining the first step with this patient. This tends to reduce the likelihood of a grindingly abrasive set of mutual role-relationships that just might foster bad or dangerous things happening as a result of the initial sessions.

The experiential therapist tends to decline therapist roles, including those that invite patients to do bad and dangerous things so that the therapist can deal with these crises. Some therapist roles include heightened vigilance for indications that the patient might fall into a suicidal depression, act out destructive impulses, become grossly psychotic. The moment therapists spot these indications, the role propels them into appropriate action. Such roles feed on bad and dangerous possibilities. In contrast, to avoid this vicious cycle, the experiential therapist declines roles, including any stance that involves "doing something" about patients who may go crazy, kill themselves, or harm others. Since the role invites, builds, and capitalizes on what the therapist sees as potentially bad and dangerous, declining the role washes away most of these threats.

Although it may seem paradoxical, the first step in the session tends to reduce the possibility of bad and dangerous things happening by intentionally entering into the scenes and the actual moments of strong bad feeling. When the session opens, a patient may be on the edge of falling apart or erupting into violence, but as we identify and enter into a scene of strong feeling, the likelihood diminishes.

In the second step, welcoming and appreciating the accessed deeper potential further serve to diminish the possibility of the patient's doing bad and dangerous things. It seems that the more there are integrative good relationships between the person and her deeper potentials, the less there is a likelihood of dire consequences.

In the third step, the patient can actually let go of the ordinary and continuing personality, and can effect the radical shift into being and behaving as the deeper potential. I find that the person who is the deeper potential—who is fully being this deeper potential—is even less likely to do bad and dangerous things than the ordinary, continuing person. Each step progressively reduces the threat of harmful states or behaviors.

One of the features of the third step is to give the person several opportunities to be this new inner experiencing, and to do so in a number of situational contexts, including the painful and unpleasant scenes and situations from the first step. Once again, the likelihood of injurious behaviors is softened and diminished.

In the fourth step, the person has opportunities to be and to behave as the inner experiencing in prospective scenes and situations. The probability of actually being and behaving as this new person increases, whereas the probability of doing bad and dangerous things symmetrically diminishes. If he is ready and inclined to be and behave as this new person in the extratherapy world, he rehearses being this way "for real," refining and modifying it till it feels right for both patient and therapist. The patient then has a chance to have negative feelings about the possible new way of being and behaving, to take different positions for or against it. Seriously considering the prospect of actually carrying out the new way of being and behaving is subjected to these checks and balances to provide for the practical likelihood of carrying it out in a way that feels right. The final substep is the commitment to carrying it out. If actually trying it out in the session is accompanied with good bodily sensations, in both therapist and patient, then the patient is inclined to do it for real. If the feelings are not especially good ones, are only moderately good, or even are bad ones, in either therapist or patient, then the guideline is not to do it. I have yet to complete Step 4 with the patient intent on undertaking some new way of being and behaving while I am filled with awful bodily sensations. Almost always, we both have quite delightful bodily sensations, or they are at least good and pleasant.

By following the ordinary procedures of an experiential session, there is little or no likelihood of bad or dangerous consequences from a session.

HOW CAN YOU STUDY AND LEARN FROM YOUR OWN WORK?

If you want to improve your experiential skills, and you should, there are some practical ways to do this by studying and learning from your own work.

Study and Learn from Your Experiential Sessions with a Partner

One way of learning experiential therapy is to have sessions with a partner. Choose someone who is also interested in learning this therapy, and who is roughly at your level of experience and expertise. Choose someone whom you can trust. It is probably sensible to choose someone who is not a part of your own personal life, not someone you live with, not someone who is a friend or a coworker.

Have regular sessions every week or so. Alternate your being the therapist and your being the patient. Since the purpose is to learn the skills, it pays to record the session so that the two of you can study how well you did. On the other hand, even though the purpose is to develop skills, just about every part of the session deals with the sensitive and the highly personal. Accordingly, it is exceedingly important that you both respect the guideline of readiness. This means that the one who is being the therapist and the one who is being the patient are both quite open to ending the session at whatever point seems warranted. At any time in the session, and for whatever reason, each party is perfectly free to stop.

In this kind of cotherapy, it is quite common for the partners to talk about the skills and the therapy before and after the sessions. You may, for example, decide that you will begin with just the opening instructions and the patient's finding some opening scenes of strong feeling. At the outset, you may agree to stop at that point. After the session, which may only last a short time, play the tape and discuss what seemed to work or not work, both from the perspective of the therapist and that of the patient.

By working with a partner, you can practice being the therapist. You can try out the skills in a way that is somewhat safer than working with a patient. Both of you are seeking to learn. But you can also learn when you are in the role of patient. It makes it easier to learn the skills when the nagging bad feeling of being tense and scared actually is replaced by an energetic giddiness as you play out new ways of being and behaving in the fourth step. It is impressive when you are actually living in a scene and you are crying. The skills become alive when you come up with a memory from when you were three years old, or when the image of your father suddenly becomes real and you are genuinely being six years old and you are with him in the car. It is impressive when you are in eighth grade, sitting in class next to your boyfriend, having the same thoughts and feelings that seemed to be there when it was actually happening. You can actually see and feel what the methods achieve in the patient when you are the patient.

Study and Learn from Your Own Sessions

It is probably helpful to tape all your sessions or at least most of them. I use these tapes partly to help me write brief notes about the session for the patient's file. However, I also tape all my sessions so that I can study and learn how to become a better experiential therapist. After each session, I spend about 15 minutes or so studying some part of the tape, and then I rewind the tape and use it for the next patient. Every so often, I also take an hour or so, later, to go over a whole session to study and to learn. I follow this routine today. I suggest that you follow a similar routine.

How can you learn from what you did well?   To study and learn by yourself, spend a little time after each session to see what you think worked for you in this session. If you study with a partner or a small group, it is probably more workable to study a taped session. In either case, try to mark down a simple sentence or two that identifies what seemed to work. Try to figure out what you did, when you did it, and what it helped bring about in the patient. As you build up a list of specific things that worked for you, you are gradually identifying and defining a way for you to do therapy. This method is effective whether you are learning experiential therapy, whether you are learning some other kind of therapy or, more likely, whether you are developing your own particular style of therapy or variation on some other approach (Mahrer, 1988c, 1992a). It is a simple and straightforward way of learning how to do therapy, especially as you grad- ually refine, modify, and organize the points you mark down to serve as a framework based on what works for you.

Whether you spend a few minutes or so after a session, or you study your tape with a partner or small group, start by identifying one place where you were impressed with the change in the patient. If you are learning experiential therapy, look for when you were impressed that the patient achieved a given substep in one of the steps. Then go back and try to identify what you did right, what seemed to work.

How can you learn from your mistakes?   If the whole session was awful, or if you believe that a particular part of the session was no good, do your best to identify the problem. Usually, this is easier to do when you go over that part of the session with a partner, a small group, or a teacher. Identifying the problem can be hard, partly be- cause it is more useful to look for what you did to set up the problem, rather than fo- cusing on when it reached unmanageable proportions. Because it is difficult to rectify a problem that has grown so very large, it is more practical to identify what you did wrong to bring about that problem in the first place.

Some trainees point to this place on the tape, and want to know what to do when the patient does this or that. What do I do when the patient won't agree to closing her eyes? What do I do if the patient won't consider behavior change? What do I do when the patient just drifts from one scene to another? We can begin where something seems to be wrong, and try to fix it. However, I prefer to look for what the therapist did to help bring about the problem. It turns out that the therapist had a pretherapy minisession with the patient and was almost pleading with the patient to try this offbeat therapy, together with a promise that if she wanted to shift back to their usual face-to-face treat- ment, he would shift back, even after a few minutes. Then he told her to move her chair parallel to his and to close her eyes the whole time. That is when she said she felt more comfortable with her eyes open. The payoff is higher if you look for how the therapist created the problem as compared with what to do once the problem has been created.

Suppose that the problem seems to be that the patient has a very hard time being the inner experiencing in Step 3. When you look for what you did to set up this prob- lem, you, or your partner, group, or teacher, go back a bit. "What happened in Step 2?" It turns out that you skipped this step or that you never came close to achieving what this step is designed to achieve. It is important to locate when you did the wrong thing to create the problem that you face.

I find that the payoff is also considerably higher if you look for your own mistakes instead of turning accusingly toward the patient. Once we come across some problem or difficulty in the session, most therapists have an unending resource of excuses that involve the patient. Essentially, the therapist is blaming the patient. These therapists explain the problem by talking about the patient's resistance (Mahrer, Murphy, Gagnon, & Gingras, 1994), her tendency to drift from topic to topic, his need to stay away from strong feeling, how hard it is to work with borderlines, how patients with this personality makeup tend to be like this, how fearful this patient is of getting too close to threatening material, how this patient is fearful of therapy because he has this or that personality dimension, condition, or psychodynamic. The rush to put the blame on the patient is doomed to success, no matter what kind of jargon system you use for your explanation. However, the payoff in terms of your getting better is quite slim. You may be as accurate as you can be in labeling the patient, in accusing the patient of being whatever way you choose. However, if you want to get better, let that line of justification go and look for what you yourself did or did not do to set up and foster the problem. Almost always, you can find what you did wrong, and you can do something about it.

How can you learn with a partner, small group, or teacher?   You can study and learn by yourself, but it is much easier, for many, to do these things with a partner, a small group, or especially with a teacher (Mahrer & Boulet, 1989). In this format, it is helpful if you prepare the part of the session you want to study. Pick out something that seemed to work, a part of the session that you are honestly proud of, a part that you either believe shows you are getting better or that you are simply impressed with and want to show off. Or you can select a part that contains some problem, something you feel you had better study carefully. Play 10 or 15 minutes of the tape that includes the part you have preselected to study.

I like to teach in a small group of four to six therapists, with plenty of discussion. My job is to show the therapist how to become a better therapist. There is little or no delving into the personality of the therapist because that is the job of the therapist and her own personal therapy. In general, I leave it up to the therapist to set the agenda. Will we be trying to study what seemed to go well, or will we be poking around to see what went wrong? If we are trying to see what the therapist did right, we study the tape and try our best to figure out what the therapist seemed to do that worked. I do most of the work, usually, but the others are free to figure out what I am trying to figure out.

Trying to see how the therapist got into that problem is harder. When we uncover what the therapist did wrong, we commonly find that she is not especially clear on what step she is in, or where she is in this step. To a large extent, many problems are created because the therapist is not programmed to achieve this particular step or drifts over to accomplishing something other than this immediate step. Using simple restatements of the patient's feeling may not be especially effective in enabling the patient to welcome and appreciate the inner experiencing in Step 2. Attaining Step 3 requires that some earlier life incidents be found, and it is hard to find them if you are geared instead toward tracking the patient's feelings.

Much of what I do as a teacher ends up with the identifying of some skill. Here is what you seemed to do that worked. Here is what you seemed to be heading toward, here is where you should have been heading, and here are the ways of working in the right direction. Here is where you pulled away, and here is what you might have done to continue in the right direction. Here is what you did, and it worked; how about trying these other methods now that you seem relatively proficient in using this way? I study the therapist's tape to try and deepen and broaden the therapist's skills and competencies. And I am always on the lookout for better ways of doing this therapy.

Start Doing Experiential Therapy and Do Your Best to Improve

Start doing experiential therapy when you are reasonably sure that you are ready. Generally, this means that you have studied this book carefully and have had a sufficient number of sessions with a partner to feel ready to start. A reasonable test is that in your sessions with a partner you were adequately programmed toward achieving the four steps. It is important that you can proceed through the four-step format without having to stop, pull out, and try to think what step is next.

You are doing experiential therapy when most of your sessions go through all four steps. You may accomplish the four steps well or only barely, but this is your goal. You should be able to accomplish the four steps after studying this handbook and after accomplishing the four steps in work with your partner. This is your first plateau, and you should reach it fairly soon after starting work with patients.

From then on, you can improve. Learning and improving should be something you do for the rest of your career. Becoming a better psychotherapist is a matter of explicitly dedicating some time every week or so to your own improvement. You may do this for 10 or 15 minutes after most of your sessions, or you may do this once a week or so, especially in meetings with a partner, training group, or teacher. Regardless of the format, study and learning and getting better should occur as long as you do psychotherapy.

It is essential that you use just about every session to enable you to get better. My concern is that you consistently and regularly improve, no matter what level you are at when you start. My concern is that you are better, two or six months from now, or even every few weeks or so. It is good if you spend a few minutes or so after each session, trying to figure out what seemed to work, and writing that down. It is also helpful to meet regularly with a partner or group to study and learn from your sessions. With regular study and practice, you will gradually increase your skill and competence.

As you use this handbook, you can expand your own methods of obtaining each of the steps. As you listen to others' tapes, you can find additional methods to include in your own work. As you add methods and study your own sessions, you are engaging in a steady program of improvement, and that is the goal.

Practice, Practice, Practice

Practicing from study of your own tapes can be quite different from practicing with tapes of fine therapists. Whether you have found what to practice through study of your own tape or by locating it with a partner, group, or teacher, you will typically have a chance to practice something you did relatively well or to practice what you could and should have done right.

Right here, in the moment of strong feeling in Step 1, you could have allowed yourself to be the other person. The patient was leaning toward being this other person, and you could have used that method. Practice using this method. In Step 2, you only seem to use a few of the methods. Try practicing one other method. Actually spend some time trying it out, practicing until you become somewhat skilled.

Right here you made a mistake. In Step 3, you failed to enable the patient to enter into the scene and to be the new person in play, in pretense, in fantasy. You tried to get the patient to be the new person in reality, and that did not work. Go back to where you invited the patient to be the new person, and this time do it correctly. Practice doing this until you can do it relatively well.

In Step 1, you were unable to see a scene given to you by the patient's words. He is creating a scene in which an acquaintance is leaning forward, with that disbelieving look on his face, and saying, "You did . . . what!?" Practice allowing yourself to see that scene until you can literally see that person, can literally be right here with that other fellow, can see this as real and immediate and present.

Right here you knew that you had trouble staying aligned with the woman who touched her female lover's breast and was aroused. You are a woman, and yet you have not had such an experience. Practice. Let yourself go over and over the patient's words until you have this experiencing. This is something you can practice until you can adequately feel what the patient is feeling.

When you practice from tapes of fine therapists, you have a criterion to shoot for. You have the therapist showing you what you could accomplish. When you study your own tapes, you lack that advantage. However, you have the advantage of seeing when and where you can improve. If you already do that reasonably well, then you can do even better with that skill. If you did not do well right here, then this is where you have to improve. Nevertheless, whether you study tapes of fine therapists or your own tapes, learning includes simple and straightforward practice.

CHAPTER SEVEN

Step 1. Being in the Moment of Strong Feeling and Accessing the Inner Experiencing

This chapter, along with the next three chapters, serves as a manual for implementing the four steps. This chapter will show you how to go through Step 1. You attain this step when you and the patient are living and being in a moment of strong feeling, and you access, actually receive, the deeper potential or inner experiencing.

YOU ARE PROGRAMMED TOWARD THE SCENE OF STRONG FEELING, THE MOMENT OF STRONG FEELING, AND THE INNER EXPERIENCING

By "programmed," I mean that it will become almost second nature for you to find and enter the scene of strong feeling, find and go further into the actual moment of strong feeling, and then access the inner experiencing. Being programmed means you have mastered the actual skills and substeps so that you can perform them almost without conscious thought in much the same way that pianists, surgeons, and dancers master their techniques. First you are programmed to find a scene of strong feeling, then to locate the actual instant or moment of strong feeling, and finally to access the inner experiencing.

Being programmed also means that you are ready to accept whatever the patient offers you. Step 1 is, in this sense, an adventure. After the opening instructions, you are moment-to-moment ready to receive whatever the patient presents in this session and to use it for accessing the deeper potential.

GIVE OPENING INSTRUCTIONS

The session starts with your giving the opening instructions.

What Position or State Are You in as You Give the Opening Instructions?

You are in the aligned position or state. Almost all of your attention is out there, ready to see whatever appears when the patient says something in some way. Your eyes are closed, your attention is directed in front of you, not toward the patient. You are positioned so that when your instructions are over and the patient talks, it is as if the patient is a part of you; the patient's words seem to come from inside you or some part of you.

What Are the Purposes and Goals of the Opening Instructions? What Indicates That the Opening Instructions Were Successful and Effective?

Your instructions are successful and effective when they enable the patient to have a scene of strong feeling. If your opening instructions are just about perfect, the patient is facing a scene of strong feeling. The scene is vivid, immediate, real, and present; the feeling is strong—it may be pleasant or unpleasant, but it is strong.

The aim is not to pressure or force the patient to have a scene of strong feeling. Instead, the instructions invite the person, show the person what to do and how to do it, provided that the person is ready and willing. In this sense, the instructions are similar to those used in many forms of meditation and contemplation where the person directs attention onto some object: a candle flame, a gurgling brook, the back-and-forth movement of air through the nostrils, a word or phrase, a symbol or picture. Your instructions are similar, except that the patient is to find something that is accompanied with strong feeling.

If your instructions are successful and effective, the patient will be seeing some scene of strong feeling, and will symmetrically attend less and less to your instructions. In this sense, your instructions are paradoxical, because the more the patient follows your instructions the less the patient will hear what you are saying.

What Are the More or Less Standard Opening Instructions?

There are a few parts of your opening instructions that get the patient set for following your instructions. Tell him that you will be showing him what to do, and how to do it. Tell him that he is to see whatever comes to his mind when you talk. If he thinks of just one thing, that is fine. If he thinks of two or three things, that is fine. Don't censor anything. Don't decide that this or that is not important. Even if whatever he sees or comes to mind seems to have nothing to do with the words you say, that is just fine.

Ask him to get ready to see whatever he sees, whatever comes to mind. He has to be set. Is he ready? When he is ready, then you can begin telling him what to look for. There are at least three ways to phrase the opening instructions for what to see. You may emphasize one, or you may include all three in the opening instructions.

Some ways to highlight what the patient is to attend to.   One way is to ask the patient to look for the biggest thing that bothers him, worries him, troubles and concerns him. There is something that makes him feel bad, awful, rotten. It may be something about the way he is, or something happening in his life, maybe something he does. It may be something about him that he doesn't like or wishes would go away. It may be something inside, some way that he is. It may be something that eats at him, plagues him, is always on his mind, worrying him. This first way can show the patient how to get right at the

,heart of the pain, hurt, bad feeling. It can bypass much of the ordinary "talking about" this and that and can help the patient go directly to the very core of the matter.

A second way is to direct the patient's attention to when he has a genuinely strong feeling, when he feels really bad, or really good, some time when the feeling is very strong. It is when you feel awful, rotten, miserable, terrible. It is a time when you feel fantastic, happy as can be. Keep the terms relatively loose and general. This second way enables the patient also to get some scene, some situational context, some time of strong feeling.

Third, the instructions may emphasize the feeling first, and then the time when this feeling is quite strong. Direct the patient's attention to a feeling:

> *You are having a strong feeling . . . the feeling in you is wonderful, so nice, so pleasant . . . the feeling in you is awful; it feels terrible, really bad . . .*

Then direct the patient's attention to a time when this feeling is very strong. Once the patient has identified the special feeling, invite the patient to think of or to see whatever comes to mind when you name or describe the feeling as strong, as powerful. You may say:

> *What is probably the worst feeling that you have? I mean the feeling that tears you apart, the kind of awful feeling you can have, but you never want to have. Maybe it happened recently. Maybe it started to happen. Maybe it happened in a jolt, and it drives you wild, crazy, awful. Having this feeling is your personal hell . . . What am I describing? When does it happen?*

These are the three more or less standard things to emphasize in the opening instructions. You highlight the powerful bother, trouble, concern, the thing that plagues her. You highlight the time, the scene, the situation when the feeling is strong. Or, third, you first highlight the strong feeling, and then when and where this feeling occurs, the scene or situational context.

Some helpful guidelines in giving the opening instructions. It is generally helpful to emphasize the present, scenes of strong feeling that are in the current life. But keep this only as a gentle emphasis. Leave some room for the patient to use something that happened long ago. He immediately sees the time when he was an adolescent, and the soldiers shot his whole family.

The instructions give the patient an opportunity to go directly to all those things that may be dramatic, frightening, central, weird, out of the ordinary. Highlight scenes and issues that are compelling, uppermost, central. Give the patient plenty of room to go right to the heart of the painful and unhappy matter.

As you are saying the opening instructions, your own words will often bring examples to mind. Allow yourself to cite these examples as they come to you. Sometimes the examples are broad-stroked and rather general. You think of times when the patient is alone, or with friends, or going somewhere, or with the family. Sometimes the strong-feelinged scenes that pop into your mind are far out, unusual, outrageous, whimsical, silly. If these come to you, you may cite them, even as coming to your own mind, right here and now, even though, as you say, you have no idea where these came from.

Your opening instructions are gentle and easy, sensitive and delicate. Make sure that you leave plenty of room for the patient to see whatever is there for her to see, or to bring up anything that she may be inclined to bring up. Be careful not to impose your own selected scene or attentional center, your own predetermined agenda or treatment plan. You may know something dramatic that you think the patient ought to be focusing on, and you may perhaps mention it, but do not force him to use that topic or scene or attentional center. Try to leave plenty of room for the patient to attend to whatever the patient is ready to attend to. Do not exert your own will.

Sometimes there is already some strong-feelinged attentional center even before you start with your opening instructions. As he settles into the chair, he is obviously ready to bellow or to cry or is in a state of shock or despair. Or, as soon as she sits down and closes her eyes, she starts:

> *I won the Symonds Award! Best in the whole country. Fantastic!*

or he says:

> *I'm going to cry . . .*

and he starts crying hard. Just accommodate. The patient is following the instructions before you give them. That is fine. Do not interfere by reciting the instructions.

What Are Some Topics That May Be Included in the Opening Instructions?

There are at least two ways to use these topics. One way is to include some of these topics as part of your more or less standard opening instructions. A second way is to go to some of these topics when the standard opening instructions seem to come up with little or nothing.

> 1. *There is some feeling in you right now. I invite the person to attend to whatever feeling is here in her right now:*

There may be some feeling right now, so just let it get stronger. Just let it happen. Show it. Give in to it, if that is all right. Let yourself be angry, violent, furious, mad as hell. If you feel like crying, then cry. If you feel like screaming and yelling and roaring, then do it. If you feel like laughing, then laugh. Go ahead. If you feel like curling up like a little baby and whimpering, go ahead. If you feel ready to fall apart, to let go, to go to pieces, to become a berserk lunatic, go ahead.

Encourage the person to open up and to have any kind of feeling that is here right now. Almost always, having the feeling also displays something the feeling is about, some attentional center, some context, some scene.

> 2. *It happened very recently, another one of those times when you hardly even knew you felt bad, and you didn't do anything, you didn't say anything, you didn't do anything at all, you just let it happen.*

The emphasis is on catching recent scenes and times that do not stand out, where there was no flagrantly manifested bad feeling, no dramatic situation to whip up a bad feeling. Instead, these are the times when nothing much happens. The situation comes and goes swiftly, without fanfare. There is a look, a few words, nothing especially incendiary. Similarly, the inside feeling is quiet, muted. Not much happens. Typically, the inside feeling is more like a closing off, a stopping, a blocking of feeling, an antifeeling. The person actually does little or nothing.

It is as if the feeling just occurs, and then slowly festers or oozes. Afterward, the person usually just feels bad, but without any explicit scene or incident as the offender.

Instead, the person slides into a state of generally being at loose ends, disgruntled, depressed, fretting, somewhat tense, grumbling, bothered and annoyed about everything and anything.

It is important that the patient make an explicit effort to catch whatever scenes simply appear, because few will be easily recollected. Emphasize that whatever it was probably occurred recently, and that the patient did little or nothing. There was just an inside spark of a feeling that was hardly noticed.

> *3. After the last session, you did what you decided to do, and with the same good feeling.*

You are highlighting the new way of being and behaving that the patient was ready and willing to be and do at the end of last session. You may say:

> *You bought a dozen red roses for the old woman next door, and gave them to her, and you felt friendly and warm when you did this.*

Or you say:

> *You took your mother out to lunch, and you felt so open and straight, a little firm, when you told her you love her and she's the greatest mother in the world, but no more showing up at your place just like that! Call first!*

I tend to include this topic in the opening instructions of just about every session. This is a regular part of the opening because it is almost essential that the new way of being and behaving actually takes place, and also because its occurrence or its not being carried out often are scenes of strong feeling, just what the opening instructions seek. It is common that patients are very pleased and happy about carrying out the new way of being and behaving, or can feel awful about not doing it or doing it in a way that simply did not feel good at all.

I include this topic so regularly that patients come to expect a kind of report about how it went, for better or for worse. Occasionally, the patient says:

> *I knew you were going to ask about that, and yes, I did it and it was fantastic!*

> *4. You had that same, strong, bad feeling in the same, awful situation.*

Give the patient plenty of room to attend to the same attentional center or scene of strong bad feeling from the last session, or from the last several sessions. This is another topic that I include in the opening of almost every session.

It is important to start with the previous scenes of strong bad feeling, to give the patient plenty of opportunity to go to these same scenes, or to note that these central scenes are no longer occurring or with little or no bad feeling. Even if the actual scene occurred some time ago, give the patient plenty of room to see if he is still drawn toward that scene with the same bad feeling. It is important and helpful to include this as a regular topic, and to give the patient ample opportunity to attend to the bad-feelinged scenes from the previous session or sessions.

> *5. It's when you were being the kind of person you're terrified is really you. You may bring forth this topic by saying:*

> *You are scared to death of ending up being this kind of person. You are afraid that this is the kind of person you really are, and it's awful, and it started to show. It is*

horrible. It's like getting a glimpse of the kind of person you really are, the kind of person you are scared you'll end up being.

6. *It's one of the worst feelings you have ever had, a time when the feeling was probably one of the worst you've ever had.*

You are describing a time when the feeling was devastating, tore the patient apart, was so awful that the patient would never want to undergo such a feeling again:

It was so scary, so miserable, so racking, that it stands out in your mind. It was probably one of the worst times in your whole life. It may have happened recently, or some time ago, or many years ago. It may have happened only once or twice, or that worst feeling may have happened over and over again.

7. *You had a dream, in the last day or so, and you had strong feelings in the dream.*

The helpful thing about a dream is that it generally provides a ready-made scene of strong feeling (Mahrer, 1989c, 1990a). This saves a lot of work in the first step of the session, for dreams are marvelous in providing times when patients have strong feeling. You do not have to search around for a scene, especially when it is often hard to find a ready-made scene of strong feeling. I often include dreams in opening instructions, and I let patients know what kinds of dreams are useful for experiential work (Mahrer, 1989c):

8. *Your whole life, from the time you were little, there was something about you, something about the kind of person you've always been, that keeps you from being happy, that makes you feel bad:*

It is the thing that has been wrong with you your whole life. You've always sensed that there is something wrong with you, something about you that is different from the way others are, something that has always been wrong about you. It's always stopped you from being happy. It's always made you feel bad, given you bad feelings. People who knew you sensed that thing about you, reacted to you as being like that. All your life, the people that disliked you knew that there was something funny about you, something they disliked. Your whole life, you try, you do your best, but it's always for nothing; it never works out. There's never been someone who really cares about you, is genuinely interested in you; you just cannot be really close and intimate, at least for long. Whatever you do, you're never quite sure of yourself, never really confident like lots of other people are. You can't ever really show your feelings, never really express yourself right; it never comes out quite the way it should. Whatever you do, it's never quite good enough, never just right. What times come to your mind, times when you have the same awful feeling?

9. *There are some changes you are noticing lately, changes in you, changes in the way you are, in the way others are with you:*

These may be changes that you like. They make you feel good. They may be changes that bother you, that make you feel bad. They may be big changes, or they may be little changes, ones that maybe only you are noticing. Something different is happening in how you are, in the ways you act, in your feelings, in the ways you are with people. Things are getting worse. Things may be getting better. People are being different with you. People are reacting differently with you. It feels good. It feels ominous, scary, bad. These changes are happening recently. They may have been happening over the past months or more.

These are some useful topics to use in the opening instructions. You may think of other topics, but these are some of the main ones I use in many of the opening instructions, including some that I include in just about every session.

What Do You Do if the Opening Instructions Are Unsuccessful and Ineffective?

Provided that you are positioned correctly to receive whatever comes from the patient; provided that you are well into the aligned position as you give the instructions; and provided that you did a reasonably good job of giving the opening instructions, the patient will usually get a scene, will be attending to and describing it, and will be having a measure of the strong feeling. But suppose that you finish the opening instructions and none of this occurs?

Feel free to repeat the instructions, and this time try to be clearer, to do a better job. You may say:

All right, I'm ready to try again, if you are. Is this all right?

If, after doing the best you can in modifying the opening instructions, the patient still gets nothing, allow yourself to consider winding to a stop. It does not pay to push, to try forcing the patient to come up with something. Be willing to end the session. After about 15 to 25 minutes, you say:

OK, well we can wind to a close today. If you're not ready, that's fine . . . Now, about another session . . .

Almost always, you schedule another session.

Do you inquire into why the patient is not following the opening instructions? Shouldn't you try to find out what may be happening? There are two reasons why I leave all of this alone, why I may simply allow the session to wind to a close. One reason I do not probe is that I want to have a successful, effective session. If she is not ready to follow the opening instructions, I cannot force her to. Second, if I start attending mainly to the patient, trying to probe into her unreadiness or unwillingness, then I have plunged into a face-to-face role-relationship, and that is not experiential psychotherapy. Accordingly, if the patient is essentially not ready or willing, I let this be. I do not push. And I am ready to wind the session to a close.

Sometimes your opening instructions are followed by a prolonged silence. It is as if the patient is thinking, weighing this or that. With your attention out there, after 5 or 10 seconds, your screen will tend to diffuse away. You may say:

Say it out loud. Just keep talking, whatever it is, talk. Say it. Anything. Forget about pauses or silences . . . OK?

Sometimes the patient will open by talking directly to you, with little or no feeling, and without attending out there, to a scene of strong feeling. Under these conditions, give the opening instructions again. Give him plenty of opportunity to have a scene of strong feeling.

You have completed giving the opening instructions. Now the patient will say something.

WHEN THE PATIENT TALKS, FEEL THE FEELING AND SEE THE SCENE

When the patient talks, when the patient says and does something, you are generally quiet. You are listening. How do you listen? What do you listen for? You are looking out there to see whatever scenes are put there by what the patient is saying and doing. You are also having the feeling that occurs in you when you are aligned, when you see the scene and the patient's words are coming from inside you.

While it is very important to see the scene, the feeling that you have is critical. It is the feeling that will lead you to finding the scene of strong feeling. The feeling is your guide, your direction-finder, the thing you use to find the scene of strong feeling, whether it is this scene right here, or whether it is some other that you will find by using this guide. Accordingly, both the feeling and the scene are important, but of the two, it is the feeling that is more important.

Be Fully Aligned with Patient So You Can Feel the Feeling and See the Scene

As the patient talks, it is absolutely essential that virtually all of your attention is directed out there. You are looking out there, in front of you. At the same time, you are postured so that everything that comes from the patient is coming from inside you. The sounds, the words, the intonation, everything that the patient is doing and saying is coming from some part of you.

As the patient starts to say something, your eyes are closed, and you are ready to see whatever her words bring forth to see. When she says: "my mother . . . ," you see mother. If she says, "down at the cottage," you see an image of down at the cottage. Furthermore, these words are coming from you, from inside you. You are saying these words, and you are seeing what these words put here for you to see.

You will see scenes.   As all of your attention is out there, you will receive and see all kinds of scenes, images, objects, situations. You will see people, flowers, headaches, landscapes, babies. You will be with a woman at a table, you will be sitting alone in your room, you will be arguing with a devil or a neighbor or a best friend.

You are so sensitive to what is produced out there that, without trying, without effort, these scenes may be produced fresh as the patient talks:

> *My brother is staying with us . . . [an image of brother being in the house] . . . and he knew my wife before I did [an image of brother sitting and talking with Ann, some years ago] . . . He's always liked her [scene of brother being with Ann, and thinking out loud that he likes her a lot] . . . And he says, "Ann is really something!" [Scene of brother leering at Ann, touching her body, and Ann enjoying the sexual attention] . . .*

Sometimes the scenes quickly replace one another. Sometimes a scene remains relatively stable.

The scene may consist only of some focused attentional center, some thing, a defined object. He says:

> *This damned headache just comes whenever it wants. It's always there, like it can get me whenever it wants.*

You "see" a headache, a defined thing. It lurks about and then strikes whenever it wants. You may see a cartoon character that is the headache.

The attentional center can be whatever the patient focuses on. If the patient says:

My depression is destroying my life. It'll never let go. The drugs don't get near it,

see the depression, dancing around the effects of the drugs, grabbing hold of his life, never letting go.

This fear is something I just damned want to get rid of. I am going to get rid of it!

Picture the fear. Maybe you see the fear all worried and scared about the threats. Maybe you see it rolling its eyes and regarding the patient as full of bluffs, empty threats.

Patients often talk about some feeling. By being aligned, you will be able to "see" the feeling that the patient is talking about, referring to, attending to. When you listen in this way, the referred-to feeling takes on a form and a shape. It may be a shimmering green blob or a cartoonlike character. But it is a thing, something you see.

You will feel feelings.   Something very special happens when you are aligned with the patient in a scene of strong feeling, and the patient's words are coming in through you. The something very special is that you feel feelings.

You feel the feeling because as she is describing a scene of strong feeling, you are in that scene, and her words are coming from inside you. She says:

My father just told me no, he wasn't coming to the party, and he just walked out!

Not only are you seeing him say that he isn't coming, but you are saying these words. As you are saying:

My father just told me no, he wasn't coming to the party, and he just walked out!

something will happen inside you. It may be disbelief, outrage, anger, being slapped in the face by him. You will feel some feeling.

Because you are so aligned, you are probably more sensitively receptive to the scenes evoked by the patient's words than she is. Also, you are probably more receptive to the feelings than she is. You have feelings because you are in the scene put there by the patient's words coming in and through you, and because her words are coming in and through you as you are being in that scene.

Use Whatever Feeling and Scene Are Occurring in You

Get yourself as aligned as you can. When the patient talks, make sure that practically all of you is attending out there, and the patient's words are wholly coming from you, in you, and through you. Once you are aligned, trust whatever scenes and feelings occur in you. There are no other data for you to use.

Use whatever scene is here.   Use whatever scene is here for you. It may be vague and diffuse. That is all right. You may just see a finger or a face or a piece of candy. Use it. You may get a rush of scenes, one right after the other. Use them. Use whatever scenes are here.

The scene you get may be stimulated by the patient's words, but the connection may be hard to trace. The scene just seems to appear. The patient says:

. . . so, yes, I am going to do it, for me! I damned well can do what I want!

You may see a scene of being at the office, just walking around, being with his colleagues. Or you may see a friendly force or agency, pushing him to do something, but tolerantly going along with his wanting to do whatever he wants. The scene you get may sometimes seem to come from almost nowhere. Use whatever scene is here, for you, right now.

Just be aligned and let the scenes appear, no matter how disconnected or farfetched the scene may seem to be when you listen to the tape. He may ostensibly be talking about problems at the office as he says:

Well, no one really liked him when he was head of the department for a year while Todd was in London, but I think he's easier to talk with now. Sam and Betty agree with me, but I don't know . . . I still can't, don't, really trust him. Maybe that's just me . . .

You may be seeing the fellow he is talking about, seeing what it is like talking with him. But you may get other scenes. You may see a man enjoying his massive erection, or you see a lion attacking an antelope, or you see the patient looking in a bathroom mirror, and there are big yellow dots all over his face and neck. You use the images you get when you are thoroughly aligned. Because you are so fully aligned, there is virtually no removed part of you to think:

What weird things! What are these? How do these relate to what he is saying? They don't at all!

You use the scenes and images that you get.

Use the scenes that are here even if the patient's words seem to be weird and crazy from the vantage point of the therapist who is outside, external, face-to-face. The patient opens by saying:

I can make others do whatever I want. It's because of the apple. I have always known what they think, and now I can make them think any way I want. I am Willa, and I was burned. A witch. That's my former life. And I was a princess, but the snake killed me. I have the soul, the power . . . They send me messages in the newspaper. It is always the headlines on the front page. They are my people. I have come to live on earth as the messenger. I have the key to all the people on this planet. I am the first one. If I fail, then the earth is doomed, and there will be no more life on earth . . .

You have scenes. You see scenes. All you see are the scenes.

Because you are aligned, you do not have thoughts about, or reactions to, whatever scene is put here for you. You do not have such thoughts as:

She is not ready for this scene . . . This is like the scene she mentioned last session . . . She is indirectly trying to convey messages to me about my pushing her too hard about her hesitancy in trusting me . . . This relates to her childhood relationships with her stepmother.

You just get scenes, no private stream of thoughts.

Use whatever feeling occurs in you.   When you are aligned, when there is some scene before you, and when the patient's words are coming in and through you, you will almost certainly have some kind of feeling. Use that feeling, whatever it is.

KDS

Do not try to apply clinical reasoning to turn the feeling you get into some other feeling. Do not reason that patients with this depressed feeling really have underlying hostility. Do not try to convert the bad or scary feeling into one that is better, more acceptable, easier to handle, not so bad or scary. If he is in a scene in which he inadvertently touches the lady on her breast, and the feeling you get is frozen shock and embarrassment, do not interpret this into rampant sexual feelings. Merely receive and use whatever feeling occurs in you. There is no removed therapist who weighs whether or not this is the right feeling, or who does things to get some other feeling from this immediate feeling. You get the feeling that you get.

On the other hand, use the feeling that occurs in you rather than the feeling that the patient says she is having. The patient says:

Two months ago I had an abortion, and ever since I felt depressed, like killing myself. I feel so damned depressed.

As you are saying these words, the feeling you get may indeed be overwhelming depression, heavy unhappiness, total gloom. But the words also may be accompanied with a feeling of spitted-out anger, wholesale annoyance, erupting violence, and this is the feeling you get. A patient may say that he is feeling tight, tense, anxious:

I failed my medical specialty exam. I get so tense, even thinking about it. My whole body gets anxious for any kind of test. I feel so tense . . .

Yet, as these words come through you, the feeling is one of crying, giving up, inability to cope, enveloping depression. This is the feeling you use, whether or not it is the feeling referred to by the words.

You are so closely aligned that the feeling you get is subtly determined by the way the words are said, by the intonation, the manner, the vocal quality. He says, referring to the old cat:

She's been gone two days. I know some day she won't come back.

Spoken in one way, the feeling is one of steeling oneself for the awful thing, tearful disbelief, forlorn sadness. Spoken in another way, the feeling is one of devilish hope, wicked expectancy, good riddance. She is describing her mother coming to her home, and the usual first thing mother does:

She opens the door and sniffs. Cigarettes! Then she gets the look on her face, always the same look.

Spoken in one way, the feeling is cuddling mother, loving her, enjoying her. Said in another way, the feeling is tightness, ready for the fight, the confrontation.

How do you know if you are accurate and objective in the feeling that you get? The answer is that you are accurate and objective if you get the feeling by being fully aligned. In other words, this is not much of an issue, once you are aligned. If several therapists listen to the recording, and all are reasonably aligned, they will tend to have just about the same feeling. You use the feeling that you get. It is sufficiently accurate and objective when you are in the aligned state.

Perhaps the most helpful guideline is that your attention should always be "out there," with as much attention as possible directed out there. When you do this, it is easy to position yourself so that the patient's words are coming in and through you. When you are aligned, things are right with the world, and the feeling that you get is reasonably accurate and objective.

In other words, when the feelings are objective and accurate, you will probably not be having thoughts that your feelings are objective and accurate. Most likely, you will only know when your feelings and scenes are not accurate. Your patient is saying:

> *I am going to kill him. He does enough harm to me and my daughter. I know where he lives. I'd like to put an end to that bastard, and I've got the gun to do it.*

You will have a hint that your feelings are not especially objective and accurate when you are having external, removed, private thoughts about her actually killing her ex-husband, and thoughts about your testifying in court. You can know when your feelings and scenes are probably not objective and accurate, but you will probably not consciously think that this feeling seems to be objective and accurate.

Never, but never, do you seek confirmation or verification from the patient. Doing so almost demands that the patient pull out of the scene and into having a conversation with you in which each of you is attending mainly to the other. If he answers your question, you both are becoming entwined into a role-relationship trap. For example, he says:

> *Yeah, I guess I feel something like that. Yeah, that's right. I'm amazed that you can know me so well. It's like you really understand . . .*

You are no longer both looking out there, looking for a scene of strong feeling. Whether the patient says you are correct or incorrect will not help either of you in verifying the accuracy and objectivity of the feeling that you got. All in all, asking the patient for verification is useless and interferes with the work.

When the patient talks, you are to feel the feeling and see the scene, and you use whatever scene is here and whatever feeling occurs in you.

Be Sensitively Receptive to Implied Feelings and Scenes

When you are thoroughly aligned with the patient, you can be supremely sensitive and receptive to feelings and scenes that are implied in what the patient is saying and doing. You don't know or think that this feeling and scene are implied. You are merely in a state of being sensitively receptive to these implied feelings and scenes.

Be receptive to the wickedly pleasurable, implied feelings and scenes. When you are fully aligned, you can be sensitive to what is implied, to wicked pleasures, devilishly delightful, deliciously tabooed feelings and scenes. Typically, these are masked, disguised, hidden behind ostensibly bad feelings:

> *I had no idea that it was that late! I thought it was only around two or so, and it was after five! I left him waiting at the airport for three hours!*

He is oozing guilt and embarrassment, and the feeling is wicked pleasure at leaving him stewing there at the airport.

> *I didn't mean to blurt out that Peg was pregnant! I don't know what got into me! Honest!*

Wicked pleasure. Underneath the shock or the excuse or the dismay can be implied feelings of sheer wicked pleasure, nastiness, secret delights, exciting feelings of tabooed satisfaction.

Being aligned enables you to be free of the conspicuous surface bad feeling, and thereby to receive the wickedly pleasurable implied scene and feeling. She is bathing in bad feeling as she is telling about doing so terribly at rehearsal, how she played so miserably:

> . . . *it threw everyone off! . . . they couldn't play! How terrible I am. What a failure. The others hate me! I have no talent at anything.*

If you set aside the conspicuous surface feeling, what is the scene and what is the feeling? It is a nasty, mischievous, devilish little gnome cackling:

> *I just love being lousy! Do I shock you all? Do I shock you all? Do I screw up your rehearsal? I do? Ha ha ha ha ha!*

While the patient feels bad, you can listen by letting the conspicuous, surface bad feeling go and, instead, being receptive to the wickedly pleasurable, implied feelings and scenes.

Be receptive to the implied, exaggerated, caricatured, catastrophized, tragicomic extremes.   Being sensitively receptive means that you can be sensitively receptive to the absolutely extreme scenes constructed by the patient's words. Be open to the exaggerated, caricatured, catastrophized, tragicomic extremes. There is no law that the constructed scenes must be within straitlaced constraints. He says:

> *Sometimes I feel like I am going to lose my mind; I'll go off the deep end.*

If you open up the ceiling, what scene do you get? Do you picture him a raving lunatic, screeching in a dungeon of the bowels of an insane asylum? Do you see him as a dancing elf on the top of the monument, crazy as a loon? Do you see him plunging downward, off the deep end, a body with no mind?

When she says, "I am scared of getting old. I'd die first," what scene do you get? Can you see her around 97, scraggly and bony, with about a hundred disheveled hairs on her head, shaking and trembling, grotesquely ugly, holding a rope tied into a noose, and trying vainly to get up on a dilapidated, shaky, old kitchen chair? Be sensitively receptive to the extreme scenes brought forth in you by the naively received words of the patient.

Be receptive to the other side implied by the hopes and goals, yearnings and wantings, insistent assertions of what is certainly true.   When you are wholly attending out there, and when the patient's words come in and through you, you may be receptive to the other side of what the patient seems to be reaching for or insisting is really true:

> *I want to be closer to my husband . . . The thing I want from therapy is to feel closer to people . . .*

The seeking for closeness, intimacy, and oneness may be said in such a way that implies the awful other side, the lurking isolation, separateness, distance, emptiness, imprisonment in a self that is forever far from others, that can never be known by others

(Angyal, 1965; Fromm, 1956; Laing, 1975; Mahrer, 1982, 1978\1989d; May, 1968). Be receptive to the possibility of the feeling of desperate isolation and aloneness.

Patients voice their yearnings, their precious hopes and goals for therapy. You should at least be open to the implied other side, to the dashed hopes. It is as if the other side is saying, ". . . but I know it will never happen!" The patient says, "I want to be successful in my work," and the implied other side says, "But I know it will not happen." The patient says, "I want to understand my son, to be closer to him," and the other side says, "But I know that will never happen." He says, "I want to have good sex, like we had years ago," and the implied other side says, "But I know that will never happen." The desperate "efforts after" are often filled with the implied other side that knows they are nothing more than desperate efforts after.

Often, patients will insist on something being unquestionably true, as if there is some inner critic or disbelieving opponent who knows that it is not true at all. For example, she says:

> *This time, the marriage is going to work! I know it! Fred is the right man for me. Finally. This marriage is going to work!*

It is as if there is some implied other part that knows this marriage is headed for a breakup like the last two; it's not going to work. The older man is insisting on how wonderful it is to be old.

> *Don't have to worry so much. I like being old. Don't have to struggle. I'm happier now.*

It is as if he is arguing against some inner agency that is bent on telling him the truth:

> *You're old! You're an old man! It's over, kiddo!*

You can feel the feeling and see the scene by being sensitively receptive to the whole range of implied feelings and scenes.

How Do You Feel the Feeling and See the Scene . . .

Some relatively common conditions occur when you have given the opening instructions and are aligned with the patient. Here are some special guidelines for some of these conditions.

When the patient is simply being in a feeling state with no explicit scene?   He is simply crying, with little or no indication of any explicit scene or attentional center, perhaps punctuated with occasional words such as, "Oh God . . . What's the use . . . I feel so awful . . ." Sometimes she may just wallow in a state of anger:

> *Well, fuck! God damn! Sometimes I could just kill someone! I take it, all my life! Sometimes there's just a damned limit! Shit! It's not worth it! Damn!*

Sometimes there is just a feeling state with no explicit scene. Sometimes there is a feeling state and a headlong rush from one fragment of a scene to another and on and on to many others. Sometimes the patient seems to be caught in a dreamlike state, drifting here and there in a kind of ethereal world of fleeting metaphors, images, fantasies.

The important thing is to get the feeling, and this is generally easy because the patient is wallowing in the feeling state. But it helps to see whatever scenes seem to be occurring when you are bathed in this feeling state. Just let yourself be sensitive to whatever scenes the patient's words convey. Even if the words only give little cues or hints, let them construct whatever scene they provide for you. Then search. Look for when this feeling happened or when these scenes may have occurred.

When the patient is attending to an entity that is a self, a problem, a personal quality, a feeling?   What the patient is attending to does not have to be a thing in the external world like a washing machine or her brother or the new car. It is common that the patient is attending to something that has no generally accepted form and shape. Yet it is here, the focal center of attention. Patients spend a lot of time attending to things such as: their selves, their problems, their personal qualities, their feelings.

Your attention is focused on your self. It is a real thing, an entity that you actually see. Or the patient may literally see herself. She sees herself sitting in the corner, reading, or she stands over here and sees herself over there, talking to her friend. A fair amount of what patients say tends to define and construct a self, a real thing that you can witness. It is here in front of you, put there by the patient's own words.

When patients construct a self out there, the therapist is sensitive to the feeling that is occurring. There may be a feeling of being in love with the self; it is so precious and kissable. The feeling may be one of avuncular protection, watching over, being here to help the needy little self. The feeling may be one of hating, of repulsion toward that self.

In the same way, patients often will define a problem, or a personal quality, about which they have some kind of feeling. Allow the attended-to problem or problematic quality to assume a form and shape. When you are aligned, you can see these problems and problematic qualities as having a tangible form and shape. It is as if they become real, and you are privy to the feeling as the patient is attending to them.

Be receptive to the actual characteristics of the problem or problematic quality as he says:

> *It's my temper. It just flares up. I have no idea when it's going to come. Nothing can stop it! I tried drugs. My doctor gave me drugs. But they didn't even have any effect!*

Can you see the temper? When you see it, and with the patient's words coming in and through you, you have a feeling, perhaps one of pride in the little bugger, pride in its toughness and invulnerability to things like drugs.

Patients talk about problems by endowing them with qualities and characteristics. If you didn't know that she was talking about a problem, you could easily think that she was talking about a person or some actual thing. This applies to any kind of problem: my alcoholism, my being oversexed, this tension, my fear of being abandoned, my agoraphobia, my dependency, my attraction to little girls, my nail-biting. Whatever the problem, it is given form and shape as patients attend to it and say:

> *I've had it for years . . . It is getting stronger lately . . . I got it after the war in my country . . . I've tried just about everything, but nothing does any good . . . Where could it have come from? . . . It takes me over and I have no idea when it's going to happen . . . I really want to get rid of it . . . If it keeps up, I just don't know what I'll do . . . I think I can live with it, but I've got to keep in control, always . . . It's wearing me down . . .*

When patients are keyed onto the problem, you can actually see it. Once you see it, you can also have the accompanying feeling of having a long-term buddy and confidante, someone you always fight and bicker with, nevertheless, have stayed with for many years. The feeling is one of reluctant pride in its toughness, its single-mindedness. The feeling is bitching and carping about it, incessant whining and complaining about it. There is a feeling of being bad and wicked, of being punished by it, of somehow deserving it as a curse, a penance for your essential badness. The feeling is absolute satisfaction and fascination with it; let's study everything about it, know every detail about it. The feeling is one of struggle, of back and forth fighting, of having a worthy opponent with whom you can fight for years and years, keeping a running score of who is winning, who is on top, winning the contest. Once the patient focuses on the problem, be receptive to its form and shape, and especially to the feeling that is here as the patient talks about it, attends to it.

In much the same way, patients attend to personal qualities and personality characteristics. Much like their "self" or their "problem," patients can focus on their temper, loyalty, tendency to fall in love, never liking anyone getting too close, sense of humor, cheapness with money, sheer talkativeness, laziness, having to have everything in order, bossiness, toughness, ability to handle pressure, and loads of other personal qualities. Added to this pot of personal qualities are hundreds of personal qualities contributed by psychotherapists, especially those with a psychodynamic bent. Patients can attend to their ambivalence, aggressive drive, weak ego, anal retentiveness, obsessive tendency, genital inhibitions, regressive tendency, repression of impulses, resistances, compulsions, narcissism, exhibitionism, masochism, projections, and on and on.

Be receptive to the feeling that is here as he is attending to personal qualities and characteristics. Be receptive to the fascination as the patient and therapist collude in endless exploration, discovery, and exciting analysis of almost every aspect of one personal quality and characteristic after another.

In much the same way, a patient may be attending to a feeling, talking about and focusing on the feeling. Listen so as to allow this feeling to be its own entity, a thing with form and shape. See the feeling that is attended to. He says:

> It's a terrible feeling. I wish I could get rid of it, but I can't. It's always there. Soon as I wake up, I feel lost, confused, never sure about anything. Its always there and I can't get rid of it. Tried lots of things. I don't know what causes it. Damn.

As he says these words, slowly, there is a feeling of giving up, of helplessness, of no longer struggling against it.

Use the feeling that is occurring in you, as the patient's words come in and through you, rather than the feeling that he says he is having. The patient indicates that he had poisoned his brother's dog:

> I feel sad. He was always causing trouble, but somehow I miss him, and I feel sad about his not being here. I've been feeling sad about him lately.

The feeling accompanying these words may be sadness. But the therapist may get some other feeling such as a tension, a threat of being accused, a trying to get around the implied accusation.

Patients may describe what they are feeling, but there usually is quite a difference between the feelings they refer to and the feelings in the person who is saying the words:

> I am feeling so free, easy, spontaneous, and this is good because it is new for me. I like having this feeling. It is so fresh.

Some therapists might conclude that the patient is feeling free, easy, and spontaneous, and the evidence is that the patient said so. However, experiential listening might yield a feeling of quiet bitterness, a removed unexpressed anger. Feelings are often the focal center of attention. Listen for the feeling in the person who is saying the words, and not for the feeling that the patient talks about or refers to.

Yet the same guiding principle applies. Attend to whatever is put there for you to see, the scene, the focal center. Feel the feeling in you as the patient's words come in and through you. You do this for everything, even when the attentional center or scene involves a self, a problem, a personal quality, or a feeling.

When the patient's private and removed words are cast in the context of the scene? Your attention is almost predominantly out there. You see things. This means that you may well be living and being in some scene. When he says:

Sam opens the door, comes in, and just announces that he won't be paying his share of the rent any more . . . .

What do you see? Do you see Sam opening the door, coming in, and announcing that he won't be paying his share of the rent any more? Suppose that he continues, almost with no pause:

That bastard! What a helluva nerve!

As these words are coming in and through you, are you still attending to Sam, hearing Sam say words about not paying his share of the rent? If you are right here with Sam, then are the words about his being a bastard included or excluded from the scene? In the experiential way of listening, these "private thoughts" may be open and public. Sam hears you. Now what is the feeling in you? Is it a feeling of being confrontational, yelling at Sam, openly exploding at him? The feeling is quite different once the private words are opened into the alive and real scene. These little asides, these comments, yield some intriguing new feelings when they are not taken out of the ongoing scene.

My father is getting old. I remember last week, he had trouble just holding the paper up. His arms are so thin. He has to sit just right and prop the paper on his lap. But then he can't see too well, and I offered to read the paper to him . . . God, I love him . . .

When he says, "God, I love him," are these words said out loud to his father? If so, the feeling may be one of showing your love, expressing your warmth and love.

Listen for the feeling by allowing the out-of-scene private thoughts and asides to occur in the context of the ongoing scenes. Sometimes the feelings come from the words being said out loud. Sometimes the words are blurted out as if the patient is no longer in the scene, but you can receive the feeling by remaining in the scene. You are thereby open to a rich set of feelings, some open and shown in the scene, some hidden and private, but poured into the context of the scene.

When the patient's words seem to be addressed toward the therapist?   I say "seem to be" addressed toward the therapist because the patient's words are received differently when the therapist is attending out there, with the patient's words coming in and through the therapist, as compared with when the therapist is face-to-face, attending mainly to the patient. When you are aligned, the patient's words occur within the context that is out there. This context makes it easier to hear the words differently than if you were face-to-face. You "miss" hearing the patient talking to you, to the extent that you are truly aligned.

In any case, try to keep your attention out there. Always look out there. The feeling you get is with your attention directed out there, no matter what the patient says. For example, suppose he says:

> *I better not tell you her name cause I think you know her.*

As I say these words, I am with some other person, possibly a therapist type, and the feeling is being risky, lightly tantalizing, provoking, seductive, mischievous. I can receive the feeling because I am the one, along with the patient, who is saying the words.

Occasionally, the patient's words come across as addressed directly at you, and you are face-to-face with the patient. You no longer see out there. No longer are the patient's words coming in and through you. Instead, you are attending mainly to the patient. When this happens, you are no longer in a position to feel the feelings and see the scenes. You may do your best to return to the aligned posture and go back to work.

So far, the patient is talking. You are essentially quiet. The main thing going on in you is that you are seeing some scene, some thing, person, object, attentional center out there. You are also having a feeling. The feeling is essential. After you have given the opening instructions, you are programmed to listen and to see the scene and feel the feeling. You now see a scene and feel a feeling. What do you do?

KEEP SEARCHING UNTIL THE PATIENT ARRIVES AT A SCENE OF STRONG FEELING

If your instructions were just about perfect, and if the patient were fully ready and willing, the patient would start right out by having a strong feeling in the context of some scene. After your excellent opening instructions, she immediately goes to a scene of strong feeling:

> *I got up! I really got up! My sister's boyfriend was acting like a damned obnoxious asshole! Making remarks about her being a social worker. I wasn't nice!! I got up! And I said, 'OK, you asshole, I've had enough. If I stay longer, I'll kick your ass in, you damned asshole'—and I actually left!*

It would be delightful if we found a scene of strong feeling as soon as the opening instructions ended. But that does not happen often.

Your aim is to find a scene of strong feeling. From the moment you finish giving the opening instructions, you listen for the scene and the feeling, and you try to find a scene of strong feeling. This is your mission, your goal. You accomplish this by being programmed to achieve this goal, and by using whatever feelings lead you to find a scene of strong feeling.

You Are Programmed to Find a Scene of Strong Feeling

By "programmed," I mean that you are set or geared to find a scene of strong feeling. You know what the immediate feeling is. You have some idea of what the scene or context or attentional center is. The question that guides what you say, almost every time you say something, is "What is the scene, the time, the context, in which this immediate feeling is strong?" Your program is this simple. The scene may be the scene that you have right now. Or it may be that this feeling is strong in some other scene. In any case, whether it is this scene or some other one, you are quietly programmed to find a scene of strong feeling.

Use the feeling to look for the scene in which this feeling is strong.   You get the feeling that is here right now. When you talk, you ask the patient to find some scene, some time or place, when this feeling is strong. Just about each time you talk, you should identify the feeling, identify the scene, and then invite the patient to find a scene where this feeling is strong. You and the patient are quite free to go further into this immediate scene, or to pursue some other time and place when this feeling is strong. It may be somewhere here, in this general scene, or it may be any other time, any other place. The possibilities are wide open, but you are looking, searching, seeing what scene is the one in which this feeling is strong. The feeling is being the victim, helpless, done to, and the immediate scene is here with mother, in the kitchen, with mother criticizing me: "When is this feeling strong, this feeling of being the victim, helpless, done to, maybe here with mother or any other time at all, recently, long ago?"

Show him what to do. Be clear, both in what he is to do and what you both are looking for. Be clear in describing the feeling: "It's a feeling of being mean, cruel, uncaring, heartless." "It is the feeling of being free, liberated, light, able to do what I want." Be clear about what you mean by "scene." Let him know that you are looking for some time, some situation, where the feeling is strong. It may be here in this general scene that is present right now. It may be one that occurred quite recently, or one that happened in the past year or so. You may open the possibilities to include any time in the person's life, even when he was a little boy. No matter whether it is recent or remote, you are looking for a time, some scene, when this feeling is strong.

The opening scene may be one in which the feeling is somewhat mild or rather strong. She is crying and the scene is being in her apartment, in bed, with thoughts racing through her head, thoughts about bloody eyes, rotting bodies, entrails. The feeling is crying, being helpless, weak, vulnerable. You say:

> *Yes . . . cry . . . cry . . . feeling like just crying more. Yes. Do it . . . And feeling so help- less, weak, vulnerable . . . When this feeling is so full, so . . . strong . . . when is it? Here? With all these thoughts about bloody eyes, rotting bodies . . . or . . . any time . . . Some other time . . .*

Her crying deepens, and she says:

> *My sister . . . She was killed by the soldiers . . . they stabbed her . . . over and over . . . And my mother and me, we were screaming . . . [hard crying] . . . My baby . . .*

Always look for when the feeling is strong, whether this means going further into this general scene or, as is more common, looking elsewhere.

Leave room for the scene to be right here in this general context. You say:

> *Don starts right out with a nasty shot at you. A look! Hello, pea-brain . . . and the feeling is tightness, like being hit, right in the pit of your stomach. When is it that you've had this feeling really strong? It's very strong, this feeling. It may be here with Don, or some other time . . .*

She says:

No, it's with Don, . . . he's with me and my sister, and the waiter hands the bill to me, cause I asked for it, and he just grabs it from my hand, says I can't add—and he doesn't even pay the bill! He says it's right and tosses it off to me!

The net result is that, just about each time you say something, you describe the feeling, the scene, and you invite the person to look for when this feeling is strong, either somewhere in this scene or elsewhere. If, until you find a scene of strong feeling, about 70 to 80 percent of your statements include these elements, you are doing what you should be doing. On the other hand, if only about 10 to 20 percent or so of your statements include these elements, then you are not doing an especially good job of enabling the patient to find a scene of strong feeling.

The process is quite simple, mainly because you are so programmed. You give the opening instructions. The patient talks. You get a feeling and a scene. Then you work with the patient to find the scene in which this feeling is strong.

What do you do when the feeling is relatively strong, and there is no special scene? After the opening instructions, the patient talks, and you get a relatively strong feeling. However, there is no special scene, the scene is not even vaguely present, or there is a rushed concatenation of scenes. Whether the feeling is bad or good, all you get is the relatively strong feeling and no special scene. What do you do?

With your attention out there, search for a scene of strong feeling. It may seem to make sense that you will access the inner experiencing when the patient is screaming, wailing, pounding, undergoing powerful feeling. However, I do not find that the inner experiencing accesses when a feeling is merely strong. I find that the main thing is that the strong feeling merely gets stronger. I want to open up or get at or access an inner experiencing, and that seems to require a situational context. Therefore, your job is to put this strong feeling into some scene, to find a scene of strong feeling.

When the patient is in a state of sheer strong feeling, it seems useful to search for some recent incident, some relatively recent time or scene (Mahrer, 1972). If your search for recent scenes seems to yield little or nothing, open the window and look for scenes from a while ago. It is easy for patients to drift in some strong-feelinged state for days or months or years. You may have to go to some time ago, but there is almost always some situational context in which this feeling is strong. Actively search. There is some time when the feeling of being very gloomy, very sad, is very strong. He scans the past weeks, a month or so ago. Nothing. Go back. Look for some time, perhaps six months ago, a year or so ago, a time that simply comes to mind when he wallows in the strong feeling of being sad, gloomy. It was almost a year ago. He wanted to be one of the athletes who tries to qualify for the Olympic track team. Maybe there was a chance. However, when he came in seventh in the local trials, he knew he was not even good enough to try to go to the next few rounds. The dream was over. Afterward, alone, he cried. It really hurt.

A bad feeling can persist all by itself for months or years. However, to be useful, it helps to find some appropriate scene. For example, he is walking along the street and a shot rings out. The young fellow lounging against the outdoor telephone booth is hit. There is pandemonium as others rush to the bloodied young fellow. The patient was almost pulverized with feeling, but it was all inside. However, from that moment, he was filled with a feeling of being at loose ends, anxious, gloomy, frightened, low. Your job is to start from this pervasive feeling, which occurs everywhere and nowhere, and to go to some fitting scene such as the one in which the young fellow is shot.

When the feeling is moderately strong, and there is no defined scene, use the feeling to find a scene of powerful feeling. Often this scene occurred recently. Often you have to go back months or years to the last time the feeling was powerful.

Are some kinds of feelings and scenes especially useful? Are some "dangerous"? Are there some kinds of feelings or some kinds of scenes that are better, more appropriate, more helpful or useful? Are recent scenes and feelings better than earlier ones? Are "traumatic" incidents better than just ordinary incidents and feelings? The general answer is no. Just look for a scene of strong feeling.

I have a moderate preference for two kinds of scenes. One is from more or less recent life. I find that it is helpful to look for and to identify current times when feelings were quite strong. The other kind of preference is for scenes of excruciatingly powerful feeling. These could have occurred at any time, from a year or so ago or from when the patient was a young adult, adolescent, child, or infant. It was when his father beat him up, when the patient was 11 years old, and then his father walked into the other room, locked the door, and shot himself. It was two years ago, when he saw his wife in the street, dead, in a pool of blood, and the neighbors not only saw nothing, but had him sent to the mental hospital because he truly insisted that he had seen what he had seen.

Almost every patient has several such times of wrenchingly catastrophic feelings. However, and this is why such times are so very useful, it is almost a rule that these catastrophic incidents are rarely used. It is as if these terrible scenes are insulated, enveloped with a generalized bad feeling, and talked around. But they are almost never used. When these scenes of powerful feeling are not used, then the consequence is often that there is a mild or moderate bad feeling state from then on.

What about feelings where the patient seems on the verge of going crazy, falling apart, plunging into craziness? The patient is terrified of his flesh turning into millions of worms. He is shrieking about falling into a pit of lunacy. She is sobbing as she is being enveloped by madness, and cannot stop what is happening. He is pleading to make the visions stop or he knows he will be berserk. She is horrified by the pounding imminence of the very end of her existence and going out of her mind. Are there limits on the feelings when they involve the patient's sinking into a pit of madness and trying desperately to avoid the horrible consequences, calling out for help against the crazy catastrophe? The answer is no. If you are programmed to find the scene of strong feeling, you use all of this to find scenes of strong feeling.

Virtually any scene or feeling is usable to find a scene of strong feeling. When you are aligned and work toward finding such a scene, few if any scenes or feelings seem to encourage patients to become savage, insane, to do dangerous things, to become deranged evil monsters. Are some scenes or feelings "dangerous"? My answer is no. The answer is no from the theory of experiential psychotherapy as well as in terms of what has actually occurred, and not occurred, in sessions.

You Are Fully Aligned with the Patient in Finding a Scene of Strong Feeling

You are essentially programmed to find a scene of strong feeling. You are wholly aligned with the patient in the search. This means that you are wholesomely undergoing the feeling, receiving and having the feeling, practically filled with the feeling. This means that you are attending out there, living and being in the scene. And you are also dedicated and programmed to finding a scene of strong feeling.

You feel, have, and show this immediate feeling to at least a moderate degree.   You are like an extremely sensitive feeling meter, plugged into the patient. As the feeling is occurring in the patient, it also is happening in you, except that it is happening at least moderately in you. If it is relatively low or mild in the patient, the feeling is happening more fully in you. If the feeling is occurring moderately or strongly in the patient, it is happening to at least that level in you. Indeed, you are feeling as much or more than the patient is.

Furthermore, when you talk, no matter what you are saying, you are giving voice to the feeling. In you, the feeling is here to at least a moderate degree. You show the feeling. It shines forth as you talk, and with at least moderate strength and fullness. You may be describing the feeling or saying something about the scene or telling him what to do. Whatever you are saying, the feeling is showing in you to at least a moderate degree.

This is a departure from the way most therapists talk. Your job is to be so aligned that you plug into the immediate feeling that is here in you. Then, all the time that you are looking for a scene of strong feeling, you are having and voicing this feeling to at least a moderate degree. You are the alive version of the feeling that is stirred up in you. What you say comes out as if you are being the voice of the feeling of being proud of, respectful of, admiring. Or your voice comes from the feeling of jealousy, green competition. Or your voice is jaw-clenched anger and violence. You are the alive feeling because this feeling is happening in you. You are this feeling. You are this feeling to at least a moderate degree, as you look for a scene of strong feeling.

If you are with your brother's little boy, and the feeling is being disgusted with the little brat, everything you say oozes with this feeling. Your voice is radiant with disgust as you search for when this feeling is strong:

> *At the table here, and watching little Jerome eat. The little monster. It's a feeling of real pure disgust! Yech! What a repulsive little kid! When is it that a feeling like this is strong? Disgust! Is it specially sometime with the little kid. Or any other time, with anyone, and the feeling is, "Actually, I can't stand this person! What an obnoxious sonuvabitch!"*

Each word that you say is as if the feeling of disgust were talking, and with at least a moderate feeling of disgust.

It may be a good feeling, or it may bad, hurtful, painful. But whatever its nature and content, you feel it rather strongly, fully, saturatedly, as you talk, no matter what you are saying as you search for the scene of strong feeling. The feeling may easily switch almost each time the patient talks. You feel, have, and show whatever feeling is here, and at least a moderate degree. Right now, the feeling is envy, jealousy, competitiveness. Soon it is anger and annoyance. Then the feeling is being powerful, strong, very firm. You are continuously searching for the scene of strong feeling, and you are continuously feeling, having, and showing the immediate feeling to at least a moderate degree, even as it moves from one feeling to another.

You are continuously and fully attending out there, fully being in this immediate scene. All the time that you are looking for a scene of strong feeling, being aligned means that virtually all your attention is continuously and fully out there, and it means that you are just about fully living and being in this immediate scene. Practically none of your attention is on the patient, or on your own private, removed thoughts. All your attention is out there.

Searching for the scene of strong feeling means that you literally see the scene as you talk, and you literally are being in this context. Say these words, and be in the scene you are describing:

> *Here at the desk, sitting, and the report is done. Just sitting here. The report is on the desk. Done . . .*
>
> *Being in bed, just a little boy, seven or eight. Lying in bed, and the thing is hard, this thing, my penis, and touching it. Wow! No one better come in. Kind of watching. No one better come in. It's hard. It feels . . . good . . .*

As you say these words, you are seeing out there, and you are living and being in the scene.

All your attention is out there, even when you address the patient. You say:

> *This feeling, when is it strong? Really full, inside you, even if it doesn't show, or it shows. Yeah. Somewhere, maybe here with them. Or some other time, somewhere else . . .*

As you talk, your attention is always out there, even when you merely ask if it is all right to search.

> *Is it all right to look around, to see when this feeling is strong? After all, it's a bad feeling, you know, feeling put down, like you're no good, not really worth anything. It's painful. But is it all right?*

With these words, addressed toward the patient, your attention is directed out there, and it is out there all the time.

One of the nice consequences is that because you are attending out there, being and living in this immediate scene, the patient is pulled to also be attending out there, being and living in the scene. Indeed, it seems almost essential that you are attending out there, if you want the patient to be able to find a scene of strong feeling.

You are fully aligned as the patient's words are addressed to you.   In searching for the scene of strong feeling, there will be occasions when the patient's words may be received as addressed to you. Stay aligned. Always keep your attention out there, and keep the patient's words coming in and through you. Finding the scene of strong feeling can occur when you are aligned; it probably cannot be found when you give up the aligned position (Mahrer, 1984, 1985a, 1986f).

It is common that the patient will attend out there for a bit and then say something that is aimed toward the therapist. She says:

> *Don kept getting at me, says I'm too aggressive, I'm too short-tempered. I fly off. He was after me for three days. You've seen other patients like me. Do they get better?*

If the therapist is external, face-to-face with the patient, the therapist will hear these words as being said to the therapist, as part of the ongoing interactive relationship. But something quite different may be occurring when the therapist is aligned, with most of the attention out there. Mainly, the therapist is still looking out there, seeing the scene and feeling the feeling. Even when the patient says:

> *You've seen other patients like me. Do they get better?*

You are looking out there. You may still be seeing Don, and the feeling may be a pocketful of pride at being aggressive, short-tempered. Or you may be seeing another person, a therapist type, with complaining Don in the background, and the feeling is one of asking for approval, being accepted, told that I really am all right. When the therapist is aligned, the patient's words occur in the context of the scene, and the patient's words are coming in and through the therapist. Saying that the patient is talking directly to the therapist is "true" when you are external, face-to-face. It is not necessarily true when you are aligned.

When you are aligned, the useful scenes will be out there, especially those accompanied with some feeling. Many other therapists value and emphasize the therapist-patient relationship. The face-to-face therapist tends to lose our data, and the aligned therapist tends to lose opportunities to deal with relationship data. The moral is to remain in the aligned posture.

What do you do if you are no longer aligned with the patient? There are at least two conditions in which you are no longer aligned with the patient. One is when you find yourself attending mainly to the patient who is over there, saying words directly at you. You are no longer looking out there. The patient is saying:

Why did you say that? You know how that hurts me? I hate being reminded of that!

Or he is saying:

Well, the thing is, I can be any way here with you. You're not like other people. Hell, you're not like anyone! Are you this way? I mean, are you so close to people? You know what I mean? I never met anyone like you . . . You're weird! I mean, in a nice way. Aw, you know . . .

You can say that it is the patient who pulled you out of being aligned. You may also say that you allowed yourself to be in the external position, attending mainly to the patient. In any case, the first condition is when you are no longer aligned. You are here, separated from the patient, attending mainly to the patient. What do you do?

One thing you can do is to try to minimize the damage and get back into being aligned with the patient. You may say:

OK! I'm sorry! I will never say that again, ever, I promise . . . Now, how can we get back to work? Oh yeah. It's mother! She's checking up on you again, and the feeling is tight. Watch out. Be careful! Are you ready? Go ahead!

Or you say:

No! I'm not like this except with you! But, thank you. Now, where were we? Oh yes, this feeling of how nice it is to be really open, even about how you feel about someone. If this nice feeling is strong, strong, then where is it that you feel this? Somewhere. Where?

You should get back to being aligned. If you are unsuccessful, if you and the patient work your way into a position where you are both attending mainly to one another, you are almost certainly unable to find a scene of strong feeling. You may as well declare this session a failure and wind it to a close.

There is a second condition in which you are no longer aligned with the patient. This is when the patient is simply silent, especially for long periods, or when what the patient says is so neutral, dead, flat, that you cannot even get a hint of some scene and some feeling. If there is even a slight whisper of some life in the patient's words, you can get a sense of some kind of scene and feeling. On the other hand, a patient may occasionally mumble a few words that are barely audible, with essentially no feeling, and interspersed with long silent periods. When this occurs, you will lose the aligned posture. You see nothing out there. You have no feeling at all. What can you do?

One possibility is to try and start again. Invite him to keep saying and doing things, to talk, to make noises. If there are silences, tell him to keep talking. Tell him to talk louder. Explain that your aim is to see what is there, whatever is here as he talks. If it seems timely, repeat the opening instructions. If you fail, however, and you cannot see anything or feel anything, then again consider winding this session to a close, because you will almost certainly be unable to find a scene of strong feeling. Not in this session at least.

You May Float from Feeling to Feeling, Scene to Scene, Always Aligned and Programmed to Find a Scene of Strong Feeling

After your opening instructions, the patient may almost immediately provide a scene of strong feeling. But that is not common. Usually you search for a scene in which the feeling is strong, and this search may well take you through a series of scenes and feelings. You are to float along with the patient in going from feeling to feeling, scene to scene. However, it is a guided, directional floating. You are always aligned, and you are always programmed toward finding the scene of strong feeling. In this important sense, you are by no means engaged in a floating that is free, aimless, disconnected, endless. The floating is always programmed toward scenes in which this feeling is strong.

Float from feeling to feeling.   You have the feeling that is here in you right now. Generally, it remains pretty much the same feeling. But it may also give way to some other feeling. When this happens, you follow the immediately present feeling, looking for where and when this feeling is strong.

After the opening instructions, the scene is one of sifting through some of your husband's papers; he died nine years ago, and the feeling is being scared of him, being the little girl who does bad things. When you describe this feeling, and look for when this feeling is strong, you are in a new scene—he is screaming at you about misplacing his papers, and there is a hard core of resisting him, fighting him, being the bad little girl. The feeling is relatively similar, but it takes a somewhat more defined form and shape as you continue searching for a scene in which it is relatively strong.

Often the feeling will give way to a new feeling. As you search for when this immediate feeling is strong, and as you are having this feeling in a scene, a new feeling occurs with the same or greater strength of feeling. You float from this feeling, in this scene, to the new feeling that is here in this new scene.

The opening scene is one in which she is in the car, driving her husband to the mall for Saturday shopping. Her opening feeling is a kind of light chirping at him for his carping and complaining about the way she takes care of things. She is feeling that she has a whining little boy that she has to take care of. As you look for when this feeling is stronger, she remains in this scene, and he is interrogating her about exactly when she took his shirts in to the cleaners, and why she didn't take them in a few hours earlier so that they could be ready today instead of next Monday. As you go further into this scene, the feeling changes and becomes one of grimness, of being tied up, of growling. The feeling shifts as you move further into a scene in which the initial feeling occurred.

The scene may be accompanied with relatively strong bad feelings. As you pursue the more explicit scene of bad feeling, the feeling itself may shift to an altogether different one. She is lightly crying as she is picturing herself, always alone, friendless, going for days without talking to anyone. The feeling is awful. Yet, as you look for a scene of strong feeling and she actually sees herself as a weird creature, sitting alone in the park, absolutely cut off from every human being, the feeling shifts to something quite different. Now it is a rumbling hatred, a growling rage, or there is a strange feeling of calm, a kind of inner stillness, or there is a powerful feeling of lightness, drifting, a freedom from all connections. You just never know what the next feeling will be.

Sometimes there are no shifts in feeling and other times there are many. In any case, you are free to float, and your floating from feeling to feeling is always in the direction of finding when and where this particular feeling is strong.

Float from scene to scene.   You are almost always in some scene. In looking for the scene of strong feeling, you invite the patient to look more deeply into this general scene, or to leave it and look anywhere for some time when this feeling is strong. You are free to float, either down into this general scene, or over to any other scene. Whether the feeling is mild or strong, whether you remain with it or shift to another, the search for a time when this feeling is strong will often lead you into new scenes. Herein lies the adventure, the excitement of discovery, because you almost never know where you will end. Whether you move from the initial scene to one more, or whether your pursuit leads you into and out of a series of scenes, the journey can be an adventure, and the eventual scene of strong feeling can be a surprise.

The new scene may be found by going deeper into this general scene. It is as if the new scene is nested somewhere inside this general scene. You open with the general scene. Here is the meeting of the board, but almost half the board is missing. The feeling is being tight, anxious, scared. Then you look for when this feeling is strong, and he says:

> *The chair doesn't even seem fazed by half the board missing . . . He just starts, and I'm wondering where the hell they are! They hate me. I never thought I was the one they wanted. They preferred some other guy. They didn't want to come . . .*

With these words, you are in a new scene in which the missing board members are together, in some other room of the department, heads together, whispering all sorts of viciousness about you, like how they never wanted you in the first place. Your programmed floating carries you to this new scene, a kind of spinoff within the general scene.

The more common sequence is from this initial scene to some other, and perhaps on to still other scenes. Yet your continuous direction is toward finding the scene in which this immediate feeling is strong.

Sometimes the patient goes from one scene to another, all rather recent, and all involving a woman who hurts him in some way. As you move from one scene to another, always leave room for staying in this scene or looking elsewhere, perhaps from any time in his life. With this invitation, he begins crying:

> *My mommy was in the hospital, and she came back home, and I put my arms around her, and I tell her that I love you . . .*

He starts to cry harder and is soon sobbing. Always leave the window open to other and earlier times when the feeling is strong.

The opening instructions often lead to statements that are problem situations or statements about problems. In following the opening instructions, the patient says:

I can get so depressed that I start having thoughts about killing myself. Its gets that bad . . .

Looking for a scene of strong feeling can penetrate down further into some scene or it can take you off to some other scene. If he says:

I can get so depressed that I start having thoughts about killing myself. It gets that bad.

Suppose that the feeling is one of being scared, frightened, helpless, and the attentional center is that looming depression. Floating can take you further into that scene. You say:

Yes! God, it is scary! That depression. I see it getting bigger! When is this scary feeling really strong? When is this?

He says:

Just a couple of days ago. I was . . . I just got up. In my bedroom. I woke up and then I . . . It's the cancer. I think . . . Why live. Why not just end it all? I just sat on the floor, and I had all kinds of thoughts about killing myself. Shit! Why not?

Here is a further scene within or tied to the earlier scene. Floating can draw you further into whatever the patient cites as the thing that is frightening, troublesome, worrying, or it can take you to some other feelinged scene. Even when you start with some ostensible problem scene, you can go off to some altogether new scene.

Once we open with a problem statement or situation or feeling, there is no guarantee that we will stay here. Typically, by following the feeling, we depart to other scenes. Our journey can lead us down into or far away from the initial scene that she saw as her "problem" scene. Here is perhaps a graphic illustration of the difference between sheer naming of some "problem" and the pursuit of a scene of strong feeling. Sometimes we arrive at a very particular scene inside the general statement of the problem. Usually, however, we depart by using the feeling to take us to some other scene of strong feeling. Trying to identify a "problem" is almost always irrelevant to the finding of a scene of strong feeling (Mahrer, 1967a, 1967b, 1986f). When many therapists might believe they have a fairly good notion of what the problem is, the experiential therapist is typically still looking for the situational context in which this feeling is strong.

In this programmed floating from scene to scene, the time frame can be wide open. You may go from today to childhood, or from today to recently and then to childhood, or from recently to adolescence and then back to today. The scene may be from any time in the patient's life, and the sequence may involve any periods of life. Give the patient plenty of room to go to any period at all. The feeling of being hounded, not being able to escape, can then yield a scene when you are eight years old, lying on your bed, trying to go to sleep. You are pushing the pillows against your ears to mute the voices inside your head. This scene opens into another that occurred when you were an adolescent; you are riding on the subway, and you know that all the people in the car not only know your thoughts, but the people sneer at and ridicule you for having those thoughts.

You can go from feeling to feeling, and from scene to scene, but you are continuously aligned and continuously programmed or geared to find a scene of strong feeling.

How Do You Know When You Have Found a Scene of Strong Feeling?

If your opening instructions are very good, and if the patient is ready and willing to do what your instructions invite him to do, he may go directly to a scene of strong feeling. But this is uncommon. Usually you go from scene to scene and feeling to feeling until you do find a scene of strong feeling. How do you know you have it? There are some guidelines to help you know that you have found a workable and useful scene.

One is that the scene is relatively specific and explicit. You are attending directly to a big eye, right before you, dripping with blood. Or you are in the corner store, fascinated by the young woman standing rigidly by the frozen foods. It is not a scene if it is quite loose, abstract, vague, and generalized. It is not enough for the scene to be one in which the client says:

I drink too much. I am alcoholic . . .

It's when I'm with my sister. Damn, she bothers me . . .

I can't get close to people. I never could, with anyone, even with my family . . .

All I have to do is just think about a plane, and I get tense, I mean I can hardly breathe . . .

I get in fights, I yell. I know I shouldn't. But I'm getting tired of always being the bad one . . .

The scene should be relatively specific and explicit, relatively fixed, stable, and present, rather than merely a fleeting part of a fluid series of scenes.

Second, the scene is compelling. It grabs you, pulls you. It is real. It engrosses you. It has such vividness and immediacy that you are not in a position to start looking elsewhere for a scene of strong feeling. Both you and the patient are preponderantly attending to it, drawn into its absorbing presence and realness.

A third guideline is that the feeling in you is relatively strong, definitely present in you. It need not be powerful. You need not be screaming or crying or transfixed with hatred, but the feeling is relatively strong. If there is only mild feeling in you, you have not yet found the scene of strong feeling. Trust your own level of feeling. When it is relatively strong, you may well be at the scene you can work with. If it is low, you have more work to do.

This is how you can identify a scene of strong feeling. But remember that there is no law saying you must stay with this scene. You may proceed to look for some other scene of strong feeling. In any case, the scene you select should adhere to these guidelines.

The process is gentle. There is no pressure, no forcing, no trying to get the patient to do what you want, no use of "interventions." You are continually asking if this is all right, checking with the patient, seeing if she is ready and willing. There is a gentleness in floating from one scene or feeling to another as you show the patient how to move toward finding such a scene of strong feeling. What you both do is therefore accomplished with little effort, push, pressure, strain.

The process is also powerful. When you start the session, the patient may have some kind of bad feeling, but it is rare for the patient to be in a particular scene of strong feeling. Typically, patients start with some kind of generalized, unfocused bad feeling. The process then brings the patient to a scene of strong feeling. This is new. It is an accomplishment, a discovery. Not only is the feeling strong, but the process for finding the scene is powerful.

ENTER INTO THE SCENE OF STRONG FEELING

First you give the opening instructions. Then you work with the patient to find a scene of strong feeling. Once you find the scene, both of you are simply to enter into the scene. Be in it. Live and exist in this scene.

Sometimes the two of you have already entered into the scene. As soon as you find the scene, she is crying as she holds her grandfather's hand, in the hospital. He is dying of cancer, and she is literally being in this scene. Or he is on the phone when the colleague notifies him that he got the appointment, and the patient is ecstatic:

I got it! It's mine! I really got the appointment!

As soon as you find the scene of strong feeling, the patient may have already entered into it. The scene is alive, real, and present, and the patient is living in the scene.

But suppose that you have only found the scene of strong feeling. The patient is not living and being in the scene. Your job is for both of you to be living and being in this scene of strong feeling.

Show the Patient How to Enter into the Scene

You are fully ready and willing to enter into this scene. Indeed, it is likely that you are already partly in the scene. Perhaps the main way to show patients how to enter into the scene is for you to enter in. If you enter in, it helps the patient to enter in. If you hold back, stay outside, are not fully ready and willing to enter in, then it is hard for the patient to do so. Let yourself go right into the scene so that it is alive and real. This is your ability as a therapist. It is almost essential. Your attention is wholly on the scene, and you are to be able to enter in more easily and more fully than most patients can.

Here are the elements that may be used to show the patient what to do and how to do it.

Lock in the scene. The actual incident or scene may have spanned 20 minutes or only a few seconds. In any case, freeze the scene. Put it on hold. You may say:

Your father is eating the corn and yes, it drives you wild, especially since, as usual, you aren't saying anything. But look at the old goat! If we're going to make this real, let's put it on hold. Just freeze it, all right? I want to just look around here a bit, so let's lock in this scene. OK, Dad? You're going to have to sit here and keep chomping!

Let's live in this scene as if it's really happening, right now. Try to be in this scene as if you are really living in it. You say:

Try and make it real. You are in bed, and right over there is auntie. See the red hair? Her body is very close to yours. She is trying to go to sleep. Talk like it is happening right now. Present tense. "This perfume is overwhelming. I think I am going to gag!" Keep it present tense. "My God, I wonder if she snores! I will never do this again, never!" If you talk, say it directly to her, whether or not she can hear you. "If you push over to my side of the bed, I'm out of here! Auntie, I don't even like you all that much, much less wanting to sleep with you! Yech!" Put all your attention on everything you see. Really look at it. See it. Be very aware of being here, under the covers, and with good old auntie right here, next to you. Put all your attention on her. Look at her. See the wall? See what's around you in the room? Look at it carefully. The more you see each little thing, the more you can be right here.

Feel the feeling.   You say:

It helps if you go ahead and feel the feeling. Here you are, walking down the street with your boss, and you are very uncomfortable. The feeling is being so damned aware, vigilant, scared of doing something wrong. You can be in this thing here if you go ahead and let yourself be this way. Just be it. Show it. Have this feeling. "I am scared that I'll say something stupid. Hell, everyone will know I am trying to suck up to the big boss. Oh God, maybe I'll fall off the curb or say just the wrong thing. I'll try to act like I'm not scared. HELP! Oh shit, what am I going to do." Feel it out loud. Let yourself feel it, have it.

It is easier for the patient to be in the scene, having the feeling, if you invite him to have the feeling. Therefore, simply invite him to go ahead and have the feeling right now (Mahrer, White, Soulière, Macphee, & Boulet, 1991). Of course, you are undergoing the feeling even as you speak. You are the voice of the feeling as you are showing the patient how to feel the feeling.

Describe everything in detail.   You say:

I am looking at your father, sitting there, eating, ravaging the corncob. I want to be right here, actually living here, being here, with him. I want to have the same exact feeling you have, and I want to have this feeling right here, sitting at the table. If you are going to really be right here, then describe everything that you can, everything that you can see and smell and hear, and what's going on around you, everything that is outside and everything inside. What you are thinking, and what may be going on inside your father. Maybe you can have some idea of what is going on in him.

Let me see. I'll start, but I'm probably wrong. I see him sitting right across from me, just the two of us. Right? Wrong? . . . And you're pretty quiet, not saying anything. But you're having things going on inside. Yeah? . . . You go ahead. Describe everything around you here. Like when this is, evening. And in the kitchen? . . . Oh, dining room. Ha! That makes it more disgusting.

It is essential to solicit and to honor patient's readiness and willingness.   She may be poised on the edge of entering into the scene. She may even be leaning toward entering it. Even if she knows what to do and how to do it, there is still one essential element required for her to enter into the scene—her readiness and willingness. If you do not call on and honor her readiness and willingness, it is very hard for her to enter into the scene.

You need her cooperation, her readiness and willingness. One way or another, ask if this is all right:

Are you ready to do this? Is it all right to do it this way?

Just about everything she is to do to enter into the scene requires that she be ready and willing to do it. Is it all right to go into this scene, to make it real and alive?

Be quite open about the reasons for hesitating or even for declining. If the feeling is a bad one, be open about a decision to go into a scene when the feeling is painful. Say that it will probably mean having this awful feeling again, maybe even more. If the scene involves that terrible look on your father's face, the hateful look that pulls and compels you, it means letting yourself be the awful victim of that look, maybe getting swept into it (cf. Binswanger, 1958a; Condrau & Boss, 1971; Gendlin, 1962; Mahrer, 1978a; Needleman, 1967a, 1967b).

Before, during, and after you show the person what to do and how to do it, make sure that you solicit the person's cooperative readiness and willingness. Without this, you will probably fail to enter into the scene of strong feeling.

What Do You Do if Patient Does Not Want to Enter the Scene, or Departs to Some Other Scene?

You have shown him what to do and how to do it. You have solicited his cooperation, his readiness and willingness. He declines:

No, I don't want to . . .

Why? What for? It was awful! She made me feel like shit! . . .

I'd rather not. No . . .

If he declines, honor his preference not to enter into the scene. Accept his choice. Do not push. Do not try to get him to do what he is not ready and willing to do. Give him plenty of room to look for some other scene of strong feeling. You may indicate that you yourself are quite ready and willing. But if the patient says no, then no it is. Honor the patient's unreadiness and unwillingness.

Sometimes the patient will enter into the scene a bit, or for a while, and then depart for some other scene. She is coming out of the small lake, feeling so very aroused, all-over sensual, and she stands on the shore, full of sexual feelings. Then, quickly, she says:

. . . my sister and I used to swim all the time. Every time we had, I mean when we stayed at the beach when we were kids . . .

If you are drawn out of the scene, no longer feeling so sensual, here on the shore, you may honor her unreadiness and unwillingness. You may provide her with plenty of room to find some other scene, if she wishes. But suppose that you are still living and being in this scene, still on the shore, feeling sensual. If this happens, then her words about her sister are being said as you are in the scene, on the shore, feeling sensual. It will probably not occur to you that she is somewhere else. You will likely just invite her to be here, on the shore, with you.

You have given the opening instructions, found a scene of strong feeling, and entered into this scene. Typically, all of this proceeds right along, and we may have taken up to 20 minutes or so. Now that you are living and being in the scene of strong feeling, you are geared to discover and to be in a moment of strong feeling.

DISCOVER THE MOMENT OF STRONG FEELING

Once you have entered into the "scene" of strong feeling, you are to find the "moment" in which the feeling is strong. This is a fluid, simple, natural process. You are looking for the instant, the moment, when the feeling is strong.

Discovering the Moment of Strong Feeling is Rare and Powerful

It is easy to say that first you find a scene of strong feeling, then you enter in and try to discover the actual moment of strong feeling. However, this is also a rare and powerful journey. It is rare because almost no patients ever go beyond scenes or situations of strong feeling. If you listen to hundreds of hours of therapy, it is rare that patients ever dig inside some moment of strong feeling to look for a tiny precise moment in which the feeling peaked. Patients have plenty of other things to do. It is rare because almost no therapists go beyond scenes or situations of strong feeling. In most approaches, there is no reason to press further. Therapists get what they need by staying at the level of the sheer scene or situation. If you listen to hundreds of hours of therapy, it is rare that therapists even seem to want to go beyond these scenes and situations.

Yet discovering the moment, the precise instant, of strong feeling is powerful. It is the royal road down inside the person, down into the deeper domain. Something powerful happens when you begin searching for precisely when the feeling is happening. You are entering the territory of the deeper potential. The main reason for starting with a scene of strong feeling is to discover this precise moment.

Discovering the moment of strong feeling can be thought of as a matter of meticulous searching, but in an alive scene of strong feeling. You know that the scene of strong feeling is when your mother is talking to you on the phone. You are in this scene. If you search for the exact moment when the feeling was strong, you suddenly discover it is when you ask if she got your letter explaining about your leaving the job, and your mother pauses! That's when it was! During this damned pause!

Finding the Moment of Strong Feeling Is Almost Always a Surprising Discovery

If you are looking for what is happening in the actual moment when the feeling is strong, dreams are usually a lot easier to work with than real-life experiences. In many dreams, the moment of strong feeling is right here, relatively easy to locate. I am floating along in this bathtub, way above the ground, and the moment of strong feeling is when I realize I can steer this thing just by leaning forward or to the side and back; when I realize I can steer this baby, that's when I am excited as hell!

But real-life experiences are usually different. Almost without exception, you may have some idea of what is happening in the scene of strong feeling, but that is as far as you get. You almost never have any idea what is occurring in the exact moment of strong feeling. You know that the bad feeling was when you were a little girl and your aunt held you under the water. You freaked out. You can remember much of what happened in that scene. However, the chances are rather high that you have no idea about the precise moment of strong feeling. You are still upset about the argument you and your husband had, standing by the telephone in the kitchen, fighting about the way he acted like a simpering idiot on the telephone, excessively happy, laughing like a silly little boy. You may be living and being in this scene. However, you probably have no idea exactly what was occurring when the feeling was strongest, in some instant within this general scene. When is the instant when the feeling is strongest? That is hard to say.

In the scene, whether the feeling is good or bad, looking for and finding the actual moment of strong feeling is usually an adventure of discovery. You have no idea what this moment is. All you know is that somewhere in this scene is a moment of strong feeling.

It is exceedingly rare to penetrate far enough into these scenes to find the precise moments of strong feeling. The feeling itself tends to block you from discovering the actual moment. Whether the feeling is good or bad, the feeling seems to act like a protective buffer, keeping you away from entering further and deeper into discovering the actual moment of strong feeling. For many patients and therapists, almost all the pulls are away from the scene, to talk about it, to understand it, see what caused it, discuss how it is similar to other times, do things to reduce it. But you go further. You venture into new territory. You discover the precise moment of strong feeling.

What Do You Do to Discover the Moment of Strong Feeling?

You and the patient are living and being in a scene of strong feeling, at least to some degree. You are both geared to discover the moment of strong feeling. What do you do to accomplish this?

Fully be in the scene of strong feeling, and with strong feeling.   The great advantage of living and being in the scene of strong feeling is that it is the doorway to the moment of strong feeling. You can find this moment by living and being in this scene.

Remember that you are holding the scene; it is fixed. This allows you to enter into it almost all the way, to inspect it, look around in it. You are a little girl, sitting in the bathroom, watching your father shave. You know that he will be leaving this afternoon to go back to Detroit and his new wife. You are already missing him, and he won't be back again for perhaps six months or so. In this sustained scene, you can savor it, live and be in it, even more than when it actually happened.

Actively search for the moment of strong feeling.   You find the moment of strong feeling by actively searching for it. Somewhere in this scene is the moment when the feeling is strongest. You look for when and where this is. Nor can you succeed by yourself. You need the cooperation of the patient. You must live and be in this scene, have the feeling, and invite the patient to join you in searching for the moment of strong feeling. You don't know where it is. You certainly cannot find it by yourself. The patient has to guide you. The patient must be ready and willing to search around to see just when and where this feeling is strong:

Are you ready? It is here somewhere. Is it all right to look around?

The patient is the important one in this search. You follow. The scene is this telephone call when she is talking to her friend, hesitant to talk with her, trying so hard to be social. Inside, she is frightened, fearing that her friend will hate her for what she did. But when is the moment of strong feeling? You both search. The active search leads to a moment before she actually reached the friend, just dialing, and living in a momentary vision of her friend, hateful, vindictive, full of fury at the patient, and yet, in the moment, the patient decides to go ahead, face it. It is always the patient who leads, who is the important one in the search, while you provide the programmed energy to maintain the search.

You are programmed to carry out the search, even if the patient is caught up in the feeling. Entered into the scene, he is in the throes of saturnine depression, and he is alone in his apartment. He is so full of the depressed feeling that he can barely move. Yet you are searching. When is it worst? What is going on when it is strongest? You look around, you probe, you and the patient are to find the moment when this feeling is strongest.

No matter what the scene or feeling are like, you are to search for the precise moment of strong feeling. It is here somewhere. No matter how much you are pulled to get out of this scene or to stay away from probing, your job is to search, to join with the patient in actively searching for the moment of strong feeling.

Clarify and probe into the details to discover the moment of strong feeling. Actively searching for the moment of strong feeling includes clarifying what is here as you move closer and closer to discovering the moment of strong feeling. It is a matter of filling it in, probing into it, making it clearer, seeing and hearing what is present. The search includes going deeper, progressive clarification. The wonderful feeling is in a scene when the two of you are touching one another, both very aroused. Looking for the moment of strong feeling means clarifying everything in and around what may be the moment of strong feeling. Clarify the noises, the utterances, the bodily movements, the touchings, everything that is occurring inside, the feel of the skin, exactly what every detail is like.

The scene of strong feeling is when mother is yelling at the patient's younger brother. She's got him backed into a corner. What corner does it seem to be? Just look. Patient says:

Like in the front entry, by the closet, I don't know.

Mother is yelling at him. About what? What is she saying?

I don't know! She's always after him, and she screams at him!

Just listen, let it come to you. Just listen. What seems natural?

Where are your damned mittens? Did you lose them again? She's always screaming at him, yeah, about the mittens! Jesus Christ!

As you get closer to the moment of strong feeling, clarifying some immediate detail may release a sudden new image that is nested or contained in the detail. You and Stan, your supervisor, are walking along in the corridor. This is the scene of strong feeling. As you and the patient clarify more and more of what is happening, getting closer and closer to the moment of strong feeling, you arrive at a point where Stan mentions your project, your pet project, the one you cherish. Stan says:

I have taken another look at the thing you're working on, well, thinking about . . .

Bam! Clarifying the exact words releases a flash image of Stan sitting at his desk, disdainfully canceling your proposal, writing a nasty, cryptic note on your brief. Here is the moment when the feeling is strongest.

It is relatively common that movement from the scene of strong bad feeling to the very moment of strong feeling is accompanied with a letting go of the bad feeling that was there in the scene. In a way, this is a bonus of going further and deeper into the scene. Almost all you have to do is to clarify the details of the scene, and the awful feeling diffuses. The closer you come to the moment of strong feeling, the more the bad feeling may both intensify and diffuse away. Paradoxically, identifying the moment of strong feeling is a way of freeing a patient of the bad feeling accompanying the scene.

How Do You Know When You Have Discovered the Moment of Strong Feeling?

Usually, there are three indications that go together. One is that you find a very particular moment, an instant, an alive, real, immediate, present moment. Second, it is a new moment, a discovered moment. Whether you discovered it by focusing further down inside the scene, or by probing until a new moment is released, there is a newness, a sense of discovery. Third, there is a burst or a shift of strong feeling.

In the scene, you are at your mother's house, and the whole family is here. You feel pretty good, especially when you first arrive, and many of the people greet you, hug you, kiss you. In searching to find the moment of strong feeling, you are drawn toward when your old uncle kisses you. He has cancer, and everyone knows that he will probably die soon. Then you discover the instant. As you kiss, he touches your tongue with his tongue! Here is the moment, and there is a burst of feeling in you. That mischievous sonuvagun!

Often the moment of strong feeling occurs when you focus attention on some precise detail that was there all along. Looking slowly and carefully allows the detail to be held, fixed; it gives a kind of special immediacy to this instant. You knew that you were terribly upset by little cracks and barbs from your mother as the two of you talked over the phone. In describing the scene, you mentioned a lot of what she said. Now, looking for the moment of strong feeling, you go over what she said. When you go slowly over her words you arrive at her saying:

Do you have any news for me?

That does it! Here is a release of feeling in this instant. The moment takes on an immediate life of its own. You know that she means:

Are you pregnant?

She is talking in code. You are supposed to know what she is alluding to. You tighten up. This moment is alive and real. It is the moment of strong feeling.

The moment may be defined by a sudden outburst of feeling. As you go over the scene in the bus, taking the passengers from the airplane to the airport, the moment is punctuated by the burst of laughter as you discover the instant when the bus lurches a bit and you are thrust up against the lovely woman (cf. Mahrer, Markow, & Gervaize, 1992; Mahrer, Markow, Gervaize, & Boulet, 1987). This moment is suddenly defined, discovered, and identified by the burst of strong feeling. Sometimes the patient is absolutely drawn in to the moment so fully that he is actually living and being in it. Having entered into the scene, the patient identifies the moment of strong feeling by wholly being in it, for real, and with sharply heightened feelings. It is just after the funeral of your younger brother, who died of cancer. You risk putting your arm around your mother, and she draws back from you, glaring at you. Instantly, the patient is wholly living and being in this moment. She screams out:

> *You never liked me! You never even looked at me. GOD, ALL I EVER WANTED IS*
> *FOR YOU TO LOOK AT ME—JUST SEE THAT I AM ALIVE!*

She is totally living and being in this alive, fixed, exceedingly real moment.

What Is the Value and Use of Discovering the Moment of Strong Feeling?

The main value and use of discovering the moment of strong feeling is that you and the deeper potential are practically touching one another. You are very close to the deeper potential. You can feel its breath. The whole purpose of the opening instructions is to get to this moment of strong feeling. The whole purpose of finding and entering into a scene of strong feeling is to get into this moment. Once you discover it, you are holding hands with the deeper potential. It is here somewhere in this moment of strong feeling.

This is what makes the actual moment of strong feeling so priceless, and yet it is always within hand's reach. Almost every day, most people have scenes of strong feeling. Yet you can spend a whole lifetime without going from the scene of strong feeling to discovering the moment of strong feeling. I regard that as sad. Just about every night, dreams give us gifts of strong-feelinged scenes; just about every day we are in scenes of strong feeling. Yet it is the rarest of persons who uses any of these scenes to discover the hidden moments of strong feeling. And once you find the moment of strong feeling, you can hold the deeper potential in the palm of your hand. This is what makes this moment so valuable and so very useful.

ACCESS THE INNER EXPERIENCING

This is the jewel of Step 1, the culminating achievement. Whether it is called the deeper potential or the inner experiencing, the aim is to access it, to receive it, to sense and touch it. From inside the moment of strong feeling, you can pluck the inner experiencing.

You are in the moment of strong feeling. Somewhere in this moment is the doorway to the inner experiencing. The question is where. It is exciting and frustrating to know that the deeper potential is here, somewhere in this moment. How do we find it? What do we do, once we discover and are in the moment of strong feeling, to access the inner experiencing?

There are three ways to access the inner experiencing:

1. You can access the inner experiencing by placing yourself in the right position or location. When you are in the right place, you are accessing, receiving, sensing, having, and undergoing the inner experiencing. I will describe these positions or locations.
2. You can access the inner experiencing by actively strengthening or heightening the experiencing. Even though the feeling is already strong, you can actively and deliberately strengthen or heighten the sheer ongoing experiencing, and that accesses the inner experiencing. I will show you how to do this.

3. You can access the inner experiencing by including suddenly released new elements into the moment of strong feeling. This new element, whatever it is, alters the moment of strong feeling, changes the moment of new feeling, yields a new moment of strong feeling. The inner experiencing is accessed in this new moment of strong feeling.

These are the three ways of accessing the inner experiencing in the moment of strong feeling.

Where Is The therapist Located, in the Moment of Strong Feeling?

Figure 7.1 gives a picture of what is happening in the moment of strong feeling. In daily living, the deeper potential is ordinarily safely below the operating domain. It is far inside you. What is so precious about this moment of strong feeling is that the deeper potential has now partly intruded into the operating domain. It is touching you. Figure 7.1 illustrates how the deeper potential has partially entered the operating domain.

In the moment of strong feeling, the patient is almost certainly stuck inside the operating potential. But the therapist does not have to be stuck inside the operating potential, and this provides the opportunity to access the inner experiencing. The therapist has the golden gift of being free to be in any of the locations given in Figure 7.1. More bluntly, a therapist who is stuck inside the operating potential will almost certainly not be able to access the inner experiencing; a therapist who is in any of the four locations given in Figure 7.1, has a good chance of accessing the inner experiencing.

All four locations have one thing in common. They enable the therapist to be literally in touch with the deeper potential. The patient is almost totally bound by the disintegrative relationship to the deeper potential, and this acts to keep the patient from accessing the deeper potential. From the vantage point of the operating potential, there are usually frightening and unpleasant pictures of the deeper potential filtered through the disintegrative relationship. It is almost assured that, in the moment

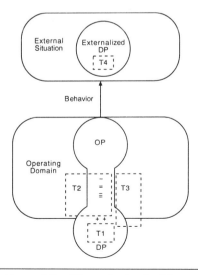

FIGURE 7.1   Locations of the Therapist in the Moment of Strong Feeling

of strong feeling, the operating potential's glimpse of the encroaching deeper potential will be awful, grotesque, monstrous, and accompanied with bad feelings. Accessing the deeper potential means that the therapist must be in other locations that provide much more direct touching of the deeper potential.

One location is down inside the bowels of the deeper potential. This is indicated as T1 in Figure 7.1. You not only receive and access the inner experiencing, you are ensconced inside it. In the moment of strong feeling, you are actually inside the deeper potential. While she is horrified and feeling repulsed by her lying to her lover about her husband and lying to her husband about her lover, the therapist is inside the deeper potential, having a wonderful time:

> *They'll never know! Fooled them both! Damn, I'm clever! Ha!*

Second, you may be solidly situated inside the bad feeling, well within the core of the awful feeling. This is indicated as T2 in Figure 7.1. Where the patient is generally having the bad feeling and pulling away, drawing back from having the bad feeling too much, you are blithely ready, willing, and eager to plunge deep inside the awfulness of the bad feeling. It is as if you are saying:

> *I want to plunge all the way inside this bad feeling, to wallow inside the very worst of the bad feeling, so take me deep inside its black inner hole. What is it that is so very scary, horrible, the absolutely worst possibility?*

The patient is feeling just awful as he signs the agreement for his old and sickly mother to be placed in "the home," the place for old people. He is shaking with the awfulness of it. As the therapist plunges deeper and deeper into these terrible feelings, the nadir is reached with a monstrous picture of mother dying, being cut off, alone, and dead. This image softy hovers above the accessed inner experiencing of being free of her, out of her grasp, liberated from her.

The third location is alongside the patient. It is as if one foot is inside the deeper potential while the rest of you is alongside the patient. You are close to the patient, but you are able to see what is happening without being jaundiced by being inside the operating potential and having its disintegrative bad feelings. She is feeling guilty and defensive as she is horrified that she inadvertently got into bed with the attractive visitor, rather than with her husband, when she came home very early in the morning. You are in a position to witness what is happening, to receive the exciting sexual experiencing, but without her bad feelings. This is indicated as T3 in Figure 7.1.

The fourth location is inside the externalized deeper potential. This is indicated as T4 in Figure 7.1. In the moment of strong feeling, he is feeling so terrible as his uncle is yelling at the patient's father. Virtually all his attention is riveted on the uncle. He is so magnetized by the uncle that he almost senses what the uncle is thinking, feeling, intending. When you take the next step and enter into the uncle, you are located at T4 (Figure 7.1) and you are accessible to the inner experiencing of putting down the little father, being superior to him, commanding him. This is the externalized deeper potential.

How Do You Know When You Have Accessed and Received the Inner Experiencing?

You are in the moment of strong feeling. You are in one of the locations for receiving the inner experiencing. How do you know when you have accessed the inner experiencing? The answer is that something new is actually occurring in you. This shift is the inner experiencing.

The intense bad feeling is not the inner experiencing.   In the moment of strong feeling, and especially as you are using methods for accessing the inner experiencing, the feeling may be good. However, the feeling is usually bad, often intensely bad. The patient may be wailing, screaming, shaking, in the pit of depression, sobbing, terrified. This is not the inner experiencing. This may be the awful feeling accompanying the operating potential, the terrible feeling of the screechingly intense disintegrative relationship with the deeper potential. But it is not the inner experiencing.

In the moment of strong feeling, you are about three years old, standing in the crowded mall. You know your mommy is gone, and the feeling is awful. You are lost, abandoned, and you begin to sob. The feeling is strong. But feeling scared and lost and alone is not the inner experiencing. You are 16 years old, and the two men are grabbing your arms and legs, pinning them down on the bed. You are terrified about being raped. Your whole body aches, hurts, is twisted and full of pain as they maul you, hit you. The feeling is awful. This terrible feeling is not the inner experiencing. You are sitting in the car, and your companion is relentlessly berating you, saying how selfish you are, how cold, sterile, unfeeling. Inside, your whole body is wrenched and locked. You feel miserable. This is not the inner experiencing.

In the moment of strong feeling, you may be having a feeling that is quite strong and quite bad. This strong bad feeling is not the inner experiencing.

The inner experiencing is something new and different that occurs in you.   No matter what you are feeling in the moment of strong feeling, the inner experiencing is almost always something new and different. Wait for the shift, the new experiencing in you. This is the inner experiencing. In the moment of strong feeling, you are by yourself in the cemetery, at the small tombstone of your grandmother. The strong feeling is one of painful disbelief, surrounded by swirling memories of her drinking and laughing and loving you. Then, suddenly, as you use the methods, you start sobbing. Big baby tears are pouring down your face. Herein lies the inner experiencing, contained in the new experiencing in you as you are openly, unabashedly sobbing.

It is understandable that the inner experiencing will occur as something new and different. In the moment of strong feeling, you are typically undergoing the operating potential, and a main purpose or goal of the operating potential is to provide a safe little whiff of the deeper potential while, at the same time, ensuring that the deeper potential remains inside, kept down, barricaded. Therefore, when you are undergoing the deeper potential, it will be new and different.

There is a good feeling in you, and there is a shift in the immediate situation.   When you access the inner experiencing, it feels good. There is a burst or release of good feeling in you, that indicates you have come into contact with the inner experiencing. Indeed, it means that you are beginning to undergo the inner experiencing.

Isn't it strange that the feeling is good? After all, the patient's relationship with the deeper potential is exceedingly negative. If the patient were to somehow have a peek into the deeper potential, she would see something awful, something she would certainly not want to be. But you have moved out of that disintegrative relationship. You are in a position to reach, to be touched by, the deeper potential, and this feels so good. The good feeling may occur for just a moment, in a kind of little burst, but the feeling is good. Even if you are not wholly being the deeper potential, not being it all the way, even if you are only near to it, the feelings are good ones. They are feelings of excitement, of aliveness, of tingling, of vibrancy. They are the good feelings of actualization.

Because you are in contact with the deeper potential, it is common that while you are having the good feeling of actualization, the patient is having the bad feeling of disintegration. In other words, you are actually undergoing the deeper potential, whereas the patient is drawing back from it, relating to it disintegratively (Mahrer, 1962a, 1970a, 1970b; Mahrer & Pearson, 1973a, 1973b).

The burst of good feeling and the shift in the situational context almost always occur together. When the situational context shifts and the burst of good feeling happens, you are accessing the inner experiencing. When you access the inner experiencing, there is a burst of good feeling and the situational context shifts. They go together. In the moment of strong feeling, she is being slapped by her angry father. Then, as you access the inner experiencing, there is a new sense of strength, an unreachable inner core of strength, and with this there is a burst of good feelings, and the situational context shifts. You are now observing your removed and feckless father, doing what he can but unable to reach you, even with his slapping.

Trust and use the new experiencing that occurs in you.   The data that you trust and use consist in what is occurring in you as you are located in the right position and as you use the methods of accessing the inner experiencing. It is your experiencing. When this experiencing happens inside you, you can have some trust in the presence of the inner experiencing. There will be bodily sensations in you. Something is now alive, moving, carrying forward, shifting, stirring in you. There is a new life in you, very much as if you sense the baby inside you, only it is the inner experiencing. This is what you trust and use.

Ordinarily, you will have the inner experiencing before the patient does. Ordinarily, what is occurring in you is closer to the inner experiencing than what may be occurring in the patient. You cannot ask the patient. You cannot find out from the patient what inner experiencing is present in her. Asking the patient only removes both of you from being in the moment of strong feeling and accessing the inner experiencing. Besides, her description of what is occurring in her does not bring either of you closer to accessing the inner experiencing.

These are the ways that you can know you have accessed and received the inner experiencing. But there are methods to use. Once you are in the moment of strong feeling, there are three methods to access the inner experiencing. The balance of this chapter describes these three methods of getting the inner experiencing. Once you are in the moment of strong feeling, you can access the inner experiencing by (a) being in a proper or receptive location, (b) heightening and strengthening the experiencing, or (c) inserting the new element that appears.

Access the Inner Experiencing by Being in a Receptive Location, in the Moment of Strong Feeling

You and the patient have achieved a great deal by being in a moment of strong feeling because the inner experiencing is here somewhere. Now that you are in the moment of strong feeling, put yourself in a proper location to receive the inner experiencing. It is here somewhere.

Make sure that you are not inside the operating potential. That location won't do. You cannot easily have access to the inner experiencing when you are with the patient inside the operating potential. As indicated in Figure 7.1, there are other places for you to be located to receive the inner experiencing.

Access the inner experiencing by being inside the deeper potential; or by being alongside the patient, free of the bad feeling.   The two locations are given as T1 and T3 in Figure 7.1. In both locations, you are located so that you are free of the operating potential, free of the bad feeling, and much closer to the deeper potential.

You may be situated inside the deeper potential (T1, Figure 7.1). Or you may be alongside the patient, but with one foot touching the deeper potential (T3, Figure 7.1). In each position, you can be in touch with the inner experiencing. You can sense the inner experiencing. You can receive it. In each of the following examples, patient and therapist are living in a moment of strong feeling and the therapist accesses the inner experiencing by being inside the deeper potential or by being alongside the patient. In these locations, you are free of the disintegrative bad feelings.

He is a minor official in the large department. His boss went out of town and left him with the responsibility for getting particular information from four section heads. The moment of bad feeling is when they are at the meeting, and he is saying that two of them did not fill in the form properly, so he cannot revise the equipment budget for the next six months. As he is saying this, he is feeling terrible, not belonging, disliked by the section heads, out of his proper role. None of them are looking directly at him. In this moment, free of the bad feeling, and alongside the patient, you witness him interacting with the four section heads. The whole scene shifts, takes on a new meaning. Something stirs inside you. It is an experiencing of bawling them out, exerting power over them, being the critical authority. It feels so sweet.

She is looking for her grandmother in grandmother's old house. It is afternoon. Grandmother should be around. It is so quiet. Grandmother is not on the first floor, yet the doors are unlocked, both front and back. This is strange. The moment of strong feeling is when she goes up the narrow stairs and is just opening the bedroom door. She is gripped with tension, and the pressure fills her. Is grandmother dead? Is she on the floor, head smashed, blood all over the cream-colored carpet? This is a moment of panic. In this newly created scene, you are inside the activated deeper potential, and you receive something within. It is the inner experiencing of violence, murder, wholesale destruction. It feels exciting.

You and your father are sitting in the living room. On the low table is an old-style model airplane that your nine-year-old son just freshly glued. Your father has come for a visit. He reaches out to grab the delicate airplane model, and the moment of strong feeling is when your arm suddenly grabs father's outstretched fingers in mid-air. The patient feels bad, especially when his father yanks back his hand and turns away, annoyed. However, in this instant, right alongside the patient, what is activated in you is a sense of being the strong one, the ruggedly protective father lion, the one who won't let his father do anything bad to the child. It feels good.

He feels awful as he is standing on the street corner. He was to have met the client at 4:30 to go a few blocks to an office so that they can sign the papers. It is now 5:10, and he is frantic. The office is undoubtedly closed at 5:00. He is almost certain that he told the client the wrong location, and the client is probably frantically waiting at some other corner. Alongside the patient, in the moment, free of the bad feeling, you sense an inner glow: being devilish, stick it to him, screw him up, wreak havoc.

There are many occasions in which the patient is having awful feelings in the moment of strong feeling. The patient is appalled at herself, or depressed and gloomy, or full of guilt, or feels wrong, sick, crazy. Yet, in this very moment, the therapist is in the deeper potential or alongside the patient, and the therapist is quite free of these bad feelings. Instead, the therapist accesses a good-feelinged inner experiencing. She feels awful when in the moment of strong feeling, the man whose ass she is caressing at the party turns out to be someone other than her husband. She is shocked and is horrified here in the moment. He feels terrible when his mother pounds on the upstairs floor with her cane, and in the moment of strong feeling, he cannot jump up and serve her because he suddenly has a wrenching clamping up of the thigh muscles in both legs. She feels rotten and horrified when her sister calls to talk to mother, and the patient suddenly realizes that mother's plane came in three hours ago; the patient forgot to pick up her mother at the airport. Yet in each case, the therapist actually has an inner experiencing that is almost joyous, partly because the therapist is located so as to be free of the bad feeling that the patient is having at this very moment.

In the moment of strong feeling, the feeling may be quite enjoyable. The inner experiencing is accessed when the therapist is inside the deeper potential, and the inner experiencing is distinguished from the good feeling. For example, he is terribly attracted to the lovely colleague. At the departmental party, he looks over at her, across the room. She is looking directly at him, grinning. The moment is when their mutual gazes lock together. In this instant, the therapist is inside the deeper potential, and the experiencing is the magic of shared love and affection. It swells inside, and feels wonderful.

Access the inner experiencing by being inside the other person. In some moments of strong feeling, the inner experiencing is housed within the other person, and not within the patient. Sometimes the other "person" is a thing such as the cancer, the headache, the fetus, the heart, or even the fear, the "problem," the cat, the snake, the dagger, the precious jewel.

In experiential theory, as in some other theories, what is deeper inside the person may occur in the form of some external agency or person or thing. This is indicated as the externalized deeper potential in Figure 7.1. Accordingly, the useful location for the therapist is within this externalized deeper potential, indicated as location T4 in Figure 7.1. By being inside this externalized deeper potential, by being inside the other person or thing, in the moment of strong feeling, the therapist can thereby receive the inner experiencing.

There are some friendly clues for when the therapist gets inside the other person or thing as the one that houses the inner experiencing:

1. In the moment of strong feeling, the other person and not the patient seems to be the main character, the active one, the doer.
2. Often the other person is highly compelling, with the patient's attention drawn toward, riveted onto and into the other person.
3. Usually the other person is seen exceedingly clearly and vividly, in minute detail.
4. Generally, the patient seems to have access to, to know, what the other person is like, the other person's thoughts and feeling, intentions and wants. The

patient often goes so far as to voice the words as if the other person were saying them, or even to speak as and for the other person.

5. Sometimes, the patient's own center of gravity seems to shift toward the other person. It is as if the person's own identity diffuses and the patient somehow almost becomes the other person.

In other words, you get inside and be the other person when some of these conditions are pulling you to get inside the other person. You do not simply decide to try and access the inner experiencing by getting inside the other person. Furthermore, you can either get inside the other person by yourself or you can invite the patient to go there with you. In either case, the patient must first provide you with at least some of the clues. Often you do not have to ask the patient to get inside of and to be the other person. In the moment, the patient adopts the other person's perspective, talks as the other person, is inside the other person.

She is 14 years old, living with her aunt. In the moment of strong feeling, she has just come straight home from school and she is facing auntie. The patient is riveted on the aunt, describes every detail of how the aunt is perched on her throne, barking out orders. The patient has described the aunt so minutely that the aunt is practically alive and real:

> *And she's so inconsistent! I think she just is excited about having a slave. "First go to the deli and get salami. Make sure it's the right kind! Go to Edna's and return her iron. Don't lose the iron! You lose everything! And go there first cause Edna likes to take a nap in the afternoon. Then go to the hardware store, and then to the deli on your way home. It's miles away, but of course that doesn't matter . . ."*

These words are poured out in the moment of strong feeling, and you are drawn inside the aunt as these words allow you to receive the inner experiencing of being the controlling boss, dictating orders, commanding.

She is only about seven years old, and the moment of strong feeling is in the big old attic of her older cousin's house, way out in the country. She has never felt comfortable with Mark. He always seems too quiet, impassive. The moment is when he has her down on the floor, has something metal around her ankles, and it hurts. She is screaming in fright, and Mark is just sitting, his knees drawn up under his chin, gazing blankly at her. She rivets her attention on him, focusing on his face, describing the look in such detail that her own self seems to recede away. She is magnetized by him:

> *He's very clever, and planned this cause he has the music so loud that even if anyone did hear, it would seem like music, the opera, and that doesn't seem to matter anyhow because he seems like he isn't going to hurt anyone, just have something. Yeah, own something, like something of your very own. No one wants to be with him. There are no friends, and even in the family no one barely talks to him, so now he has something of his very own, like a pretty bird, with red hair . . . not going to hurt it . . . just having something . . .*

There are tears in the therapist's eyes, and the patient pauses, lightly sniffling, crying. There is an inner experiencing of being so very alone, without anyone, nothing of my own. Without trying, or hardly being aware, the therapist had drifted into being Mark, the older cousin.

The other person may occur as some thing, for example as the cancer in his lung. The patient's attention is almost completely transfixed onto the cancer. He is hypnotized by the cancer, and as he keeps describing the cancer, he seems to lose his own identity and virtually to become the cancer. His voice changes. He speaks as the thing that is the cancer:

> *It just knows eating, killing, it destroys whatever is there . . . Not even caring . . . It doesn't care, and nothing can stop it. Nothing. It is impervious, invincible. Try anything. Chemicals. Nothing can affect it, it's a powerhouse. Anything can die but it stays on. It grows and nothing can even reach it . . .*

As he rasps out these words, and as the therapist is being the cancer, there is an inner experiencing of being inviolate, invincible, unreachable. It feels absolutely wonderful.

Access the inner experiencing by being wholly inside the bad feeling, and by penetrating into the very core of the bad feeling.   In each of the other ways of accessing the inner experiencing, the therapist has been in a location that intentionally frees the therapist of the bad feeling that is occurring in the moment of strong feeling. These have been locations T1, T3, and T4 in Figure 7.1. Another location is one in which the therapist is exceedingly ready and willing to go right into the heart of the bad feeling, to undergo the bad feeling all the way, to plunge into the very core of the bad feeling, to allow the bad feeling to show its most grotesque and twisted face, to wallow down inside the worst possible meaning of the bad feeling, to wholly surrender to the absolute abyss of hellish feeling. This location is given as T2 in Figure 7.1. Once we penetrate into the very core of the bad feeling, we will arrive at the deeper potential, the inner experiencing. As indicated in Figure 7.1, the bad feeling is the gateway into the inner experiencing. This is the avenue we travel.

When you finally go through the worst of the bad feeling, the inner experiencing is almost always a surprise, a discovery. You have essentially no idea of what the deeper potential is. All you have is a working faith that penetrating down into the bad feeling will yield the deeper potential. This means that the surprise, the discovery, consists of both the occurrence of the deeper potential, and its particular nature.

As you undergo the bad feeling, you are looking for the terrible scene that is illuminated by the bad feeling. What is the awful possibility, the catastrophic scene that is inside the worst feeling? The more you actually search out the hell that is implied in the bad feeling, the closer you come to the inner experiencing. What does the awful feeling imply, point toward?

The moment of strong feeling is after the car pulls alongside him on the country road, both cars going fast. The fellow to his left screams something at him. Although he doesn't know what he was saying, the patient is filled with panic. In the actual moment of strong feeling, right after the scream, the other fellow is facing him, both cars careening along, and the patient is shaking. In the frozen moment, the therapist is yelling, voice full of panic:

> *So you're scared as hell—he's gonna do something?. . .*

The patient is panic-stricken, terrified. Therapist is yelling:

> *What's so scary? Something is . . . what?*

He babbles in panic, and ends by yelling.

I'm scared that something awful's going to happen . . . Like . . . SMASHING . . . JUST RAMMING THAT FUCKING CAR!

With these exploding words, the therapist is almost giddy as she receives the inner experiencing of going aggressively out of control, being physically violent, crashing and bashing and smashing.

The moment of bad feeling is when he is in the supervisor's office, being told what to do to revise the report. His job is to write reports that his supervisor corrects and modifies, and then the patient is to revise them accordingly. But he has awful moments of being handcuffed by tightness and tension. He is terrified by going blank when his supervisor is going over his report with him:

I can't think! Richard is pointing to that section and he is saying things, and I am scared to death 'cause I can't make out what he's saying! Jesus, there is something wrong with me!

The therapist blurts out:

All right, let's be this all the way. What is so awful about this? It is awful, but what is so awful?

I'll just be sitting here with this frozen look on my face? I'll be so dizzy I'll pass out on the floor?

What is so terrifying? Let's let it happen. Richard will know that you're a stupid idiot? He'll tell everyone that you're a raving lunatic? What?

The patient is shaking and screeching. We are both wallowing deeper and deeper into the awful feeling, just letting it happen. Then, he shrieks

I WON'T BE ABLE TO DO WHAT HE SAYS!

The patient has entered a new state of catastrophically horrible feeling. Together with him, the therapist plunges even further into this imminently grotesque and hellish possibility, and is now free of the wrenching bad feeling. In the therapist is a stirring of something new, something that feels quite delicious. It is an inner experiencing of utter defiance, of refusal, of not doing it, of not doing what he says.

How despicable for a man in his position to have a secret cache of pornographic videos, and to vigorously masturbate, complete with grunts and groans, as he is transfixed by the video. The moment of strong feeling is not as he ejaculates, but afterward when he is overcome with self-disgust and loathing. As we both lived in this moment, wallowing in these awful feelings, traveling along the line of the worst feeling, we finally arrived at the excruciating payoff. He is painfully screaming:

. . . SOMEONE MIGHT SEE . . . MY WIFE . . . HER MOTHER . . . OH GOD!

Having disgorged this scene, he is feeling properly torn apart and out of his mind with terror. The therapist, however, is facing wife and mother squarely, the naked essence of exposed sexuality, displaying his sexuality to them. This is the inner experiencing.

You can access the inner experiencing by living and being in this immediately ongoing moment of strong feeling, and by using one of the four locations. But the proper location is only one way of accessing the inner experiencing.

Access the Inner Experiencing by Actively Strengthening the Experiencing

You and the patient are in a moment of strong feeling, and you are having the immediately ongoing experiencing. You are being weak and passive, or fiercely tough, or being drained, used, deprived, or being critical, hurting, or being the chosen one, the wonderful one, the prized one. Whatever the nature of the surface experiencing, the method is to strengthen it, let it intensify, deepen, open it up all the way.

Say it over and over. Do it louder and louder. Make it more and more intense. Let it become fuller inside, totally saturating you. Actively strengthening the experiencing can be quiet, inside, more saturated and intense inside, or it may be open, public, shown, with loudness and volume.

When you actively strengthen the immediately ongoing experiencing, this accesses the deeper potential. This is the key to this method: Actively and deliberately strengthening the experiencing is an effective way of accessing the inner experiencing.

In the moment of strong feeling, the experiencing is being critical, hurting, attacking. Your job is to undergo this experiencing much further, much more intensely, much more deeply. No matter how strong is the experiencing, you are to allow it to be much stronger in you. You speak with the voice of the actively stronger experiencing. But in addition, you invite the patient to actively strengthen the experiencing in the moment of strong feeling by saying it louder, feeling it more, following your own lead as you are the voice of the stronger experiencing. Invite the patient to be this experiencing much more, to throw himself into being this experiencing. When the operating, surface, ongoing experiencing is actively strengthened, then the inner, deeper experiencing will be accessed.

In the moment of strong feeling, she is about 7 years old, tears pouring all over her face, as she tries to tell her mother that her cousin, who is 20 years old, got into bed with her and made her touch his penis and tried to stick it inside her. She is frightened and terribly agitated as she is trying to get her mother to listen, but mother is taking the side of the cousin. The little girl is crying hard as she is yelling:

How could you let him do that to me!? HELP ME!

Mother is coldly impassive. The therapist is feeling hurt, angry, and terribly lost, as he shows the patient how to show this much more, with much greater strength. When the patient opens up this experiencing all the way, the therapist is now in touch with and receiving something new. It is an inner experiencing of being utterly vulnerable, defenseless, fully dependent, an innocent little baby, and the surrounding feeling is peaceful, quiet, harmonious.

He is in his sister's apartment, and the moment of strong feeling is when he puts his arms around her. She is feeling so bad about the way she is with her son, and she is huddled and crying. The ongoing experiencing is one of comforting, consoling, caring for. When the therapist invites the patient to open up this experiencing even further, to actively strengthen this experiencing, the patient exaggerates and heightens this experiencing until a new element stirs inside the therapist. It is a newfelt sense of oneness, of melding with, of complete closeness. It is a wonderful experiencing, accompanied with wonderful feelings.

She has been in a mental hospital twice in the past year or so, and each time was after her husband had left on a trip. She is in the apartment, alone, before going crazy and ending up in the hospital. The moment of strong feeling is when she is shaking, cannot stand up, her head is swirling, and she has visions of him crashing, being in an accident, having a heart attack. She is panic-stricken. Living in the exact moment, the therapist invites her to let the panic get absolutely full. At first she is merely breathing rapidly, trembling, and shaking. As she actively opens up the panic, she becomes full of terror at the deranged things she might do. With even stronger feeling, she shifts into something else, moaning, throaty groans, and she is suddenly writhing in sensual excitation, touching her body on the bed, being consumed with sexual feelings. This is the accessed inner experiencing.

The terrible moment of strong feeling is when he is at an airport. He left his home city, is now at a second airport, and is to take another plane to go to the final destination. He thinks he has time for a cigarette, and he starts to find a place to smoke. Then it happens. He feels woozy, lost, has no idea where he is, almost feels like crying, seems to not know who he is, what he is doing here. Things seem both speeded up, and slowed down, flashing, out of control, crazy. It is awful. This is the moment. When both therapist and patient actively strengthened this experiencing, he fell into a vortex of dizzy swirling, becoming ever more helpless, retreating even more out of himself. With a full crescendo of feeling, he withdrew out of himself, and suddenly is giggling like a maniac:

> NO! NO NO NO NO NO! [Giggling] I'M ABOVE THEM, FLOATING ABOVE THEM. LOOK AT LITTLE CLAUDE. POOR LITTLE CLAUDE. YOU'RE CRAZY, CLAUDE . . . HA HA HA. I AM FREE . . . HA HA HA . . .

There is an accessed inner experiencing of being free, letting go of who I am, no longer being me, freedom, liberation, escaping from. It is so very peaceful.

Once you have entered into the moment of strong feeling, you can access the inner experiencing by being in the proper location and simply receiving it. Or you can actively strengthen the ongoing experiencing and access the inner experiencing that is heated up and that shines forth. There is a third way of accessing the inner experiencing in the moment of strong feeling.

Access the Inner Experiencing by Inserting the New Element

As you are living and being in the moment of strong feeling, a whole new element will often appear. It may be a feelinged outburst, a feeling-laden thought or idea, a new and critical element of the immediate situational context. These suddenly occurring new elements can make a significant difference in what is occurring in the moment. They alter the moment, sometimes drastically. They may open up an entirely new moment. In any case, the inner experiencing is accessed in the new moment that is released by inserting the new element.

Insert the feelinged outburst into the moment of strong feeling; release the implied new moment.   The new element may consist of a feelinged outburst. The patient bursts into tears, suddenly gets mad, cracks up with laughter. These feelinged outbursts were not parts of the original moment of strong feeling. They are added elements. There are two ways that these added elements can help you to access the inner experiencing. One way is simply to include the feelinged outburst into the moment of strong feeling. Suppose the tears or the sudden outburst of anger actually occur in the moment of strong feeling. That would probably change things a great deal, release a whole new moment. The second way is to allow the feelinged outburst to release an implied new moment, to explode the moment of strong feeling into a released new moment. The feelinged outburst essentially unlocks an implied new moment of strong feeling.

He lives with a woman who had been hospitalized years ago, and she is under drug therapy. She becomes full of panic when she can't call him at work. He stays at home after work and takes care of her. The moment of strong feeling is when a friend calls and asks if he would come ice skating with a few friends. He asks the woman, as he holds the phone, and she says nothing, but puts her head down. In this instant, he feels trapped, cornered. Then, as if outside this moment, he says:

I am like a damned slave! I can't even breathe! I deserve a little freedom!

The therapist says:

YOU BETTER NOT SAY THIS. IMAGINE SAYING THIS. HEY, WOMAN, I'M LIKE A DAMNED SLAVE. HA!

Immediately the patient bursts out:

OH GOD, SHE'D DIE! SHE'D FLIP OUT! SHE'D LOSE IT.

Get the picture? See her going completely bonkers? Here is the moment that is released. In this new moment, the inner experiencing is driving her crazy, off the deep end, driving her out of her mind.

The moment of strong feeling is when she is about 16, and she snuck her boyfriend into her room. In the middle of the night, right after sex, her father knocks on the door and demands to know what's going on in there. Her boyfriend dives under the covers, and her father says, "Well?" in a demanding, angry tone. She is panic-stricken. This is the moment. As we are living and being in this moment, she says:

He might come in! My God! He might come in!

The therapist says:

Yeah? So? I got it! He bursts in, and . . .

She shrieks:

HE'D DIE! HE'D HAVE A HEART ATTACK RIGHT ON THE SPOT. HIS LITTLE GIRL . . . FUCKING . . . HE'D DIE!

In the new moment, released by this outburst, the inner experiencing is shocking them, being sexually wild, grossly exhibiting oneself, shocking the hell out of.

He is a little boy, and he has a bad cold. His father is a physician, and the father comes into his bedroom, sits down on the bed, and touches his forehead, his neck, and his face. The moment of strong feeling is when the little boy is being touched on the face by his father. As the patient is detailing exactly what is occurring in this moment, he suddenly bursts into hard crying. He is saying nothing, just sobbing. With this inserted into the revised moment of strong feeling, the therapist has, inside, an inner experiencing of soft crying, showing warm and caring love, being close and lovingly expressive.

She is at the family gathering. There are about eight people, including her brothers, their wives, two aunts and uncles. The agenda is what to do about mother, now that father is dead, and mother is without money and is gloomy and crying a lot. The moment of strong feeling is when they run out of ideas, and there is a pause. No one knows what to do. She is agitated. As she is living and being in this moment, describing detail after detail, she is whining:

> *I know I should be offering to care for mom, and they're trying, but they are all older, and Hilda is so wealthy that she doesn't know what to do with all her money. No one comes up with anything. Just a lot of hand-wringing. Sam is looking away. Don and his wife are acting like it is all a boring game, and they are just being nice. They have no idea what to do! [Then comes the feelinged outburst.] THEY COULD DO SOMETHING IF THEY GOT OFF THEIR FAT ASSES!*

As the therapist senses what it is like to yell these words in this way in the moment of strong feeling, there is a released pocket of inner experiencing. It is a glow of being firm, sure of herself, strong, openly and directly frustrated.

Insert the feeling-laden private thought into the moment of strong feeling.   You and the patient are living and being in the moment of strong feeling. Then, suddenly, the patient has a feeling-laden thought. This thought is private, hidden, inside. But suppose that it is inserted into the ongoing moment. That changes the moment, perhaps drastically. The inner experiencing occurs in what is stirred inside the therapist when this feeling-laden thought is poured into the context of the moment of strong feeling.

He is a little boy, in the basement of the house, playing, and his father is fixing the wiring in the ceiling of the basement. He asks if he can help, and his father barks out, "No!" He feels hurt, intrusive, unwanted. As we are in this moment of strong feeling, the patient voices a private thought:

> *He doesn't love me. He never touches me or holds me or anything!*

Within the immediate context, it is as if this is said out loud, to father. The very moment is suddenly changed. Saying this out loud, inserting this into the ongoing moment, the therapist is resonating with an inner experiencing. It is the inner stirring of a sense of being openly critical, challenging, being accusatory.

Sometimes the private thought is a reaction to the way the person is being, and is a wholly new element. He is at the board, explaining to the department heads his brand-new plan for reorganization. It is brilliant. He is enjoying a sense of being the leader, the superior one, the genius. Living in the moment of strong feeling, he blurts out a private thought:

> *My God! I sound like a pretentious bastard! Who the hell do I think I am?*

Did he really say this in the moment? No. Inserted into the context of the moment of strong feeling, the whole context is altered, and with this comes the inner experiencing of being able to step away from and tease oneself, to poke fun at oneself.

Insert the suddenly unlocked or released new scene.   This usually happens in one of two ways. In one, you are living and being in the moment of strong feeling and then some entirely new element of the scene pops out, comes into focus. The missing crucial detail is now found. Suddenly, you know exactly what you were holding in your hand, you know who that other person was, you know exactly where all this is taking place. This entirely new element renders the scene altogether different, and with this, the inner experiencing is accessed. In the other way, this suddenly emerged new element shifts you dramatically to a connected or related scene that shoots out of the immediate moment of strong feeling. It is as if your being so fully in the moment of strong feeling catapults you off to this related scene and therein lies the accessed inner experiencing.

The moment of strong feeling is when she is in the midst of intercourse, carried away with strong sexual feelings. Her eyes are wide open, and she is grinning. Suddenly, she catches a whole new element. Yes! That's it! She fills in the missing detail of her husband's exact words:

What's wrong with you?

With this new element, a whole new moment is unlocked and released. In this radically altered new moment, the inner experiencing is being a sex-crazed, lewd slut, a sexual monster.

He is a little boy, sitting cramped at his desk, trying to write the letters of the alphabet as his mother is leaning against him, to his left. She is berating him, yelling how bad he is, what an awful child he is. In the moment of strong feeling, he is struggling to write the letters properly, and he is feeling stupid, berated, dumb, yelled at. The more we fill in what is exactly occurring in this moment, the more we arrive at precisely what he is writing. First, it is the letter B, then G. Then we see lines on the paper. He is doing something that is the reason for her screaming. What is it? Suddenly it appears. He writes B wrong! It is backward! Then he writes G way above the line! Mother goes crazy! With the new, critical element, there is a radically altered scene. It appears very suddenly, and in this sudden new instant,the therapist is touched inside with a new inner experiencing: driving her crazy, infuriating her, provoking her. It is almost deliriously wicked and delicious.

DENOUEMENT

It seems almost glib to say that you have accessed an inner experiencing, that some deeper potential has been brought forward, and that you are in touch with it, sensing it, being touched by it. It seems almost glib because what you and the patient have achieved is quite remarkable. You may only be in touch with it for three to six seconds or so, perhaps longer. But most people go through their entire lives without being close enough to what lies inside to actually sense it, to access the deeper potential.

But you cannot just reach inside and pluck the inner experiencing. You must show the patient how to find a scene of strong feeling, something she attends to that is accompanied with strong feeling. You must be wholly aligned with the patient. Once you find a scene of strong feeling, you must live in it, and you must look for the elusive and priceless moment of strong feeling. By being in this moment in the right away, you can access the inner experiencing, and this is the goal of this first step.

This chapter is long. This is not because there are lots of complicated substeps. Actually, the structure of Step 1 is rather simple and straightforward. It is long because most therapists are not especially familiar with this way of opening a session, and I wanted to be quite clear about what you do and how you do it. More than merely providing an introduction, I wanted to enable you to carry out the first step and to access a precious deeper potential or inner experiencing.

CHAPTER EIGHT

Step 2. Integrative Good Relationship with Inner Experiencing

Step 1 ends with the accessing of the inner experiencing. Ordinarily, the patient's relationship with this accessed inner experiencing is quite bad. The word I use is "disintegrative." This chapter shows you how to enable the patient to move from a disintegrative bad relationship to an integrative good relationship with this inner experiencing. By the end of Step 2, the patient feels good, integrative, welcoming, appreciating, about the inner experiencing (Figure 3.1, p. 82). This chapter shows you how to accomplish this change.

In one sense, Step 2 is easier than Step 1. In Step 1, patients rarely start by being in a moment of strong feeling. You have to give the opening instructions, then you must locate a scene of strong feeling, then you have to enter into the scene, then you must find a moment of strong feeling, and finally you can access the inner experiencing in that moment of strong feeling.

In Step 2, the important material is typically right here. You work with the inner experiencing and the person's relationship with the inner experiencing, and these are right here before you. In this important sense, the work of Step 2 is a lot easier than the work of Step 1. In Step 2, you can simply go ahead and apply the methods for moving the bad disintegrative relationship to a good, integrative relationship.

When Do You Move to Step 2, to Enable the Patient to Have an Integrative Good Relationship with the Inner Experiencing?

At the very end of Step 1, there is an instant or two in which you accessed the inner experiencing. It is stirring in you. This is when you switch to Step 2. There is no pause, no fanfare of switching from Step 1 to Step 2. As soon as you are receiving the inner experiencing, in Step 1, you switch to using the methods of Step 2. It happens that quickly, and that automatically.

Typically, at the end of Step 1, there is an instant when the patient is quite close to the inner experiencing and, just in that instant, is momentarily free of the disintegrative relationship. In this instant of accessing the inner experiencing, the patient is getting a foretaste of what can be accomplished in the second step. In this instant, you have simultaneously achieved Step 1 and you have also begun Step 2.

What Are the Aims, Goals, and Uses of Step 2?

The aim, goal, and use of Step 1 is to be in a moment of strong feeling and to access the deeper potential or inner experiencing. What are the aims, goals, and uses of Step 2?

To make it easier to move on to Step 3.   Step 2 increases the chances of having a reasonably successful Step 3. In Step 3, the patient is to get inside of, literally to "be" the deeper potential. Essentially, the patient is to become a whole new person, the deeper potential, that the person has spent his whole life successfully not being. To accomplish Step 3, it is almost essential that the patient have a welcoming and appreciative relationship toward the deeper potential. If you can be somewhat friendly and accepting toward the deeper potential, you will perhaps be able to let go of your self and literally become the deeper potential. If you absolutely hate that deeper potential, if you want to have nothing to do with it, if you don't even want it close by, then the chances of having a successful Step 3 are rather slight.

To achieve an integrative relationship between the person and the inner experiencing. Another way of describing the aims and uses of Step 2 is that this step enables the person to have an integrative relationship with the inner experiencing. What is meant by "integrative"? It means that the person genuinely welcomes and appreciates the deeper potential, loves it, cherishes it, feels good about it. At the very least, the deeper potential is kept around. It is allowed to remain close to the person, to be near. It is not pushed back down again, kept out of awareness. I am not referring to a little bit less fear or fright of it. I do not mean a kind of wary tolerance or a shaky neutrality. I am referring to a newfound state of integration where the patient feels very welcoming and very appreciating toward the deeper potential, a state that is accompanied with feelings of closeness, warmth, peacefulness, inner harmony, a sense of wholeness, a sense of togetherness, tranquillity. This constitutes a radical shift in the person's relationship to the inner experiencing.

Do you welcome and appreciate every inner experiencing, or only certain worthy ones? Are you to welcome and appreciate every deeper potential, or should you discriminate, push for integration with some deeper potentials but not with others? The answer is that Step 2 is for all deeper potentials. There is no division into those that are to be integrated and those that are not to be. Once a deeper potential is accessed at the end of Step 1, Step 2 is to enable the patient to relate to it integratively. No conditions. There are no deeper potentials that are judged as bad, as having to be controlled and watched, as not worthy of integration.

Are there circumstances that justify skipping Step 2? Suppose that there are good feelings at the end of Step 1. Do you still go through Step 2? Suppose that the patient has a sudden outburst of hard, strong laughter that accompanies the accessing of the deeper potential in Step 1. The feelings are great. You still go through Step 2. The good feelings of actualization are different from the good feelings of integration, of inner peace, harmony, oneness. Even if Step 1 ends with a burst of good feeling, go through Step 2. In short, just go through Step 2 all the time, regardless of the nature of the deeper potential or the accompanying good feelings.

Just how momentous an accomplishment is Step 2?   How big a change is it to go from essentially fending off a deeper potential to welcoming and appreciating it? Step 2 is a momentous accomplishment, a powerful and radical change in the person's relationship with the deeper potential. The patient has probably spent just about his whole life sealing off and being barricaded against the deeper potential. Whenever the deeper potential even approached the operating domain, the person pushed it down, sealed it off. Now things are quite different. The person can leave the deeper potential be. The person can actually welcome and appreciate the deeper potential. This is a momentous change.

It is almost too easy to say that the relationship has changed from disintegrative to integrative. That gives little or no picture of the actual change in the patient. Consider the inner experiencing of complaining, bitching, moaning, and groaning. Toward the end of Step 1, this was accompanied with bad disintegrative feelings. She was unhappy, depressed, bitter, tight. At the end of Step 2, she was light and happy, chuckling and jesting, caviling, and bantering in a kind of happy complaining, bitching, moaning, and groaning. The shift from disintegrative to integrative relationship with the inner experiencing can be a momentous shift.

Most patients never come close to seeing their deeper potentials. They spend most of their lives fearing and hating something vague and fuzzy. Therefore, because they fear and hate whatever it is, pictures of "it" must be monstrous. They aren't sure what the inner experiencing is, but it deserves to be feared and hated, otherwise the person might just kill someone, or carry out cruelly inhuman acts, or do something terrible. Right here, in this session, these awful pictures will be replaced with a set of more integrative pictures. Like magic, the person has given up these awful pictures, and has a much more integrative set of pictures. Step 2 accomplishes a great deal.

Aside from the actual nature of the deeper potential, aside from whether or not the deeper potential deserves to be so hated, sealed off, relationships between operating and deeper potentials are hatefully disintegrative. By the end of Step 2, the relationship is to be converted to one that is blissfully welcoming, appreciating, integrative. That which you absolutely hated is now fully loved and accepted. Is this a momentous change? I think so.

In a rather important way, Step 1 has been quite clever. It managed to access the deeper potential by either avoiding or by plunging into the patient's disintegrative relationship. That is, the whole aim of getting into a scene of strong feeling, getting into a moment of strong feeling, and then using the methods of accessing the inner experiencing is to bypass the disintegrative relationship, or to plunge headlong into this bad relationship. Indeed, the disintegrative relationship serves almost as a torch or direction-finder. However, once the therapist has accessed the inner experiencing, the disintegrative relationship remains. Accessing the deeper potential does not automatically set aside the patient's awful relationship toward it. That job still has to be done. It is the responsibility of Step 2 to do this job. It is a momentous change.

What Are Some Almost Essential Guidelines for Achieving Step 2?

This chapter will provide you with methods you can use. They are useful, workable, effective. If you want to increase the chances of using these methods successfully, there are some helpful guidelines that you can follow.

You are programmed to attain an integrative good relationship with the inner experiencing. The instant you access the inner experiencing in Step 1, you switch to a program of attaining an integrative good relationship with the inner experiencing. You are instantly geared toward attaining Step 2. This means that whatever the patient says and does is grist for attaining Step 2. In Step 1, you were programmed toward accessing the deeper potential. No longer. Everything that comes from the patient, and everything that comes from you, is aimed toward achieving a more integrative relationship with the inner experiencing.

Your attention is wholly and consistently out there. Just as it was throughout the first step, your attention is wholly and consistently out there throughout Step 2. No matter what methods you use, your attention is to be out there. Attending mainly to the patient will prevent you from attaining Step 2.

Typically, your attention is focused on the inner experiencing itself or on the situational context in which the inner experiencing is occurring. Some of the methods count on the therapist attending mainly to the inner experiencing itself, to keeping it around, to seeing what it is like, to noticing its characteristics, how it feels. Some of the methods count on the therapist's seeing the situational context in which the inner experiencing accesses. In any case, your attention is always and fully out there, not on the patient.

Many of the methods can be used within the context of the moment of strong feeling. All you have to do is to remain in this situational context. In one instant, you are living and being in the moment of strong feeling to access the inner experiencing. In another instant, you are in Step 2; you are still living and being in the moment of strong feeling, only now you are using some of the methods of welcoming and appreciating the inner experiencing that was just accessed.

Accessing the inner experiencing means that it is now relatively nearby. It is active, stirring, present within you. Some of the methods of Step 2 consist of pouring attention onto this inner experiencing. Whatever its nature proves to be, you are to keep your attention fastened onto it (Mahrer, White, Soulière, Macphee, & Boulet, 1991). See it. Attend to what it looks like. Attend to how it is affecting you. Keep your attention on this immediate inner experiencing, no matter whether the feelings are bad or good. If you attend mainly to the patient, you will probably have a hard time using the methods of welcoming and appreciating the inner experiencing.

The methods are to be carried out by you and the patient together, not by you alone. If the methods are carried out well, both you and the patient will be active, involved, both doing something. Sometimes the patient is doing it mainly, and you are going along with her. Sometimes you may be the main one to do the work, yet the patient shares in the task, helps you, participates with you.

The warning is that you are not to be the one who carries out these methods by yourself. Welcoming and appreciating the inner experiencing does not mean you are doing the talking while the patient is silently listening. These methods are not "interventions," things you do to or at the patient. Both of you must participate in their use.

Because you and the patient are carrying out these methods together, there will be lots of occasions when you will be having and expressing strong feelings, generally good feelings. You will be saying things like, "You are good at this! . . . Good! . . . Oh, this is great! . . . You really do this well! . . . This is fun! . . . Yes! Yes!" Since this step involves undergoing a good integrative relationship with the inner experiencing, you will likely be laughing, chuckling, giggling, chortling.

You must be fully welcoming and appreciative of the inner experiencing. It is essential that you are thoroughly welcoming and appreciative of the inner experiencing, indecently and unabashedly integrative toward it. No matter its nature, you love it. There are no conditions or clauses. You simply do not have the right to judge whether or not the inner experiencing is acceptable. From the instant you access the inner experiencing in Step 1, you are thoroughly taken with it. You really have no option. You start out hopelessly integrative, and you continue being this way through Step 2.

You are already welcoming and appreciating toward that which is stirring in you at the end of Step 1. You probably don't know what it is, yet. But you are integrative toward whatever is deeper, and toward this particular inner stirring. What you find to welcome and appreciate is easy because you are already in a welcoming and appreciating state.

You do not meet the inner experiencing through a disintegrative relationship, and then try your best to make it tolerable. This is like getting a sneak preview of the disintegrative deeper potential, and then trying to see it in some sort of positive light. It is like viewing the label through a disintegrative relationship. If the label says, "being cold and mean, hurting others, being crassly manipulative," then you consider yourself justified to pass this one by. If you access and greet the inner experiencing through a disintegrative relationship, you have virtually disqualified yourself from attaining Step 2. If what you see is repulsive fecal matter, trying to see its integrative good aspect is already doomed to failure. You are to be fully welcoming and appreciating of the inner experiencing before, during, and after your relationship helps define what it is.

Use a package of methods, rather than relying on one or two. There are about eight methods for welcoming and appreciating the inner experiencing. Try to use a number of methods rather than relying on a consistent one or two, both in a particular session and over a series of sessions. Most of the methods are designed to work together, so it is easy to combine a fair number.

From session to session, study the methods that you use. Compare the ones you use with those described in this chapter. Then you can begin incorporating the methods that you tended to bypass. There is one exception. Make sure that in each session you use the method of naming and describing the inner experiencing. This is practically essential.

The integrative relationship makes it easier to use the methods, and using the methods increases the integrative relationship. With most of the methods, you start out with a low or moderate degree of integrative relationship. Using the methods tends to increase the integrative relationship, and that in turn tends to make it easier to use the methods. If you listen to a competent therapist and patient in Step 2, the therapist starts with some level or degree of integrative relationship. Then the therapist uses methods that tend to increase the integrative relationship a bit, and that enables the therapist to go further with the methods. The therapist and patient work together to attain a kind of self-propelling force in which there is more and more integrative relationship and more and more effective use of the methods.

This process works in complementary ways. The more fully and well you use the methods, the more fully and well you are probably living and being in the scene; the more fully and well you are living and being in the scene, the more fully and well you will tend to use the methods. The net result is that increasing the integrative relationship and using the methods go hand in hand with one another in a kind of cumulative working crescendo.

Effective use of the methods calls for strong feeling.   In Step 1, it is almost necessary that there be strong feeling in order to be in a moment of strong feeling and to access the inner experiencing. It is very hard to attain Step 1 without strong feeling. The same thing holds for Step 2. It may be feasible to use some of the methods without strong feeling, but generally it seems that attaining Step 2 involves use of strong feeling.

All of this has been prefatory to introducing the methods of enabling the patient to attain an integrative good relationship with the inner experiencing. The balance of this chapter deals directly with the methods.

LET THE INNER EXPERIENCING BE, AND SAVOR THE BODILY SENSATIONS

Using this method means that you have to freeze the moment when the inner experiencing accesses, when the patient is sensing, having, undergoing the inner experiencing, when the inner experiencing is quite present, close, nearby, within touch. When this happens, keep the moment frozen, in suspension. Now turn your attention to the inner bodily sensations. Savor the felt bodily sensations that are occurring right now in you. Your attention goes inward, into your own sense of warmth in your hands, the electrical quivering across the skin, the lightness in your head, the quickening of your heartbeat, the slow rolling sensation inside your chest. Pay attention to what these sensations feel like, their weight, movement, color, texture.

You are to let the inner experiencing be. This means keeping it present. The only work that is involved in this method is to attend to how this inner experiencing affects you, its impact on your own bodily sensations. Letting the inner experiencing be is a quiet, simple, gentle, naive process. You do not move away from the inner experiencing to try to grasp its symbolic meaning, or how it relates to something else. You do not look for other times and places where it has occurred, or its similarity to or difference from other things about you, other qualities or characteristics. You do not recoil from it, deny it, or fend it off. You merely let the inner experiencing be and you describe the nature of the immediately ongoing bodily sensations. You may say:

> *What's it feel like inside your body? . . . Where are the feelings in you, mainly? In the chest, head, legs? . . . Here is what is happening in me . . . Is this what's happening in you? . . . Describe it so I can have it too, just like it's happening in your body . . .*

How is this integrative? How does doing this mean that there is a welcoming and an appreciating of the inner experiencing? There are at least two ways in which this method acts to allow the relationship to become more integrative. One is that the inner experiencing is kept present. It is to remain right here. You and it are in direct and interactive relationship with each other. It is kept right here. It is not allowed to fall back into the deeper domain. Second, by describing the immediately present inner bodily sensations in you, your relationship with the inner experiencing inevitably becomes more welcoming and appreciating. This change seems to occur whether the bodily sensations are good or bad, pleasant or unpleasant. Merely having and describing the ongoing bodily sensations moves you, perhaps ever so slowly, in the direction of an integrative relationship (cf. Gendlin, 1961, 1962, 1964, 1969).

By checking the inner bodily sensations, the patient may get direct indications that, for example, it feels good, welcomed, appreciated:

> *I think I'm grinning ear to ear . . . I know that I feel so light inside, and my chest feels strong . . . Damn, it feels good . . . Whatever this thing is, I don't know, it sure feels nice. Real nice . . .*

Sometimes, the patient gets indications of what is no longer present, of the absence of the disintegrative feelings:

> *It's gone! I mean, I'm not tensed up inside. Holy shit! My whole insides were tight, and my back was hurting as usual. It's gone! What the hell!*

You may use this method in the moment of strong feeling at the end of Step 1. The instant you access the inner experiencing, you can freeze the moment and turn to the nature of the internal bodily sensations. Or, you can use this method with any other situational context or scene that occurs in the course of Step 2, in conjunction with any other method.

Consider some examples in which you have just accessed the inner experiencing in Step 1, and you immediately use this method of welcoming and appreciating the accessed inner experiencing. In this moment, you don't even have an explicit idea of how the inner experiencing can be named and identified. But here it is.

At the end of Step 1, the scene of strong feeling is when she is in intercourse, her eyes are wide open and she is grinning. Her husband blurts out:

> *What's wrong with you?*

With this, the instantly released new moment contains and accesses the inner experiencing: a sex-crazed, lewd, slut, a sexual monster. She hisses:

> *Yessss!*

You and she are fully being in this moment, and now you are both breathing very hard, wholly giving in to the writhing, throbbing, full-bodied sexual craziness. You breathe it out with passion:

> *HOLD IT! Yesss! YESSS! YOU FEEL WHAT IT'S LIKE INSIDE? IN YOUR BODY? INSIDE! INSIDE! WHAT'S HAPPENING IN THE BODY? YESSS. INSIDE THE BODY . . . WHAT'S IT LIKE?*

She hisses:

> *Rumbling . . . it's going on by itself, rolling . . . OH OH . . . Wonderful! . . . INSIDE . . . INSIDE ME . . . OWNING IT . . . IT'S MINE . . . HA HA HA . . . Strength . . . lots of strength . . . Oh yes, gyrating . . . quivering . . . I don't even want to stop it . . .*

You are having bodily sensations too, and you want to see if they are similar to hers:

> *In me it's pretty much all over my body. Is that the way it is for you too, or are they mainly on the arms or chest or . . .*

She says:

Yeah, well, mainly in the hips . . . ! Uh huh!

In Step 1, there is a moment when the inner experiencing is now accessed. Your boss is out of town, and you are to get the information from the four big department heads. They had not provided you with the information you needed in time for you to revise the equipment budget. In the actual moment, you are in a small room, having called the meeting to get the information. None of them are looking directly at you, and you have just told them again what you need. There is a pause, and you are waiting. Although you haven't identified the inner experiencing yet, it consists of bawling them out, exerting power over them, being the superior authority. In this instant, you immediately switch to using this method of Step 2:

Right now, inside. Just hold it! Right now something is happening in my body. But what's going on inside you? What's it feel like inside?

The patient says:

It feels . . . good . . . Solid. You know, I feel strong. Breathing is nice, even. I'm looking at them, and they're looking down or away, and there's a little . . . uh . . . nice . . . A little tingling, sort of? Yeah, tingling. Yeah, all over my skin. It's nice.

In the moment of strong feeling, at the end of Step 1, she is a little girl, around seven years old, alone with her older cousin Mark, in the attic of Mark's old house, in the country. She is his prisoner. There is some kind of metal around her ankles. She is attending fully to Mark. He is quiet, sitting, his knees drawn up under his chin, gazing blankly at her. She is riveted, magnetized onto him:

. . . he seems like he isn't going to hurt anyone, just have something. Yeah, own something, like something of your very own. No one wants to be with him. There are no friends, and even in the family, no one barely talks to him, so now he has something of his very own, like a pretty bird, with red hair . . . not going to hurt it . . . just having something.

The inner experiencing is being so very alone, without anyone, nothing of my own. Although you have not yet identified or described this inner experiencing, you sense it accessed in you. If you let this inner experiencing be, if you savor the bodily sensations, what do you find? You begin, quietly:

If you hold this, just keep everything right here, still, where are the feelings mainly, in your body?

She replies:

I'm crying.

Yeah, me too, and . . .

Just feel warmth, over my face and chest, inside. Mainly warmth, warm, on my chest, and soft . . . and good, it feels good. I like the feeling . . . Good.

This may be the initial Step 2 method you use as soon as you access the inner experiencing in Step 1. However, it is also common to use this method later on in Step 2, while using other methods. In this second way of using this method, the patient is carrying out some other Step 2 method. Then you say:

All right, now just stop. Hold this. Freeze it for a minute or so. OK? . . . Now check your body. Just check inside. Where are the things happening in your body? Where are there things going on mainly. In your head? Stomach, hands? And what is it? What's it like inside your body?

Or you start describing what it is like for you.

Wait a minute! Just hold it! You know what's happening inside my body? No, you don't. Well, it feels good. My chest is so nice and warm. Really warm . . . and . . . my feet are hot. They're hot . . . Is this just me? What's going on inside your body right now?

BE OPENLY WELCOMING AND APPRECIATING TOWARD THE INNER EXPERIENCING

You may use this method the instant you receive the inner experiencing at the end of Step 1, before you have identified what it is. Or, you may use this method later on in Step 2. In either case, you are attending directly to the inner experiencing, and the method consists of simple and direct welcoming of it, appreciating of it, loving and cherishing of it. It is as if you say directly:

I love you. I think you are marvelous. What a wonderful thing you are.

You are fully welcoming and appreciative toward that inner experiencing. You are to show how very much you are genuinely fond of it, how much you love it, and to do so quite openly and candidly. You are openly and directly to cherish this inner experiencing. There are no limits. Whatever the nature of the inner experiencing, you are to show your absolute treasuring of whatever it is:

You sonuvugun! There is this thing in you—a veritable coldness, hardness, toughness. Ha! It's great! What a quality! Sonuvugun! Look at that!

Carrying out this method requires at least two things in the therapist. One is that you must genuinely love and cherish this quality, this inner experiencing, this deeper potential. Your love of this quality has to be real. It cannot be faked. You may have already named and described the inner experiencing, or you may simply be facing it, not yet named and identified. In either case, your genuine relationship toward this inner experiencing has to be one of wholesale love and treasuring. Second, you must show your integrative feeling, and the more openly and expressively the better, for this method to work.

Very often, there is a burst of laughter in you or in the patient, or in both of you together, the instant the inner experiencing is accessed in the moment of strong feeling at the end of Step 1. This sudden burst of joyful laughter is usually the simple expression of welcoming and appreciating the inner experiencing. Step 1 accessed the inner experiencing. The outburst of laughter is the expression of this method in Step 2. As you burst into welcoming and appreciative laughter, you say:

You provoked her! You drove your mother CRAZY!

You WHAT! You almost let her go—and down she goes! You bastard! You're mean! No one fucks around with you!

you are saying that all their desires should be loved merely because they desire them.

you are accepting
you don't that
people want

274   The Practice of Experiential Psychotherapy

Good for you! He's all confused now! He doesn't know what to do! Good for you! You're great! Wonderful!

It's your brother-in-law! Sidney? Oh that's great! He sounds like he's a great fuck! "Jesus Christ, I thought you were my husband! What the hell are you doing in his bed?"

You poured it right over his head? In front of everyone? That's delicious! Don't mess with Rita! Oh that's great! I can see the look on his face! You're marvelous!

In an instant, you have achieved Step 1 access to the inner experiencing, and you are openly expressing your wholesale joy about the suddenly accessed inner experiencing in the opening of Step 2.

In the moment of strong feeling in Step 1, he is nine years old, sneaking through the woods at the back of his house to avoid his boyfriend's seeing him. His boyfriend lives directly across from the front of the patient's house. The patient is going out the back of his house, through the woods, to get to the house of his other friend who lives around the corner. He can't go out the front because the friend from across the street would see him. As he is sneaking out the back, there is an instant where the inner experiencing opens up: being sneaky, lying, deceitful. When it bursts forth, you crack into laughter, even though, in the moment, the patient is not feeling happy. Through your laughter you say:

You're hiding! You're fooling him! You're lying! You really are something! And you pulled if off! Some quality! A real thing in you! Being sneaky, deceitful, lying! And in good old Jerome! Honest, a good boy! Ha ha ha! Boy, you're great! And successful. Pretty damned clever! Good for you!

The patient is now laughing hard:

Well, I didn't want Chuck to see me!

Chuck'll never know what lies inside his best buddy: sneaky, deceitful, lying!

No! He trusts me!

Idiot!

Yeah!

In the moment of strong feeling, in Step 1, patients will occasionally betray a delicious feeling in relationship toward the suddenly accessed inner experiencing. She forgot to meet her husband's uncle at the airport. First, the inner experiencing accesses: being mean, giving it to him, making him sweat. Then she blurts out:

I never liked him anyhow!

In the height of the moment, you switch immediately to this Step 2 method:

You like it! I heard you! You loved it! You got a mean, nasty streak in you—and you damned well like it! I got proof! Good for you! Oh this is delicious! You are mean! You are really nasty! You can actually enjoy being a mean nasty woman! Oh you are just fantastic! Good for you!

Direct expressions of integrative welcome and appreciation may be forthcoming the instant you get the inner experiencing in Step 1, or at any other time in Step 2. You are simply cherishing and treasuring this quality in the person. It is most common, perhaps, to show your welcome and appreciation of this quality when you have named and identified the inner experiencing. In any case, the essence of the method is simply to say, openly and directly, how much you truly like this quality, this inner experiencing. You say:

> *You know, this honesty in you, this openness. Good for you. It's a great thing in you. You have this quality of being so open and honest. You can be genuinely pissed off at her and you show it, and then you can really feel close and intimate with her, and you show it too. Good for you.*

The situational context is one in which she is four years old. Her uncle is forcing her to be quiet, to sit still. But she is writhing and squirming and fighting him. Then she actually spits in his face! The inner experiencing is accessed, and you both have identified a deeper quality of being tough, unstoppable, a real mind of her own, an unquenchable spirit:

> *So look at the guy! He stopped! He came across something he never expected! This kid's tough! Congratulations. I love this thing in you. It's a great tough streak. I think it's just wonderful. Damn! I love this thing in you. What a fantastic thing. Don't mess with this kid. She's tough. Wonderful.*

In general, let yourself cherish and treasure the inner experiencing. Genuinely enjoy it. Show how much you love this potential for experiencing, this deep-seated inner streak. Let him know how wonderful it is, what an absolute treasure it is. It is essential that you love this inner experiencing in the person, and that you say this openly and directly, with good integrative feeling.

NAME AND DESCRIBE THE INNER EXPERIENCING

Essentially this method simply consists of both you and the patient identifying what this inner experiencing is, its nature and content. You are to name and to describe what it is like, and this helps make the relationship integrative.

Using this method is just about essential in carrying out Step 2. Almost certainly, you will use a package of methods in Step 2. But make sure that this is one of the methods. I cannot conceive attaining Step 2 without this method.

When Is It Useful to Name and Describe the Inner Experiencing?

You may use this method as soon as you have accessed the inner experiencing at the end of Step 1. You are living and being in the moment of strong feeling, and you are touched by the inner experiencing. Go ahead and name and describe it. Or you may use other Step 2 methods, and then name and describe it. If you use this method the moment that the inner experiencing accesses, you say:

> *A-ha! A little being kind of rejecting here, a little pushing away. "Just stay away, little man, I have no particular use for you!" There must be a little streak of this inside you somewhere. Maybe. Probably.*

Oops! What have we here? I do believe we have uncovered a little bit of being the lit-tle jewel, the precious little one, the treasured little precious boy. Yes, indeed! Inside this solid and responsible personage is this little tiny quality here. Deeply hidden and not showing much, but here it is. Out in the open. Very interesting . . .

What Is Integrative-Enhancing about Naming and Describing the Inner Experiencing?

There are at least two ways in which this, and most of the methods, serve to help inte-grate the relationship between the patient and the inner experiencing. One is that the inner experiencing is kept around. It is kept present and alive. During most of the pa-tient's life, the inner experiencing has been locked within the deeper domain, sealed off. Not now. As long as you attend to it, try to name and describe it, the net effect is that the inner experiencing is kept right here, and this promotes the integrative rela-tionship. Second, naming and describing the inner experiencing is integrative because you are using integrative words in identifying it. Why will your words be integrative? The answer is that your own relationship to the inner experiencing is itself unabashedly integrative. You love the inner experiencing, and because you love it, the words you use will convey and express this integrative relationship.

How Do You Name and Describe the Inner Experiencing in Ways That Are Welcoming and Appreciating?

According to experiential theory, the deeper potential is construed as having a neutral nature or content, if we can conceive what the deeper potential is like in and of itself. No inner experiencing is intrinsically or essentially bad or evil unless your relation-ship is disintegrative. Accordingly, the methods you use in Step 1 to access the deeper potential will reveal something good. If you are inside the deeper potential, or if you penetrate down through the bad feeling, or if you use any other way of accessing it, the deeper potential occurs as something good, something welcomed and appreciated. This means that the words you use for the inner experiencing will name and describe something good that you are sensing, receiving, or knowing through an integrative relationship.

There are a number of helpful and useful guidelines for naming and describing the inner experiencing in ways that are welcoming and appreciating, that further the integrative relationship. One has already been mentioned. That is, you must love, cher-ish, treasure the inner experiencing. In addition, it helps if you preface your descrip-tion by acknowledging that it is your own impression of the inner experiencing. It is your own attempt to try and identify what it is. It is certainly not truth. You are not giv-ing your elevated interpretation of what the inner experiencing is really like. You are going to give your best description of what it is. You say:

You know what I think? I think there is this thing in you. It's like something that knows what it's like to be a little older, wiser, seasoned. That's the way it seems to me. Who knows? I may be way off, but that's how I'd describe it.

Here is the way this feeling seems to be in me. It's like a kind of strength, a firmness, a toughness. Yeah, that's sort of what it seems like. Yeah, those words seem pretty close.

I want to see if I can describe what this feeling is like. I'm not sure, but let's see if I can start to identify it. It's my impression any way . . .

Identify the inner experiencing as something inside, something deeper, an inner quality or characteristic, quite separate from his ordinary, on-the-surface, continuing way of being:

There is this thing inside you, you know, a deeper thing about you, a little quality or inside streak in you, kind of deep . . .

Well, it's not part of the way you are, not the way you ordinarily are. Not the way you act and think and feel. Something deeper, inside . . .

It's like there's this little thing inside you. It's not you. More like a quality, inside. If it could talk, it would say something like: "Well, what about ME? Huh? No one thinks about ME. Well, dammit, someone ought to think about me, 'cause I deserve it!"

You know what this deeper thing is like? It's mad, or at least it knows what it's like to be mad. "I get pissed off! Sometimes I could just kick shit out of things! Yeah! I am mad, MAD!"

Invite the patient to name and describe the inner experiencing too, and arrive at an honestly mutual, negotiated description. You may invite the patient to start, or you may start, but the understanding is that both of you will work together. Sometimes the patient will come up with better words. Use them. You say:

I am going to try and describe it, but see what you think. Use your own words . . .

All right, let's see how we can describe this feeling inside. You want to start? What is it like for you? No, let me start. I think I got a good handle on it. Then you go.

When she describes it, she says:

It's like I'm better, better than they are. Not better than anyone, but special, a little. That's what it feels like.

When you describe it, and the patient agrees, you say:

OK, yeah. That seems to get it.

When the patient modifies the description a bit, you may say:

Yes, that's it! Like being elevated, competent, a little better, kind of special. Yeah. Does that seem to do it? It does it for me. I think that's it.

Keep naming and describing the inner experiencing until you arrive at a kind of thumbnail sketch of this inner quality. You may say:

Let's keep going till we can describe it enough that a fine character actor could actually be this thing, you know, act it, carry it off.

Use several words or phrases, rather than just one or two. Make sure that you use only general classes of behaviors, rather than specific behaviors, and general classes of situations, rather than a specific situational context. You say words like being aggressive, standing your ground, pressing on, rather than saying that you are forcing the politician to tell the number of jobs created by her proposed housing policy.

What Are Some Examples of How to Name and Describe the Inner Experiencing?

Here are some examples of the actual words used in naming and describing particular inner experiencings in given sessions: being caring, protecting, nurturing, watchful over; being provocative, driving the other one mad, getting the other one upset, I get you all worked up; taking over, controlling, being in charge, owning, dominating; being appreciated, treasured, cherished, the loved and admired one; being vigilant, on guard, watchful, alert to; touching, caressing, contacting, fondling; pulled back, distant, unreachable, separated from; sexual explosiveness, blasting sexuality, sexual thrusting, pounding; being attractive, sexually appealing, sexually admired; sexually oozing, wallowing in sexuality, writhing in sexuality, sexual slithering; confronting, daring the other one, one-against-one, me against you; being powerful, strong, mighty; craving it, wanting it to be my own, compelled by it; being special, elevated, looked up to, esteemed, superior.

Notice how the right words provide a picture of the inner experiencing: being honest, open, not hiding; giving of self, showing self, fully open; being protected, shielded, watched over; serene, tranquil, peaceful; tormenting, abusing, torturing; bringing it out, creating, opening it up; accusing, protesting, criticizing; being weird, a character, different from others; having it, owning, making it my own; evaluating, judging, assessing; whining, grumbling, never pleased; being fascinated, entranced with, intrigued by; gentle, soft, yielding; impotent, feckless, passive; pampered, needy, provided for; complaining, bitching, protesting at; rejecting, saying no, pushing away; being out of control, unrestrained, having boundless energy; lonely, away from others, being alone; respected, admired, regarded as something special; being criticized, picked at, put down; being awkward, a screwup, irresponsible, incompetent; setting free, delivering up, releasing; put on a show, being entertaining, exhibit oneself; loving, being intimate with, caring for; attacking, killing, destroying; being ruthless, uncaring, cold-blooded; self-confident, sure of oneself, capable; being candid, frank, transparent, guileless; being trapped, cornered, nowhere to turn; being dilapidated, rundown, used, worn; being confused, lost, helpless, bewildered; being superficial, thin, pretense, no depth; independent, on my own, autonomous; awe, wonder, gawking at, fascinated with.

The aim is to name and describe what the inner experiencing is in this person in this session. If you are coming close to capturing what it is like, you are helping to welcome and appreciate this inner experiencing.

INVITE THE PATIENT'S AGREEMENT OR DISAGREEMENT WITH THE PRESENCE OF THE INNER EXPERIENCING IN THE PATIENT

The idea is that you name and describe the inner experiencing, and the patient is invited to agree or disagree that this inner experiencing is present, inside. When you name and describe this inner experiencing in some detail, the patient is forced to see it, to witness it, to regard it. One way this method works is by keeping the inner experiencing defined, identified, and therefore exceedingly present. It almost does not matter if the patient agrees or disagrees, for the inner experiencing is kept alive, defined, and present, and that is all it takes to use this method to promote an integrative relationship with the inner experiencing.

This method may be used either before or after you name and describe the inner experiencing. That is, you may preface your own or the conjoint description of the inner experiencing by inviting the patient to be ready to agree or to disagree with its presence inside the patient. Or you may finish naming and describing the inner experiencing, and then say:

> *Well, what do you think? Is it a part of you or not? Is this something you know, or not? You want to agree that it is there, deep inside you, an inner, deeper quality, or do you want to say that it is not a part of you, no way, not me?*

You may first use some other method, and then you say:

> *Now go ahead and deny that this is in you, somewhere. Go ahead! Show how you are just a tense, anxious guy who is frightened to death of having orgasms. Now's the time. It is your show. Go right ahead. This I would like to see!*

You may treasure this inner experiencing as you accuse her of having this deeper quality:

> *You Sonuvagun! You have this little streak, way inside you, and it knows damned well what it's like to provoke the hell out of someone; a little pissiness, a shit-disturber. You can get someone as upset as hell. So what do you think? Yes? No? You got this deep inside you—or no way, not at all? What do you think?*

You may explicitly alert the patient that you are going to name and describe the inner experiencing, and it is up to the patient to determine if that is something deep inside the person or definitely not:

> *You can say yes or you can say no. You can say, "Uh huh, I think so. Sure." Or you can totally disagree. "Me? No way. Absolutely not. Must be someone else. Not in me. No way. Not even very deep, way inside. No way." OK. Ready? There is something inside you, a quality that can say things openly, honestly, it is transparent, open, straightforward. It can say, "I like you . . . You scare me . . . You come on too strong . . . I am attracted to you . . . I am jealous of you . . ." All right. It's your turn. What do you think? You agree? You disagree? Well?*

Explicitly invite the patient to have an argument with you:

> *I am going to say that you got this in you, maybe kind of deep, but it is there in you. Then you can argue and insist that there is nothing like it inside you. Prove that there is not even the slightest possibility of that in you. All right? Agreed? Ready?*

Then go ahead and describe the inner experiencing. Insist that there is something like this deep within the patient. You may tell the patient how to argue, how to deny its presence inside:

> *You say no! I am not that way at all! There is nothing like that in me. It is all a lie. I am kind, loving, sweet, considerate. I protest! I am registering a denial, playing this game under protest. Go ahead! Insist there is nothing like that inside you.*

Have an enjoyable argument.

Openly invite the patient to prove that you are wrong. Make wildly unsupported claims as your own proof:

> *You are distanced, separated, by yourself, not part of a group, you are not a belonger.*

Claim as proof that he has people like this in his world and he hates them:

> *Your weird younger brother Oswald is like that and you can't stand him! That's proof that I am right!*

Argue that he never is this way, that he works hard to be a part of the family and that he has loads of friends:

> *See! That proves it! You work hard to make sure that this is nowhere in your life! Your kids love you and they trust you. That proves I'm right. I think . . . Maybe not . . .*

Force the patient to come up with proof that there is no such inner quality in him:

> *Wait a minute! That doesn't prove anything at all. It's deeper in you. Of course it doesn't show! I can't lose!*

Chide and play with the patient to show how invested you are in getting her to admit that the inner experiencing is somewhere inside her:

> *Look, you don't have to like it! You don't even have to tolerate it in you. Just admit that it's there inside you. Please! Admit that there is a quality in you of being a passive wimp, of not having the balls to fight back; you can't even stand up for yourself. Come on, there must be a tiny little pocket of something like this in you. Right? For God's sake, don't fight me on this!*

Take over the patient's role in wholly denying the presence of the inner experiencing. Bound up and down as you disclaim its presence.

> *Oozing with sexuality? Writhing with sex? Full of sexual feelings? Ha! I laugh! That, sir, is so far from the truth that I won't even honor it with a denial. But of course I deny it. You will never get me to acknowledge even a tiny smidgeon of anything so vile, so gross, so utterly not in me. The charges are false, and I dare anyone to prove otherwise! OK, I think I did pretty well. Now, you go ahead and disagree that there is even a whiff of anything like that in you. Go ahead . . . Well?*

Often the patient will simply agree with the presence of the inner experiencing:

> *Yeah I know . . . No, I'm not going to argue . . .*

Often the patient will waffle around, trying hard not to agree, but he will usually agree:

> *No! I HATE being like that! It's just not the way I was brought up. Oh, Jesus, I wish I had! I know I'm like that, and I don't like it! It's a helluva way to be. But I know I'm like that . . .*

Often he will think of all sorts of times that confirm the presence of the inner experiencing. Typically these are times from long ago:

> *Just a passive little wimp? A little washrag? No balls? Hell, yes, I got that. I spent my whole life fighting that. I remember how my Dad used to correct me when I talked. Damn, that drove me crazy, and I'd never say anything? And my sister used to twist the skin on my arms and I'd cry like a baby! Damned right I knew what that was like. I hated it! I know I can always feel that way. I am never going to let that happen again!*

Occasionally, the patient will simply deny that there is anything like that in him. He is serious and firm. You described it as a being cold, hard, vicious, uncaring.

No, I am not like that.

He is deadly serious. What do you do? Use the other methods that are available. If you try these other methods and none of them work, you may agree with the patient.

I think you are right. There is nothing like that in you. See how agreeable I am? Course I still think there is this thing in you, you know.

Most patients will agree that this is present inside. You can help this to occur by inviting the patient to describe just what the inner experiencing is. Even in the rare session where the patient would like to deny its existence, at the very least you and the patient have seen it, attended to it, and that alone works toward welcoming and appreciating what the patient insists is not present.

DO YOU KNOW WHAT IT IS LIKE TO BE THIS INNER EXPERIENCING IN A WAY THAT FEELS GOOD?

The method simply consists of inviting the person to think of times when he felt good with this inner experiencing. You may look around in his current life. Perhaps there is some time in his life today when he has this inner experiencing in a way that feels good. Or, you may look over his whole life. As far back as you can remember, have there been times when you had this experiencing, and it felt good? The important thing is whether the patient seems to know what it's like to have this experiencing in a way that feels relatively good, whether it happens in his life today or happened some time ago.

How is this method useful? How does it help to bring about an integrative relationship with the inner experiencing? One way is that the inner experiencing is kept around. Both you and the patient are looking at it, attending to it, even as you are weighing whether there is some time when the patient knows what it is like to enjoy, to feel good with, the inner experiencing. If the answer is yes, then merely noting that, savoring the memory, tends to promote a good integrative relationship with the inner experiencing. If the patient cannot recollect a time when he enjoyed and felt good with the inner experiencing, you can still use this to enhance the integrative relationship.

What a pity that you have missed something so wonderful in your life! You have been deprived of the valuable inner thing, or somehow managed to sidestep and lose fine opportunities to feel good with and to enjoy the inner quality in you.

In several ways, then, this method helps to promote an integrative relationship with the inner experiencing.

There are some guidelines that help in using this method. Patients will often come up with times when you merely incline them toward recollecting such times:

Well, yes, you know. Like in an emergency. My father-in-law, the rabbi, he's such a spoiled brat. A couple of weeks ago we were in their apartment and my mother-in-law fell. So I guess I took over, and I yelled at him to call 911. That little baby was headed out of the apartment! He gets people to take care of him. I yelled, "Call 911 dammit!"

and he did. I was in charge, taking control. And yes, it felt wonderful. But I'm never that way. That's just not me . . .

If you describe the inner experiencing well enough, patients can sometimes find times.

Make sure that the patient realizes that the feeling need not be powerful. Enjoying it can mean having nice little feelings:

It maybe just felt kind of good inside. Maybe didn't even show so someone outside can see. It just felt good inside. Kind of nice. You know, inside feeling of being soft, gentle, sweet, and it feels good inside, maybe even a little, nothing bombastic.

She says:

OK, yeah. What I think of is Missy, our cat. She gets up on the bed at night, and in the morning, and I just stroke her, once or twice, and she purrs, and that's how I feel. I guess I do know that feeling. I know what it's like . . .

It helps when you are reasonably convinced that such times have indeed occurred in the patient's life. Keep the window open to times when she did enjoy that experiencing:

I know that you know what it's like. Maybe it happened only a little bit. Maybe when you were just a kid, but think, some time when you felt very good. It's like, "I did it! I accomplished it! I got it done!" And it felt great, really great . . .

She says:

You know what I'm thinking? I once tried to run all the way to school. I must have been seven, eight? And I couldn't run fast, but I chugged my way, and I got all the way to school! Yes! I felt that way! Just like that! . . . Oh, and I made one of those things . . . a soapbox . . . a racer, with wheels! I did it with my brother Todd, and we worked together. Yes! It's when I got in it and sailed down the street and it worked! Yes! That's two times, and they felt marvelous!

Encourage her to search, and join with her in looking:

OK, so keep looking. Some time when it felt absolutely delicious. Just walking away, letting go. I've had it. Come on, keep looking. Any time will do. Whatever comes to your mind, as long as it felt good. Hmm. How are you doing? Anything?

You may come up with scenes that simply appear to you. Toss them in.

You said goodbye to some guy, and it was like a whole freedom descended on you. Free, free at last! I got out of this! . . .

A final guideline you may use is outright challenge to come up with some time when he enjoyed the inner experiencing:

All right, so let's see. Do you even have the slightest idea of what it's like to have fun being a complaining whiner? Where it's fun, and I mean fun, bitching and complaining. About anything. A loud complainer! In the last week, month, six months, I'll bet there hasn't been ten minutes when old David bitched and yelled and complained and thoroughly enjoyed himself! Shit! I don't think you have any idea what this is like? Well? See! You don't. All right, go back five years, ten years. Anytime in

your whole damned life! You are bitching, bellyaching, complaining, moaning, criti-
cizing, and it feels wonderful! Do you even have the slightest idea of what that feels
like? Have you known it—ever? Maybe. So what do you think?

Sometimes the patient will scour her recent life and conclude that she just can't
find any times when she had that feeling and enjoyed it. Go back further. Look around
in childhood:

I remember! I got one! Yes! I am three years old, and I got some squash, and I told my
mom I wasn't going to eat it, and she said OK! I felt great! I'll never forget how fan-
tastic that felt! I said no! No! It was one of the best times of my life!

She is exuberant.

Sometimes you do have to go back many years to find even a few instances of thoroughly enjoying the inner experiencing. Think of some time when it felt just exciting
and wonderful to be fighting against, one-on-one, combating against the other:

And felt good? Christ, I feel terrible! That's my problem! I am scared to death of that!
I am loyal, a team member. I got no push. I can go back a hundred years. Me? Me feel
good about that? That would be . . . NO! YES! I used to! I did! Oh my God! I haven't
thought about this . . . I used to be a competitive kid. I mean little kids. Sure! We'd
arm wrestle. And games. Checkers. We'd play in the summer every day on my front
porch. We'd yell at each other. We'd go one-on-one. I loved it! I remember when we'd
wrestle. Oh yes! In the backyard. Jimmy's backyard. I wasn't specially good, but we'd
take turns. I loved combating, and one-on-one. Yes! And it was wonderful! But that
was so many years ago. What happened? Something happened to me! What a differ-
ence now! Ha! I changed! I was better then!!

The inner experiencing may be one the patient is not attracted to. It may even be
rather loathsome. It is the sense of gotten home free, gotten out of something, not being
caught. The patient can hardly admit that the inner experiencing is present, and certainly not one that is accompanied with good feelings:

Do you even have an inkling of what it can be like to enjoy this awful, nasty, terri-
ble feeling? If we talk about it quietly, even in whispers. Ssshhh. Do you even know
what that is like, in a secretly enjoyable way?

She says, almost giggling, secretively, hushed:

I brought a guy into my room when I was 16, and he left around five in the morning,
and at breakfast no one knew. I just sat there, and no one knew! I was very good! I
was very quiet. Sex was fantastic. Ssshhh.

You do know what it's like, I mean to feel very good about this sense of being home free,
not getting caught.

Little Miss Goody Goody. No one knew.

You are terrible.

Yes I am, and it felt fantastic . . .

Ha!

INVITE PATIENT TO VOICE POSITIVE AND NEGATIVE REACTIONS TO THE INNER EXPERIENCING

The gist of this method is to provide the person with plenty of opportunity to voice her positive reactions and her negative reactions to the inner experiencing, how wonderful and valuable it is, how bad, evil, awful, grotesque such an inner experiencing is. If she likes the inner experiencing, that contributes to the good, integrative relationship with the inner experiencing. On the other hand, even if she is voicing her quite honest and open negative reactions to the inner experiencing, she is retaining it, keeping it around, maintaining its presence. In addition, somehow, even if she is saying how awful it is, something seems to move the relationship toward one that is positive, integrative.

Provide Plenty of Room for the Patient to Voice Positive or Negative Reactions to the Inner Experiencing

With your own eye on the inner experiencing, give the patient plenty of room to love it, to feel good about it, or to regard it as disastrous and awful, as something she would like to get rid of, as menacing and dangerous:

> *Do you like it? Is it awful? Is it appealing to you? Is this something you wish would just go away?*

Give her plenty of space to give her positive or her negative reactions to the inner experiencing. She loves this quality in her, even if it rarely shows itself.

> *I'd love to be pissy, to say no. I wish I could be more defiant, and stand up for myself. I'd love to be able to say no. That'd be great!*

Ask her why, how. She can explain:

> *It'd feel better. That's why. It'd feel more . . . natural . . . I think it would be great if I could tell my father-in-law to piss off. I'm not your little girl! Leave me alone! Saying no? That'd be fantastic! I've always admired friends who can resist, and they do it . . . like it feels good. I can't! I wish I could!*

You describe the inner experiencing, and see how he feels about it:

> *All right. You know there's this thing in you. It is kind of self-contained, by itself, autonomous. It does things by itself. So what do you think about this? You like it? Hate It? Does it appeal to you? What do you think?*

He is not sure:

> *I don't even know what that's like. It doesn't seem like me . . . It's scary . . . I love being with Jenny . . . and the kids . . . I don't know . . . My brother's like that. He's all alone, and he . . . he's a writer . . . But he has no one. I've always been with people. I'm not like Ted . . . I don't think I like it . . . No . . . I don't know . . .*

How does she feel about this inner experiencing of being deceitful, hiding, doing things behind their back?

> *You know something? I wish I could be like that! I should be! I am so damned . . . goody goody! You know what I do? I smoke secretly! Oh yes! I drive off once in a while*

and have a smoke! And no one knows. I love it! I just can't do it openly! And I buy sexy lingerie! Well, I always try it on and never really buy it. I don't buy it. But I try it on! Damn! Yes! Why not? I wish I could be that way for real! When my son hides things, I can't get mad at him! I wish I could do it! He hides little things. I find them. I don't hide anything! I should! Yes, dammit! I wish to hell I could be that way more! Why not!

The inner experiencing is being tough, firm, saying it directly. You may simply be curious about how he feels about this quality:

It's in you, all right. You know it. I know it. There it is. But how do you really feel about it? Because you aren't like this in any open and impressive way. It's not the way you are. In fact, it's just not a part of the way you are, or have been, probably since you were put together. So what do you think? You have something against this? Maybe. You probably do. What do you think?

He pauses, and then:

I'd give anything to be like that. No, it's not the way I am. I'd do anything to be like that . . . I think . . .

The inner experiencing is being openly aroused, reveling in erotic sensations, celebrating sexuality, throwing oneself into wholesale sexual feelings. How does he feel about this? Is it appealing? Is this bad? Is it the source of all his troubles and problems?

Well, to be truthful, I don't like it. It is actually quite bothersome to me. All my life I knew that I get very aroused. Too much. Much too much. I always knew there was something wrong. I should not have such sexual feelings. Not so much anyhow. Sure, I want to have sexual feelings. I want to be normal. I am afraid of becoming like . . . A Mr. Hyde, you know? In Jekyll and Hyde? I know that I feel sexual, but I am very hesitant to acknowledge it in front of my wife, even my wife, and when it comes to others, I think it is the worst thing . . .

Challenge Patient to Deliberately Oppose Your Positive Reactions to the Inner Experiencing

Deliberately set up a friendly, open, integrative encounter or argument. You will regard the inner experiencing as wonderful, pleasing, appealing, and you challenge the patient to regard it as awful, dangerous, bad. The patient is to see the inner experiencing as his mortal enemy, as the terrible thing that it is (cf. Mahrer, 1978/1989d):

Ready? All right. This thing in you is absolutely wonderful. It can say, "Get the hell out of here! . . . Just leave me alone! . . . Go away!" It knows what it's like to be rejecting, to get rid of all the bad things that own you, that imprison you. It's a wonderful thing in you! Just fabulous! All right, now you say how rotten it is, how awful such a quality is. No one should have anything like that. Then we can argue. Great. Let's argue. Your turn . . .

The inner experiencing is being present, being noticed, being special, being the center of attention. She is still living in the moment of strong feeling when she is the only one at the big Christmas table who is not dressed formally, and she is the only one to drink the red wine, and her plate is clean while all the others are in the middle of eating and talking, and she is the only quiet one, eating and drinking. She is definitely not enjoying the inner experiencing. You say:

So here is the deal. I am going to convince you how fantastic this thing is in you—being noticed, being special, being the center of attention. That's my job. OK? You are to hate this thing in you. You think how terrible it would be to be like that. Then we can have a great argument. Ready? . . . You are blessed to have something in you, being the special one, being noticed. I know 48,000 people who would kill to have this quality in them . . . If you knew how to use it, you could be so happy . . . I mean really happy, being noticed. See me! Oh here I am, you lucky people! I am here! It is I . . . I am so special. You all know how very special I am . . . Yes, look at me . . . Oh how wonderful this is . . . Well, that's pretty good for openers. It's your turn. Show me how rotten and awful this thing is in you. Being special, bad! Being the center of attention? Rotten! Go ahead . . .

You can hop up and down with your energetic praise of the inner experiencing:

Just a minute! I got my eye on this thing in you. Yes, it's deeper, and yes you are bothered by it. It's a being cold, leave me alone, not responding, not being warm and gentle, a haughtiness, above it all, a cold superiority. Now you don't like this thing, right? You think it's a source of unhappiness, right? It's something you wish you could eradicate, right? You want to "understand" it, right? You want to understand its history and how it ever got started in you, right? Then you can maybe get rid of it, right? Well, listen buster! I'm going to defend it. I am going to say how wonderful it is. I think this thing is wonderful. In fact, I think it's better than you are! Yes! I don't think you deserve to have this great inner quality. In fact, I am going to take it right away from you—you'd like that—and I'm going to give it to a deserving guy, one who knows how to use it properly. I think this quality is too good for you! So what do you think of that? Huh? And remember, I am just opening, just starting . . .

Outdo the Patient in Voicing Powerfully Negative Reactions to the Inner Experiencing

Whether the patient's reactions are somewhat positive or especially somewhat negative, you may outdo the patient in exaggerated, overblown, negative reactions to the inner experiencing. In the moment of strong feeling, what accesses is being oppositional, defiant, refusing. In giving his reactions, he is somewhat hesitant:

Well, I don't know . . . She wouldn't understand . . .

You say:

Of course she wouldn't! Being that way is awful! You should never be that way to your sweet, kindly, old mother—you rat! Basically, you're a rotten kid. You are oppositional, defiant, refusing, and that means you're sick! You got a social disease! You are mentally ill! A nut! A BAD BOY! Thank God, it is a streak that is deep inside you. Maybe we can cauterize it away. Or find out what's causing this terrible thing in you and do something about it. Can you imagine what would happen if this rotten thing in you even starts showing itself? Horror of horrors! Your life would be finished! Your mother would have a heart attack and die, and it'd be your fault! No one would like you! No one! You know the way you are worried about not having any sex with Justine? Well, that would be taken care of cause she'd leave you in a month! Your whole life would be miserable? Ha! By the way, how am I doing?

Portray how the inner experiencing might well show itself, and be dramatically explicit in how this would mess up her life:

Some possibility in you. Being passive, gentle, vulnerable, sensitive? Oh my God, this could be your ruination! You are the chair of the whole damned department! Just imagine what would happen if one of your staff yells at you, or is mean to you. You'd be hurt, and you'd show it. You'd burst into tears and fall to your knees in forgiveness. All someone has to do is be nice to you, and you'd start panting like a puppy. That's the end of your career. You know what the rest of you would say? "Maria, what's happened to you? You lost your mind? You're turning into a baby, a passive little wimp! The job's too much for you?" And you're supposed to be the tower of strength in the family. That's your job for Christ's sake! If you start being passive, gentle, vulnerable, everyone'll think you flipped! Get a hold of yourself, Maria, this thing in you is trouble, so seal it off. Kill it. Don't let anyone know this is in you. Maybe it isn't. Maybe it's all a big mistake.

Explain how there simply is no room for this inner experiencing. There is nowhere in your current world that the inner experiencing could occur. Explain that the patient has spent years carefully crafting a particular kind of life and being a particular sort of woman, and therefore, the inner experiencing will have to find some other host because there is no place for it here:

Being exceedingly honest, open, showing everything, never hiding anything? Come on, that would be so alien that no one would recognize you. You have done a great job of keeping it all in, not even telling your husband much. You are always quiet and scared inside. Just where would you be open and showing everything? With Sam? Nope? With your two sisters? No way. At work? Impossible. I'm sorry! There is no room in your life. Get a diary. Maybe that'll work. Just make sure you hide the diary, and don't tell anyone that you pour out all your feelings in a diary.

Give voice to what some other opposing part of him would say:

Let's go slow here, George. This thing in you, this wicked little devil, this little streak of pure nastiness. What happened to Mr. Nice Guy? Remember you are a basically nice guy, kindly, forgiving, understanding. This isn't you. It's awful, horrible. No one'd recognize you. Well certainly no one'll like you. You used to be sweet. Not now! This is not good old George. What's going to happen to good old George? Tell me that? Huh? He's finished? No more good old George? Don't you think about anyone but yourself? Think of kindly George, the nice guy. So what's he supposed to do? I think you'd better think again about this disgusting thing in you. So don't show this terrible streak in you. You can have one nasty thought a day, but only one, and keep the thought to yourself. Don't admit it openly. Don't show it, ever! Don't let anyone know there is even such a thing in you. Just watch it!

Almost always, the consequence is a movement toward a more integrative relationship toward the inner experiencing. This seems to occur even when he joins you in voicing powerful negative reactions to the inner experiencing, sometimes in playfulness and sometimes in genuine seriousness. It can be exuberantly integrative to fully voice all the negative reactions to the inner experiencing.

Challenge Patient to Try to Have a Negative Reaction after Attaining a Full-Blown Integrative Relationship with the Inner Experiencing

What is critical here is the timing. There are lots of Step 2 methods that provide the patient with an opportunity to have a full-blown, positive, integrative relationship toward the deeper potential. Whatever method you use, the timing is when she is thoroughly enjoying the inner experiencing. She may be joyously laughing about the inner experiencing. Challenge her to go ahead and feel rotten about it, feel frightened about it, feel awful about it. Hate it. See it as monstrous. Very often, she will fail. She will be unable to switch back to bearing the hoary old disintegrative relationship toward the inner experiencing.

In the course of Step 2, she is coming to love her own inner experiencing of being rejecting, pushing away, not caring. She plays with this experiencing, enacts it, jokes and laughs about it, carries it out with playful exaggeration. When the patient is in the midst of celebrating this new integrative relationship, the therapist invites her to return to the bad-felinged scene she brought up in the beginning of Step 1. She was hurt and angered by her mother's never calling her, never asking how she is, never showing any interest in her. The challenge is to have a negative reaction to this inner experiencing:

> *All right, so you like this thing in you, even fun, right? Being rejecting. You! Pushing others away. Not caring. Bad bad. Now go ahead and hate it. That's right, feel miserable about it. After all, if your mother doesn't call and has absolutely no interest in you, isn't that awful? Go ahead. Feel rotten about your mother rejecting you, pushing you away, never calling, not ever giving a damn about you. Hell, she's better at this than you are! So go ahead. Feel rotten about having this thing in you. Feel miserable about it. No! I got a better idea. Your mother doesn't even call when you get that great promotion to the board. Nothing! Go ahead and cry about that. Feel miserable. She doesn't love you. Hell, she barely knows you exist. So feel rotten.*

She mutters lightly:

> *I can't . . . I am the same way. Shit . . .*

Step 1 started with his being in a scene of being upset with some of his neighbors in the apartment building. So much noise! He couldn't say anything because that would only provoke them further. He was stuck. He was grumpy. He was frustrated. In Step 2, we were actually enjoying the inner experiencing of being angry, destructive, aggressive, attacking. One method after the other brought him toward a good, integrative relationship with this inner experiencing. Then the therapist says:

> *I am looking directly at this thing in you: attacking, aggressive, angry, destructive. Wow! So go ahead and hate it. Feel anguished about having this in you. Being like this is terrible. Go ahead, that big noisy family in your building? Loud . . . and smelly . . . and they don't give a damn for the neighbors. Feel rotten that there's something in you that really would like to be destructive. I mean could explode the shit out of them. Here's your chance to feel bad. All right, go ahead. Look at that quality inside you, and show how terrible it is. Feel bad!*

He laughs:

> *I can't do that! I think I'll just visit them with my mafiosa buddies, ha ha!*

In a way, this is a kind of acid test. Once you have a good, integrative relationship with the inner experiencing, try to have a disintegrative relationship with it. Fear and hate this inner experiencing. It is very hard to do so.

What Do You Do if the Patient's Reaction to the Inner Experiencing Is Manifestly and Fundamentally Negative?

One way that the patient can manifest a negative, disintegrative reaction to the inner experiencing is by sinking into an extended silence. If the reaction is so disintegrative, and if the patient does envelop himself in a cloak of silence, you cannot be fully aligned. You see little or nothing out there. Things come to a standstill. You may try to keep your attention in front of you and invite him to talk:

> *Wait a minute! I don't know where I am. Do something. Say it out loud. You're think-ing about something, seeing something. What is it?*

There are occasions when the patient is dead-set against the inner experiencing. Her reaction is powerfully and deeply negative and disintegrative. She is facing the inner experiencing, and everything in her draws back in fear and hate of the inner ex-periencing of being coldly revengeful, vindictive, getting at them, hating them, mak-ing them pay:

> *What good is that? I've tried all my life to fight that. It'll kill me. I would rather die . . .*

She means it. What can you do? One answer is to join with her and concur. Just make sure that her attention is on the inner experiencing. It is essential that you both attend directly to the inner experiencing, even if her reaction is fundamentally disintegra-tive. Join with her. Agree with her:

> *I think you're right . . . This thing is only going to make for more trouble. Do not let yourself feel this vindictiveness. If you are revengeful, you'll only get into trouble. Making them pay! Can you imagine? You'd only start another hundred-year war. Hate breeds hate. There could be no peace, no happiness. You can kill them and they'll kill you. On and on. I agree. Just seal it off. Forget it. Don't be this way.*

The inner experiencing is going berserk, wild, having a crazy tantrum, getting out of control. That is absolutely forbidden as far as she is concerned:

> *But how is that going to help me when my ex-husband comes and makes trouble?*

She says this in a dead, mechanical, lifeless way:

> *I couldn't be that way . . . He'd have me locked up . . . So what good is it?*

Don't try and get her to bear an integrative relationship toward the inner experienc-ing. If her relationship is solidly disintegrative, honor that:

> *Yeah, I agree. It sure as hell would be of no help. I can see him over, and I can just imagine your going berserk, losing your cool. You'd scream and yell, and wave your arms, and bring up all sorts of things, and just generally have a fit, and for what? Nothing. He'd be the same. He'd still make trouble. Nothing would change. I agree with you. This thing in you is no help. Put a cap on it. Maybe after he's gone, you*

can think about maybe you should have just gone uncorked, a raving lunatic, but keep it to yourself. Yep, you're right.

Do not try to force the person to embrace an inner experiencing that he hates, that he finds scary and bad, alien and repulsive. If this is his reaction, and if he sticks to having this reaction, do not try to press on to Step 3. If the patient draws back from and hates the inner experiencing from the end of Step 1, if the patient fights against even naming the deeper potential, considers it a disgusting quality, do not try to fool the patient. Do not try to "get" him to come around to being somewhat accepting and integrative toward it. There is no law that you have to go on to Step 3, or even that you have to reach Step 2. You attained Step 1, and nothing in Step 2 seemed to invite the person away from a steadfast and well-anchored fear and hatred of the deeper potential. There are good grounds for you and the patient to consider winding the session, to a close. Does this mean that there can be sessions where you complete Step 1, and that is that? You do not complete Step 2? There can be sessions like this. If you cannot attain Step 2, if the patient's relationship is absolutely disintegrative, then do not try to force the patient through Steps 3 and 4. After all, this is just one session. There can be others.

PICTURE BEING THE INNER EXPERIENCING IN A WHOLESOMELY INTEGRATIVE WAY

The essential part of this method is that you and the patient allow yourselves to see pictures of the inner experiencing, of the patient being the inner experiencing, and in ways that are wholesomely integrative. What you see may be realistic or exceedingly unrealistic, serious or playful, but always in ways that are integrative.

You are able to generate these pictures, these images, because your relationship to the inner experiencing is positive, loving, wholesomely integrative. It is easy for you to generate these pictures. This means that the burden lies mainly on you, in this method, rather than mainly with the patient. If you use other methods first, and the patient's relationship becomes integrative, then you may count on the patient to come up with these integrative pictures. But ordinarily your relationship to the inner experiencing is far more integrative than the patient's, and therefore the responsibility for this method falls mainly on your shoulders.

You may carry out this method in a way that is quite realistic, and in actual situations, with the patient herself as the one you see being and carrying out the inner experiencing. But if you want to be safer, to keep some distance between the patient and the inner experiencing, then you can use this method in a way that is silly, far-out, burlesqued and caricatured, unrealistic; you can use situations that are quite distorted, unreal, fantasy; and you can picture, not the patient, but rather a clone, a twin, an actor, someone other than the patient.

The scenes and situations may come from those occurring in Step 1. For example, a Step 1 scene was saying goodbye to the young woman who was the baby-sitter until he was four years old. He loved her. The inner experiencing was showing his feelings, crying openly, pleading with her:

Now I know that this didn't happen, and it probably couldn't, cause you were just a little boy, but I can see that little kid just bursting into big huge warm tears, all over his face. His little arms are outstretched, and he goes to her, wraps his arms around her legs, and clasps. "No! You can't leave me. I love you. You are my Mommy! Take me with you! I'll entertain you. I can dance! I'll cook breakfasts! I'll be your lover! I am so wonderful. Let me be with you!" Well, it's possible . . . No, I guess it isn't.

The Step 1 scene consisted of her older brother strongly hinting at wanting her to give him $5,000. He always pleads for money, and he never pays it back. The inner experiencing is being cold, hard, ungiving, uncaring:

Just imagine an actress, sort of looks like you. Sam has just said, ". . . and all it takes is five thousand." Watch that actress. She's good. She looks directly at him, one eyebrow goes up. She has a slightly bemused look on her face. And she says, in a sort of chilling way, "You got to be kidding." Then she pauses. The ball is in Sam's court. She feels wonderful. It feels great being cold, hard, ungiving, uncaring. The whole audience applauds. "Good for you lady. You didn't cave in to the sniveling older brother." All but one person in the audience. You writhe in your seat, moan and groan, and start screaming out: "I'll give you the money! I will! I really will!" I prefer the actress.

Timing can be very important. At the end of Step 1, the instant you access the inner experiencing, in the moment of strong feeling, it is often common that there is a momentary burst of good feeling. In this instant, if you can freeze it, the patient is feeling quite good, even excitedly happy, about being this way and doing what she is doing. In this moment, she is at the printer, and she notices the critical detail. She screwed up in the cover of the brochure! With horror, she notices that the title reads:

An Exhibition of Russian Works of Art Executed 1980–1990.

Oh my God, how did that word "executed" get in there? The vivid scene is being at the printer, and both of you have just burst into laughter at the double meaning of the word "executed." The inner experiencing is being a troublemaker, creating havoc, causing massive trouble:

I can see you there! Well, not really you, but this troublemaker! She notices the key word and, yes, she grins a little mischievous grin. See it? Come on! Watch that woman! And you can almost see her thinking, "Why not? Hee hee hee! I'll do it!"

The patient is laughing hard:

And inside! First page! Fifty painters lined up against the wall, and the guns aimed at them! She'd drive the whole government crazy! She's causing an international incident! DO IT. DO IT!

She continues the hearty laughter.

The scene need not be from Step 1. Merely allow yourself to imagine him being the inner experiencing in more or less simple little scenes from his current life. You may picture the person being this way unrealistically or realistically, as long as your picture is one born of an integrative relationship. It also helps to see it clearly and in detail:

Yes! There is something that is able to be a cuddling little baby, a wee baby. So picture this. And I'm going to describe it lovingly, in a way that you can feel good about. So here goes. You are over at your Mommy's place, just sitting, you know. Then something comes over you. Now watch this. The kid says, "Listen, Mom, sometimes I feel like a little kid. I know I'm 218 pounds, but sometimes I feel like a little kid." And you go over to the couch, where she's sitting, and you put your head on her lap, and you coo like a little kid. "Boy, this sure feels good. You think I flipped? I feel like a little baby. Hold me! Ah, Mom, this feels so good!" That's the kind of guy that I picture. What a guy! It is fun, so there must be some kind of law against it.

Her inner experiencing is just letting go, smashing, bashing, exploding.

I got it! I see what you could be like. But I'm going to make it easier so you won't get scared. You see some actress who looks like you? Got that? She's in a room with her boyfriend. Got that? She's in his kitchen. See her? He's standing there, taunting her. Ready? This is going to be wild. This woman screams out, "WHAT? WHAT? OK, KIDDO, THAT'S IT." And she grabs a dish and heaves it at him. POW. Another dish. SMASH. WHAM. She's going wild, and she goes over to him and clobbers him right on the kisser. WHACK. He tries to get away, and she tackles him! Down on the floor! She rips off his shirt. RIP. And she pours a whole pitcher of water on his face! POUR. SWISH. And she has a fit. Kicking with her feet on the floor, and beating the floor. And she's screaming, "I'VE HAD IT WITH YOU, YOU FUCKER. WHY THE HELL DO I PUT UP WITH YOU." And she gets up, and this guy runs like hell out of the apartment. Then she bellows: "I'M THE GREATEST. I CAN SCARE THE SHIT OUT OF THAT BASTARD. HA HA!" What a woman!

Sometimes the patient is able to picture someone from his current life who is that way, or someone from the past who was that way. Not only is the person able to be that inner experiencing, but the person radiates a sense of integration. Being that way seems right, good, almost fun:

Dan is that way! He is not afraid to touch someone, and when he does it it's great! Yeah, it's easy and natural for him. I can't. Hell, I don't. But he can. Well, hell, I wish I could be like him.

There is usually someone who is the optimal exemplar of the inner experiencing, some current or childhood friend, a sister or uncle or someone. Describing how the person is this way helps to enhance the integrative relationship.

When you see one picture, you will probably see another, and then another, in a kind of festival of pictures. Leave room for the patient to join in as you are propelled from one picture to a bunch of pictures. He jumps in:

You know what I thought of? Telling my Dad how much I respect him! Ha! Can I see that? . . . My sister can! She does it. I don't. Let's see. I see me sitting in his office. Yeah, I'd be in his office, and I can see me telling him that he had that plumbing store for . . . since I was a kid, and he did it himself, and it's a good store, and I would tell him that I respect the way he made that store a good one, and . . . he loves baseball, and he showed me how to throw a curve ball, and he showed me how to bat . . . I think I'm crying . . . I never talked to him like that . . . I can see me doing it . . . God, it's like watching myself . . . Really doing it. I never . . .

ACT OUT THE INNER EXPERIENCING IN A PLAYFULLY INTEGRATIVE WAY

Of all of the methods, this one is perhaps the most challenging and demanding for the patient. In all the other methods, the patient remains essentially the person that she is, and she relates more integratively to the inner experiencing. In this method, the patient goes much further. She is to act out the inner experiencing in a playfully integrative way.

Help the patient carry out this method by carefully explaining the purpose and what she is to do, and by respecting her choice to go ahead and do it or not. Your explanation may be rather short. Explain what the purpose is:

Just to get a sense of what it can be like to be like this.

Explain that it is mainly just pretending, that it is to have fun, that it is quite unrealistic, that she can just throw herself in it. Give her plenty of room to say yes or no. Be quite honest and up front. Then the chances will be fairly high that she can carry out this method rather well.

The Aim Is to Attain an Integrative Relationship with, Rather Than Literally Being, the Inner Experiencing

This method overlaps with what you want to achieve in Step 3. In both this method and in Step 3 the patient is enacting, giving voice to, being the inner experiencing. However, there is a difference that is both subtle and important.

In Step 3, you want to enable the person to let go of the person that she is, to disengage from her ordinary, continuing person, and instead to be the inner experiencing. She is literally to become a whole new person who is the inner experiencing. In contrast, in this Step 2 method, the person is free to remain essentially the person who she is. She need not give up or disengage from this person. Instead, she is still "herself" as she playacts, role-plays, assumes the guise of, the inner experiencing. She need not literally become the whole new person of the inner experiencing. The goal of using this method is for the patient to move closer to having an integrative relationship with the inner experiencing. The goal of Step 3 is for the person literally to "be" the inner experiencing. So the goal of this method is somewhat different from, and somewhat less ambitious than, the goal of Step 3.

Emphasize Playacting, Pretending, Unreality

You are only playacting. It is, of course, not for real. It is sheer pretending, fantasy, pretense. It is a game. You are not really to be this way. You are not really going to be this inner experiencing. The purpose is to give you a chance to feel a little friendlier with this experiencing inside you.

Acknowledge that this inner experiencing is not really the way the person is. Consider the inner experiencing something alien, perhaps a nice alien thing or a not especially nice alien thing, but alien it is:

It is not you. You are not a thoroughly nurturing soul, a provider of succor, a caregiver. It is not something that you ordinarily feel. Yes, it is perhaps a nice quality. Yes, it perhaps can be the way you can be. No, it is not something you ordinarily feel around the streets. So you will pretend. You will playact. You will play the role of being this kind of a guy, but we both know it is unreal.

Sometimes the agent of the inner experiencing is the other person. Especially in the moment of strong feeling at the end of Step 1, the inner experiencing is shown in and is carried out by the other person. Often the therapist takes the role of the other person, gets inside the skin of the other person, to access the inner experiencing. Occasionally, at the end of Step 1, the patient is likewise inside the other person. In any case, the patient is now deliberately to get inside the other person to act out the inner experiencing. In a way, this makes it easier for the patient to act out the inner experiencing because being the other person can contribute to the sense of playacting, pretending. This is often the case when the inner experiencing is not especially attractive. It consists of being demanding, childish, loutish, me first, me only. At the end of Step 1, this inner experiencing is carried out by the brother who is lounging on your couch, being this way. Playact your brother who is to be this character. The patient jumps in:

> *Feed me! Give me a special meal! I want a turkey sandwich. I want it NOW. Come on! When is Star Trek on? Turn it on. What channel is it on? I want it now!*

Usually, the patient is herself in the scene, only role-playing the inner experiencing. However, you can add to the quality of merely playing and pretending, of unreality, by inviting the patient to be a whole new character in the scene. If the scene included the patient and one other person, now it is to include an additional third person. As this added person, she may even talk to the patient in that scene. Maybe she will just talk to the other person, or to both of them. Show the patient, Nancy, how to be this third new character. This is really pretending, really playacting:

> *See Nancy? See her being with that old fat guy in the book store? Well, suppose that YOU are now here. You are going to act out being this tough coot, this no-nonsense woman, this "don't give me any shit" lady. Here you are, looking at Nancy and the old guy. So pretend. Just pretend that you are this woman. OK?*

Emphasize Exaggeration, Slapstick, Burlesque, Clowning

The patient is to playact the inner experiencing in a way that emphasizes exaggeration, slapstick, burlesque, clowning. There are to be heavy elements of the farcical, the caricatured, the far-out, the wildly unrealistic, the silly, the whimsical, the overblown. Do it way out of proportion. Do it all the way, and then beyond.

The inner experiencing consists of violence, physical assault, wholesale destructiveness. The scene is one in which her husband cuts her off, stops her from talking. They are in a restaurant, and the couple they are with ask about her legal work on a particular case she is defending. After she says that she has been working on it night and day, her husband snaps out:

> *That's enough!*

Suddenly there is a taut silence:

> *Do it in slapstick! Clown it out! Be wildly exaggerated! Burlesque it!*

She erupts:

> *I GRAB THE PITCHER OF WATER. THERE! ALL OVER YOU. I STAND UP. STRAIGHT. YOU BASTARD. YOU DAMNED BASTARD. EVERY WOMAN IN THIS PLACE IS GOING TO TEAR YOU APART. OK, WOMEN, LET'S TEAR SHIT OUT OF HIM. I JUST RIPPED OFF YOUR EARS. SMASHED YOU IN THE MOUTH. RIP OFF YOUR PANTS. THERE. POW. SMASH. WHAMP! MORE WATER. I WANT PITCHERS OF WATER. THERE. NOW YOU DAMNED WELL SAY YOU'RE SORRY OR ALL US WOMEN ARE GOING TO BEAT THE CRAP OUT OF YOU!*

When you accessed the inner experiencing at the end of Step 1, he is carrying out the inner experiencing of being disgusted with himself, criticizing himself, bawling himself out. Furthermore, it was accompanied with good feelings. That is all right. Only now he is to go much further. Wholly exaggerate the acting out of the inner experiencing. Do it in a wildly caricatured way. Go berserk in burlesquing the inner experiencing. He enters into the scene, and is the new person who sees himself in the scene:

> *You idiot! You damned fool. What the hell is wrong with you? I am grabbing you by your nose! Say something! Explain yourself! I am shaking you up and down. Talk! You are awful! You got no balls! You are a wimp! I'm gonna tell Sally and Ben and Christine! Everyone has to know! GRRRR! I am slapping your face, back and forth, back and forth. You are piss poor protoplasm! You are rotten to the core! You are NOTHING! And that is my decision. We are going to line you up and shoot you! You are executed! BAM. YOU'RE DEAD!*

The inner experiencing is being helpless, no power, totally victimized, powerless. The Step 1 scene was when her father took her along on a short trip with some other men. It was winter, and one by one, they ritually jumped into a small lake. No other children. The strong feeling came when her father took off her coat. Underneath there was a bathing suit. He suddenly lifts her up to throw her into the lake. She was shocked when he lifted her up and was poised to throw her in. During that moment, she simply went limp and had no inkling of what was about to happen. In using this method, she is to burlesque being helpless and powerless. Just exaggerate being this way so that she actually clowns being a powerless victim:

> *Daddy, I have no idea how this bathing suit got on me. And now you have me in your hands and there is a grim and determined look on your face. But I don't even see this because I automatically swoon. I am a very passive little girl. I don't even think. So do what you want with me. Whee! Oh, you are throwing me into the icy cold water. Like a lump of dirt. I am just a passive little thing here. Up, up, in the air, and down, down, into the icy cold water. Take me to a fiery pit and throw me in. Rip off my arms and legs. I am surprised that I wasn't raped when I was five, last year. I am little me. Passive and a perfect little victim . . .*

Emphasize Wholesale Wallowing in, Throwing Oneself into, the Acting out of the Inner Experiencing

Emphasize to the patient that he is to simply throw himself fully into acting out the inner experiencing. Help him to just wallow in it 150 percent. Jump into the playacting:

> *Think something like, "Oh, what the hell!" Immerse yourself into it all the way. Once you decide to do it, just go ahead and do it.*

There is a heavy element of volition, deliberateness, intentionality.

There is also a heavy element of acting it out with energy, intensity, exuberance, activation. The patient is to throw himself completely into acting out the inner experiencing. There is loudness and volume, powerfulness, fullness, wholesale saturation.

There are lots of inner experiencings that the patient might like and admire, even though he is not that way in his everyday life. But there are perhaps more inner experiencings that are not fun. He may not be overjoyed to discover a deeper potential for being useless, feckless, inept, a general screwup, or an experiencing of being pushed away, repulsed, not wanted, rejected. When you are working with inner experiencings that are no fun, are trouble, are apparently sources of unhappiness, then just help him throw himself into them. Celebrate them. Don't fight the inner experiencing. Don't try to water it down, or try and see how to do it a little bit, or in some acceptable way. He is to throw himself into being it all the way. Be the most useless fellow around, the most feckless, inept, general screwup. He is to be the total and complete expression of it.

It it as if you say the following to him:

> *You can throw yourself into any kind of inner experiencing at all. It may be light years away from the kind of person you are, so far afield from your ordinary ways of being that no one would even suspect that inner experiencing is inside you. The inner experiencing can be so vile, so grossly repulsive, that you could never conceive actually being that way. Of course that inner experiencing is monstrous. Of course it is totally out of kilter with the way you are. So just throw yourself into it. Wallow in it.*
>
> *It is an old, run-down, thirdhand motor scooter. Your buddy is trying to see what is wrong with it, and maybe it can be made to run again. You are to be a very particular kind of character: totally useless, absolutely feckless, thoroughly inept, a general screw-up. You are going to 'help' your buddy with the scooter. Actually, you are going to ruin the motor scooter, knock over your buddy, get oil over him, lose parts, bend and dent other parts, and generally turn the whole affair into a shambles. You accomplish all this by thoroughly throwing yourself into being this inner experiencing.*

And he does:

> *"I'll help." Oops! Sorry! I didn't mean to knock it over! Let me help! Let me help! What's this piece? Shit! I dropped it. And all those little things came out. Were they important? Where'd they go? Oh shit! I dropped all the oil on you! Here, take off your shirt. Well, it's dirty anyhow . . . No! I never fixed things in my life! Somehow, no one ever lets me help them! I wonder why? My hands are full of oil, and I'm dropping everything. Oops!. I didn't mean to hit your glasses . . . I broke them? Sorry! . . .*

She is the head of a large government department, and here she is, in the big store, caught stealing a sweater. She glimpses a couple of acquaintances over there, watching. Horrors. The inner experiencing is having something wrong with her, being sick, crazy, weird, peculiar. When she throws herself totally into being it, just wallowing in it, she says:

> *Oh what the hell! Hi, ladies! I am a nut? No one knows, but I go in and out of the looney bin! I am a crazy . . . a weirdo . . . I steal things from stores, and I usually get caught. I've got a whole closet of stolen stuff! Loads of stuff! I am psychiatric. There is something seriously wrong with me! I AM PECULIAR, WEIRD, CRAZY . . . I AM DERANGED . . . I GOT A SCREW LOOSE! BABABABABABA! I AM A WEIRDO! Watch out for me!*

Emphasize Fun, Pleasure, Enjoyment

The idea is to have sheer fun doing this. Do it with pleasure, enjoyment, raucous good humor, exuberance, silliness, happiness, giddiness. When you are showing the patient what to do and how to do it, emphasize that he is to have absolute fun acting out the inner experiencing, that he is to do it till there is undiluted sheer pleasure.

When you use this method, there can be an apparently magical switch from very bad feelings to exceedingly good feelings. At the end of Step 1, the inner experiencing is being mean, nasty, cutting, and the one who is carrying out this inner experiencing is her husband while she is the unhappy recipient. Her relationship to this inner experiencing is quite unpleasant; it is much easier to fear and hate this in her, or in her husband. In using this method in Step 2, you invite her not only to get inside of and to be in the role of her husband, in that scene, but you emphasize having fun, pleasure, and enjoyment in playacting the inner experiencing of being mean, nasty, cutting. In the course of doing this, she belts out:

> *And don't you dare to interrupt me cause you are an idiot! You are a dummy! I am the doctor, and you are just a nurse! You depend on me! If it weren't for me, you'd be nothing! NOTHING!*

When she is acting out this inner experiencing, the feelings are delightful fun, sheer pleasure, wholesome enjoyment. It feels good. The feelings have switched dramatically.

Emphasize the Challenging Invitation

Doing and being the inner experiencing can be set up as an outright challenge, a test. If the patient did it a little bit, the challenge is to do it much more. If he did not do it, the challenging invitation is to do it now. The challenge is to see if the patient can actually get a taste of what it can be like to be this inner experiencing:

> *Can you do it fully? Can you do it so that you actually can enjoy it, feel great doing it? You know it's not for real. We're here in the office. We're just playing, pretending. It's not for real. Paul isn't really here. He can't really hear you. No one'll really know if you do it. So go ahead. I challenge you!*

The challenge can include seeing what might happen if the patient acts out this inner experiencing:

> *Maybe it'll be a surprise. Maybe you will feel terrible because something awful happens. We know that the inner experiencing is screaming, exploding, smashing, and bashing. So here is the challenge. You are in Don's Jeep when he announces that he is leaving you for good. Let's see what happens when you start screaming and exploding, right here in the car. Are you game? It may be awful and that is the end of your whole world. Maybe worse! Maybe Don'll not even hear you. Maybe it'll make everything all better. Are you up to seeing what happens? How's that for a challenge? You up to it?*

In the committee meeting, the chair mentioned the new proposal, but never even hinted that the proposal was Laura's, and Laura did nothing in the actual moment. She just felt bad, numb, frozen, taut, tight, tense, anxious, and she did nothing. The inner experiencing is being overlooked, passed over, not credited, not being acknowledged. The challenge that you invite the patient to accept is to act out this inner experiencing:

> *I am looking at the chair. I see her. So I am now going to issue you a challenge, Laura. Keep watching the chair. OK? Here is the challenge. I dare you to show,*

openly, publically, grossly, what it is like to be overlooked, passed over, not ac-
knowledged at all. You have the guts to playact it, to act it out? I challenge you! Ha!

Emphasize the Leap into Doing It Right Now

You show the patient what to do and how to do it so that he can do a stellar job of acting out the inner experiencing in a playfully integrative way. Once the patient is ready
and willing, you then emphasize the leap into doing it right now. His attention is out
there. So is yours. Both of you are primed and set to leap into doing it. It is a sudden
and complete shift into doing it. There is no question.

When you and the patient are primed and ready, with your attention out there,
you say:

ALL RIGHT. WHENEVER YOU ARE READY . . . GO AHEAD . . . NOW!

Or you say:

WE ARE READY. THE NEXT VOICE YOU WILL HEAR IS TED DOING IT.
TAKE IT AWAY TED. NOW!

Or you say:

WE ARE READY. HERE WE GO. OK, GO AHEAD AND DO IT . . . NOW!

Do It For and With the Patient

Doing it for the patient means that you act out the inner experiencing. You model it.
You are skilled at doing it quite well. You have sheer fun doing it. You exaggerate doing
it. You wallow wholesomely in doing it. Indeed, you are superb at this. It is easy for you.
You may model it before the patient does it, or you may model it after the patient has
a crack at it. You say:

Wait a minute! That seems like too much fun. I want a chance . . .

Or you say:

All right. You did pretty well. My turn. Step back and watch this . . .

Doing it with the patient means that you join with the patient in doing it. You are
both acting it out. You may simply echo what the patient says. You may go a bit further.
You may finish something the patient says. You may be a clone, a part of the patient, taking turns. Your voice quality is loud, excited, happy, as you both are acting out the inner
experiencing.

Doing it with the patient can mean that you have reactions to the patient's doing
it. You say:

Good . . . Great . . . Yes! . . . More! . . . Oh, this feels just fantastic . . . You are very
good at this! . . . I like this! I love this!

You may give voice to other parts of the patient, or you may actually be the responding other person. The scene is at the dining room table. You are here, and your
sister-in-law and brother-in-law are sitting to your right and left. Across from you is your
husband and his mother. She is obnoxious, especially when she eats by making those
piggish sounds with every bite. It drives you wild. It drives your husband wild. But he

enforces a rule that no one is to mention anything, and as usual no one does. All we hear is smack, slosh, slurp. On and on. In the actual scene, the patient said, "Excuse me," went to the bedroom, had a cigarette, thought violent thoughts, and returned to the table. If the inner experiencing had its way, she would have shoved her mother-in-law's face down into the plate, screamed, "This is driving me crazy!" and put her nose up against her mother-in-law's nose, growling, "You are obnoxious!" When the patient is acting this out, the therapist is drawn toward expressing the outraged reactions of the husband, the brother-in-law, and the sister-in-law: "HOW DARE YOU?!" "No! You have no right to say that to her!" "You are BAD." Give voice to the other persons in the scene. Escalate your voicing these reactions to enable the patient to bring forth even more forceful acting out of the inner experiencing.

The Criterion Is Integrative Bodily Sensations

When do you stop? How do you know that you have succeeded in this method? The criterion is the presence of integrative bodily sensations. The patient is to keep on acting out the inner experiencing until you get the right kinds of bodily sensations. For one thing, if there were any bad bodily sensations, they should be gone. There is essentially no tightness, heaviness in the legs, lump in the throat, queaziness in the stomach. These unpleasant bodily sensations are gone. But the real criterion is the presence of integrative bodily sensations. There are bodily sensations that go with inner peacefulness, inner harmony, togetherness, solidness, oneness, tranquillity. If these kinds of bodily sensations are present, you have succeeded. If you have not, keep on going till these sensations are present. He says:

> I feel . . . good. I don't know. Where? . . . Everywhere . . . Kind of . . . all together . . .
> I don't know. Hard to say. But it feels good . . .

It is very hard to bring back the bad, disintegrative feelings when the patient is acting out the inner experiencing in a playfully integrative way. You might invite the patient to return, or to try and return, to having the bad feelings. You may say, "Well, just for old times' sake, go ahead and feel rotten again, you know, like when the boss passed you right by, never even mentioned that it was your proposal, never even acknowledged you. You felt rotten. See if you can feel rotten again!" Once she has attained the criterion good feelings, it can be very difficult to return to the former bad disintegrative feelings.

CONCLUSION

Step 1 culminated in your accessing the inner experiencing. From this moment, you shift into Step 2, and use any or all of these eight or so methods to help bring about an integrative good relationship with the inner experiencing. The process is rather simple and straightforward. While this chapter covered a lot of territory, in actual operation all the second Step is to accomplish is that the patient feels integratively good about the accessed inner experiencing. This Step may be accomplished in 10 to 20 minutes or so. You may only have used a few of the methods, or perhaps a fair number, but when you are done the patient now has a good, integrative relationship with the inner experiencing. His relationship with it has become more welcoming, appreciating, more integrative. You are ready to move on to Step 3.

CHAPTER NINE

Step 3. Being the Inner Experiencing in Earlier Scenes

The goal of Step 3 is to enable the person to "be" the inner experiencing. Quite literally, the patient is to let go of being the ordinary person who she is. She disengages from being the thinking, feeling, behaving, experiencing person who she is. She is to undertake the remarkable leap out of the person who she is, and she is to be this radically new person, the inner experiencing. This is the same deeper potential for experiencing that was accessed in Step 1 and welcomed and appreciated in Step 2. She is literally to shift into being this whole new person who speaks, sees, thinks, feels, is, the inner experiencing. These are the purposes and aims of Step 3.

This shift from the operating domain, from the person that you are, into being the qualitatively new person, the inner experiencing, is a magnificent feat. Most people remain the same person, in the same operating domain, their entire lives. According to experiential theory, the notable exceptions occur in dreams (Mahrer, 1971a, 1989c). In ordinary daily functioning, deeper potentials are activated and rise toward the operating domain. Then the person does whatever is necessary to make sure that the deeper potential retreats back down into the deeper domain, where it is supposed to be.

In Step 1, the person accessed the inner experiencing, came close enough to bathe in its glow. In Step 2, the person welcomed and appreciated its presence, its nature. In this third step, he will truly be a whole new person. He will be undergoing the wonderful feelings that accompany the sheer being of the deeper potential, the wonderful feelings of actualization: bodily excitement, aliveness, vitality, vibrancy, the bodily tinglings of actualization. In addition, there are no further bad feelings of the disintegrative relationship with the deeper potential. These disintegrative feelings are left behind, gone. So too are the painful ways of being and behaving, and the external world that colludes in accommodating that pain. Step 3 is truly a marvelous accomplishment.

What Are Some Almost Essential Guidelines for Achieving Step 3?

The overall program is that you find earlier life scenes, and then you invite the person to be the new person, the inner experiencing, in these earlier life scenes. The program

300

first gears you to find some earlier life scenes that you can use. Then the program gears you to enable the person to be the inner experiencing in these scenes.

In Step 1, you probably used some earlier scenes in the patient's life. In the present step, you also use earlier life scenes. What is the difference? The difference lies in the purposes and uses. In Step 1, you may have used earlier life scenes to find the moment of strong feeling and then to access the inner experiencing. The earlier scene is a means of getting at the inner experiencing. In Step 3, you also use earlier life scenes. But you are using them as contexts in which the patient can literally be the inner experiencing. Accordingly, both steps use earlier life scenes, but for quite different aims and purposes.

You use earlier life scenes mainly because they are more useful than current life scenes. Simply by virtue of their being cast within the context of the past, these scenes are usually safer and more useful for enabling the patient to be the inner experiencing. Even if the scene occurred a few months or years ago, or if it was accompanied with bad feeling, I find the earlier scene is still more useful than trying to have the patient be the inner experiencing in current life scenes.

It is almost essential that you are skilled in the methods of finding earlier life scenes and in enabling the patient to be the inner experiencing in these scenes. Indeed, you are so skilled that you can play with these methods, move gracefully from one method to another, use a package of methods.

You openly and directly show the patient what to do, how to do it, what you are trying to accomplish. You essentially prepare the patient for this step and for how to achieve this step. You make sure that you obtain the patient's cooperation, readiness, and willingness. When you start Step 3, explain what it is for:

> *Now the important thing is to have a chance to "be" like this, to see what it's like to feel "I'm the favorite. I am. I am! I am the chosen one, the prized one. I am the little jewel." Just a chance to see what it's like to actually be like this . . .*

Explain the important substeps:

> *We have to find some time, go back into your past, maybe a while ago, to look for some time, some time from your past . . .*

Try to be simple and clear. The patient must know what to do and how to do it. Most important, the patient must be ready and willing:

> *Is this all right? Are you ready?*

Remember that it is the patient who is absolutely essential in accomplishing this step. You cannot do it by yourself. You are merely the one who shows him what to do and how to do it, and who does it along with him.

Make sure that you go through Step 3 right along with the patient. When you search for some earlier life scene, you search right along with the patient. When you enter into being the inner experiencing, you are doing this right along with the patient. Even when you are giving instructions, addressing the patient, your attention is always and consistently out there, seeing and being in the scene, being the inner experiencing. This means that Step 3 is largely carried out in the present tense. The scenes are immediate, right here, vivid, alive. You are living and being in this scene in the immediate present, or, rather, you have entered into this past scene as if you and the patient are truly living in it right now. There is little or no being anchored in the present and looking back onto events and incidents that are remembered some time ago.

Which earlier life scenes do you use? One answer is that you may first go into some period of life, such as early childhood, and then find scenes that you can use. Another answer is that you may go directly to different kinds of useful earlier life scenes. In any case, it is helpful to use a number of different earlier scenes so that the patient has plenty of opportunities to be the inner experiencing fully and with good feelings.

HOW CAN YOU FIND AN EARLIER SCENE?

To show you how to find some earlier scene to use in giving the patient a chance to be the inner experiencing, I will describe one way that I use quite often. Later, I will explain a number of other ways to find earlier scenes.

Sometimes you don't have to use the method described in this section. Sometimes the patient will almost spontaneously find early scenes in the course of Step 2. If you wish, you may use these scenes. She says, in Step 2:

> I used to be that way. When I was little, I was the family show-off. I was! Some of the videos they took make me look like a spoiled brat. I used to play the piano when I was little. I remember. I was very little. My aunts always wanted me to play. I always felt like I was special, the talented one . . .

Especially when Step 2 points the person toward the past, she will likely find an earlier scene, and you are free to use this in Step 3.

How Can You Enable the Patient to Be in an Earlier Period of Life?

One way of finding an earlier scene is to start by showing the patient how to be in some earlier period of life. Instead of directly trying to remember some earlier time, first show the patient how to be an older child, an adolescent, a very young child, in her 20s. Once the patient can literally be a child, it seems to be much easier to find childhood scenes and incidents, rather than to try as an adult, to recollect childhood scenes and incidents (Mahrer & Schachter, 1991).

How do you select some earlier life period? It helps to select some relatively large period such as adolescence, or during your 20s, or when you were an older child around 7 or 8 to around 11 or 12 or so, or when you were just a little girl under 5 or 6. You may select a period by using some significant event as a dividing line, such as before your father died when you were 8, or after your parents divorced when you were 14, or before the family moved from Japan when you were about 16, or after you left home when you were 19.

I like to sample most of these general life periods, to be reasonably open and flexible, and not to favor some particular period. A patient may be inclined to go back to the terrible period, during his early adolescence, when his whole family was killed in the fighting in his city. Those times compel the patient, and we may use that period in some sessions, but I like to open up the early life to include other periods as well.

In experiential theory, an important period occurs about a year or so before conception to a year or so after birth (Mahrer, 1978/1989d). Accordingly, I occasionally emphasize this period. Typically, the important figures to attend to are the parental figures, rather than seeing the events of this period through the eyes of the infant, especially before conception. Some other approaches also use this period, especially the events around birth (cf. Janov, 1970), or events around pregnancy, conception, or earlier (cf. Grof, 1976; Rank, 1929). Some approaches may highlight this period if something serious occurred, such as mother dying in childbirth, or your twin being born dead, or your being seriously injured at birth. I am inclined merely to emphasize this general period, whether or not something extraordinary occurred during this time.

Sometimes, the patient will have a scene as soon as you mention some general period. You mention childhood, and before you can continue, he says:

> *I see my girlfriend Louise. We're walking together to school. We were always together. We were best friends . . .*

He says, almost immediately:

> *I'm about four, yes, four. That's when we moved to the apartment where I grew up. It's the eighth floor, and my Mom and Dad showed me my room. I remember staring out the window. I'll never forget looking down and seeing the snow on the ground. Maybe it's the first time I was ever so high. I can remember this like it just happened . . .*

You merely mention adolescence, and she says:

> *I see something! I'm about 14, and my cousin comes over, to the back yard, and he introduces me to this gorgeous boy . . .*

You may use these spontaneous scenes.

Once you select some period of life, you can show the patient how to be in this period by concentrating on some ordinary, common images from that period. Tell him that you are going to name some things. All you want him to do is to see them, and in this way he will be able to be in the period. You say:

> *So I am going to name some things. You see them. See them carefully, and look at them. This lets you be a little boy. You can be a little boy . . . Ready?*

Tell him to see the street where he lives when he is a little boy.

> *Stanley Drive. Just a little street. Curved, and we live at the end of the street, where it curves.*

Tell him to see the corner store:

> *Is there a store near where you live?*

> *Yes, and I see the lady who runs it. Mrs. Chang. She smiles a lot, and she gives me cookies.*

Tell him to see the front of his house:

> *There's a front porch. It's a white house, and there's a big tree in front . . .*

Tell him to see who lives next door:

> *The next apartment. God, people moved in and out . . . Jeffrey. He was my friend. He lives in the next apartment. Beekman. That's his name. He had a brother and a sister . . .*

Tell him to see his room:

What do you see in your room?

My sister and I have this room. She's older. She has the top bed. There's a desk in the room. It's hers.

Ask him what he likes doing by himself when he's a little boy, playing, by himself.

I used to throw a tennis ball against the front steps . . . Jeez, I'd do that for hours. By myself . . .

Ask him to see the bathroom:

What was it like?

I used to sit on the toilet and see faces, little faces, on the floor. There were little tiles, and I used to look down and see faces. I remember there was a face of an old man, I used to think it was the devil. It was right down there . . .

Look at your favorite toys, one of them, some toy you liked.

When I was really little I had this ball, a . . . what do you call them . . . the kind of thing with a castle in it, you could hold it in your hand, and turn it upside down, and it's like snow inside . . .

See your friend, a friend, just see him . . . her.

Louis . . . Louis Rippner . . . What a great guy. He lived across the street and we used to make a snow fort. Yeah . . .

Did you have a dog? You did? Look at your dog. Just see your dog.

She's a little white poodle, and she used to sit on my Dad's lap when he'd read. That's her place. What's her name? Uh . . . Gerty! Yeah. That's a funny name. I loved her. Just a little white mutt . . .

The more he sees these ordinary, personal images, the more he is being in this period. Sometimes he actually starts talking like a child. Clarify what he sees. Get the sights, sounds, colors, smells. Get his feelings and thoughts as he sees the bed when he was a little boy. No matter what general period you select, guide him to see these simple little images, and to do so by being a child, in his 20's, any period that seems appropriate. When you select a few of these images, you are enabling him literally to be in an earlier period of life.

Once You Are Being in an Earlier Period of Life, How Can You Show the Patient How to Find Earlier Scenes?

Merely by being in an earlier period, he may almost spontaneously find some scene, some time. You can use these. When she is being a young adult, say between 18 and 25 or so, she may suddenly say:

I see my boyfriend Frank. Yeah! We're on motorcycles, and I remember we used to love taking little trips. I think I knew more about cycles than he did!

He is being a little boy, and he says:

You know what I remember? It just came to me. I remember I'm five or six and I'm on a bus, going to camp or something, and my Dad gave me a compass. I think it was the only time he gave me something, well, not like at Christmas or something. A compass. I stared at the compass. It was something. I'm sitting on the bus and just looking at it . . .

You may use these scenes.

However, if you follow this method, you will give the patient instructions on how to come up with a scene. Give instructions for how to find a scene by using either the inner experiencing or the general features of the scene from Step 1. The purpose of this section is to describe what to include in the instructions.

Use the first thing that comes to your mind.

Tell her to trust the first thing that comes to her mind, no matter what it is, regardless of whether it seems to have anything or nothing to do with the words you say.

Just trust and use whatever pops into your mind. Do not try to think of why this image or scene is here. Whatever you see, whatever you think of, use it. Use whatever comes to mind, even if it is not really an incident or a scene. You may simply see a ring, an eye, a toy soldier, a little bird, a washcloth, some person, a shoe. Whatever it is, use it. It doesn't even matter when it occurs, when you are a teenager, or it may be from when you were around four or five. That is all right. Whatever you see right off, whatever just shows up, trust it. Use it.

Sometimes she is more or less familiar with whatever comes to mind. However, lots of times the incident or image that pops into mind is new:

Where did that come from? . . . I don't think I ever thought of that? . . . Well? Where the hell? What made me think of that?

I find that this surprise quality makes looking for an earlier scene fun. It is an adventure.

Don't censor or think about it. Whatever comes to your mind, use it. Use anything that appears. Don't think that it should somehow be important or some significant time. Don't start judging it in any way. Don't try and decide whether it has anything to do with whatever you are concerned about. Don't judge that it is mundane, not a scene full of feeling. Don't censor anything because it is embarrassing or bad or makes you feel like mentioning it is going to ruin everything.

On the other hand, if the patient is dead-set against using some time, honor his unwillingness, his decision. Do not force him to reveal whatever he is very reluctant to use.

You may get two or three things. That's fine. Mention whatever comes to you.

Sometimes the scenes come in bunches. She may get two or three right away, or she gets one and then one or two more. Give her plenty of room to mention all of them.

It's funny. I saw the playground, the park. I used to go there just about every day in the summer. I'd play basketball. And I saw Jerry. He wasn't even my best buddy. But I knew him. And I also saw Evelyn. I haven't thought of her in years. We'd hang around together, sitting on the grass and talking. She was a hoot. I liked her. All of a sudden. All these things. From the summers. They're just there.

Use whatever comes to your mind, even if it is vague or you just see one little thing.

He may see something down in there, underneath something, and he isn't quite clear what "underneath" refers to. Or what the person is holding seems nice, something special, but he isn't sure what it is. Sometimes the person will come up with a fragment, something relatively clear, but devoid of a context. She sees a page in a book, a page with a diagram of the eye. He sees a little toy microscope, or a dagger with a serrated blade. All these images are useful, no matter how vague or fragmented they are (cf. A. Freud, 1937; Grof, 1976).

It may be a fantasy, a daydream, a story about your mother or father.

Let the patient know that he may come up with fantasies he had from this period of life. He remembers always having a fantasy of some man living secretly in the attic, the empty crawl space. There was a time when he had a secret companion, Luke, and no one ever saw Luke, but he would play with Luke and tell his parents things that Luke believed or said. She had wonderful fantasies about her father when he was a reporter on a newspaper in India, and how he got married to his first wife, before she died and he came to Canada.

You may see you, or you may actually be you, or maybe you just see someone else, not you at all.

The patient is free to be herself or to see herself. She may see herself sitting by the pool when she was in her early 20s, or she may literally be the one who is sitting by the pool. On the other hand, she may simply see someone else, and she may or may not have been in the scene:

Well, that's my aunt Sally. I see her on an airplane. She traveled a lot for the government.
What you think of, whatever comes to mind, may feel good or it may feel bad.

Give the patient plenty of room to come up with images and scenes that feel good or that feel bad. Some patients just gear themselves to look for bad images and scenes, or just for good images and scenes.

Sometimes the feelings are good. Sometimes bad. Sometimes there are no feelings at all, just things you see. All of these are fine.
OK. Ready? Here we go . . .

The aim is for the patient to be poised to receive whatever appears when you then describe the inner experiencing or the general features of the scene. The patient's attention is largely out there. It is as if he is set to see whatever pops into his mind (Mahrer, 1952, 1956, 1969).

You will be describing either the general features of a scene or the inner experiencing. In either case, talk slowly, almost hypnotically. As you talk, allow yourself to see the evoked images and scenes. Keep your attention out there. Say the words two or three times if that helps. You may use the same words repeatedly, or you may vary them slightly. But do not rush. Take plenty of time to say the words slowly. Essentially, you are either going to describe the inner experiencing or you are going to describe the general features of a situational context.

Find earlier scenes by describing the inner experiencing.   The general idea is that the patient is in some period of life, attention out there, ready to see whatever comes to mind as you say words. As you describe the inner experiencing, he will see things, scenes, times, incidents.

Tell him that you are going to be describing the inner experiencing. Typically, I use the word "feeling" instead of "inner experiencing" or "deeper potential." Then go ahead and describe the inner experiencing. You say:

There is a feeling of making something, creating something, fashioning something . . .

You say these words once again, and then she says:

I see something . . . Just a little girl . . . I'm in a sandbox or something. Sand. Yeah, a sandbox, a big one. At someone's house, and I'm making a castle . . . and tunnels. A tunnel going to the castle.

You say the inner experiencing slowly.

Fighting . . . there's a feeling of fighting, hitting at, pushing and hitting . . .

He says, almost immediately:

I saw it as soon as you started . . . I don't know how old I am. Little. And some bigger boy . . . I don't know who he is. Don't know where I am . . . He knocks me down. I'm on the ground. I see the ground and I'm knocked down. I don't know why he did it . . .

You describe the inner experiencing:

You're having a feeling of not caring, just giving in, letting it take you over.

Almost as soon as you finish, she says:

Yes! Oh yes! I went to this bar and I am about . . . 17. Yes! This guy I'm dancing with . . . slow dancing . . . He is kissing my neck. I am getting so aroused! I get limp! I'm there with my girlfriend. It's Montreal. I dragged her to this place, and I met this fellow. I almost passed out! It was wonderful!

You say:

The feeling is being close, the two of you, real buddies . . .

She says:

I see the girl . . . Karen . . . We're playing cards on her front porch. And I see the dog my Dad gave me. Something happened. I only had him for a few weeks, and then he was gone. I still don't know what happened! My Mom said I was mean to him, but I don't remember anything . . .

Quite often, the images and scenes may have little or no apparent connection with the words you say to describe the inner experiencing. You describe the inner experiencing with these words:

The feeling is being powerful, very strong . . .

That is about as far as you get, and the patient bursts into tears:

Oh God! Andy! My little boy! . . . [There is more sobbing.] There was something wrong with him . . . I put him in an institution when he was three . . . and . . . I haven't seen him . . . He's 13 . . . Haven't seen him in almost five years . . . [More hard sobbing]

Sometimes the scene is accompanied with very good feelings. You describe the inner experiencing:

It's a feeling of doing what I want, yeah! You can't make me! . . . No!

She says:

Oh yes! I see my mommy. She tells me to get the hairbrush so she can spank me, and I said, "No I won't!"

Then she laughs delightfully. Or you say:

It's a great feeling of being special, admired, a precious jewel, like that . . . Very nice . . .

He comes up with a particular time:

Yes! Well! I am in the living room, and my mom has a bunch of her ladyfriends over, and I'm telling . . . ha ha ha . . . It's so silly . . . I'm explaining to them how some fish can swim upstream. That's the big thing, and I go on and on, and they are listening . . . Christ . . . like they are really impressed [he laughs heartily] . . . Like a little Einstein . . . But I loved it . . . I loved it . . .

Usually, the patient is geared and poised to see herself or to be herself. However, you can position the patient to be ready to see someone else. You say:

It may be someone else, not you. Get ready to see someone else. I'll say the words, and you see whoever just shows up, any one at all. OK? Ready? . . . This person has the feeling of being a real loser, a fuckup, an incompetent . . .

He says:

My Dad! In the front yard! He's trying to fix Claude's bike, and it's all in pieces, and he can't fix it. Everyone's laughing at Dad. He can't do it! Only Dad's not laughing. No way! He's mad. He's really mad!

You give the introduction and then you say:

A leader, the organizing one, knows what's what . . .

She says:

Jane. My friend Jane. She is in charge . . . and she's good. We just naturally turn to her, like if someone's got some trouble at work? Jane. Everyone calls Jane . . .

You can find an earlier scene by describing the inner experiencing. But this is only one way.

Find earlier scenes by describing the general features of the Step 1 scene.   In Step 1, you found a scene of strong feeling. Then you probed further and deeper into this scene to find the moment of strong feeling. In Step 3, you can find an earlier scene by using that scene of strong feeling. As the patient is poised and ready to see something, describe the general features of this Step 1 scene of strong feeling and use whatever pops into the patient's mind.

Preface this by telling the patient what you are going to do. You may say:

I am going to describe the time you mentioned earlier, you know, the thing you started with, when you were giving that talk in parliament. I'll describe it in general, and you just stay being a little kid and see whatever comes to you. Whatever. Ready? Ready to see whatever comes to mind?

Your job is to describe the general contours or features of the Step 1 scene, the scene of strong feeling. Keep your description general to allow the patient to find a concrete scene. You say:

There are people, maybe three or five or so, planning and talking about doing something together.

Emphasize the overall features of the Step 1 scene:

There is an accident, and someone is hurt.

You are alone, in a strange room.

You and one other person are together, and there is touching. You two are touching one another . . .

In the Step 1 scene, the feeling was probably good or bad, but in using this method, omit any mention of the feeling. This gives the description more power to find earlier scenes.

You say:

There are a couple of people in a kind of small, enclosed place . . .

He gets a scene:

A closet. My cousin and I are in a closet. We're hiding. We're in her house! That is fun. Shelly and I are . . . We took some cookies, we had a bunch of cookies, and we hid in a closet . . .

If you keep the description just a bit more general than the Step 1 scene, but yet close enough to pull some scene, it is often surprising what scenes you elicit. The scene may be one that is accompanied with good feelings or bad feelings, but patients are often surprised by the scenes that appear. Here are a few examples of scenes that seemed so surprising:

You describe the general features:

Something is in your mouth and feels good and, at the same time, there is a rubbing, some kind of rubbing.

He blurts out:

Yes! What do you know! . . . A baby. I'm a baby . . . About one or two, two, maybe older. I used to put my left thumb in my mouth and suck my thumb and . . . This is something! . . . I would rub the little nipple thing, the button, or whatever it's called, on my other ear, my right ear. My Mom did everything to try and get me to stop . . . No! I did that when I was older too! This is silly! My God!

The patient may be shown how to open up to earlier scenes that do not necessarily involve the patient.

It may involve you. Or you may see someone else, not you at all. So what you see may just involve someone else. All right . . . ?

Then you give the general features of the scene:

Some people are arguing, really having it out . . .

He says:

My mom and dad . . . yelling at each other. Screaming. And they're . . . You can hear them all over the house. It's about mom's drinking, and she's yelling at dad to leave her alone. But they're both yelling, and it seems like they're going to kill each other.

When you and the patient are in her 20s, you describe the scene as follows:

Someone or some people are trying to get this person to do something, and this person won't, just isn't going to do it . . .

Here is the scene that pops into her mind:

Yes! That's Jenny! [She starts laughing.] She's a character! When . . . If she doesn't want to do something . . . like they wanted her to stay later after work and go drinking after . . . She says . . . "Nyaa!" Then she cracks up and laughs hard.

HOW CAN THE PATIENT BE THE INNER EXPERIENCING IN THE EARLIER SCENE?

The grand shift is from being the person that he is, disengaging from this person, and getting inside the inner experiencing and being this whole new person. The earlier scene is merely the context. The critical accomplishment is for the patient to become this whole new person, the inner experiencing (Mahrer, 1970d, 1972a, 1975a). How do you enable the patient to be the inner experiencing?

Find and Be in the Part of the Scene When There Is a Feeling

Usually the scene includes some incident or series of little things, or it is a general situation. You are to try and find the time, in the general scene, when there was some feeling. The feeling may be good or bad. Mainly, you want to find when the feeling was relatively pronounced.

Your attention is almost fully out there, on the scene. With your attention out there, invite her to look for when there was a feeling in the scene. You say:

Yes . . . Here at gramma's house. Sunday dinner. The big meal, and the whole family's here. You're all at the table, and the meal is on . . . When is it that there is some feeling in you? . . . Some feeling . . . Any feeling . . .

She finds the time:

I'm looking at my uncle Sid, my aunt's husband. Everyone says my aunt was lucky to marry him, and I'm looking at him. Seeing his eyebrows. [A little giggle, light.] They're curvy, like a half circle . . .

The scene is being in the bathroom, with the razor blade, just about ready to kill himself.

When is there a feeling? Here in the bathroom . . . There is some time when the feeling is stronger . . .

He says, quietly:

Well, yes . . . I think I'm going to do it. I'm running the razor blade over my wrist, and feeling like what's the use . . . Then I hear the door. That's when Joan comes in. That's when something happens. I freeze. Yeah. Stops. I get scared. And I put the razor away and I turn on the water loud . . .

It helps to fill in some of the vague spots, the bigger holes.

Well, my dad is spanking me, and I guess I did something bad . . . I mean when he's spanking me . . . Uh . . . where? I think . . . I don't know . . . Oh, yeah . . . In the living room, and he got me over his lap, and . . . I called him something . . . What? . . . I called him a fucker!! . . . He walloped me! But I felt good calling him a fucker. He shouldn't have hit me!

Trying to get when the feeling is strong can mean detailing and clarifying, which in turn pulls you more into being in that part of the scene.

My mom called and said that my wife . . . Christ I forget her name . . . Lisa! God, I was only 19. Well, mom said that Lisa did something, and . . . Oh now I remember! . . . Lisa is screaming in the background! I could hear her swearing! Yeah, that's when I think I knew this marriage is over. I didn't say nothing. I closed my eyes and thought about how the hell I'm gonna get out of this marriage . . . and get away from both of them. They're driving me crazy!

Which Person Is the Patient to Be in the Earlier Scene: Himself, the Other Person, or a Whole New Figure?

The patient can be himself in the earlier scene. When you are on the phone, talking to your mother, and you can hear your wife screaming in the background, it makes sense that you can be yourself in this scene. Once you find the scene, and the time when the feeling was stronger, the most conspicuous answer is that you can be yourself is that scene. But this is not the only answer.

The patient may also be the other person in that scene. Since the aim is for the patient to "be" the inner experiencing, it really does not matter whether he is himself, listening to his mother and hearing his wife in the background, or whether he takes the role of his mother or his wife. The key ingredient is that he is to be the inner experiencing, and therefore it may be more useful for him to be the inner experiencing as his mother or as his wife. The choice is up to the therapist and the patient.

How does the therapist determine when it might be useful for the patient to be the other person in the scene? One answer is that it may be the other person who is much better suited as the inner experiencing. Suppose that the scene is playing chess with the fellow from Chile. That fellow waits for the patient to make the first two moves, and then the fellow laughingly chides the patient:

I think it'll be all over in three more moves!

You both laugh. If the inner experiencing is being cocky, arrogant, sure of yourself, then the other fellow seems better outfitted as the agency of the inner experiencing.

It may be useful to be the other person when the patient is merely a quiet, removed observer, almost out of the action. In the scene, the neighbor is showing the patient's parents the magic trick that was included in the party material. Everyone is laughing and having fun. The patient is just one of about five little kids, sitting and watching, outside the group. The inner experiencing consists of being entertaining, the center of attention, the showman. While the patient may be herself in that scene, it may be easier and more useful to take the role of being the neighbor. There are lots of scenes in which the patient is a removed observer. Leave open the possibility that the patient can be the other person in these scenes.

There is another possibility that is useful. Instead of being himself or someone else, the patient may enter the scene as a whole new figure. Essentially, the patient is to be a new figure who is the essence of the inner experiencing. This is relatively easy, it is fun, and it is effective in enabling the patient to be the inner experiencing. The patient is this live new figure, a new element. In the actual scene, there is the patient who is watching television. There is also the patient's slightly older sister. Now there is a third person who is the inner experiencing. This new person lives in the scene. She talks to the patient and to the older sister. In an important sense, introducing this added element is appropriate because she is indeed something new. She is the inner experiencing, and this was not present in the original scene.

In the earlier scene, she is a little girl, and the older man is in bed with her, touching her body, and showing her how to touch his penis. In the recollected scene, she did what he said, and in going back into this scene, the patient is sobbing, scared, shaking. The inner experiencing is being an evil goddess, vindictive, revengeful. Show her how to be a whole new figure in the scene. Now there is the little girl, the man, and the new figure who is the inner experiencing. The patient is this new figure. The stage is set for the patient to be the inner experiencing as this whole new figure.

The important goal is for the patient to live and be in the scene, in the time when the feeling seemed to be relatively stronger. In accomplishing this, the patient may enter into herself or some other person, or she may become the embodiment of the inner experiencing, and enter into the scene as this whole new figure.

What Can the Therapist Do to Enable the Patient to Be the Inner Experiencing in the Earlier Scene?

There are some useful guidelines to help the patient be the inner experiencing in the scene.

Tell the patient that the aim is to see what it is like to be the inner experiencing.   Be open, direct, and honest in telling the purpose and goal that is to be accomplished. Without fanfare or elaborate justification, simply tell him that the aim is for him to see what it is like to "be" the inner experiencing:

> *It gives you a chance to taste and sample what this feeling is. It gives you a chance to be this quality in you, to have this feeling.*

And that is all you do want to accomplish. It is as simple as that.

Some patients have known that experiencing, but perhaps not with wonderfully good feelings. Many patients have little or no memory of having this experiencing in a way that felt good, or perhaps only once or twice in their lives:

> *You can barely remember any time when you felt safe and warm and loved and cud-dled. Right? So it's going to be a big change. Just for you to get a taste of what that's like. So get ready. This can be something kind of new for you. Ready . . . ?*

Emphasize the playfulness, the bigger-than-life exaggeration, and the wholesome, fun, en-joyable unreality in being the inner experiencing. Being the inner experiencing is defi-nitely not to be serious or even realistic. That can make being the inner experiencing too difficult. Instead, emphasize the importance of having fun. It is to be sheer play. It is fantasy. It is burlesque and caricature. It is pretending. It is to be wholesome pleasure. Make it absolutely unreal, bigger-than-life. Emphasize the fanciful. The deeper poten-tial may have been accompanied with awful feelings in Step 1, and Step 2 may have achieved its goal of welcoming and appreciating the deeper potential to some degree. Even so, being the inner experiencing in Step 3 should be made easy, and this guide-line is designed to accomplish that.

Suppose that the inner experiencing is described as losing it, having something taken away, letting it go. The early scene is one in which you are about six years old, and your older brother has a friend lounging in your lower bunk. Acknowledge that it can feel awful to have your special place taken by a stranger, to lose your bed, to feel ripped off, like it was removed from you. Of course this feels rotten. Now you can go ahead and totally exaggerate. Just play. You are the sort of kid who plays with losing it, having something special taken away. Once you acknowledge the truth of the inner experi-encing, go ahead and engage in playful exaggeration, in unrealistic burlesque.

Sometimes a patient may be hesitant or reluctant to disengage from the person that she is and to be the inner experiencing in this scene. Or the patient starts, be-comes ensconced in being the inner experiencing, and then suddenly pulls back into being the old patient. I find that these problems are minimized when you provide a wholesome context of play, pretense, unreality. Being the inner experiencing "for real" is understandably hard. Doing it in this kind of helpful context seems to be much eas-ier and reduces the problems of hesitancy or of pulling out.

Invite and honor the patient's readiness and willingness to be the inner experiencing in this scene. The patient's own readiness and willingness are essential. Before the pa-tient is to enter into the scene and to be the inner experiencing, ask if she is ready. You must elicit her wholesale cooperation:

> *Is this all right? Are you ready to do this?*

Do not try to get her to do this. Do not use pressure. If she is ready and willing, it can be done. If she is not ready and willing, being the inner experiencing will probably not be accomplished well.

Almost always, the patient will be ready and willing. There is typically an eager readiness to be the inner experiencing in this scene. But suppose it is one of those in-frequent times when the patient is not ready and willing. What do you do? He may be expressly unwilling to live and be in the scene itself, or to be that inner experiencing in that scene. In either case, accept and honor the patient's unwillingness. You may look for some other scene that is more acceptable. The only kind of pressure that I sometimes use is to invite the patient to be the inner experiencing in the scene, but to try it just for five seconds or so.

> *No more. Just five seconds or so. That's all. Then stop, or I will stop. How does that sound?*

If the patient is still hesitant or reluctant, I simply leave it be.

The scene is several years ago, when that man was alone with her in the corridor of her apartment house, and he started grabbing her, roughing her up, grabbing at her breasts. The inner experiencing is being crazy, uninhibited, going wild. She pauses, and then says:

> *I don't think I want to do that . . .*

Honor her reluctance.

You are to be aligned with the patient throughout Step 3. From the beginning to the end of Step 3, you are to be thoroughly aligned with the patient. This means that virtually all of your attention is out there. You are seeing the scene. You are living and being in the scene.

Being aligned means that the two of you are so fused, so merged together, so intertwined, that the patient's words and your words actually intermingle, with the words of each being over and under the words of the other. If you two have somewhat similar voices, a listener would have a very hard time knowing who is saying what.

Being aligned means that you freely and spontaneously come up with all sorts of new behaviors to carry out in the scene. The inner experiencing is being deceptive, sneaky, fooling them. The scene is when she is about 11 and she and Sally steal little things from a department store. When she is being the inner experiencing in the scene, you come up with all sorts of notions of what to do:

> *Work together with Sally. On the signal—that prearranged look between you—Sally passes out! Clunk! She faints! Everyone comes running and . . . you know what you do?*

She says:

> *Yeah! I grab all the cosmetics and stick them in a big bag, and walk out!*

And you say:

> *Yes! Great! You got it!*

Being aligned means that the therapist is literally being the inner experiencing in the scene, right along with the patient. The therapist joins with the patient in doing it and being it. Sometimes the therapist does it a little independently. You and the patient are little girls, sitting on the floor with the coloring book. The inner experiencing is being captivated, entranced, awe-struck. She is being this way as she colors in the duck. You say:

> *I look at the picture. So pretty . . . Oh oh . . . It's like the duck is almost . . . alive . . . It's moving a little . . . I am staring at it . . . Look . . . it's starting to move a little . . .*

When you become increasingly aligned, there is a point beyond which you are truly living and being in the early scene. You are truly sitting on the floor, and the coloring book is real. It is unquestionably real. You are not living in this scene a little, or pretending that you are a little girl, sitting on the floor with the coloring book. Something happens, and it is real. When you can accomplish this, when the scene is alive and real for you, it is so much easier for the patient to live and be in this childhood scene.

Show the patient what to do and how to do it in order to be the inner experiencing in the scene.   Show the patient how to be in the scene and how to be the inner experiencing in the scene. Make the scene alive and real by detailing pieces and bits of the scene. Go over the inner experiencing to make sure he knows the way he is to be. Describe the inner experiencing in plenty of detail. Show him how to put his attention fully into the scene. Explain how to talk directly to the other person. Make sure that the patient talks in the present tense. Tell him what words to start with, and how the words are to be said. Do all that you can to show him how to be the inner experiencing in the scene.

It is a joint venture, with the two of you pulling each other into being in the scene. You are 11 years old, in the tent with Gerald:

I don't think you can stand up in this tent. It's small, right?

Yeah, and we're both in sleeping bags . . .

I want to make this so real, so I'm lying on my back, and we're talking.

I think I'm saying how I wish I could be home in bed . . .

So talk. Tell him. Hey, Gerald . . . Jerry? . . . Jerry, I want to go home . . .

I think I'm going to pee! Oh God, I gotta pee! . . . Oh shit, I don't like it here . . .

If the scene takes place in childhood, the patient's childhood language may have been different from the language he is speaking now, with you. It makes it more real and alive if you suggest that when he is the child again, talking to his mother, he speak in the language they spoke. You will be carried along for the ride, even though you may have no idea what he is saying to his mother (Mahrer, 1985c).

There is a magical switch: The person in the scene is replaced by, or complemented with, this whole new person.   The patient is to be the whole new person in the scene. You may invite the new person to replace the patient, or you can invite the new person to enter the scene as an added figure. For example, in the scene the patient is lying in bed, shivering and racked with terrible feelings, scared that she may have to go back to the hospital. Her husband is on the phone, talking to the patient's sister about his worries and concerns for the patient. The inner experiencing is being frustrated at, yelling at, being angry. You say:

See Helen there on the bed? Suppose that there is some kind of magical shift, and you are actually here in the bedroom. Helen is over there on the bed, and you are standing here in the bedroom, brimming over with frustration, full of yelling at. You can be one angry person! And you can pour it all out at anything or anyone you can find. At pitiful old Helen, at her husband, her sister, the terrible circumstances, anything at all . . .

It is often harder when the patient is to replace herself in the scene. How do you accomplish this? The general idea is to invite the patient to picture a sudden shift in which the new person suddenly replaces the old person. The following examples show how this may be done.

> *So there's you in the group, sitting. There is a magic bolt of lightning, a flash. Ssshhh. It's quiet. No one can see it. It takes a minisecond or less, and when it happens, the old fellow—the old you—is very suddenly replaced. You know who's here? You!*
>
> *Now let's freeze this scene right here. You are sitting in the car, driving along with all of them in the car. Then something happens inside you. In a flash, there is a whole change! The old Sam is gone. Wap! And here's this new guy! No one in the car saw the switch. It happened automatically. Zap!*
>
> *Karen is sitting at the table, and her husband is glaring at her. Karen feels rotten. Let's hold this moment. Then something inside starts happening. Karen slowly changes . . . changes . . . and she becomes a whole new person. Then, here is a whole new Karen! No one knows her. A big switch! And here is the new Karen . . . confident, self-confident, sure of herself. There's been a magical switch, and now you are this whole new Karen!*
>
> *You are six years old, sitting at the table, and daddy is glaring at your sister's chair. Louise is late! As usual! And you are tight. Oh God. Then, something magical happens. You are gone! And in your place is a whole new Julie. No, she's nothing like you. She can tease her daddy, she can be playful with her daddy, she can kid her daddy. Wham! You're gone, and here is this whole new Julie . . .*

Ready? Do it . . . now!   The switch into actually being and behaving as the inner experiencing is to occur now, suddenly. It is to happen totally and completely, and right now. It is like deciding to jump into the water, and then going ahead and doing it right now. You, the therapist, are to be primed and ready for the patient to make this switch and, quite literally, to be and behave as this inner experiencing right now. He is primed and ready. You say:

> *. . . and then you . . . GO AHEAD. DO IT. NOW!*

> *All right. You are right here, standing next to the door, looking directly at the door. And then . . . when you are ready, GO AHEAD AND . . . DO IT!*

> *OK, whenever you are ready to be this whole new Jack, GO AHEAD . . . NOW!*

> *You are looking at your Dad. See him. AND DO IT . . . GO!*

The patient is to be the inner experiencing until the feelings are full and wonderful. The patient is to keep being and behaving as this inner experiencing in the scene until two things happen. One is that the sheer experiencing is full, intense, strong, powerful, saturating, fully felt throughout most of the body (Ellenberger, 1958; Janov, 1970; Levitsky & Perls, 1970; Mahrer, 1975a, 1987b, 1989c; Maupin, 1965; Ouspensky, 1957). The other is that the feelings are the wonderful, bodily felt feelings of actualization: energy, aliveness, excitement, tingling, vibrancy, activation, exuberance.

When the feelings are full and wonderful in you, or when they are definitely not full and wonderful in you, choose a moment when there is a pause, and say:

OK, now check your body. I want to see if we're having sort of similar things happening inside . . . What's happening in your body? Where are things happening in you body? Face? Chest? Where? And what's it like?

If the bodily sensations are not especially full or wonderful, tell the patient to keep going.

Yeah, me too. It feels all right, not great. So let's do it again, till the feelings are full and wonderful! . . . Do it again, louder, with more feeling! And have fun, make it feel fantastic!

Show her how to be the inner experiencing fully and with great feelings. Join her. Do it for her. Keep doing it and being the inner experiencing until the feelings in the body are full and feel wonderful.

When she does it fully and wonderfully, check your bodies again. She says:

It's all over! Oh, I'm tingling! Damn, this feels good! My head feels light, and . . . my whole body's . . . I don't know . . . warm and light . . .

With some kinds of experiencings, the feelings can be good ones without being loud or raucous. Consider the experiencing of being full of awe, wonder, reverence, rapture. The scene may be from a few years ago when you saw the newborn baby, and just stared at her, almost like witnessing a miracle. When the experiencing is full and the feelings are wonderful, there need be no loud noises or flailing of arms and legs. It may be quiet. Bodily sensations are alive, tingling, vibrant, but quiet.

How can you use the other person to help the patient be the inner experiencing? There are at least a couple of ways that you can use the other person in the scene. One is to invite the patient to allow the other person to accommodate, to go along with, even to participate in, the patient's being the inner experiencing. This is usually a great deal to ask of the patient:

Come on, let your mother go along with your being this way. What the hell. Give it a try . . .

Most patients insist that the other person has to remain being just the way that allows the patient to feel miserable. It can be almost inconceivable that the other person can change.

Here is a test. Try and let your mother be different. Look, if you're going to be different, a big change, see what it's like if you let her be altogether different too! Not the way she really is. A whole different person. Forget about how your wife really is. Just for now, for your sake, everyone is going to be altogether different, you, and Angela. OK? Willing to let her go along with this?

Another way to use the other person is for you, the therapist, to voice the other person. This helps to heat up the interaction. He is well into being the inner experiencing with his father-in-law, and he is saying:

I HATE when you call me that! DON'T YOU EVER DO THAT OR I'LL SMASH YOU. I'LL KNOCK YOU DOWN AND BEAT THE SHIT OUT OF YOU. DO YOU UNDERSTAND?

The attention shifts over to the father-in-law. You say:

Oh Oh. I know what he'll say. "*YES I WILL! I'LL CALL YOU ANYTHING I WANT.*"

Or you speak as the father-in-law:

WHAT? JUST TRY, YOU LITTLE WIMP! I'LL WIPE THE FLOOR WITH YOU!

Typically, this galvanizes the patient's being the inner experiencing.

How can you use an earlier scene in which the patient felt good being the inner experiencing?   In some earlier scenes, the patient felt good being the inner experiencing. Use these scenes to enable the patient to feel the inner experiencing much more fully, and to use all sorts of new behaviors in being the inner experiencing. For example, the inner experiencing is gentling, befriending, bringing around into friendship. In the actual scene, he is a little boy, playing alone in the front yard, and the big neighborhood dog appears. It is the terror of the neighborhood. For some reason, he just reaches out and pets the big bear. It feels good. Your work starts here and goes much further. Have much more fun stroking the big dog. Embrace him, run and play with him, scold him for scaring the people in the neighborhood. Sit on him. Growl at him. Go walking with him.

Start with scenes in which the experiencing felt good. Go much further, both in undergoing the inner experiencing and also in exaggerating and burlesquing by carrying out all sorts of additional behavior.

Being the inner experiencing actively dilates and changes the earlier scene and its meaning.   Recollected early scenes seem to have a relatively persistent form and shape. This is the way you remember it. However, when the patient goes back into these scenes, and when the patient is the inner experiencing in these scenes, something dramatic ordinarily happens. The scene grows, more details appear. The incident changes, and there is generally a significant shift in what is remembered. Perhaps even more importantly, the scene takes on a different meaning. It is as if almost everything about that scene is open to change when the patient is being the deeper potential in that scene.

Some theorists say that even the act of recalling an earlier incident is an active process during which parts of the earlier incident may be modified and synthesized (Pribram, 1971, 1980). If, in addition, the patient is being the inner experiencing in that incident, then it is even more likely that the earlier incident will be modified and new parts synthesized. He remembered throwing the ball and breaking the third floor window, the only window on the third floor of this side of the house. He remembered this incident vividly. He remembers being shocked that the ball smashed the window, he remembers his father spanking him so very hard, and he remembers the terrible feeling of being a hated troublemaker. However, things change significantly when he enters into this scene as the inner experiencing of being self-confident, self-assured, sure of himself. For one thing, he now senses someone to his left, and then this person emerges as his older sister, challenging him to throw the ball over the roof. She says:

I can do it! Can you?

Here is a whole new piece of the incident. With this new piece, and with being the inner experiencing in the scene, the whole meaning of the incident changes. It is less connected to a feeling of being a rejected troublemaker, the way he had always remembered it. Now there is a connected sense of the sisterly challenge, the feeling of being taunted.

All she recalls of the awful incident is her uncle driving her home after ballet practice. She is six years old, and the vivid part of the memory is her struggling to resist and say no when he grabs her left hand and tries to put it on his stiff penis while he is driving. The memory opens and closes there. However, when she is being the inner experiencing of the evil goddess, the one with magic power, she vividly recalls something else. As soon as she gets home, she tearfully tells her mother what her uncle did, and her mother screams at her:

> *Don't you ever make up stories like that! I never want to hear anything like that from you!*

The whole meaning of the incident has shifted, changed dramatically, at least from the perspective of the whole new person.

Being the inner experiencing can also open up altogether new possibilities for what the patient might have done in the earlier scenes. It is as if there are whole new options where before there may have been none, or so it seemed. The inner experiencing is being free, liberated, able to do what you want. The recollected scene is waking up on Saturday mornings when he lived with his grandmother after his parents were killed in the accident. He lived with grandmother from the time he was 12 years old. On Saturdays, all his friends played baseball or just hung out with one another. For him, Saturdays were chore days. He had assigned chores throughout the entire day, every Saturday, and he did them dutifully. In being the inner experiencing, he says:

> *On Friday, I call gramma's sister, Betty. Invite gramma for a weekend! She's always saying she'd like to spend a weekend with you. She says you two don't spend enough time together. Done! So it's Saturday morning, early, seven, and guess who's outside? Henry! With a basketball. Come on over to the park! You got it! I am free! Free at last! My people are free! Aw shit! I should have done something!*

Most patients seem to remember these earlier scenes in more or less one way, with a relatively persistent meaning. Being the inner experiencing in these scenes can make for changes in what is now apparently remembered, and also in the apparent meanings of the earlier events. These changes may be accompanied with feelings that are good or bad. Likewise, the changed meanings may be pleasant or unpleasant. In any case, being the inner experiencing in the earlier scenes seems often to dilate and change the earlier scene and its meaning.

What do you do if the patient is swept into being the old experiencing in the earlier scene? There are occasions when the patient is drawn into being the old, painful experiencing in the earlier scene. In the scene, she is outside the car, stranded on the country road, and some man is grabbing her wrists, twisting her and pushing her down on the ground. Her mother is somewhere in the woods, with mother's boyfriend, and the patient is frantically screaming at her younger sister to get away, run to mommy. The inner experiencing is being commanding, ordering, being the boss. However, once the patient enters into the earlier scene, she slides back into being the old experiencing:

NO. NO . . . LEAVE ME ALONE . . . [Then she bursts into shrieking and hard sobbing] MOMMY . . . MOMMY . . . Mommy . . .

What do you do?

Many earlier scenes are painful. Some are excruciatingly agonizing. Entering back into these scenes can bring the patient close to undergoing the painful feelings again. The methods typically enable the patient to decline this option, and to be the inner experiencing instead. If, however, the person is swept into undergoing the old and painful experiencing, then offer her the opportunity to be a whole new person, the inner experiencing, in that scene. She is living in the scene. She has stopped crying. Everything is subsiding. You have gone through the excruciating pain along with her. Now you are ready to enable her to be the inner experiencing. You say, quietly:

There is a whole different little girl in you. Altogether different. She is . . . commanding! SHE KNOWS WHAT IT'S LIKE TO ORDER! TO BE THE BIG BOSS HERE. Yeah! Now is it all right for her to have a go at this . . . ?

You may provide the guidelines and instructions for her to be the little girl, but this time as the inner experiencing. Or you may invite this whole new person to enter into the scene when the man is grabbing the patient, and the patient is frantically yelling to her younger sister. In either case, patients almost regularly are able to go back into the scene and to be the inner experiencing:

HEY THERE, LET HER GO! SIT DOWN! WHAT THE HELL DO YOU THINK YOU ARE DOING? . . . I AM IN CHARGE NOW. YOU GOTTA DEAL WITH ME! NOW EXPLAIN YOURSELF BEFORE I PUT YOU IN JAIL! . . .

Sometimes the patient will pour so much attention into the focal center of attention that rather unusual bodily sensations will occur. He is being a little boy of around five, in the bathtub with his younger sister. Suddenly the sister becomes exceedingly real and he is compelled by her presence. This is when he has strange bodily sensations in which his lips become thick and protruding, his whole body is very heavy, and his fingers seem like they merge into one another in a web. Since I am geared to being the inner experiencing, I generally allow all this to happen in me and then, when it seems to subside, I turn to the work of being the new inner experiencing.

In this third step, you have found an earlier scene, and you have enabled the patient to be the inner experiencing in this scene. This is a magnificent achievement. But, if you and the patient are inclined, you can either augment or replace this way of finding earlier scenes. There are additional ways of finding still other earlier scenes to enable the patient to be the inner experiencing.

HOW CAN YOU FIND OTHER SCENES IN WHICH THE PATIENT MAY BE THE INNER EXPERIENCING?

The aim is to provide the patient with other scenes from relatively recent or from quite remote times in her life, and thereby enable her to be the inner experiencing. Whether you use just one of these other kinds of scenes, or several of them, the aim is to enable the patient to let go of the person that she is, and to live and be as the inner experiencing.

What Are Some Helpful Guidelines for Finding Other Scenes and Being the Inner Experiencing in These Scenes?

You may use the first way of finding earlier scenes, which has already been described, or you can go directly to earlier scenes using the methods given in this section, or you may do both. Sometimes I skip the first way and go directly to finding earlier scenes by using one or more of these topics. Either option can provide you with earlier scenes, and that is the aim.

Patients will occasionally just simply bring up other scenes. Indeed, you may almost count on other scenes being accessible once the patient has been the inner experiencing in one early scene (Mahrer & Schachter, 1991). This is sometimes referred to as "state-dependent" memory wherein each part of the personality is described as having its own, relatively independent, package of memories (Braun, 1983; Erickson, 1980; Erickson & Rossi, 1979; Rossi, 1986), consistent with Penfield's (1952, 1975) suggestion that memories may be seen as packed into one or several storehouses, and what Palombo (1978, 1980) refers to as "regression in the service of remembering."

Make sure to encourage him to use whatever scenes, or even fragments of scenes, come directly and quickly to mind. Tell him to use these, even if they seem to be spontaneously irrelevant, vague, piecemeal, or even if he gets two or three things. In a way, this is fun, because he will see things that just seem to pop in.

Hey! I see my piano teacher! What do you know? He was a real nut, and I liked that guy . . .

Once the patient is being the inner experiencing in the context of one scene, you may help anchor the patient into remaining as this inner experiencing in looking for other scenes. You may address her as this new inner experiencing, and say:

I am going to talk to you as if you are this whole new person. Just stay being the person you are now. So, Julie, Julie who can be awestruck, seeing something for the first time, who can be impressed and staring at it anew . . .

Once the patient is this new person, she can continue as this new person while you replace one scene with another. Suppose that she starts with being this whole new Julie, and she is this new person who watches herself sitting at the kitchen table with her grandmother. The little girl is feeling glum because she has to spend the weekend with her grandmother, and the new person, the inner experiencing, is present now, and talking to both the little girl and the grandmother. When she completes the work in this scene, you simply introduce another early scene. You say:

Remember when Julie was 7 years old and she was lost in the woods? That was such a terrible time for her. She was crying . . . Now here you are, with her. See her? So keep on, do whatever you want. Go ahead . . .

You can be the inner experiencing, and come up with all sorts of other scenes that come to you, most of which did not occur in her life. But if they appear to you, you may cite them. If the inner experiencing is being silly, whimsical, giddy, let yourself be this inner experiencing, and describe any scenes that you do see:

You know what I see? You are in this restaurant, a very posh place, all dressed up, a formal affair, and you're at this table with your husband and another couple, and you have this overwhelming desire for a juicy hamburger and a cold beer, and you burst out with . . . all sorts of things that come from a feeling of being silly, whimsical, giddy . . . Anyhow, this is what I get. Anything coming to your mind?

She says:

I remember when my dad's fly was open! The four of us went to this high-class restaurant. My uncle, he's rich, he invited us. I must have been about eight . . . Dad was dressed in a suit. I didn't think he had a suit! And he's standing by the . . . waiting for the waiter to seat us, and . . . his fly's wide open! [She can barely restrain herself from gales of hearty laughter] . . . I can't remember . . . what happened! . . .

One of the most exciting guidelines has to do with options for who the patient is to be in being the inner experiencing. Consider an earlier scene in which he is about five, living with his grandfather over the summer, and he is watching his grandfather plant some flowers in a garden. The inner experiencing is being loving, holding close, fondling lovingly. If the patient is going to be this inner experiencing, then whom is he to be? The range of options is exciting:

1. He may be himself, the little boy who is watching his grandfather, only now he is to be the inner experiencing.
2. He may be the grandfather. As the grandfather, being the inner experiencing may be in relation to the flowers, and perhaps to the little boy who is with him.
3. He may be a third identity in the scene who embodies and exemplifies the inner experiencing. As this added third person, the undergoing of the inner experiencing may be in relation to the little boy or to the grandfather, or to both.

Sometimes, in being the inner experiencing, the patient is stopped by what he clings to and virtually insists is the way the other person would be or would respond. The inner experiencing is being critical, nasty, tough, sharp. The scene is when he is pouring wine for his mother-in-law, and she snaps:

That's enough!

In trying to be the new person in that scene, he blocks and stops:

But I can't! She'd . . . She'd get mad! I couldn't do it!

Be free enough to allow the patient to go ahead and be the inner experiencing anyhow, or especially because his mother-in-law would be that way. Or, you may invite him to switch over to being the inner experiencing as the mother-in-law:

Right! Let's switch over to being the old bag. Yes, she's critical! Let's be her. Get inside her skin. Switch over to being her . . . And now . . . Yes! Jerome!

STOP THAT! WHO THE HELL DO YOU THINK YOU ARE? I SAID STOP! YOU UNGRATEFUL BASTARD . . .

Once the patient has been the inner experiencing, it is relatively common that he will take a grander view of much of his life in a way that has been referred to as insight or understanding or expanded awareness. Patients will see trends, connections, patterns. They will see their lives from quite new and different perspectives. Notice that these instances of insight and understanding are the consequences, not the causes, of having been the inner experiencing, indications that the patient has effectively been the inner experiencing.

Once the patient has been the inner experiencing fully and with good feelings, it is very hard to return to being the old person with the painful feelings. The original scene may have included terrible feelings. It may have occurred when he was an adolescent and, as usual, his father is home, drunk, fighting, lying in bed yelling and crying. After the patient is the whole new person in that scene, challenge him to revert to the painful feeling:

> *Go ahead, he is lying on his bed, dressed, reeking from booze, drunk again, a scary mess. Go ahead! Feel tight and scared and like it is somehow your fault . . . Dum de dumm . . . Well? I am waiting. Feel shitty!*

He says:

> *I CAN'T . . . I don't feel like that!*

The old bad feeling is gone when the patient is being the new person fully and with good feelings.

Step 3 involves finding earlier life scenes and then being the inner experiencing in these life scenes. Whether or not you start by being in some earlier life period, there are other ways to find earlier life scenes. Here are some useful ways.

Look for Other Times When the Patient Was Being the Inner Experiencing

Once she has been the inner experiencing in one scene, guide her into looking for other times when she had this experiencing, or something relatively similar:

> *It may have felt good or maybe not so good, but you had this same kind of feeling. Maybe you've had this kind of feeling a lot. Maybe not. Maybe just once, some exception . . . so look around . . . other times when, yes, you knew what this feeling is like . . . Yeah?*

Patients may come up with times that are from current life. The inner experiencing is described slowly:

> *. . . and maybe you had just a little bit of it, a feeling of cracking up, going bonkers, everything's falling apart. Yeah?*

She says:

> *Lately! Yeah, lately! I woke up, couple of days ago, and . . . I thought I was at home, you know, when I grew up! I forgot I was married and had grown kids. Christ! I look over at Joe, and for a few seconds I didn't know who the hell he was. And it happened when I was driving along on the freeway. It was yesterday afternoon. I couldn't remember where the hell I was going! I thought like getting off so I could figure out where I was headed for . . . But it's funny. I wasn't scared or nothing. It was funny. I mean really funny. I'm so damned organized. I'm like a computer . . . I was with George, in the car, and I started to laugh. I told him I forget where the hell we're going, and I said I thought I was losing my mind . . . Actually, it's fun . . . I think!*

Show her how to throw herself into a full feeling of cracking up, going bonkers, simply falling apart. In the course of her doing so, she says:

. . . So who the hell are you? . . . George? Who's George? . . . What are you doing in my car? . . . Where are we? What am I doing? . . . I wanna ice cream cone! I want a big chocolate ice cream cone! PLEASE DADDY. CAN I HAVE ONE PLEASE? I WANNA ICE CREAM CONE . . . HERE! YOU DRIVE! NO! WAIT! LET'S FLY! I ALWAYS WANTED TO FLY . . . LET'S FLY AWAY. I WANNA GO TO GREECE . . . LET'S GO TO GREECE! . . . WATCH OUT! THERE'S A FISH HERE. MY GOD! YOU'RE A FISH! I ALWAYS KNEW YOU WERE A FISH. . . . HEY FISH . . . LET'S GO TO GREECE . . . WHEEEEEEE! . . .

Sometimes the evoked scenes are recent, but usually they are from years ago. You say:

Just any time that comes to mind, any at all, when you had even a little bit of this feeling, maybe just inside, a little, not even much. A feeling of being powerful, explosive, unleashing massive power . . .

She says:

As soon as you started. Yes! I'm with Norma, and we're kids. Kids! And we have tomatoes. Norma had them. Lots. And we throw them against the wall! Splat! The side of the building, used to be the hardware store! [She starts laughing.] We smashed those suckers all over the wall!

With Edward, you say:

I'll bet there are other times when you at least know what this feeling is like. No way, can't make me do it. I won't I won't.

Edward says:

Not today. No. I am not like that. Never . . . But I used to be, I think . . . When I was a kid. They sent me to a counselor in school! I know! My mom and dad would tell stories about me, when I was a baby. I wouldn't eat that warm cereal with lumps in it! Shit! I used to dump it on the floor! I don't remember, but they'd tell stories about me . . . I hate that stuff. Oatmeal! Yech! I haven't had any in . . . since I was a kid! Hell, maybe I never had any oatmeal! I don't remember . . .

Show him how to be in the kitchen with the oatmeal, and how to be the exaggerated experiencing. He does this with gusto, and continues:

. . . Oatmeal all over! On the floor! All over the walls! . . . HEY MA. LOOK UP AT THE CEILING. OATMEAL. NO ONE CAN GET ME TO DO NOTHIN! AND I HATE MY NAME. HAROLD. SHAROLD. OK, IT'S YOUR FATHER'S NAME. SO YOU USE IT. NO LONGER SELMA. YOU'RE HAROLD. AND I'M ROCKY . . . AND STAY OUT OF MY ROOM . . . AND NO MORE BATHS . . . AND I'M NOT EVER GOING TO GRAMMA'S HOUSE . . . I WANT TO BE WITH GIRLS . . . THE NEXT TIME YOU GO TO GRAMMA'S, BRING ME A LOAD OF CONDOMS . . . AND I'M NOT GOING TO DO ANYTHING . . . NO NO NO . . .

Look for One of the First Times When the Patient Felt the Inner Experiencing

Show the patient how to follow a directed, intentional search for one of the first times that he had the inner experiencing. Describe the inner experiencing slowly and carefully, while the patient is geared to find some early time when it happened. It need not be the first time, just one of the earliest times that he remembers having this experiencing. It is the active, directed search that is important, so whatever time comes to mind is the one to use.

The patient listens to your instructions, is geared to receive one of the first times he had the experiencing you describe:

> . . . *You're doing it secretly, no one is to know, it is a bad thing* . . .

She immediately says:

> *Sandra, the devil, and me. I always thought Sandra was a devil . . . We were six or seven, and we'd look for cigarette butts on the sidewalk. Never told anyone. We'd go downtown, about five blocks from our houses, and we'd always find three or four butts. Then we'd go behind the hardware store and smoke . . . You know, I can't remember where we'd get matches from!*

Here is a wonderful opportunity to enjoy the inner experiencing of being secretive, a bad thing, no one is to know. When you show her what to do, she enters into that scene behind the hardware store, and revels in being the inner experiencing:

> *Listen, Sandy . . . You're a devil, right? I know that . . . I want to be a devil too . . . And so does my brother . . . He's a little crazy . . . When we finish smoking, let's go in the alley by your place, and get a doll of Mrs. Hawkins and stick pins in . . . I want to arrange for her to die . . . yesssss . . . And no one'll know that we are devils . . . Everyone thinks I'm sweet little Ann Marie . . . Ha ha ha . . . Then we can take the body and carve it up and eat it . . . Yeechhh! I don't want to eat it . . . We'll bury it in pieces . . . Now let's steal a pack of cigarettes . . . and I'll take some beer from home . . . I want to have a secret group. You, me, and my brother . . . and . . . we'll all go to the cave and put stuff on our skin and dance . . . slowly . . . I want to be a devil . . .*

Look for One of the Worst Times When the Patient Felt the Inner Experiencing

The patient is geared to search for one of the worst times when she had this inner experiencing. Make sure that the patient is quite free to use any time that comes to mind, as long as she sets herself to receive one of the worst times. Sometimes this yields a scene easily and readily. You describe the inner experiencing:

> . . . *the feeling is being crazy . . . out of your mind . . . something is wrong* . . .

She says, right off:

> *I heard voices . . . in my head . . . like hissing . . . I could barely make out the words . . . mad . . . angry voices . . . screaming at me . . . and once it was so loud and so scary that I was sitting in an alley and I had my hands over my ears, and something*

was happening . . . I think the voices were taking me over . . . And I opened my eyes and a cop was standing next to me . . . He must have thought I was crazy . . . I was . . . I felt crazy . . . Christ, I think I was out of my mind . . . Those voices were . . . so real . . .

Often, he will be set to find some worst time, but he has a hard time finding such a time. After all, he may spent have years dedicated to erasing incidents in which the feelings were so rackingly painful. If you want to help him find some of these worst times, mention some scenes that spontaneously come to mind as you are describing the inner experiencing. After he says that he is not coming up with anything, you say:

One of the worst times when this feeling is terrible . . . Someone is invading your space . . . trying to get much too close into you . . . It's driving you crazy . . . Hmm. Well . . . I'm getting something . . . You're just a little boy, and you did something bad, and your mother, your aunt, someone is saying what you are like, as if they know what you are thinking, and you aren't saying anything, but you feel awful . . .

He then remembers a time:

Yes . . . Well, not that. It was when I was at the public library, in high school. I was having trouble in school. I don't know why I was there. But this old guy, a bum, he smelled, and he . . . was a bum . . . He sat real close to me and . . . God, his mouth smelled . . . He said he knew I was not very smart, and not talented in anything like sports or anything, and I shouldn't go to college. I should try and get a job. He scared the shit out of me cause that's what was driving me crazy, and I couldn't talk to my mom and dad about it. I thought I'd pass out . . . I . . . He walked away. That fucking old bum . . . He knew what I was thinking! That's all I remember, but it's like he's the devil, and I . . . it was like a nightmare . . . I thought I was going crazy . . . I . . . All my life I am still scared of that . . .

You may invite the patient to celebrate the worst feeling, to wallow in it in a flagrantly dramaticized way. She describes when the worst feeling occurred:

I was at a ski . . . There was this older woman. She came into my room and she was so tall, skinny. But she held my arms, and I . . . I let her . . . Not sex or anything . . . She twisted my arms and she hurt me . . . She grabbed my arms on the bed and squeezed me so hard . . . [She is crying.] I just let her . . . Wanted her to go away . . . [Now she is crying hard.]

As she is crying, give her an opportunity to just simply surrender to the inner experiencing of being helpless, passive. Show her how to celebrate this experiencing, to be it fully and with good feelings. When she is ready, she begins:

Here I am . . . on the bed . . . go ahead . . . here . . . take the other arm . . . twist it off . . . I'll do whatever you want . . . [She hums a bit and then singsongs her words.] I'm so passive . . . I'm just a helpless little girl . . . I look like a grown kid, but I am just a little girl . . . I'm so glad you came in . . . You want to turn me into a pretzel? Move my whole body? . . . Twist off my arms and legs . . . Oh yes . . . Do it to me . . . That feels good . . . Are you enjoying yourself? . . . I'll just glue myself to you and you can do whatever you want . . . Tell me what you want me to do . . . Yes . . . Whatever it is . . . I am just a helpless little girl . . . da da da dumdedum . . .

Both she and the therapist wallow in being this inner experiencing, fully, inventively, and with good feeling.

Accept and use whatever situational context the patient finds when he follows your instructions, no matter how bizarre or creative it may seem to be. As you give the instructions, he starts breathing rapidly, and describes what it is like being inside the womb:

> *. . . I know she hates me already, and she's jerking and I'm supposed to be born . . . But it's squishing me! Yaaa! It hurts! . . .*

Or he tells about seeing the bloody eye. It is a thing, a thing with a mind of its own, and it is trying to swallow his will, to take away his essence.

> *It knows that I am frail. Not much will, and it's got all that blood, still, not pouring out . . . At me . . . Like I'm its victim . . .*

Or he tells about being a baby, and the huge billowing buttocks are squashing his face:

> *It's pressing down on me . . . All over my face . . . It's settling in, down on my head . . . White. It's white. I can't breathe . . . I'm just floating . . . My arms are straight out . . . Just floating and I can't move . . .*

Look for Ways in Which the Patient Virtually Ensures That He Is Not the Inner Experiencing

Show the patient how to look for ways that virtually deny, oppose, hide, and ensure that he is absolutely not the inner experiencing. This produces scenes from the patient's current life, or perhaps even lifelong ways characteristic of most of his life.

Suppose that the inner experiencing is being utterly trusting, entrusting oneself to others, putting oneself in others' hands. Invite her to find scenes by saying:

> *There are things about you, the kind of person that you are, really are, today, that make sure you do not have that feeling, no, not at all . . . Think of times when you were growing up, your whole life, times that proved you're not that way at all . . . When you are growing up, there are some things that made sure you didn't become that kind of person at all. You wouldn't have that kind of feeling . . . Your whole life, you were not that kind of person, not at all. You were maybe the opposite. A whole different kind of person . . . If I talked to people who knew you when you were a kid, or people in your life today and I said, "Jane is trusting, she entrusts herself to others, she puts herself in others' hands." And they'd say, "Jane? Our Jane? You must be kidding. No way, Jane is . . ."*

She pauses. Chuckles. Then, quietly and evenly, says:

> *No, I am definitely not like that now and I think I was never like that. My whole life I was small, tough, and very rigid. No one would ever describe me as trusting. Now if you had said "bossy, tough, very smart, the one who runs everything," that's me. They'd all recognize me. I was class president all the time. And I am head of the law firm today. I am quite different from that . . .*

Regardless of the nature of the inner experiencing, patients can arrive at ways that virtually ensure that they are not the same way. He says:

Strong, competitive? Better than others? All my life, my father made fun of me as a sissy. He played football, and he hated that I was so sickly, had weak muscles. Other kids . . . I couldn't even play sports. I never did. Not real sports . . .

She starts laughing.

Not me. I'm too fat. Plain. Sexy? Seductive? That's a joke . . . I think I've had sex ten times in my whole life! And the main feeling I had was grateful. They never lasted. The last guy kept telling me to relax! I am not sexy. I am anything but sexy . . .

He says:

No way. Never . . . I am not tough. I never yelled at anyone. I'm a nice guy. Everyone likes me. My patients swear by me. I am the kindest doctor in Ottawa. Nurses love me. I've been nice from the time when I was . . . my whole life. I remember when my brother took my bicycle and wrecked it. My dad smacked him . . . I knew how my brother felt! I wasn't mad. I really wasn't . . . It's like I became someone who isn't tough . . . I am the opposite . . . A nice guy . . .

She starts laughing quite hard:

That is easy! I am definitely not responsible. I am the least organized person I know! . . . I never have any money . . . I have no records . . . Income tax time is a nightmare . . . I lose everything . . . I even forget where I parked the car! . . . A couple of weeks ago I called my husband. I told him that the car was stolen! I thought I took it shopping for a Valentine's card. He didn't answer and I thought he was going to kill me. Then he was laughing at me. He had the car! . . . I am a disorganized mess . . .

You may invite her to replace the mixed-up, disorganized person on the phone, frantic about losing the car, or to enter that scene as a third entity, the inner experiencing of being in charge, responsible, organized. She is drawn toward being this third added figure in the scene, and she begins:

Denise darling, I know you're confused. Just give me the phone. Thank you dear. Hello, Gregory? We both know your dim-witted but lovable wife is a nut. Well, I am going to take care of her for a while . . . Now here is what I want you to do . . . Oh, I got something better . . . I'm at work. Yes! WE ARE GOING TO HAVE REGULAR MEETINGS EVERY MONDAY MORNING. THIS PLACE HAS BEEN ALL MIXED UP FOR LONG ENOUGH. I AM GOING TO SET THE AGENDA BEFOREHAND AND I WILL MAKE MINUTES OF OUR MEETINGS . . . AND I AM GOING TO POST A CHART OF WHO'S WORKING WITH WHAT CLIENTS . . . THAT WILL TAKE CARE OF EVERYTHING . . . Oh, yes, now Denise, you are going to open a checking account with your name on it, no more joint accounts . . . And I am going to teach you how to keep the budget . . . I mean the accounts . . . Wait just a second! I said budget . . . Beginning tonight, you are going to spend one week doing the bills, and you will do it together with Gregg. I will do one bill with Gregory, and then you will do it for one week. Now practice telling all of this to Gregg. Go ahead. Try and act like a grown-up . . . I know you can do it . . .

As the new inner experiencing, speaking with the voice of the sense of being powerful, dynamic, strong, she talks to the self who was always held in and depressed, sickly and weak. As this new inner experiencing, she talks to that other self in a scene from years ago, when she begins to do some sexual exploration with an equally held in and depressed, shy and withdrawn boy. She is being this new inner experiencing as she is not only being powerful, dynamic, and strong, but also chiding the old self as being a kind of mistake. She says:

> *Why don't you two start yelling! Orgasms are great. Have them! It's all right to make noise! I'm going to get in there with you two and get some aliveness here! DO SOME-THING. GRAB EACH OTHER. HAVE A POWERFUL ORGASM. THEY'RE WONDERFUL! . . . Linda! You're such a wimp! You poor kid . . . You became the wrong person . . . You never had to be such a sickly frail thing . . . so damned scared and depressed! THAT WAS CRAZY. YOU SHOULD HAVE BEEN ME, OR I SHOULD HAVE BEEN AROUND . . . MY GOD! I BECAME THE WRONG PER-SON! WHAT A MISTAKE I MADE!*

Look for Times When the Patient Could and Should Have Been the Inner Experiencing

The times might refer to more or less particular incidents, or they might refer to whole chunks of the person's life. Sometimes it seems as if the person could and should have been this way just about her whole life, but she wasn't. As far back as she can remember, she was not this way, not this kind of person. Throughout her childhood, she wasn't that way at all, although maybe she came slightly close here and there. Sometimes either you or the patient can stand back and see that the person simply was not the person she could and should have been:

> *I think you led the wrong life! You were the wrong person!*

She says:

> *If I was that way, I wouldn't have been the dumb little girl . . . I never would have gotten pregnant . . . I never would have worked as a nurse! My whole life would have been different. Oh my God!*

Leave the window wide open so that the person can see quite specific times when she could and should have been the inner experiencing, or when much of her life could and should have been different.

Get the patient ready to look back a few years or so, or throughout most of her life, and to be ready to see whatever comes to mind when you say words such as these:

> *There were times when you could have been powerful, dynamic, strong . . . when you should have been like this . . . but you sure as hell weren't. Maybe you even felt you should have been . . .*

Without missing a beat, she says:

> *Oh yes . . . Oh yes . . . My whole marriage. With Tom . . . Every day . . . I'm think-ing of when he brought his mother to come live with us, and I was pregnant, and I put up with her drinking and her nagging at me . . . I remember when she wanted Tom to drive her to her sister's and spend a week with . . . at her sister's farm . . . I was . . . They never even asked me. They . . . Tom let me know that he'd be gone . . . And I just cried . . . Yeah, I did . . .*

As soon as you invite her to continue being this powerful, dynamic, strong person, and you say:

OK, Do it!

She breaks out of the starting gates:

WHOA. STOP. EVERYBODY STOP . . . I AM A PARTNER HERE. NOT ONLY IS TOM NOT GOING TO DRIVE YOU UP THERE AND SPEND A WEEK WITH YOU . . . YOU ARE GOING TO LIVE THERE! WITH YOUR SISTER. YOU ASKED TO . . . I'LL GET YOU A BUS TICKET AND YOU ARE GOING TO SPEND A WEEK THERE AND TOM AND I ARE GOING TO HAVE IT OUT LIKE TWO ADULTS. WE WILL DISCUSS IT RATIONALLY! AND THAT OLD BAG ISN'T GOING TO BE LIVING WITH US ANY MORE. OR I'M OUT OF HERE. AND SINCE I MAKE AS MUCH MONEY AS YOU DO, I GOT A RIGHT TO DECIDE WHO THE HELL LIVES IN OUR HOUSE . . . I'M BRINGING IN MY SISTER AND HER TWO KIDS CAUSE SHE JUST GOT DIVORCED, AND THE WHOLE BUNCH CAN LIVE HERE TOGETHER . . . WE'RE GOING TO MOVE OUT AND GET A GREAT APARTMENT FOR US . . . AND THAT'S JUST FOR OPENERS . . .

You simply say:

Some time when you should have been loving and close, intimate, or you could have been this way . . .

He says:

Uh . . . uh . . . I'm thinking of Liz . . . Liz and I have been married for seven years . . . I can't remember ever . . . I don't . . . Jesus Christ . . . I remember when we were first married and she was pregnant and lost the baby, and I . . . I never . . . I felt so sorry for her, and . . . [He is crying, lightly.] . . . I should have held her and loved her . . . I should have . . .

You quietly invite him to be this new person, after detailing the scene sufficiently:

Go ahead.

He does:

Oh Liz, you poor darling . . . I love you so much . . . Yes . . . I'm so sorry . . . [He is crying more.] I am so sorry . . . Oh my little girl . . . I haven't ever told you how much I love you . . . Liz, I love you . . . I love you so much . . . What can I do? . . . Liz . . . Liz . . . I'm so sorry for the way I've been . . . I love you so much . . . so very much . . . my darling . . .

Use the Bad-Feelinged Scene from Step 1

In Step 1, you found some scene in which the feeling was relatively strong. Usually, the feeling was a bad one. Even if you used this scene in Step 2, seriously consider using this same scene in Step 3. Indeed, I suggest that you use this scene quite regularly in this step. There are some reasons for such heavy reliance on using this scene in Step 3.

One is that there usually is a close relationship between the inner experiencing and the Step 1 scene of bad feeling. Generally, the inner experiencing was housed inside of that Step 1 scene. Second, being the inner experiencing in that bad-feelinged scene provides a sample, a taste of how the patient might have been that is free of the bad-feelinged operating potential, free of the accompanying bad feelings, free of the behaviors that constructed and maintained the external situation. Third, being the inner experiencing in this step leads quite naturally to Step 4 in which the patient is enabled to become a person who is free of the bad-feelinged scenes of Step 1. This is a major goal of experiential therapy. Ideally, in one session, the patient is to be able to be free of, to let go of, the Step 1 scene of bad feeling. In achieving this important goal, using this Step 1 scene in this step is almost essential. It should, therefore, be a regular part of Step 3.

The awful scene, in Step 1, just occurred a few days ago. Her mother had been upset by continued wrangling with her ex-husband, and, for the first time, mother hatefully accused the patient of always siding with her father against mother. The mother was crying and attacking as she said something like:

I always put up with your lying . . . You've always been cold and heartless. You only think of yourself!

The patient was devastated. Throughout Step 3, the patient sampled being the inner experiencing: unglued, falling apart, being a lunatic, a crazy one. She loved being this newfound inner experiencing, and she thoroughly enjoyed being this way in the Step 1 scene with her mother. It felt wonderful being this new person. At the height of her being this new person after her mother attacked her, the therapist says:

Now go ahead and feel rotten. Go on! Lordy Lordy! Your mother has just said things that are awful! Right? When it happened, you were mortally wounded! Right? So go ahead and feel awful . . . I want to hear this . . .

She tried, fumblingly:

She hurt me . . . She didn't have to say those things . . . Oh shit. I can't!

Then she laughs:

I can't do it! Isn't that something?

It helps to use the bad-feelinged scene from Step 1 after the patient is being the inner experiencing fully and with good feelings in some other scene. You say:

Well! You can certainly bitch and complain and be critical! [Now insert the Step 1 scene.] So here you are in the bar. You are an old fart, 48, just about 50, and all the people in this singles bar are kids, in their 20s, with one or two in their 30s. And here you are, an old fart, balding, fat, in lousy shape, except for an old fart. No one looks at you. You are not the attractive guy you were 30 years ago! So go ahead, see what it's like! Bitch! Complain! Be critical! Go ahead!

He starts:

What the hell am I doing here . . . with all you children . . . Yeah, I think some of you are younger than my boy! I don't belong here . . . I'M AN OLD MAN. AND FAT. WHAT THE HELL AM I DOING HERE? GET THE HELL OUT OF HERE, YOU OLD FART. GO FIND PEOPLE YOUR OWN AGE . . . SHIT! GO PLAY WITH THE KIDDIES ON THE PLAYGROUND . . . FIND AN OLD LADY AND BITCH

AND MOAN ABOUT THE GOOD OLD DAYS WHEN YOU WERE YOUNG . . .
BYE EVERYBODY! . . . THE OLD FART IS LEAVING . . . LIKE HE SHOULD . . .

In the Step 1 scene, he was so depressed that he had taken a gun, not yet loaded, and sat, crying, wallowing in thoughts of killing himself. The inner experiencing is being furious, not taking any more shit, making drastic changes, especially in his relationship with his business partner. He had been this inner experiencing in an earlier childhood scene. He drenched himself in this inner experiencing, and the feelings were exhilarating. Now it is time to be this inner experiencing in the bad-feelinged scene from Step 1. You show him how, and he reenters the scene, but this time as the new entity, the person who is this inner experiencing, and who addresses the unhappy slob. He says:

> *Andrew!! You sonuvabitch! Go ahead and kill yourself! You deserve it! Five years you let that bastard fuck up the business, and all you did was feel bad! WELL, DO SOMETHING! TAKE THE GODDAMNED GUN AND KILL SAM! IT'S ABOUT TIME! BLAST HIS FUCKING HEAD OFF! YOU IDIOT! YOU'RE KILLING YOURSELF! IF YOU DON'T! I'LL TAKE THE GUN AND SHOOT YOU! DO SOMETHING! DON'T JUST MOPE AROUND! GET A LAWYER! TELL SUZY WHAT'S HAPPENING! DO SOMETHING, YOU SHITHEAD!*

The bad-feelinged Step 1 scene is one in which he comes home, hears lots of noise coming from his study, goes in, and there is his girlfriend's 13-year-old daughter, with five other friends, lounging in his study, laughing and drinking beer. His girlfriend and daughter had moved into his house just a few weeks before. He was a confirmed bachelor physician, had never lived with a woman, and he started the session in a state of dismayed shock. The inner experiencing is a flagrant defiance, rebelliousness, disobedience. In the session, he threw himself into this inner experience in the context of a scene from childhood, and he was giddy with being this inner experiencing when the therapist says:

> *And now for something completely different! You are the well-esteemed doctor Claude, in this big, beautiful home, with all the expensive furniture in your prized study . . . and you walk in, and here in front of you are . . . Oh my God . . . kids! Beer! Teenagers on your leather couch! Here you are . . . the most rebellious, defiant, disobedient kid on the block! Go! Do it!*

He continued being this whole new person in the Step 1 scene. He exulted in being this new person. He belted it out. He stayed as this new person throughout this whole third step.

Use Catastrophic Incidents

Sometimes, in other approaches, these are called "traumatic" incidents. They are times in which the feelings were powerful, excruciatingly painful. They are catastrophic incidents that are indelibly planted in the patient's mind. It is helpful to go back into these incidents and to enable the patient to be the inner experiencing in these scenes. You may use the same catastrophic incident with a number of different inner experiencings, in a number of different sessions.

Most of these incidents are from some time ago, probably during childhood. It is when your father got you to suck his penis, and this occurred repeatedly. It was when your legs were ripped to shreds in the accident, and ever since that childhood time you have been in a wheelchair, with stumps for legs. It was when you were a child, and you saw your mother stab your sister to death. It was when you were only about three, and saw your father's face, sad, receding into the dark shadows, and you never saw your father again because he threw himself off the roof and died. It was when you were about 11 and the bear mangled your right arm.

Sometimes the catastrophic incidents are more recent. It was last year, when the doctor told you that you had cancer, and you may as well prepare to die in a year or so, maybe less. It happened four years ago when you were suddenly overcome with a terrible terror that something happened to your son in the woods behind your home. Petrified, you frantically ran into the woods and saw a pool of blood and his sock. When the neighbors went with you back to the spot, there was no blood, no sock. Your son was fine, and within a few days you were in the mental hospital. It happened three years ago when you were walking along downtown, and the two men beat you, knocked you down, kicked you until you were almost senseless, and you have been altogether different since then. It was three years ago when you found your apartment ransacked, everything broken or stolen, and the words, "you don't belong in this country" sprayed on the wall.

Standing here in your apartment, shocked and frozen as you stare at the words on the wall, you show her how to be the inner experiencing of being cold, hard, calculating in this catastrophic scene. You say:

So here you are, standing in the apartment, and you are this cold critter, hard, calculating . . . It's your turn now . . . Whenever you are ready, go ahead.

She continues with the steely cold voice:

I am going to find out who did this . . . I will take my time and track them down . . . [She speaks slowly, assuredly.] There are fingerprints. Carefully, painstakingly, I am going to track them down . . . There are others from my country. Men who have been detectives, policemen, killers. We will plan together, slowly, very carefully. [She is almost hissing, and she is oozing the inner experiencing.] And we will find them. We will know what to do with these animals. We will teach them a lesson. No one dares to treat Chinese like this. It will take time. We will find them . . .

Use the same catastrophic early scene in different sessions. In one session, you have one inner experiencing, and you are likely to get somewhat different inner experiencings in other sessions. Typically, by using the same catastrophic scene with a number of inner experiencings the catastrophic early scene tends to be altered, softened, changed. Its lingering effects are no longer so painful, so enduring. The pain seems to leave these catastrophic events. Maybe a better way of putting it is that the event seems to change because you have gone through the event in a whole new way. Yet the main reason for going back is to enable the patient to be the new person.

Use Earliest Scenes with Parents as the Main Figures

The main figures in the scene may not necessarily include the patient. They may include parental figures, or even older brothers or sisters or grandparents or others. The scenes may be from any time in the patient's life.

Every so often, I am drawn toward using scenes that make sense in the experiential theory of human beings, scenes that may be outside of most of the ones used those in many other approaches, but perhaps are less unusual than those in some approaches. I occasionally look for scenes that occurred in a period from approximately a year or so before the patient was conceived to a year or so after birth. In these scenes, the important figures that I use are the parents, and sometimes someone else such as a grandmother or an older brother. I tend to favor scenes in which these other figures are attending to the infant, or to the baby who is in the womb. Sometimes the scenes do not even include the patient.

Patients readily can shift to such a perspective, and they can come up with scenes:

My mom and dad made me on their wedding night, on their honeymoon. They had sex before, but they went camping on their honeymoon, and that's when they conceived me. Yeah, I can see them together. Alone. Camping . . .

My dad was in the delivery room, and he got so excited when I came out that he started shaking, and then he passed out. He always had to be the center of attention! That sonuvagun!

My mom told me that she breast-fed me, and dad used to get so embarrassed. So mom whipped out a tit and fed me at dad's parents' place. At the table! Mom is a clown! And nobody tells her not to do something!

Well, I was the fourth kid, and it happened so fast that I was born at home. First time for mom. It was in the middle of the night . . .

Mom never said. Not directly. But I think my father was her boss. They had an affair for about six months, and I can see her and her boss in his apartment. I visited there. I met him!

When mom was pregnant, that's when dad left. They broke up. That's when they separated. She said that the day he moved out she just sat with me and talked to me . . . I mean, you know . . . That must have been terrible for her . . .

When I was born, my mom went back to work, and my father took care of me. He stayed home and did everything. He fed me, and that's when he did a lot of writing . . . I can see him, me sleeping, and he's in the kitchen, working on the books that he wrote when I was a baby . . .

Start with these scenes and use them as contexts for being the inner experiencing. The patient may be the patient, or the baby, or some added new person. These scenes may be unusual, but they can be useful.

CONCLUSION

The singular purpose of Step 3 is to enable the patient to disengage from the person she is, and literally to be the inner experiencing. This is the purpose no matter what earlier scene you use, no matter how you find earlier scenes to use. Let yourself be flexible. Find and use a number of earlier scenes. You may start by having the patient be in some earlier scene you use, no matter how you find earlier scenes to use. Let yourself be flexible. Find and use a number of earlier scenes. You may start by having the patient be in some earlier life period and then find an earlier scene by means of the general features of the Step 1 scene or by means of the inner experiencing. You may skip this and go directly to other earlier scenes.

Whatever method you use to find earlier scenes, the important point is for the patient to be the inner experiencing fully and with good feelings. This step ends when the patient has been the inner experiencing in two or four or six or so earlier life scenes. This step ends with the patient being the inner experiencing. This is a remarkable achievement.

CHAPTER TEN

Step 4. Being and Behaving as the Inner Experiencing in the Present

By the end of Step 3, a remarkable change has occurred in the patient. He is being a new person. Of course, he is being this new person in the context of scenes that occurred a little while ago, or even long ago, but he is now a qualitatively different person. Even further, he is essentially free of being the old person with the bad feelings in those particular kinds of scenes and situations which were the centerpiece of Step 1. All in all, quite a remarkable change has occurred. We now turn from Step 3, in which the patient is being and behaving as the inner experiencing in earlier life scenes, to Step 4, in which the patient is enabled to be and to behave as the inner experiencing in the present, the world of today, tomorrow, and from then on.

What Are the Aims and Purposes of Step 4?

The simple but general way of answering this question is that the aim and purpose of this culminating step is to enable the patient to become a more integrated and actualized new person. What had been deeper, inside this person, is now an integrated and actualized part of a new person. The patient leaves the session as a different person, and is this different person in the person's different world.

The context shifts from the past to the present, to the whole world that is here when you and the patient open your eyes, the session is over, and the person is and lives in the extratherapy world. What the two of you have accomplished in the session is enabled to continue out beyond the session, into an extratherapy world that is also qualitatively changed. It is the world that goes with the new person. It is no longer the old world of the old person who entered the session.

To accomplish this, you need Step 4 because there is, in the experiential theory, no built-in force that leads one toward integration and actualization (cf. Maslow, 1968; Rogers, 1970; Tauber, 1960). It takes work to enable the new person to live and be in the present, to enter the prospective new world of the new person. This is the work of Step 4. Instead of the person being the inner experiencing in the context of earlier life scenes, the whole new person is to live and be in the context of present and prospective scenes. This is a simple but general way of describing the goals of Step 4. What are the explicit, working aims and purposes of this step?

The patient is to play and sample being the new person who is the inner experiencing in prospective scenes.   Your job is to enable the patient to have a taste of what it is like to be this whole new person, to think, act, feel, and experience as this whole new person who is living and being in the world outside the office. But the emphasis, in this first aim or purpose, is on play, on sampling, on providing a safe context for the new person. The context is loosened, opened up, deliberately allowed to be playful, unrealistic. The present and prospective scenes are to be lighter, friendly, playful, unrealistic, because the aim is to allow the new person to have a chance to come alive in the present world. Even in play, in unrealistic sampling, the new person enters into the extratherapy world of the present.

What is the criterion? How can you tell if you and the patient have succeeded? You can tell by paying attention to what happens in the session. The criterion is either met or not met right here in Step 4. If she is being the inner experiencing in present and prospective scenes, if the experiencing is full and the feeling is good, this opening purpose and aim are accomplished.

The patient is actually to be the new person who is the inner experiencing in the real extratherapy world.   We now go beyond fun and games, beyond play and fantasy, beyond playing and sampling what it is like as the inner experiencing. We now confront the serious, exciting possibility of actually being and behaving as this new person in the real extratherapy world. We move from playful sampling to realistic rehearsal. We are ready to suppose that the new person is really going to live and be in the extratherapy world. The opportunity is for this new person to remain perhaps, from now on, to persist and to endure, to live in and to construct a new external world.

Step 4 prepares the new person to be present in the actual world, and symmetrically, being in the actual world anchors the new person. The aim is to be this new person, and it is the actual world that enables this to occur. Indeed, being the new person is more important than merely behaving in new ways, regardless of the nature or worth of the new behaviors. It is being the new person that is uppermost, that is the aim and purpose of Step 4, and of using the extratherapy world to accomplish this goal.

The change may be slight or across the board. The change may be in one safe little situation or in virtually all situations. The change may be within the context of the extant extratherapy world, or some significant changes may be made in that world.

First the patient is to rehearse being and behaving as this whole new person in a true dress rehearsal. We can then make modifications and revisions in what to do, how to be, in the prospective scenes and situations. Then the new person faces the possibility of being ready, of being committed, of resolving to be and behave as this whole new person in this defined prospective scene, in several prospective scenes, or perhaps everywhere, and for real.

How can we determine if this aim and purpose have been achieved? How do we tell if we are successful and effective? There are at least two ways:

1. We can tell by seeing what happens right here at the end of this fourth step. Has the rehearsal been successful and effective? Is the new person genuinely committed to being and behaving in the rehearsed scenes and situations? If the answer is yes, this indicates that this aim and purpose have been accomplished.

2. We can tell by seeing who and what the patient is in the beginning of the next session. If the patient is essentially the same person as in the beginning of this present session, then we have failed. On the other hand, if the patient is being and behaving as this new person, then here is an indication of success and effectiveness. The opening of the next session can reveal the new person or the continuing old person. If the new person is here, then this aim and purpose were achieved.

The patient is to be the new person who is free of being the old potential with the bad feeling in those scenes.   In the first step, the patient may have identified a scene of bad feeling. One of the aims and purposes of Step 4 is for the patient to be free of being the old operating potential with the bad feeling in particular scenes. By being the new person, the patient is thereby free of being the old operating potential with the bad feeling in those scenes. Even further, Step 4 can enable the new person to let go of the bad-feelinged scenes, the bad-feelinged behaviors, and the bad feelings themselves.

What are the indications that this has been achieved? There are at least two:

1. In the session itself, in Step 4, the patient has a chance to do something about the bad-feelinged scenes that may occur tomorrow or next week or so. The very situations themselves may be revised, done away with, altered, so that they are no longer present in the same way. This can be achieved in the session so that the new person can see whether or not she can be free of being the old person with the bad feeling in prospective scenes.

2. The second indication lies in the opening step of the next session. If the patient is the same old operating potential, with the same bad feeling in the same scenes, then the present session was unsuccessful and ineffective in achieving this aim and purpose. This is both a stringent and ambitious goal. Yet it is important, in the opening of the subsequent session, to give the patient plenty of room to see whether the bad-feelinged scene is still present or has disappeared because the new person is now free of that scene.

What Are Some Helpful Guidelines for Achieving Step 4?

If you are going to achieve these goals, it is just about essential that you follow these guidelines:

Complete Steps 2 and 3 reasonably well before going on to Step 4.   Step 2 helped make the patient's relationship with the deeper potential more integrative. Step 3 gave the patient a chance to get inside of and to be the deeper potential. If Steps 2 and 3 were done reasonably well, then the way is open to do Step 4. If Steps 2 and 3 were not done well, if they were rather unsuccessful, then do not try to force the patient to go through Step 4. The simplest and easiest guideline is that if you do not do a reasonably good job in Steps 1 through 3, do not even start Step 4. Consider drawing the session to a close. There can always be another session tomorrow. Or perhaps you might tiptoe over Step 4, lightly touching on the possibility of new ways of being and behaving in the imminent extratherapy world, but do no serious work on Step 4.

Move to Step 4 when the patient has achieved Step 3 quite well, or when the patient naturally turns to the present.   Suppose that she has been the inner experiencing in several scenes from earlier life, in Step 3. At this very moment, she is being the inner experiencing in an earlier life scene, and she is being the inner experiencing fully and with good feelings. Here is a precise point when you may shift over to Step 4. There is no marquee that lights up and says that Step 3 is completed, mainly because you are always free to use some other earlier life scenes. However, after several times of being the inner experiencing fully and with good feelings, you may move into Step 4.

Occasionally, the patient herself will switch to the present. She finishes being the inner experiencing in an earlier life scene and then says:

This is the way I should be . . .

If I was like this, my husband would have a fit! . . .

It would be wonderful if I could be this way . . .

I could never do that. Never. Oh, would I get into trouble!

In effect, the patient has shifted over to the Step 4 involvement with the imminently present.

The therapist is probably the most important determinant of the nature and extent of the change that can occur.   The therapist can determine that there may be essentially no change at all, or perhaps some slight change, or a wholesale, transformational change. Even before you start Step 4, a therapist may foreclose the possibility of virtually any change in the person in this session. Or the therapist may have predetermined to allow a limited kind of change in the way the patient deals with her husband's pushings, but that is about the only kind of change that is to be considered. On the other hand, the therapist may be open to the possibility of sweeping and transformative changes in the patient, in the patient's ways of being and behaving, and in the situational contexts of the patient's life.

The experiential therapist is to leave open the distinct possibility of full and complete changes, transformational changes, in this session. Leaving this possibility open, allowing for the greatest possible change, is the responsibility of the therapist. If the therapist starts with a limited ceiling on the nature and the extent of change, for this person in this session, that is the limit of what can be achieved.

When Steps 2 and 3 have been accomplished well, and when the therapist is competent in the Step 4 methods, it is exciting how much change can be accomplished. No matter how much the therapist may be inclined to see the determinants of change as residing substantially in both therapist and patient, or to blame the patient if there is little or no change, the therapist is the most important determinant by far. The success and effectiveness of this step depend almost exclusively on the therapist's skill, competence, and entrenched beliefs about just how much of what kind of change can be attained in this session.

The therapist is to picture the patient being the inner experiencing in prospective scenes.
The therapist is to regard the patient as the new person, as the inner experiencing. Indeed, the patient was the new person, in Step 3, in the context of earlier life scenes. Now the therapist is to continue regarding the patient as being the new person, only now in the context of prospective life scenes. This means that the therapist can, all by herself, picture the patient being the inner experiencing in all sorts of scenes and situations from tomorrow or next week. This is the test. Can you literally see the patient as the inner experiencing, being and behaving in scenes from the extratherapy world? You may choose scenes that are real or sheer playful fantasy. You should be able to picture the patient, in all sorts of scenes and situations, being and behaving as the inner

experiencing. Indeed, you should be able to come up with these scenes and to invent all sorts of behaviors. You should be able to produce loads of pictures of the patient being the inner experiencing in all sorts of extratherapy situations. If you are truly aligned with this person, if your own entrenched beliefs allow you to do so, and if you are competent, then you should be able to see pictures of your patient being the inner experiencing from the time she leaves the session.

The therapist is to be the inner experiencing, and so is the patient.   Throughout Step 4, the therapist remains thoroughly aligned with the patient. This means that the therapist is the inner experiencing, speaks with the voice of the inner experiencing, and looks out on the world through the eyes of the inner experiencing. Furthermore, the therapist is the inner experiencing from start to finish of Step 4.

Since the patient is usually the new person at the end of Step 3, this means that both therapist and patient are being the inner experiencing in Step 4. It is as if two cohorts are working together, two people who are both being the inner experiencing.

This means that the therapist talks to the patient who is the new person, not as the former old person who started the session. It is as if the therapist is saying, "Well, hello! I am glad that you are here. Our next task is to stay this way, and to live and be in the extratherapy world."

Step 4 goes much more easily when the patient is the inner experiencing. In this sense, one of the helpful things about Step 3 is that the new person is present when you begin Step 4. When this happens, it is so much easier and effective for this new person to find situations and new behaviors for being this new way in the forthcoming extratherapy world. It is even more productive and more effective when both therapist and patient are being the new person, the inner experiencing. Not only can they join forces in doing the work of Step 4, but there is an integrative togetherness in both being the inner experiencing. They may take turns in carrying out the work, and they can do so in a delightfully integrative way.

The new behavior is to be carried out by the new person, not by the old personality. The new behavior may be as simple as buying some flowers and leaving them with a note, for the lady next door. If may consist of letting your friend finish his rambling story, and doing so without interruption. It may consist of reaching out and caressing the face of your daughter, saying, "I love you." Even with such simple and concrete behaviors, it is essential that the behaviors be carried out by the new person, and not just by the old personality.

Perhaps the main purpose of the new behavior is to enable the new person to live, to be, to be present. The new behavior is to serve the inner experiencing, to bring it forth. If the old personality carries out the behavior, the behavior has failed to accomplish its purpose. In this sense, the important consideration is what the person is experiencing as the new behavior is being carried out. If it is the inner experiencing, then the new behavior is doing its job.

The effect or the consequence of some new behaviors may seem to be similar, whether it is carried out by the new person or the old personality, especially if we look at the distal effects and consequences, and not at the effects on the person himself. The light is turned on, whether it is the new person or the old personality who turns it on. The lady next door gets the flowers, regardless whether the behaving one is the new person or the old person. However, many behaviors are quite different, depending on who is carrying them out. Caressing and holding the other person can vary a great deal depending on who is doing these things. Declining the other person's invitation to supper or asking the neighbor to help you, or washing the woman's back as she is standing with you in the shower, all of these behaviors can be quite different depending on whether they are being carried out by the new person or the old person. Indeed, the more carefully the behaviors are described, the more they may be substantially different behaviors, depending on who is carrying them out.

The therapist's attention is consistently and fully out there. Your attention is consistently and fully in front of you, directed out there throughout Step 4. At least two considerations highlight the importance of your attention being out there.

One is that your attention being out there makes it easier for the patient to remain as the new person throughout this step. If you withdraw your attention from out there, it is quite tempting for you to lapse into talking to the old personality. You may not do this, but it seems to be easier to retain the patient as the new person when your attention is consistently and fully out there.

Second, some of the methods call on you to peer into the future to see how the patient can be and behave. You have to envision the new person in prospective scenes. You see scenes and new behaviors. You will also see the patient being this new way in the future scenes. These methods almost require that your attention be consistently and fully out there.

Playing and sampling precede getting serious about really being-behaving as the inner experiencing in the extratherapy world. First you play and sample what it is like to be the inner experiencing. This introduces the patient to what it can be like to be and behave as the new person in the extratherapy world. It also makes it easier for the patient to then move on to the more serious phase of actually living and being as this new person in the real world. In Step 3, the emphasis is on merely being the deeper potential, on seeing what it is like to let go of being the old person and to be the new person. Step 3 is therefore carried out in a context of unrealistic play, exaggeration, throwing oneself fully into the silliness, the burlesque. This wholesome context continues when you move from Step 3 to the first phase of Step 4, because you have the same purpose, namely, for the person to gain a taste and a sample of what it is like to be this inner experiencing. Then you can move to more serious consideration, more the way the person might really be in these prospective scenes. First being the new person in wholesome, unrealistic play makes it much easier to then move to the more serious and realistic examination consideration of how the new person might really be in the extratherapy world following the session.

Just about every session should culminate in the patient's being and behaving as the new person in the real world. It is almost a rule that if the patient carries out the new way of being and behaving in the real world, actual changes will continue to occur. Symmetrically, if the patient does not carry out the new way of being and behaving, there will essentially be no change. At the very end of the session, the patient should be on a kind of high, quite ready, eager, and geared toward being and behaving as this new person. The new way of being and behaving may be wholesale and transformational, or it may be reduced to a safe little token. Otherwise, the patient remains the old personality. Actual changes do not occur automatically, even if you went through Steps 1,

2, and 3 quite well. Step 4 is essential, and being-behaving as the new person, in the real world, is likewise essential.

This means that you must do at least two things to virtually ensure that he is the new person who behaves as the new person in the extratherapy world. At the end of this session, he is to be the new person who is quite committed and eager to be this new person in the extratherapy world. Second, in the beginning of the next session, check up. The opening instructions can focus attention on scenes of carrying out the new way of being and behaving, being free of the old bad-feelinged scenes, or scenes of having botched up the job or of having skipped it altogether.

WHAT METHODS ARE USEFUL FOR THE PATIENT TO PLAY AND SAMPLE BEING-BEHAVING AS THE INNER EXPERIENCING IN PROSPECTIVE SCENES?

The emphasis here is on sheer playing, with the emphasis on fantasy, unreality, exaggeration, caricature, burlesque, whimsy, and slapstick. It is definitely not being the inner experiencing for real. Make it clear that the purpose is for her to get a playful sample of being the whole new person in prospective scenes. It is a safe sample, a way of trying out this new possibility in a context of fun, free of reality constraints.

Usually, the patient is already being the new person. There are methods that are more suitable when the patient is being the inner experiencing. Other methods are more suitable if the patient slides back into being the old personality. Consider both sets of methods as ways to enable the patient to play and sample being the new person in prospective life scenes.

When the Patient Is Being the New Person Who Is the Inner Experiencing

The person who is here with you is the new person. This is whom you address. Pretend that the person who is here is really the new person, not the patient who was here in the beginning of the session. You talk to this new person. You may do this as a matter of course, or you may put a flag on your addressing the new person:

> *I am going to talk to this new woman, because I am very glad that you are here.*

You may go even further in celebrating and highlighting the presence of the new person:

> *So I am fortunate, ladies and gentlemen, to be here, having this interview with the famous Jerry Malinowski. Well, Jerry, you are elite, looked up to, known by just about everyone. You are the new owner of the famous Fairmount restaurant. Now Jerry, I understand that this is the fourth world-renowned restaurant that you have under your belt—ooops, sorry . . . But what is it like for such a well-known person to be the owner of so many famous restaurants?*

Here are some methods to use when the patient is being the new person. Each of these methods enables the patient to play and sample being and behaving as the inner experiencing in prospective scenes. Use any of the methods. Use several of the methods.

Invite the new person into a wholesale transformation.   The idea is relatively simple. Here is a whole new person. Stay being this whole new person from now on. There is no law that prohibits the new person from being here from this point on. Here is the door into a complete, total transformation:

> *Something happened in the session, and you are now this whole new person. Is there something so preposterous about continuing as this whole new person? After all, it feels good. And the old worries and troubles are gone. There are some real advantages from remaining here. You have been hidden for a few decades or more. So what!*

Suppose that the deeper potential is being high-minded, above pettiness, being responsible. In the session, you went back to times when he was eight years old, and he pretended that he was the high judge of all the world; people brought the most important matters to him for his weighed decision. Step 3 involved his switch into being this new person. Now, in Step 4, the method consists of inviting him to stay being this person all the time, everywhere, a wholesale transformation (Mahrer, 1993b).

The therapist is the key to whether such a grand and sweeping change is possible, even in play, fantasy, make-believe. Can you conceive the patient being a wholly transformed person? You should. If you cannot, you may be doing your patient a disservice. More practically, if you cannot even conceive the patient undergoing this wholesale transformation, then both you and the patient will probably have a hard time with this method. If you can easily picture this radical shift, right here, right now, then the patient at least has a chance of succeeding with this method. Welcome this new person, and couple the greeting with an invitation for a full transformation:

> *Hello! Here you are. Well, how about being here full-time, all the time, everywhere . . . I understand that you are going to be around for about 40 years or so, right? That's good. That's very good!*

Explain how this means a wholesale transformation in the very being, the very essence, of the person. Instead of being the new person in this or that situation, it means being this whole new person all the time, everywhere. It is a whole new person who stands on the corner, waiting for your friend to come pick you up. It is a whole new person who wakes up in the morning, who holds the glass of juice, who listens as the friend tells him about the basketball game, who smokes the pipe, who reads the paper.

Invite the new person to define what is to be different.   As you are talking with this new person, invite this new person to designate what things are to be different. It is the new person who does the talking:

> *Well, to begin with, no more smoking, and I am going to lose 30 pounds, and I dump Louise and move out of that crappy apartment . . . for starters!*

The patient may define changes in him and changes in his life. The important point is that he is literally being the new person as he is defining how and where things are going to be different.

Since you are talking to the new person, you are entitled to be curious about where this new person intends or wants changes to occur. You may suggest places in which you can picture changes occurring, and invite the patient herself to take a turn:

I can picture you being quite different with David. I mean very different. If he doesn't come home, I don't think you'd much put up with it. Well, right or wrong, that's what I see. Your turn . . .

Or you may try and envision the new person:

Yes, I think I got it! Your sculpture is everywhere—galleries across the country, and in front of lots of big buildings, and . . . I see your picture in the paper . . . Some kind of award . . . Well, those are my pictures. What do you picture, I mean when life becomes ideal? where do you get these things

Insert the new person into specific prospective scenes and situations.   The patient is being the new person in the Step 3 situation. He is well and truly being the inner experiencing. As he is being this new person, in a flash, remove the Step 3 scene and replace it with the prospective scene. You have to preselect a very specific scene, and place the new person in this whole new scene.

The work for the therapist is to preselect the prospective scene, and then replace the Step 3 scene with the prospective scene. At the end of Step 3, she is in a scene in high school. You then insert her in a prospective scene:

It is going to happen three or four days from now. You are at David and Lynne's place, and it is around seven at night. Maybe you are thinking about leaving, or perhaps staying a while. Lynne looks directly at you and candidly says that she would like you to stay and participate in sex with them. She says quite openly that they are both very attracted to you, and ask if that would be acceptable to you. And then . . . get ready . . . you say to Lynne . . .

Invite the new person to talk to and interact with the old personality.   The new person is to be with the old personality in a scene that can occur tomorrow or next week or so. In this method, the new person is literally inserted into the imminent future, and is talking to and interacting with the old personality. It almost does not matter what the new person says and does, provided that he is being the new person in these prospective scenes. Furthermore, it almost makes little difference what the prospective scene is. It may be a dramatic scene, filled with feeling, or it may be a mundane little moment when he is showering or having tea tomorrow.

You invite him to talk to the new Sam:

So here you are, sitting alone with Sam, just the two of you. See him sitting there, holding the paper, but his mind is on the job, the job. What do you want to do about Sam? You know, the way Sam is a nice guy, but he never lets himself take the big leap, anything about getting the kind of job he could have, and would be happier in. Much happier. So you are you, so look at him. What do you say?

Sam starts right off.

Sam, listen Sam. Wait about three days, four days, then you damned well call Jack Oakes, and you ask him if you can have lunch with him to talk about your plan for reorganization. Just let him know that you'll bring along a short summary of the reorganization. That'll do it!

You say to Ellie:

Now it is today, and Ellie is 42 years old, a prominent specialist in town, respected by most of her colleagues. You see her at the hospital, walking along the corridor? Can you see her? I can . . . You are also in the corridor, and you are watching her walking along . . . See her . . . She is tight as usual, kind of pulled in. Nice . . . Tight, very tight. Now it's your turn. Tell her what sorts of changes you would like in her life. You are this forceful, pushy, a little big aggressive kid, only you are 42 big ones. So keep your eyes on tight old Ellie, and start telling her what you think of her, and all the little and big changes you think she should make in her life . . .

These are some useful ways to enable to patient to play and sample being the inner experiencing in prospective scenes, provided that the patient is already being the inner experiencing.

When the Patient Reverts to Being the Old Personality

Unfortunately, you may find yourself starting Step 4 with the patient as the old personality, and not the inner experiencing. This is unfortunate because playing and sampling as the new person in prospective scenes virtually requires that the patient be the new person who is the inner experiencing.

Even when the patient slides back into being the old personality, you are to remain steadfastly as the inner experiencing, with your attention mainly directed out there. However, there are things you can do, provided the old personality is ready and willing, so that the patient can get a playful sampling of being the inner experiencing in prospective scenes.

Give the patient plenty of room to see being-behaving as inner experiencing as appealing or unappealing.　It is really up to the patient whether this new way of being and behaving is appealing or unappealing, but it is up to you to cast the choice within the context of the imminent future. It is as if the patient is literally looking into the next few days or weeks or so, and deciding that it is attractive or repulsive to be and to behave in that way. To decide, it helps if you paint a picture of just what it is that the patient might regard as appealing or unappealing. This gives the patient plenty of room to react in one way or another:

So what do you think? Yes? No? Maybe? In a little way? Once in a while? Absolutely not?

Emphasize that this is just to give the patient a chance to play, to imagine. It is certainly not for real. Just to see what it is like, to get a little taste and sample. Since you are speaking with the voice of the inner experiencing, you say:

Naturally, I think being this way is great, and nothing can be better. But you're the important one, so is it even a little appealing or is it just damned repulsive? What do you think?

Do a little defining of the context. Point him toward the next few days or so:

So here's the thing. With Jan. Maybe just playing. It would mean being a whole new guy. Sharing, genuinely accepting and welcoming her, opening everything up to her.

That would change everything all right. No matter how she is, what she does. Oh that would be a big change! How does that sound to you? Remember, this is just imagining, but you can't even imagine if the whole idea drives you crazy. Is it appealing, awful, just to exaggerate it and see what the hell it can be like? What do you think?

The therapist is the one who plays and samples being-behaving as the inner experiencing in prospective scenes.   The patient does not have to be the one who is the inner experiencing. You do it for her. You are the one who models it for her, who is the wholesale inner experiencing on behalf of or instead of the patient. You may declare this quite openly:

I am going to do it! Yes! Oh here is my chance! . . .

May I do it? Ok? I want a chance. It'll be fun!

You may set the stage for your being and behaving as the inner experiencing. Then go ahead and do it in playful and whimsical fantasy. You may even go further and proclaim that you are really going to do it:

You know, if this quality inside you could talk, here is what it would say: "I am going to go out and get Carol an engagement ring! Right! Of course, I'll arrange to be able to exchange it if she says no way, or wants some other one. Right! I am going to do it tomorrow, after work. During lunch and after work . . . First I'll get it and then ask her to marry me." "Darling, will you marry me? You make more money than I do, so it'll pay off . . ." Does that scare you? Yes? Say, if it does, you move out and I'll do it. Come to think of it, I damned well will do it!

As the voice of the inner experiencing, you command the patient:

Go to a store and get yourself some nice shirts! And take your wife with you! Get pants that aren't torn at the bottom, and that your wife picks out, not you. You don't know how to dress! Learn to dress better. After all, you're almost 11 years old. Older? You're 40 years old! So dress better. You look rotten . . .

Invite the patient to observe the new person who is the inner experiencing.   When the patient has reverted to being the old personality, you need not try to dislodge him. However, you can set the stage by explaining that he is to put his attention on the actor who is made up to look just like him, or a twin who looks like him, or a clone of him, or some other form of him. All the patient has to do is to observe this other person. Your instructions may explicitly situate the patient 10 or 15 feet away from the look-alike. The patient may be present in the scene, or he may be in the audience, watching as in a play, or he may be invisible. You say:

He is tall like you, and has that cavernous, sepulchral voice like yours, and he wears the same distinctive glasses like you, and he also has those big boney hands like yours. All in all, that person looks very much like you.

You may even explain that this allows the patient to not risk having to be the inner experiencing:

This way is safer. You can just be you. You can at least take a look at what someone just like you can be like. You can even sit back and not like it, or scoff at it, or be very critical. But you can still see it.

Then you are to describe exactly what the look-alike is like, and what the look-alike does. Make sure that you describe this so carefully that the patient is virtually hypnotized into being and behaving as the inner experiencing. This means that you yourself must wholly be the inner experiencing, and wholly undergo precisely what you are describing. If the inner experiencing is being close and loving, you may take 10 minutes or more just detailing what it is like, inside and outside, for the look-alike to caress the face of her little daughter who is sleeping. You are so excruciatingly detailed that the patient is drawn in to being and behaving as this inner experiencing.

One way to distance the patient from the look-alike is to do so within the context of playful unreality. You may go even further by picturing the look-alike as being optimal, the ideal version of the inner experiencing:

> *Just to make it easier, I am going to describe that guy as ideal, the perfect version of this quality in you, even if you don't especially like that thing in you.*

The more you concretely detail the idealized form of the inner experiencing, the more the patient is safely distanced from the person he is observing; yet he is still gaining a whiff of what life could be like as this optimal version of the inner experiencing.

Invite the patient simply to go ahead and throw himself into being-behaving as the utterly new person. This is indeed an invitation, because you are relying wholly on the patient's readiness and willingness to go ahead and accept your invitation. You are virtually saying:

> *Oh, what the hell, why not just simply throw yourself into being this completely different person? I know it's not the way you are. You know it. Everyone who ever knew you knows it is not you. So go ahead and just take a big leap. What the hell!*

Make sure that you highlight the absolute unreality of being and behaving in this way. It is to be sheer nonsense, whimsy, silly play. It is pretense. Make it easier for the patient by inviting her to speak in a mock voice, the exaggerated version of the inner experiencing, making fun of the way the inner experiencing could or would speak. Use a weird and incorrect accent if that helps.

Invite her to do it for only 5 to 10 seconds, just enough to see what it is like. Show her how you would do it. Do it for 5 or 10 seconds or so, and tell her that you will tell her when 5 or 10 seconds are up. Then she can return to her ordinary self and even be repulsed by what she did.

You may make it easier by providing an impossibly unrealistic version of how the person changed into being the new person:

> *You went right out of your mind, flipped, went bonkers, and changed into this guy . . . You were hit by a friendly little bolt of lightning . . . Someone slipped a drug into your hot dog . . . You were hypnotized . . . Something weird came over you . . . and you turned into this whole different guy for about 10 seconds . . .*

Regardless of what method you use, regardless whether the patient is being the new person or reverted back to being the old person, your aim is for the patient to get a taste, a playful and unrealistic sample, of what it is like to be the inner experiencing after the session, in the extratherapy world. The patient has the chance to be the new person in the context of a present and future world that is stretched into pretense and nonsense, into mere play.

If we could simply just get this playful taste and sample in some direct way, that would be nice. But we need methods that will enable this to happen. This section has described a number of methods you can use. Whichever method you use still means that you have to select a scene in which the method is to be used, and some behaviors that the new person is to carry out. The next two sections suggest how you can get the prospective scenes and how you can select prospective behaviors.

HOW CAN YOU GET PROSPECTIVE SCENES?

You need to get or find prospective scenes in which the patient can sample being the inner experiencing. The scene should be one that can enable the patient to be the inner experiencing in a way that is playful, unrealistic, whimsical, burlesqued, caricatured, exaggerated. Here are some ways you can use to get these prospective scenes.

Build Prospective Scenes from Those Already Used in the Session

Start from scenes you have already used in the session. Select a few of these scenes and use them to build scenes in the next few days or so.

Build prospective scenes from those used in Step 3.   Start with scenes that you used in Step 3, and see how these scenes can be placed in the next few days or weeks or so. With a little inventiveness, you and the patient can construct imminently future scenes. For example, in Step 3 you found times in the past when the patient had been the inner experiencing of being warm and close, intimate and socked in with her close buddy during adolescence. Now let's look ahead, over the next few days or so. Picture being with someone with whom you can be genuinely close, very intimate, and socked in. Who comes to mind right away? Linda! Sure! We create a scene in which she and Linda have a few beers at Linda's apartment.

She had located a scene, in Step 3, in which she and her friend have stolen little items from stores. You inquire if she perhaps does this today. She groans:

> Not much. Yes. Awww. Once in a while . . . Not much . . . Well, I took some shoelaces . . . Just once. Uh, a couple of weeks ago . . . [And then, with a muted confession.] I think I might steal something again. I do . . . I will . . . Yes . . .

So we build a prospective scene in which she steals a few choice items from a favorite store.

In Step 3, you went to early childhood, to bending down and looking at things upside down with your head between your legs. You can do this tomorrow. You and your dad used to go to baseball games together. Can you arrange something like that for the next week? The earlier scenes involved hilarious pillow fights. How can you do something like this in the next few days? With some creative readjustments, you may be able to build prospective scenes from many of those that were used in Step 3.

Build prospective scenes from those used in Step 1, especially the scenes of bad feeling. In the first step, the patient generally identifies scenes of relatively strong feeling. Usually the scenes are accompanied with bad feeling. Occasionally, the scenes are with good feelings. You may use these scenes to build prospective scenes. If you concentrate on the bad-feelinged scenes from Step 1, there are several ways to build prospective scenes.

Invite the patient to peer ahead, into the next few days or weeks or so, and you describe the bad feeling or the bad-feelinged scene from Step 1. Get the patient ready to see whatever appears. You say:

> *Some man is getting too close, physically close, intruding too close, coming into your space too much . . .*

She says, almost immediately:

> *Rudy! The guy who fixes things in the apartment! Yeah, he does it. He's gonna come in and fix . . . the water pressure is low . . . Oh yeah . . . That's Rudy . . .*

When the patient is set, you say:

> *You are going to feel like you're hiding, can't say what you mean, tight inside . . .*

He answers:

> *Otto is coming from Munich next week . . . I can't talk with him! And he's staying with us for a week, again! I know it's going to happen again, same way . . . Maybe he won't come . . . [groans].*

You describe the very uncomfortable bodily sensations that go with her feeling awful:

> *You'll have those tight things in your stomach, like a tight scrunched ball, and your face feels flushed. Something is wrong!*

A short pause, and she says:

> *Yeah, my stage fright. I got to make a presentation to the section. My report. Shit. It's starting now. Just mentioning it . . .*

You can build a prospective scene merely by looking ahead to when the bad-feelinged scene is probably going to happen again in the near future. You say:

> *It's tonight or in the evening tomorrow or so. Getting ready for bed. You hate sex with him. You can't talk together. You feel caught and trapped, like living a hateful marriage. Stuck . . .*

From Step 1, you say:

> *Tomorrow morning. Wake up. First thought: "I am so bored! I hate being a doctor, doing the same old fucking thing, a hundred patients a day, in and out. Same thing. What am I going to do?" You feel like your whole family'd think your out of your damned mind . . .*

You describe the Step 1 scene of awful feeling as you both are looking into the next few days or so:

> *You are churning inside, and there are almost frantic feelings of ending it all, dying, killing yourself. Tomorrow, Friday, on the weekend. You're alone, and filled with these terrible feelings. Alone, in your car, or sitting at your place . . .*

Just about every bad-feelinged Step 1 scene can occur again in the next few days. Whatever the nature of the inner experiencing, it is helpful to enable the patient to be the new person in prospective scenes that consist of these bad feelings of the Step 1 scenes.

The prospective scene may be created by picturing how the patient can actively reconstruct the bad-feelinged Step 1 scene. It may have occurred recently or when the patient was a small child. Yet it may be reconstructed in the next few days or so. Suppose that the bad-feelinged scene from Step 1 occurred yesterday. The woman she lives with is screaming at her, and grabs a knife, yelling:

I could KILL you!

This situation may be actively reconstructed if the patient and the other woman mutually agree to reconstruct the situation. The tenor and the feelings will likely be altogether different, and the situation is only grossly similar in some main features:

Do you think she'd be willing to play it again? With or without the big scary knife?

Both of you would have to agree. It takes work to recreate the scene. Lighter maybe. No one gets hurt. What do you think? Possible? No way?"

Prospective scenes can be re-created even with bad-feelinged scenes from long ago:

Twenty years ago, your dad just started screaming at you that you took his car without asking him, and you were so terrified you just stood there and cried, and you didn't take the car at all! You were petrified! OK, so he's still around. Hell, you two never even mentioned that thing, ever. So how about setting the scene again. Tell him that he's going to have to agree to whatever you want. Tell him to start screaming about your taking the car when you were a kid, and no questions. That'll set it up again. Explain that it's going to be playtime, but he's got to cooperate, and then he has to shut up till you say whatever you say. Well, what do you think? Yes? No?

Get Prospective Scenes from the Inner Experiencing Itself

Allow the inner experiencing itself to create useful prospective scenes. Start with the inner experiencing, and let it do the work.

If you picture the patient as the optimal new person, what are the scenes in which you see this occurring?   In this way of getting prospective scenes, the burden is usually on the therapist. Let yourself picture the patient as the optimal new person, integrated and actualized. Try to allow the vision to develop. See the kind of world that supports this new person, the life around him, the situations that come from and provide for this new inner experiencing. You may work within some of the reality constraints of who and what he is, and his present world. Or you may get a little far-fetched. You can stay with him as a married man, in his late 40s, with an adolescent daughter, and a job in landscaping, living in a house in the suburbs. Within this world, how might there be prospective scenes ideally suited for a new person who is the beloved jewel, the worshipped center of attention, the one they all love? Or, you may go way beyond his present life circumstances, and picture what might be, could be.

If you stay within the general contours of his present life, just let yourself see this fellow as the beloved jewel, the worshipped center of attention, the one they all love. What scenes appear to you? Can you see him in a living room, filled with the whole family, all the uncles and aunts and cousins and all the children? They are celebrating his birthday. Everyone is simply beaming at him because they adore this wonderful person. Can you see him at work, with four or five other guys? They are relaxing, and he has just said something kind of friendly and funny. The guys are looking and grinning at him, and you can tell that they like him immensely, that they would just about do anything for him. If you go further, but still within the realm of what may be possible, what appears is his being with a husband and a wife, in their house. He has done something almost magical for them. Their house had burned down, and they had almost no insurance. The patient organized a group of neighbors, and they helped rebuild the house. Now the couple are thanking him, quietly, adoringly, gratefully, and with love.

She is in her early 30s, married to a fellow who has a small restaurant. They have two children. The inner experiencing is being wild, spontaneous, crazy. You picture her becoming this transformed new person, and you broaden the scope to see the scenes in which she is being this whole new person. What scenes do you imagine? You see pictures of her in gales of laughter, getting drunk with some other woman, someone she can be wild and spontaneous with ("My cousin Louise! Yes! We were crazy!"). You picture her grabbing someone and dancing in a rollicking, fun-loving way ("I've thought about helping in the restaurant! I'd love to be that way—with old regulars"). You picture her with a man, maybe her husband, maybe not, and she is being wild, spontaneous, crazy with him as the two are making loud noises, stripping off their clothes, touching their bodies, and preparing for a night of lovemaking ("Not my husband . . . Better Salvador! Ha!"). Stay within the general bounds of reality, but push the limits. What would the ideal circumstances be for this whole new person?

Start with the inner experiencing, and picture the new person as practically optimal, ideal. That will give you scenes, some relatively close to realistic constraints, and some dipping into unrealistic fantasy.

If you picture the completely transformed new person, what would be the most ordinary scenes, and what would be the scenes of fantasy, of daydreams? Start with the inner experiencing. Let it grow until it develops into a whole new person. You are seeing a picture of an utterly transformed person. Now see this transformed person being in the most mundane, ordinary, trivial situations.

Start with the way the person looks, the physical features. As the transformed new person who is the utterly new expression of being self-confident, self-assured, able to do it, what does this new person look like? How is she dressed? What does her hair look like? Is she fatter or skinnier than you? If you see her walking along the corridor, notice the way she walks. Literally picture this person, this whole new person, walking down the corridor. Look at her face, at the ordinary expression on her face as she is merely walking along. Describe this expression. The prospective scene is simply being this whole new person, dressed in this way, walking in this way, and with this particular facial expression as she is walking along the corridor at work.

Get the prospective scenes by seeing how this whole new person is in the most ordinary situations of everyday life. Notice the way she wakes up, looks around, moves, all before getting out of bed. Watch her get out of bed. She is not you, even though her physical features are similar. Watch the way she urinates, brushes her teeth, showers, towels herself, puts on her makeup, selects clothes, gets dressed. See this person as she drives the car, eats a sandwich. See the way she sits in a chair. How does she listen when she is talking on the telephone? What is the look on her face when she is listening to her friend tell her things? Describe how she is when she reads a newspaper. How does this kind of person sit at the table with some friends? How does she watch television as a person who is self-confident, self-assured, able to do it? How does this kind of person push a grocery cart, stand in the line to pay for food, walk out of the store?

You must be able to see this whole new person actually coming to life, and being present in this form. The inventiveness comes in your allowing yourself to see this person sitting at the kitchen table and drinking coffee, or looking in the bathroom mirror, or engaged in any of those ordinary everyday activities. You are getting scenes by seeing how the transformed person is in commonplace situations.

You can also get scenes by seeing what this transformed person does inside the patient's private realm of fantasy, of daydreams. Many patients have private daydreams of what they could be like, of the whole other person that they can be. What fantasies and daydreams surround the inner experiencing of self-confidence, self-assuredness, being able to accomplish anything? There is a terrible accident on the street, with two cars crashing into each other. It is mayhem. Then you are present, exuding your self-confidence and self-assuredness, and you organize everything. Scientists announce that a gigantic meteorite is headed toward earth, and the whole world is frantic. You enter the United Nations and you are the supreme commander, full of self-confidence and self-assurance. You are able to get scenes by starting with the utterly transformed person, and entering the realm of daydreams and fantasies, or the mundane little scenes of everyday life.

What scenes are implied in the nature or content of the inner experiencing itself?   Most inner experiencings imply some kinds of situational contexts. If you examine the description of the inner experiencing, you will usually find hints and cues about prospective scenes. They are implied by or carried inside the nature of the inner experiencing itself. This does not apply uniformly to all inner experiencings. Many descriptions give almost no hints about the kinds of situational contexts in which they occur. But others do, and you can get some idea of the prospective scenes merely by paying attention to the nature and content of the inner experiencing itself.

If the inner experiencing is resisting, defying, saying no to, you can get a dim picture of a prospective scene in which there is something out there to be resisted, defied, said no to. It may be quite diffuse, but can you picture a force, some agency, a person or thing that is impending, perhaps putting pressure on the patient, daring or challenging her to resist it, defy it, say no to it? Let yourself see something. You may see her husband, attacking whatever she believes, relishing his taking apart what she thinks, using specious reasoning and casuistry to undermine her thoughts and ideas.

If the inner experiencing is being entered into, intruded into, invaded, you can picture something doing that. You may have flashes of forceful sexual enterings into, or you may see someone simply getting much too close physically, or some stranger sitting on your front porch or lounging on your front yard. You may use your own pictures, or you may invite the patient to see whatever appears within the context of the next few days or so, but the inner experiencing itself may imply something of the prospective scenes.

Get Prospective Scenes by Actively Inserting the Inner Experiencing into the Next Few Days or So, and Seeing What Scenes Appear

You know what the inner experiencing is. Suppose that you push or project the inner experiencing into the next few days or so. There are ways to do this so that you can come up with all sorts of prospective scenes.

What would be the most outrageously impossible and inappropriate times and places for being this inner experiencing? In this phase of Step 4, you are looking for prospective scenes in which the patient can play, taste, sample, what it can be like to be the inner experiencing. Think of forthcoming times and places where it would be absolutely impossible and outrageously inappropriate to be the inner experiencing. What are the forthcoming times and places in which the patient could not, should not, would not, be this way? Those are precisely the times and places that we can use.

The inner experiencing is pure erotic, slithering sexuality, cooing seductiveness:

So let's see, where would be the place where that would be absolutely out of place? No way. Not there . . . A-ha! Lucille, your mother-in-law, is having a very formal outdoor party, with all the important people in town. It will be this Saturday. Of course, you will attend. Is that one wonderful place where you absolutely would not be this way? Good! Now you think of another. Better than mine . . .

Well, let's see now. This feeling is putting your foot down, stop it! That is it! Ending the shit! Now where could you never be this kind of person? The last place. It would mean you'd be tarred and feathered.

She says:

Right off, I thought of Edward. Sunday. We . . . he's my grandfather . . . We go to church on Sunday and then to his place for a cup of coffee and cookies or something. We've done that ever since we were married . . . [She laughs.] Yes, that would be one thing . . . I like going to church and to his apartment. The kids don't . . . And yes, that would be one place I'd never be that way . . . Oh, it would be . . . ! I don't know what . . . !

There are whole areas of one's current life where it would simply be unthinkable, maybe downright threatening and scary, even to contemplate being the inner experiencing, especially certain kinds of inner experiencings. Consider being brutal, cold-blooded, mean. He says:

Well, that's not me! I couldn't be that way! I wouldn't even want to! I'd lose my job . . . If I was like that with my supervisor I'd get transferred in a day . . . Course I'd love to squeeze his eyeballs or . . . steal that expensive pocket watch, or . . . I could never smash his Mercedes sports car!

You can think of outlandish situations that are quite inappropriate and grossly impossible. Set the patient to look ahead and see these times and places:

Ready? . . . Some time in the next few days or so . . . You are being wild, crazy, very "spontaneous," which means unpredictable . . .

He says:

There's a meeting . . . oh no! But that's what I thought of! Yeah! That would be the last place I'd ever . . . I can't even picture it . . . !

That is the scene.

What are scenes where the patient would-could-should be the inner experiencing?
Since the emphasis is on playful sampling, imaginative unreality, it can be productive fun to look for prospective scenes in which the patient could perhaps be this new way,

or possibly should be this way, or maybe would love to be this new person. This way of getting prospective scenes leaves most of the work up to the patient:

> *So suppose that you somehow were like this: violent, explosive, just blasting out. Just suppose. So where would you start, huh?*

She says:

> *I'd get Donna to get rid of David. And I sure as hell would do it! Or else! I'd fix that sonuvabitch!*

You ask him where he could or would just love to be this way, being teasing, seductive, sexual up front. He says:

> *I think Norm is attracted to me. Just a little. Yeah! I'd love to . . . oh that would be great, with Norm! I know just when I could do it, too!*

Invite the patient to look for prospective scenes when perhaps there is a little glow of the inner experiencing. It starts to happen inside. In fact, the patient would just love to be this way, all the way. You describe the inner experiencing of being loved, treasured, cherished. Then he says:

> *Larry will tell me that he looks forward to our talks. We have a long lunch together every two weeks, almost regular, and we talk seriously about work, work things. He says that . . .*

You ask her when she would get this feeling anyhow, just a bit, but only inside, a little. It is the sense of being close to, touching, holding. She says:

> *There's this lady in my apartment. She said . . . in the elevator . . . she's got cancer . . . and sometimes she looks . . . brave, I guess. I didn't . . . I wish I could just touch her arm . . . or have coffee with her and talk with her . . . And with my brother. He's so happy with his new wife . . . He came over yesterday . . . I felt good, but I should have . . . put my arms around him . . . I could be more . . . well, loving . . . I feel it, a lot . . .*

If there is even a little glow of this inner experiencing, you can use that to get a scene.

Patients can come up with prospective scenes when you give them plenty of room to look for times when they know they should be this way:

> *In the next few days or so, you know that there will be plenty of times when you should be this way. Yes you should. You might actually be this way, but probably not. You should. I'll describe the feeling, the way you can be. You think of times when you damned well ought to be this way . . . OK?*

Then you describe the inner experiencing:

> *Yes! You should be doing a little scolding here, a little being critical, telling someone they messed up a little . . .*

He then says:

> *Tonight, Lisa will have a pile of shit all around. Sure! More of her crap all over, the usual mess she leaves . . . It's all over the house! Her junk, shoes, and sweaters and*

scarfs. The whole mess. Not just in the bedroom! It's on the floor, on tables, all over the whole place!

You say:

... and the feeling is "drop it, let it go already, get rid of it" ... Why the hell should you be this way?

She snickers:

Would you believe just about everywhere? Starting with my new assignment? I HATE taking over that section for two months? I'm a damned troubleshooter, and it's awful! I should say no, once. Once? I should get the kind of position that I had two years ago. I loved it ... And smoking ... and Jeffrey ... Jeffrey ... In a minute I should tell him to pack his things, and his damned dog ... and get out ... I'm making myself miserable, and it's my own fault!

You are geared toward enabling the patient to play and sample being and behaving as the inner experiencing in prospective scenes. To accomplish this, you need to get these prospective scenes. This section has described three ways that you can get prospective scenes. You may use any of these ways. The important thing is to be able to find prospective scenes. But scenes are not enough. You also have to get behaviors the patient can use in these prospective scenes.

HOW CAN YOU GET BEHAVIORS FOR BEING-BEHAVING AS INNER EXPERIENCING IN PROSPECTIVE SCENES?

Suppose that the inner experiencing is being a buddy, a close companion, being together. Even if you select some prospective scene, such as being with your older brother at the family reunion, you still have to identify behaviors. These behaviors have several jobs to do. They usually have to set up or build the situation itself. How can the patient build the right situation at the family reunion? It would probably take more than merely being at the same place, with all the other people. He may behave in ways that put him and his brother together on the shore of the small lake near the family cottage where the reunion is occurring. Then, being alone with his older brother, what behaviors are effective to provide a full good-feelinged sense of being a buddy, a close companion, being together? What behaviors, then, would enable the patient to construct the right situation with a full sense of the inner experiencing, and would do so in a way that is accompanied with good feelings?

Here are some ways you can get behaviors of being-behaving as the inner experiencing in prospective scenes.

Use Behaviors That Were Actually Carried out in the Session

One grand source of behaviors is the whole range of behaviors that the patient actually carried out in the session. These are the behaviors that actually occurred in the session, not behaviors that the patient talks about. Nor does the behavior have to be one that occurred in the same kind of situation.

If you look back over the session, she carried out some quite impressive behaviors. She screamed in surprise and bewilderment. She swore a bloody streak. She fell into gales of laughter. She said:

I love you . . .

The answer is NO. Leave me alone . . .

I'll do whatever you want. Anything. Just name it . . .

I am the boss, and I order you to stop that damned smoking. Just give it up!

In the session, she literally cried and sobbed. She told, in detail, what happened the first time she had sex, and this was the first time she talked about that.

Especially during Steps 2 and 3, the patient behaved in ways that were perhaps out of the ordinary, for him. But he did these things. He told his father to shut up and leave him the hell alone. He caressed his sister's face and said that he loves her. He screamed with glee when he smashed the dishes against the floor. He bellowed:

For Christ's sake, THAT'S ENOUGH!

He got down on the floor as a little kid, and he had a full-blown temper tantrum. All these behaviors were essentially new for him, and all of them actually occurred in the session.

The therapist is therefore entitled to say:

You did it here! I heard it. So did you. You did it!

Here is one source of behaviors for the patient to use in prospective scenes.

Insert the New Person into the Prospective Scene, and Allow New Behaviors to Be Produced

You have some idea of what the prospective scene is. You know what the new person is like. If you therefore insert this new person into the scene, it is almost easy for new behaviors to be produced. This is creative, effective, and fun. Suppose we know that the prospective scene involves his sister, with whom the patient has been fighting for years and years. In this scene, he will be alone with her in the living room of her apartment, the inner experiencing is touching, holding, being close. Given this inner experiencing, in this scene, what behaviors might be generated? Once you know the prospective scene and the inner experiencing, you can concoct all sorts of behaviors. This is one way of generating new behaviors.

The old person will typically face prospective scenes as not at all friendly to new behaviors. The old person will have a hard time conceiving new behaviors or even admitting the possibility of any new behaviors. This is why getting some new behaviors is the job of the new person, or it is your job, or you and the new person can work productively together to get some new behaviors. You say:

It is tomorrow. You are in the elevator with Larry, and again you are overwhelmed. He stinks! Same old body odor. And you are this new person, mean, nasty, hardhearted. Can you be here? Right here in the elevator. With Larry? Yes! OK, what the hell do you do?

There are at least a couple of ways that you can invite these new behaviors, by inserting the new person into the prospective scene:

Invent behaviors that are reasonably doable, practical, realistic. The main aim is to enable the patient to play and sample being and behaving as the inner experiencing in prospective scenes. The emphasis is on play, on not being realistic. Yet the behaviors that you select may themselves be reasonably doable, practical, and realistic. Sometimes the new behaviors just pop out. You paint the prospective scene. In the next few days, her recent boyfriend comes back from his trip, and settles in her apartment again. She is the new person, seeking commitment, wanting to marry, craving mutual loyalty. So what can this new person do with Ron? Immediately she says, blurting it out with an excited screech:

Drop him! Find another guy! [Hard laughter.] A better prospect!

Here is a possible behavior.

Suppose that the prospective scene is being alone with her daughter, who is seventeen. They are sitting together, having coffee in the kitchen. If you insert the new person into this scene, what behaviors are produced? The new person is drawn into, being focused on, being interested in. Allow yourself to picture behaviors that are reasonably doable, practical, and realistic. What do you see? If you are the new person, or if you picture the new person, what may appear is this woman sitting quietly, more or less listening, not pushing the daughter, lightly inquiring into whatever the daughter seems to bring up, consistently attending to her daughter and what her daughter is saying and doing.

Suppose that the prospective scene is one in which he typically has the awful feeling. It is a few days from now. His dad is coming from Montreal for a weekend visit, and as usual, dad finds things to be bothered about. For example, his dad is short and curt with the kids; his dad can't hear most of what is said, and always looks grumpy when he can't be sure what is said. The inner experiencing is being loving, intimate, caring for deeply. When both you and the patient look for new behaviors, the two of you picture the new person deliberately sitting close to his dad when he talks, kissing his dad on the forehead and saying:

What can we do so you can hear everything, kiddo?

spending plenty of time alone with his dad, and saying "I love you."

For behaviors to be reasonably doable, practical, and realistic means that they could be done, not that they are behaviors that the patient would be ready and willing to carry out after the session. The context is still one of play, of merely seeing what it is like to be the inner experiencing. Suppose that the inner experiencing is being demonic, evil, undiluted wickedness. The prospective scene is going to his favorite hot dog stand where the proprietor is friendly, affable, but drives the patient crazy by inevitably mentioning something about the patient's being Jewish. If you insert the new person into this scene, as it probably is going to occur soon, what behaviors come forth? When you order the hot dog, you lean forward and whisper in the proprietor's ear:

If you start up with that Jewish crap, the Israeli mafia told me to let them know. They'll take care of you.

Then you lean back and grin, maliciously, oozing politeness. Or you walk up to the fellow and show him your efficient, red, portable torch. Roll your eyes around his hot dog stand. Then dripping with wickedness, you say:

> *Mention something about "Jewish" . . . and . . . poof! Gone!*

You may go further by enabling other behaviors that come from the reactions of other parts of you or to the patient to having behaved in this way. In other words, you may step aside from such behaviors and have your own integrative behavioral reactions. For example, you then say:

> *Oooo . . . that did come across as a little bit evil, no?*

Or you may say:

> *Well! That was not nice! Do you think that was nice? Sounded sort of like a little demon to me, right? Nasty nasty. How awful!*

The behavior is simply to comment on, respond and react to, the behavior you just carried out.

Invent behaviors that are wild, outlandish, zany, fanciful, silly, risky, dangerous, impractical, impossible, unrealistic.   You can get behaviors by inserting the new person into the prospective scene, and seeing what behaviors emerge. However, you can go way beyond all constraints. Once you identify a prospective scene and the inner experiencing, you say:

> *. . . and I want to picture being like this and doing all sorts of things that are wild, crazy, you should not really do, you could not really do . . . never, never . . . bad things, things that would get you into all sorts of trouble, things that are far-out, illegal, dangerous, impossible, very very risky, but one helluva lot of fun, absolutely unrealistic . . .*

The behaviors that are invented can be wonderfully useful to provide for a very full undergoing of the inner experiencing. Furthermore, they can be sheer fun and games, filled with joy and pleasure.

The inner experience is taking charge, taking care of it, being the competent boss. The prospective scene is having a meeting with her real boss whom she regards as sloughing off, not being around much, making a mess of things. You and the patient invent a bunch of things for her to say and do:

> *You're a shitty boss! . . . I'm taking over . . . Go home and stay home! . . . You should be here more! . . . Never fear! I am here! I will be the real boss!*

She and you invent behaviors such as sitting in the boss's chair and having him sit on the floor while she lectures him, dragging the poor slob to the king of the department and pronouncing herself as the replacement, then having a departmental meeting to celebrate her being the boss.

The prospective scene is walking downtown, alone, and the big, tough guy confronts you:

> *Got any spare change?*

He glares at you, and you freeze, cringe, and you are so tight that your voice squeaks out through a dry throat. The inner experiencing is being the victim, being done to, very passive. Using this way of getting new behaviors, you come up with some weird possibilities. Look down, take out your wallet, give it to him like an offering. Throw yourself on him:

Anything! It's all yours! Take it all!

Run aimlessly around the sidewalk and beseech all the people walking by:

He wants money! Give him something, anything, everything! Everyone give him money!

Take him by the hand:

My bank is a block away! Come! It's all yours! Anything you want!

Go limp; fall to the ground; lie spread-eagled on the sidewalk; pass out.

Some deeper potentials are not all fun and games. They are ones where it would be easy to have bad feelings when they are occurring. One way of undergoing these experiencings is to throw yourself into them. Juice them up. Celebrate them. Exaggerate them. For example, the inner experiencing is not belonging, not fitting in, no place for me. The instant you sense it beginning in you, clown it out. Be outrageously honest, but exaggerate the experiencing way out of proportion, and have fun doing so. She is with five or six of the important people from the firm, and they are at the restaurant, maneuvering to get the good seats at the table. Here is when the inner experiencing rumbles, is starting inside, and she belts out:

I want to get a good seat! I am important! I am one of the important ones here. NO I'M NOT. I KNOW I'M NOT. [Mock loud crying.] WAAAA. I'M NOT IMPORTANT. I DON'T BELONG WITH THE IMPORTANT PEOPLE. I DON'T FIT IN. WAAAAAA

You know what the inner experiencing is. You have identified a prospective scene and some fitting behaviors to occur in the scene. What do you do to enable the patient to play and sample being and behaving as the inner experiencing in the prospective scene?

THE PATIENT IS TO PLAY AND SAMPLE BEING-BEHAVING AS THE INNER EXPERIENCING IN PROSPECTIVE SCENES

Everything you have accomplished throughout the session is aimed at the patient's being and behaving as the inner experiencing in prospective scenes. Even if the context is play, pretending, imagining, even if the context is quite unrealistic, what you are accomplishing here is remarkable. This person will actually be a substantially new person in the present. He will be and behave as this significantly new person within the context of the external world that will be occurring when he opens his eyes, leaves the office, and walks into the extratherapy world.

He is getting a taste, a sample, of what it can be like to be this whole new person, this integrated and actualized new person who is living and being in the present, in prospective scenes and situations. In addition, he is getting a taste and a sample of how to be essentially free of the bad-feelinged scenes from Step 1. Even as a playful sample, that is quite a feat. Instead of feeling bad, hurt, pained, unpleasant, in that situation, he is being a way that is quite different, and virtually free of that bad-feelinged scene. These are remarkable accomplishments, even if they are accomplished within a context of play and unreality.

In many respects, the highlight of the session is when the patient is actually being and behaving as this new person, within the context of prospective scenes. Even if the context is one of playful sampling, this remains a highlight of the session, the culmination of all your work so far.

What Are Some Helpful Instructions?

Make it clear that the context is play and unreality, that being and behaving in this way is sheer fantasy, whimsy, pretense, as if it were happening in a dream, a fantasy, a daydream, pure comedy, theater of the absurd. Emphasize that it is absolutely not the way the patient is to be in reality, in the real world.

Make it clear that this is mainly to give the patient a chance to see what it can be like to be this new inner experiencing in prospective scenes. It is an opportunity to practice what the person has probably not had 100 hours or even 10 hours of actual experience in being like and in doing.

Make it clear that the patient is to be this way and to behave this way until the experiencing is quite full, and until the feelings are quite good. We are quite free to try it over and over, to modify what we do and how we do it, until we are being this new person fully and with good feelings.

Make it clear that the patient is to let the other person accommodate. Of course mother or the spouse or the acquaintance might never go along with the patient being this new way. Because we are highlighting sheer play and fantasy, and because the important thing is to get a taste of being and behaving in this new way, make sure that the other person cooperates.

Make it clear that the patient has to be ready and willing to do this. It is the patient who must do the work, and therefore the patient's readiness and willingness, are absolutely essential.

The instructions are for the patient to live fully in the scene. You are in the office, a few days from now, and your two colleagues come in to ask, again, about the project. This is to be so real that you and the patient are literally being here with the colleagues. Make it clear that the patient is to be the inner experience of commanding, ordering, and is to start out by pointing to the chairs and saying, in heavy-handed seriousness, "Down . . . There . . . Sit!" And then the therapist opens the gate for the patient to start. The therapist says, "Do it . . . Now!" or "All right . . . Your turn. Go ahead!"

The Patient is Literally Being and Behaving as the New Person in the Extratherapy World

This is the key, the critical feature. You have selected a scene and a behavior, all within the context of the imminent future. Now the patient is to be the inner experiencing, to live it, to be it, to get a sample of what it is like to be and to behave as this new person in the extratherapy world. The patient is not talking about it. Instead, the patient is being this new person, living in this prospective scene, and carrying out the behaviors. It is actual, real, vivid, compelling, and yet the whole context is one of playful pretending, pretense, and unreality.

You are going through this right along with the patient. Indeed, you are doing this as well or better than the patient. As the inner experiencing, you are ready and eager to be the inner experiencing, ready and eager to literally be and behave as the new person in the extratherapy world.

Some of the prospective scenes are simply likely to occur; they will present themselves to the patient. Others probably would have to be constructed by the patient. No matter what the nature of the prospective scenes, some will almost certainly occur in the next few days or so, and others are up to the patient to bring about. In either case, the patient is literally to be and behave as the new person in these scenes.

Suppose that the inner experiencing is being loving, intimate, close to. The prospective scene is being with your sister in her apartment, and the behaviors include saying over and over again, in a voice that is loud and almost musical:

I love you. I love you. I really love you . . . Yes I do,

and then sitting next to her, clasping her hands, and saying, quietly:

I think you're wonderful, and I've been too shy to tell you.

The critical point is that the patient is literally to be the inner experiencing, literally to carry out these behaviors, and literally to live in this prospective scene.

Once the patient is being the inner experiencing in the prospective scene, the behaviors are mainly to prime the experiential pump. The patient and you start with these behaviors and incorporate them in a burst of all kinds of additional behaviors. The inner experiencing is being explosive, yelling and screaming at, giving shit to, and the prospective scene is when she is in her apartment with the new guy who moved in a few weeks ago, and now his 13-year-old daughter has arrived, intending to stay here with him, for the next decade or so. The behavior, used earlier in the session, is a simple proclamation, at the top of her voice, and held for about ten seconds: "NOOOOOOO!" In actuality, she only starts here. Both you and she go much further. She is accompanied with 14 superheavyweight iron pumpers from the gym where she works out. At the top of her voice, she commands these behemoths to keep bouncing the guy on the bed, and she throws out the window item after item belonging to him and his spoiled daughter:

OUT . . . OUT . . . TAKE ALL YOUR SHIT AND GET THE HELL OUT . . . NOW! . . . AND TAKE YOUR LITTLE KID WITH YOU . . . AND FLUSH THE TOILET BEFORE YOU GO! NEITHER OF YOU KNOW HOW TO FLUSH THE DAMNED TOILET! . . . YOU'RE BOTH PIGS! YOU DON'T BELONG IN APART-MENTS . . . SO GET THE HELL OUT OF HERE!

She goes much further, suddenly inventing new things to do.

I'M GOING TO GRAB YOU . . . THERE . . . AND THROW YOU OUT THE WIN-DOW . . . THERE! . . . I'm gonna be big, strong . . . I'M GOING TO SLAP THE SHIT OUT OF YOU, HELL, I DON'T NEED THESE GUYS! BAM! POW! BAM BAM BAM! AND IF I HEAR OF YOU DOING THIS TO ANY OTHER WOMAN . . . YOU'RE TOAST, LITTLE MAN! . . . I KNOW! I'M GONNA GET ALL THE

WOMEN YOU USED, AND WE'RE GONNA TAKE YOU APART BIT BY BIT, CAUSE YOU ARE ONE ROTTEN SONUVABITCH!

But it doesn't stop here.

Once she is in the scene, being and behaving as the new person, it is common that she finds other scenes:

> *. . . and you know what? That fucking superintendent of the apartment? Herman? Yeah, Big dumb Herman. I'm going to go to his apartment. "HERMAN . . . BAM! I JUST SMASHED YOUR DOOR . . . AH, THERE YOU ARE. SIT DOWN, DOWN! YOU LISTEN TO ME, YOU STUPID IDIOT! IF THAT POUNDING IN THE DUCTS DOESN'T STOP, I'M GONNA COME UP HERE AND BURN YOUR WIG. THEN I'LL POUND THE SHIT OUT OF YOU, WITH THE HELP OF MY FRIENDS FROM THE GYM. LET ME INTRODUCE THEM . . . HAHAHA-HAHA. DO YOU UNDERSTAND—YOU THICK-HEADED BASTARD!" And oh yes, I have a thing or two to say to my brother . . .*

Suppose that the inner experiencing is being the mature one, above it all, high-minded, transcendent. She is a lawyer. If we dip into the realm of daydreams, she envisions being the supreme court justice. In her daydream, she pictures herself delivering a grand speech at a formal hearing, and afterward, at a gathering of the eminent lawyers and judges of the country, she is sitting, comfortably and graciously, talking and listening to the others in the small group around the coffee table. This is her personal fantasy. Live it. Literally be this whole new person. For three to five minutes, she is this transformed new person, actually being and behaving in this prospective scene.

How Can Other Potentials Participate in the New Way of Being?

Even though the context is unrealistic and playful fantasy, the radical switch into being the inner experiencing may still be hard for some patients, and especially with some inner experiencings. Sometimes the operating and deeper potentials are sheer opposites, and it is hard for the person to undergo such a radical shift, even in playful unreality. Sometimes the current way of being feels just fine, and a simple replacement by the inner experiencing does not sit well. There are ways to be the new person and still let the old person remain and even participate.

A simple way to accomplish this is for the person to play the role of an added person in the scene, so that there is the old patient, his sister, and the new person who can be this way with the sister and also with the old patient. As this new person, he says:

> *Just sit and watch a master show her how I feel. Don't bother me, cause I love her [and then, turning to his sister], and I do. Look, I know I've been a cold bastard, always gone, never really close. Well, I want you to know that I love you. You've been the most important person in my life. I love you. I do. I've always loved you. Just never grown up enough to tell you . . .*

In this way, the person can be the inner experiencing without dispatching away the former ways of being.

Another way is for the patient to be both the former person and the new inner experiencing. Quite often, the old operating potential is accompanied with relatively good feelings. She actually feels good being sure of herself, the decision-maker, with her own way of thinking. The deeper potential is being done to, soft, without strength. There are ways in which she can have fun switching from one to the other. As the recently appointed director of the section, she has meetings with her heads of the subsections. As the old operating potential, she says:

> *Under "new business," you will see the item on consultants. We are going to consider getting rid of all consultants. They are a complete waste of money, and I will present all my effective arguments when we come to that item. Got it?*

Then she switches over to the new inner experiencing. In a whole different voice, but again with full and good feelings, she launches out:

> *Is this all right? I'm never sure! I'll do whatever you want! Oh please say this is OK! I shouldn't be the director. It's all a giant fluke. I am so mixed up and unsure . . . Help!*

She is wildly exaggerating and being wholesomely unrealistic. Yet she is being both the old operating potential, not losing it, but also being able to switch over to the new inner experiencing.

The deeper potential consists of being tough and hard, standing one's ground and fighting. In the meeting, he allows himself to play and fantasize what it could be like to actually go ahead and be this way. He does this and then we give some other parts a chance to get into the act. The moment he finishes being this new way, he switches over and says:

> *That was good! I am progressing. What do you guys think? Am I getting better? I could never raise my voice like that . . .*

Or he can move to another old operating potential:

> *Is it over now? Everyone thinks of me as a kind-hearted guy, looking out for the other one. Is this over? Have I switched? Is there nothing left of the great old guy that I was? Well? Tell me!*

There will be times when the old person is exceedingly present, being and behaving in just the right ways that feel rotten. She will be enveloped in a cloud of numbness when someone has just given her a nasty shot. It may be her husband, her mother or sister, or one of a few people at work. She is frozen, not thinking, in suspension. In this scene, the new person is a sense of looking down on, being critical, ridiculing. What can this new person do? How can the new person coexist with the old person? A few seconds after going into shock, the new person wakes up and says:

> *I went frozen! Did you see? I just got numb? Like a dimwit, and idiot! That is terrible! What kind of a nut would just go blank? Huh?*

The new person is talking about her self, and may be talking to the people who are here, even to the one who gave her the benumbing shot.

It can be important to allow other parts to have their say. Just as soon as you are being the inner experiencing, these other parts are usually aroused. They might be pleased. They might become frightened. There is no law that only the new experiencing can occur. Practice allowing the old parts to have their say. This means that the person can go ahead and be the new person, and then go even further and be the old parts having their reactions to what the person has just done. This is the mark of a higher plateau, for each part can now get along well enough with the inner experiencing to be able to have its say. Being able to carry this out in actual behavior is a real achievement.

Being the new person, being the inner experiencing, can occur all by itself in a sort of pure form. However, there is far greater power in being able to move from the inner experiencing to one of the old operating potentials, or to move from being the old operating potential to the new inner experiencing. The trick is being able to move to the other part and to give the other part plenty of room to have its reaction. When you are being the new inner experiencing, leave room for you also to be the old operating potential, having its reaction. When you are being the old operating potential, leave room for you to be the new inner experiencing, having its say. There can always be some other part that objects, that has a disintegrative reaction. It is powerful for you to be able to move over to that other part and to voice its reaction in a friendly, integrative, playfully unrealistic way. This is a treasurehouse of an achievement and promises a substantially new person when the patient is this way in actuality, outside and after the session.

It is all play, all unrealistic fantasy. Nevertheless, the patient is literally being and behaving as the new person who can move back and forth between the new inner experiencing and the old operating potentials. She is gaining a taste and sample of what it is like to be this way in the world out there.

How Can You Use the Other Person in the Prospective Scene?

Almost always, there is some other person in the scene. The main way to use the other person is to help the patient to play and sample being and behaving as the inner experiencing in the prospective scenes. Perhaps the easiest way is to allow the other person to go along with everything, to participate cooperatively, to accommodate. In so doing, you may either describe or you may voice what the other person says and does. You say:

> *Look at him! He is whimpering! He is pleading with you! "No, please don't throw my stuff out the window! . . . THAT'S MY CAMPING GEAR . . . OOPS, THERE IT ALL GOES, OUT THE WINDOW!*

You are right here, being the inner experiencing, and looking at the other person. When you look at Herman, the superintendent of the apartment, see him as accommodating. You say:

> *He'll do it! He'll fix the ducts! "Yes, yes, yes! Anything you want. Just get rid of those big guys! And please let me have my wig!" My god, look at Herman! He's shaking! Look at him shaking!*

Whether you are just seeing the other person or caricaturing their reactions, make sure that they accommodate to the patient's playful being of the inner experiencing.

Almost always, this is seeing the other person in a way that is far from the way the other person would likely be. But the context is play and unreality, so that allows the other person to be dragged way out of character. On the other hand, you may see the other person as being much less eager to accommodate. Suppose that you see her boyfriend and her apartment superintendent as not going along at all. You can nevertheless enable the patient to have playful fun being the inner experiencing if you can either describe or give voice to the other person in a way that is helpful, allows her to be the inner experiencing. With regard to the superintendent, you say:

> *Well, I don't know . . . I just don't know . . . Suppose old Herman just stands up tall and says, "Oh yeah! Just try it! I'm going to make sure there is one helluva lot more pounding in the ducts! So what do you say to that, little lady?"*

You may imitate the voice of the superintendent. Just make sure the overall context remains playfully unrealistic.

In all these ways of using the other person, the aim is to enable the patient to playfully sample what it is like to be the inner experiencing in these prospective, and unrealistic, scenes.

Keep Going Till Experiencing Is Full and Feeling Is Very Good

Typically, you and the patient enjoy a festival of being and behaving as the inner experiencing in this scene. It is fun. It is playful. It is happily unrealistic. The two of you can go on and on, conjointly pushing one another further and further. You move from one behavior to another, and from one scene to another. It is easy to be creative and inventive, using increasingly delightful behaviors. When the patient has done it for a while, you can claim your turn.

> *Yes! And I want a rebate on the rent because dealing with you takes time, and my fee is $250 an hour!*

It is easy, inviting, and useful fun to keep this going for some time, rather than stopping after one or two statements by the patient. It is an extended chance for the patient to revel and wallow in being the inner experiencing. Ordinarily, the two of you will attain a kind of high, a plateau, on which you both can do all sorts of things to extend the being and behaving as the new person in the prospective scene.

Your aim is to keep going till the experiencing is full and the feelings are very good. When the experiencing is full, you feel it over most of your body. There might be loud noises and high volume. There might be little noise or volume, yet the experiencing is nevertheless full and saturating. Furthermore, the feeling is good, and is indicated by words such as aliveness, vitality, lightness, buoyancy, "high," vibrating, exuberance, tingling, excitement, ecstasy, energy, power, force. These words point toward particular kinds of bodily sensations that are somewhat similar to descriptions of the Nietzschean meaning of power (May, 1958a), and to a state to be achieved in some forms of meditation and contemplation (Chang, 1959; Herrigel, 1956; Kondo, 1952, 1958; Wilhelm, 1962).

How do you know when you have achieved this state? When there is a pause, check your body, and invite the patient to check what is happening in hers. You may say:

> *Yeah! All over my body, a kind of little tingling. And it feels good. Alive, sort of . . . What about you? Anything like this?*

Often the patient will indicate somewhat similar kinds of bodily sensations, and maybe even a bonus:

> *It's mainly in my arms and . . . chest . . . and I don't feel heavy . . . tired, any more. It's gone . . .*

If the experiencing is less than full, or not especially pleasant, keep going until the experiencing is relatively full, and with pleasant feelings. Your aim is to attain a state in which the experiencing is full, the feelings are very good, and then to stay in this state for some time.

In this way, you are giving the patient a chance to be this new person, to be and to behave as this new person, to gain an actual taste and sample, and to accomplish this in a way that is nevertheless safe and doable. However, it is critical that it is the new person who is carrying out the behavior. It is not enough for the old person to carry out the behavior. That is, the behaviors are to come from and to provide for the inner experiencing, and not merely to be carried out by the old person.

Invite the New Person to Be the Old, Bad-Feelinged Patient in the Prospective Scene

This is something you may do if you are so inclined. When the patient has been the inner experiencing fully and with good feeling, it is sometimes helpful to invite this new person, flushed with success, to be the old patient with the old feelings.

In a way, this is a trick. It is just about impossible for the new person to have the old bad feeling, especially if he is being the new person fully and with good feelings. It is like asking:

> Are you, the new person, flushed with being this new person, and feeling just wonderful, able to have the awful feeling of this altogether different other person, and in this or some altogether different scene?

Almost certainly, the new person would have trouble. This means that the patient is essentially free of the bad feelings in the same kind of scene that he brought up in Step 1.

Your invitation may contain elements of almost daring or challenging this new person to revert back to the old, bad-feelinged patient. You say:

> It is tomorrow. Suppose you are sitting alone in your apartment, and on the bed are pills, alcohol, plenty. Go ahead and see what it's like to be depressed, as much as you can. Talk about suicide . . .

This was the bad-feelinged Step 1 scene. He pauses and says, as the new person:

> I can't . . . Wait a minute . . . I can't do it!

Whatever the Step 1 bad-feelinged scene was, see it as occurring in the next few days or so. You may either create the prospective scene, or you invite the patient to be in the same old situation as it may occur in the next few days. You say:

> Here you are, in the car, tomorrow, and now there is a terrible urge to smash the car into someone crossing the street, anyone! Go ahead, feel crazy, overwhelmed by this powerful urge . . .

> It is Tuesday, and you are leaving the apartment. Feel that everyone in the apartment hates you, wants to do bad things to you, have meetings where they talk about you. Go ahead, feel this again, like you did earlier.

You wake up. Peg is still sleeping, and it is tomorrow morning. As usual, the voices start screeching at you. Feel helpless. Feel crazy, out of your mind, weird. Go ahead, and feel absolutely miserable! Try it out, what the hell. See what happens.

It is Friday. You are at work. It's going to happen again. Jan or Solly or Joanne will be good, smart. And now it is your turn to feel shitty: dumb, ordinary, looked down on by them, not good. And you don't do anything. Just feel it inside. Awful. So let's feel this again. Let yourself be miserable. Friday, sitting around the table. Feel rotten . . .

Patients ordinarily do not even try. They may simply indicate that they can't, that they don't feel that way. They may try and then give up. They may try for a bit, and you say:

Sorry, that's not too convincing. Want to give it another shot? Go ahead, feel rotten . . .

It is rare that the patient can slide back into the old person and again have the same bad feeling as occurred in Step 1.

What Do You Do if the Patient Reverts Back to Being the Old Patient?

Some patients, in some sessions, will simply revert back to being the old patient. Yes, the person was being the new person in and at the end of Step 3. That was safe. It included scenes from the past. But now you are living and being in the immediate future. Even if the context is play and unrealistic fantasy, there will be occasions when the person here with you is the old patient once again. What do you do?

This shift occurs generally at two places. One is when you move from Step 3 to Step 4. All you have to do is to whisper something about the real world, or the present, or what is going to happen tomorrow. Suddenly you are with the old person who was here in Step 1. Change? Are you kidding? It is the old person talking. The second place this shift occurs is in the course of Step 4. You and he may have gone through several prospective scenes, being the new person, doing it well in the context of fantasy, play, unreality. Then there is an abrupt shift and the person who is present is the old person, his whole body taut, feet firmly planted against the slightest possibility of being the new person. If this shift occurs, what do you do?

Perhaps the main guideline is for you to remain as the new person, the inner experiencing, and to continue your integrative relationship with the patient. Whether the patient is the new person or reverts back to the old person, you are to remain the integrated inner experiencing. This means that you do not try to get the patient to play and sample being the new person in prospective scenes. There is no pressure, no effortful trying to get the patient back into being the new person.

As the integrative inner experiencing, you may fully welcome and appreciate her hesitancy, her reluctance, her not wanting even to play and sample being the new person. Yes, it may be dangerous. Being this way is not good, not the way you really are. It certainly could get you into trouble. There are loads of good reasons for not being and behaving as this new person. Indeed, you may outdo the patient in finding solid considerations for not even trying to be and behave as the new person.

As the integrative new inner experiencing, you remain loving, welcoming, and appreciating, as you perhaps challenge, berate, push, and pressure the patient to be the new person:

You should be this way! No doubt about it, this is how you ought to be! . . . How dare you stop yourself from being like this! No way! Do it! What a pity! What a damned pity! It's such a marvelous quality! Stop fighting being this way! . . . You've spent 35 years not being this way. It's time to change! So do it for the next 35 years! Or, how about the next two days?

Because you are being the new person, you will tend to hear what the patient says from this perspective, rather than as a therapist who is external or who has moved over to being the old person along with the patient. Suppose that the patient says, in a more or less neutral way:

I do not do things like that.

Because you are ensconced inside the inner experiencing, what the patient says may be received and used in a way that often leads almost directly to her going ahead and being and behaving as the new person. You say:

Right . . . Well, now's the chance! . . .

Or you say:

So you haven't had much practice. Well, do the best you can. Ready?

It is much easier to receive and work with whatever the patient says when you are fully being the inner experiencing, and the net result is that the patient usually is enabled to be less unwilling and more inclined to go ahead and playfully sample being and behaving as the new person.

So far, in Step 4, you have enabled the patient to play, to get a taste, of what it can be like to be and to behave as the new person in the extratherapy world. But the context has been play and unreality. Now the work shifts. Now you become serious, because you are introducing the possibility of the new person's really being and behaving in this way.

HOW CAN YOU GO FROM PLAYING AND SAMPLING TO ACTUALLY BEING THE NEW PERSON IN THE EXTRATHERAPY WORLD?

First, the patient has a kind of playful, unrealistic taste and sample of what it can be like to be and to behave as the new person. The purpose now is to get the patient ready to be and behave as the new person in the extratherapy world. This means that the patient is to go through a very realistic dress rehearsal. As literally as possible, the patient is to be the new person, is to behave as the new person, is to select the right kind of behavior to carry out, and is to rehearse everything so carefully and so well that you have gone from playing and sampling to actually being the new person in the extratherapy world. Playtime is over.

When and how do you move to this final phase? You may move when the patient himself turns from playful unreality to the real world of tomorrow and beyond. The patient says:

I think I can really be this way . . .

That was a lot of fun, but I could never really do that . . .

Why not? Why not? I could be this way with her . . .

If I really did that, was that way with my grandfather, I think that would be fantastic!

More commonly, you move toward this final substep whenever you are ready to go from playful unreality to truly being and behaving in this way. You may introduce this switch by saying:

All right! How about really being this way with Bill tomorrow? I mean really.

You're enjoying this too much! How about doing it—for real? You ready to think about really being like this?

So what are you going to do about that really?

Now let's get serious. What do you think you would really like to do?

The sequence is important. At the end of Step 3, the patient is usually being the inner experiencing, but doing this safely within the context of earlier life scenes. It would be rather hard to go directly to a serious consideration of actually being and behaving as this new person in the real world. That is too great a leap. First, it is better to do a little bit of unrealistic playing. Then you can begin serious consideration of actually being and behaving as this new person in the extratherapy world.

How Can You Enable the Patient to Rehearse Actually Being the New Person in the Extratherapy World?

The patient is to go through a dress rehearsal, to see what it is like to be this new person in the real extratherapy world. One of the purposes of the rehearsal is to find precisely the right behavior in the right scene. The second purpose is to try it out to see if being and behaving in this way is fitting, appropriate, and works.

How do you enable the patient to get ready to rehearse the new way of being and behaving?   If the patient is ready, we can go from playing and sampling to seeing what it might be like to be and to behave this way for real. Right now, she is being the new person with her good friend, and she is playing what it is like to be zany, silly, a little weird. She just finished a shrimp cocktail before ordering the rest of the meal, and is being this new way as she clowns with the waiter to please bring her another shrimp cocktail and a piece of pumpkin pie. This is the pinnacle of playful unreality, and the experiencing is full, the feeling delightful. The therapist says:

This feels great! How would you feel about maybe being this way for real? You really want to be like this? Really be like this, do it, for real?

She says:

Yes! Yes, I would!

Then the therapist says:

All right. So let's try it out for real. Suppose it is really happening, like tomorrow. I mean for real. Let's really try it out. Remember, you haven't had much practice being this way. Right? Hell, you haven't been like this really for an hour or more in your whole life, just about, right? . . .

You may stay in this particular scene, or you may go to other prospective scenes. You may stay with these behaviors, or the two of you may proceed to find other behaviors. Either you or the new person can find scenes and behaviors for being this new person. He says:

Sarah and I are going to start having sex again! It's time!

or

I am going to change all the stuff in my place! I hate that crap, and I had it for too damned long, 20 years!

or

Yes, I am going to call my sister and start being a decent kid to her,

or

I am going to buy dad a gift that will knock his socks off: a camper!

or

That job? I am going to apply for it!

or

I'm going to tell Louise that I am sorry; of course I screwed up.

Whatever the scene, whatever the behavior, indicate that it is time to try it out for real. Let's rehearse it and see how it feels.

In general, the prospective scenes provides a context for the new person to come to life, to exist and be, in the extratherapy real world. The scenes are to enable the new person to be experienced, to be present. But suppose we consider the scenes of bad feeling. How might the new person be in these scenes when they occur in the next few days? What might the new person do to dismantle these old scenes of bad feelings? How would the new person use those scenes? You are approaching these old bad-feelinged scenes with a more realistic eye.

This new person is in a position to eliminate the bad-feelinged scene, to let it go, to dismantle important parts of the old bad-feelinged scene. It is the new person who is the one to consider how to disenfranchise the bad-feelinged situation. Here is where the new person can say:

I don't have to come home so late, work later than others, and then get mad at her cause she didn't make supper. Shit! That's dumb.

I always find a guy who isn't caring and loving, and then grumble and end it cause he's not the way I want! Gregg's OK, but he's not for me . . . I think I can stop all these fights and just ask him to leave. Friends yes, but a live-in guy, no way! . . .

I'm the one who got my mother to live in with us! My God! I don't think she wants to stay here with us. And sure as hell, Stella doesn't! And the three of us never talk about it! It's awful! We should at least talk about where mom can live. What the hell?

I never let dad talk about anything on his mind and then I feel rotten cause he won't ever be close to me. Damn! And I won't tell him anything about what I worry about. I act like the little pissy kid. Well, I'm going to stop that nonsense and be a helluva lot more honest. I am bored as hell being a doctor, and I'm going to tell him!

I live in this huge house like Linda's still alive and the kids are still here. And I cry and think about killing myself. Maybe it's time to move to a nice apartment, by my-self. . . And I can get rid of Linda's old things like her sister said. What an idiot I've been . . .

The new person can be here when the bad-feelinged scene first begins to present itself. What does the new person want to do as the bad-feelinged scene is just assembling, just starting to take shape? This is when he and you are in the elevator alone; he has not moved over to touch your shoulder yet, but you are wary. It is when your husband will burst into your room with that "I'm going to give you some shit" look on his face, and you freeze; the scene has not yet come to the high point where he is yelling at you. It is when you are alone for the whole weekend, and you have the first thoughts about having a few drinks. When these little scenes just start to occur, what will the new person do? It is rehearsal time.

In all these situations, you can help get the person ready by letting the person say whether being this new way is right, feels good. You ask if she really would like to be this way:

How about it? Do you want to be like this? Would it seem to be all right with you? Is it appealing? What do you think?

Whatever the nature of this inner experiencing, give her a chance to indicate if being this way is appealing and attractive, or perhaps not much at all. She says:

Well, I don't know . . . yes . . . Why not? Hell, it's about time, and it felt so natural . . .

If it is appealing, then get her ready to try it out for real, to rehearse being this way and seeing what it is like.

Acknowledge that actually being this way can be a big change. It may be a change that he would like. It may even seem to feel good. But it is a big change. In fact, being this way is not something he has done a lot. He has very little practice being this way. It is sort of new. So it makes sense that being and behaving this way has to be rehearsed:

So maybe we can both try it out, just to see what it's like, how it feels. Then we can change it around a little. And remember, this is going to be kind of new for you, and a big change from the way you ordinarily are, right? No?

Lay your own cards on the table. Since you are being the integrated inner experiencing throughout this step, you are, of course, in favor of actually being this new person. Say so:

I think it would be great if you just continued being this way. It's about time. After all, it sure felt fine, playing I mean. And you were this way when you were a kid, long, long ago. And you've been this way for 20 minutes or so here, so maybe it would be great just to be this way tomorrow and for the next 80 years. I think this would be marvelous! This means trying it out for real. Rehearsing it. We can try and see. Ready?

Rehearsal, refinement-modification, and further rehearsal. Then you try it out. You try it our for real. It is a rehearsal of being this new person in the prospective scene. It is as if this new person were truly to be in the scene of tomorrow or the next few days, were really being and behaving as this new person. You are to get as close as possible to try-ing out what it is like to be and behave as this new person.

Your aim is to enable the experiencing to be full and for the accompanying feel-ings to be very good. If this occurs the first time that he rehearses the new way of being and behaving, fine. Usually it takes several trials. Keep going, keep rehearsing and try-ing it out, until experiencing is full and feelings are very good.

You are free to modify and alter the behavior, to refine what is done and how it is done. Try it out and then check your body to see if the experiencing is full and the feeling very good. If the answer is no, then refine it a bit or modify it substantially. See what this is like. Keep going until the experiencing is full and the feeling very good.

The inner experiencing is giving into, being drawn into, becoming one with. He had been playing with prospective scenes of sitting in the park and watching the pi-geons, and scenes of being this way with his boss. The first scenes were almost hilar-ious as he exaggerated seeing the pigeons so intently that he became mesmerized by them, and started sensing his body becoming that of a pigeon. The second scene was outrageously unrealistic as he was at a committee meeting, chaired by the boss, and slowly slid across the table, fusing with his boss and becoming one with him. Both scenes were quite playful and utterly unrealistic. Yet experiencing was full and feel-ing very good. Would he really like to behave in these ways in these scenes? Not really.

He mentions, however, that he almost never even looks at his boss during meet-ings. He rehearsed what it can be like to look at his boss during the committee meet-ing that will occur in the next few days. As he tried this out, he murmurs:

> You prepare things well, and you're organized . . . You are . . . worried sometimes that we just oppose you . . . You look down if we don't agree . . . I'm seeing you . . . looking at you . . .

The experiencing in you is only moderate, and the feeling is a little scary, not espe-cially good. In the patient, too. So how can this be modified? He says:

> He comes into my office every so often, and is friendly. Sort of . . . Maybe . . . I could tell him to sit down and . . . Yes, I don't look at him . . . Geez . . . I could look at him . . . !

We try this out. He rehearses looking directly at his boss, and saying:

> Sit down, Sam. What's on your mind?

He tries this out, letting himself be drawn into seeing his boss, listening intently to what his boss is saying, and not having private thoughts. It is a rather full experiencing. It feels wonderful. But another scene appears, almost spontaneously.

> At night, when the kids are in bed, Kathy and I . . . I can let her talk, and I can let myself listen, and look at her . . .

He tries this out. He rehearses letting himself hold her hand as she talks, feeling what she feels, sharing her feelings. With some slight refinements of watching her every fa-cial change, he reaches a point where being and behaving in these ways provide a full experiencing and with wonderful feelings.

For Marie, the inner experiencing is saying no, protecting herself, standing her own ground. Easter was coming, and she knew her sisters would expect that she would have the big family meal at her house once again. In the context of playful unreality, she was almost ecstatic as she assembled the pushy people in the family, including mother, two sisters, and her brother, and screamed her absolute unwillingness to be the grand hostess this time, as every time, for all the big dinners and reunions. She put on a whole show of dancing out her reluctance, including loud grunts and groans, as well as ear-piercing screams of no, no, no. When we moved to what she might really do, she decided to continue being this way, and the feeling was not especially good. She modified what she might do and say. This was better, but not accompanied with great feeling. With further modifications and rehearsals, she arrived at a point where she brings together the same people, but at her mom's apartment, and she declares her retirement from being the family hostess. It is done in good humor. She invites each person to say what he or she thinks. She is laughing, but tough. She is saying:

> . . . I've had it. In fact I have had it for five years, twice a year, and even I am starting to expect that everything's going to be at my place. So this year I am abdicating . . . Who wants to take over for this year?

Experiencing is full. Does this feel all right? It feel marvelous.

It is very important whether or not the new person can allow the other person to accommodate. Will the patient be able to free the other person to cooperatively participate? In the playful sampling, this almost does not matter. Now it does. If her family rises up in a phalanx of horror, if they refuse to accommodate, this calls for some major modifications. Perhaps it means letting go of this whole scene. It almost certainly calls for serious changes and more rehearsal. Experiencing can be full and feelings can be good only when the other person seems to accommodate. Try it out. See what happens. If rehearsal indicates that the answer is yes, then this new way of being and behaving is possible. If the answer is no, then further modifications and rehearsals are in order.

When you are drawn toward the reaction of the other person, or when some other part of you comes forth and wants to say something, it is helpful to include these in the process of rehearsal and of refining how to be till it feels right. She has no real experience being genuinely critical, of saying that the other person did a bad thing. However, what arose in the session is a deeper sense of not letting things slide, of being critical, of scolding. This was new and alien for her. The prospective scene involves her older sister being at the patient's apartment, as usual, and being dirty, messy, or clumsy. Her sister puts jam away without closing the lid, borrows new books and returns them with food stains on the pages, makes coffee and spills coffee on the counter. In playful unreality, the patient had sheer fun pulling her sister's ears, giving her a mop and ordering her to go to it, and generally enjoying the inner experiencing. But what will she do when the inevitable situation occurs tomorrow?

She worked her way toward two additional behaviors. It was all right to criticize her sister:

> You clod! Here, I'll show you how to put the lid on the jam! See, you idiot! Easy, huh! Now do it right or no more jam!

However, that was immediately followed by other parts of her running around in agitated circles. She was frightened by how her sister might feel. She was fearing, and almost excited about, her sister rising up in fury. With more rehearsal and refinement, she was able to accommodate her own concerns:

Wait a minute . . . Does this mean you are going to get mad? Are we going to have a huge fight? Please say no! I can't fight with you. I don't even know how to fight!

She went on to other reactions of her own to actually criticizing her sister and felt just wonderful saying this:

You put the jam away without even closing the lid. You idiot! Here, do it this way. Easy, right? Close it a little and I won't get so damned upset . . . You know, it's hard criticizing you, or anyone. It scares the hell out of me!

Being this way, allowing herself to be the inner experiencing and also to accommodate older parts of her self, felt exhilarating. Sometimes, rehearsal and refinement involve more than just being and behaving on the basis of the inner experiencing.

Take plenty of time in looking for scenes. If you find one scene, try out the new way of being and behaving. You are always free to move on to other scenes. Often the patient will go almost spontaneously to other scenes. Whether or not that occurs, you can open up new times and places for the new way of being and behaving. The aim is to enable the new person to find all sorts of scenes for being the new person, if only to practice what it is like being and behaving as this new person.

In some sessions, the patient is drawn toward this new way of being and behaving almost everywhere, in essentially all scenes and situations. You are witnessing the possibility of an almost complete transformation. After rehearsal in one or two scenes, she says:

But I could be this everywhere! Yes! My God! I feel so different! . . . It's like I waited my whole life . . . This seems to be me! . . . I feel so different!

Both you and the patient can rehearse what it might be like to be this whole new person. You rehearse all kinds of mundane little ways of being this way, everything from the way she sits to the way she talks. Rehearse all kinds of prospective scenes, whether they seem rather small and insignificant or big and very substantial. Rehearse what life can be like if this wholesale transformation were really to occur.

On the other hand, rehearsal of the new way of being and behaving in prospective scenes may not culminate in full experiencing and good feelings. Instead, experiencing is throttled, and the feeling leans toward the unpleasant. Under these conditions, you may consider the possibility of safe, token, little behaviors in safe, token, little scenes and situations. It is like a willingness to take just tiny baby steps.

With a bit of inventiveness, both therapist and patient can come up with such safe and token behaviors, just enough to give a little whiff of the inner experiencing. Instead of saying it to the real person, playact with a friend with whom you can safely say those words. Buy the gift, even if you don't give it to her. Dress this new way in the privacy of your home, rather than at work. Instead of saying it directly to your instructor, murmur the words quietly, under your breath. Instead of shocking the family, cover the outrageous words on the t-shirt with a sweater. Do it in effigy, with a friend, with a substitute, and not with the real other person or situation. Yet the essential ingredient is that even in safe, token ways, experiencing is at least moderate and feelings are good.

How do you and patient determine whether or not to be and behave this way in the extratherapy world?   There will come a time when the rehearsal is over with. Now is the time for you and the patient to deliberately check your bodies. You say:

All right . . . Now check your body. Where are things happening in your body? Check all over. Chest, head, legs, arms, everywhere. What's happening in your body? Where are the feelings in your body?

You may start by asking the patient, or, especially if there are prominent feelings in your own body, you may mention what is happening in you.

She says:

Well! I feel great! . . . My head is light, nice, clear . . . and . . . I've got a warm glow, soft, warm . . . in my chest . . . It's nice . . .

If your bodily sensations are similar, say so. Describe where the feelings are in your body, and describe what they are like. If it seems to you that experiencing is relatively full, and if the feelings are good ones, then mention that maybe she can really be this way, maybe she could and should actually do this for real.

So maybe you could really be this way, maybe you could really do it!

Usually, experiencing is full and feelings are very good. But not always. If experiencing is not full, if feelings are not delightful, or especially if the feelings are bad, then all the indications point away from being and behaving in this way. This applies whether the new way of being and behaving seems like a major change or a very minor one, whether the behavior involves leaving the spouse, having the abortion, quitting the job, confronting the hated enemy, or whether the behavior consists of trying a new perfume, brushing your teeth once more each day, or whistling as you cross the street. You say:

Oh, I don't know . . . Doesn't feel so good to me. I don't think it's a very good idea. I think you should forget it. Not do it. What do you think?

Almost always, if the experiencing is full and feelings are good in the patient, the same thing will occur in you. Occasionally, experiencing is full and feelings are good in you, but far less so in the patient. When this happens, caution the patient against being this way and carrying out the behavior:

No way, your body says no, I say that I agree. The answer is no. So forget it.

It may happen some time, but I have yet to come across a situation where the new way of being and behaving sits very well in the patient but leaves me with awful, troubling, unpleasant feelings. It is easy to conceive such possibilities, but they have not yet occurred. For example, I can imagine a patient having full experiencing and great feelings as she rehearses slitting a child's throat, blowing up a restaurant, killing himself, or doing all sorts of things that are accompanied with terrible feelings in me. This has not happened, yet. Even after the sessions, I have yet to be significantly troubled, worried, bothered, or scared about whom the patient might be and what this new person might be doing in the extratherapy world.

The criteria include the fullness of the experiencing and the presence of good feelings. Suppose that the patient is trying out the new way of being and behaving in the context of the bad-feelinged scene from Step 1. She felt devastated when he ridiculed her face and laughed at her big nose. That was a horrible moment for her. It was the moment of awful feeling from Step 1. Now, in Step 4, she is trying out new behaviors that come from and provide for the experiencing of standing up to, being firm with, standing her own ground. Now the criteria are twofold. One involves the presence of good feelings as she is fully experiencing the inner experiencing. In addition, the criterion includes the absence of the bad feeling. She ends up with a good feeling as she is in bed with him, touching him and arousing him, and saying:

> . . . *and if you think my nose is too big, you can just do the rest yourself, you sonuvagun! What do you think of that?*

Yes, this feels good. Yes the experiencing is full. No, there is no bad feeling of being ridiculed and devastated. You say:

> *Neat! Yes, and I don't feel ridiculed and devastated. Nothing here like that. What about in you?*

Nevertheless, even when experiencing seems to be relatively full and feelings are rather good, it is often helpful for the therapist and patient to sample all sorts of misgivings, hesitations, and outright objections to the new way of being and behaving. You are, throughout this step, speaking with the voice of the integrative inner experiencing. This means you are able to invite the whole range of other parts of the patient to have their say. Indeed, you can even exceed the patient in raising all sorts of concerns about the new way of being and behaving.

You may say:

> *Just wait a minute! Think about your husband, your children, your mother and father, all your neighbors! Maybe they would not be so happy with this. What might they say? Ha! Maybe you should consult with them first. After all, they'll be affected by all these changes, right? . . . You're a good, loyal, true daughter. Well, if you really are this way and really do these things, that's not a good daughter! Think about your mother and father. Right? . . . What about Hortense and Edna at work? Maybe they wouldn't like that. Maybe they'll be offended. Think of them! . . . What would people say?*

Raise all sorts of cautions. All parts of the patient have a voice in considering the change: "This is different. You're sort of being a whole new guy, you know. I mean, you are able to let yourself be attractive, looked at, and things maybe can be different. Is this all right with you? Things can be quite different with Tammy. Maybe she'll wonder who the hell you are. And probably at the hospital too. So is this all right? Is it all right if such a big change happens? What do you think?"

Emphasize the likely difference between the patient's present life and the kind of life that she is heading toward:

> *If you keep this up, you'll have friends, and you'll be spending Sundays with your friends, riding bicycles and having coffee and laughing about things you did together. Right now you spend your Sundays sweating and shaking and getting drunk by yourself. That is one helluva big change in your life. It's big! Is this change too much for you? Maybe it's too much to ask. What do you think?*

Openly pull other parts to object. You may voice objections on their behalf:

> *What's going to happen to sweet, loyal, nice Gertrude? Is that the end of that? Well? Think about that! What do you think?*

> *Maybe what you're thinking of doing is immoral, illegal, bad, awful, uncivilized, not you, horrible, Well? Huh?*

Maybe you should wait a while. Maybe this is too fast. Maybe you should take your time. Wait a bit. It's too early. Do it later.

Maybe it won't work! How do you know that Sally will go along with this? Maybe she'll hate you for doing that. After all, she has her own feelings. Be realistic!

Just suppose it gets out of hand! Maybe you'll go too far. Once you start saying no, invoking limits, declining what they want you to do, maybe you'll go too far. You'll stop bathing, you won't pay bills, you won't obey driving regulations! You'll end up in jail or the mental hospital! So? What do you think?

Your aim is to be the integrative inner experiencing who allows other parts of the patient to voice their concerns, to invoke injunctions, to express all their objections, realistic or unrealistic. If the experiencing is full and the feelings are very good, then these are the indications for determining that the new person can be and behave in the external world. Anything less, and the decision is not to go ahead with being and behaving in this new way.

Quite often, there is an exciting settlement, a negotiated compromise that is joyful for all parts. Not only does the inner experiencing step up and occur, but related other potentials can then join in. Once the new person does what she does, the old part gives its reaction:

What a terrible thing to say! Disgusting!

Oh, I don't think I should have done that. I'm in trouble now!

If being this twofold new way feels right, checks out, then the way is open to go ahead and be this way.

I am quite concerned about the new behaviors, but I am much more concerned about who the person is who carries out the new behavior. The aim is for the new person to be the one to carry out the new behavior. When this is the case, I find myself excited and pleased about the likelihood of the patient being and behaving in this way in the extratherapy world. Then the answer is yes, go ahead and do it. On the other hand, if it is the old person who carries out the new behavior, then I am much less sanguine about going ahead. When there is anything substantially less than full experiencing as the new person, and with very good feelings, my inclination is that we are not yet ready for the person to carry out the new way of being and behaving in the extratherapy world.

What Can You Do to Keep the New Person Here Fully and from Now On?

In the first phase of this step, the emphasis is on unrealistic play. Typically, the patient can be this new person to an impressive degree, almost fully. But in the second phase, we become much more realistic. Can the patient be the new person till the end of the session and perhaps after the session ends? How remarkable this would be. Since the patient is probably being the new person when you start Step 4, what can you do to achieve the impressive goal of enabling the new person to remain throughout Step 4 and following the session?

Answering this question can elevate this therapy to an exciting higher plateau. One of the problems, in Step 4, is that the new person fades away and is replaced by the old person. I wish I knew how the new person could be fully present throughout this step, to the very end of the session. When we learn how to accomplish this, we will be entering a new departure for psychotherapy, or at least for experiential psychotherapy (Mahrer, 1986a, 1987c). Then psychotherapy would indeed be able to culminate most of our sessions with the patient being a wholly new person. There would be a transformation (Mahrer, 1993b). This therapy would have elevated to an exciting higher plateau (Mahrer, 1988c).

I believe that the problem occurs in the second part of the step, when we consider the possibility of truly being and behaving as the new person. In most sessions, the new person is here to the very end of the session, but this does not always occur. If we knew how to preserve this change, then experiential psychotherapy could do wonderful things in just about every session. This is possible (Mahrer, 1987a, 1989b). It can be accomplished. I turn for help to other experiential therapists who are at least equally fascinated with this question and with the search for answers that will elevate this therapy to a higher plateau (Mahrer, 1990b, 1990d, 1993b).

What do you do if the patient does not want to be and to behave as the new person in the extratherapy world?   For whatever reasons, he has shifted back into being the old personality. Typically, this occurs almost the moment that you move from playing and sampling, in a context of fantasy and unreality, to a more or less serious consideration of actually being and behaving in this way. He simply does not want to rehearse the new behavior. He faces a prospective world that is closed shut against the new way of being and behaving. He brings up good and proper reasons why being and behaving in this way is not in the cards, is not good, is impossible, is dangerous, frightening, awful, disastrous. He switches attention over to the therapist and says:

> *Would you ever do that? You wouldn't . . . Why are you trying to get me to do that? How would that help me? . . .*

What do you do?

The main point is that you honor and respect the person's not wanting to be this new person in the extratherapy world. You do not try to force the person to undertake this new way of being and behaving. Do not argue, threaten, punish, criticize, force, cajole, or pressure the person in any way. You say:

> *Yes, I agree with you. It makes good sense. I can picture you trying to be this way and to do things like that, and I agree. It doesn't feel right. So leave it alone. Yes. You're right.*

You may even go further and give the patient further good reasons why it would not be a good idea to be and behave in that way. Explain how it might even be more negative and more disastrous than the patient has described.

It is fitting that you can at least be welcoming and appreciative of the inner experiencing. No, the patient is not going to be this new way. However, you can indicate how much you do like this new way. You say:

> *Yes, I can understand, and I respect your not wanting to be this new person. But I still admire, no, I really like, this quality in you, this being awestruck, being surprised, like a little girl, this wide-eyed fascination with something. I still think this is the kind of person you should be. Some day maybe. Maybe.*

Honor and respect the person's unwillingness, her decision not to try out and rehearse this new way of being. You say:

You are the boss. You are the important one. If being this new way doesn't sit right, if it's not appealing, doesn't attract you, then it is not right for you. Good for you.

But typically the patient is substantially being the new person who is quite ready to be this new way in the extratherapy world.

How Can You Enable the Patient to Be Committed to Being and Behaving as the New Person in the Extratherapy World?

This is the highest and final aim of the session. The person is to be well and truly committed to being the new person and behaving in this way in the prospective scene. I mean "committed" in the sense that the person wants to do this, fully intends to do this, and is quite eager to be and to behave in this way (Mahrer, Gagnon, Fairweather, Boulet, & Herring, 1994). The commitment may be in regard to a given situation and a given behavior, or it may also spread out to include several scenes and ways of behaving.

Each session is to culminate in this final substep. It is the primary indication that the session is successful and effective: At the very end of the session, the patient is to be the new person, fully and with good feelings, and is to indicate an eager readiness and commitment to being and behaving in this way in given situations in the forthcoming extratherapy world (cf. Talmon, 1990). This state is to be achieved in each session, starting from the initial session.

Commitment means that the person says:

I am going to do it! . . .

I can't wait. I'm going to do this today . . .

Oh, this is going to be fun. Sure, I will. I will . . .

Oh yes! I don't know why I waited so long. Yes, I'm going to do it.

Tomorrow morning. That's when it's going to happen. Sure!

He'll love it. He'll love it. Not as much as me. Oh yeah. I am . . .

Just open the door and let me out! I am ready. Just watch me go!

When the patient is bent on being and behaving in this way, and because the therapist is essentially speaking as the inner experiencing, the therapist may be excused for being somewhat exuberant. The therapist may say how wonderful and how important it is for the new person to remain and to be in the extratherapy world. The therapist is happy about the commitment and about the new person being this way after the session. Talking to the new person, the therapist says:

I think it is just wonderful. I can picture you being like this, having fun and feeling great. And, yes, if you are going to be here, you have to live and do things and feel good doing them. You're being this way here, now. Stick around for a year or more, or at least a little while . . .

You may say:

Remember, being this way is kind of new for you, and actually doing it is kind of new too. So do the best you can. Maybe it'll take time to be solid and really good at being this way, right? Wrong?

Sometimes the therapist is quite excited. She says:

> *I am so damned excited. Should I go with you? I'd love to be there, with Harold and Maude. Well, good luck. Hope you feel wonderful. Damn, this feels good!*

If the patient does not carry out the inner experiencing in the extratherapy world, if there are not even a few seconds in which the new person is alive and present in the real world, then the likelihood of change is close to zero. This is when the next session starts with much the same kind of painful feeling in much the same kind of scene. This is when the session failed to produce the postsession changes that could and should occur. It is this important that the person is the new person, is able to be and to behave as this new person, following the session.

And what about the bad-feelinged scene from Step 1? The new person has little or no need for any of the parts of the old, bad-feelinged scene. The new person has little need for that old experiencing, or for maintaining those kinds of situational contexts, or to behave in just the right ways to provide for the situational contexts and the bad feelings. Not only is there a new person committed to being and behaving in new ways, but the presence of the new person means that the old patient, with the bad-feelinged Step 1 scenes, tends to fade away.

The patient may say something about the bad-feelinged scene from Step 1, but usually it is the therapist who plays out the requiem. The therapist may draw attention to the old patient who is separate from the new person. The therapist may indicate that the bad-feelinged old scenes can be left behind. The therapist can be pleased about the possibility of letting go of the bad-feelinged scene. The therapist can enjoy the new person's choice and opportunity to retain or let go of the bad-feelinged old scenes. The therapist says:

> *I can see the old Linda, feeling so shitty, having all those terrible thoughts about killing herself. Goodbye old Linda. I think all that can be over with.*

> *You know all those rotten feelings of being invaded, attacked, helpless? Well, that's not you any more . . . I think all that can be over with, especially when Otto gets all worked up and starts glaring at you and screaming at you about how terrible you are . . .*

> *When you're this way, then the old Steve is just about gone, and no more of those awful times when he goes into pubic toilets and masturbates, terrified, scared to death of being caught.*

> *Well! So what about all those terrible feelings of being out of place, not fitting in? Is it all right to let them go? No more? Things are different now, in the family. They're gone. Maybe they can be gone forever. Possible?*

> *How about Carol's getting that panic when you see the big splotches of blood that you see and you are terrified aren't really there? Are you ready to let others go to the hospital? Maybe all that is over with.*

Both of you can bid farewell to the old, bad-feelinged scenes. Both you and the patient can be the new person who can be committed to the new way of being and behaving, and who can let go of the old person with the bad-feelinged scenes.

This ends the session. You have done your job to the extent that (a) the person is fully being the integrated and actualized inner experiencing, with wonderful feelings;

(b) the inner experiencing is now a newfound part of the operating domain; and (c) this new person is eagerly ready and committed to being and behaving in the new extratherapy world of the immediate present and future. This is about as far as you can go in the session.

If you have done your job well, then the chances are rather high that the new person will be and behave in the extratherapy world. If the person does this, then change can and will likely occur. If the person does not do this, then change will be very limited, if there is any substantive change at all. It is crucial that the new person is able to be and to behave in the extratherapy world.

In this session, we simply followed the four steps that were outlined in the preface. The patient began with some scene of strong feeling and proceeded to find a given moment in which this feeling is strong. Living and being in this moment, you were able to access the inner, deeper potential for experiencing. In the second step, this person was able to welcome and appreciate that inner experiencing, to be more integrated with it. This allowed the person, in the third step, to be able to get inside and to be this inner experiencing, a radical shift in who the person is. This was done in the context of earlier life scenes. Finally, the new person remained, but the context is now the present and prospective future. First in a sense of playful unreality and then in a sense of actually being and behaving as this new person, the patient is enabled to live and be in present and prospective scenes. When the session ends, this new person can leave the office and enter into a changed world, a more integrated and actualized person who is free of the bad-feelinged scenes that were there at the beginning of the session. We have completed one session. We are looking forward to the next session.

WHAT DO YOU DO WHEN THE WORK OF THE SESSION IS OVER?

There are some windup matters to be taken care of. Suppose that the work of the session is finished. The person has turned to the extratherapy world, and is ready and willing to be this new person in carrying out this new behavior in this new situation. You have finished the work of the session. What else do you do?

Some of these matters were discussed in Chapter 6 because they are part of the practicalities of doing experiential psychotherapy. Nevertheless, now is the time that you face these concerns. There are some things for you to do when the work of the session seems to be over.

How Do You Know When to End the Session?

It may have taken an hour, usually around an hour and a half, sometimes up to two hours, but the work of the session is over. The person is, you hope, ready to be and to behave as this new person in the new extratherapy world, and is free of the bad-feelinged scene from the beginning of the session. When Step 4 is finished, you usually know that you are ready to end the session.

This is when you let go of being aligned with the person. You return to being you. No longer is your attention mainly out there, on whatever the patient is attending to. No longer are you and the patient so aligned that the words of the patient come in and through you. There is typically a drop in the energy of being aligned and being programmed to do the work. Your own thoughts and feelings return. This is when you know you can draw the session to a close.

You may say:

All right. Well, I am ready to stop. Are you?

Almost always, the patient is ready, especially when she is ready to reenter the new world as the new person:

I'm going to open my eyes . . . There.

Turn Off the Tape Recorder, and Arrange for Payment

Turn off the tape recorder. When the patient has left the office, and before the session with the next person, you will probably be reviewing some part of the tape. If the session was special in some way, you might want to save the tape to study it more carefully. Otherwise, after reviewing the part you want to review, you will get the tape ready for the next person.

Take care of the payment for this session. I typically make out a statement, give the person the statement, and get a check for this session.

Schedule the Next Session

Just about the last thing you do is to schedule the next session. If you and the person have settled into a routine, scheduling the next session may be simple.

Next week? Tuesday, 3:00? OK? Is that all right?

You initiate scheduling of the next session, whether or not you have settled into a regular schedule.

I would like to have a session on Friday. At 5:30. How does that sound to you? Is that all right?

Sometimes you may want to have a session in a few days. Sometimes you may want one in a week or two. Generally, the two of you work out a more or less regular schedule, but you finalize it one session at a time.

You may not always want to schedule another session.   Typically, this happens in the first session or so. Suppose that you and the person have spent around a half hour or so, and it seems rather clear that the person must talk directly to you, is not inclined to follow the opening instructions, and this session has not even begun to move toward Step 1. You may be willing to try again, or you may not be especially inclined to have another session. Be frank, and give the person plenty of room to have or not have any further sessions with you, at least for now.

Ordinarily, there can always be another session if the person is ready and willing.   One use of experiential sessions is to enable the person to continue becoming a qualitatively new person, to move toward becoming increasingly optimal, increasingly integrated and actualized. This can be a lifelong journey. Another use of experiential sessions is to be free of bad-feelinged scenes. If some kind of bad-feelinged scene is front and center on the person's mind, a session may be useful, not only as a window into accessing a deeper inner potential, but also as a way of freeing the person of this bad-feelinged scene.

When you want to have another session, and when the person wants to have another session, it probably makes good sense to schedule another session. If the two of you have sessions once or twice a week, or every few weeks or so, you are always free to keep on scheduling a next session, or to not schedule another session, or to schedule a session months ahead, or to do whatever the two of you agree to do. The key is whether you and the person want to schedule another session, and for when.

In one sense, sessions can occur for the rest of the person's life. How often to have sessions depends on the two of you. The person may want to return every year or so for a session, and it is common for patients to return for a batch of sessions every year or so.

How do you know when to stop having regularly scheduled sessions? Picture a session in which the juice or energy or focused inclination for this session is not here in the patient. After the opening instructions, there is nothing. For whatever reason, the person is not ready or willing to have this session. Typically, this happens every so often. If you are ready and willing to have another session, and so is the patient, then schedule one. If a few sessions in a row do not seem to be energized, if there is no inclination to move into the first step, then consider whether or not the person would like to schedule a session for months from now. Include the possibility that you can have a session whenever the person wants, whether or not it is scheduled. Remember that you are working only one session at a time, and this frees you to be quite flexible. If the person does not want to schedule another session, that is fine, as long as the person knows he or she is free to have a session at any time in the future.

Write Your Notes from This Session

There are at least three kinds of notes that will probably help in your work with this patient:

1. Mark down your impression of the scene of strong feeling, especially a bad-feelinged scene, from this session. In just a sentence or so, tell what that scene was.
2. Mark down your impression of the inner deeper potential that was accessed and used in this session. A few words and phrases will generally do.
3. Mark down the postsession commitment. What was the patient to be, what was the patient to do, and in what situational context?

These three kinds of notes make it easier to gauge the success and effectiveness of the prior session or so, and of the subsequent session or so. These notes also make it easier for you to begin the first step of the next session.

A fourth kind of note can help you become a better experiential therapist: Mark down what you learned about how to do therapy in this session. What did the session teach you? What did you discover or confirm? Your notes may open up grand and glorious new dimensions of psychotherapy, or the notes may reaffirm some small detail in carrying out a small method. Get in the habit of marking down something, big or small, about what you discovered about how to do therapy. Listen to that part of the tape to help you clarify what you think this session taught you. If the tape is truly special, save it for further and more careful study.

Study Tapes to Help You Improve

One way of improving your skill is to study tapes (Mahrer, 1979, 1987d, in press a; Mahrer & Morel, 1993). You may study tapes by yourself, or with a partner, or with a teacher (Mahrer & Boulet, in press). Once a month or so, listen to special sessions of yours, or listen to tapes of your partner, or listen to tapes of exemplary experiential therapists. Even if you study your own tapes, by yourself or with a partner or two, try to learn from careful examination of the tape.

Help to Make Experiential Psychotherapy Better

It seem that I have spent over 40 years trying to figure out how to do psychotherapy. It also seems that in the past 10 years or less I have finally figured out how to do this experiential psychotherapy. I have, in other words, gone about as far as I can go in developing this therapy. This therapy is completed, in terms of what I can do. But there is still work to do (Mahrer, 1992b). Here are some ways that you can make experiential psychotherapy better.

Discover how each session can enable transformational changes.   Each session should enable the person to attain a state in which the person is a qualitatively new person and in which the person is free of the bad-feelinged scene that was front and center in the session. Occasionally, the session contains a supremely precious transformational change in which the person moves well along the road toward being optimal, toward actualization and integration (Mahrer, 1993a). There is considerable work ahead for those who can picture nearly every session opening up such transformational changes. Discover how to increase the rate of such sessions.

Discover how to improve the four steps.   I have figured out what these four steps are and how they can organize a session; I am proud of their meaning and use. However, this also suggests that it is up to others to improve the four steps. The question is this: How can a session be organized to increase the likelihood of enabling the person to become a qualitatively new person and to be free of bad-feelinged scenes? My answer is to attain the four steps. What is a better answer?

Discover better working methods.   I have tried to find and to adapt all sorts of working methods to attain each of the four steps. Find better methods. Each of the four steps is a goal. There are probably plenty of other and better methods to attain each of these goals or steps.

Discover how experiential psychotherapy may be used by and for children and infants. In its present form, this therapy may be used with some people who are relatively young, perhaps 12 to 14 years old or so. I have in mind much younger children (up to 10 or 12 years old) and infants, from a year or so before what is called conception to a year or so after what is called birth. When I picture these infants and young children, I can see parents or parental figures following experiential principles to achieve the goals of experiential psychotherapy (Mahrer, 1978/1989d; Mahrer, Levinson, & Fine, 1976).

Just as with adults, the experiential therapist is more of a teacher, a guide, someone who shows the person what to do and how to do it. In the same way, the parents and parental figures can show infants and young children what to do and how to do it. This is in contrast with doing therapy "on" infants or young children, with applying treatment to infants or young children.

The aim is to discover how to modify experiential psychotherapy for use by and with infants and young children. This brings up the issue of how parents or parental figures can use experiential principles with newborns, or with pregnant mothers, or a year or so before conception.

Discover how experiential psychotherapy may be used for one's own self-change. According to the experiential model of human beings, parents are crucial in constituting the very foundations of the infant's personality. It would be nice if these people had some way of undergoing their own heightened integration and actualization, their own letting go of scenes of bad feeling, their own personal self-change. It would be nice if any one who wanted to undergo self-change could have some reasonably effective way of doing so, without a therapist.

Experiential psychotherapy could be made better by outfitting it to just about any person who might want to undergo this kind of self-change. There is already a way to do this when Step 1 starts with a dream (Mahrer, 1966, 1971a, 1975a, 1989c). It would be helpful to modify this therapy so that a person could start with any focal center, any scene of strong feeling, anything that is front and center on the person's mind. Picture a person undergoing self-change by himself or with a partner. This is the further work that may be done for experiential psychotherapy, preparing it for use by any person who is ready and willing, and who is inclined to learn the methods and how to use them. The changes would be good for the person, as well as for the infants, children, and others in his external world and in whose worlds the person plays a part (Mahrer, 1970c, 1986d, 1978/1989d; Mahrer, Howard, & Soulière, 1991; Rowe, 1988).

A FINAL INVITATION

Please write to me at the School of Psychology, University of Ottawa, Ottawa, Canada K1N 6N5. Corresponding about psychotherapy is important to me. Perhaps it is even more important to listen to each other's tapes, to discover more about what can be accomplished in what we call psychotherapy, to teach each other about psychotherapy, to see if we can ask the right questions.

I wrote this book as a kind of log of how far I have gone in trying to see what this experiential psychotherapy can become, what it can enable a person to be, and how to use the most fitting package of nuts and bolts to make this therapy as effective as it can be. I would very much like to talk with readers so that this psychotherapy can develop even further, either in little ways or in some larger ways that you might have in mind.

References

Adams, H. E., Doster, J. A., & Calhoun, K. S. (1977). A psychologically based system of response classification. In A. R. Ciminero, K. S. Calhoun, & H. E. Adams (Eds.), *Handbook of behavioral assessment* (pp. 185–221). New York: Wiley.

Adler, A. (1927). *Practice and theory of individual psychology.* New York: Harcourt Brace.

Adler, A. (1969). *The science of living.* New York: Anchor-Doubleday.

Albee, G. W. (1977). The protestant ethic, sex, and psychotherapy. *American Psychologist, 32,* 156–161.

Alexander, F. (1963). The dynamics of psychotherapy in the light of learning theory. *American Journal of Psychiatry, 5,* 440–448.

Alexander, F. (1965). Psychoanalytic contributions to short-term psychotherapy. In L. R. Wolberg (Ed.), *Short-term psychotherapy* (pp. 145–167). New York: Grune and Stratton.

Alexander, F., & French, T. M. (1946). *Psychoanalytic therapy.* New York: Ronald.

Allport, G. W. (1955). *Becoming: Basic considerations for a psychology of personality.* New Haven, CT: Yale University Press.

American Psychiatric Association. (1994). *Diagnostic and statistical manual of mental disorders* (4th ed.). Washington, DC: Author.

Angyal, A. (1941). *Foundations for a science of personality.* New York: Commonwealth Foundation.

Angyal, A. (1965). *Neurosis and treatment: A holistic theory.* New York: Wiley.

Ansbacher, H. L. (1965). The structure of individual psychology. In B. B. Wolman (Ed.), *Scientific psychology* (pp. 346–364). New York: Basic Books.

Ansell, C., Mindess, H., Stern, M., & Stern, V. (1981). Pies in the face and similar matters. *Voices, 16,* 10–23.

Anthony, J., & Edelstein, B. A. (1975). Thought-stopping treatment of anxiety attacks due to seizure-related obsessive ruminations. *Journal of Behavior Therapy and Experimental Psychiatry, 6,* 343–344.

Argelander, H. (1976). *The initial interview in psychotherapy.* New York: Human Sciences.

Armstrong, J. S. (1982). Research on scientific journals: Implications for editors and authors. *Journal of Forecasting, 1,* 83–104.

Atkin, S. (1966). Discussion. In R. E. Litman (Ed.), *Psychoanalysis in the Americas* (pp. 240–246). New York: International Universities Press.

Auchincloss, E. L. (1982). Conflict among psychiatric residents in response to pregnancy. *American Journal of Psychiatry, 139,* 818–821.

Barrett, C. J. (1979). Women in widowhood. In J. H. Williams (Ed.), *Psychology of women* (pp. 496–506). New York: Norton.

Barrios, B. A. (1988). On the changing nature of behavioral assessment. In A. S. Bellack & M. Hersen (Eds.), *Behavioral assessment: A practical handbook* (3rd ed., pp. 3–41). New York: Pergamon.

Beck, A. T. (1976). *Cognitive therapy and the emotional disorders.* New York: International Universities Press.

Beier, E. G. (1966). *The silent language of psychotherapy.* Chicago: Aldine.

Bell, J. E. (1963). A theoretical position for family group therapy. *Family Process, 2,* 1–14.

Bellak, L. (1981). *Crises and special problems in psychoanalysis and psychotherapy.* New York: Brunner/Mazel.

Benjamin, A. (1969). *The helping interview.* Boston: Houghton Mifflin.

Benton, A. L. (1971). Psychological tests for brain damage. In A. M. Freedman & H. I. Kaplan (Eds.), *Diagnosing mental illness: Evaluation in psychiatry and psychology* (pp. 86–102). New York: Atheneum.

Bequaert, L. H. (1976). *Single women, alone and together.* Boston: Beacon.

Berne, E. (1966). *Principles of group treatment.* New York: Oxford University Press.

Bernstein, L., Bernstein, R. S., & Dana, R. H. (1974). *Interviewing: A guide for health professionals.* New York: Appleton-Century-Crofts.

Bernstein, S. (1984). A case history demonstrating the complementary use of psychodynamic and behavior techniques in therapy. *Psychotherapy, 21,* 402–407.

Bertalanffy, L. (1966). General system theory and psychiatry. In S. Arieti (Ed.), *American handbook of psychiatry* (Vol. 3). New York: Basic Books.

Beutler, L. E. (1981). Convergence in counseling and psychotherapy: A current look. *Clinical Psychology Review, 1,* 79–101.

Binswanger, L. (1958a). The existential analysis school of thought. In R. May, E. Angel, & H. F. Ellenberger (Eds.), *Existence: A new dimension in psychiatry and psychology* (pp. 191–213). New York: Basic Books.

Binswanger, L. (1958b). The case of Ellen West: An anthropological clinical study. In R. May, E. Angel, & H. F. Ellenberger (Eds.), *Existence: A new dimension in psychiatry and psychology* (pp. 237–364). New York: Basic Books.

Bion, W. R. (1967). Notes on memory and desire. *Psychoanalytic Forum, 2,* 271–280.

Bion, W. R. (1970). *Seven servants.* New York: Jason Aronson.

Birk, L. (1970). Behavior therapy: Integration with dynamic psychiatry. *Behavior Therapy, 1,* 522–526.

Bloom, B. L. (1981). Focused single-session therapy: Initial development and evaluation. In S. H. Budman (Ed.), *Forms of brief therapy* (pp. 167–218). New York: Guilford.

Blum, H. P. (1989). The concept of termination and the evolution of psychoanalytic thought. *Journal of the American Psychoanalytic Association, 37,* 275–295.

Bokar, J. A. (1981). *Primer for the psychotherapist.* New York: Spectrum.

Bolman, W. M. (1967). Theoretical and empirical bases of community mental health. *American Journal of Psychiatry, 124,* 8–13.

Boss, M. (1963). *Psychoanalysis and daseinsanalysis.* New York: Basic Books.

Boszormenyi-Nagy, I., & Framo, J. G. (Eds.). (1965). *Intensive family therapy: Theoretical and practical aspects.* New York: Harper & Row.

Boulougouris, J. C., & Rabarilas, A. D. (Eds.). (1977). *The treatment of phobic and obsessive compulsive disorders.* Oxford, England: Pergamon.

Bowers, M., & Weinstock, W. (1978). A case of healing in malignancy. *Journal of the American Academy of Psychoanalysis, 6,* 393–402.

Braaten, L. S. (1961). The movement from non-self to self in client-centered psychotherapy. *Journal of Counseling Psychology, 8,* 20–24.

Brady, J. P. (1968). Psychotherapy by combined behavioral and dynamic approach. *Comprehensive Psychiatry, 9,* 536–543.

Brammer, L. M., & Shostrom, E. L. (1982). *Therapeutic psychology.* Englewood Cliffs, NJ: Prentice-Hall.

Braun, B. (1983). Psychophysiological phenomena in multiple personality. *The American Journal of Clinical Hypnosis, 26,* 84–92.

Breger, L. (1976). Psychological testing: Treatment and research implications. In A. P. Goldstein & N. Stein (Eds.), *Prescriptive psychotherapies* (pp. 31–39). New York: Pergamon.

Bridger, H. (1950). Criteria for termination of an analysis. *International Journal of Psychoanalysis, 31,* 202–203.

Bridges, N., & Smith, J. M. (1988). The pregnant therapist and the seriously disturbed patient: Managing long-term psychotherapeutic treatment. *Psychiatry, 51,* 104–109.

Brodbeck, M., & Feigl, H. (1968). *Readings in the philosophy of the social sciences.* New York: MacMillan.

Brown, J. F. (1936). *Psychology and the social order: An introduction to the dynamic study of social fields.* New York: McGraw-Hill.

Brush, S. G. (1974). Should the history of science be rated X? *Science, 183,* 1164–1172.

Buchanan, R. L. (1974). The widow and widower. In E. A. Grollman (Ed.), *Concerning death: A practical guide for the living* (pp. 182–211). Boston: Beacon.

Buffery, A. W. H. (1987). The promotion of neuropsychological rehabilitation: The role of the home-based personal computer in brain function therapy. In D. R. Peterson & D. B. Fishman (Eds.), *Assessment for decision* (pp. 79–100). New Brunswick, NJ: Rutgers University Press.

Bugental, J. F. T. (1965). *The search for authenticity: An existential-analytic approach to psychotherapy.* New York: Holt, Rinehart and Winston.

Buhler, C. (1968a). The general structure of the human life cycle. In C. Buhler & F. Massarik (Eds.), *The course of human life* (pp. 12–26). New York: Springer.

Buhler, C. (1968b). The developmental structure of goal-setting in group and individual studies. In C. Buhler & F. Massarik (Eds.), *The course of human life* (pp. 27–54). New York: Springer.

Buhler, C. (1971). Basic theoretical concepts of humanistic psychology. *American Psychologist, 26,* 378–386.

Buxbaum, E. (1950). Technique of terminating analysis. *International Journal of Psychoanalysis, 31,* 184–196.

Buytendijk, F. J. J. (1950). A phenomenological approach to the problem of feelings and emotions. In M. L. Reymert (Ed.), *Feelings and emotions* (pp. 127–141). New York: McGraw-Hill.

Byles, M. B. (1962). *Journey into Burmese silence.* London: George Allen and Unwin.

Cantor, G. N., & Cromwell, R. L. (1957). The principle of reductionism and mental deficiency. *American Journal of Mental Deficiency, 61,* 461–466.

Caruso, I. A. (1964). *Existential psychology.* New York: Herder and Herder.

Cashdan, S. (1973). *Interactional psychotherapy: Stages and strategies in behavioral changes.* New York: Grune and Stratton.

Cautela, J. R., & Upper, D. (1975). The process of individual behavior therapy. In M. Hersen, R. M. Eisler, & P. M. Miller (Eds.), *Progress in behavior modification* (Vol. 1). New York: Academic Press.

Cawley, R. (1974). Psychotherapy and obsessional disorders. In H. R. Beach (Ed.), *Obsessional states* (pp. 259–290). London: Methuen.

Chang, C. C. (1959). *The practice of Zen.* New York: Harper & Row.

Claiborn, C. D. (1982). Interpretation and change in counseling. *Journal of Counseling Psychology, 29,* 439–453.

Clark, A. (1982). Grief and Gestalt therapy. *The Gestalt Journal, 5,* 49–63.

Clarke, J. C., & Jackson, J. A. (1983). *Hypnosis and behavior therapy: The treatment of anxiety and phobias.* New York: Springer.

Cohen, I. H., & Pope, B. (1980). Concurrent use of insight and desensitization therapy. *Psychiatry, 43,* 146–154.

Colby, K. M. (1951). *A primer for psychotherapists.* New York: Ronald.

Combs, A. W., & Snygg, D. (1959). *Individual behavior.* New York: Harper & Row.

Condrau, G., & Boss, M. (1971). Existential analysis. In J. G. Howells (Ed.), *Modern perspectives in world psychiatry* (pp. 488–518). New York: Brunner/Mazel.

Cone, J. P. (1988). Psychometric considerations and the multiple models of behavioral assessment. In A. S. Bellack & M. Hersen (Eds.), *Behavioral assessment: A practical handbook* (pp. 42–66). New York: Pergamon.

Coriat, I. H. (1915). Stammering as a psychoneurosis. *Journal of Abnormal and Social Psychology, 9,* 417–430.

Cormier, W. H., & Cormier, L. S. (1979). *Interviewing strategies for helpers: A guide to assessment, treatment, and evaluation.* Monterey, CA: Brooks Cole.

Coyne, J. C., & Segal, L. (1982). A brief strategic interaction approach to psychotherapy. In J. C. Anchin & D. J. Kiesler (Eds.), *Handbook of interactional psychotherapy* (pp. 248–261). New York: Pergamon.

Craighead, E. W., Kazdin, A. E., & Mahoney, M. J. (1976). *Behavior modification.* Boston: Houghton Mifflin.

Crosby, J. F., & Jose, N. L. (1983). Death: Family adjustment to loss. In C. R. Figley & H. I. McCubbin (Eds.), *Stress and the family. Vol. 2: Coping with catastrophe* (pp. 75–89). New York: Brunner/Mazel.

Danziger, K. (1985). The methodological imperative in psychology. *Philosophy of the Social Sciences, 15,* 1–13.

Darroch, V., & Silvers, R. J. (1982). *Interpretive human studies: An introduction to phenomenological research.* Washington, DC: University Press of America.

Davis, J. D. (1971). *The interview as arena.* Stanford, CA: Stanford University Press.

Davison, G. C. (1977). Homosexuality, the ethical challenge. *Journal of Homosexuality, 2,* 195–204.

Dengrove, E. (1972). Practical behavioral diagnosis. In A. A. Lazarus (Ed.), *Clinical behavior therapy* (pp. 85–115). New York: Brunner/Mazel.

de Shazer, S. (1985). *Keys to solution in brief therapy.* New York: Norton.

de Shazer, S. (1991). *Putting difference to work.* New York: Norton.

Deutsch, F. (1949). *Applied psychoanalysis.* New York: Grune and Stratton.

Dollard, J., & Mowrer, C. H. (1947). A method of measuring tension in written documents. *Journal of Abnormal and Social Psychology, 42,* 3–32.

Ekstein, R. (1965). Working through and termination of analysis. *Journal of the American Psychoanalytic Association, 13,* 57–78.

Ekstein, R. (1976). Psychotherapy in America and Europe: The two shall meet. In H. Argelander (Ed.), *The initial interview in psychotherapy* (pp. 9–19). New York: Human Sciences.

Elke, F. (1947). Specialists interpret the case of Harold Holzer. *Journal of Abnormal and Social Psychology, 42,* 99–111.

Elkind, S. N. (1992). *Resolving impasses in therapeutic relationships*. New York: Guilford.

Ellenberger, H. F. (1958). A clinical introduction to psychiatric phenomenology and existential analysis. In R. May, E. Angel, & H. F. Ellenberger (Eds.), *Existence: A new dimension in psychiatry and psychology* (pp. 92–124). New York: Basic Books.

Elliott, R. (1984). A discovery-oriented approach to significant change events in psychotherapy. Interpersonal process to call and comprehensive process analysis. In L. N. Rice & L. S. Greenberg (Eds.), *Patterns of change* (pp. 249–286). New York: Guilford.

Ellis, A. (1962). *Reason and emotion in psychotherapy*. New York: Lyle Stuart.

Ellis, A. (1967). Goals of psychotherapy. In A. R. Mahrer (Ed.), *The goals of psychotherapy* (pp. 206–220). New York: Appleton-Century-Crofts.

Ellis, A. (1977). Fun as psychotherapy. *Rational Living, 21*, 2–6.

Ellis, A. (1981). The use of rational-emotive humorous songs in psychotherapy, *Voices, 16*, 29–36.

Enright, J. (1970). An introduction to Gestalt techniques. In J. Fagan & J. L. Shepherd (Eds.), *Gestalt therapy now* (pp. 107–124). New York: Harper & Row.

Erickson, M. H. (1980). Hypnotic psychotherapy. In E. Rossi (Ed.), *The collected papers of Milton H. Erickson on hypnosis. IV. Innovative hypnotherapy* (pp. 35–48). New York: Irvington.

Erickson, M. H., & Rossi, E. (1979). *Hypnotherapy: An exploratory casebook*. New York: Irvington.

Evans, I. M. (1985). Building systems models as a strategy for target behavior selection in clinical assessment. *Behavioral Assessment, 7*, 21–32.

Farrelly, F., & Brandsma, J. (1974). *Provocative therapy*. Fort Collins, CO: Shields.

Feather, B. W., & Rhoads, J. M. (1972). Psychodynamic behavior therapy. *Archives of General Psychiatry, 26*, 496–511.

Feigl, H. (1953). The mind-body problem in the development of logical empiricism. In H. Feigl & M. B. Brodbeck (Eds.), *Readings in the philosophy of science* (pp. 612–626). New York: Appleton-Century-Crofts.

Feigl, H. (1958). The "mental" and the "physical." In H. Feigl, M. Scriven, & G. Maxwell (Eds.), *Minnesota studies in the philosophy of science, Vol. 2: Concepts, theories, and the mind-body problem* (pp. 370–497). Minneapolis: University of Minnesota Press.

Feldman, M. P., & Peay, J. (1982). Ethical and legal issues. In A. S. Bellack, M. Hersen, & A. E. Kazdin (Eds.), *International handbook of behavior modification and therapy* (pp. 231–261). New York: Plenum.

Fenichel, O. (1945). *The psychoanalytic theory of neurosis*. New York: Norton.

Fenichel, O. (1953). Psychoanalytic method. In H. Fenichel & D. Rapaport (Eds.), *The collected papers of Otto Fenichel: First series* (pp. 318–330). New York: Norton.

Ferenczi, S. (1955). *Final contributions to psycho-analysis*. New York: Basic Books. (Original work published 1927)

Ferster, C. B. (1967). Classification of behavioral pathology. In L. Krasner & L. P. Ullman (Eds.), *Research in behavior modification* (pp. 212–241). New York: Holt, Rinehart and Winston.

Feyerabend, P. (1975). *Against method*. London: Verso.

Fiester, A. R., Mahrer, A. R., & Giambra, L. M. (1974). Shaping a clinic population: The dropout problem reconsidered. *Community Mental Health Journal, 10*, 173–179.

Fine, R. (1971). *The healing of the mind*. New York: David McKay.

Firestein, S. K. (1969). Panel report: Problems of termination in the analysis of adults. *Journal of the American Psychoanalytic Association, 17*, 222–237.

Firestein, S. K. (1978). *Termination in psychoanalysis*. New York: International Universities Press.

Fleming, J., & Benedek, T. (1966). *Psychoanalytic supervision*. New York: Grune and Stratton.

Foley, A. R., & Sanders, D. S. (1966). Theoretical considerations for the development of the community mental health concept. *American Journal of Psychiatry, 122*, 985–996.

Frank, J. D. (1959). The dynamics of the psychotherapeutic relationship: Determinants and effects of the therapist's influence. *Psychiatry, 22,* 17–39.

Frank, J. D. (1961). The role of influence in psychotherapy. In M. J. Stern (Ed.), *Contemporary psychotherapies* (pp. 17–41). New York: Free Press of Glencoe.

Frank, J. D. (1973). *Persuasion and healing.* Baltimore, MD: Johns Hopkins Press.

Franks, C. M. (1983). Behavior therapy: An overview. In C. M. Franks, G. T. Wilson, K. D. Brownell, & P. C. Kendall (Eds.), *Annual review of behavior therapy: Theory and practice* (Vol. 9, pp. 1–38). New York: Brunner/Mazel.

Freud, A. (1937). *The ego and the mechanism of defense.* London: Hogarth.

Freud, S. (1937). Analysis terminable and interminable. In J. Strachey (Ed. and Trans.), *The standard edition of the complete psychological works of Sigmund Freud.* London: Hogarth.

Frieze, I. H., Parsons, J. E., Johnson, P. B., Rubler, D. N., & Zellman, G. L. (1978). *Women and sex roles: A social psychological perspective.* New York: Norton.

Froeschels, E. (1943). Pathology and therapy of stuttering. *Nervous Child, 2,* 148–161.

Fromm, E. (1947). *Man for himself.* New York: Rinehart.

Fromm, E. (1956). *The art of loving.* New York: Harper & Row.

Fromm, E., Suzuki, D., & Dimartino, R. (1960). *Zen Buddhism and psychoanalysis.* New York: Harper & Row.

Fromm-Reichmann, F. (1958). *Principles of intensive psychotherapy.* Chicago: University of Chicago Press.

Gendlin, E. T. (1961). Experiencing: A variable in the process of therapeutic change. *American Journal of Psychotherapy, 15,* 233–245.

Gendlin, E. T. (1962). *Experiencing and the creation of meaning.* New York: Free Press of Glencoe.

Gendlin, E. T. (1964). A theory of personality change. In B. Worchel & D. Byrne (Eds.), *Personality change* (pp. 100–148). New York: Wiley.

Gendlin, E. T. (1969). Focusing. *Psychotherapy: Theory, Research and Practice, 6,* 4–15.

Gendlin, E. T. (1972). Therapeutic procedures with schizophrenic patients. In M. Hammer (Ed.), *The theory and practice of psychotherapy with specific disorders* (pp. 333–375). Springfield, IL: Charles C. Thomas.

Gendlin, E. T. (1973). Experiential psychotherapy. In R. Corsini (Ed.), *Current psychotherapies* (pp. 317–352). Itasca, IL: Peacock.

Gendlin, E. T. (1974). Client-Centered and experimental psychotherapy. In D. A. Wexler & L. N. Rice (Eds.), *Innovations in client-centered therapy* (pp. 211–246). New York: Wiley.

Gendlin, E. T. (1981). *Focusing.* New York: Bantam.

Gendlin, E. T. (1984). The client's client: The edge of awareness. In F. R. Levant & J. M. Shlien (Eds.), *Client-centered therapy and the person-centered approach* (pp. 76–107). New York: Praeger.

Gendlin, E. T., Beebe, J., Cassens, J., Klein, M., & Oberlander, M. (1968). Focusing ability in psychotherapy, personality, and creativity. In J. M. Shlien, H. F. Hunt, J. D. Matarazzo, & C. Savage (Eds.), *Research in psychotherapy* (Vol. 3, pp. 217–241). Washington, DC: American Psychological Association.

Gill, M., Newman, R., & Redlich, F. C. (1954). *The initial interview in psychiatric practice.* New York: International Universities Press.

Gillman, R. D. (1982). The termination phase in psychoanalytic practice: A survey of 48 completed cases. *Psychoanalytic Inquiry, 2,* 463–472.

Glatzer, H. T. (1972). Treatment of oral character neurosis in group therapy. In C. Sager & H. Kaplan (Eds.), *Progress in group and Family therapy* (pp. 148–170). New York: Brunner/Mazel.

Glauber, I. P. (1953). The nature of stuttering. *Social Casework, 34,* 95–103.

Glover, E. (1955). *The technique of psychoanalysis.* New York: International Universities Press.

Goldfried, M. R., & Pomeranz, D. M. (1976). Role of assessment in behavior modification. In A. P. Goldstein & N. Stein (Eds.), *Prescriptive psychotherapies* (pp. 41–54). New York: Pergamon.

Goldstein, A. P., & Stein, N. (1976). *Prescriptive psychotherapies.* New York: Pergamon.

Gordon, I. (1967). *A parent education approach to provision of early stimulation for the culturally disadvantaged.* Gainesville: University of Florida, Institute for Development of Human Resources.

Gottman, J. M., & Leiblum, S. R. (1974). *How to do psychotherapy and how to evaluate it: A manual for beginners.* New York: Holt, Rinehart and Winston.

Gould, S. J. (1981). *The mismeasure of man.* New York: Norton.

Goulding, M. M., & Goulding, R. L. (1979). *Changing lives through redecision therapy.* New York: Grove.

Goulding, R. L., & Goulding, M. M. (1978). *The power is in the patient.* San Francisco: Transactional Analysis Press.

Greenberg, L. S., & Johnson, S. M. (1988). *Emotional focused therapy for couples.* New York: Guilford.

Greenberg, L. S., & Safran, J. D. (1987). *Emotion in psychotherapy.* New York: Guilford.

Greenson, R. R. (1966). Discussion. In R. E. Litman (Ed.), *Psychoanalysis in the Americas* (pp. 263–266). New York: International Universities Press.

Greenwald, A. G. (1975). Consequences of prejudice against the null hypothesis. *Psychological Bulletin, 82,* 1–20.

Greenwald, H. (1975). Humor in psychotherapy. *Journal of Contemporary Psychotherapy, 7,* 113–116.

Gregory, I., & Smeltzer, D. J. (1977). *Psychiatry: Essentials of clinical practice.* Boston: Little, Brown.

Grof, S. (1976). *Realms of the human unconscious.* New York: E. P. Dutton.

Grotjahn, M. (1970). Laughter in psychotherapy. In W. M. Mandel (Ed.), *A celebration of laughter* (pp. 181–214). Los Angeles: Mara.

Gullick, E. L., & Blanchard, E. B. (1973). The use of psychotherapy and behavior therapy in the treatment of an obsessional disorder. An experimental case study. *Journal of Nervous and Mental Disease, 156,* 427–431.

Hackney, H., Ivey, A., & Oetting, E. (1970). Attending, island and hiatus behavior: Process conception of counselor and client interaction. *Journal of Counseling Psychology, 17,* 342–346.

Haigh, G. (1949). Defensive behavior in client-centered therapy. *Journal of Consulting Psychology, 30,* 3–18.

Haley, J. (1963). *Strategies of psychotherapy.* New York: Grune and Stratton.

Haley, J., & Hoffman, L. (1967). *Techniques of family therapy.* New York: Basic Books.

Halgin, R. P. (1985). Teaching integration of psychotherapy models to beginning therapists. *Psychotherapy, 22,* 555–563.

Halpern, H. (1965). An essential ingredient in successful psychotherapy. *Psychotherapy: Theory, Research and Practice, 2,* 177–180.

Havens, L. L. (1978). Explorations in the uses of language in psychotherapy: Simple empathic statements. *Psychiatry, 41,* 336–345.

Havens, L. L. (1986). *Making contact: Uses of language in psychotherapy.* Cambridge, MA: Harvard University Press.

Heidegger, M. (1963). *Being and time.* New York: Harper & Row.

Herrigel, E. (1956). *Zen in the art of archery.* New York: Pantheon.

Hersen, M. (Ed.). (1986). *Pharmacological and behavioral treatment: An integrative approach.* New York: Wiley.

Hersen, M., & Bellack, A. S. (1988). *DSM-III and behavioral assessment: A practical handbook.* New York: Pergamon.

Hill, C. E. (1990). A review of exploratory in-session process research. *Journal of Consulting and Clinical Psychology, 58,* 288–294.

Hill, C. E., Carter, J. A., & O'Farrell, M. K. (1983). A case study of the process and outcomes of time-limited counseling. *Journal of Consulting Psychology, 30,* 3–18.

Hill, H. (1945). An interbehavioral analysis of several aspects of stuttering. *Journal of General Psychology, 32,* 289–316.

Hobbs, N. (1962). Sources of gain in psychotherapy. *American Psychologist, 17,* 741–747.

Holt, H. (1968). The problem of interpretation from the point of view of existential psychoanalysis. In E. F. Hammer (Ed.), *Use of interpretation in treatment* (pp. 240–252). New York: Grune and Stratton.

Horowitz, L. M., Sampson, H., Siegelman, E. Y., Weiss, J., & Goodfriend, S. (1978). Cohesive and dispersal behaviors: Two classes of concomitant changes in psychotherapy. *Journal of Consulting and Clinical Psychology, 46,* 556–564.

Hugdahl, K. (1981). The three-systems model of fear and emotion: A critical examination. *Behavior Research and therapy, 19,* 75–86.

Jackins, H. (1962). *Elementary counselor's manual.* Seattle, WA: Rational Island.

Jackins, H. (1965). *The human side of human beings: The theory of re-evaluation counseling.* Seattle, WA: Rational Island.

Jackson, D. D. (1957). The question of family homeostasis. *Psychiatric Quarterly, 31,* 79–90.

Janov, A. (1970). *The primal scream.* New York: Dell.

Jung, C. G. (1933). *Modern man in search of a soul.* New York: Harcourt Brace.

Jung, C. G. (1962). The detachment of consciousness from the object. In R. Wilhelm (Ed.), *The secret of the golden flower: A Chinese book of life* (pp. 122–127). London: Routledge and Kegan Paul.

Kahn, M. H., Mahrer, A. R., & Bornstein, R. (1972). Male psychosexual development: Role of sibling sex and ordinal position. *Journal of Genetic Psychology, 121,* 187–196.

Kanfer, F. H. (1985). Target selection for clinical change programs. *Behavioral Assessment, 7,* 7–20.

Kanfer, F. H., & Busemeyer, J. R. (1982). The use of problem-solving and decision-making in behavior therapy. *Clinical Psychology Review, 2,* 239–266.

Kanfer, F. H., & Saslow, G. (1969). Behavioral diagnosis. In C. M. Franks (Ed.), *Behavior therapy: Appraisal and status* (pp. 417–444). New York: McGraw-Hill.

Kantor, J. R. (1942). Preface to interbehavioral psychology. *Psychological Record, 5,* 173–193.

Kantor, J. R. (1953). *The logic of modern science.* Bloomington, IL: Principia.

Kantor, J. R. (1957). Events and constructs in the science of psychology. *Psychological Record, 7,* 55–60.

Kazdin, A. E. (1985). Selection of target behaviors: The relationship of the treatment focus to clinical dysfunction. *Behavioral Assessment, 7,* 33–47.

Kelly, G. A. (1955). *The psychology of personal constructs* (Vols. 1 & 2). New York: Norton.

Kelly, G. A. (1967). A psychology of the optimal man. In A. R. Mahrer (Ed.), *The goals of psychotherapy* (pp. 238–258). New York: Appleton-Century-Crofts.

Kempf, E. J. (1915). The behavior chart in mental diseases. *American Journal of Insanity, 71,* 761–772.

Kierkegaard, S. (1944). *The concept of dread*. Princeton, MA: Princeton University Press.

Kiesler, D. J. (1971). Experimental designs in psychotherapy research. In A. E. Bergin & S. L. Garfield (Eds.), *Handbook of psychotherapy and behavior change: An empirical analysis* (pp. 36–74). New York: Wiley.

Killinger, B. (1976). The place of humor in adult psychotherapy. In A. J. Chapman & H. C. Foot (Eds.), *It's a funny thing, humor* (pp. 87–113). New York: Pergamon.

Klein, M. H., Dittman, A. T., Parloff, M. B., & Gill, M. M. (1969). Behavior therapy: Observations and reflections. *Journal of Consulting and Clinical Psychology, 33,* 259–266.

Kleinplatz, P. J. (1992). The pregnant clinical psychologist: Issues, impressions and observations. *Women and Therapy, 12,* 21–37.

Kondo, A. (1952). Intuition in Zen Buddhism. *American Journal of Psychoanalysis, 12,* 10–14.

Kondo, A. (1958). Zen in psychotherapy. *Chicago Review, 12,* 57–64.

Korchin, S. J. (1976). *Modern clinical psychology.* New York: Basic Books.

Kratochwill, T. R. (1985). Selection of target behaviors in behavioral consultation. *Behavioral Assessment, 7,* 49–62.

Kuhn, T. (1970). *The structure of scientific revolutions* (2nd ed.). Chicago: University of Chicago Press.

Labov, W., & Fanshel, D. (1977). *Therapeutic discourse: Psychotherapy as conversation.* New York: Academic Press.

Laing, R. D. (1962). *The self and others.* Chicago: Quadrangle.

Laing, R. D. (1975). *The divided self.* London: Tavistock.

Laing, R. D. (1982). *The voice of experience.* New York: Pantheon.

Laing, R. D., & Esterson, A. (1970). *Sanity, madness, and the family.* New York: Penguin.

Lakatos, I. (1976). *Proofs and refutations.* London: Cambridge University Press.

Lambie, D. Z., & Weikart, D. B. (1970). Ypsilanti: Carnegie infant education project. In J. Helimuth (Ed.), *Disadvantaged child* (Vol. 3, pp. 85–112). New York: Brunner/Mazel.

Langs, R. (1979). *The therapeutic environment.* New York: Jason Aronson.

Lazarus, A. A. (1976). Toward a flexible or personalistic system of psychotherapy. In A. P. Goldstein & N. Stein (Eds.), *Prescriptive psychotherapies* (pp. 99–113). New York: Pergamon.

Leary, T., & Gill, M. (1959). The dimensions and a measure of the process of psychotherapy: A system for the analysis of content of clinical evaluations and patient-therapist interactions. In E. A. Rubenstein & M. B. Parloff (Eds.), *Research in psychotherapy* (Vol. 1, pp. 62–95). Washington, DC: American Psychological Association.

Lennard, H. L., & Bernstein, A. (1960). *The anatomy of psychotherapy: Systems of communication and expectation.* New York: Columbia University Press.

Leon, R. L. (1982). *Psychiatric interviewing.* Amsterdam: Elsevier Science.

LeShan, L. (1977). *You can fight for your life.* New York: Evans.

Levis, D. J., & Hare, D. J. (1977). A review of the theoretical rationale and empirical support for the extinction approach of implosive (flooding) therapy. In M. Hersen, R. M. Eisler, & P. M. Miller (Eds.), *Progress in behavior modification* (Vol. 4, pp. 185–223). New York: Academic.

Levy, J. (1986). The working through process during the termination of analysis. *Current Issues in Psychoanalytic Practice, 3,* 121–148.

Levy, L. H. (1963). *Psychological interpretation.* New York: Holt, Rinehart and Winston.

Lewis, C. S. (1960). *The four loves.* New York: Harcourt Brace.

Lief, V. F. (1972). The medical examination in psychiatric assessment. In A. M. Freedman & H. I. Kaplan (Eds.), *Diagnosing mental illness: Evaluation in psychiatry and psychology* (pp. 106–112). New York: Atheneum.

Linn, L. (1972). Clinical manifestations of psychiatric disorders. In A. M. Kaplan & H. I. Kaplan (Eds.), *Diagnosing mental illness: Evaluation in psychiatry and psychology* (pp. 113–181). New York: Atheneum.

Lopata, H. Z. (1969). Loneliness: Forms and components. *Social Problems, 17,* 248–261.

MacDonald, M. L. (1984). Behavioral assessment of woman clients. In E. A. Blechman (Ed.), *Behavior modification with women* (pp. 60–93). New York: Guilford.

Mahrer, A. R. (1952). A clinical study of set in intraserial learning. *Journal of Abnormal and Social Psychology, 47,* 478–481.

Mahrer, A. R. (1956). The role of expectancy in delayed reinforcement. *Journal of Experimental Psychology, 52,* 101–106.

Mahrer, A. R. (1957). Potential intelligence testing. *U. S. Armed Forces Medical Journal, 8,* 684–692.

Mahrer, A. R. (1958). Potential intelligence: A learning theory approach to description and clinical implication. *Journal of General Psychology, 59,* 59–71.

Mahrer, A. R. (1962a). A preface to the mind-body problem. *Psychological Record, 12,* 53–60.

Mahrer, A. R. (1962b). The psychodynamics of psychiatric hospitalization. *Journal of Nervous and Mental Diseases, 135,* 354–360.

Mahrer, A. R. (1962c). Psychodiagnostic preference by professional affiliation and length of experience. *Journal of Clinical Psychology, 18,* 14–18.

Mahrer, A. R. (1963). Psychological symptoms as a function of psychiatric hospitalization. *Psychological Reports, 13,* 266.

Mahrer, A. R. (1966). Analysis of a fragment of a dream. *Voices, 2,* 40–41.

Mahrer, A. R. (Ed.). (1967a). *The goals of psychotherapy.* New York: Appleton-Century-Crofts.

Mahrer, A. R. (1967b). The goals and families of psychotherapy: Discussion. In A. R. Mahrer (Ed.), *The goals of psychotherapy* (pp. 270–287). New York: Appleton-Century-Crofts.

Mahrer, A. R. (1967c). The psychological problem inventory. *Psychological Reports, 20,* 711–714.

Mahrer, A. R. (1969). Childhood determinants of adult functioning: Strategies in the clinical research use of the personal-psychological history. *Psychological Record, 19,* 39–46.

Mahrer, A. R. (1970a). Interpretation of patient behavior through goals, feelings, and context. *Journal of Individual Psychology, 26,* 186–195.

Mahrer, A. R. (1970b). Motivational theory: Foundations of a personality classification. In A. R. Mahrer (Ed.), *New approaches to personality classification* (pp. 239–276). New York: Columbia University Press.

Mahrer, A. R. (1970c). Self-change and social change. *International Journal of Interpersonal Development, 1,* 159–166.

Mahrer, A. R. (1970d). Some known effects of psychotherapy and a reinterpretation. *Psychotherapy: Theory, Research and Practice, 7,* 186–191.

Mahrer, A. R. (1971a). Personal life change through systematic use of dreams. *Psychotherapy: Theory, Research and Practice, 8,* 328–332.

Mahrer, A. R. (1971b). An emerging field of human relations *International Journal of Interpersonal Development, 2,* 105–120.

Mahrer, A. R. (1972a). Theory and treatment of anxiety: The perspective of motivational psychology. *Journal of Pastoral Counseling, 7,* 4–16.

Mahrer, A. R. (1972b). The Human Relations Center: Community mental health from a motivational perspective. *Corrective Psychiatry and Journal of Social Therapy, 18,* 39–45.

Mahrer, A. R. (1973). Defining characteristics of a humanistic program of community change and a specimen: The facilitation of self-competence in the neonate. *The Ontario Psychologist, 5,* 45–50.

Mahrer, A. R. (1975a). Metamorphosis through suicide: The changing of one's self by oneself. *Journal of Pastoral Counseling, 10,* 10–26.

Mahrer, A. R. (1975b). Therapeutic outcome as a function of goodness-of-fit on an internal-external dimension of interaction. *Psychotherapy: Theory, Research and Practice, 12,* 22–28.

Mahrer, A. R. (1978a). Experiential psychotherapists: A prognostic test and some speculations about their personalities. *Psychotherapy: Theory, Research and Practices, 15,* 382–389.

Mahrer, A. R. (1978b). Sequence and consequence in the experiential psychotherapies. In C. L. Cooper & C. Alderfer (Eds.), *Advances in experiential social processes* (Vol. 1, pp. 39–65). New York: Wiley.

Mahrer, A. R. (1978c). The therapist-patient relationship: Conceptual analysis and a proposal for a paradigm-shift. *Psychotherapy: Theory, Research and Practice, 15,* 201–215.

Mahrer, A. R. (1978d). Turning the tables on termination. *Voices, 13,* 24–31.

Mahrer, A. R. (1979). An invitation to theoreticians and researchers from an applied experiential practitioner. *Psychotherapy: Theory, Research and Practice, 16,* 409–418.

Mahrer, A. R. (1980a). Research on theoretical concepts of psychotherapy. In W. Demoor & H. R. Wijngaarten (Eds.), *Psychotherapy: Research and training* (pp. 33–46). Amsterdam: Elsevier/North Holland Biomedical Press.

Mahrer, A. R. (1980b). The treatment of cancer through experiential psychotherapy. *Psychotherapy: Theory, Research and Practice, 17,* 335–342.

Mahrer, A. R. (1980c). Value decisions in therapeutically-induced acute psychotic episodes. *Psychotherapy: Theory, Research and Practice, 17,* 454–458.

Mahrer, A. R. (1982). Humanistic approaches to intimacy. In M. Fisher & G. Stricker (Eds.), Intimacy (pp. 141–158). New York: Plenum.

Mahrer, A. R. (1983a). An existential-experiential view and operational perspective on passive-aggressiveness. In R. D. Parsons & R. J. Wicks (Eds.), *Passive-aggressiveness: Theory and practice* (pp. 98–133). New York: Brunner/Mazel.

Mahrer, A. R. (1983b). Fully experiencing the therapist's ailments. *Voices, 19,* 33–35.

Mahrer, A. R. (1984). The care and feeding of abrasiveness. *The Psychotherapy Patient, 1,* 69–78.

Mahrer, A. R. (1985a). The essence of experiential therapy. *The Humanistic Psychologist, 13,* 12–13.

Mahrer, A. R. (1985b). Introduction to symposium on therapeutic laughter. *Psychotherapy in Private Practice, 3,* 59–61.

Mahrer, A. R. (1985c). My alienness and foreignness: Therapeutic problems and no-problems. *Voices, 21,* 19–24.

Mahrer, A. R. (1985d). *Psychotherapeutic change: An alternative approach to meaning and measurement.* New York: Norton.

Mahrer, A. R. (1986a). A challenge to communication therapy: The therapist does not communicate with the patient. *Journal of Communication Therapy, 3,* 97–114.

Mahrer, A. R. (1986b). Humanistic psychologists decline to be guests in the medical household. *The Humanistic Psychologist, 14,* 5–10.

Mahrer, A. R. (1986c). Introduction to symposium on dreamwork in psychotherapy: Fading art or resurgence? *Psychotherapy in Private Practice, 4,* 107–108.

Mahrer, A. R. (1986d). Is human destiny tragic? Psychoanalytic and humanistic answers. *The Humanistic Psychologist, 14,* 73–86.

Mahrer, A. R. (1986e). Psychotherapy research as the thoughtful study of psychotherapy by psychotherapists *Voices, 22,* 89–90.

Mahrer, A. R. (1986f). *Therapeutic experiencing: The process of change.* New York: Norton.

Mahrer, A. R. (1987a). Clinical exchange on the case of "the diplomat." *Journal of Integrative and Eclectic Psychotherapy, 6,* 102–105.

Mahrer, A. R. (1987b). The depth of dreams: Some data and a model. *Psychiatric Journal of the University of Ottawa, 12,* 73–75.

Mahrer, A. R. (1987c). If there really were a specialty of psychotherapy: Standards for post-doctoral training in psychotherapy. *The Humanistic Psychologist, 15,* 83–94.

Mahrer, A. R. (1987d). Joining the dreamer in having the dream. *Psychiatric Journal of the University of Ottawa, 12,* 76–81.

Mahrer, A. R. (1987e). Relationships between an experiential therapist's personal and professional lives. *Psychotherapy in Private Practice, 5,* 95–97.

Mahrer, A. R. (1987f). These are the components of any theory of psychotherapy. *Journal of Integrative and Eclectic Psychotherapy, 6,* 28–31.

Mahrer, A. R. (1988a). The briefest psychotherapy, *Changes, 6,* 86–89.

Mahrer, A. R. (1988b). Discovery-oriented psychotherapy research: Rationale, aims, and methods. *American Psychologist, 43,* 694–702.

Mahrer, A. R. (1988c). My pilgrimage toward an experiential psychotherapy. *Pilgrimage, 14,* 16–21.

Mahrer, A. R. (1988d). Research and clinical applications of "good moments" in psychotherapy. *Journal of Integrative and Eclectic Psychotherapy, 7,* 81–93.

Mahrer, A. R. (1989a). The case for fundamentally different existential-humanistic psychologies. *Journal of Humanistic Psychology, 29,* 249–262.

Mahrer, A. R. (1989b). Clinical exchange: The case of naivete. *Journal of Integrative and Eclectic Psychotherapy, 8,* 367–369.

Mahrer, A. R. (1989c). *Dreamwork: In psychotherapy and self-change.* New York: Norton.

Mahrer, A. R. (1989d). *Experiencing: A humanistic theory of psychology and psychiatry.* Ottawa: University of Ottawa Press. (Original work published 1978)

Mahrer, A. R. (1989e). *Experiential psychotherapy: Basic practices.* Ottawa: University of Ottawa Press. (Original work published in 1983)

Mahrer, A. R. (1989f). *How to do experiential psychotherapy: A manual for practitioners.* Ottawa: University of Ottawa Press.

Mahrer, A. R. (1989g). *The integration of psychotherapies: A guide for practicing therapists.* New York: Human Sciences.

Mahrer, A. R. (1990a). The experiential approach to the case of the "diplomat." In N. Saltzman & J. C. Norcross (Eds.), *Therapy wars: Contention and convergence in differing clinical approaches* (pp. 41–48). San Francisco: Jossey-Bass.

Mahrer, A. R. (1990b). Existential psychology and psychotherapy. In R. J. Hunter (Ed.), *Dictionary of pastoral care and counseling* (pp. 382–384). Nashville, TN: Abingdon.

Mahrer, A. R. (1990c). Experiential psychotherapy. In J. K. Zeig & W. M. Munion (Eds.), *What is psychotherapy? Contemporary perspectives* (pp. 92–96). San Francisco: Jossey-Bass.

Mahrer, A. R. (1990d). Points of contention and convergence. In N. Saltzman & J. C. Norcross (Eds.), *Therapy wars: Contention and convergence in differing clinical approaches* (pp. 59–61). San Francisco: Jossey-Bass.

Mahrer, A. R. (1990e). The role of dreams in psychotherapy. In S. Krippner (Ed.), *Dreamtime and dreamwork* (pp. 41–48). Los Angeles: Jeremy P. Tarchev.

Mahrer, A. R. (1991a). The care and feeding of a psychotherapy research team. *Journal of Psychiatry and Neuroscience, 16,* 188–192.

Mahrer, A. R. (1991b). Experiential psychotherapy, simple phobias, and a recasting of prescriptive treatment. *Psychotherapy, 28,* 448–451.

Mahrer, A. R. (1992a). Postdoctoral education and training for the practice of psychotherapy. *Psychotherapy in Private Practice, 10,* 111–128.

Mahrer, A. R. (1992b). Shaping the future of psychotherapy by making changes in the present. *Psychotherapy, 29,* 104–108.

Mahrer, A. R. (1993a). The experiential relationship: Is it all-purpose or is it tailored to the individual client? *Psychotherapy, 30,* 413–416.

Mahrer, A. R. (1993b). Transformational psychotherapy sessions. *Journal of Humanistic Psychology, 33,* 30–37.

Mahrer, A. R. (in press). Studying distinguished psychotherapists: A humanistic approach to discovering how to do psychotherapy. *Journal of Humanistic Psychology.*

Mahrer, A. R., & Bernstein, L. (1958). A proposed method for measuring potential intelligence. *Journal of Clinical Psychology, 14,* 404–409.

Mahrer, A. R., & Bornstein, R. (1969). Depression: Characteristic syndromes and a prefatory conceptualization. *Journal of General Psychology, 81,* 217–229.

Mahrer, A. R., & Boulet, D. B. (1987). An experiential session with Edward and his "obsessional" thoughts and fears. *The Psychotherapy Patient, 3,* 143–158.

Mahrer, A. R., & Boulet, D. B. (1989). The postdoctoral plan for the education and training of counsellors. *Canadian Journal of Counselling, 23,* 388–399.

Mahrer, A. R., & Boulet, D. B. (in press). The experiential model of on-the-job teaching. In C. E. Watkins, Jr. (Ed.), *Handbook of psychotherapy supervision.* New York: Wiley.

Mahrer, A. R., Boulet, D. B., & Fairweather, D. R. (1994). Beyond empathy: Advances in the clinical theory and methods of empathy. *Clinical Psychology Review, 14,* 183–198.

Mahrer, A. R., Dessaulles, A., Gervaize, P. A., & Nadler, W. P. (1987). An indictment of interpretation: The elevated role of the therapist as grand interpreter. *Psychotherapy in Private Practice, 5,* 39–51.

Mahrer, A. R., Edwards, H. P., Durak, G. M., & Sterner, I. (1985). The psychotherapy patient and the initial session. *The Psychotherapy Patient, 1,* 39–48.

Mahrer, A. R., & Fairweather, D. R. (1993). What is "experiencing"? A critical review of meanings and applications in psychotherapy. *The Humanistic Psychologist, 21,* 2–25.

Mahrer, A. R., Freedheim, D. K., Norcross, J. C., Stern, E. M., & Weitz, R. D. (1989). Where are the psychotherapy breakthroughs? A roundtable of journal editors. *Voices, 25,* 83–92.

Mahrer, A. R., Gagnon, R., Fairweather, D. R., Boulet, D. B., & Herring, C. B. (1994). Client commitment and resolve to carry out post-session behaviors. *Journal of Counseling Psychology, 41,* 407–414.

Mahrer, A. R., Gagnon, R., Fairweather, D. R., & Cote, P. (1992). How to determine if a session is a very good one. *Journal of Integrative and Eclectic Psychotherapy, 11,* 8–23.

Mahrer, A. R., & Gervaize, P. A. (1983). Impossible roles therapists must play. *Canadian Psychology, 24,* 81–87.

Mahrer, A. R., & Gervaize, P. A. (1984). An integrative review of strong laughter in psychotherapy: What it is and how it works. *Psychotherapy, 21,* 510–516.

Mahrer, A. R., & Gervaize, P. A. (1985). Humanistic theory of development. In T. Husen & T. N. Postlethwaite (Eds.), *International encyclopedia of education: Research and studies* (pp. 2350–2353). New York: Pergamon.

Mahrer, A. R., & Gervaize, P. A. (1986). The steps and methods in experiential psychotherapy sessions. In P. A. Keller & L. G. Ritt (Eds.), *Innovations in clinical practice: A source book* (pp. 59–69). Sarasota, FL: Professional Resource Exchange.

Mahrer, A. R., Howard, M. T., & Boulet, D. B. (1991). A humanistic critique of psychoanalytic termination. *The Humanistic Psychologist, 19,* 331–348.

Mahrer, A. R., Howard, M. T., Gervaize, P. A., & Boulet, D. M. (1990). When the spouse is dead: The alternative approach of experiential psychotherapy. *The Psychotherapy Patient, 6,* 49–70.

Mahrer, A. R., Howard, M. T., & Soulière, M. D. (1991). Do psychotherapists have anything to contribute to social change? *Psychotherapy in Private Practice, 9*, 85–98.

Mahrer, A. R., Lawson, K. C., Stalikas, A., & Schachter, H. M. (1990). Relationships between strength of feeling, type of therapy, and occurrence of in-session good moments. *Psychotherapy, 27*, 531–541.

Mahrer, A. R., Levinson, J., & Fine, S. (1976). Infant psychotherapy: Theory, research and practice. *Psychotherapy: Theory, Research and Practice, 13*, 201–215.

Mahrer, A. R., Mason, D. J., Kahn, E., & Projansky, M. (1966). High complainers versus low complainers: Patterning of amount of self-reported symptomatology. *Psychological Reports, 19*, 955–958.

Mahrer, A. R., & Morel, C. (1993, February). How to become an even better counselor than you are now. *Counseling and Educational Psychology Guidepost*, 34–35.

Mahrer, A. R., Murphy, L., Gagnon, R., & Gingras, N. (1994). The counsellor as a cause and cure of client resistance. *Canadian Journal of Counselling, 28*, 125–134.

Mahrer, A. R., & Nadler, W. P. (1986). Good moments in psychotherapy: A preliminary review, a list, and some promising research avenues. *Journal of Consulting and Clinical Psychology, 54*, 10–16.

Mahrer, A. R., Nadler, W. P., Dessaulles, A., Gervaize, P. A., & Sterner, I. (1987). Good and very good moments in psychotherapy: Content, distribution, and facilitation. *Psychotherapy, 24*, 7–14.

Mahrer, A. R., Nadler, W. P., Gervaize, P. A., & Markow, R. (1986). Discovering how one therapist obtains some very good moments in psychotherapy. *Voices, 22*, 72–83.

Mahrer, A. R., Nifakis, D. J., Abhukara, L., & Sterner, I. (1984). Microstrategies in psychotherapy: The patterning of sequential therapist statements. *Psychotherapy, 21*, 465–472.

Mahrer, A. R., & Pearson, L. (1973a). The directions of psychotherapeutic change: Creative developments. In A. R. Mahrer & L. Pearson (Eds.), *Creative developments in psychotherapy* (pp. 1–14). New York: Jason Aronson.

Mahrer, A. R., & Pearson, L. (1973b). The working processes of psychotherapy: Creative developments. In A. R. Mahrer & L. Pearson (Eds.), *Creative developments in psychotherapy* (pp. 309–329). New York: Jason Aronson.

Mahrer, A. R., & Roberge, M. (1993). Single-session experiential therapy with any person whatsoever. In R. A. Wells & V. J. Giannetti (Eds.), *Casebook of the brief therapies* (pp. 179–196). New York: Plenum.

Mahrer, A. R., & Schachter, H. M. (1991). How to use the patient's past: An experiential alternative, some discoveries, and a theory of the past. *Psychotherapy in Private Practice, 8*, 1–11.

Mahrer, A. R., & White, M. V. (1988). Do behavior therapies own behavior change? Introduction and an experiential answer. *Journal of Integrative and Eclectic Psychotherapy, 7*, 385–391.

Mahrer, A. R., White, M. V., Soulière, M. D., Macphee, D. C., & Boulet, D. B. (1991). Intensive process analysis of significant in-session client change events and antecedent therapist methods. *Journal of Integrative and Eclectic Psychotherapy, 10*, 38–55.

Mahrer, A. R., & Young, H. H. (1962). The onset of stuttering. *Journal of General Psychology, 67*, 241–250.

Mahrer, A. R., Young, H. H., & Katz, G. (1960). Toward a psychological rationale for understanding the effects of anti-depressant medication. In C. L. Lindlay (Ed.), *Cooperative studies in psychiatry and research approaches to mental illness* (pp. 131–134). Washington, DC: Veterans Administration.

Malan, D. H. (1982). *Individual psychotherapy and the science of psychodynamics*. London: Butterworths.

Mann, J. (1973). *Time-limited psychotherapy*. Cambridge, MA: Harvard University Press.

Marmor, J. (1971). Dynamic psychotherapy and behavior therapy: Are they irreconcilable? *Archives of General Psychiatry, 24,* 22–28.

Marshall, W. L., Gauthier, J., & Gordon, A. (1979). The current status of flooding therapy. In M. Hersen, R. M. Eisler, & P. M. Miller (Eds.), *Progress in behavior modification* (Vol. 7, pp. 87–117). New York: Academic.

Marx, M. H. (1951). The general nature of theory construction. In M. H. Marx (Ed.), *Psychological theory* (pp. 3–19). New York: Macmillan.

Mash, E. J. (1985). Some comments on target selection in behavior therapy. *Behavioral Assessment, 7,* 63–98.

Mash, E. J., & Terdal, L. G. (Eds.). (1981). *Behavioral assessment of childhood disorders.* New York: Guilford.

Maslow, A. H. (1963). Fusions of facts and values. *American Journal of Psychoanalysis, 23,* 117–131.

Maslow, A. H. (1968). *Toward a psychology of being* (2nd ed.), New York: Van Nostrand-Reinhold.

Maslow, A. H. (1970). *Motivation and personality* (2nd ed.), New York: Harper & Row.

Masson, J. M. (1984). *The assault on truth.* New York: Farrar, Strauss, and Giroux.

Masson, J. M. (1988). *Against therapy.* New York: Atheneum.

Maupin, E. W. (1965). Zen Buddhism: A psychological review. *Journal of Consulting Psychology, 29,* 139–145.

May, R. (1958a). Contributions of existential psychotherapy. In R. May, E. Angel, & H. F. Ellenberger (Eds.), *Existence: A new dimension in psychiatry and psychology* (pp. 37–91). New York: Basic Books.

May, R. (1958b). The origins and significance of the existential movement in psychology. In R. May, E. Angel, & H. F. Ellenberger (Eds.), *Existence: A new dimension in psychiatry and psychology* (pp. 3–36). New York: Basic Books.

May, R. (1961). *Existential psychology.* New York: Random House.

May, R. (1968). The daemonic: Love and death. *Psychology Today, 1,* 16–25.

May, R. (1989). *The art of counseling.* New York: Gardner.

McConville, B. J. (1976). Opening moves and sequential strategies in child psychotherapy. *Canadian Psychiatric Association Journal, 21,* 295–301.

McGeoch, J. A. (1933). Formal criteria of systematic psychology. *Psychological Review, 40,* 1–12.

McLemore, C. W., & Hart, P. P. (1982). Rational psychotherapy: The clinical facilitation of intimacy. In J. C. Anchin & D. J. Kiesler (Eds.), *Handbook of interactional psychotherapy* (pp. 227–247). New York: Pergamon.

McWilliams, N. (1986). Patients for life: The case for devotion. *The Psychotherapy Patient, 3,* 55–69.

Meehl, P. E. (1978). Theoretical risks and tabular asterisks: Sir Karl, Sir Ronald, and the slow progress of soft psychology. *Journal of Consulting and Clinical Psychology, 46,* 806–834.

Meichenbaum, D. H. (1977). *Cognitive behavior modification.* New York: Plenum.

Menninger, K. (1958). *The theory of psychoanalytic technique.* New York: Basic Books.

Meyer, V., Levy, R., & Schnurer, A. (1974). The behavioral treatment of obsessive-compulsive disorders. In H. R. Beech (Ed.), *Obsessive states,* (pp. 233–258). London: Methuen.

Millon, T. (1981). *Disorders of personality: DSM III: Axis II.* New York: Wiley.

Mindess, H. (1971). *Laughter and liberation.* Los Angeles: Nash.

Mindess, H. (1976). The use and abuse of humor in psychotherapy. In A. J. Chapman & H. C. Foot (Eds.), *Humor and laughter: Theory, research, and applications* (pp. 180–197). London: Wiley.

Morgenstern, K. P. (1988). Behavioral interviewing. In A. S. Bellack & M. Hersen (Eds.), *Behavioral assessment: A practical handbook* (pp. 86–118). New York: Pergamon.

Mullan, H., & Sangiuliano, I. (1964). *The therapist's contribution to the treatment process.* Springfield, IL: Charles C. Thomas.

Nadelson, C., Notman, M., Arons, E. I., & Feldman, J. (1974). The pregnant therapist. *American Journal of Psychiatry, 131,* 1107–1111.

Narboc, N. (1981). Why did the therapist cross the road? *Voices, 16,* 55–58.

Nathan, P. E. (1981). Symptomatic diagnosis and behavioral assessment: A synthesis? In D. H. Barlow (Ed.), *Behavioral assessment of adult disorders* (pp. 1–11). New York: Guilford.

Needleman, J. (1967a). Preface. In J. Needleman (Ed.), *Being-in-the-world: Selected papers of Ludwig Binswanger* (pp. XIII–XVII). New York and London: Harper Torchbooks.

Needleman, J. (1967b). The concept of the existential a priori. In J. Needleman (Ed.), *Being-in-the-world: Selected papers of Ludwig Binswanger* (pp. 9–31). New York: Harper Torchbooks.

Neil, J. R. (1979). The difficult patient: Identification and response. *Journal of Clinical Psychiatry, 40,* 209–212.

Nelson, R. O., & Barlow, D. H. (1981). Behavioral assessment: A synthesis? In D. H. Barlow (Ed.), *Behavioral assessment of adult disorders* (pp. 1–11). New York: Guilford.

Newton-Smith, W. H. (1981). *The rationality of science.* London: Routledge and Kegan Paul.

Noyes, A. P., & Kolb, L. C. (1967). *Modern clinical psychiatry.* Philadelphia: Saunders.

Nydes, J. (1966). Interpretation and the therapeutic act. *Psychoanalytical Review, 53,* 469–481.

O' Leary, K. D., & Wilson, G. T. (1987). *Behavior therapy: Application and outcome.* Englewood Cliffs, NJ: Prentice-Hall.

Orne, M. T. (1969). Demand characteristics and the concept of quasi-controls. In R. Rosenthal & R. L. Rosnow (Eds.), *Artifact in behavioral research* (pp. 97–128). New York: Academic Press.

Ornstein, R. E. (1971). "Turning off" awareness. In C. Naranjo & R. E. Ornstein (Eds.), *On the psychology of meditation* (pp. 142–169). New York: Viking.

Osipow, S. H., & Walsh, W. B. (1970). *Strategies in counseling for behavior change.* New York: Appleton-Century-Crofts.

Ouspensky, P. D. (1949). *In search of the miraculous.* New York: Harcourt, Brace, Jovanovich.

Ouspensky, P. D. (1957). *The fourth way.* London: Routledge and Kegan Paul.

Ownby, R. L. (1983). A cognitive behavioral intervention for compulsive handwashing with a thirteen-year-old boy. *Psychology in the Schools, 20,* 219–222.

Palombo, S. R. (1978). *Dreaming and memory.* New York: Basic Books.

Palombo, S. R. (1980). The cognitive act in dream construction. *Journal of the American Academy of Psychoanalysis, 8,* 185–201.

Parkers, C. M. (1972). *Bereavement: Studies of grief in adult life.* New York: International Universities Press.

Patterson, C. H. (1968). Relationship therapy and/or behavior therapy? *Psychotherapy: Theory, Research, and Practice, 5,* 226–233.

Patterson, C. H. (1974). *Relationship counseling and psychotherapy.* New York: Harper & Row.

Paul, G. L. (1967). Strategy of outcome research in psychotherapy. *Journal of Consulting Psychology, 31,* 109–119.

Paul, G. L. (1969a). Behavior modification research: Design and tactics. In C. M. Franks (Ed.), *Behavior therapy: Appraisal and status* (pp. 29–62). New York: McGraw-Hill.

Paul, G. L. (1969b). Outcome of systematic desensitization: II. Controlled investigations of individual treatment variations, and current status. In C. M. Franks (Ed.), *Behavior therapy: Appraisal and status* (pp. 184–219). New York: McGraw-Hill.

Paul, I. H. (1978). *The form and technique of psychotherapy.* Chicago: University of Chicago Press.

Paul, G. L. (1987). Rational operations in residential treatment settings through ongoing assessment of client and staff functioning. In D. R. Peterson & D. B. Fishman (Ed.), *Assessment for decision* (pp. 145–203). New Brunswick, NJ: Rutgers University Press.

Penfield, W. (1952). Memory mechanisms. *Archives of Neurology and Psychiatry, 67*, 178–191.

Penfield, W. (1975). *The mystery of the mind.* Princeton, NJ: Princeton University Press.

Perls, F. (1970). Four lectures. In J. Fagan & I. L. Shepherd (Eds.), *Gestalt therapy now* (pp. 130–149). Palo Alto, CA: Science and Behavior Books.

Peterson, D. R. (1968). *The clinical study of social behavior.* New York: Appleton-Century-Crofts.

Peterson, D. R. (1987). The role of assessment in professional psychology. In D. R. Peterson & D. B. Fishman (Eds.), *Assessment for decision* (pp. 5–43). New Brunswick, NJ: Rutgers University Press.

Peterson, J. A., & Briley, M. P. (1977). *Widows and widowhood.* New York: Association.

Plant, J. S. (1922). Rating scheme for conduct. *American Journal of Psychiatry, 1*, 547–572.

Polanyi, M. (1958). *Personal knowledge: Towards a post-critical philosophy.* Chicago: University of Chicago Press.

Pollack, J., & Horner, A. (1985). Brief adaptation-oriented psychotherapy. In A. Winston (Ed.), *Short-term dynamic psychotherapy* (pp. 42–60). Washington, DC: American Psychiatric Press.

Popper, K. (1968). *The logic of scientific discovery.* London: Hutchinson.

Pratt, C. C. (1939). *The logic of modern psychology.* New York: Macmillan.

Pribram, K. (1971). *Language of the brain: Experimental paradoxes and principles in neuropsychology.* New York: Brandon House.

Pribram, K. (1980). Cognition and performance. In A. Routtenberg (Ed.), *Biology of reinforcement: Facets of brain stimulation reward* (pp. 11–36). New York: Academic Press.

Rachman, S. J. (1982). Obstacles to the successful treatment of obsessions. In E. B. Foa & P. M. G. Emmelkamp (Eds.), *Failures in behavior therapy* (pp. 35–57). New York: Wiley.

Rachman, S. J., & Hodgson, R. J. (1980). *Obsessions and compulsions.* Englewood Cliffs, NJ: Prentice-Hall.

Rafferty, F. T. (1966). The community is becoming. *American Journal of Orthopsychiatry, 36*, 102–110.

Raimy, V. C. (1948). Self-reference in counseling interviews. *Journal of Consulting Psychology, 12*, 153–163.

Rank, O. (1929). *The trauma of birth.* New York: Harcourt Brace.

Rebec, G. V., & Anderson, G. D. (1986). Regional neuropharmacology of the anti-psychotic drugs: Implication for the dopamine hypothesis of schizophrenia. *Behavioral Assessment, 8*, 11–29.

Reider, N. (1972). Metaphor as interpretation. *International Journal of Psycho-Analysis, 53*, 463–469.

Rhoads, J. M., & Feather, B. F. (1974). The application of psychodynamics to behavior therapy. *American Journal of Psychiatry, 131*, 17–20.

Rice, L. N. (1974). The evocative function of the therapist. In D. Wexler & L. N. Rice (Eds.), *Innovations in client-centered therapy* (pp. 289–312). New York: Wiley.

Rice, L. N. (1984). Client tasks in client-centered therapy. In R. L. Levant & J. M. Shlien (Eds.), *Client-centered therapy and the person-centered approach* (pp. 261–277). New York: Praeger.

Rice, L. N. (1990). Person-centered. In N. Saltzman & J. C. Norcross (Eds.), *Therapy wars: Contention and convergence in differing clinical approaches* (pp. 56–58). San Francisco: Jossey-Bass.

Rimm, D. C., & Masters, J. C. (1974). *Behavior therapy: Techniques and empirical findings.* New York: Academic Press.

Ripley, H. S. (1972). Psychiatric interview. In A. M. Freedman & H. I. Kaplan (Eds.), *Diagnosing mental illness* (pp. 3–19). New York: Atheneum.

Robbins, E., Stern, M., Robbins, L., & Margolin, L. (1978). Unwelcome patients: Where can they find asylum? *Hospital and Community Psychiatry, 29,* 44–46.

Robbins, W. S. (1975). Termination: Problems and techniques. *Journal of the American Psychoanalytic Association, 23,* 166–176.

Robertiello, R., & Forbes, S. (1970). The treatment of the masochistic character disorder. *Journal of Contemporary Psychotherapy, 2,* 3–12.

Roe, A. (1970). Community Resources Centers. *American Psychologist, 25,* 1033–1040.

Rogers, C. R. (1951). *Client-centered therapy.* Boston: Houghton Mifflin.

Rogers, C. R. (1957). The necessary and sufficient conditions of therapeutic personality change. *Journal of Consulting Psychology, 21,* 95–103.

Rogers, C. R. (1966). Some learnings from a study of psychotherapy with schizophrenics. In A. Goldstein & S. Dean (Eds.), *The investigation of psychotherapy* (pp. 5–13). New York: Wiley.

Rogers, C. R. (1970). *On becoming a person.* Boston: Houghton Mifflin.

Rohrbaugh, J. B. (1979). *Women: Psychology's puzzle.* New York: Basic Books.

Rose, G. H. (1969). King Lear and the use of humor in treatment. *Journal of the American Psychoanalytic Association, 17,* 927–940.

Rosenbaum, R., Hoyt, M. F., & Talmon, M. (1990). The challenge of single-session therapies: Creating pivotal moments. In R. A. Wells & V. J. Giannetti (Eds.), *Handbook of the brief psychotherapies,* (pp. 165–189). New York: Plenum.

Rosenberg, S., & Curtis, J. (1939). The effects of stuttering on the behavior of the listener. *Journal of Abnormal and Social Psychology, 49,* 143–148.

Rosenheim, E. (1974). Humor in psychotherapy: An interactive experience. *American Journal of Psychotherapy, 28,* 584–591.

Rosenthal, R. (1966). *Experimenter effects in behavioral research.* New York: Appleton.

Rossi, E. (1986). *The psychobiology of mind-body healing: New conceptions of therapeutic hypnosis.* New York: Norton.

Rothenberg, A. (1987). Empathy as a creative process in treatment. *International Review of Psycho-Analysis, 14,* 445–463.

Rotter, J. B. (1942). A working hypothesis as to the nature and treatment of stuttering. *Journal of Speech Disorders, 7,* 263–288.

Rotter, J. B. (1954). *Social learning and clinical psychology.* New York: Prentice-Hall.

Rowe, D. (1988). Preface. *Counselling and peace* (pp. 1–5). Warwickshire, United Kingdom: British Association for Counselling.

Sands, W. L. (1972). Psychiatric history and mental status. In A. M. Freedman & H. I. Kaplan (Eds.), *Diagnosing mental illness: Evaluation in psychiatry and psychology* (pp. 20–40). New York: Atheneum.

Sarason, S. B. (1988). *The making of an American Psychologist: An autobiography.* San Francisco: Jossey-Bass.

Saretsky, T. (Ed.). (1981). *Resolving treatment impasses: The difficult patient.* New York: Human Sciences.

Saul, L. J. (1958). *Technique and practice of psychoanalysis.* Philadelphia, PA: Lippincott.

Schachtel, E. G. (1959). *Metamorphosis.* New York: Basic Books.

Schauble, P. G., & Pierce, R. M. (1974). Client in-therapy behaviors: A therapist's guide to progress. *Psychotherapy: Theory, Research and Practice, 11,* 229–234.

Schefft, B. K., & Lehr, B. K. (1985). A self-regulatory model of adjunctive-behavior change. *Behavior Modification, 9,* 458–476.

Schilder, P. (1953). *Medical psychology.* New York: International Universities Press.

Schlesinger, H. J. (1976). Diagnosis and prescription for psychotherapy. In A. P. Goldstein & N. Stein (Eds.), *Prescriptive psychotherapy,* (pp. 67–75). New York: Pergamon.

Shoenberg, B. (Ed.). (1970). *Loss and grief: Psychological management in medical practice.* New York: Columbia University Press.

Schroeder, T. (1925). The psycho-analytic method of observation. *International Journal of Psychoanalysis, 60,* 467–479.

Schuchter, S. R. (1986). *Dimensions of grief: Adjusting to the death of a spouse.* San Francisco: Jossey-Bass.

Schulberg, H. C., & Baker, F. (1970). The caregiving system in community mental health programs: An application of open-systems theory. *Community Mental Health Journal, 6,* 437–446.

Schwab, J. J. (1960). What do scientists do? *Behavioral Science, 5,* 1–27.

Schwartz-Borden, G. (1986). Grief work: Prevention and information. *Social Casework, 67,* 499–505.

Searle, J. R. (1976). A classification of illocutionary acts. *Language in Society, 5,* 1–23.

Seguin, C. A. (1965). *Love and psychotherapy.* New York: Libra.

Selvini-Palazzoli, M., Bascolo, L., Cecchin, G., & Prata, G. (1978). *Paradox and counterparadox: A new model of the therapy of the family in schizophrenic transition.* New York: Jason Aronson.

Selvini-Palazzoli, M., Bascolo, L., Cecchin, G., & Prata, G. (1980). Hypothesizing-circulating-neutrality: Three guidelines for the conduct of a session. *Family Process, 19,* 3–13.

Shane, M., & Shane, E. (1984). The end phase of analysis: Indicators, function, and tasks of termination. *Journal of the American Psychoanalytic Association, 32,* 739–772.

Silverman, P. R. (1981). *Helping women cope with grief.* Beverly Hills, CA: Apex.

Silverman, W. H., & Beech, R. P. (1979). Are dropouts, dropouts? *Journal of Community Psychology, 7,* 236–242.

Silverstein, G. (1977). Homosexuality and the ethics of behavioral interventions. *Journal of Homosexuality, 2,* 205–211.

Simkin, J. S., & Yontef, G. M. (1984). Gestalt therapy. In R. J. Corsini (Ed.), *Current psychotherapies* (pp. 279–319). Itasca, IL: Peacock.

Simonton, O. C., Matthews-Simonton, S. S., & Creighton, J. (1978). *Getting well again.* Los Angeles: J. P. Tarcher.

Singer, E. (1965). *Key concepts in psychotherapy.* New York: Random House.

Snyder, W. U. (1945). An investigation of the nature of non-directive psychotherapy. *Journal of General Psychology, 33,* 193–223.

Spiegel, R. (1972). Management of crises in psychotherapy. In G. D. Goldman & G. Striker (Eds.), *Practical problems of a private psychotherapy practice* (pp. 93–117). Springfield, IL: Charles C. Thomas.

Stern, R. (1970). Treatment of a case of obsessional neurosis using thought-stopping technique. *British Journal of Psychiatry, 117,* 441–442.

Stevens, S. S. (1935). The operational definition of psychological concepts. *Psychological Review, 42,* 517–527.

Stevens, S. S. (1939). Psychology and the science of science. *Psychological Bulletin, 36,* 221–263.

Stieper, D. R., & Wiener, D. N. (1965). *Dimensions of psychotherapy.* Chicago: Aldine.

Stigliano, A. (1986). An ontology for the human sciences. *Saybrook Review, 6,* 33–63.

Stone, G. C. (1979). Psychology and the health system. In G. C. Stone, G. Cohen, & N. E. Adler (Eds.), *Health psychology: A handbook* (pp. 88–103). San Francisco: Jossey-Bass.

Suinn, R. M. (Ed.). (1970). *Fundamentals of behavior pathology.* New York: Wiley.

Sullivan, H. S. (1953a). *Conceptions of modern psychiatry.* New York: Norton.

Sullivan, H. S. (1953b). *The interpersonal theory of psychiatry.* New York: Norton.

Szasz, T. S. (1988). *The ethics of psychoanalysis.* Syracuse, NY: Syracuse University Press. (Original work published 1965)

Talmon, M. (1990). *Single session therapy.* San Francisco: Jossey-Bass.

Tauber, E. S. (1960). Sullivan's conception of cure. *American Journal of Psychotherapy, 14,* 666–676.

Tennov, D. (1975). *Psychotherapy: The hazardous cure.* New York: Abelard-Schuman.

Thorp, T. R., & Mahrer, A. R. (1959). Predicting potential intelligence. *Journal of Clinical Psychology, 15,* 286–288.

Thorpe, S. A. (1987). An approach to treatment planning. *Psychotherapy, 24,* 729–735.

Ticho, E. (1972). Termination of psychoanalysis: Treatment goals, life goals. *Psychoanalytic Quarterly, 41,* 315–333.

Toukmanian, S. G. (1990). A schema-based information processing perspective on client change in experiential psychotherapy. In G. Lietaer, J. Rombauts, & R. Van Balen (Eds.), *Client-centered and experiential psychotherapy in the nineties* (pp. 309–326). Leuven, Belgium: Leuven University Press.

Troemel-Platz, S. (1980). "I'd come to you for therapy": Interpretation, redefinition, and paradox in Rogerian therapy. *Psychotherapy: Theory, Research and Practice, 17,* 246–257.

Urada, S. F. (1977). Counseling the bereaved. *Counseling and Values, 21,* 185–191.

Vanaerschot, G. (1990). The process of empathy: Holding and letting go. In G. Lietaer, J. Rombauts, & R. Van Balen (Eds.), *Client-centered and experiential psychotherapy in the nineties* (pp. 267–293). Leuven, Belgium: Leuven University Press.

Van Dusen, W. (1957). The theory and practice of existential analysis. *American Journal of Psychoanalysis, 11,* 310–322.

Van Hoose, W., & Kottler, J. (1977). *Ethical and legal issues in counseling and psychotherapy.* New York: Wiley.

Volkan, V. D. (1975). "Re-grief" therapy. In B. Schoenberg, I. Gerber, A. Wiener, A. H. Kutscher, D. Peretz, & A. C. Carr (Eds.), *Bereavement: Its psychosocial aspects* (pp. 33–50). New York: Columbia University Press.

Wachtel, P. (1980). What should we say to our patients? On the wording of therapists' comments. *Psychotherapy: Theory, Research and Practice, 17,* 183–188.

Watson, J. B. (1912). Content of a course in psychology for medical students. *Journal of the American Medical Association, 53,* 916–918.

Watts, A. W. (1960). *This is it and other essays on Zen.* New York: Random House and John Murray.

Watts, A. W. (1961). *Psychotherapy east and west.* New York: Ballantine.

Weiner, I. B. (1975). *Principles of psychotherapy.* New York: Wiley.

Weiss, S. S., & Fleming, J. (1981). On the teaching and learning of termination in psychoanalysis. In H. R. Beiser et al. (Eds), *The annals of psychoanalysis* (Vol. 3, pp. 37–55). New York: International Universities Press.

White, M. (1993). Deconstruction and therapy. In S. Gilligan & R. Price (Eds.), *Therapeutic conversations* (pp. 22–61). New York: Norton.

White, M., & Epston, D. (1990). *Narrative means to therapeutic ends.* New York: Norton.

Wilhelm, R. (1962). *The secret of the golden flower: A Chinese book of life.* London: Routledge and Kegan Paul.

Williams, H., & Barber, L. (1971). Description of an infancy curriculum for character development. *Character Potential, 5,* 99–106.

Wilson, F. E., & Evans, I. M. (1983). The reliability of target-behavioral selection in behavioral assessment. *Behavioral Assessment, 3,* 15–32.

Wischner, G. J. (1950). Stuttering behavior and learning: A preliminary theoretical formulation. *Journal of Speech and Hearing Disorders, 15,* 324–335.

Wolpe, J. (1969). *The practice of behavior therapy.* New York: Pergamon.

Wolpe, J., & Lazarus, A. A. (1966). *Behavior therapy techniques.* New York: Pergamon.

Woodger, J. H. (1952). *Biology and language.* Cambridge, England: Cambridge University Press.

Woody, R. H. (1976). Issues in application. In A. P. Goldstein & N. Stein (Eds.), *Prescriptive psychotherapies* (pp. 55–65). New York: Pergamon.

Zaro, J. S., Barach, R., Nedelman, D. J., & Dreiblatt, I. S. (1977). *A guide for beginning psychotherapists.* Cambridge: Cambridge University Press.

Author Index